TRANSLATING MAYA HIEROGLYPHS

This book is published as part of the Recovering Languages and Literacies of the Americas initiative. Recovering Languages and Literacies is generously supported by the Andrew W. Mellon Foundation.

SCOTT A. J. JOHNSON

TRANSLATING MAYA HIEROGLYPHS

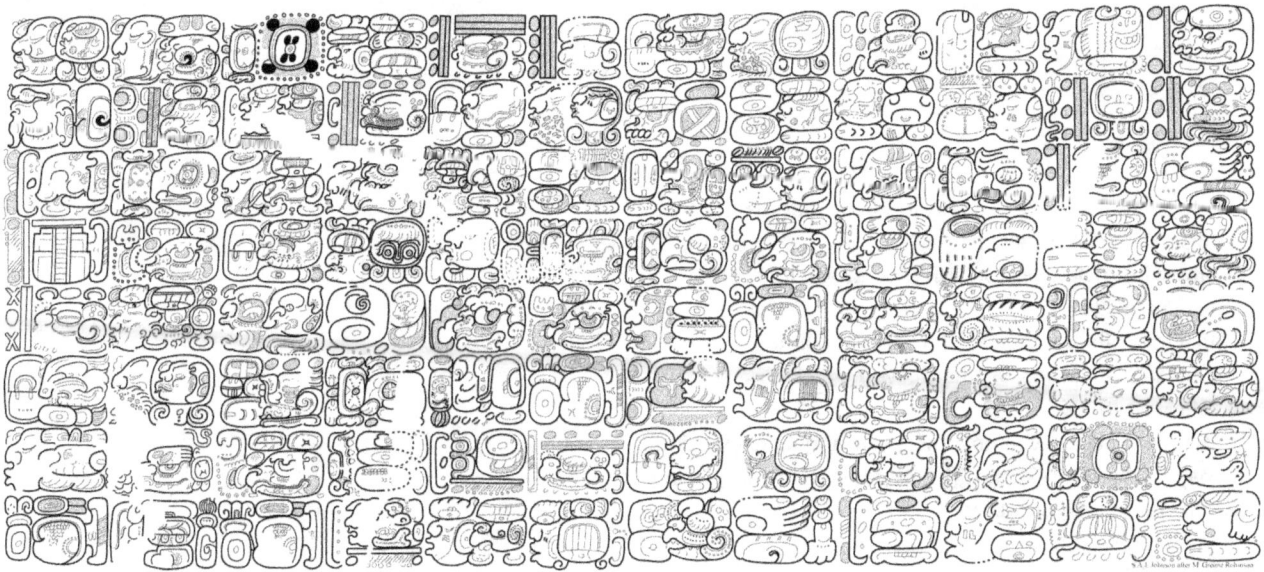

University of Oklahoma Press : Norman

Library of Congress Cataloging-in-Publication Data
Johnson, Scott A. J., 1983–
    Translating Maya Hieroglyphs / Scott A.J. Johnson.
          pages cm
    Includes bibliographical references and index.
    ISBN 978-0-8061-4333-0 (hardcover)
    ISBN 978-0-8061-5121-2
1. Maya language—Grammar. 2. Maya language—Writing.
3. Maya language—Syntax. 4. Translating and interpreting.
5. Inscriptions, Mayan. I. Title.
    PM3969.J64 2013
    497'.42711—dc23
                                                    2012041253

The paper in this book meets the guidelines for permanence and durability of the Committee on Production Guidelines for Book Longevity of the Council on Library Resources, Inc. ∞

Copyright © 2013 by the University of Oklahoma Press, Norman, Publishing Division of the University. Manufactured in the U.S.A.

All rights reserved. No part of this publication may be reproduced, stored in a retrieval system, or transmitted, in any form or by any means, electronic, mechanical, photocopying, recording, or otherwise—except as permitted under Section 107 or 108 of the United States Copyright Act—without the prior written permission of the University of Oklahoma Press. To request permission to reproduce selections from this book, write to Permissions, University of Oklahoma Press, 2800 Venture Drive, Norman OK, 73069, or email rights.oupress@ou.edu.

I dedicate this book to Linda Schele and her belief that epigraphy should be open to everybody, but also to Lauren, for her constant support and encouragement.

CONTENTS

List of Illustrations *xi*
Drawing Credits *xiii*
List of Tables *xv*
Acknowledgments *xvii*
Abbreviations *xix*

INTRODUCTION 3

0.1. Why This Book Is Needed 3
0.2. Today's Major Controversies 4
0.3. How This Book Is Laid Out 4
0.4. A Brief History of the Maya 5
0.5. A Short History of Maya Decipherment 8
0.6. Where Glyphs Are Encountered 11
Further Reading 12

1. THE NATURE OF THE SCRIPT 15

1.1. Glyph Blocks 15
   Exercise 1.1. Schematic Depiction of Glyph Blocks 18
   Exercise 1.2. Piedras Negras, Stela 3 19
   Exercise 1.3. Palenque, Tablet of the 96 Glyphs 20
1.2. Reading Order within an Inscription 21
1.3. Reading Order within a Glyph Block 25
   Exercise 1.4. Main Signs and Affixes from Piedras Negras, Stela 3 28
1.4. Common Inscription Format 33
1.5. Logograms 34
   Exercise 1.5. Identify Logograms 34
1.6. Syllabograms 36
   Exercise 1.6. Identify Syllables 42
   Exercise 1.7. Identify Syllables II 43
1.7. Semantic Determinatives 45
1.8. Numeral Classifiers 48
1.9. Transcription 50
   Exercise 1.8. Syllabic Spellings 53
   Exercise 1.9. Transcribe, Transliterate, and Translate 54
1.10. Transliteration 55
1.11. Translation 56
Further Reading 57

2. SPELLING AND LANGUAGE 59

2.1. Sounds in Classic Mayan 59
    2.1.1. Consonants 59
    2.1.2. Vowels 60

2.2. Synharmony 62

2.3. Disharmony 62
    Inset Box 2.1. Key Controversy: Disharmonic Spellings of Complex Vowels 64
    Exercise 2.1. Synharmonic Transliterations 67
    Exercise 2.2. Disharmonic Transliterations 68

2.4. Phonetic Complements 69

2.5. "New" versus "Old" Orthography 70

2.6. Language(s) Represented Glyphically 71

Further Reading 72

3. DATES AND NUMBERS 73

3.1. Numbers 73
    Exercise 3.1. Numerals 78

3.2. Long Count 81
    Inset Box 3.1. Key Controversy: Long Count Correlations 86

3.3. Calendar Round 87
    Exercise 3.2. Calculate Calendar Round Dates 92
    Exercise 3.3. Identify Calendar Round Dates 93

3.4. Supplementary Series 94
    Exercise 3.4. Identify Supplementary Inscription Elements 100

3.5. Distance Numbers 101
    Exercise 3.5. Identify Distance Numbers 106
    Exercise 3.6. Reconstruct Dates: Yaxchilan, Hieroglyphic Stairway 3 110
    Exercise 3.7. Reconstruct Dates: Piedras Negras, Stela 3 111
    Exercise 3.8. Reconstruct Dates: Palenque, Tablet of 96 Glyphs 112
    Exercise 3.9. Reconstruct Dates: Piedras Negras, Altar 2 113
    Exercise 3.10. Reconstruct Dates: Palenque, Hieroglyphic Stairway 114
    Exercise 3.11. Inscription Date Reconstruction: Palenque, Sarcophagus 115
    Exercise 3.12. Reconstruct Dates: Palenque, Palace Tablet 117

3.6. Short Counts 119

4. BASIC GRAMMAR 121

4.1. Prepositions *121*
    Exercise 4.1. Identify Prepositions *123*

4.2. Pronouns *124*
    Exercise 4.2. Identify Pronouns *134*
    Exercise 4.3. Pronouns *135*
    Exercise 4.4. Pronouns II *136*

4.3. Nouns, Noun Suffixes, and Morphosyllables *137*
    Exercise 4.5. Derived Nouns *142*
    Inset Box 4.1. Key Controversy: Plural Markers *143*
    Inset Box 4.2. Key Controversy: Morphosyllables *145*
    Exercise 4.6. Identify Titles *151*

4.4. Adjectives and Adverbs *152*
    Exercise 4.7. Derived Adjectives *153*

4.5. Word Order in Classic Mayan *155*
    Exercise 4.8. Noun Phrases *157*

4.6. Stative Clauses and Particles *158*

4.7. Complete Examples *160*
    Exercise 4.9. Piedras Negras, Stela 3 *162*
    Exercise 4.10. Piedras Negras, Altar 2 *163*

Further Reading *164*

5. VERBAL GRAMMAR 165

5.1. Transitive Verbs *166*
    5.1.1. Active *166*
    5.1.2. Passive *169*
    5.1.3. Mediopassive *169*
    5.1.4. Antipassive *170*
    5.1.5. Imperative *170*
        Exercise 5.1. Transitive Verb Voices *172*
        Exercise 5.2. Transitive Verb Voices II *173*
        Exercise 5.3. Transitive Verb Voices III *174*

5.2. Intransitive Verbs *175*
    5.2.1. Root *175*
    5.2.2. Derived *175*

5.3. Positional (and Causative) *178*
    Exercise 5.4. Intransitive Verbs *179*
    Exercise 5.5. More Intransitive Verbs *180*

5.4. Inchoative *181*

5.5. Affective *183*

5.6. Stative Particles *183*

5.7. Expressing Time *184*
    Inset Box 5.1. Key Controversy: Aspect versus Tense *185*

6. PUTTING IT ALL TOGETHER 193

6.1. Piedras Negras: K'inich Yo'nal Ahk II and Lady K'atun Ajaw *194*
    6.1.1. Piedras Negras, Stela 1 *194*
    6.1.2. Piedras Negras, Stela 3 *199*
    6.1.3. Piedras Negras, Stela 8 (Partial) *206*

6.2. Palenque: Dynasty and K'inich Janaab' Pakal *210*
    6.2.1. Palenque, Sarcophagus Lid *210*
    6.2.2. Palenque, Hieroglyphic Stairway (Partial) *215*

APPENDICES

APPENDIX I. GRAMMAR *219*
    I.1. Pronouns *219*
    I.2. Verbs *220*
    I.3. Prepositions *222*
    I.4. Adjectives *223*
    I.5. Adverbs and Enclitics *224*

APPENDIX II. CATALOG CORRESPONDENCE *225*
    II.1. Catalog Numbers and Drawings *225*
    II.2. Transcriptions and Catalog Numbers *232*

APPENDIX III. BASIC VOCABULARY *236*
    III.1. Classic Maya Calendar *236*
    III.2. Classic Maya Verbs *244*
    III.3. Classic Maya Colors *246*
    III.4. Classic Maya Titles *247*
    III.5. Classic Maya Animals *249*
    III.6. Classic Maya Family Relations *252*
    III.7. Classic Maya Emblem Glyphs *253*
    III.8. Classic Maya Objects *254*

APPENDIX IV. LEXICON *257*
    IV.1. Classic Mayan to English Lexicon *257*
    IV.2. English to Classic Mayan Lexicon *333*

APPENDIX V. CALENDAR PROGRAMS *359*

APPENDIX VI. HOW TO DRAW MONUMENTS AND TEXTS *362*

Glossary *365*
References *367*
Exercise Answer Key *372*
Index *381*

ILLUSTRATIONS

0.1. Map of the Major Maya Sites 6

1.1. Traditional Labeling Scheme for Glyph Blocks 16
1.2. Glyph Blocks from Palenque, Hieroglyphic Stairway 17
1.3. Reading Order of Glyph Blocks and Separated Block Pairs 22
1.4. Schematic Depiction of Proper Reading Order of Glyph Blocks 23
1.5. Reading Order of the Inscription from Palenque, Hieroglyphic Stairway 24
1.6. Reading Order within a Glyph Block and Common Labels 26
1.7. Combinations, Conflations, and Infixes 27
1.8. Equivalent Affixes and Main Signs 29
1.9. Thompson Example: 1.528:116 30
1.10. Reading Order within a Block Inscription from Palenque, Hieroglyphic Stairway 32
1.11. Reading Order for Glyphs Commonly Situated behind Other Glyphs 33
1.12. Examples of Common Logograms 35
1.13. Totum pro Parte 36
1.14. Syllabary of Currently Deciphered Glyphs 37
1.15. Polyphonic Glyphs 45
1.16. Polyvalent Glyphs 46
1.17. Semantic Determinatives 47
1.18. Numerical Classifiers 49
1.19. Transcription, Transliteration, and Translation 50
1.20. Piedras Negras, Stela 3 51

2.1. Phonetic Complements 69

3.1. Bar-and-Dot and Head-Variant Numbers 75
3.2. Long Count Glyphs and Head Variants 82
3.3. Tzolk'in Day Names 89
3.4. Haab' Month Names 90
3.5. Glyph G (Lords of the Night) 95
3.6. Glyph F 96
3.7. Glyphs Z and Y 96
3.8. Glyphs E and D 96
3.9. Glyph C 96
3.10. Glyph X 97
3.11. Glyph B 97
3.12. Glyph A 99
3.13. 819-Day Cycle 99
3.14. Distance Number Introductory Glyph and K'in Variants 101
3.15. Distance Number Examples 102
3.16. Date Indicators and Period Completions 103
3.17. Date Examples 104
3.18. Dates and Distance Numbers from Yaxchilan, Lintel 21 107
3.19. Dates and Distance Numbers from Naranjo, Stela 24 108
3.20. Short Count Date 119

- 4.1. Prepositions *122*
- 4.2. Personal Pronouns *125*
- 4.3. Pure Nouns *137*
- 4.4. Noun Suffixes *139*
- 4.5. Noun Suffixes Showing Possession *144*
- 4.6. Titles *146*
- 4.7. Animals *149*
- 4.8. Emblem Glyphs *150*
- 4.9. Family Relations *150*
- 4.10. Adjectival Endings *152*
- 4.11. Adjectives and Colors *154*
- 4.12. Noun Phrase Construction *156*
- 4.13. Stative Clauses and Particles *159*
- 4.14. Pronoun Examples *161*

- 5.1. Transitive Verb Markers *167*
- 5.2. Transitive Verb Examples *168*
- 5.3. Transitive Verb Construction *171*
- 5.4. Intransitive Verb Markers *176*
- 5.5. Intransitive Verb Examples *177*
- 5.6. Other Verb Markers *181*
- 5.7. Other Verb Examples *182*
- 5.8. Temporal Verb Markers or Adverbs *188*
- 5.9. Verb Time Examples *190*

- 6.1. Piedras Negras, Stela 1 *195*
- 6.2. Piedras Negras, Stela 3 *201*
- 6.3. Piedras Negras, Stela 8 *207*
- 6.4. Palenque, Pakal's Sarcophagus Lid *211*
- 6.5. Palenque, Hieroglyphic Stairway *216*

DRAWING CREDITS

All drawings except exercise 3.12 were vectorized by the author (most after other drawings or photographs).

Maya Map: vectorized after Google Earth satellite image.

Aguateca, Stela 1: vectorized after Graham 1967: figure 3.

Aguateca, Stela 2: vectorized after Graham 1967: figure 5.

Aguateca, Stela 15: vectorized after Eberl 2000.

Chichen Itza, Temple of the Initial Series: vectorized after Krochock and Schmidt 1989.

Dos Pilas, Hieroglyphic Stair 4: vectorized after Houston 1993: figure 4-11.

Naranjo, Altar 1: vectorized after Graham 1978: 103–104.

Naranjo, Stela 24: vectorized after Graham and von Euw 1975: 63–64.

Naranjo, Stela 29: vectorized after Graham 1978: 77–78.

Naranjo-area, Vessel: vectorized after Kerr Drawing Database Number 1398 1998.

Palenque, Hieroglyphic Stairway: vectorized drawing after Schele 1996: figure 1.

Palenque, Palace Tablet: image in exercise 3.12 copyright Merle Greene Robertson, 1976; everywhere else the drawing is vectorized after Greene Robertson 1985: figure 258.

Palenque, Sarcophagus Lid: vectorized after Greene Robertson 1983: 170.

Palenque, Tablet of 96 Glyphs: vectorized after Greene Robertson 1991: figure 264.

Palenque, Temple of the Cross Tablet: vectorized after Greene Robertson 1991: figure 9.

Palenque, Temple of the Inscriptions: vectorized after Greene Robertson 1983: figure 96.

Palenque, Temple of the Sun Tablet: vectorized after Greene Robertson 1991: 95.

Piedras Negras, Panel 3: vectorized after Kettunen and Helmke 2010: figure 8.

Piedras Negras, Stela 1: vectorized after Montgomery 2000; and Stuart and Graham 2003: 15–20.

Piedras Negras, Stela 3: vectorized after Montgomery 2000; and Stuart and Graham 2003: 24–28.

Piedras Negras, Stela 8: vectorized after Montgomery 2000; and Stuart and Graham 2003: 43–49.

Piedras Negras, Stela 10: vectorized after Stuart and Graham 2003: 53–55.

Seibal, Stela 10: vectorized after Graham 1996: 31–32.

Tikal, Stela 31: vectorized after Montgomery 2000.

Tonina, Monument 139: vectorized after Graham and Mathews 1999: 168–69.

Tortuguero, Monument 6: vectorized after Bricker 1986: 66.

Yaxchilan, Hieroglyphic Stairway 3: vectorized after Graham 1982: 169.

Yaxchilan, Lintel 2: vectorized after Graham and von Euw 1977: 15.

Yaxchilan, Lintel 14: vectorized after Graham and von Euw 1977: 37.

Yaxchilan, Lintel 21: vectorized after Graham and von Euw 1977: 49.

Yaxchilan, Lintel 25: vectorized after Graham and von Euw 1977: 55–56.

TABLES

2.1. Classic Mayan Consonant Sounds *60*
2.2. Classic Mayan Vowel Sounds *61*
2.3. Modified Spelling Rules Used in This Book *63*
2.4. Synharmonic and Disharmonic Spelling Results *63*
2.5. Lacadena and Wichmann's Complex Vowel Spelling Rules *65*
2.6. Correspondence of Complex Vowel Spellings *66*
2.7. Correspondence of Old and New Orthography *70*

3.1. Vigesimal Math and Conversion *74*
3.2. Minimum Attributes of Number Variants *77*
3.3. Long Count to Day Number Conversion *83*
3.4. Abbreviated Day Number to Gregorian Year Conversion *84*
3.5. Complete Day Number to Gregorian Year Conversion *85*
3.6. List of Correlation Coefficients *86*
3.7. Calculating Tzolk'in Position *88*
3.8. Calculating Haab' Position *91*
3.9. Calculating Lord of the Night Position *95*
3.10. Indicating Dates through an Inscription *105*
3.11. Short Count Names and Their Equivalent Long Counts *120*

4.1. Morphosyllables *145*

5.1. Common Abbreviations *165*
5.2. English Tense and Voice *184*
5.3. Verb Paradigm Indicating Relative Time *187*

6.1. Piedras Negras, Stela 1 Chronology *196*
6.2. Piedras Negras, Stela 3 Chronology *200*
6.3. Piedras Negras, Stela 8 Chronology *206*
6.4. Palenque, Pakal's Sarcophagus Lid Chronology *212*
6.5. Palenque, Hieroglyphic Stairway Chronology *217*

ACKNOWLEDGMENTS

This book would not have been possible without the influence, support, and encouragement of many people from academia and from my personal life. Thank you to Paul Zimansky, who introduced me to the world of ancient scripts and their decipherment, and Norman Hammond, my undergraduate advisor at Boston University, who had me read (among other epigraphy classics) all 347 pages of Thompson's *Maya Hieroglyphic Writing: An Introduction* in a single week before sending me to learn more from Marc Zender. Marc was then at Harvard and became my first glyph teacher and later my friend. He has the rare talent of explaining a complex concept in a way that is easy to understand without being overly pedantic. I must thank Marc for his support and critical feedback on this project and others. This book is more balanced and complete because of Markus Eberl and Victoria Bricker, who were at Tulane University when I began my graduate studies there. Markus is a meticulous scholar, and our discussions about glyphic controversies made me realize that no textbook would be complete without explaining both sides of today's issues. Although Victoria retired the year before I began at Tulane, her critiques of my drawings and some sections of the text made me work hard to improve them. A great deal of appreciation is due to the Tulane Glyph Group and the students in my glyph class in the spring of 2010, especially David Chatelain. I first got the idea to start this project over two years ago because there was no complete introductory glyph textbook. My class used the first draft of this text and was a great focus group, helping to ensure that the explanations were clear to beginners. Thanks must also go to the University of Oklahoma Press: Alessandra Jacobi Tamulevich, my editor; Julie Rushing, Emmy Ezzell, Julie Allred, Anna María Rodriguez, and Emily Jerman, the poor graphics editors who had to deal with the mountain of figures in this project; Kathy Burford Lewis, who had to copyedit a book about an obscure language; and especially the two anonymous reviewers of this work, who gave me useful feedback and polite corrections of the manuscript. Thank you to David Greene and the estate of Merle Greene Robertson for permission to republish her beautiful drawing of the Palenque Palace Tablet. Finally, I must thank my graduate advisor, Will Andrews. I did not tell him about this project until it was nearly completed, because I could have been working on my doctoral dissertation instead. Nonetheless, he has been encouraging and supportive of my finishing this book (as quickly as possible).

I would not be who I am today without the support and influence of my friends and family. First, thanks to my parents, Gerald and Kelly, and stepmother, Cindy. My father has been a strong example of hard work and making the right decision, although it may be difficult. My mother has encouraged me to be creative (although my sister, Jamie, is the real family artist) and to pursue whatever career makes me happy, even if it is not the profitable one. Finally, I must thank my wife, Lauren, and her family for their emotional and material support while I completed this project. As Lauren will tell you, I have multiple projects going on at once, some of them more feasible than others. A complete hieroglyphic textbook is a huge undertaking, especially while completing a dissertation, but Lauren never faltered in her support of it.

ABBREVIATIONS

Parts of speech are indicated by the following abbreviations:

adj	adjective
adv	adverb
div	derived intransitive verb
icv	inchoative verb
n	noun
ncl	numeral classifier
num	numeral
partic	participle
prep	preposition
pron	pronoun
pv	positional verb
riv	root intransitive verb
tv	transitive verb

TRANSLATING MAYA HIEROGLYPHS

INTRODUCTION

Welcome to the world of ancient Maya writing. Some of you may be archaeologists, looking for further insight into Maya culture. Others may be budding epigraphers, starting your study of this immense topic. Many of you are likely lay readers, pursuing this topic out of personal curiosity. Indeed, many important advances in the fields of Maya epigraphy and archaeology have been made by nonprofessionals with a passion for all things Maya. This book is designed to fit the needs of anybody who is interested in learning to read Maya hieroglyphs.

0.1. WHY THIS BOOK IS NEEDED

The study of Maya glyphs for too long has been the realm of specialists. Maya epigraphers have made giant strides in deciphering hieroglyphics in the last four decades. Archaeologists, however, have not always embraced the study of glyphs for a number of reasons. The state of decipherment has advanced to the point that Maya hieroglyphics should not be understood by epigraphers alone; nor should archaeologists be allowed to continue without a stronger understanding of the complex writing system of the culture that they are studying.

Epigraphers are (and will continue to be) engaged with advancing our understanding of Maya hieroglyphic writing. Current epigraphic debates center on a number of important issues, such as the expression of time, complex vowels, and morphosyllables. Without debates about complex linguistic and epigraphic issues, we would not have reached our current state of understanding. The problem has been that specialists have left the rest of the Mayanists behind. These debates may seem arcane to the average reader. To understand the current state of decipherment and read glyphs at a state-of-the-art level, you must work through decades of literature and unpublished correspondence. Most nonspecialists do not have the time to do this.

This book is intended to give the nonepigrapher an insight into this writing system not afforded by modern literature. It is not intended to make the role of experts obsolete. Epigraphers will always be responsible for advancing our understanding of how the Classic Maya expressed themselves graphically. This book is intended to foster appreciation on the part of archaeologists and others who would otherwise regard glyph studies as esoteric.

Mayanists have been able to gain an initial understanding of glyphic writing from a number of other sources. The handbooks from the Texas Maya Meetings and European Maya Conference have been excellent sources. Glyph guides and dictionaries also have been readily available from the Foundation for the Advancement of Mesoamerican Studies Incorporated website (www.famsi.org). John Montgomery's *How to Read Maya Hieroglyphs* (2002) was an excellent resource when it was published. Important strides have been made since then, and a few cloudy issues have been clarified. Much of this progress came in Søren Wichmann's *The Linguistics of Maya Writing* (2004), written for an audience of specialists. Michael Coe and Mark Van Stone's *Reading the Maya Glyphs* (2005) is likely the most popular published work that provides practical reading instruction. There are a few important differences between that work and this one. This textbook integrates formal linguistic information regarding grammar. It includes an extensive lexicon as well as many worksheets and exercises and is presented in an instructional format that introduces glyphs in a language-focused way. Although epigraphers have written reference books for one another or to explain the history of Maya epigraphy, none has written a book specifically to teach the topic at an introductory but comprehensive level.

0.2. TODAY'S MAJOR CONTROVERSIES

Although epigraphers have made significant advances in decipherment in the last few decades, a number of important debates remain. Recently it has been suggested that Maya writing used tense (past, present, and future) to express differences and change in time. Others have proposed that Maya writing employs the aspectual system (completed actions vs. incompleted actions) found in modern Maya languages. Another debate centers on how the words written in hieroglyphics were actually spoken by the ancient Maya. Some question whether certain vowel pronunciations existed during the Classic period and how they may (or may not) have been represented glyphically. Scholars also argue over whether or not certain signs can "flip" their usual value in certain contexts. Yet another area of contention is the representation (or lack thereof) of plurality in the written script. The thing that must be kept in mind is this: how much will the resolution of these debates change the way in which the average person translates and understands glyphic inscriptions? For instance, an important phonological difference between the sounds *h* and *j* in the Maya script has recently been demonstrated. This resolved a long-standing debate in the field but did not significantly change the actual meaning of many translations. Although the resolution of these debates will further sharpen our understanding of the Maya writing system, for the most part the largest puzzle pieces have already fallen into place. Enough progress has been made in this field to warrant the creation of a definitive resource and textbook.

0.3. HOW THIS BOOK IS LAID OUT

The format of this book is similar to that of other textbooks commonly used to introduce students to a modern foreign language. It is not simply a reference volume (a few excellent handbooks are already available). This text is laid out in a linguistically oriented fashion, unlike other books arranged in sections based on art-historical themes.

Each section of this book covers related topics and grammatical issues. These sections are short and easily understood. Examples from real and hypothetical inscriptions are used to illustrate the subject under consideration. Real inscriptions show the variety and scribal virtuosity common in Maya writing. Hypothetical inscriptions are employed as examples of grammatical forms that are rarely expressed in real glyphic inscriptions. This serves to give students a feeling for the full writing system that might have been expressed on perishable media, such as codices.

Because the Maya writing system has not been fully deciphered, current debates and controversies must be addressed. Inset boxes throughout the text outline and explain the relevant arguments and evidence for each disputed issue. To be comprehensive, a textbook must carefully weigh the pros and cons of any academic argument relevant to the material. To be practical, the text must adopt one position or strike a compromise. The decision to take a certain side of an argument is explained in the inset boxes. These topics will probably be resolved and updated in later editions.

Every chapter has associated exercises, which complement and reinforce the material covered in the text. Some exercises come directly from real inscriptions, while others are more grammatically oriented. This will allow practice in identification in real-world situations as well as fostering a strong basic understanding of the language.

Finally, suggestions for further reading are included at the end of many chapters. In attempting to cover every major aspect of the Maya script, it was not possible to go into detail on a number of interesting topics. Some people may not be interested in the minutiae of the field, but these resources are provided for those who wish to purse independent study.

The appendixes are an important part of this book. They offer (mostly in tables and lists) much of the "quick reference" material needed when attempting a translation. The appendixes provide most prominent vocabulary and glyphs as well as a comprehensive lexicon. They also include information on calendrical programs and Thompson numbers.

The Maya script is visually complex. Many drawings and figures were created for this book. Some of these glyph blocks, inscriptions, and phrases have been taken directly from real monuments. In these instances, the inscription is identified in the accompanying text. When the provenience is not specifically noted, individual glyphs have been drawn from multiple sources and arranged to create the necessary glyph blocks or inscription. All drawings except exercise 3.12 were vectorized in a process described in appendix VI.

0.4. A BRIEF HISTORY OF THE MAYA

The Maya have been fascinating scholars and lay audiences alike for hundreds of years. In the mid-1800s the first books describing the sites, people, and history of this culture became available. Although the ideas and reconstructions have changed significantly over the decades, a more complete and unified picture of Maya culture has slowly emerged. Today we have many books describing the Maya and various aspects of their culture. Robert Sharer and Loa Traxler's *The Ancient Maya* (2006) is often considered the most comprehensive. Started in 1946 by Sylvanus Griswold Morley, this book is now in its sixth edition. It is continually improved and updated as new discoveries are made. The book is nearly 1,000 pages long, though, and may be too extensive for the nonspecialist. Michael Coe has published his eighth edition of *The Maya* (2011), a more modest treatment that nonetheless gives the reader a broad introduction. Simon Martin and Nikolai Grube synthesized the information from hundreds of monuments in their book *Chronicle of the Maya Kings and Queens* (second edition, 2008), which traces the history of the Maya as recorded on their own monuments. Other popular books (such as those by Norman Hammond, Arthur Demarest, and Linda Schele and David Freidel) are listed at the end of this chapter.

Figure 0.1. Map of the Major Maya Sites (southern Mexico, Guatemala, Belize, Honduras, and El Salvador)

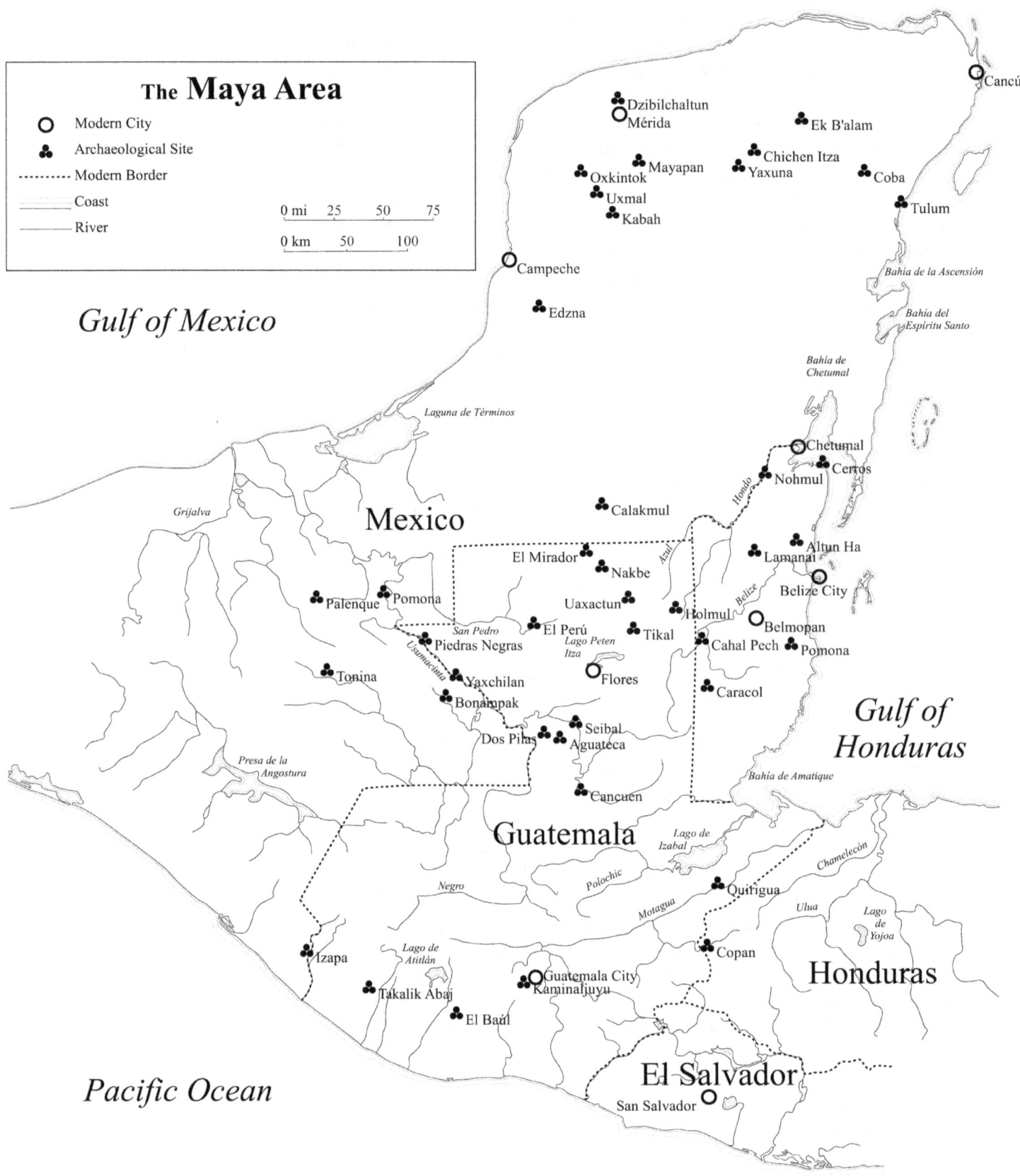

The Maya area extends from Yucatan, Mexico, to the Pacific coast of Guatemala (from north to south) and from the Isthmus of Tehuantepec to western El Salvador and Honduras (from west to east). Modern Guatemala, Belize, and Mexico contain the majority of Maya sites (**see fig. 0.1**). The geology varies from flat, karstic limestone in the north to volcanic mountains in the south. The region contains a wide variety of environments, from wetlands and rain forests to scrub brush and highlands. Most of the area is quite hot and subject to seasonal rainfall.

The Maya, like all pre-European inhabitants of the New World, are descended from northeastern Asiatic groups that entered into the Americas across the Bering Strait at the very end of the Pleistocene. Although the exact date of the first habitation of the area is not clear, evidence of human occupation dates back to the Paleoindian period (11,000–8000 BCE). This early time is characterized by nomadic hunter-gatherers, the exploitation of megafauna, and sites with only short-lived activity. The Ladyville site in modern-day Belize, for instance, has evidence of occupation before 9000 BCE, consisting of a lanceolate-shaped projectile point but no permanent structures. The Archaic period (8000–2000 BCE) witnessed a fundamental change in lifeways across Mesoamerica. During this period, there was a reduced reliance on hunting large game and an increase in exploitation of plant resources, at first by gathering and collecting. At the end of the Archaic period, we find evidence for moderate-scale maize-based agriculture, pottery, and sedentism: the basis for later Maya civilization (although the earliest evidence of maize itself currently dates back to around 5000 BCE).

The Maya, as a cultural unit, really came into being in the Preclassic (or Formative) period (2000 BCE–250 CE). Intensive maize agriculture was practiced in the Maya area from 2500 BCE. Complemented by beans and squash, maize formed the basis of the Maya physical and imagined world. A complex society was forming. Agriculture usually requires a sedentary lifestyle. Sedentism and agriculture encourage a higher population density, which in turn requires more agriculture to support itself. Groups tend to become more socially complex; some centralization is needed for better organization of the finite resources of an area. Leaders can emerge and begin to dominate societies. Societies become stratified over time, and craft specialization becomes common. As the society changed from nomadic or seminomadic to fully sedentary stratified groups, a complex culture emerged across Mesoamerica. Early pan-Mesoamerican features included linguistic similarities, a common calendar, divine rulership, and monumental architecture, among others. Major Maya sites of this time include El Mirador, Nakbe, and Kaminaljuyu, although many sites that would become large in later times were already occupied. Large towns, massive construction, ritual deposits, and complex pottery became hallmarks of the Maya culture during this time. The earliest Maya writing found so far also dates to the late Preclassic period. The site of San Bartolo, Guatemala, a rather small site in the Peten, has recently yielded recognizable Maya glyphs dating between 300 and 150 BCE. Although not yet readable, they appear to be related to later Maya writing. The Preclassic period ended with a collapse of most major sites around 100 CE. During this time, populations declined, sites were abandoned, and little or no construction took place. The major sites of the Preclassic did not recover, and new powers emerged in the Classic period.

During the Classic (250–900/1100 CE), the most recognized aspects of Maya culture flourished. The large, densely occupied sites returned, social stratification became even more pronounced, and monumental architecture became commonplace at most sites.

The rulers of this time were considered to be divine or at least in close communication with the divine. This is seen in the title *k'uhul ajaw*, "holy ruler," one of the most common epithets on Maya inscriptions. Large carved monuments were erected at many sites in this period. Traditionally the Classic was defined by the occurrence of dated stone monuments, but new dates have been found, reaching back to 37 CE (El Baúl, Stela 1) in the Maya area or 32 BCE at Tres Zapotes (Stela C). The latest dated monument is from 909 CE at Tonina (Stela 101). Major sites covered the landscape throughout this time. Many of them are well-known today, including Tikal, Calakmul, Palenque, Piedras Negras, Yaxchilan, Copan, Quirigua, Cancuen, and many more. The political interactions and relationships among these sites and their rulers were complex. Only recently have Mayanists come to understand the complicated history of the area with the aid of deciphered texts. The Classic period ended with another collapse. This transition took place over a long time, probably from the mid-700s through 900 CE. Although it did not affect all areas in exactly the same way, the collapse was associated with decreased construction, smaller populations, and the end of monumental inscriptions.

Following the Classic period came a time traditionally referred to as the Postclassic. This name is misleading, because considerable social complexity, monumental architecture, and knowledge still existed in many parts of the Maya world. Chichen Itza rose to dominate the regional landscape of the Northern Lowlands, building a trading empire. The Aztec empire in north-central Mexico was growing. The Maya area appears to have experienced a focus on long-distance trade and commerce rather than the maintenance of the divine-kingship apparatus. Although powerful rulers almost certainly existed, monuments were not built or inscribed in their honor. In some areas, rulership may have been shared by a council instead of an individual. Large sites and dense populations are still found throughout the Postclassic, but with some significant changes. The quality of art declined, although mass production increased. Classic Maya art was distinctive, but in the later period it showed a marked increase in influence from north-central Mexico. Though inscribed stone monuments were not created, writing on perishable media and murals continued to some extent. Unfortunately, much of the surviving corpus from this period was purposefully burned by the Spanish after the conquest.

0.5. A SHORT HISTORY OF MAYA DECIPHERMENT

The history of the decipherment of Maya hieroglyphic writing has been thoroughly chronicled in a number of books. The most complete account is given by Michael Coe in *Breaking the Maya Code* (1999). Coe has had personal connections and associations with many of the major players in the modern history of decipherment. The book is well written and tells a rather compelling story of the decipherment of the Maya script. The study reveals the personalities of various scholars through the recounting of major events and turning points in Maya glyph studies. I will give only a brief account of the history here, with the hope that those who are interesting in learning more will avail themselves of Coe's work. Much of the story has also been summarized by the television program *Nova*, in an episode entitled "Cracking the Maya Code," available online from the Public Broadcasting Service (http://www.pbs.org).

The history of Maya decipherment begins with the conquest of Latin America by the Spanish in the 1500s. Missionaries who accompanied the conquistadors recorded important contact-period observations of the indigenous culture. The goal was not to support and preserve the culture but rather to subvert it. With a greater knowledge of their culture, the friars thought, it would be easier to convert the local inhabitants to Christianity. One such missionary was Fray Diego de Landa (1524–79), a Franciscan friar and later bishop of Yucatan. Landa is both a hero and villain in the history of decipherment. As friar of Izamal, Yucatan, he was responsible for the rounding up and burning of all indigenous manuscripts or codices. He later described this infamous event: "We found a large number of books in their letters and because they had nothing in which there was not superstition and lies of the devil, we burned them all, which they regretted to an amazing degree and which caused them sorrow" (Sharer and Traxler 2006: 126, quoting Landa 1938).

In 1562, after fifteen years in Izamal, Landa was recalled to Spain to account for his actions, which some authorities found to be overzealous. During this time in Spain, he wrote *Relación de las cosas de Yucatán* (A Relation of the Things of Yucatan: Landa 1938). This book-length defense of his actions describes the "idolatrous" practices of the local Yucatecans as justification. Although Landa destroyed perhaps thousands of irreplaceable manuscripts, he did provide one of the best descriptions of indigenous life shortly after conquest, including religious and ritual practices. Furthermore, he recorded what would turn out to be the Rosetta Stone of Maya decipherment. In an interview with a high-ranking Maya named Juan Nachi Cocom, Landa solicited what he called an "A, B, C" of the Maya writing system. Unfortunately, his manuscript was not recognized for what it was for nearly 300 years.

In the meantime, a number of explorers crisscrossed the Maya area, discovering sites and publishing descriptions and drawings of monuments. The enigmatic "Count" Jean-Frédéric Maximilien de Waldeck (1766?–1875) drew dramatic versions of the monuments of Palenque in the 1830s. Waldeck claimed that he was a member of the nobility, of French and British ancestry, and had fathered a son at the age of eighty-four. The only sure thing about his life, aside from his visit to Palenque, is that he died in Paris in 1875 (supposedly from turning his head too fast to observe a passing woman). John Lloyd Stephens (1805–52) and Frederick Catherwood (1799–1854) explored many sites in their two popular travel books *Incidents of Travel in Central America, Chiapas, and Yucatan* (1841) and *Incidents of Travel in Yucatan* (1843). Catherwood's hyperaccurate drawings of monuments and sites (aided by a camera lucida) were the best representations to date. Stephens explored many ruined sites, describing and mapping them in great detail. He also correctly mused that the glyphs were historical in nature and lamented that they could not yet be read. Importantly, Stephens recognized the local inhabitants as the descendants of the builders of the ruins. Many other academics of the time believed that the sites represented the cities of the lost tribes of Israel, Phoenicians, Atlanteans, or Hindus.

In 1864 Abbé Charles-Étienne Brasseur de Bourbourg (1814–74) discovered an abridged copy of Landa's *Relación* in a royal archive. Fifty-four years earlier, Alexander von Humbolt had published five pages of a codex, one of the three remaining preconquest Maya documents. Constantine Samuel Rafinesque (1783–1840) deduced the numeral system from these saved books (which were probably loot from the conquest) and meager publications, and Ernst Förstemann (1822–1906) identified astronomical calculations. Although a number of people attempted to read the codices using Landa's alphabet, including Brasseur de Bourbourg and Léon de Rosny, no real progress was made.

In the mid-1900s decipherment began to yield fruitful results. John Eric Sydney Thompson (1898–1975) published *Maya Hieroglyphic Writing: An Introduction* in 1950. This monumental volume argued forcefully that Maya writing was not phonetic; each sign was endowed with meaning independent of language. Thompson was an expert in Maya culture, iconography, and archaeology. His arguments were vehement and sometimes vitriolic. He viewed the Maya as peaceful stargazers in a society devoted to ritual and time-worship, all of which was recorded on their monuments and books. Thompson harshly disapproved of any arguments for phoneticism or historical content in the inscriptions. It was no surprise that he reacted strongly when a young Soviet scholar, Yuri Valentinovich Knorozov (1922–99), published a paper in 1952 purporting to read signs in the Dresden Codex phonetically. Thompson refuted Knorozov's hypothesis on methodological, academic, and politically ideological grounds. Knorozov was a trained linguist and had worked with Chinese and Japanese writing. During World War II, he discovered a book in Berlin, which contained line drawings of the three known Maya codices and a suggestion that these codices were impossible to read. Using Landa's alphabet, Knorozov made the observation that the system might be syllabic, not alphabetic: one sign might represent a consonant-vowel combination (similar to Japanese). When Landa had asked Juan Nachi Cocom to write the sign for the letter *b*, he had instead written the sign for the sound *be*; *m* was written with two signs, *e-me*, approximating the Spanish pronunciation of the letter: *eme*. Using this logic and a Yucatec dictionary, Knozorov was able to find spellings such as *tzu-lu* near a picture of a dog (*tzul* in Yucatec). He correctly surmised that the last vowel of words spelled in this way was unpronounced, as most Maya words ended with consonants.

Because of Thompson's strength of personality and reputation, Knorozov's breakthrough was only adopted by a few. Another scholar was able to change Thompson's mind about the content of the inscriptions, however. Tatiana Proskouriakoff (1909–85) was Russian by birth but had emigrated to the United States with her family when she was six. As an architect with the Peabody Museum's project at Piedras Negras, she became interested in a strange pattern of dates on the inscriptions of the site. A series of large stone monuments at Piedras Negras all followed a similar pattern: a seated individual framed by an inscription. She noticed that three glyphs were repeated on each monument in the same order. Furthermore, the last date on one monument coincided with the middle date on another. Proskouriakoff therefore suggested that the last date on each monument recorded the death of the ruler. The middle date on another monument recorded the ascension of the new ruler (always soon after the death of the previous ruler), and the first date must record his birth. She was able to trace the dynasty of Piedras Negras. At first Thompson opposed her argument, but he quickly realized that she was right and lent her his full support.

After Thompson's death in 1975, more scholars openly employed Knorozov's method and hypothesis. Most notably, a series of meetings at the site of Palenque (Palenque Round Tables) improved on Knorozov's readings and traced the lineage of the rulers of Palenque over a number of years. Linda Schele (1942–98) emerged from this group as a charismatic leader in the field. An art instructor by training, she worked tirelessly to advance the decipherment of Maya hieroglyphs. She started the University of Texas Maya Meeting workshops and influenced many modern experts. Unfortunately, she died of cancer at an early age. Today the field is dominated by a few well-known individuals, although the number of proficient epigraphers throughout the world is growing. David

Stuart (1965–) is probably the most famous Maya epigrapher today. He was introduced to glyphs at a young age as the son of another prominent Mayanist and has published scores of influential articles and books; he currently teaches at the University of Texas at Austin. Stephen Houston (1958–) is another leading figure in Maya epigraphy. After first working in the Maya area as a researcher at the Peabody Museum at Yale, he is now a professor at Brown University. Nikolai Grube is a German researcher responsible for a number of important decipherments and is the co-author of *Chronicle of the Maya Kings and Queens;* he teaches at the University of Bonn, Germany. Other prominent figures in the world of epigraphy today include Alfonso Lacadena, Simon Martin, Marc Zender, Michael Coe, John Robertson, Barbara MacLeod, Matt Looper, Robert Wald, David Mora-Marín, Victoria Bricker, John Justeson, Terrence Kaufman, Martha Macri, Søren Wichmann, Eric Boot, Stanley Gunter, Alexandre Tokovinine, Markus Eberl, Harri Kettunen, Christophe Helmke, and many, many more. The modern world of Maya epigraphy is a difficult one to enter. The discussions of the most current subjects are often highly specialized, and reference materials are not commonly available to the lay audience. These scholars have published the most up-to-date thoughts on Maya epigraphy and are responsible for many of the major discoveries and advances of the last few decades. This book attempts to present the current state of the field as defined by these experts.

0.6. WHERE GLYPHS ARE ENCOUNTERED

Hieroglyphs are most commonly found on three media. The most imposing are the large stone monuments known as **stelae** (singular **stela**). Ranging in height from one or two to five or six meters, these monuments often are covered in writing, especially on the sides and back. They were erected by the ancient Maya to commemorate major historical events, such as the birth, ascension, and death of royalty; the ending of major calendar periods; the defeat or success of military campaigns; and many more occasions. The writing on stelae is carved into the stone. It is currently thought that scribes painted guidelines on the monuments before masons etched the words into stone (we have found half-completed stelae with faint traces of these lines). The glyph forms found here are less fluid than glyphs found on other media, as is true in stone-carving around the world. The information inscribed on stelae is formal. The majority of examples in this book are drawn from carved monuments and stelae.

Hieroglyphic texts are also found on pottery. Technically speaking, painted glyphs are not inscriptions, which by definition must be carved into a background medium, but the term "inscription" is often used to describe any hieroglyphic text. Pottery was primarily decorated with paint, producing more fluid and calligraphic texts. Although stelae may have also been painted, that does not seem to be the primary means of decoration. The painted texts on pottery can contain more personal and informal information than is found on large public monuments. We find many individual names and even dialog on painted vessels. One commonly found text is the Primary Standard Sequence, which is a formula that describes the vessel, the type of food or beverage that it contained, the name of the owner, and even the name of the person who made it. Texts on pottery are often accompanied by beautifully painted scenes from ancient Maya court life or mythology. We will look at a few examples of texts from pottery in this book as well.

The ancient Maya also wrote on books, called **codices** (singular **codex**) by Maya scholars. Only three undisputed examples of these fig-bark books are known to exist today. They are known as the Dresden Codex, Paris Codex, and Madrid Codex, each taking its name from the city in which it is stored. These remaining books are divinatory almanacs, probably used by Maya priests to forecast astrological and astronomical events. Many more books existed when the first Europeans entered the New World, but they were burned by Diego de Landa in the mid-1500s. Like the pottery texts, glyphs in codices were painted. A thin layer of fine plaster was applied to the fig-bark paper to make a smooth, white writing surface (just as modern magazines utilize kaolin, a compound found in porcelain, to achieve their glossy texture). Some pottery is even decorated in what is called "codex style": the format of the scene and text on the pottery is similar to the known codex format and style. It is sad to think of the history and cultural information lost in the burning of the codices. Even with our current understanding of hieroglyphic writing, only a small portion of the texts remain: those that were carved or painted on nonperishable or incombustible materials.

A number of other media carry hieroglyphic texts. Like stelae, carved monuments and panels are stone tablets with inscriptions and scenes. Stucco can also be carved to bear inscriptions. Murals are often accompanied by painted glyphs describing the people and actions in the scenes. Painted texts can be found on the walls of tombs or other protected spaces. Lintels made of wood or stone, sometimes covered with plaster, often had inscriptions covering their downward-facing surface. Small objects carry "name tag" inscriptions, identifying their owner and purpose.

Many published resources are available to scholars looking for inscriptions (see Further Reading at the end of this chapter), including *The Corpus of Maya Hieroglyphic Inscriptions*, published by Harvard University's Peabody Museum (1975–present). Drawings can also be found online, at sites such as the Foundation for the Advancement of Mesoamerican Studies Incorporated (http://www.famsi.org), the European Association of Mayanists (http://wayeb.org), and the Corpus Project at Harvard University's Peabody Museum (http://www.peabody.harvard.edu/CMHI/index.php). The amount of inscriptions accessible on the Internet represents a quantum leap beyond what was available to scholars only fifteen years ago.

FURTHER READING

Maya Culture and History

Coe, Michael D.
2011   *The Maya*. 8th edition. New York: Thames and Hudson.

Demarest, Arthur
2004   *Ancient Maya: The Rise and Fall of a Rainforest Civilization*. Cambridge: Cambridge University Press.

Hammond, Norman
1988   *Ancient Maya Civilization*. New Brunswick, N.J.: Rutgers University Press.

Houston, Stephen D., and Takeshi Inomata
2009   *The Classic Maya*. Cambridge: Cambridge University Press.

Martin, Simon, and Nikolai Grube
2008 *Chronicle of the Maya Kings and Queens.* 2nd edition. New York: Thames and Hudson.

Schele, Linda, and David Freidel
1990 *A Forest of Kings: The Untold Story of the Ancient Maya.* New York: William Morrow and Company.

Sharer, Robert J., and Loa P. Traxler
2006 *The Ancient Maya.* 6th edition. Stanford, Calif.: Stanford University Press.

Maya Decipherment

Coe, Michael D.
1999 *Breaking the Maya Code.* Revised edition. New York: Thames and Hudson, New York.

Pope, Maurice
1999 *The Story of Decipherment: From Egyptian Hieroglyphs to Maya Script.* New York: Thames and Hudson.

Robinson, Andrew
1985 *Lost Languages: The Enigma of the World's Undeciphered Scripts.* New York: McGraw-Hill.

Maya Hieroglyphs and Iconography

Coe, Michael D., and Mark Van Stone
2005 *Reading the Maya Glyphs.* 2nd edition. New York: Thames and Hudson.

Marcus, Joyce
1992 *Mesoamerican Writing Systems: Propaganda, Myth, and History in Four Ancient Civilizations.* Princeton, N.J.: Princeton University Press.

Montgomery, John
2002 *How to Read Maya Hieroglyphs.* New York: Hippocrene Books, Inc.

Schele, Linda, and Mary Ellen Miller
1986 *The Blood of Kings: Dynasty and Ritual in Maya Art.* New York: George Braziller; Fort Worth: Kimbell Art Museum.

Stone, Andrea, and Marc Zender
2011 *Reading Maya Art: A Hieroglyphic Guide to Ancient Maya Painting and Sculpture.* London: Thames and Hudson.

Stuart, David
2005 *The Inscriptions from Temple XIX at Palenque.* San Francisco: Pre-Columbian Art Research Institute.

Wichmann, Søren (editor)
2004 *The Linguistics of Maya Writing.* Salt Lake City: University of Utah Press.

1. THE NATURE OF THE SCRIPT

Maya hieroglyphic writing is a regular and comprehensible system. What may at first appear to be a confusing morass of symbols becomes clear when it is divided into its constituent parts. This book takes a divide-and-conquer approach to understanding the hieroglyphs because it is the easiest and most methodical way to learn a system that may seem impossibly foreign. The best place to start is with the basics. This chapter describes how to divide a Maya text into individual glyphs in the correct reading order. It then explains the different types of glyphs and how they function in the script. Finally, it shows a systematic way to convert a Maya inscription into the Latin alphabet. Examples occur throughout this chapter, with corresponding exercises. By tackling each section one at a time, you should be able to move on to actual text analysis and translation in short order.

1.1. GLYPH BLOCKS

A **glyph block** is a discrete group of glyphs that constitutes an entire word or verb phrase. These blocks are set apart graphically as a square or rectangle, as seen in **figure 1.1**. In some instances, especially on pottery, they may have a more rounded or free-form shape. Glyph blocks are easy to differentiate from one another because of the space between them. Furthermore, glyphs that make up glyph blocks appear to be attached to one another. The blocks are laid out in a grid-like pattern. Although there are exceptions to every rule in Maya writing, these conventions are generally followed.

Maya epigraphers have devised a standard labeling system for inscriptions in order to specify particular glyph blocks. Because glyph blocks create a grid system, they are labeled much like sectors on a map. Across the top of an inscription, each column is labeled from left to right in ascending alphabetical order: A, B, C, and so on. Each row is labeled from top to bottom in ascending numerical order: 1, 2, 3, and so forth. Thus any glyph can be identified by referring to its column letter and row number: B2, for instance, is the glyph block located in the second column from the left and second row from the top. Sometimes a monument has more than one contiguous inscription. In this case, the main inscription is labeled first and independent glyph blocks or inscriptions are labeled second. The same letter (column label) cannot be used more than once on the same monument, even if the inscriptions on the monument are separate or appear on different sides. If the inscription contains more than twenty-six columns, the letters continue with A', B', C', and so on. Numbers (row labels), however, are started anew for each new contiguous glyph block.

Figure 1.1 shows schematic inscriptions. Each square represents one glyph block. As you can see, the letters across the top label each column and the numbers along the left-hand side label each row. Each block is individually labeled with its alphanumeric position, which can be used to identify a particular glyph. Notice that the numbers start over at one for the supplementary inscription to the bottom right of the top inscription, but the letters do not repeat.

Figure 1.2 is a real inscription from Palenque's Hieroglyphic Stairway. The columns are labeled from A to D and the rows from one to six. There are clear spaces between all of the glyph blocks, emphasized by lines in this example. The glyphs within each block appear to be stuck together. Internal divisions are visible in a few of the blocks (such as B5 and D3), but they are still considered part of the overall glyph block because of the general lack of space between these divisions.

Now it is time for you to try to identify and separate glyph blocks. **Exercise 1.1** features a schematic, theoretical representation of an inscription. In this case, it is relatively easy to divide the inscription into discrete blocks: label the columns and rows accordingly in **exercise 1.1.1**. The next two exercises come from real inscriptions. **Exercise 1.2** represents Stela 3 at Piedras Negras, which describes events in the life of one of the site's important historical figures (see chapter 6). Try to separate the glyph blocks and to label each row and column correctly in **exercise 1.2.1**. **Exercise 1.3** comes from the Tablet of 96 Glyphs at the site of Palenque, one of the most beautiful examples of Maya hieroglyphic writing. Unfortunately, the tablet was broken when a worker's pickax hit it during excavation. Just as in the first two exercises, try to delineate the glyph blocks and to label each row and column. These inscriptions and others are used as exercises throughout the book.

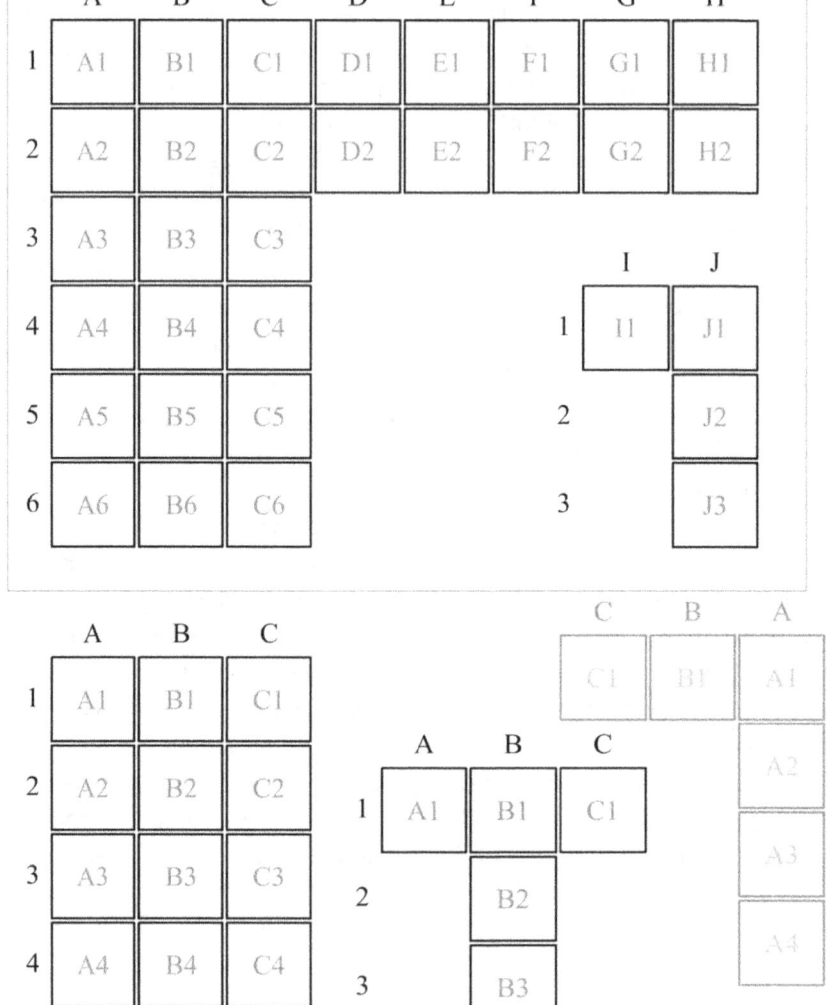

Figure 1.1. Traditional Labeling Scheme for Glyph Blocks (ascending letters for columns from left to right, ascending numbers for rows from top to bottom)

Figure 1.2. Glyph Blocks from Palenque, Hieroglyphic Stairway (rows and columns labeled according to accepted epigraphic conventions, with added lines demarcating the glyph blocks)

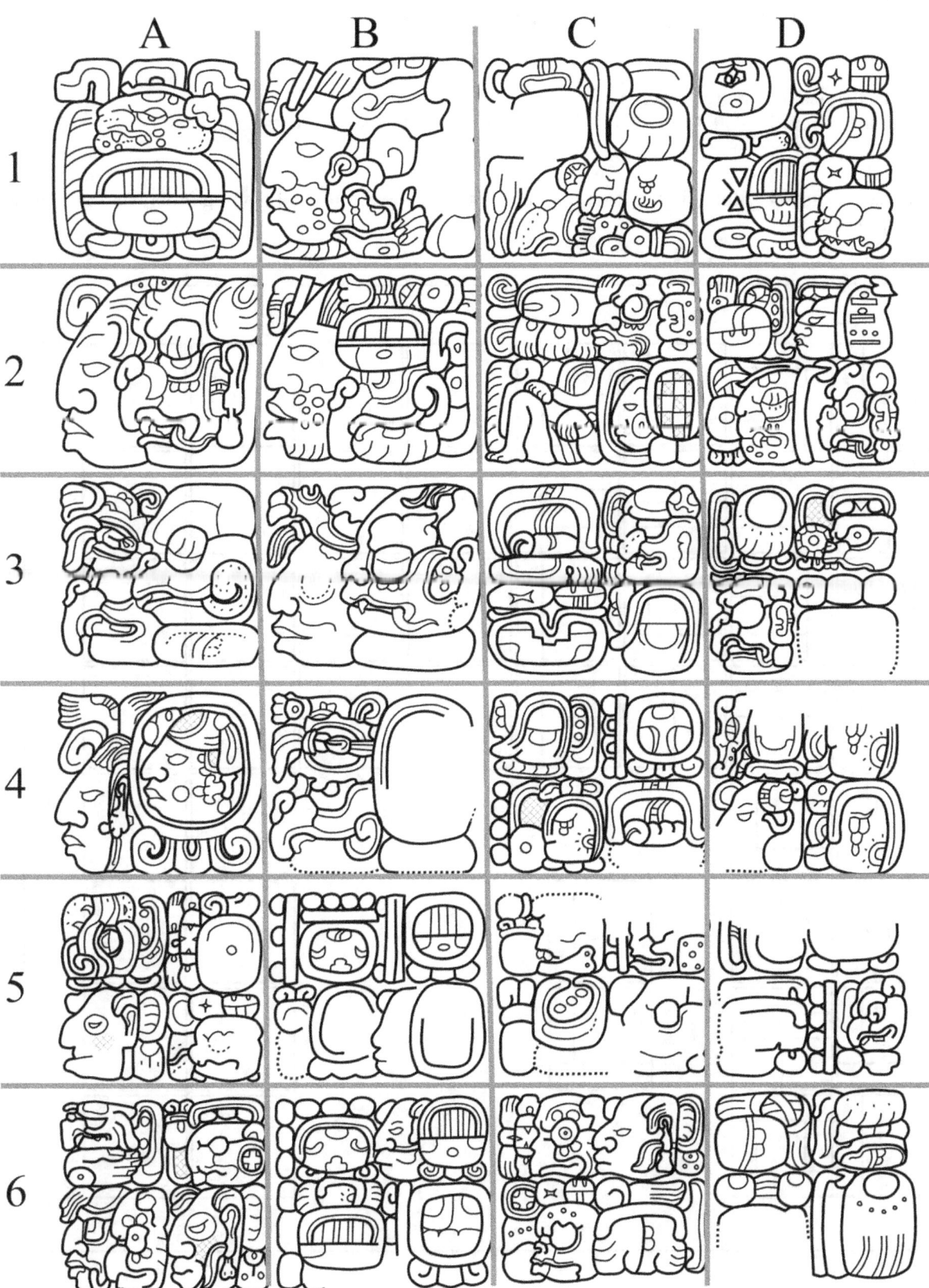

18 THE NATURE OF THE SCRIPT

Exercise 1.1. Schematic Depiction of Glyph Blocks

Exercise 1.1.1
1. Label each row and column according to accepted conventions.

Exercise 1.1.2
1. Draw lines delineating "paired columns."
2. Using numbers from 1 to 50, label the reading order of glyph blocks; circle the numbers.

Exercise 1.1.3
1. Number each segment within the first four columns with the correct internal reading order; start at 1 in each new glyph block.

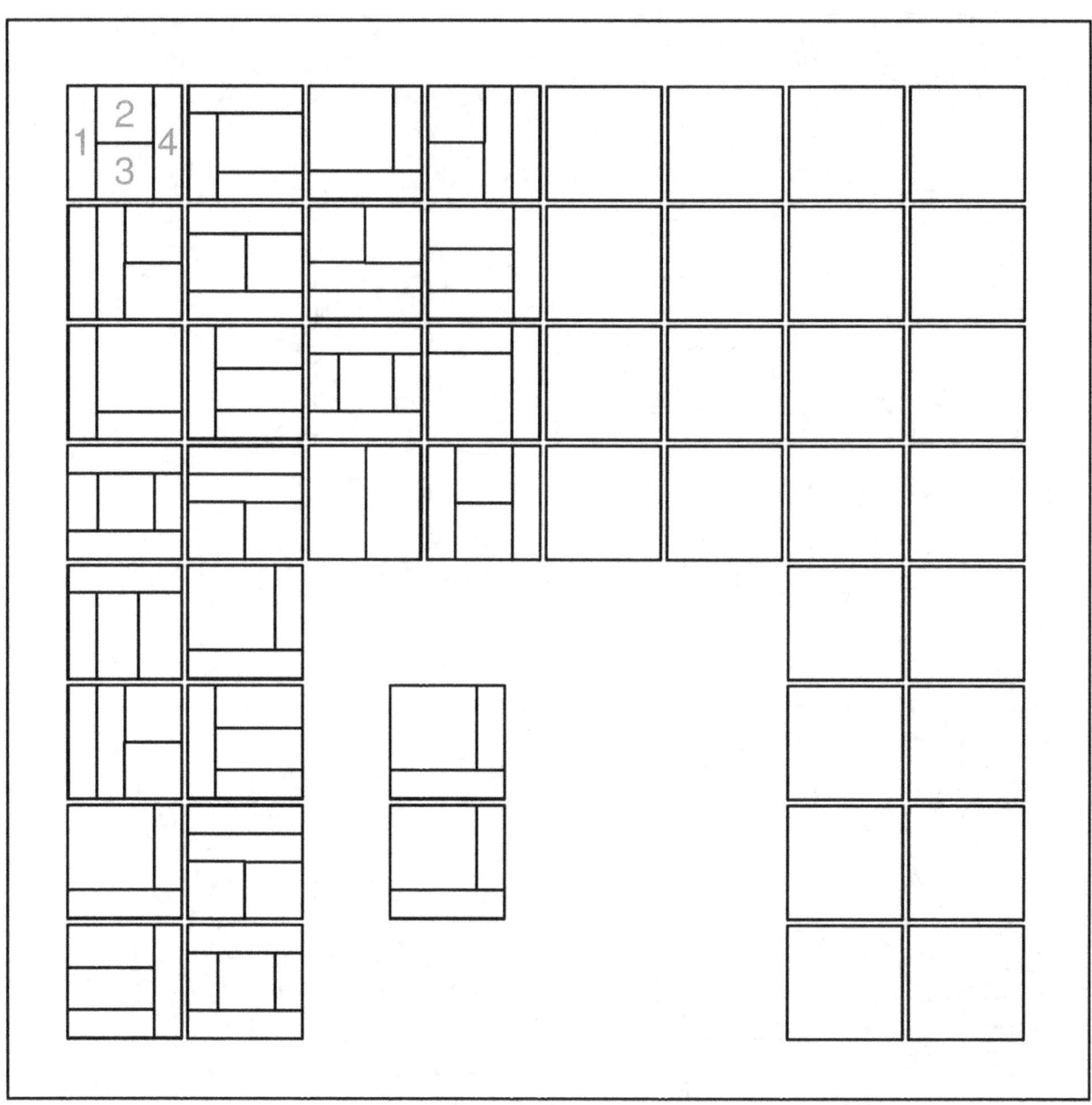

1.1. GLYPH BLOCKS

Exercise 1.2. Piedras Negras, Stela 3

Exercise 1.2.1
1. Draw a square around each glyph block.
2. Label each row and column according to accepted conventions.

Exercise 1.2.2
1. Draw lines delineating "paired columns."
2. Using numbers from 1 to 48, label the reading order of glyph blocks; circle the numbers.

Exercise 1.2.3
1. Number each segment within the glyph blocks enlarged on the right with the correct internal reading order.

Note: I have highlighted the glyph divisions with thick border lines and thin internal lines.

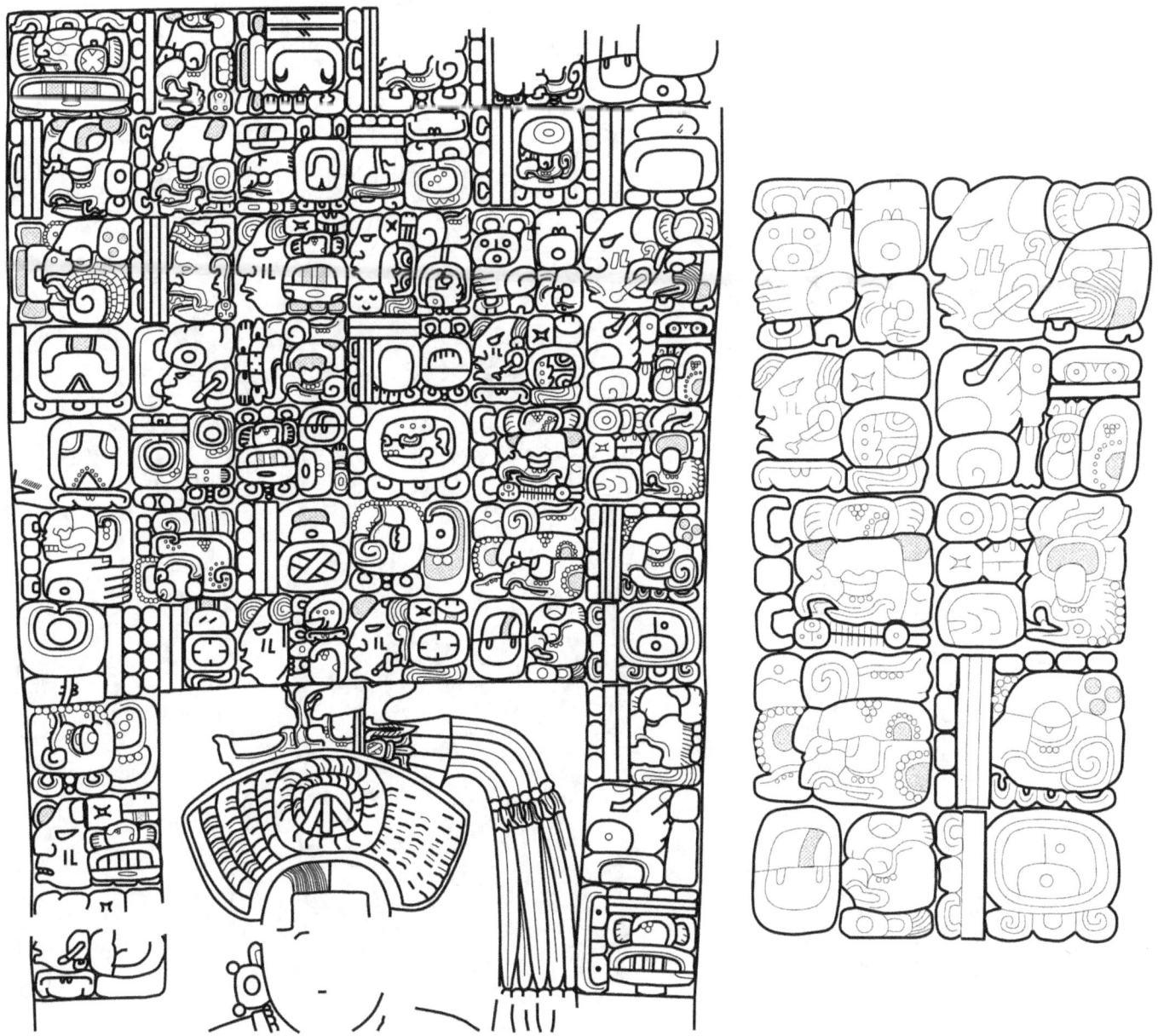

Exercise 1.3. Palenque, Tablet of the 96 Glyphs

Exercise 1.3.1
1. Draw a square around each glyph block.
2. Label each row and column according to accepted conventions.

Exercise 1.3.2
1. Draw lines delineating "paired columns."
2. Using numbers from 1 to 96, label the reading order of glyph blocks; circle the numbers.

Exercise 1.3.3
1. In the boxes on the right, draw and label twelve syllables found in this inscription.

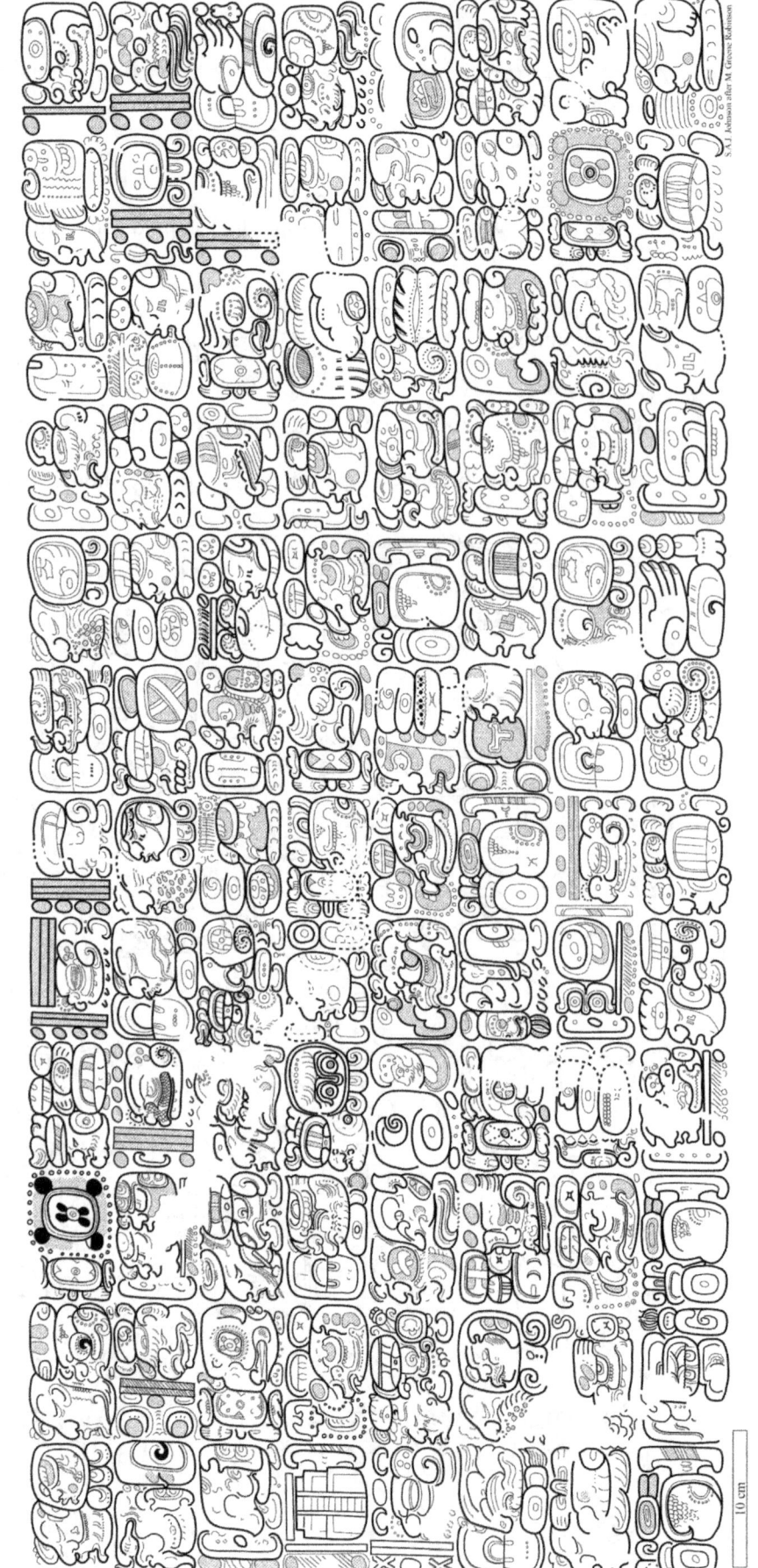

1.2. READING ORDER WITHIN AN INSCRIPTION

Inscriptions are generally laid out in contiguous sections of glyph blocks in a systematic fashion. Over time, the reading order of glyph blocks and individual glyphs will become second nature to you. Anywhere from one to several hundred glyphs can be strung together to record historical or mythical events. A monument may display a single inscription or a number of separate inscriptions. The largest and most prominent inscription (hereafter called the **main inscription**) may contain the principal calendrical information and prominent events. If a scene is depicted on the monument, a number of smaller inscriptions (**supplementary inscriptions**) are often embedded within the scene. These inscriptions frequently bear the name and titles of the person who appears closest to the inscription. In the vast majority of cases, the script is read from left to right and from top to bottom.

Although the overall shape of inscriptions may vary, they are internally divided into paired columns of glyph blocks. A vertical line can be placed after every other column, pairing the first and second, third and fourth, fifth and sixth, and so on. Starting at the top left of the inscription, the first glyph block (usually A1) is read, followed by the block to the right (B1), before moving down and to the left one block (A2) and continuing the zigzag motion down the paired columns. At the bottom of the pair of columns, the inscription continues at the top left of the next pair of columns and proceeds as before (**see fig. 1.3 and 1.4: C1, D1, C2**, and so on).

Sometimes the inscription contains an odd number of columns, resulting in a final column without a pair. In this case, the glyphs in the single column are simply read straight down. Although this often happens in a final column, it can also happen in the middle of the inscription when a text frames a scene (as shown in **fig. 1.3**), creating a "T" or inverted-"L" shape. Instances of right-to-left writing in Maya hieroglyphs are exceptionally rare and easy to identify. Common head-variant glyphs (discussed in section 1.3) always face into the reading order: if heads are facing to the left, you read from left to right. As noted, there are exceptions to every rule. But do not be daunted. The vast majority of inscriptions are regular and relatively transparent in their layout. Over time, it becomes easier to deal with irregular and novel inscriptions.

Figure 1.5 shows the inscription from the Hieroglyphic Stairway at Palenque again, highlighting the correct reading order of the glyph blocks with a zigzag arrow. Please delineate the double columns in **exercises 1.1.2 and 1.2.2**. Then label the reading order of each glyph block, starting at the upper left for each inscription. Remember that single lines are read straight down and supplementary inscriptions are read second.

Figure 1.3. Reading Order of Glyph Blocks and Separated Block Pairs

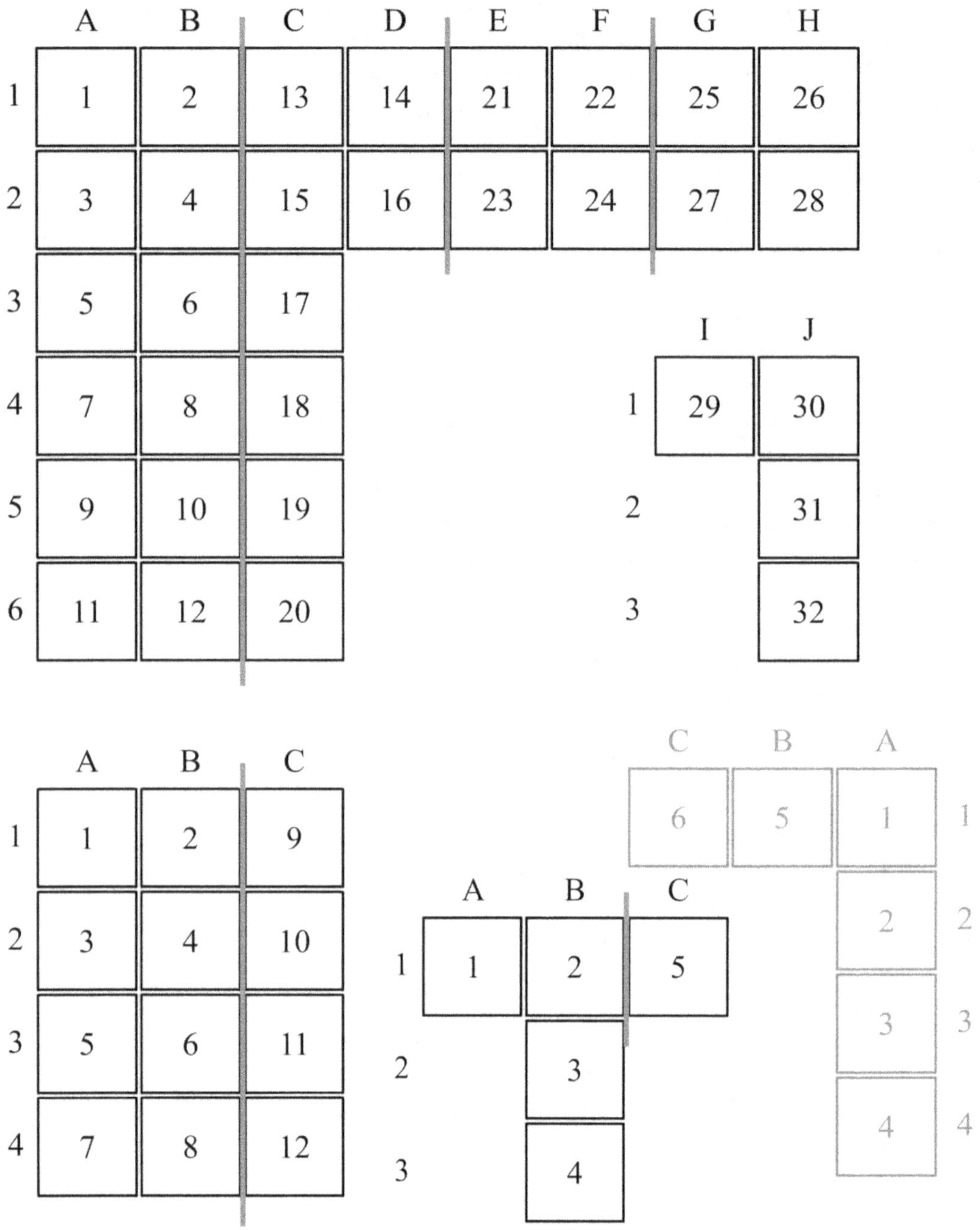

1.2. READING ORDER WITHIN AN INSCRIPTION   23

Figure 1.4. Schematic Depiction of Proper Reading Order of Glyph Blocks

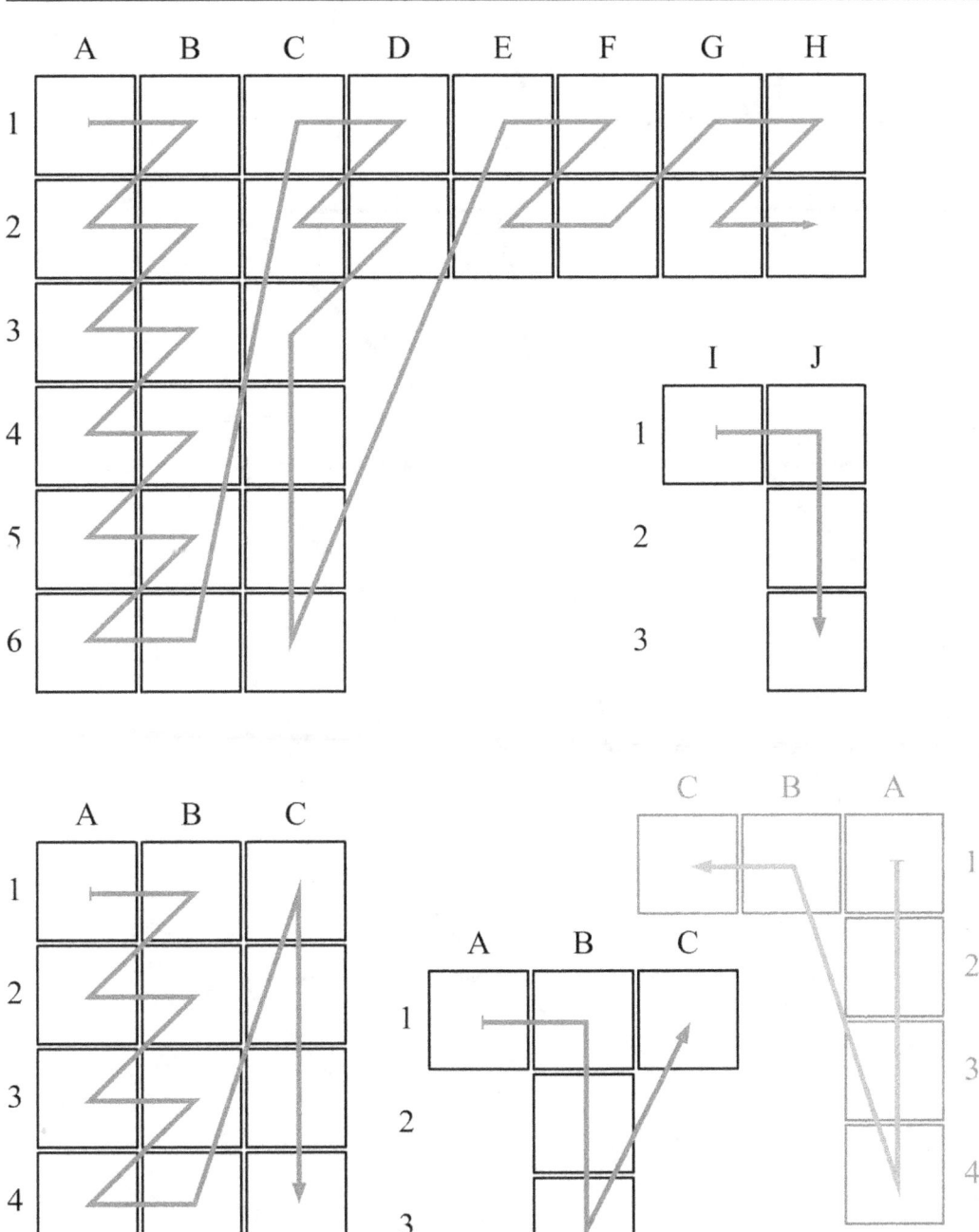

Figure 1.5. Reading Order of the Inscription from Palenque, Hieroglyphic Stairway (indicated by the arrow below)

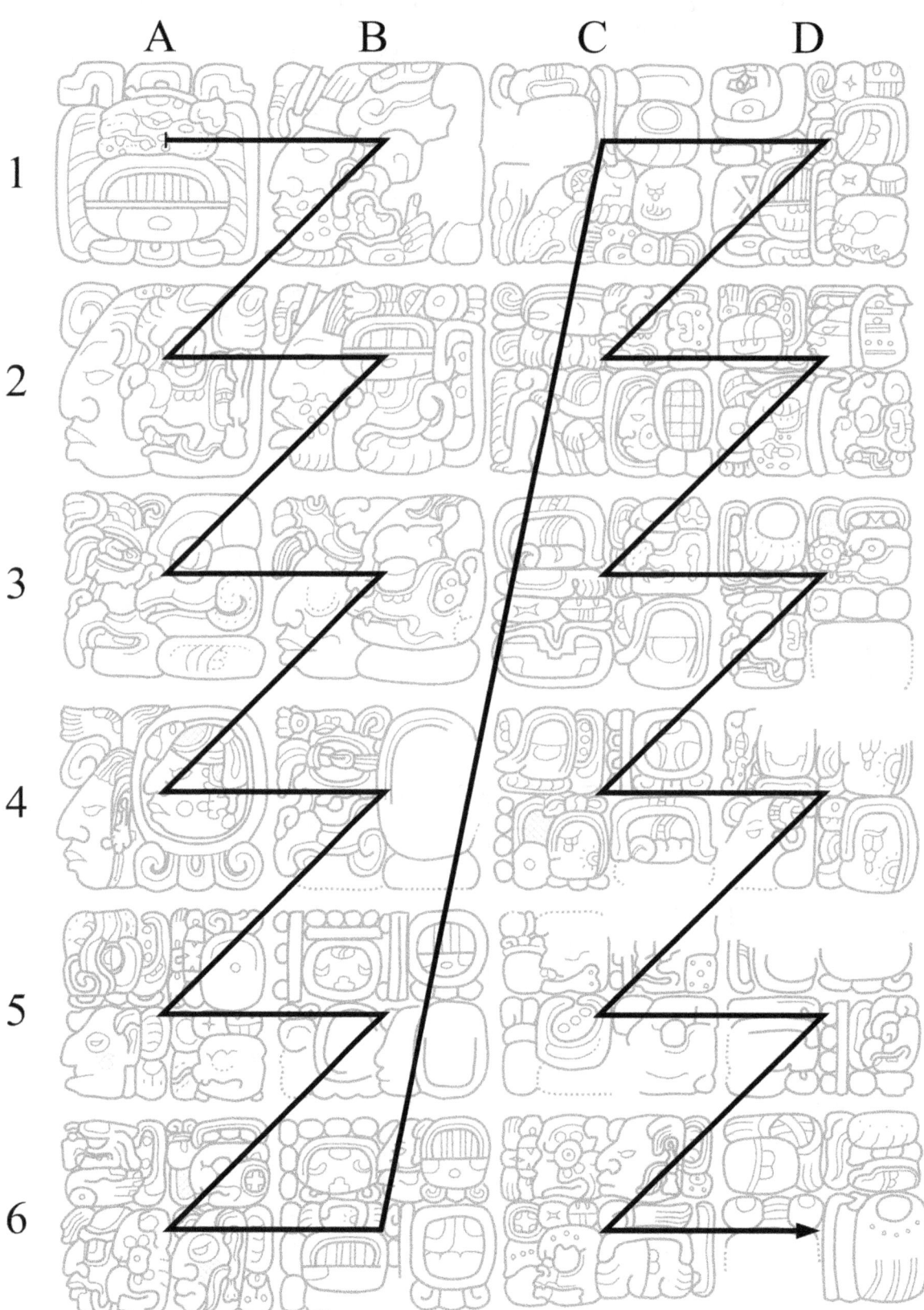

1.3. READING ORDER WITHIN A GLYPH BLOCK

To talk about the reading order within a glyph block, it is necessary to become familiar with the conventions and nomenclature describing the glyphs that make up any given block. There are two main categories of signs: main signs and affixes. A **main sign** is the large, square glyph (or glyphs) that appears to be the focus of a glyph block. These signs are twice as big as the smaller, rectangular affixes. Main signs can be nouns, root verbs, numbers, adjectives, adverbs, or phonetic signs. Abstract main signs do not resemble any readily apparent object. Other main signs, such as the **PAKAL**, "shield," sign, depict the item they represent. Another set of main signs is known as **head variants,** which appear to be the personification of the represented word. The **TUN**, "stone," head variant, for instance, resembles a monster with fissures and iconography identical to that of mountains and caves represented in Maya art.

An **affix** is a smaller, rectangular glyph that appears to be attached to the main sign (**fig. 1.6**). An affix to the left of the main sign and oriented vertically is called a **prefix**. A horizontal affix located above the main sign is a **superfix**. A horizontal affix located below the main sign is a **subfix**. A vertically oriented affix to the right of the main sign is a **postfix**. Finally, an **infix** is a sign (either an affix or a main sign) placed inside the boundaries of a main sign. Similarly, in a **conflation** two glyphs are melded together and appear inseparable. This differs from an infix, where one glyph is simply reduced and placed whole within another glyph. **Figure 1.7** shows a number of common conflations and infixes. Affixes can be nouns, numbers, verbs, prepositions, pronouns, verbal suffixes, phonetic signs, and a whole host of other parts of speech. Although a glyph block could consist solely of affixes, it usually contains a main sign. Note also that affixes have main sign equivalents that are interchangeable, depending on the scribe's preference. Some of the common equivalent affixes and main signs are shown in **figure 1.8**. Think of it as capital and lowercase letters: "HoUSe," "hoUsE," and "hOusE" all spell "house," with variant signs. Because of the flexibility and free-form nature of hieroglyphic signs, scribes could vary the inscription to suit their aesthetic tastes. Maya scribes are well known for their virtuosity and inventiveness. Unfortunately, this may make sign identification difficult for beginners. Try labeling the type of sign (main sign, prefix, postfix, superfix, or subfix) found in each of the glyph blocks in **exercise 1.4.1**, an excerpt from Piedras Negras, Stela 3.

Maya scribes often substituted a smaller affix to represent the larger main sign, which made it possible to represent words in a variety of ways. One important principle is **pars pro toto,** which literally means "part for the whole" in Latin. A small part of the main sign can be used to stand for the complete meaning. This is similar to an abbreviation in English: "no." commonly stands for the complete word "number." **Figure 1.8** shows common affix–main sign equivalents. It is clear that many affixes use a small part of the main sign (usually a head variant) to represent the whole, often by exaggerating or enlarging this part. The scribe can also represent a whole idea through **truncation**, where a part of the main sign is cut off and used as a free affix. A **reduction** simply scales the main sign down into a smaller affix. These principles allow for a flexible representation of any Maya word but also make life more complicated for the epigrapher. Instead of learning one sign that stands for the sound *u,* epigraphers must be aware of the dozen or so signs that can represent it. Although the signs are all graphically distinct, they often have a common distinguishing feature.

Figure 1.6. Reading Order within a Glyph Block and Common Labels

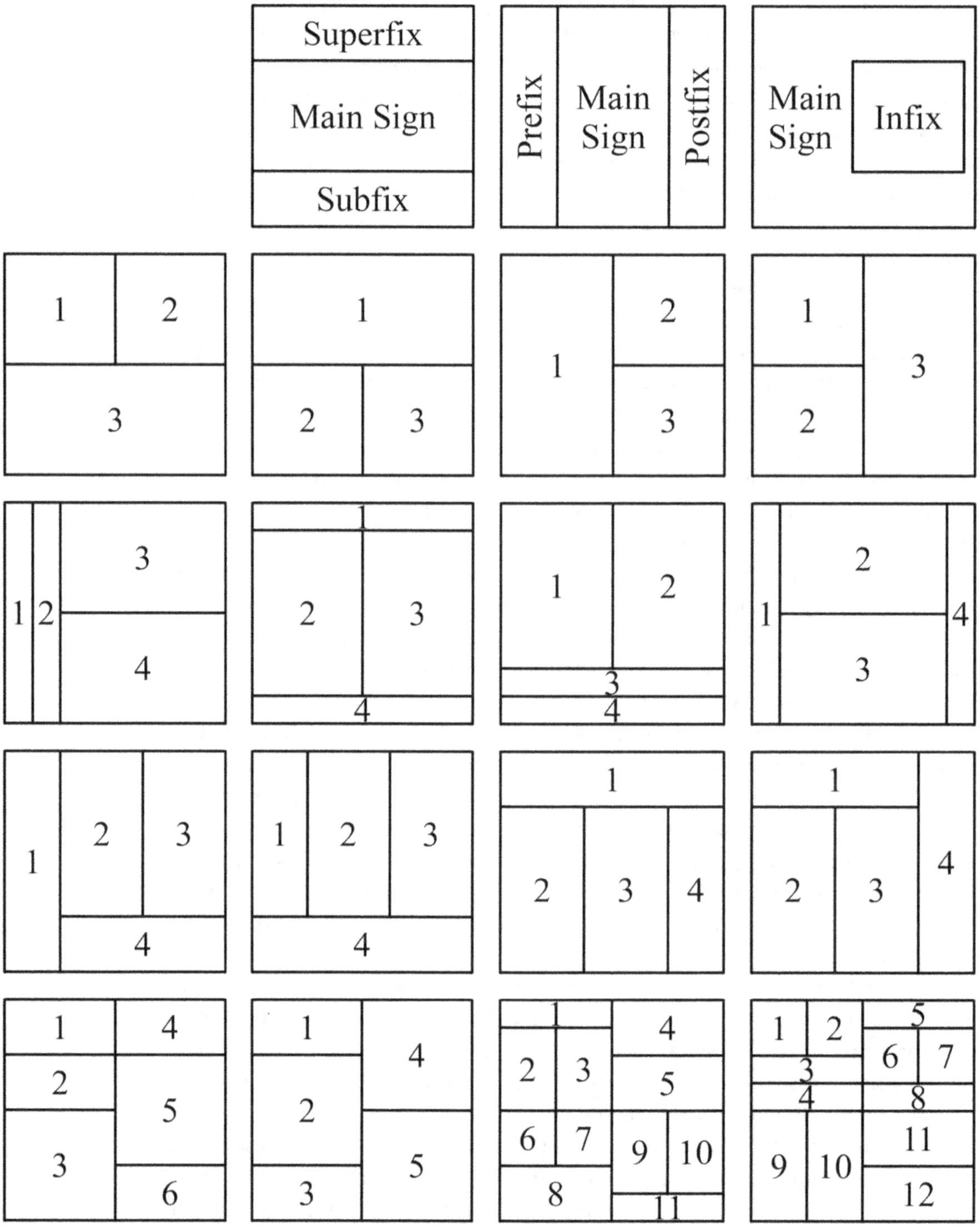

Figure 1.7. Combinations, Conflations, and Infixes

Combinations

CH'AK-ka
ch'ak
chop

Conflations

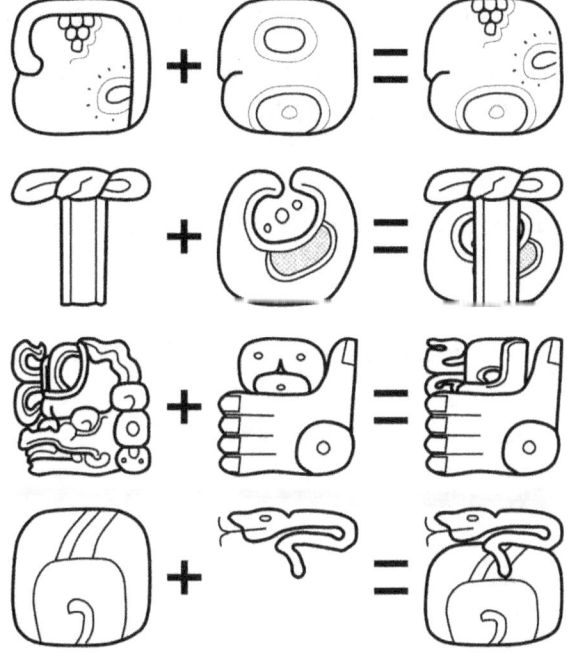

CHUM-TUN
chum tuun
stone seating

JOY-ja
johyaj
is encircled/bound

CH'AM-K'AWIL
ch'am k'awiil
grasp [the] K'awil [scepter]

LOK-yi
lokiiy
emerged already/after

Infixes

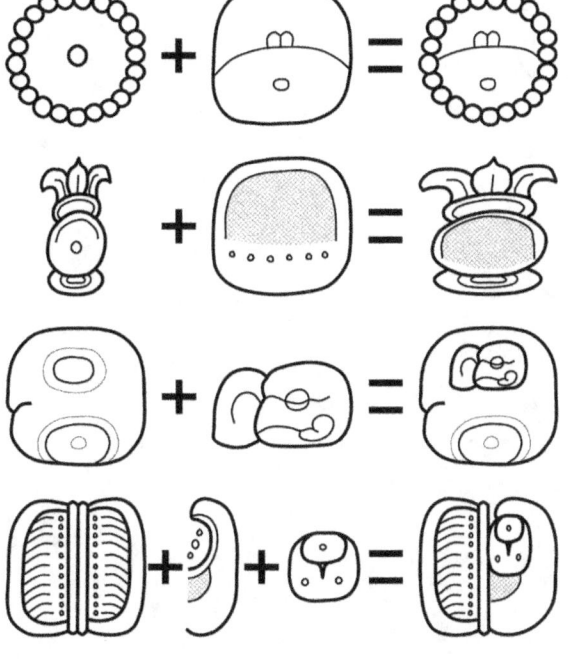

mo[lo]
mol
Mol (month name)

tz'a[pa]
tz'ap
plant, erect

CHUM[mu]
chum
seat

sa-ja[la]
sajal
sajal (subordinate title)

28 THE NATURE OF THE SCRIPT

Because of the visual complexity and variability of Maya inscriptions, epigraphers needed a consistent way to transcribe glyphic inscriptions into a Western script. This happened before the phonetic nature of the Maya script was understood. Hence numbers (instead of a transcribed pronunciation) were employed to represent each glyph. The most widely used system was developed by J. E. S. Thompson and outlined in *A Catalog of Maya Hieroglyphs* (1962). Thompson numbers affixes from 1 to 500, main signs from 501 to 999, and head variants (or "portraits" as he calls them) from 1,000 to 1,299. He prefaced each number with "T-," and they are still called "T-Numbers." Although we now know that some variants of a single number are entirely different glyphs and other glyphs that he considers separate are in fact variations of the same glyph, this system still enjoys widespread use. Thompson's glyph drawings are included in appendix II.

Exercise 1.4. Main Signs and Affixes from Piedras Negras, Stela 3

Exercise 1.4.1
1. Label each glyph as a Main Sign, Prefix, Postfix, Superfix, Subfix, or Infix. Remember that each glyph block (especially compound ones) may contain more than one.

Exercise 1.4.2
1. Draw and label twenty syllables from the inscription on the left in the boxes on the right.

Figure 1.8. Equivalent Affixes and Main Signs

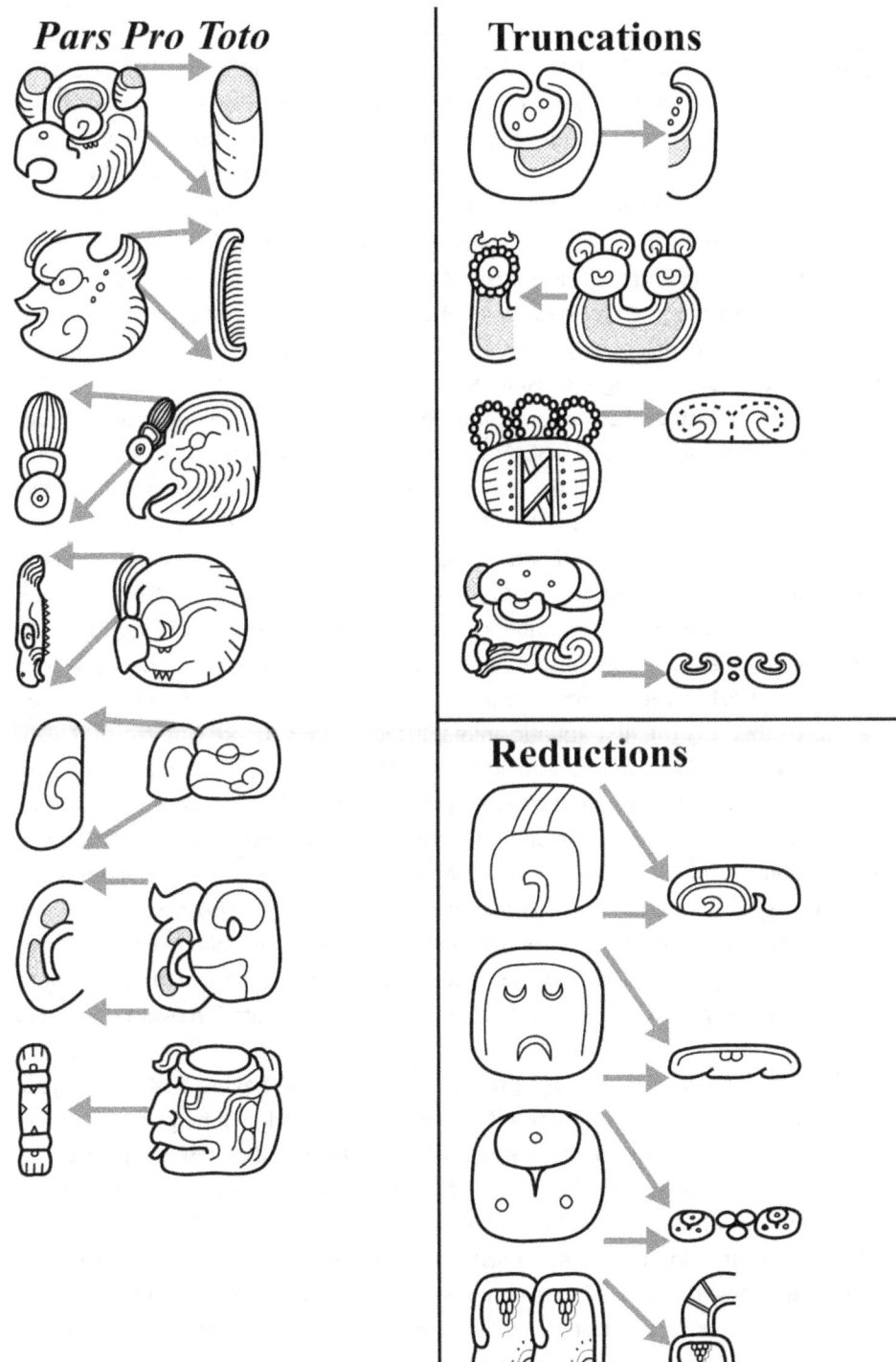

Figure 1.9. Thompson Example: 1.528:116

1.528:116   u-TUN-ni
             utuun
             his stone

In order to give an accurate description of each glyph block, Thompson devised a system to record each number to indicate its relative position within the block. The numbers are listed in the correct reading order. Each glyph on the same horizontal register is separated by a period. To show the vertical arrangement, the numbers from each row are separated by a colon and infixed signs are indicated in brackets. For instance, the number 1.528:116 shown in **figure 1.9** can encode the prefix (1), main sign (528), and subfix (116), indicating their relative positions. Furthermore, Thompson's catalog lists the use of each affix and main sign from the known inscriptions of the time. It is easy to find many instances of a desired glyph using this catalog. Beware of the descriptions provided for each glyph, however, which are not based on modern phonetic readings but are iconographic interpretations. Although they are occasionally right, the majority are no longer considered valid.

Martha Macri, Matthew Looper, and Gabrielle Vail published *The New Catalog of Maya Hieroglyphs* (Macri and Looper 2003b; Macri and Vail 2009), which catalogs the glyphs based on appearance, such as "birds," "body parts," "hands," and other categories. While Thompson placed similar-looking glyphs together in his numbering system, the *New Catalog* uses a three-digit alphanumeric code. The code is not sequential but thematic: the first digit of the code corresponds to the type of sign (such as animals); the second defines the subcategory (such as aquatic, snake, lizard, monkey, dog, jaguar, deer, or mixed subcategories); and the third is a serial number. In this system, for example, T-25 is coded as AA1. While the T-Number only tells us that this is an affix, the *New Catalog* code tells us that it is the first aquatic animal listed in the catalog. One major advantage of the *New Catalog* is that it benefits from a half-century of glyph scholarship. Today epigraphers have a better understanding of functional differences between specific glyphs (Thompson sometimes lumped multiple glyphs together under one T-Number, which can cause confusion). Even more important than the value of an updated labeling system is the information that accompanies each entry. While Thompson's numbers may still be seen in some publications, his interpretations of each glyph are widely discounted. Each entry in the *New Catalog* provides the most up-to-date reading and interpretation of the glyph as well as a history of the glyph's interpretation over the last 450 years.

Serious students of Maya hieroglyphs would benefit from having both the original *Catalog* and the *New Catalog* on their reference desks. The original helps to locate the occurrence of glyphs across the Maya world, while the *New Catalog* offers the most current and complete information for each glyph. Appendix II includes many of the most common glyphs with their T-Number and *New Catalog* code.

Just as the entire inscription has a distinct reading order, each glyph block is read systematically. Most glyph blocks are composed of two or more constituent glyphs. Although this may seem complicated, it will become easy to parse each glyph block into the correct order. Start in the upper left-hand corner. The glyph occupying this corner is read first, whether it is horizontal, vertical, or square. The next glyph is to the right, unless the first glyph covers the entire top of the block or the glyph to the right covers the entire right side. If so, the next glyph is the left-most glyph below the first. Continue reading the next glyph to the right, unless it covers the entire right side. The last glyph read should be the one that covers the bottom-right corner, regardless of whether it is horizontal, vertical, or square. This can be somewhat confusing but is relatively clear with a few examples, as shown in **figure 1.6**.

Some may find the following steps clearer:

1. Read the glyph in the upper left corner.
2. If the first glyph covers the entire top of the glyph block, go to No. 6; else go to No. 3.
3. If the glyph to the right covers the entire right side of the block, go to No. 6; else go to No. 4.
4. If there is no glyph to the right, go to No. 6; else go to No. 5.
5. Read the glyph to the right of the last glyph, then go to No. 3.
6. If there are no glyphs below the last glyph read, go to No. 8; else go to No. 7.
7. Read the left-most glyph below the already-read glyph(s), then go to No. 3.
8. If the glyph read last covers the bottom right corner, the block was likely read correctly.

Sometimes a Classic Maya scribe compressed a lot of information into a single glyph block. This looks like two or four glyph blocks stuck together. Although the reading order may look daunting, think of it as two or four separate glyph blocks. For a double glyph block, read the left and then the right half. For a quadruple glyph block, read the top-left quarter in normal reading order first then move to the top-right, bottom-left, and bottom-right quarters in turn. These exceptions are illustrated on the bottom row of **figure 1.6**. The correct internal reading order for an inscription from Palenque's Hieroglyphic Stair is shown in **figure 1.10** (even quadruple glyph blocks in A5, B5, A6, and B6). Please number each segment in **exercises 1.1.3 and 1.2.3** with the correct reading order for each glyph block. **Exercise 1.1.3** is relatively straightforward because the glyphs are easy to differentiate, while the excerpted glyphs to the right in **exercise 1.2.3** may be more difficult to parse before you have learned what each glyph is.

As with every rule, there are a few exceptions. Although the reading order presented here is generally observed, some particular glyphs may appear at the top of the glyph block but are read last. The reason for this is that the glyph seen at the top is only part of a larger glyph that is conceptually situated behind the rest of the glyphs, in three dimensions. Therefore, read the glyphs situated behind the other glyphs last. **Figure 1.11** has some common examples of these glyphs.

Figure 1.10. Reading Order within a Block Inscription from Palenque, Hieroglyphic Stairway
Internal glyph block reading order indicated below.

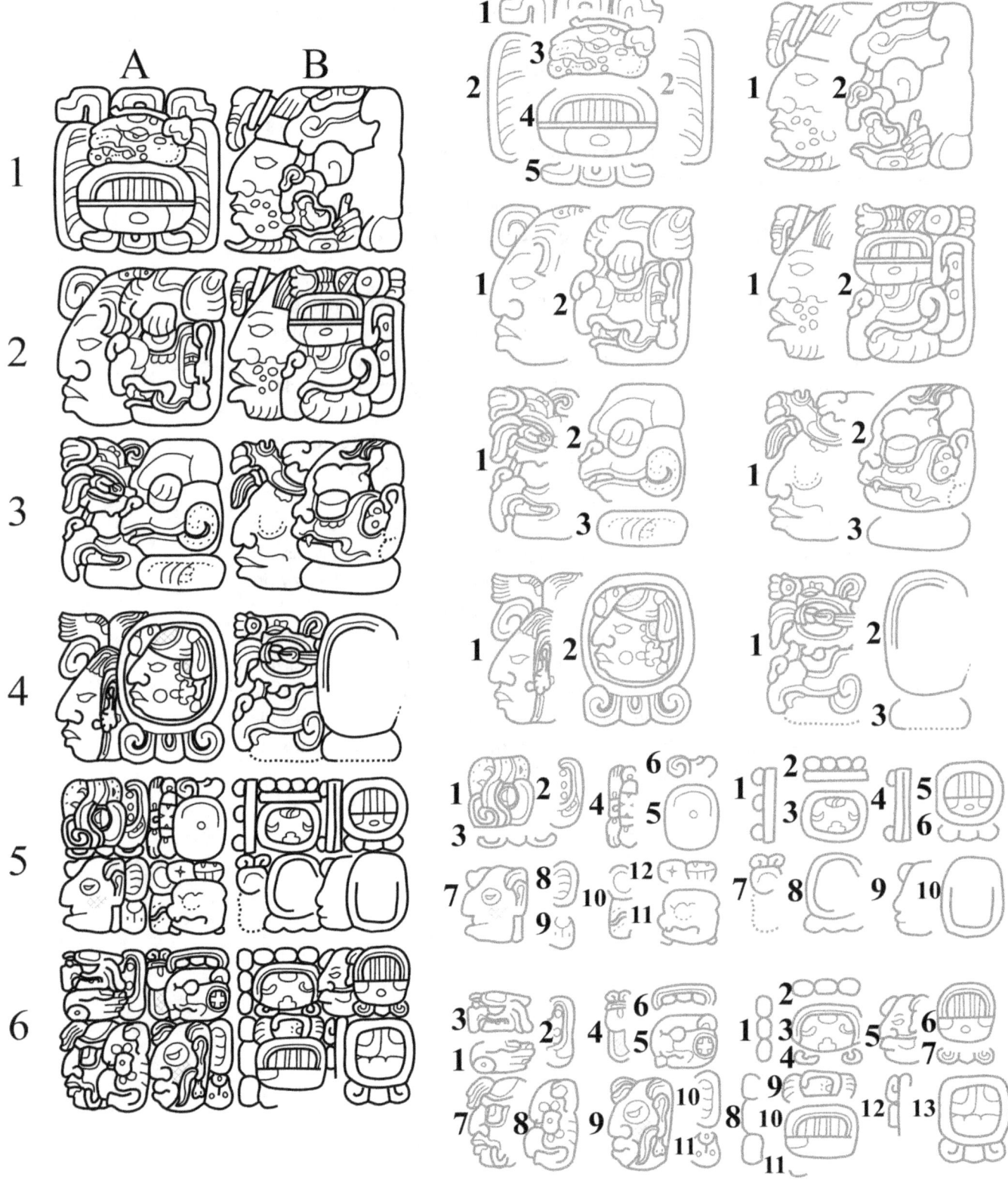

Figure 1.11. Reading Order for Glyphs Commonly Situated behind Other Glyphs

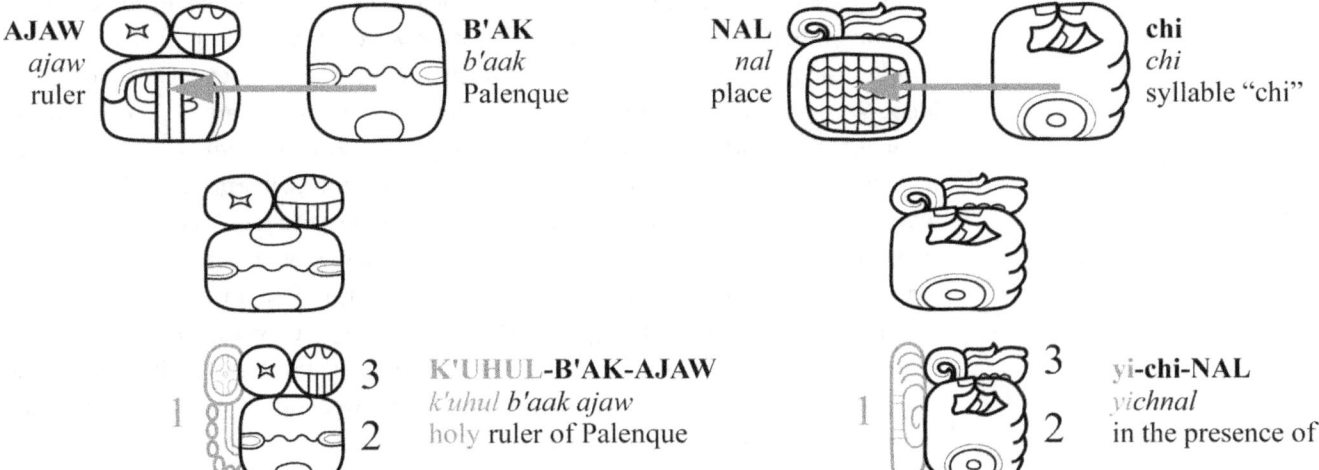

1.4. COMMON INSCRIPTION FORMAT

Most Maya inscriptions follow a general pattern of discourse. A date is given through either a Long Count or Calendar Round date (both discussed in chapter 3). The date is followed by the action taking place and the objects and/or people involved. The next event is then indicated by another date, and so on. The dates act as a framework to organize the events in an inscription. An English example that approximates this pattern would be: "On 19 October 1469 CE, Ferdinand of Aragon and Isabella of Castile married. Twenty-two years, eleven months, and 23 days later, on 12 October 1492 CE, Christopher Columbus sighted the New World. Twenty-six years, four months, and 28 days later, on 12 March 1519 CE, Hernán Cortés landed in Tabasco. Seven months and 27 days later, on 8 November 1519 CE, Cortés arrived in Tenochtitlan."

34 THE NATURE OF THE SCRIPT

1.5. LOGOGRAMS

A **logogram** is a sign that represents a word or idea but does not directly indicate pronunciation. "Logogram" literally means "written word or idea" (from the Greek *logos*, "word/idea" and *gram*, "that which is written"). These are sometimes called logographs, ideograms, or ideographs, but in Maya studies the word "logograms" is most popular. In English, for instance, the ampersand, "&," is pronounced and means "and" but originally comes from a ligature of the *E* and *t* of the Latin word *Et*. It represents the idea and word "and" but does not indicate it phonetically like the word "and" itself. Many people think that Chinese is written with logograms, but most modern characters actually have a phonetic component and are therefore not technically logograms.

In Mayan, a logogram is a sign that stands for a complete word or idea. Logograms represent nouns, verbs, adjectives, adverbs, or numeral classifiers. They are often the main sign in a glyph block but can also be an affix, depending on the choice of the scribe. To give readers a clue to the correct pronunciation of the word, Maya scribes added phonetic complements to a logogram that echo the first and/or last sound of the word with a syllabogram (discussed in the next section). Because logograms do not represent pronunciation, the words encoded in them can be modified by adjoining syllabograms to indicate their correct pronunciations, such as in the conjugation of verbs. This is also seen in English. For example, the logogram "9" represents the word "nine." If we add a final *th*, making it "9th," however, we know that the pronunciation changes to "ninth"; the phonetic signs modify the logogram. Take a look at some logograms highlighted in **figure 1.12**. These are just a few of the hundreds of logograms that you will learn throughout this book. Many of the signs are easy to remember, because they look just like their meaning; others are so abstract that they must simply be memorized, as in any other writing system. Do not worry about memorizing them now. Try to identify the logograms laid out in **exercise 1.5**, using **figure 1.12** for comparison.

Exercise 1.5. Identify Logograms

1. Identify the following logograms (using fig. 1.12).

1.5. LOGOGRAMS

Figure 1.12. Examples of Common Logograms

 **AJAW** *ajaw* ruler

 **CHAN** *chan* snake

 **K'AB'A** *k'ab'a* name

 **SAK** *sak* white/resplendent

 **AJAW** *ajaw* ruler

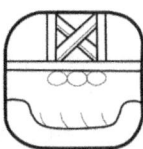 **CHAN** *chan* heaven/sky

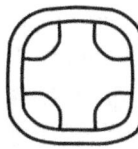 **K'AN** *k'an* yellow, precious

 **TUN** *tuun* stone

 **AK** *ahk* turtle

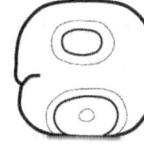 **CHUM** *chum* to sit

 **K'AWIL** *k'awiil* K'awil

 **TZAK** *tza'k* to conjure

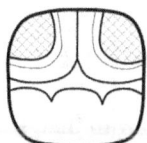 **AK'AB'** *ak'ab'* to conjure

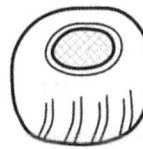 **HA'** *ha'* water

 **K'IN** *k'ihn* day/sun

 **TZUTZ** *tzutz* to end, terminate

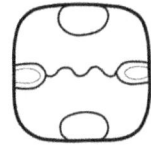 **B'AK** *b'aak* bone, captive

 **HUL** *hul* to arrive

 **K'UH** *k'uh* god

 **TZ'AK** *tz'ahk* to accumulate

 **B'ALAM** *b'ahlam* jaguar

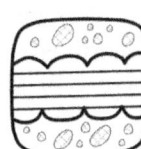 **HUN** *hu'n* book

 **NAH** *naah* house

 **YAX** *yax* blue-green/first

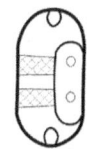 **CHAK** *chak* red

1.6. SYLLABOGRAMS

A **syllabogram** is a sign that represents a phonetic syllable (combination of a consonant and a vowel). It comes from the Latin *syllaba,* meaning "syllable," and *gram,* meaning "that which is written." This is also called simply a syllabic sign or syllable in Maya studies, although the latter is too general and implies only the phonetic value, not the written component. All syllabograms are made up of consonant-vowel (CV) combinations. There are so-called pure vowels, but these are technically fronted by a glottal stop, represented by the apostrophe ('). Because they can be written 'a, they may still be considered a CV combination. This is mostly a semantic argument that does not change the pronunciation of the pure vowels; indeed many epigraphers do not represent the leading glottal stop of vowel-initial words. Syllabic signs are seen today in the Japanese writing system. The *hiragana* syllabary is used to represent particles, inflections, and some words and can be used to spell complete words to aid in pronunciation (which are then called *furigana*). The *katakana* syllabary is used to spell foreign words. All of these tasks are carried out by syllabic signs in Maya writing as well.

The modern Maya syllabary is given in a grid of twenty consonants combined with five vowels, as seen in **figure 1.14**. Some syllables use signs that can also be read as logograms. Sometimes graphic clues indicate whether the sign should be used as a logogram or syllabogram, but in many cases this is only clear from the context. Although there are one hundred possible combinations, only eighty-six are currently attested. For example, only two *t'V* syllabograms are currently known: *t'u* and *t'o* (there are no accepted *t'a*, *t'e*, or *t'i* syllabograms). A number of the signs are derived from objects that begin with that sound, a principle known as **totum pro parte**, meaning "whole for a part." The complete head of an iguana (*huj*) represents the syllabic sound *hu;* the turtle (*ak'*) loans its head to the syllabic sign representing *a;* and the cushion (*pop*) is used to represent the syllabogram *po,* as seen in **figure 1.13**. Although a number of syllabograms can be traced back to an object with a similar known pronunciation, this seems to be the exception rather than the rule at this point in Maya epigraphy.

Using the syllabary found in **figure 1.14**, complete **exercises 1.6 and 1.7** by identifying syllables isolated from a number of inscriptions. After you are familiar with these exercises, try to pick out syllables from inscriptions in **exercises 1.3.3 and 1.4.2**, in which you must not only find these syllables but draw and label them yourself.

Figure 1.13. *Totum pro Parte* (pronunciation derived from the whole word)

a
a
[syllable derived from *ak'*, "turtle"]

hu
hu
[syllable derived from *huj*, "iguana"]

b'a
b'a
[syllable derived from *b'aah*, "gopher"]

po
po
[syllable derived from *pop*, "mat" or "cushion"]

Figure 1.14. Syllabary of Currently Deciphered Glyphs (page 1 of 5)

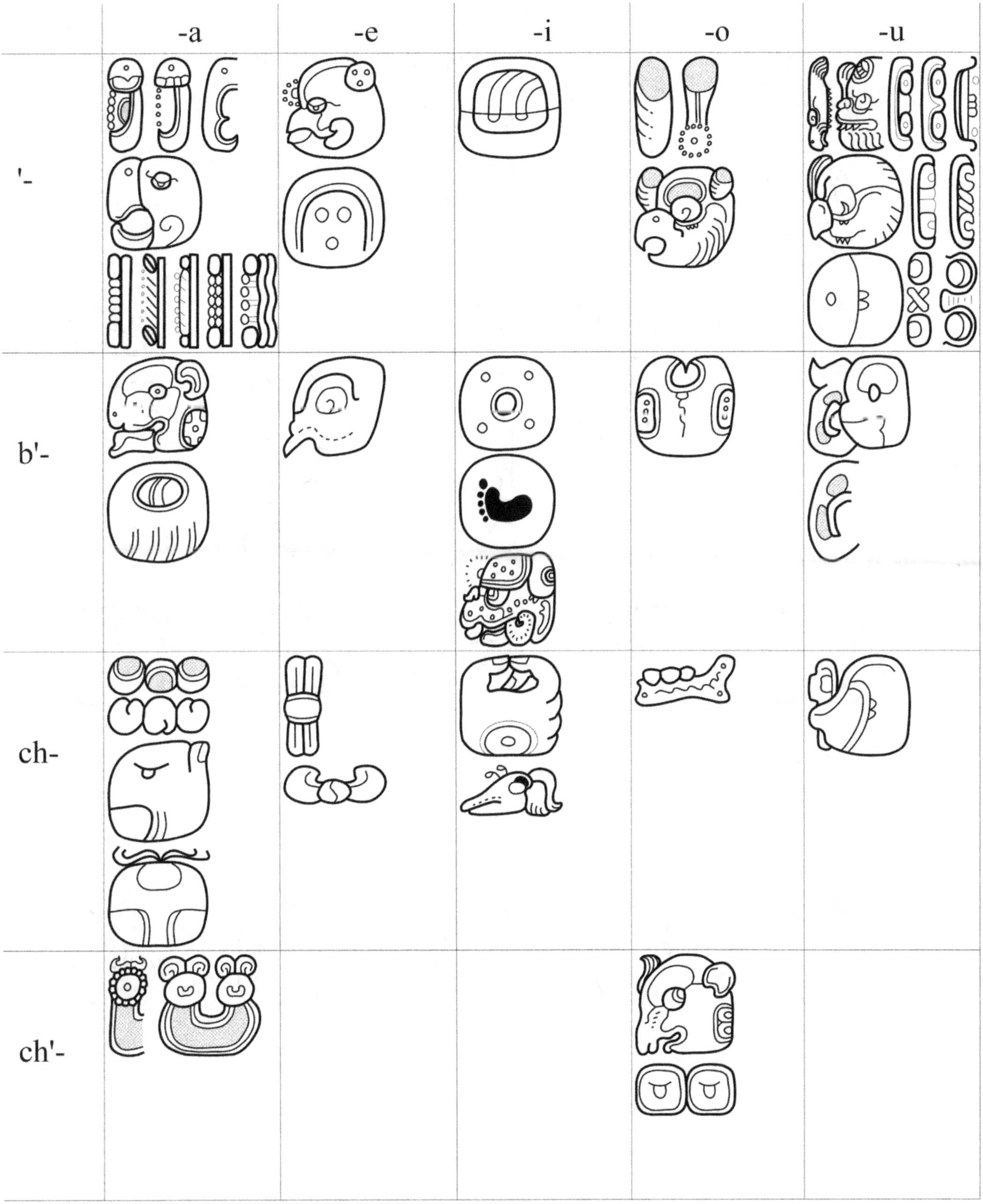

	-a	-e	-i	-o	-u
'-					
b'-					
ch-					
ch'-					

Figure 1.14. Syllabary (page 2 of 5)

	-a	-e	-i	-o	-u
h-					
j-					
k-					
k'-					

Figure 1.14. Syllabary (page 3 of 5)

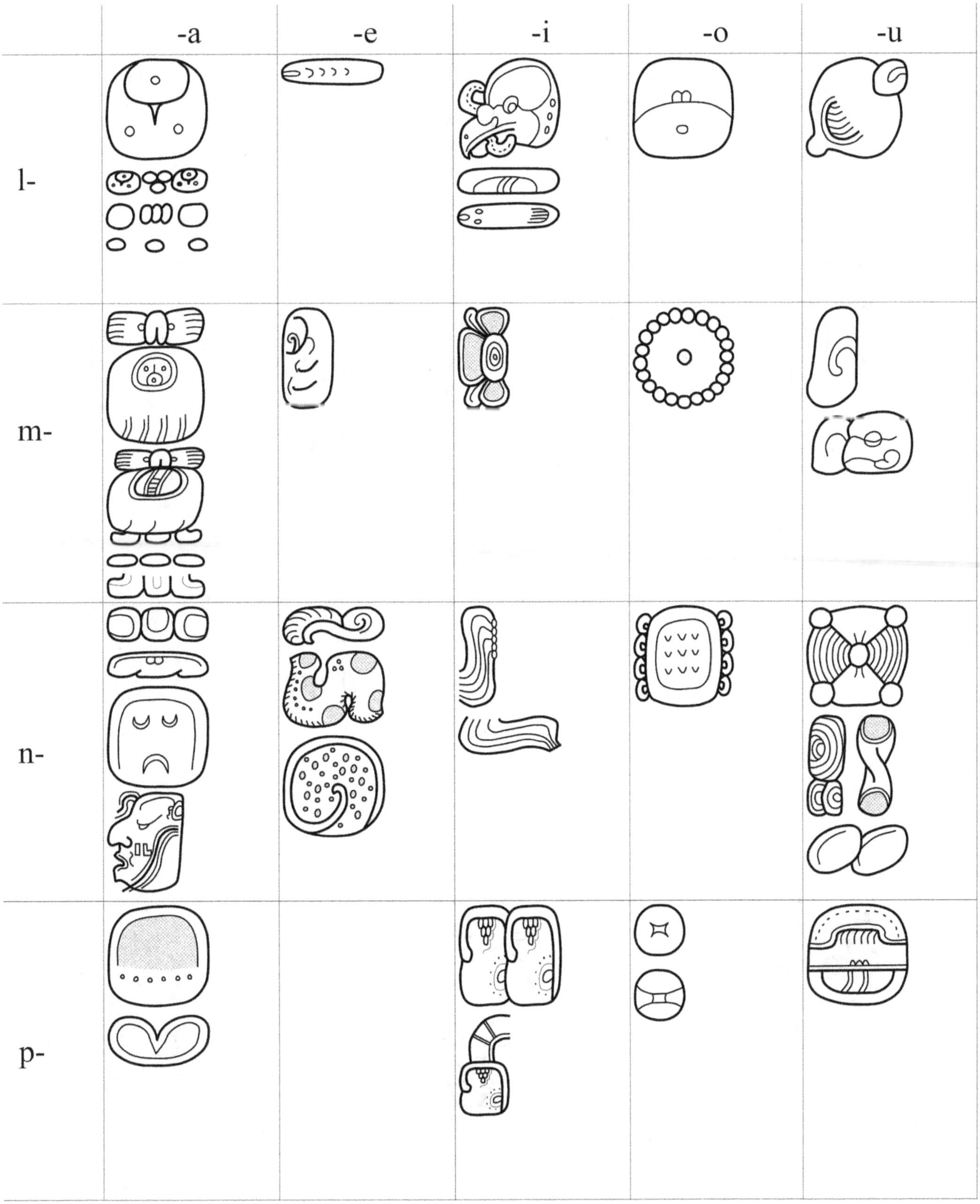

	-a	-e	-i	-o	-u
l-					
m-					
n-					
p-					

Figure 1.14. Syllabary (page 4 of 5)

	-a	-e	-i	-o	-u
s-	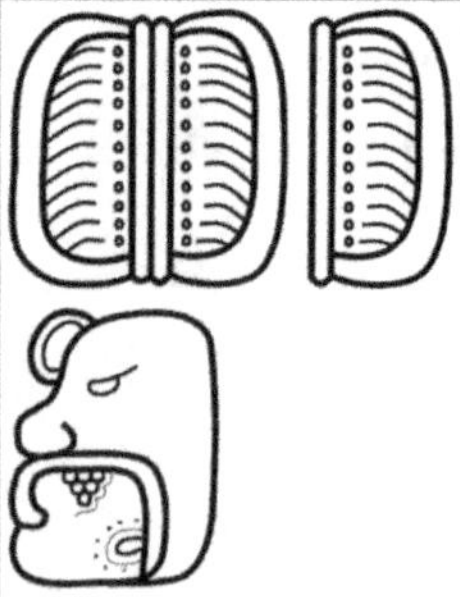	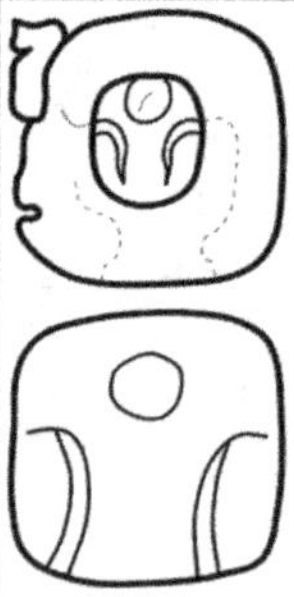			
t-	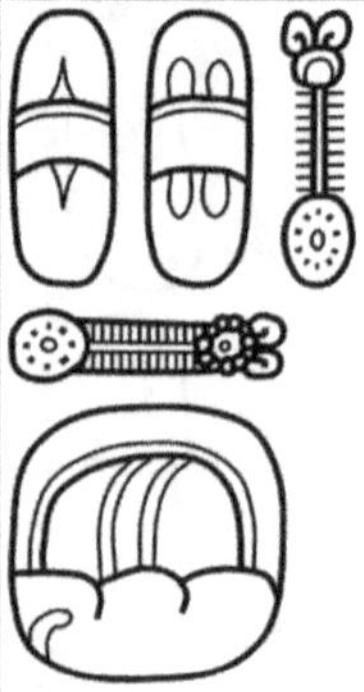	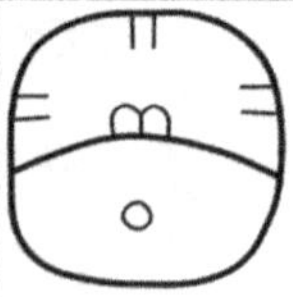			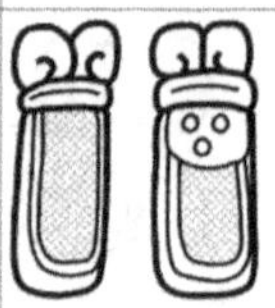
t'-					
tz-			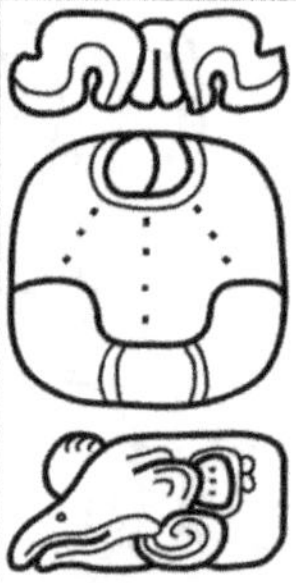		

Figure 1.14. Syllabary (page 5 of 5)

	-a	-e	-i	-o	-u
tz'-					
w-					
x-					
y-					

THE NATURE OF THE SCRIPT

Exercise 1.6. Identify Syllables

1. Identify the following syllables.

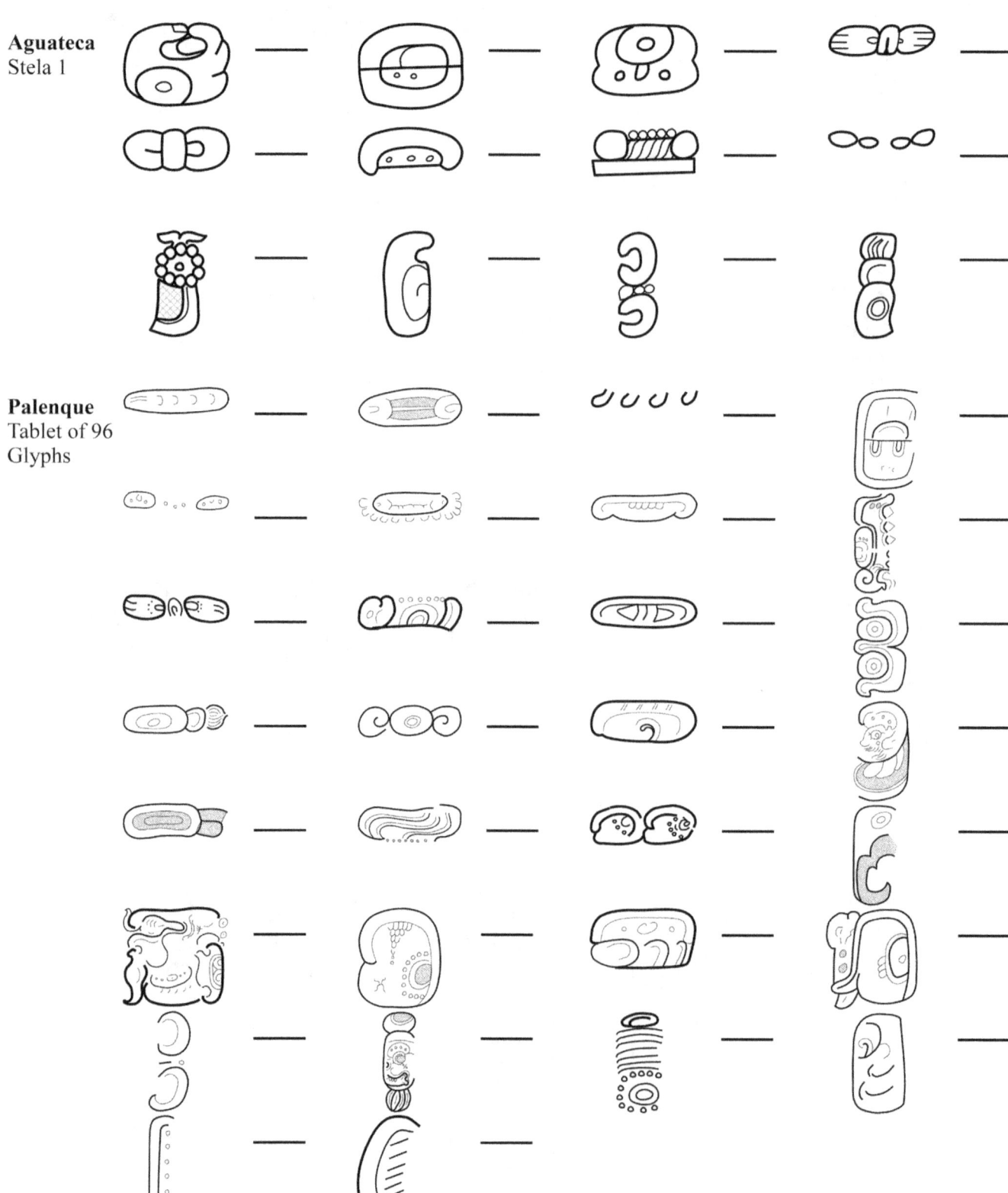

Exercise 1.7. Identify Syllables II

1. Identify the following syllables.

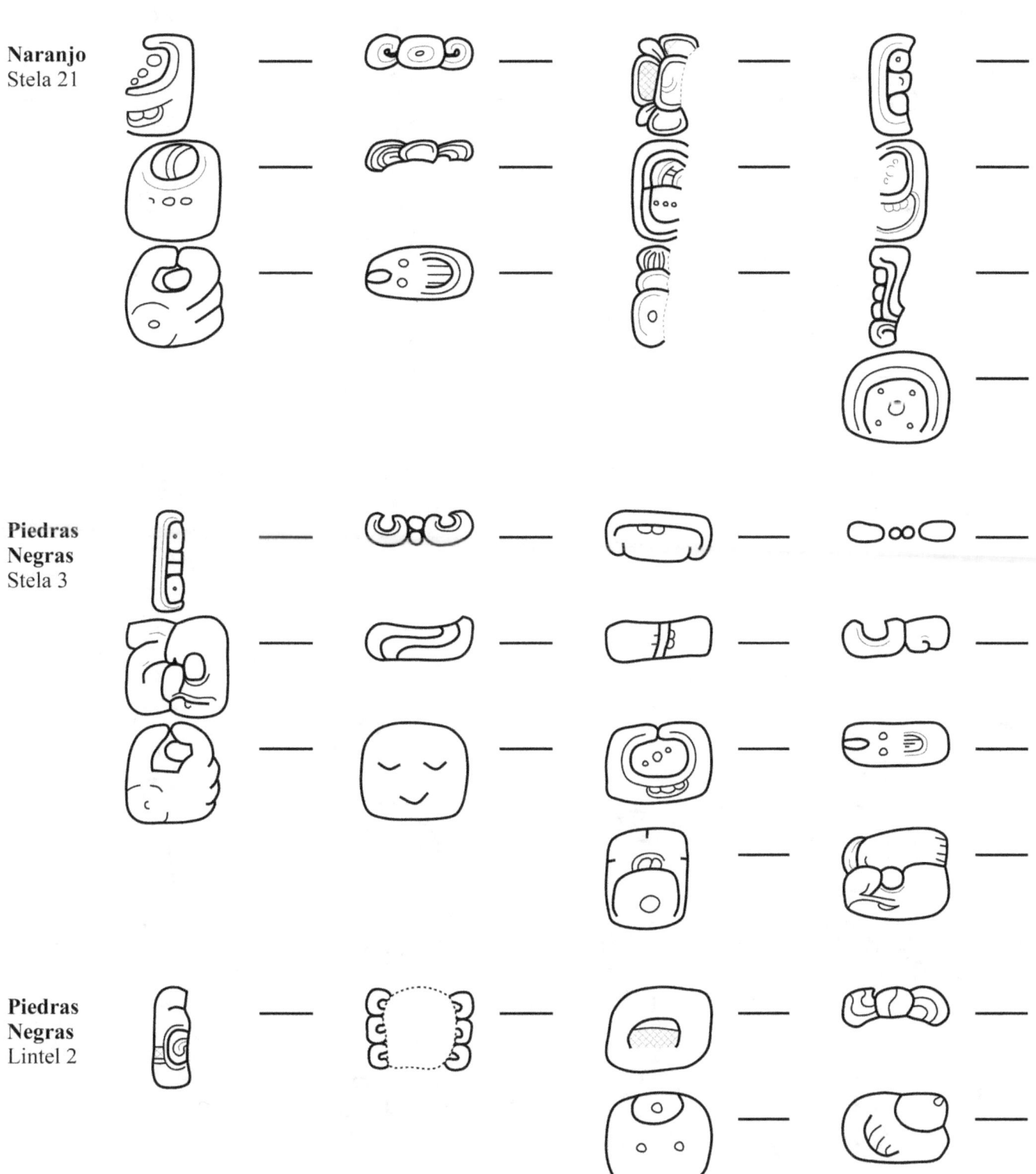

Exercise 1.7 (continued)

Yaxchilan
Lintel 21

Chichen Itza
Temple of the
Initial Series

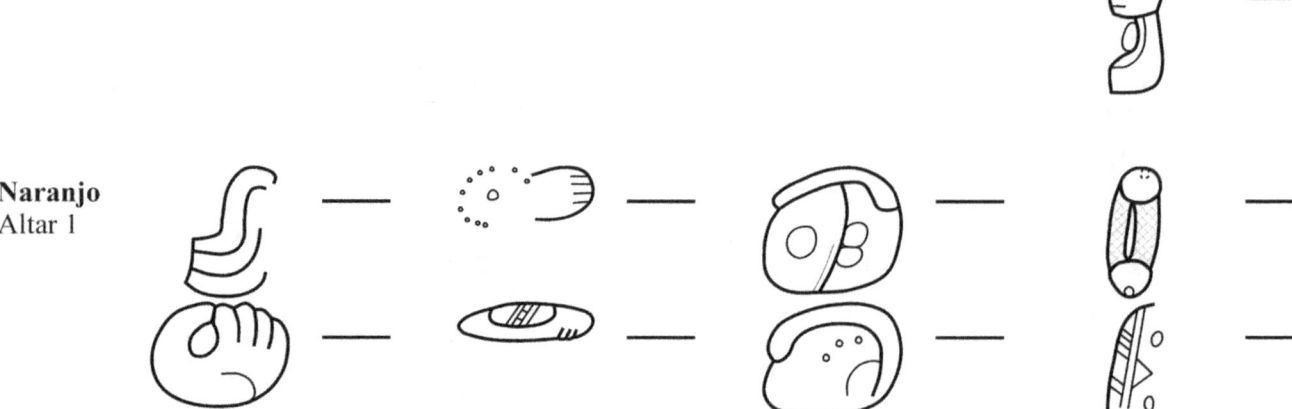

Naranjo
Altar 1

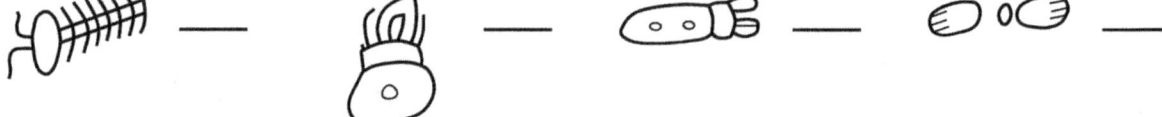

Seibal
Stela 10

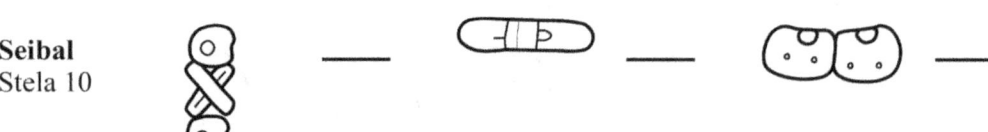

1.7. SEMANTIC DETERMINATIVES

A **semantic determinative** is used in logographic writing systems to differentiate between signs with ambiguous meanings. Egyptian hieroglyphics make extensive use of semantic determinatives, which can indicate whether a word has to do with men, women, gods, motion, places, ideas, or other things. Determinatives are not generally pronounced: they are only to assist the reader in identifying difficult glyphs. Oddly, Mayan does not employ many determinatives. In a writing system with more than a few polyvalent signs (see the following paragraph), semantic determinatives would have been useful for removing ambiguity. Maya writing does have a number of polyvalent signs but no extensive system of semantic determinatives.

Some words with the same pronunciation have several different meanings. This property is called **polyvalence**. English has some polyvalent words, such as "hear/here," "there/their/they're," "to/too/two," and others, which are differentiated by spelling but not by pronunciation. The spelling does not always differentiate between polyvalent signs in Classic Mayan, but it can. A number of Classic Mayan examples are shown in **figure 1.16**, such as **CHAN**, which can mean "snake," "four," or "sky." Polyvalence is semantic: the pronunciation is identical, but the meaning is different. This is similar to, but quite different from, the phonetic principle of **polyphony**, where a single sign represents multiple sounds and/or words. The sign T-528 can be transliterated as **TUN, KAWAK,** and **ku,** and it also forms a major part of **pi** and **JATZ'**. T-528 and other polyphonic signs are shown in **figure 1.15**. Polyphony can be seen in English words, such as "tear" and "lead," which can be verbs or nouns of quite different meanings ("to rip" versus "teardrop" and "to guide" versus "the element Pb").

The one true semantic determinative in Maya writing is the cartouche surrounding the Tzolk'in Day Name. This aspect of the calendar is explained in greater detail in chapter 3. Suffice it to say here that some signs take on a different meaning when surrounded by this cartouche (seen in **fig. 1.17**) than when they appear alone. The cartouche determines the meaning. There are a few other examples of signs that indicate the meaning of logograms. It is difficult to separate out what is a semantic determinative and what is

---

Figure 1.15. Polyphonic Glyphs

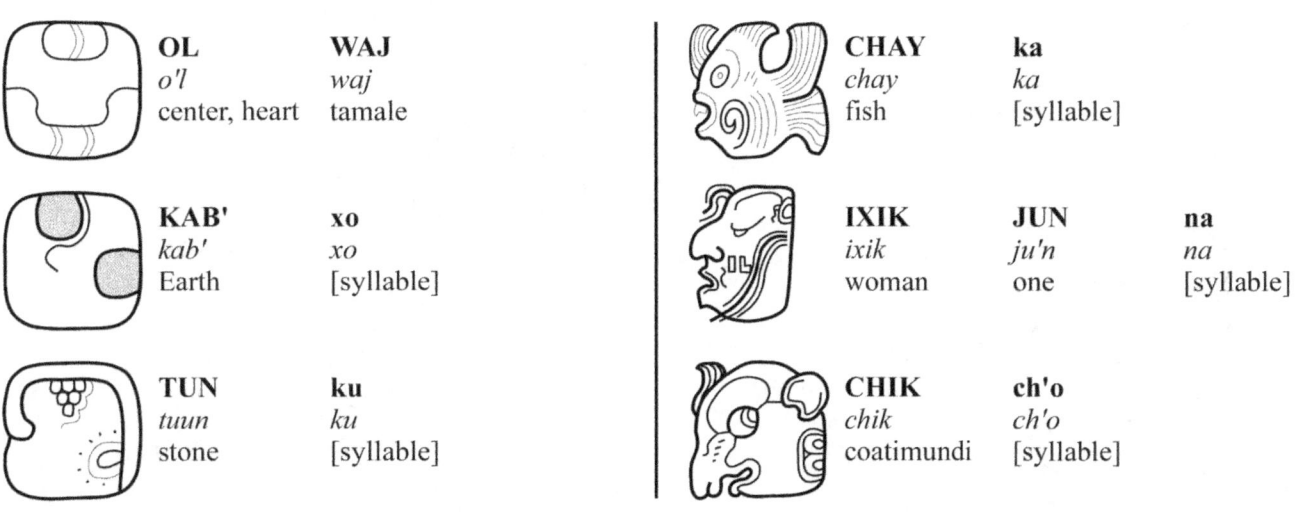

simply part of the main glyph, because of the highly complex and artistic nature of Maya writing. For instance, **b'a**, **HA'**, **ma**, and **t'u** appear to be similar because they all share the same main glyph body. The only differentiating factor is the sign infixed in the upper circle (shown in **fig. 1.17**). Is this a semantic determinative that indicates the reading of the infixed glyph or are these to be classified as different glyphs, even though they share an identical body? Most epigraphers feel that they are entirely separate glyphs. Indeed, in Thompson's *Catalog* three of the four are given their own numbers (501, **b'a**; 556, **HA'**; and 502, **ma**).

Figure 1.16. Polyvalent Glyphs

AL
al
1) child of mother (n)
2) to say (tv)
3) to throw (tv)

B'AH/b'a
b'ah/b'a
1) first, head (adj)
2) self, image (n)

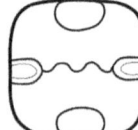

B'AK
b'aak
1) capture, seize (tv)
2) captive (n)
3) bone (n)
4) heron (n)

CHAB'
chaab'
1) beehive, bee, honey (n)
2) anteater (n)
3) supervise (tv)

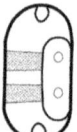

CHAK
chak
1) red (adj)
2) great, big (adj)
3) tie up (pv)

 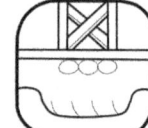

CHAN
chan
1) four (num)
2) snake (n)
3) sky (n)

KAB'
kab'
1) earth (n)
2) bee (n)
3) make it happen, supervise (tv)

K'AN
k'an
1) yellow (adj)
2) seat, bench (n)
3) precious (adj)
4) ripe (adj)
5) jewel, collar (n)

K'IN
k'in
1) hot (adj)
2) sun (n)
3) day (n)
4) festival (n)

NAL
nal
1) ear of corn (n)
2) place (n)
3) person (n)

TZ'AK
tz'ak
1) whole (adj)
2) add, accumulate (pv)
3) things; count of things (ncl)

YAX
yax
1) green/blue (adj)
2) first (adj)
3) precious, sacred (adj)

1.7. SEMANTIC DETERMINATIVES

Figure 1.17. Semantic Determinatives

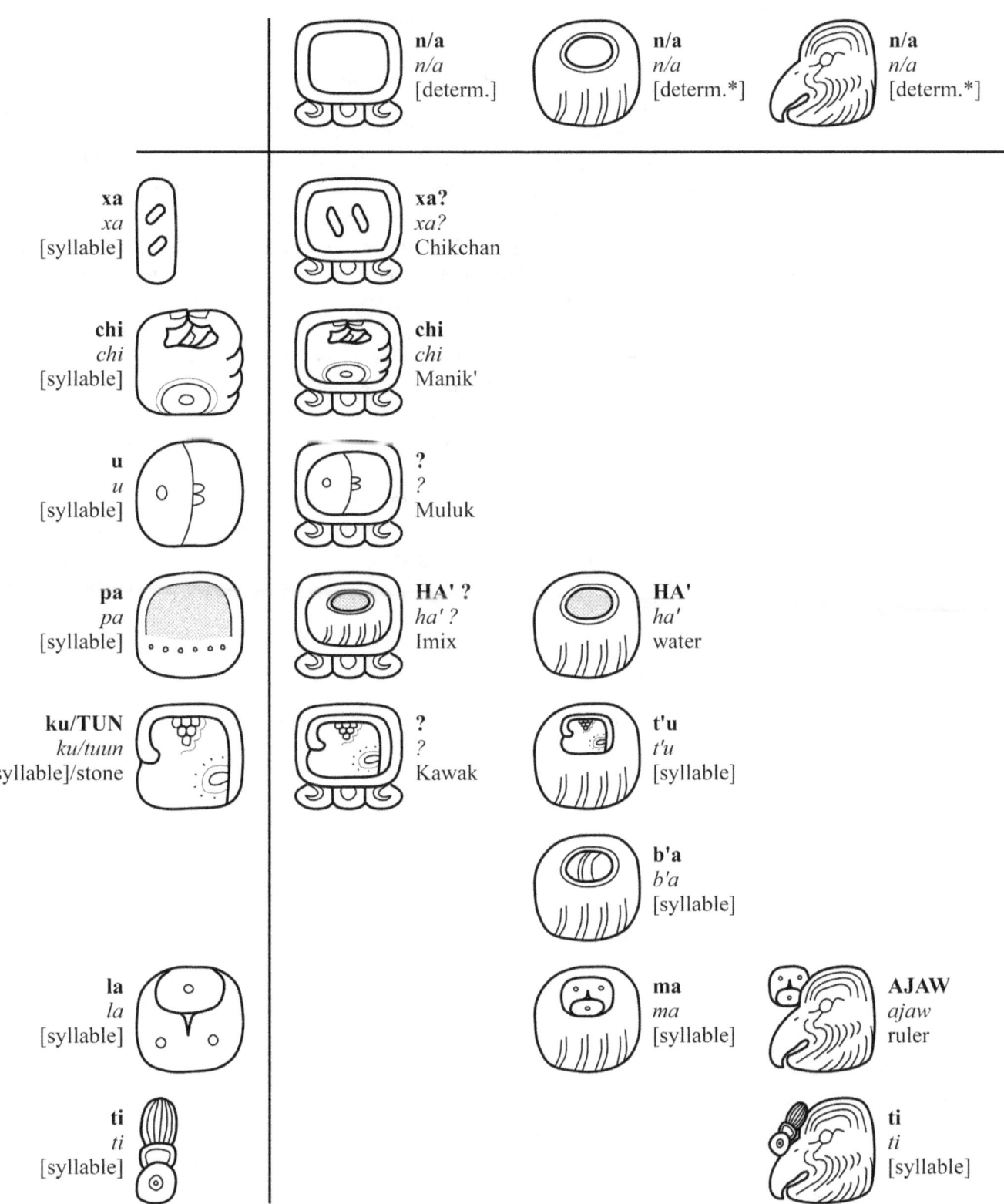

* Possible, but unlikely determinative.

1.8. NUMERAL CLASSIFIERS

A **numeral classifier** is a phonetic component appended to a number to indicate what it counts or what class of things it counts. Technically, the Long Count period names are numeral classifiers: *k'in, winik, haab', winikhaab',* and *pih* (discussed in chapter 3). More numeral classifiers are shown in **figure 1.18**. The meaning of some classifiers is relatively transparent. **PET,** for example, is the verb "to round" and adjective "round" by itself; when following a number, it indicates that the number is a count of round things. Other numeral classifiers are more abstract. **TE',** for instance, means "tree" or "wood" on its own but as a numeral classifier indicates a count of time periods.

The numeral classifiers in Classic Mayan are a necessary part of speech. We currently know about a dozen classifiers, but there were likely more. The transcription and transliteration follow the usual conventions (as explained in sections 1.9 and 1.10), but sometimes the most straightforward way to translate a numeral classifier into English is to remove the word "count of" from the definition. For instance, an inscription reading 9-tu-ku . . . , transliterated (pronounced) as *b'olon tuk* . . . , might be translated as "9 piles [of] . . . " Some classifiers may be better translated as adjectives: 9-mu-lu . . . , *b'olon mul* . . . , "9 stacked . . . " Others might just as well be left out or placed in parentheses for the English translation, such as 9-TZ'AK . . . , *b'olon tz'ak* . . . , "9 (things of) . . . " In translating between any two languages, there are always areas where the overlap of grammar and/or vocabulary is not perfect. In this case, the translator must make the best sense of the original meaning in the target language.

Figure 1.18. Numerical Classifiers

-mu-lu
-mul
count of stacked or mounted objects (ncl)

-na-ka
-nak
count of living beings (ncl)

-PET
-pet
count of round things (ncl)

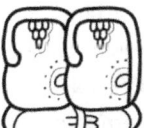
-pi-ki
-pik
count of 8,000 (ncl)

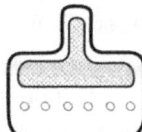
-TAL / -ta-la / -la-ta
-tal / -lat
count of elapsed periods, ordinals, or days (ncl)

-TE'
-te'
count of time periods (ncl)

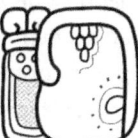
-ti-ki-li
-tikil
count of beings (ncl)

-tu-ku
-tuk
count of piles (of 20) (ncl)

-TZ'AK
-tz'uk
count of living things (ncl)

-ye
-ye
count of divine objects (ncl)

1.9. TRANSCRIPTION

A **transcription** is the systematic recording of hieroglyphics into Latin characters. It is the first step of a translation and identifies the correct reading and order for each glyph. Transcriptions should be the closest representation of what is actually recorded in an inscription. Just as the English written script only approximates the sounds said aloud, the Maya script is not a perfect record of speech. For example, the numeral "2" does not record a phonetic sound in the way that the word "two" does; the numeral is used in many languages and may indicate *zwei, dos, ni, sh'taim,* or other words. Furthermore, English spelling is influenced by fossilized archaic pronunciations and heavy French influences. Students often complain that English spelling is not necessarily a good guide for pronunciation. This is exactly the case in Maya inscriptions, which imperfectly record Classic Mayan speech.

A number of conventions are used to transcribe inscriptions. First, transcriptions are written in **boldface** type. Syllabograms are written in lowercase letters, while logograms are written in all capital letters. Numbers are written with Arabic numerals. All of the glyphs contained in one glyph block are connected by hyphens. The word for "jaguar," *b'ahlam,* is the example most often used to explain this principle. This word can be spelled purely logographically as **B'ALAM.** It can be given by a logosyllabic spelling (a combination of logograms and syllabograms), such as **b'a-B'ALAM-ma.** Alternatively, it can be spelled syllabically: **b'a-la-ma.** As you can see from **figure 1.19**, the transcription accurately transposes what we see in the glyphs into a user-friendly alphabet. Clearly this is not necessarily a clean pronunciation, because it often includes extra vowels or redundant syllables. As explained in the discussion of spelling (chapter 2), superfluous vowels and syllables are contained in parentheses to indicate their status: **(b'a)-B'ALAM-(ma)** and **b'a-la-m(a).**

Figure 1.19. Transcription, Transliteration, and Translation

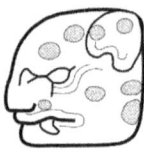
B'ALAM
b'a[h]lam
jaguar

CHUM[mu]
chum
to seat

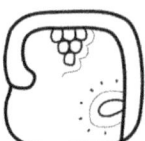
~~**TUUN**~~ / **TUN**
tuun
stone

(b'a)-B'ALAM-(ma)
b'a[h]lam
jaguar

²ka-w(a)
kakaw
chocolate

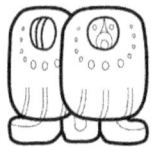
b'a-la-m(a)
b'a[h]lam
jaguar

1.9. TRANSCRIPTION

Figure 1.20. Piedras Negras, Stela 3 (transcription, transliteration, and translation)

In Figure:

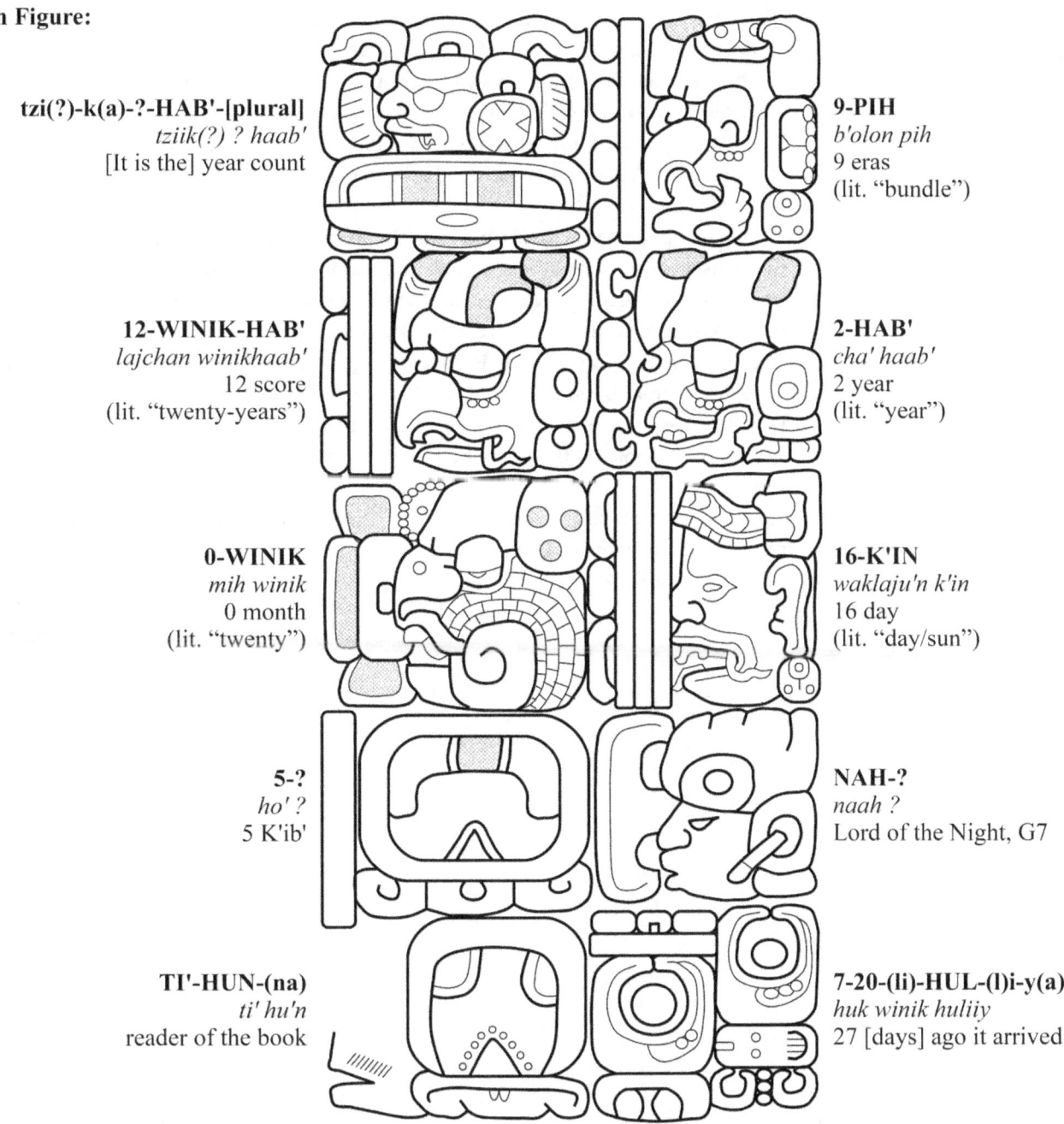

tzi(?)-k(a)-?-HAB'-[plural]
tziik(?) ? haab'
[It is the] year count

9-PIH
b'olon pih
9 eras
(lit. "bundle")

12-WINIK-HAB'
lajchan winikhaab'
12 score
(lit. "twenty-years")

2-HAB'
cha' haab'
2 year
(lit. "year")

0-WINIK
mih winik
0 month
(lit. "twenty")

16-K'IN
waklaju'n k'in
16 day
(lit. "day/sun")

5-?
ho' ?
5 K'ib'

NAH-?
naah ?
Lord of the Night, G7

TI'-HUN-(na)
ti' hu'n
reader of the book

7-20-(li)-HUL-(l)i-y(a)
huk winik huliiy
27 [days] ago it arrived

In Text: (short words or phrases)

… spelling it **HUL-(l)i-y(a)**, read *huliiy*, meaning "it had arrived," or "… ago it arrived."

In Block: (long phrases or complete inscriptions)

… the ISIG and Long Count of Piedras Negras, Stela 3, which reads in part:

tzi(?)-k(a)-?-HAB'-[plural] 9-PIH 12-WINIK-HAB' 2-HAB' …
tziik(?) ? haab', b'olon pih, lajchan winikhaab' cha' haab' …
[It is the] year count 9 era, 12 score, 2 year …

Other conventions are also used in transcriptions. Glyphs that are completely contained within another glyph (infixed glyphs) are indicated in brackets. **Figure 1.19** shows this at work: **mu** is contained within the **CHUM** glyph, transcribed as **CHUM[mu]**. Diacritical marks are also indicated in the transcription. The most common is the "doubling mark": two small dots in front of a sign whose value should be doubled. This is indicated by a superscript 2, as in [2]**ka-w(a)** in **figure 1.19**, which really corresponds to **ka-ka-w(a)**: *kakaw,* "chocolate." Eroded glyphs are indicated by an ellipsis (. . .) in place of the unreadable glyphs. Glyphs that are not yet understood can be transcribed simply as a question mark. A question mark can also be added after a word that has a questionable reading or spelling.

Classic Mayan contains complex vowels. Some epigraphers indicate this feature in the transcription, while others do not. For example, some would transcribe **TUUN** in **figure 1.19**, where others would write **TUN**. This book uses the latter, because it does not impose reconstructed vowel complexity in the realm of transcription. Interpretation of phonetics and pronunciation is done in the next step: transliteration. Transcriptions should be a no-frills, simple record of what is seen in the inscription, not an interpretation. A real example is seen in **figure 1.20**. Using the syllabary in **figure 1.13**, transcribe each of the syllables in the left-hand column of glyphs in **exercise 1.8**. Then, using the correct reading order, put these syllables into the transcription blanks in the right-hand column of that exercise to spell out some common Maya words. You can repeat the same process in **exercise 1.9.1**.

1.9. TRANSCRIPTION

Exercise 1.8. Syllabic Spellings

1. Use the syllabary chart to assign values to the glyphs in the left-hand column, which syllabically spell the associated logograph. Copy the values from the syllabic spellings to the text accompanying the logogram on the right. Do not worry about spelling rules that are covered later, but do observe proper reading order.

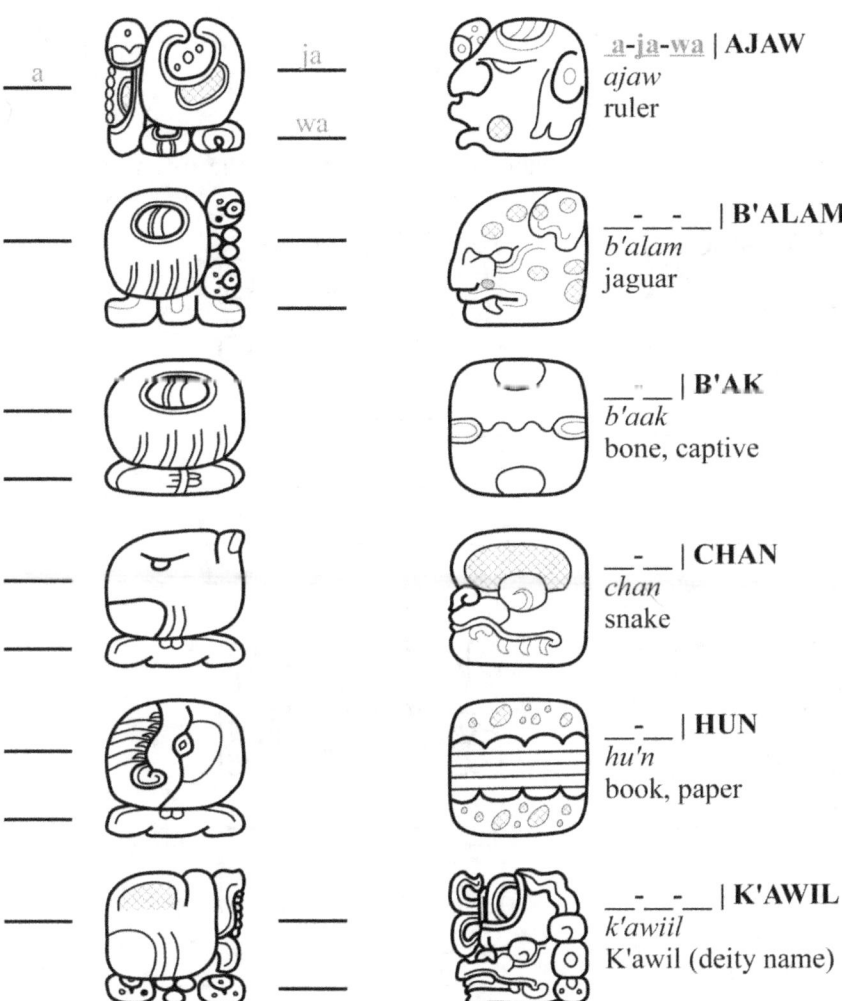

54 THE NATURE OF THE SCRIPT

Exercise 1.9. Transcribe, Transliterate, and Translate

Exercise 1.9.1: Transcription
1. Use the syllabary chart and logogram transcriptions given below to assign values to the glyphs in this exercise. Copy the values from the glyph block spaces to the proper transcription below. Be sure to observe proper reading order and transcription conventions.

Exercise 1.9.2: Transliteration
1. Using your answers from exercise 1.9.1 and the vocabulary below, transliterate each of the six short phrases, observing proper transliteration conventions.

Exercise 1.9.3: Translation
1. Using your answers from exercises 1.9.1 and 1.9.2 and the vocabulary, translate each of the six short phrases, observing proper translation conventions.

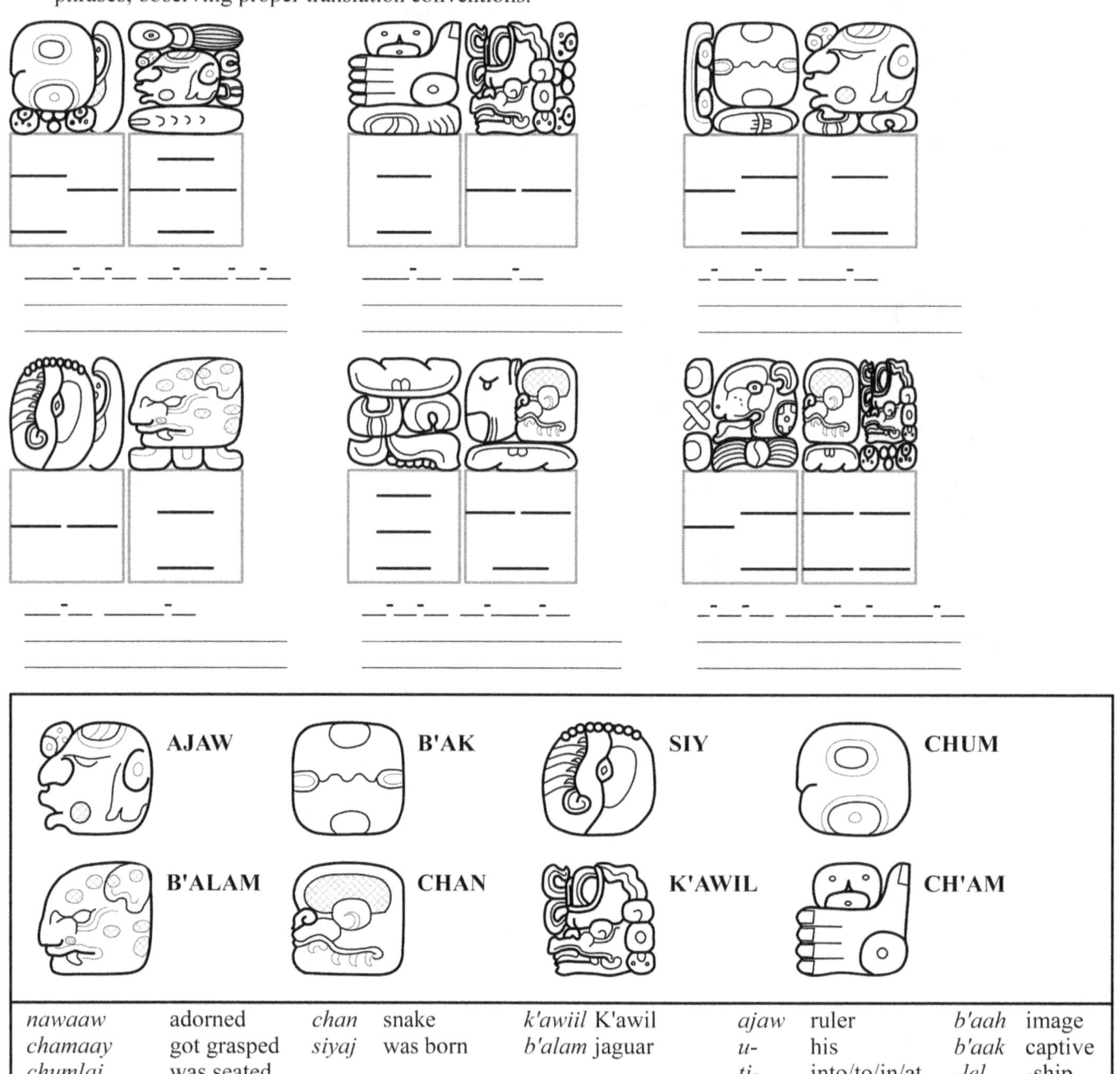

nawaaw	adorned	chan	snake	k'awiil	K'awil	ajaw	ruler	b'aah	image
chamaay	got grasped	siyaj	was born	b'alam	jaguar	u-	his	b'aak	captive
chumlaj	was seated					ti-	into/to/in/at	-lel	-ship

1.10. TRANSLITERATION

A **transliteration** is the conversion of a transcription into the reconstructed spoken language Classic Mayan. Unfortunately, nobody who speaks the language of the inscriptions has survived the thousand or so years since the collapse. Some modern Maya languages are thought to be closely related to the languages of the inscriptions, especially Ch'olan languages such as Ch'ol, Cholan, and in particular Ch'orti' (Houston et al. 2000). Classic Mayan is reconstructed by specialists, using systematic methods to derive the hypothetical pronunciation of words and sounds. It is this reconstructed pronunciation that is expressed in a transliteration. Most sounds are indicated glyphically (reconstructed sounds, such as complex vowels, are discussed in chapter 2). The "spelling" used in transliterations and transcriptions should follow the so-called new orthography (also discussed in chapter 2): for example, **AJAW** and *ajaw*, not **AHAU** and *ahau*.

Transliterations use a number of conventions to express the reconstructed spoken word. First, transliterations are written in *italics*. Unlike transcriptions, they do not differentiate between logograms and syllabograms or include any other indications of how the inscription is written glyphically. Transliteration smooths out the often awkward appearance of transcriptions. In the examples shown in **figure 1.19**, "jaguar" may be transcribed (**b'a**)-**B'ALAM**-(**ma**) or **b'a-la-m(a)**. The transliteration of both of these transcriptions would be *b'alam*. Anything that is not explicitly stated in the glyphs is placed in brackets. Some scholars reconstruct an infixed *-h* in this word, giving instead *b'a[h]lam*. Brackets are placed around the *h* to show that it is reconstructed. Because this *h* is not indicated glyphically, it is based on historical linguistic reconstruction, as discussed in chapter 2. In other instances, where it is clear that a complete word was meant but a syllable has been left out, it can be added in brackets. This must be done judiciously, however; this "underspelling" principle can be abused. To be safe, it must only be done in cases where the missing syllabogram or logogram is almost always present or clearly implied by context.

Just as with transcriptions, an ellipsis (. . .) is used to indicate eroded glyphs. A question mark can be used in place of a word to indicate the pronunciation of a glyph that is not yet known or directly after a word that is not well attested. Finally, everything is written out phonetically. For instance, numbers, which are transcribed with Arabic numerals, are written out fully in the transliteration. More examples are given in **figure 1.20**. Using the word bank included in **exercise 1.9**, you can fill in the transliterations that correspond to the transcribed glyphs in **exercise 1.9.2**.

1.11. TRANSLATION

A **translation** is the conversion of the recorded Classic Mayan into understandable English (or any other language). Epigraphers make use of both the transcription and transliteration to produce a correct translation of an inscription. A perfect, one-for-one translation of one language to another is rarely possible. Some phrases, words, and constructions are not shared by two languages. For instance, in modern Maya languages (and likely in Classic Mayan) time is not expressed in terms of past, present, and future tense. Instead, time is expressed by way of aspect: a verb is either completive or incompletive (finished or ongoing). How do we correctly translate between two entirely different systems? This topic and similar ones are covered in chapters 4 and 5.

The actual expression of a translation has its own conventions as well. Translations are written in plain text, as seen in **figure 1.19**. In a body of text, the translation is often placed in quotation marks, but this is not necessary in figures or in a block of translation, as shown in **figure 1.20**. As with transcriptions and transliterations, an ellipsis (. . .) can indicate eroded text and a question mark can indicate a questionable or unknown reading. Otherwise, the translation largely follows standard written English guidelines and the style of the individual epigrapher. Now try to complete **exercise 1.9.3**: translate the transcribed and transliterated Maya glyphs into English. This is just a short foretaste of the complexity of Maya hieroglyphic translation covered here.

These are some general rules for the expression of transcription, transliteration, and translation in Maya epigraphy. This textbook (and the field of Maya epigraphy) largely follows the standards described by George Stuart in *A Guide to the Style and Content of the Series Research Reports on Ancient Maya Writing* (1988). This book differs in a few minor aspects, but they are in line with what has become common usage in the more than twenty years since this standard was created. For instance, an unidentified sign in the 1988 standard is transcribed with an *x,* whereas many epigraphers now use a question mark. Stuart identifies underspellings with an asterisk preceding the reconstructed glyph, whereas this textbook places them in brackets. For the most part, most Maya epigraphers working today use conventions similar or identical to the ones described here.

FURTHER READING

Conventions

Stuart, George
1988   *A Guide to the Style and Content of the Series Research Reports on Maya Hieroglyphic Writing.* Washington, D.C.: Center for Maya Research.

Stuart lays out the systematic representation of transcriptions, transliterations, and translations in this well-known and often cited work.

Short List of Publications with Hieroglyphic Texts

Beetz, Carl P., and Linton Satterthwaite
1981   *The Monuments and Inscriptions of Caracol, Belize.* Philadelphia: University Museum, University of Pennsylvania.

Graham, Ian, Peter Mathews, Eric Von Euw, and David Stuart
1975–present   *Corpus of Maya Hieroglyphic Inscriptions.* Cambridge, Mass.: Peabody Museum of Archaeology and Ethnology.

This huge undertaking has been working for over thirty years to document and publish clear drawings and photographs of unpublished and difficult-to-find inscriptions from sites across the Maya area.

Greene Robertson, Merle
1983   *The Sculpture of Palenque.* Princeton, N.J.: Princeton University Press.

This work has beautiful illustrations of the rich tradition of panel and stucco carving at Palenque.

Houston, Stephen D.
1993   *Hieroglyphs and History at Dos Pilas: Dynastic Politics of the Classic Maya.* Austin: University of Texas Press.

Marcus, Joyce
1987   *The Inscriptions of Calakmul: Royal Marriage at a Maya City in Campeche, Mexico.* Ann Arbor: University of Michigan, Museum of Anthropology.

Morley, Sylvanus G.
1938   *The Inscriptions of Petén.* Washington, D.C.: Carnegie Institution of Washington.

This work is quite old but still useful, especially if you are looking for examples of calendrical information (the project was primarily interested in recording dates across the Peten).

2. SPELLING AND LANGUAGE

Spelling (transliteration) is important in translating Maya hieroglyphic texts because it records the minutiae of the Classic Mayan language. Despite this, spelling rules might be seen as unimportant, because in theory it would be possible to translate an inscription directly from the transcription, without the transliteration. Spelling rules are still changing as epigraphers continue to make new and important advances. Words are often spelled quite differently today than they were even ten years ago. Because of spelling variability over time, this is not a topic that must be mastered except by professional epigraphers. Learning to transliterate and spell correctly, however, is an achievable goal.

The spelling rules laid out here will help convert the raw transcription of an inscription (in **boldface**) into a reconstructed transliteration of Classic Mayan (in *italics*) as it is currently understood. These spelling rules are slightly simplified and conservative: they reflect the consensus on aspects of transliteration and spelling in the field of epigraphy today. Some aspects that are not as well understood are discussed here, but I do not recommend using them until they have gained wider acceptance or uniformity across the field.

2.1. SOUNDS IN CLASSIC MAYAN

The human vocal tract can only produce a finite number of sounds, but these can be combined in a seemingly infinite number of sequences. Mayan has vowels and consonants, just like all other languages. The alphabetic system used in English represents each vowel and consonant with its own symbol, although combinations of symbols are used to represent phonemes for which it has no one single letter (*ch*, *sh*, etc.). The Maya script, in contrast, represents complete words or consonant-vowel pairs with individual glyphs (see sections 1.5 and 1.6 of chapter 1). These words and syllables are made up of combinations of five vowels and twenty consonants. But it is not that simple.

2.1.1. Consonants

Classic Mayan has twenty consonants: *b', ch, ch', h, j, k, k', l, m, n, p, p', s, t, t', tz, tz', x, w,* and *y*, as laid out in **table 2.1**. Although some of these consonants must be represented by two Latin letters (*ch* and *tz*), they constitute only one sound each. Six of these consonants are glottalized (*b', ch', k', p', t', tz'*). A glottalized consonant may seem difficult or foreign to a native English speaker at first. Many people already glottalize word-final consonants at the end of an emphatic sentence. For instance, an upset youngster might cry, "I am not!" emphasizing the final *t*. The *t* may sound "spit out" or sound as if the word is abruptly cut off. This comes from the rapid closing of the vocal cords and forcing air out of the throat and mouth. To try this for yourself, say "cheese" as you normally do. Say just the first *ch* exactly the same way a few times. Notice how the sound trails off and feel

Table 2.1. Classic Mayan Consonant Sounds

Classic Mayan	IPA	English Equivalent	Classic Mayan	IPA	English Equivalent	Classic Mayan	IPA	English Equivalent	Classic Mayan	IPA	English Equivalent
b'	bʔ		k	k	cat	p	p	pop	tz	t͡s	jug
ch	t͡ʃ	cherry	k'	kʔ	work?*	p'	pʔ		tz'	t͡sʔ	
ch'	t͡ʃʔ	porch?*	l	l	line	s	s	sat	w	w	way
h	h	high	m	m	milk	t	t	tap	x	ʃ	sheep
j	x	loch or German *ich*	n	n	nap	t'	tʔ	not?*	y	j	you

Note: IPA = International Phonetic Alphabet.

* Word-final consonants in English are sometimes glottalized to add emphasis: "I don't want to go to work!" may have a glottalized final *k*, which sounds "spit out" or as if the sound is cut off abruptly.

the breath coming from your lungs. Now close your glottis: take a breath and hold it by lightly clenching in your larynx (windpipe) and make the *ch'* sound with the air trapped in your mouth. It should sound shorter, sharper, and less breathy than the previous unglottalized *ch*. Another difficult sound for native English speakers is the *j*. It is not the *j* of "jelly," but rather like the *ch* in Scottish "loch" or German *ich*. Make an *i* sound as in the English word "me," holding the final position of your mouth. Now breathe out through your mouth sharply, feeling the friction caused in the back of your mouth. By practicing you can produce the *j* sound of Mayan. Do not worry if you cannot pronounce all of the sounds correctly. The important thing is to understand the important differences between glottalized and unglottalized consonants. For instance, the verb *ch'ak*, "to chop," differs significantly from the adjective *chak*, "red."

2.1.2. Vowels

The five vowels in Mayan (*a, e, i, o,* and *u*) have four variations each, for a total of twenty possible vowel sounds, as shown in **table 2.2**. This may sound complicated, but think of the difference between "fate" and "fat": two vowel sounds are represented by one vowel sign (although the final *e* of "fate" gives us a clue to the changed pronunciation, a feature found in Maya writing as well). In Classic Mayan, as currently reconstructed by some epigraphers, each vowel can be short, long, glottalized, or aspirated. It is worth mentioning that some reconstructions include more complex vowels, such as glottalized long (VV') as well as intervocalic-glottalized long (V'V) vowels, which can also be aspirated (VV'h). Only the four principal variations are used here.

A short vowel, represented in English as a single letter (*a, e, i, o,* or *u*), is only pronounced for a brief amount of time: a single "beat" within the utterance of the word. A long vowel, represented with the doubling of the letter (*aa, ee, ii, oo,* or *uu*; other scholars sometimes represent long vowels with a colon, *a:* or with the International Phonetic Alphabet [IPA] triangles, *aː*), holds the vowel sound longer: two "beats" in the word. English used to have this distinction in words such as "bet" and "beet." It was lost during the Great Vowel Shift (Jespersen 1907), when different vowel sounds came to replace differences in length.

The third vowel variation involves a glottal stop and is currently debated among epigraphers (see inset box 2.1, Key Controversy: Disharmonic Spellings of Complex Vow-

2.1. SOUNDS IN CLASSIC MAYAN

Table 2.2. Classic Mayan Vowel Sounds

Short Vowel			Long Vowel			Glottalized Vowel			Aspirated Vowel		
Classic Mayan	IPA	English Equivalent	Classic Mayan	IPA	English Equivalent	Classic Mayan	IPA	English Equivalent (Cockney)	Classic Mayan	IPA	English Equivalent
a	a	father	aa	a:	car (Boston: cah)	a'	aʔ	hatter (ha'er)	ah	aʰ	ahh!
e	e	late	ee	e:	play	e'	eʔ	nettle (ne'le)	eh	eʰ	bleh!
i	i	me	ii	i:	fee	i'	iʔ	little (li'l)	ih	iʰ	whee!
o	o	mold	oo	o:	row	o'	oʔ	bottle (bo'le)	oh	oʰ	ohh!
u	u	rude	uu	u:	boot	u'	uʔ	button (bu'on)	uh	uʰ	ooh!

els, for a discussion of this debate). A glottalized vowel, represented with an apostrophe after the vowel (*a', e', i', o',* or *u'*; other scholars sometimes represent glottalized vowels with a sign similar to a question mark without a dot [IPA], *aʔ*, or the number seven, *a7*), is a vowel whose utterance is terminated by a closing of the vocal chords. This is seen in English words such as "uh-oh" and "little" (in some dialects people drop the *tt* out of "little" in speech, saying something close to *li'l*). This distinction is important in Classic Mayan to distinguish otherwise identical-appearing words. **CHAK**, for instance, can be the name of the rain deity, *chaak,* or the color red, *chak,* depending on the length of the vowel.

The final variation is the aspirated vowel. This is represented by an *h* inserted between a vowel and a consonant. Aspiration is the "breathy" sound of gradually releasing air after a sound. You will notice in a number of words that an *h* is inserted into the reconstructed pronunciation (*k'a[h]k',* "fire," for instance). This is based on principles of historical linguistics and epigraphers' reconstructions of individual words. The current opinion is that the inclusion of *h* between a vowel and a consonant in a word is not regularly indicated by the glyphs themselves. Therefore words that require an infixed *h* must be learned. The Maya script, like any other writing system, is an imperfect representation of the spoken word; just think of the strange spellings of many English words. An infixed *h* is not absolutely necessary to translate the meaning of any given word and will neither invalidate nor decrease the accuracy of a translation. But an accurate transliteration is an important part of the analysis of any Maya inscription.

2.2. SYNHARMONY

Synharmony, defined by Yuri Knorozov (1952), occurs when the final vowel of a word matches the preceding vowel: that is, in a CV_1C-CV_1 or CV_1-CV_1 word, the vowels match. Most Mayan words end with a consonant, so writing Mayan with syllabic signs, which all end in vowels, would be problematic. Synharmony is a clever principle that circumvents this problem, as the final vowel in a synharmonic spelling is not pronounced. For instance, in order to write the word "jaguar," *b'ahlam,* the scribe, using syllables, would write **b'a-la-ma;** the final vowel matches the preceding vowel, so it is not pronounced. An unpronounced vowel is often placed in parentheses in transcriptions to indicate its silent status: **b'a-la-m(a).** This does not happen only with pure syllabic spellings; logograms with a phonetic complement also evince synharmony. Taking the "jaguar" example again, a scribe would write **B'ALAM-ma** to indicate *b'ahlam;* the **-ma** syllable echoes the final sound of the word for the reader but is not to be pronounced again. In this case, the entire final syllabic sign can be placed in parentheses: **B'ALAM-(ma).**

2.3. DISHARMONY

Disharmonic spellings occur when a word ends with a vowel that does not match the previous one: that is, in a CV_1C-CV_2 or CV_1-CV_2 word, vowels 1 and 2 do not match. As noted, the final vowel drops out of synharmonic spellings, allowing Maya scribes to write CVC words with a syllabic system. As in synharmony, the word-final disharmonic vowel also is unpronounced. Unlike the synharmonic final vowel, it actively changes the nature of the preceding vowel. Just as the English word "fat" differs from the word "fate" because of the silent word-final *e,* disharmonic word-final vowels in Classic Mayan might indicate a **complex vowel** within the word. Although the exact nature of this complex vowel is still debated (**see inset box 2.1**), it is relatively clear that the disharmonic spelling is intentional and important for understanding Classic inscriptions.

This book has adopted spelling conventions simplified from the rules of Alfonso Lacadena and Søren Wichmann (2004). Although there are four vowel "colors," V, VV, V', and Vh, only the first three appear to be indicated by the final vowel of a word. The infixed *h* is not usually indicated glyphically; its presence must be reconstructed and therefore placed in brackets (at least in the first instance). Although an infixed *h* is rarely spelled out glyphically and it is not usually necessary to differentiate similar-sounding words, it is nevertheless reconstructed in transliterations in this book. Beginning students do not need to master and memorize which words require an infixed-*h,* but this is an important part of current epigraphic debates.

Here is how the spelling of vowels works. A synharmonic spelling indicates a simple short vowel, *V,* or sometimes an aspirated vowel, *Vh,* as in Rule 1 in **table 2.3**. A disharmonic spelling indicates a complex vowel. Only three vowels end a disharmonic spelling: *a, i,* and *u;* they indicate either a long vowel (VV) or a glottalized vowel (V'). If a disharmonic spelling ends in **Ci**, it indicates a long vowel (Rule 2 in **table 2.3**). For instance **B'AK-(ki)** ends with an *i*-final syllable, indicating a long vowel: *b'aak,* meaning "bone" or "captive." Obviously the *i*-final syllable of a **Ci-Ci** word does not indicate a long *i,* because it is synharmonic. In this case, an *a*-final syllabic sign is used when the preced-

Table 2.3. Modified Spelling Rules Used in This Book

Rule 1:	$CV_1\text{-}CV_1$ →	CV_1C (or $CV_1[h]C$)	
Rule 2:	$CV_1\text{-}Ci$ →	CV_1V_1C	where $V_1 \neq i$
	$Ci\text{-}Ca$ →	$CiiC$	
Rule 3:	$CV_1\text{-}Cu$ →	$CV'C$ (or $CV'[h]C$)	where $V_1 = i, a$
	$CV_1\text{-}Ca$ →	$CV'C$ (or $CV'[h]C$)	where $V_1 = e, u, o$

Table 2.4. Synharmonic and Disharmonic Spelling Results

		Silent Vowel (CV-C<u>V</u>)				
		a	e	i	o	u
Spoken Vowel (C<u>V</u>-CV)	a	a (or a[h])		aa		a' (or a[h])
	e	e' (or e[h])	e (or e[h])	ee		
	i	ii		i (or i[h])		i' (or i[h])
	o	o' (or o[h])		oo	o (or o[h])	
	u	u' (or u[h])		uu		u (or u[h])

ing vowel is *i* to indicate a long vowel, such as in **AHIN-(na)** or *ahiin*, meaning "caiman." A glottalized vowel is indicated by *u*-final syllabic signs after words with *i* or *a* as the preceding vowel or *a*-final syllabic signs after words with *e, u,* or *o* as the preceding vowel. This is seen in words such as **7-si-p(u)** or *huk si'p* as the name of the deity "Seven Sip"; **b'a-k(u)** or *b'a'k*, which means "child"; **CH'EN-(na)** or *ch'e'n* for "cave"; **hu-n(a)** or *hu'n* for "book"; and **pi-xo-l(a)** or *pixo'l*, which means "hat." The glottalized vowel pattern may also sometimes indicate an aspirated vowel, *Vh*. It might seem strange that this aspirated vowel "flavor" is apparently free-floating. Throughout Maya writing (and other systems), so-called weak sounds are often underrepresented or left out. The Classic Mayan word for "zero," *mih*, is usually only spelled **mi**, leaving the final aspirated sound for the reader to add. **Table 2.4** indicates the resultant vowel from any combination of vowels using the same rules as in **table 2.3**, just displayed in a different way. Use this information to complete **exercises 2.1 and 2.2**. Synharmonic transcriptions are given in **exercise 2.1**: transliterate them using Rule 1 from **table 2.3** (do not worry about the infixed-*h* right now). In **exercise 2.2** you must use Rules 2 and 3 to spell the transcribed disharmonic words.

BOX 2.1. KEY CONTROVERSY: Disharmonic Spellings of Complex Vowels

Disharmonic spellings were once thought to be conventional deviations from the synharmonic pattern or underspellings (when a final sound is not specified by the glyphs). For example, **hu-na** or **HUN-na** may have been a type of underspelling of *hunal*, "headdress," where the reader adds the final *l* from context and knowledge of the script. This is similar to abbreviations in many modern languages.

While convention and underspellings may be at work, two recent hypotheses have been put forward to explain disharmonic spellings (CV_1-CV_2 or CV_1C-CV_2) in Classic Mayan inscriptions. Stephen Houston, David Stuart, and John Robertson (2004: 84) suggest that "disharmony marks additional, medial elements within roots," meaning vowel length. Vowel length is the differentiation (in some languages) in the amount of time a vowel is pronounced. In glyph studies, this is generally represented by a doubling of the vowel: *a* → *aa*, although *a:* or *a:* would be a more traditional linguistic transcription. The difference is important, for example, in **CHAK**, *chak*, "red" and **CHAK**, *chaak*, "rain deity." In Houston, Stuart, and Robertson's model, a disharmonic spelling suggests either a long vowel (VV) or sometimes another complex vowel (Vh) in the CVC root.

Alfonso Lacadena and Søren Wichmann (2004: 110) "propose that glottal stops were indicated by means of the disharmonic spelling patterns" seen in numerous glyphic examples. While their model also represents a long vowel by disharmonic spellings, it differs from the view of Houston et al. (2004) on the representation of the other complex vowels: Vh and V'. Houston et al. (2004: 95) suggest that the glottal stop was phased out of Classic Mayan and does not appear. Furthermore, they suggest that *h* is indicated as an irregular disharmonic or synharmonic spelling. Lacadena and Wichmann (2004), in contrast, suggest that the glottal stop not only was still present but is indicated by specific disharmonic spellings. Additionally, they believe that *h* is not indicated by synharmonic or disharmonic spellings but rather rarely indicated by the addition of a logogram or syllabic sign that contains /h/ (Lacadena and Wichmann 2004: 103).

Both models are built on Classic Mayan words reconstructed from colonial and modern Maya languages. Because of the nature of historical linguistic reconstruction, the authors are able to reconstruct the same glyphic spellings in different ways, each of which may be argued to be correct. For instance, the word "book," spelled **hu-na,** is reconstructed by Houston et al. (2004: 88) as *huun* and by Lacadena and Wichmann (2004: 144) as *hu'n*. They all cite a number of modern Maya languages to support their reconstruction as valid. At present it is nearly impossible to know which hypothesis (if either) is accurately representing Classic Mayan vowels. Importantly, in the majority of cases, these differences will not affect the meaning of the word; both parties translate **hu-na** as "book." In the end, this is a semantic argument: the final translation is rarely (if ever) affected by the minor differences in transliteration spelling.

Robertson et al. (2007) recently have devised an updated set of spelling rules, using a completely different methodology. Instead of sticking to purely linguistic and epigraphic arguments, they make use of "universals and logic." They attempt to show, by way of logical proofs, the possible complex vowel spellings of Maya writing. In this 2007 work, they do accept the presence of the glottalized vowel (V') in the Classic script (a marked change from the Houston et al. 2004 article). They even go so far as to offer spelling rules. A fair portion

Table 2.5. Lacadena and Wichmann's Complex Vowel Spelling Rules

Rule 1:	CV_1-CV_1	→	CV_1C or $CV_1[h]C$	
Rule 2:	CV_1-Ci	→	CV_1V_1C	where $V_1 \neq i$
	Ci-Ca	→	CiiC	
Rule 3:	CV_1-Cu	→	CV'C, CV'[V]C, CV[V]'C, or CV'[h]C	where $V_1 = i, a$
	CV_1-Ca	→	CV'C, CV'[V]C, CV[V]'C, or CV'[h]C	where $V_1 \neq i, a$

of Robertson et al. (2007) is a critique of Lacadena and Wichmann (2004); but in the end, many of their rules agree with them in part. Unfortunately, the spelling rules in Robertson et al. (2007) are so inclusive that they are not predictive. For instance, a **Ca-Ca** transcription could result in the vowel spellings *CaC, CaaC, CahC,* or *Ca'C*. Again, we must rely on their reconstruction of each word for the correct spelling. In this scenario, it is impossible to reconstruct the transliteration from the glyphs alone.

A chronological factor also affects this debate. Because languages change over time, what may have been the pronunciation at the beginning of the Classic period may have changed significantly by the end of the Classic, circa 800 years later. Although many vowel variations are presented in table 2.5, they may not all be present at the same time. Furthermore, glyphic spellings change over time. For example, **CHAPAT**, "centipede," was initially complemented by **-tu,** yielding *chapaa'[h]t*; later by **-ti,** reconstructed as *chapaa[h]t*; and finally by -**ta,** resulting in *chapa[h]t*. There may not be one canonical spelling, but the meaning remains the same throughout. Modified spelling rules of Lacadena and Wichmann (2004) are used for the purposes of this book for three main reasons. First, taking a neutral stance and indicating the difference in transliteration every time would be cumbersome and confusing. For example, for every complex vowel, I could transcribe both options, *huun/hu'n*, or mark the vowel differently, *hu*n*; but these solutions would be awkward. Second, one major disadvantage of the argument of Houston et al. (2007) is that their spelling of each complex vowel is not predicted by the glyphic spelling. For instance, a word with a **Ci-Ci** transcription could represent a *CiC, CiiC, CihC,* or *Ci'C* spelling with no way for the student to know which is meant except to trust and memorize their reconstruction. Third, the draw of the model of Lacadena and Wichmann (2004) is the simplicity of the rules, which describe the data well and are easy to learn and implement.

It is important to remember that this debate is about the nature of the vowels, not the meaning of the words. Regardless of the side of the debate that we choose, the meaning should stay the same. The use of Lacadena and Wichmann's rules here is not an absolute endorsement of their correctness. Their argument is merely the simplest current model that seems to fit the data. The most parsimonious solution often proves to be correct. As this debate continues, editions of this book will be updated to reflect the current state of affairs.

continues

BOX 2.1. KEY CONTROVERSY (continued)

Table 2.6 lays out possible disharmonic or synharmonic spellings with the resulting vowel according to Houston et al. (2004), Lacadena and Wichmann (2004), and the newer Robertson et al. (2007: 10). A few combinations, such as **Ca-Ce**, are not attested in the script and are marked with an em dash (—). Complete differences are marked with the "not equal" sign (≠), complete agreements are marked with an "equal" sign (=), and possible agreement is marked with an "approximation" sign (≈). For those keeping score, out of a possible twenty-five, Houston et al. (2004) and Lacadena and Wichmann (2004) completely agree twelve times, possibly agree six times, and totally disagree seven times. Lacadena and Wichmann (2004) and Robertson et al. (2007) completely agree eight times, possibly agree fifteen times, and totally disagree twice. This may be a small sign of progress.

Table 2.6. Correspondence of Complex Vowel Spellings

	Houston et al. 2004		Lacadena and Wichmann 2004		Robertson et al. 2007
Ca-Ca	CaC	≈	CaC, CahC	≈	CaC, CaaC, Ca'C, CahC
-Ce	—	=	—	=	—
-Ci	CaaC, CahC	≈	CaaC	≈	CaaC, Ca'C, CahC
-Co	—	=	—	=	—
-Cu	CaaC, CahC	≠	Ca'C, Ca'hC, Caa'C, Caa'hC, Ca'aC	≈	Ca'C, CahC
Ce-Ca	CeeC	≠	Ce'C, Ce'hC, Cee'C, Cee'hC, Ce'eC	≈	CeeC, Ce'C, CehC
-Ce	CeC	≈	CeC, CehC	≈	CeC, CeeC, Ce'C, CehC
-Ci	—	≠	CeeC	≈	CeeC, CehC
-Co	—	=	—	=	—
-Cu	CeeC, CehC	≠	CeCu[l, m, n]	≠	CehC, CehC
Ci-Ca	CiiC	=	CiiC	≈	CiiC, Ci'C, CihC
-Ce	—	=	—	=	—
-Ci	CiC, CihC (CiiC)	≈	CiC, Ci[h]C	≈	CiC, CiiC, Ci'C, CihC
-Co	—	=	—	=	—
-Cu	CihC	≠	Ci'C, Ci'hC, Cii'C, Cii'hC, Ci'iC	≈	Ci'C, CihC
Co-Ca	CooC	≠	Co'C, Co'hC, Coo'C, Coo'hC, Co'oC	≈	CooC, Co'C
-Ce	—	=	—	=	—
-Ci	CooC	=	CooC	≈	CooC, CohC
-Co	CoC	≈	CoC, CohC	≈	CoC, CooC, Co'C, CohC
-Cu	—	=	—	≠	CohC
Cu-Ca	CuuC	≠	Cu'C, Cu'hC, Cuu'C, Cuu'hC, Cu'uC	≈	CuuC, Cu'C, CuhC
-Ce	—	=	—	=	—
-Ci	CuuC	=	CuuC	≈	CuuC, CuhC
-Co	—	=	—	=	—
-Cu	CuC, CuuC, CuhC	≈	CuC, CuhC	≈	CuC, CuuC, Cu'C, CuhC

( ) denotes attested but less-common spellings

[ ] denotes consonants that complete an underspelling

2.3. DISHARMONY

Exercise 2.1. Synharmonic Transliterations

The transcriptions and translations of some common synharmonic vocabulary words are shown here. Transliterate the vocabulary in the spaces using the spelling rules in table 2.5 and add parentheses as needed to transcriptions (remember that unpronounced final vowels and syllables are put in parentheses).

<u>Titles:</u>

a-ja-wa _____ ruler (n)

b'a-ka-b'a _____ first of the earth (n)

ch'o-ko
CH'OK-ko _____ youth, heir (n)

IXIK-ki _____ woman (n)

ma-ma _____ grandfather, ancestor (n)

sa-ja-la _____ ajaw subordinate (n)

WAY-ya _____ companion spirit (n)

<u>Animals:</u>

b'a-la-ma _____ jaguar (n)

CHAN-na _____ snake, sky (n)

MO'-o _____ macaw (n)

<u>Adjective:</u>

LAKAM-ma _____ big, great, wide (adj)

<u>Colors:</u>

AK'AB'-b'a _____ darkness, night (n)

CHAK-ka _____ red (n), great (adj)

K'AN-na _____ yellow (n), precious (adj)

<u>Objects:</u>

CHAN-na _____ sky/snake (n)

ka-b'a _____ earth (n)

ka-ka-wa
²ka-wa _____ chocolate (n)

KOHAW
ko-ha-wa _____ helmet (n)

K'IN-ni _____ sun, day (n)

la-ka _____ plate (n)

PAKAL-la _____ shield (n)

pi-tzi _____ ball game (n)

po-mo _____ incense (n)

TAJ-ja _____ torch (n)

TZ'AM-ma
tz'a-ma _____ throne (n)

tz'i-b'i _____ writing (n)

u-k'i-b'i _____ drinking vessel (n)

u-xu-lu _____ carving, sculpture (n)

WITZ-tzi _____ mountain, hill (n)

SPELLING AND LANGUAGE

Exercise 2.2. Disharmonic Transliterations

The transcriptions and translations of some common disharmonic vocabulary words are shown here. Transliterate the vocabulary in the spaces using the spelling rules in table 2.5 and add parentheses as needed to transcriptions (remember that unpronounced final vowels and syllables are put in parentheses).

Titles:

B'AK-ki
b'a-ki   _____   bone, captive (n)

b'a-hi
B'AH   _____   image, first, head (n)

ch'a-ho-ma   _____   incense scatterer (n)

ITZ'AT-ti
i-tz'a-ti   _____   sage (n)

Animals:

OK-ki   _____   dog, foot (n)

SUTZ'-tz'i
su-tz'i   _____   bat (n)

Deities:

K'AWIL-la   _____   K'awil (n)

Objects:

HUN-na   _____   book, paper (n)

NAB'-b'i
na-b'i   _____   pool of water, lily (n)

NAH-hi
na-hi   _____   house (n)

OL-la   _____   center, heart (n)

TOK'
to-k'a   _____   flint, obsidian (n)

TUN-ni   _____   stone (n)

OTOT-ti   _____   house (n)

2.4. PHONETIC COMPLEMENTS

Syllabic signs are often used as **phonetic complements,** which indicate the pronunciation of a logogram. Usually the phonetic complement echoes the first and/or last sound of the logogram, although a complete phonetic spelling sometimes follows a logogram. The most common example of this is the spelling of "jaguar," *b'ahlam*. The logogram **B'ALAM** is often prefixed by the **b'a-** syllabogram and/or postfixed by the **-ma** syllabic sign, as seen in **figures 1.19 and 2.1**. This pronunciation-aid is often superfluous, but in some cases it indicates important distinctions. For instance, "snake" is often represented by the word *chan* in Classic Mayan. At the site of Calakmul, however, the logogram for snake is usually prefixed by the syllabogram **ka-,** indicating that the word should be pronounced *kan*, a northern (Yucatec) pronunciation (**see fig. 2.1**). Specifically spelling out *kan* at Calakmul may indicate a conscious effort on the part of the scribes to highlight their regional dialect as distinct from their Ch'olan adversaries in the Peten, much like the British and American spellings of certain words (such as "centre/center" and "theatre/theater").

Figure 2.1. Phonetic Complements

B'ALAM
b'a[h]lam
jaguar

CHAN
chan
snake

B'ALAM-(ma)
b'a[h]lam
jaguar

(ka)-KAN
kan
snake (Yuc.)

2.5. "NEW" VERSUS "OLD" ORTHOGRAPHY

In the body of literature surrounding Maya hieroglyphics, some words may be spelled differently in various contexts. For example, the Tzolk'in day and Haab' month names are spelled differently than they are transliterated. The reason behind this disconnect is the use of traditional colonial spelling versus modern orthography. The term "orthography" simply refers to the proper use of letters and spelling in a written language. Most glyph-related terms and glosses were written with the same orthography as Colonial Yucatec and Spanish, which had been used for over four hundred years. For instance, the word *winik* would have been spelled *uinic* in the traditional orthography. Most recent epigraphers have switched to a more English-based spelling system. Although some might argue that it is more phonologically accurate than the traditional spelling, the International Phonetic Alphabet (IPA) could have been used if accuracy was the goal. The pronunciation is the same: just the spelling has changed. Furthermore, the glottal stop and vowel complexity were not always represented in the old orthography, depending on the author, but they are always present in the new orthography. There are also spelling differences as well as minor vowel discrepancies, but it is usually clear what word is being written in either orthography. The letters that represent equivalent sounds are given in **table 2.7** for reference.

Table 2.7. Correspondence of Old and New Orthography

Old	IPA	New
c	k	k
h	h or x	h or j
dz	t͡s	tz
u	w	w

2.6. LANGUAGE(S) REPRESENTED GLYPHICALLY

Throughout this book, the language written on stone monuments is referred to as Classic Mayan. This is a neutral way to refer to the written language. Stephen Houston, John Robertson, and David Stuart (2000) have argued that the language represented glyphically is related to the Ch'olan family of Maya languages (including the still-spoken Ch'ol, Chontal, and Ch'orti'). They label this language "Classic Ch'olti'an." Specifically they argue that the Classic language was an "Eastern Ch'olan" language that became the colonial-era language known as Ch'olti', which is a direct ancestor of the modern Ch'orti' language. It does appear that a Ch'olan language is represented in Maya hieroglyphic writing, but it may not be the only one. Examples of some Yucatecan influences on local glyphic spellings occur, especially later and in the Northern Lowlands. Yucatec sounds differ systematically from those of Ch'olan languages. For instance, a Ch'olan *t* is pronounced *ch* by a Yucatecan speaker, and a Ch'olan *ch* changed to *k* in Yucatec. Indeed, it appears that Calakmul specifically spelled its emblem glyph with the Yucatecan pronunciation, **(ka)-KAN** or *kan* for "snake" instead of the Ch'olan *chan*. This may have been a meaningful way for the northern center Calakmul to separate itself from its southern Ch'olan enemies. It is also possible that a "Western Ch'olan" language was represented at sites such as Palenque. Indeed, systematic differences are seen between eastern and western glyphic spellings. For instance, the positional verb *chum*, "to seat," may be inflected **CHUM-la-ja** in the east, producing *chumlaj*. The same verb may be spelled **CHUM-wa-ni**, read *chumwaan*, in the west, meaning "he/she sat." Furthermore, hieroglyphic writing probably spans more than 1,300 years, so changes that occurred over time are represented in glyphic spelling. In short, the linguistic variety represented glyphically is more complex than can be contained in any single language. Therefore, for the purposes of this book, the language represented on carved stone monuments (which by definition come from the Classic period) is best referred to as "Classic Mayan." There are regional and temporal differences in the language. For a review of the scholarly debate, see Wichmann (2006).

> **FURTHER READING**

Synharmonic and Disharmonic Spellings and Their Implications

Houston, Stephen D., David Stuart, and John Robertson
1998 Disharmony in Maya Hieroglyphic Writing: Linguistic Change and Continuity in Classic Society. In *Anatomía de una civilización: Aproximaciones interdisciplinarias a la cultura maya,* edited by A. Ciudad R., Y. Fernández, J. M. García C., M. J. Iglesias Ponce de León, A. Lacadena G. G., and L. T. Sanz C., pp. 275–96. Madrid: Spanish Society of Maya Studies.
2004 Disharmony in Maya Hieroglyphic Writing: Linguistic Change and Continuity in Classic Society. In *The Linguistics of Maya Writing,* edited by S. Wichmann, pp. 83–99. Salt Lake City: University of Utah Press.

These are the original publications in which Houston, Stuart, and Robertson argue for their disharmonic spelling paradigms.

Lacadena, Alfonso, and Søren Wichmann
2004 On the Representation of the Glottal Stop in Maya Writing. In *The Linguistics of Maya Writing,* edited by S. Wichmann, pp. 100–164. Salt Lake City: University of Utah Press.

This article argues for a different vowel reconstruction for disharmonic spelling, including a postvowel glottal stop. This is in direct opposition to the idea proposed by Robertson et al. 2007.

Robertson, John, Stephen D. Houston, Marc Zender, and David Stuart
2007 *Universals and the Logic of the Material Implication: A Case Study from Maya Hieroglyphic Spelling.* Research Reports on Maya Hieroglyphic Writing, No. 62. Washington, D.C.: Center for Maya Research.

This is the latest article in the disharmonic spelling debate. Robertson, Houston, Zender, and Stuart propose an updated set of disharmonic spelling rules, which are more broad than those initially proposed in 1998 and 2004.

Regional Differences in the Glyphs

Wichmann, Søren
2002 *Hieroglyphic Evidence for the Historical Configuration of Eastern Ch'olan.* Research Report on Ancient Maya Writing, No. 51. Washington, D.C.: Center for Maya Research.
2006 Mayan Historical Linguistics and Epigraphy: A New Synthesis. *Annual Review of Anthropology* 35: 279–94.

Languages Represented Glyphically

Houston, Stephen D., John Robertson, and David Stuart
2000 The Language of the Classic Maya Inscriptions. *Current Anthropology* 41(3): 321–56.

Lacadena, Alfonso
2000 Nominal Syntax and the Linguistic Affiliation of Classic Maya Texts. In *The Sacred and the Profane: Architecture and Identity in the Maya Lowlands,* edited by P. R. Colas, K. Delvendahl, M. Kuhnert, and A. Schubart, pp. 111–28. Acta Mesoamericana, Vol. 10. Munich: Verlag Anton Saurwein.

Macri, Martha J., and Matthew G. Looper
2003 Nahua in Ancient Mesoamerica: Evidence from Maya Inscriptions. *Ancient Mesoamerica* 14: 285–97.

3. DATES AND NUMBERS

Dates create the structure of many Maya inscriptions. Most monumental inscriptions start with a full date, giving us the exact day an event happened, and other related events tied to that initial day. The Maya are well known for their complex calendar, with which they accurately tracked astronomical cycles, predicted eclipses, and understood the universe as well as or better than their contemporaries. Just as the Gregorian calendar uses a number of cycles (days of the week, months, days in a month, and years) to pinpoint one day in history, the Maya calendar also used a number of cycles.

3.1. NUMBERS

Numbers are easily recognizable and will help you divide an inscription into discrete sentences or phrases. Like most Western number systems today, the Maya used place notation to express large numbers. The number 1,492 has one 1,000 ($10^3 \times 1$), four 100s ($10^2 \times 4$), nine 10s ($10^1 \times 9$), and two 1s ($10^0 \times 2$). We know the relative value of each number because of its position in relation to the other numbers: each unit is ten times larger than the one to its right. The Maya also had the concept of zero, which is essentially a placeholder in a place-notation system, well before the Western world. Unlike most Western number systems, which are based in groups of ten (sometimes called base-10 or decimal), Maya numbers are base-20 (sometimes referred to as vigesimal). Although this may sound strange or difficult, especially for those who do not enjoy math, it is really as easy as the Western system once you learn how it works. Because each place can go from 0 to 19, a dot is used to separate significant places. For instance, the number 1.13.12 has one unit of 400 ($20^2 \times 1$), 13 units of 20 ($20^1 \times 13$), and 12 units of 1 ($20^0 \times 12$). Each position to the left raises increases the unit value 20-fold (just as it increases by 10 in a decimal system). The vigesimal number 1.13.12 would be converted to 672 in the decimal system ($[1 \times 400] + [13 \times 20] + [12 \times 1]$), although the conversion between the systems is only needed for correlating the Maya calendar with the Western one. You can do addition and subtraction with the Maya vigesimal system just as easily as with the decimal system with just a little practice. For instance, adding the numbers 1.13.12 and 3.6.14 is easy. By adding 12 to 14, you get 26, which is 6 more than the 20 that can be held in any one place, so the 20 is converted into 1 of the next-highest place (to the left) and the 6 is left in the 1s place. Similarly, the 20s place is added up to 20 (1 + 13 + 6), which again hits the maximum amount for this position, so 20 is converted to 1 in the next-highest place, leaving zero for the 20s. Finally, the 400s are added up to equal 5 with no need to go to the next highest place. If you like to double check your arithmetic, you can convert all of the numbers to decimal and use a standard calculator (672 + 1,334 = 2,006). For your convenience, **table 3.1** can be used to convert vigesimal (base-20) numbers into decimal (base-10).

Now that we can convert vigesimal numbers into decimal numbers, let's take a look at how to recognize numbers in the inscriptions. **Figure 3.1** has two of the three types

Table 3.1. Vigesimal Math and Conversion

Vigesimal numbers can be added just like decimal numbers except that place values carry over after reaching 20, not 10.

$$
\begin{array}{ccc}
1 & 1\ 1 & 1 \\
01.13.12 & 01.13.12 & 01.13.12 \\
+\ 03.06.14 & +\ 03.06.14 & +\ 03.06.14 \\
\hline
\cancel{26} & \cancel{20} & 5 \\
06 & 00.06 & 05.00.06
\end{array}
$$

Vigesimal numbers can be converted to decimal numbers by transposing the vigesimal number into the following form, starting with the right-most number and then adding the products down. 12.04.08.18.00.15.09 is used as an example; for larger numbers, continue to increase the units size by a power of one.

$$
\begin{array}{rrrrr}
09 \times & 1 & (20^0) & = & 9 \\
15 \times & 20 & (20^1) & = & 300 \\
00 \times & 400 & (20^2) & = & 0 \\
18 \times & 8{,}000 & (20^3) & = & 144{,}000 \\
08 \times & 160{,}000 & (20^4) & = & 1{,}280{,}000 \\
04 \times & 3{,}200{,}000 & (20^5) & = & 12{,}800{,}000 \\
12 \times & 64{,}000{,}000 & (20^6) & = & 768{,}000{,}000\ + \\
& & & & 782{,}224{,}309
\end{array}
$$

---

of numerals in Maya writing: bar-and-dot and head variants. The third way to represent numbers in Maya inscriptions is with full-figure depictions. Bar-and-dot numerals are by far the most common way in which the Maya represent numbers. A dot represents a one, and a bar represents five. No more than four dots are used in one place: any number over four uses bars for each multiple of five. A combination of up to four dots and three bars is used to represent numbers from one to nineteen. One bar and three dots is eight ([1 × 5] + [3 × 1]), three bars and two dots is seventeen ([3 × 5] + [2 × 1]), and so on. Maya iconography seems to suffer from *horror vacui* (the avoidance of empty space in art). Every surface or gap is filled by frills, curlicues, or flourishes. Bar-and-dot numbers are no different. When one or two dots are used, half-moon elements are often added to fill in the vacant space, as seen accompanying the dots in **figure 3.1**'s examples of one, two, six, seven, eleven, twelve, sixteen, and seventeen. As noted, the Maya were the first society to represent zero. This was done with a flower-shaped glyph in the inscriptions and a conch shell in the codices.

The head-variant numerals are the glyphic embodiment of each number. Unlike the bar-and-dot numbers, which are like a tally, the head variants have individual attributes associated with that number. Although we may not understand the specific mythological association between a given number and its embodiment, the differences between one number and another are usually apparent. The head variants in **figure 3.1**, just like the rest of the standardized glyphs in this book, all have the minimum attributes needed to identify each number. Head variants in real inscriptions may appear more complex, but the minimum attributes should still be present.

Figure 3.1. Bar-and-Dot and Head-Variant Numbers

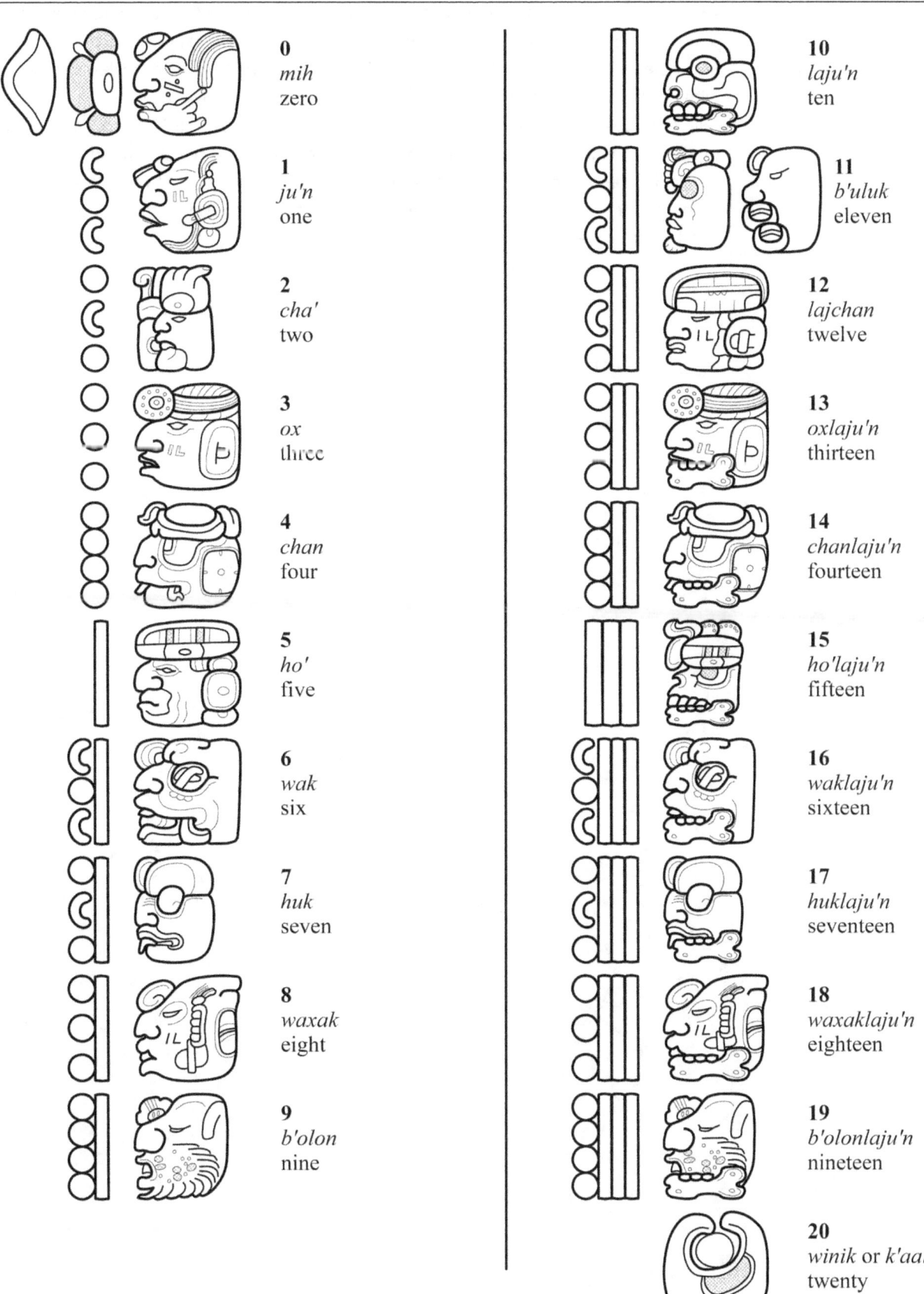

Full-figure variants, the third category of numbers, depict a complete being, not just the head, as the physical embodiment of a number. Much as in the case of the head variants, a number of minimum characteristics identify each variant as one number or another. The attributes of the full-figure depictions are identical to the characteristics of the head variants of each number. **Table 3.2** has each number from zero to twenty with its transcription, transliteration, and minimum attributes for the head variants and full-figure depictions (some descriptions drawn from Thompson 1950: 131–37). Using **figure 3.1**, **table 3.1**, and **table 3.2**, try to complete **exercise 3.1**. In 3.1.1 you must find and transcribe the numbers on five inscriptions. In 3.1.2 you are asked to complete four addition problems using vigesimal math. In 3.1.3 you must convert vigesimal numbers into the decimal system.

3.1. NUMBERS

Table 3.2. Minimum Attributes of Number Variants

Transcription	*Transliteration*	Attributes
0	*mih*	Young head, marked with three dots on the cheek Hand stretched across the lower jaw
1	*ju'n*	**IXIK/na**, woman's head, or **IXIM**, corn god's head Marked by "IL" on cheek Hair from above ear along jaw Earflare
2	*cha'*	Clenched fist headdress Female head, marked by "IL" Preceded by **SAK**
3	*ox*	Headdress with disk **IK** ("T"-shaped) sign on cheek
4	*chan*	Sun deity **K'IN** infix or patch Square, drop-eye Barbell Front tooth
5	*ho'*	Elderly male head Mouth wrinkles **HAAB'** glyph headdress
6	*wak*	Male head Ax-eye pupil Barbell Front tooth
7	*huk*	Male head Loop-eye pupil Front tooth
8	*waxak*	Maize god head Sometimes marked by "IL" Hair only on top of head Loop forehead decoration
9	*b'olon*	Jaguar-spots Male head with beard **YAX** forehead decoration
10	*laju'n*	Skull head "%" sign on cheek Visible mandible "Death-Eye" forehead decoration Three dots on upper forehead
11	*b'uluk*	Male head **KAB'** or earth markings (circle with dark crosshatching) Sometimes appears with stuffed mouth
12	*lajchan*	Young head **CHAN**, heaven sign headdress
13	*oxlaju'n*	Head of #3 with mandible Sometimes with oversized pendulous nose
14	*chanlaju'n*	Head of #4 with mandible
15	*ho'laju'n*	Head of #5 with mandible
16	*waklaju'n*	Head of #6 with mandible
17	*huklaju'n*	Head of #7 with mandible
18	*waxaklaju'n*	Head of #8 with mandible
19	*b'olonlaju'n*	Head of #9 with mandible
20	*winik* or *k'aal*	**ja/AJ** sign with a single large circle instead of three small ones in the upper portion

78 DATES AND NUMBERS

Exercise 3.1. Numerals (page 1 of 3)

1. Use these five inscriptions to complete the following exercises.

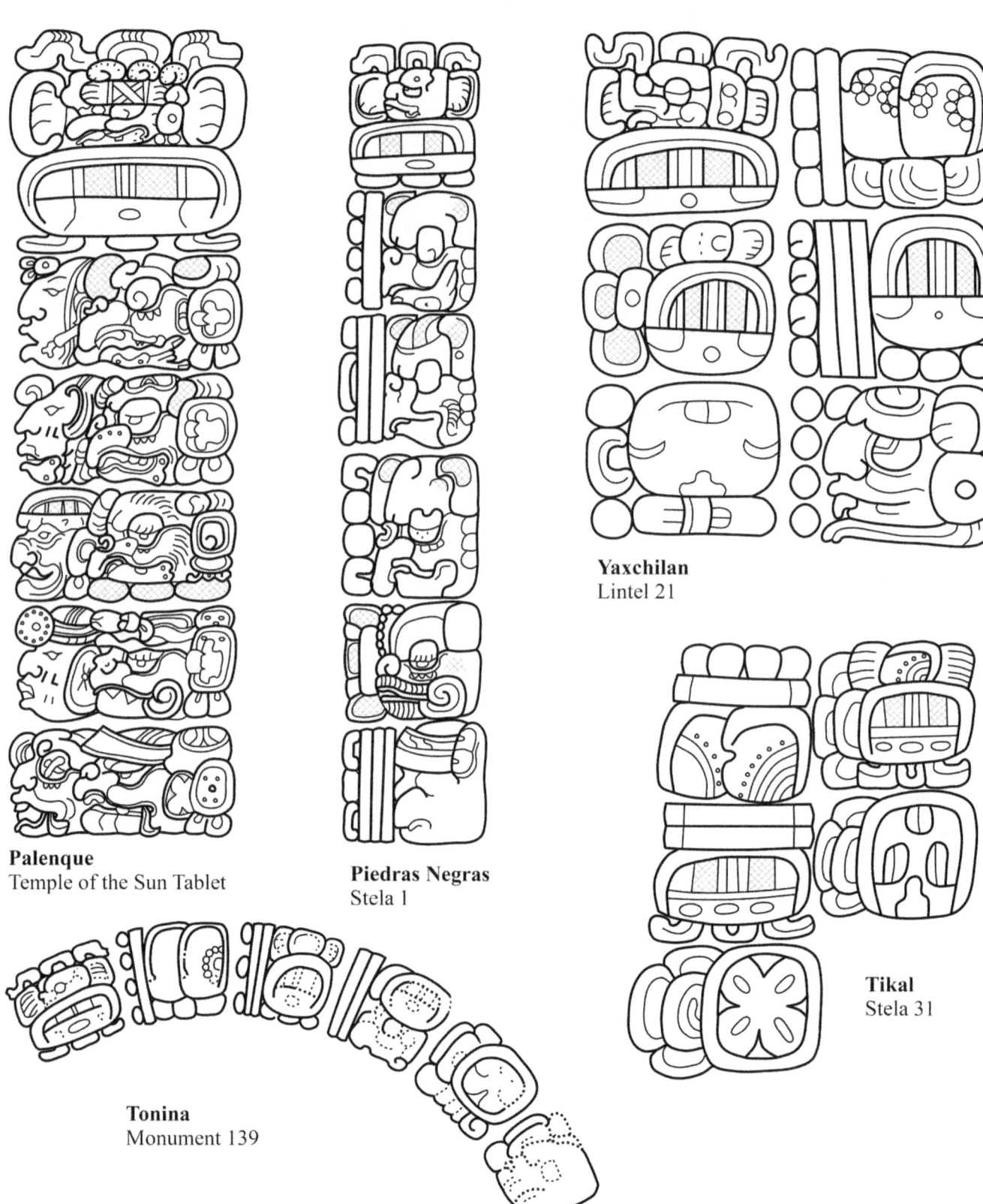

Palenque
Temple of the Sun Tablet

Piedras Negras
Stela 1

Yaxchilan
Lintel 21

Tikal
Stela 31

Tonina
Monument 139

Exercise 3.1 (page 2 of 3)

Exercise 3.1.1
1. For each of the five inscriptions, write out each number in the spaces below.

Palenque
Tablet of the Sun

___
___
___
___

Piedras Negras
Stela 1

___
___
___
___

Yaxchilan
Lintel 21

___ ___
___ ___

Tonina
Monument 139

___ ___
___

Tikal
Stela 31

___ ___
___ ___
___

Exercise 3.1.2
1. Complete the following equations, writing the answers in bar-and-dot numerals (remember that place values increase from bottom to top).

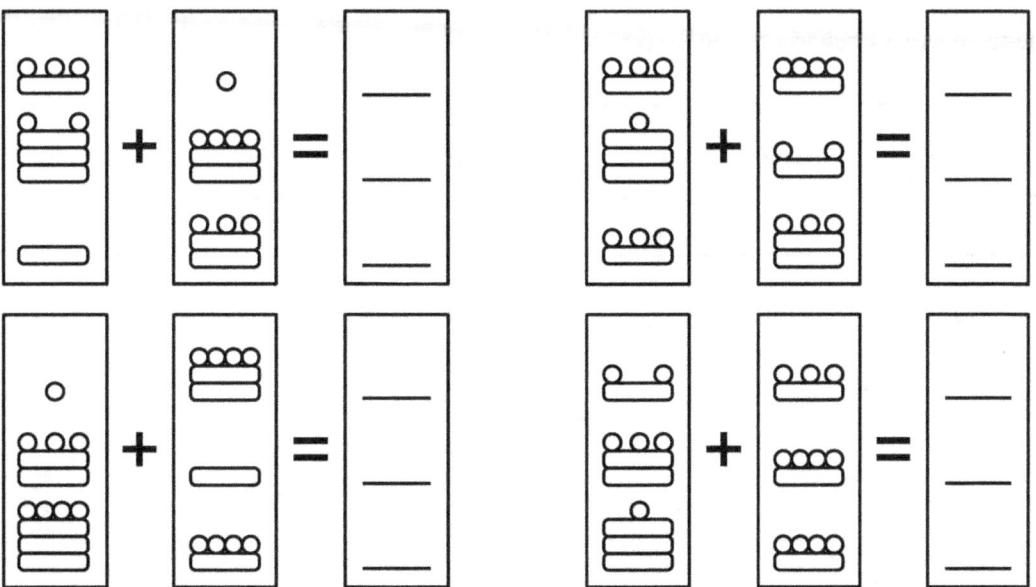

Exercise 3.1.3
1. Convert the following Maya numbers (vigesimal, base-20) to decimal (base-10) numbers.

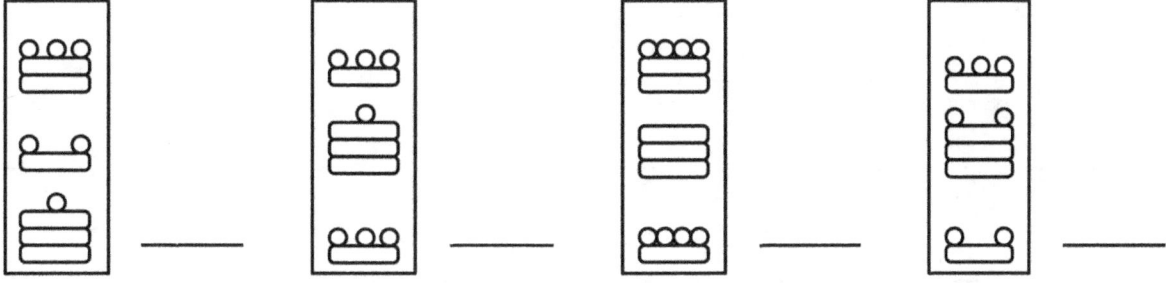

DATES AND NUMBERS

Exercise 3.1 (page 3 of 3)

Exercise 3.1.4
1. Identify the Initial Series Introductory Glyph and periods on the five Long Count inscriptions given.

Palenque
Tablet of the Sun
____
____
____
____
____

Piedras Negras
Stela 1
____
____
____
____
____

Yaxchilan
Lintel 21
____ ____
____ ____
____ ____

Tonina
Monument 139
____ ____
____ ____

Tikal
Stela 31
____ ____
____ ____
____
____

Exercise 3.1.5:
1. Transcribe the five given dates to __.__.__.__.__ format.
2. Translate each date to English.
3. Convert each date to its Day Number.
4. Convert each date to Gregorian Year using the short conversion.
5. Convert each date to an exact Gregorian Date (except for dates before 0 CE).

	1. Date Transcription	2. Translate	3. Day Number	4. Greg. Year yyyy era	5. Greg. Date dd-mmm-yyyy era
Palenque Tablet of the Sun	__.__.__.__.__	_____ _____ _____ _____	_____	_____ _____	(__-__-____)
Piedras Negras Stela 1	__.__.__.__.__	_____ _____ _____ _____	_____	_____ _____	__-__-____
Yaxchilan Lintel 21	__.__.__.__.__	_____ _____ _____ _____ _____	_____	_____ _____	__-__-____
Tonina Monument 139	__.__.__.__.__	_____ _____ _____ _____ _____	_____	_____ _____	__-__-____
Tikal Stela 31	__.__.__.__.__	_____ _____ _____ _____ _____	_____	_____ _____	__-__-____

3.2. LONG COUNT

Just as Western dates can tell you the exact time something happened, the Maya calendar can identify the precise day of a recorded event. Unlike the Gregorian system, which uses years as the major unit and smaller units (months and days) to place a particular day, the Maya calendar records history measured in days from the mythic origin of the calendar on 13 August 3114 BCE. Instead of years, it provides a complete count of days since this beginning. The Long Count date starts many inscriptions and is the basis for the computation of the dates found on Maya monuments. Most monuments take the following general format: "On the [Long Count position]th day, a [day of the week], a day overseen by lord of the night X, when the moon was in such-and-such a position, [month] [day]th, so-and-so was born. X days, Y months, and Z years later, on [day of the week], [month] [day]th, so-and-so ascended to rulership. M days and N months earlier his father died. C days, B months, and A years after he ascended to rulership, so-and-so died." In this example, the Long Count is the count of days given at the beginning, tying all later days back to this point. We will deal with other cycles (such as the day names, month names, month days, and lunar and other cycles), but first we must learn how to identify, understand, and convert the Long Count date.

The Long Count is almost always found after the **Initial Series Introductory Glyph** (ISIG) (as seen in **fig. 3.2**). This glyph can usually be found at the top left-hand corner of an inscription. It is often twice as wide and tall as the other glyphs, taking up two columns and rows. The inset head is determined by the current month. You can use this glyph to reconstruct an eroded Haab' month (discussed in section 3.3). This glyph block might be transcribed as **tzi-k(a)-HAB'**, which would have been pronounced *tziik haab'*, literally "year count"; but some epigraphers make good arguments against this specific reading. Scholars agree, however, that this glyph can be translated semantically as "on the day . . . "

The ISIG is followed by the number of days since the mythical starting-point of the calendar. This is represented by five periods based on a modified vigesimal system. The basic unit of these periods is the day, called the K'in (spelled **K'IN**, pronounced *k'ihn*, "day" or "sun"). The full-figured and head variants depict the sun or monkey deity: look for the **K'IN** sign and prominent front tooth. Each K'in is equivalent to one day (probably starting at sundown). Twenty K'in make up one Winal, the next period. The Winal glyph, spelled **WINIK** and pronounced *winik*, meant "20" because of the number of days that it contained. The head and full-figured variants depict a frog. The third period, called the Tun, has 360 days, approximating the solar year (although the Maya calculated the actual year to 365.2420 days, only 17.28 seconds off modern calculations). Only 18 Winals were needed to constitute one Tun. This is a deviation from the pure base-20 system in order to achieve a closer approximation of the solar year (360 days instead of the 400 days if 20 Winals had been used). The Tun glyph is transcribed as **HAB'** or **HAB'-b'i**, read *haab'*, meaning "year." The full-figured and head variants of the Tun appear to be the Muwan bird of the Maya month of the same name; it has a bone mandible instead of a regular jaw. The next period is called the K'atun, although it may have been spelled **WINIK-HAB'** and pronounced *winikhaab'*, meaning roughly "20-years" or "score" (as in "four score and seven years ago"). It was made up of 20 Tuns, equaling 7,200 days (close to the approximately 7,305 days in 20 solar years). The head and full-figure variant of the K'atun may be

82 DATES AND NUMBERS

Figure 3.2. Long Count Glyphs and Head Variants

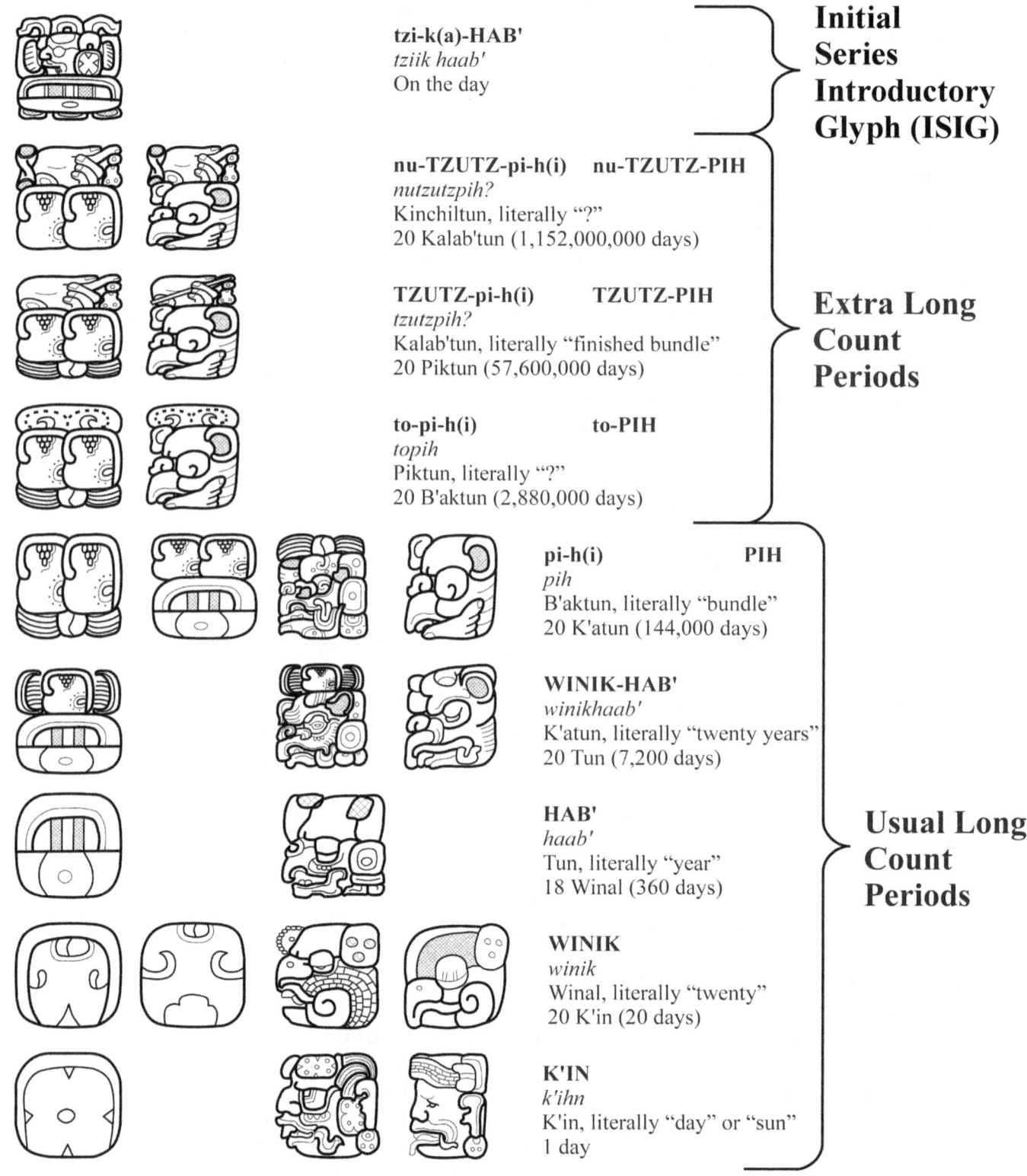

an owl or at least a bird of prey. The last standard period is what has been traditionally called the B'aktun, although it seems to be spelled **pi-hi** and pronounced *pih,* meaning "bundle." One B'aktun contains 144,000 days or 20 K'atuns. The B'aktun full-figure and head variant appears to be a bird, probably a vulture, with a human hand across the lower jaw, which makes it easily distinguishable from the superficially similar K'atun bird. Most inscriptions come from the ninth B'aktun (435–830 CE) or sometimes the late eighth (41–435 CE) or early tenth (830–1224 CE) B'aktun. This may sound confusing, but **figure 3.2** shows each period: its spelling, pronunciation, translation, value, and associated glyphs. Just as with numbers, each period has an abstract, head variant, and full-figure glyph that can be used to represent it. Usually only the five periods explained here are used, although you should be aware that many higher periods are used rarely to express events in much larger time scales. You will be able to recognize these unusual dates, so do not worry about them right now. Some of them are included in **figure 3.2**.

When you encounter a Long Count date, the first step is to transcribe it. The Long Count is written in descending order based on period length: B'aktun, K'atun, Tun, Winal, and then K'in. You only need to write the numbers, separated by periods, for each date. For example, 9.8.9.13.0 corresponds to 9 B'aktun, 8 K'atun, 9 Tun, 13 Winal, and 0 K'in. If you wanted to write this out completely, including the ISIG, it would look like this:

Transcription:
tzi-k(a)-HAB' 9-pi-h(i) 8-WINIK-HAB' 9-HAB' 13-WINIK 0-K'IN

Transliteration:
tziik haab' b'olon pih, waxak winikhaab', b'olon haab', uxlaju'n winik, mih k'ihn

Translation:
On the day 9 B'aktun, 8 K'atun, 9 Tun, 13 Winal, and no K'in.

But this does not tell us what day this corresponds to in the Gregorian calendar, so we must now calculate it. Using **table 3.3**, we can convert this to a **Day Number**, which is just the number of days that have passed since the beginning of the calendar in 3114 BCE. This example is almost the same as in **table 3.1**; but instead of multiplying the second-smallest unit by 20 it is only multiplied by 18 because of the modified vigesimal nature of the Long Count. Using this Day Number, another way to translate the passage would be: "On the 1,357,100th day."

Table 3.3. Long Count to Day Number Conversion

Transpose the Long Count date into the following form, starting with the B'aktun and continuing down to the K'in. 09.08.09.13.00 is used as an example; for larger periods, continue to increase the units size by multiplying the previous period by 20.

<u>09</u> B'aktun	×	144,000	(7,200 × 20)	=	1,296,000
<u>08</u> B'atun	×	7,200	(360 × 20)	=	57,600
<u>09</u> Tun	×	360	(20 × 18)	=	3,240
<u>13</u> Winal	×	20	(1 × 20)	=	260
<u>00</u> K'in	×	1		=	0 +
					1,357,100 days

Table 3.4. Abbreviated Day Number to Gregorian Year Conversion

1. Divide Day Number by a "vague" year and round down:
   1,357,100 days / 365 = 3,718.08 rounds down to 3,718 vague years

2. Subtract 3,114.25 years and round down again:
   3,718 vague years − 3,114.25 = rounds down to 603 CE

There are two ways to convert this Day Number into the Gregorian calendar. The abbreviated conversion (**table 3.4**) is quick and easy but will only give you an approximate year for any given Day Number. The complete conversion (**table 3.5**) is more complicated but will give you the exact day of any Long Count. As an example, we will convert the date 9.8.9.13.0.

For the abbreviated conversion, first divide the number of days (1,357,100) by the 365 days in a "vague" year to give an approximate number of years since the calendar began (3,718). Then subtract 3114.25 years and round down to convert the number of years elapsed in the Maya calendar to the modern calendar. In our example this works out to around 603 CE. This method is accurate to the nearest year.

A more accurate correlation requires a more complex computation, shown in **table 3.5**. In our example date of 9.8.9.13.0, the Goodman-Martinez-Thompson (GMT) correlation coefficient of 584,283 is added to our Day Number of 1,357,100 to reach the Julian Day Number of 1,941,383. Consult the Century Day Number chart (**table 3.5**) to find the largest Century Day Number that does not exceed the Julian Day Number. In this case, it is 1,940,206, corresponding to the seventh century (600s). This Century Day Number is then subtracted from the Julian Day Number, leaving 1,177 days remaining. This difference is divided by the 365 days of a "vague" year, giving 3.2247. The whole number 3 is the number of years into the current century (here the seventh century or 600s) that the date represents. The decimal remainder, 0.2247, is then multiplied by 365, equaling 82. We must account for the leap years elapsed in the current century. The whole year number 3 is divided by 4 and rounded down: in this case, 0.75 is rounded down to zero. If this happened to be a leap century (divisible by 400), an additional leap day would be added. In this example, the century 600 is not divisible, so a day is not added. The leap days are subtracted from the decimal remainder number of days (here 82 minus zero), leaving the number of days at 82. This is the number of days into the year that the date indicates. To figure out what month and day this represents, subtract the highest day number that does not exceed the current total day total: in this case, 59 (corresponding to March) is the highest without exceeding 82. If it is a leap year, divisible by 4, but not the end of a century divisible by 400, add one day to the Day Number if it is 59 or higher. In this case, 603 is not divisible by 4, so 1 is not added to the Day Number. This Day Number is subtracted from the day total: 82 minus 59 leaves 23 remaining days. Putting it all together, we find that the Long Count date of 9.8.9.13.0 is 23 March 603 CE. Using this same technique, please attempt **exercise 3.1.5**, where you must identify different periods as well as calculate Gregorian dates from Maya Long Counts. Almost no one does this by hand anymore. See appendix V for a discussion of useful computer programs that will calculate dates for you.

Table 3.5. Complete Day Number to Gregorian Year Conversion

1. Add GMT correlation coefficient to Day Number:
   584,283 GMT + 1,357,100 Day Number = 1,941,383 Julian Day Number (JDN)

2. Find largest Century Day Number (CDN) that is less than the Julian Day Number calculated above.
   1,940,206 CDN, 7th century

Century	CDN	Century	CDN	Century	CDN
1st (000)	1,721,060	8th (700)	1,976,730	15th (1400)	2,232,400
2nd (100)	1,757,585	9th (800)	2,013,254	16th (1500)	2,268,924
3rd (200)	1,794,109	10th (900)	2,049,779	17th (1600)	2,305,448
4th (300)	1,830,633	11th (1000)	2,086,303	18th (1700)	2,341,973
5th (400)	1,867,157	12th (1100)	2,122,827	19th (1800)	2,378,497
6th (500)	1,903,682	13th (1200)	2,159,351	20th (1900)	2,415,021
7th (600)	1,940,206	14th (1300)	2,195,876	21st (2000)	2,451,545

3. Subtract the CDN from the JDN:
   1,941,383 JDN − 1,940,206 CDN = 1,177 difference

4. Divide the difference by a "vague" year:
   1,177 / 365 = 3.2247 quotient

5. Divide the quotient into the integer and decimal:

   5.1.1. The integer corresponds to the year:
   Years (quotient integers) 3

   5.1.2. Divide years by four and round down:
   3 / 4 = .75 rounds down to 0 leap days

   5.1.3. Add 1 if century is evenly divisible by 400:
   0 leap days + 1 or 0 = 0 leap days

   5.1.4. Add century years (in parentheses) and years together:
   600 (century) + 3 (years) = 603 CE

   5.2.1. Multiply the decimal by a "vague" year:
   .2247 × 365 = 82 remainder

   5.2.2. The remainder corresponds to the days:
   Days (remainder) 82

   5.2.3. Subtract leap days (left column) from remainder days:
   82 days − 0 leap days = 82 days

6. Find the largest Day Number that is less than the days calculated above.
   59 Day Number, Month of March

Month	Day Number	Month	Day Number	Month	Day Number
January	0	May	120	September	243
February	31	June	151	October	273
March	59	July	181	November	304
April	90	August	212	December	334

7. *If* it is a leap year, add one to the Day Number *if* it is 59 or greater
   (leap years are those that are evenly divided by 4, except for centuries that are not divisible by 400):
   59 Day Number + 1 or 0 = 59 Day Number

8. Subtract the Day Number from the days calculated above:
   82 Days − 59 Day Number = 23 month day

9. Combine the year, month, and day information to get the date:
   The Long Count date refers to the 23rd (month day) day of March (month), 603 CE.

BOX 3.1. KEY CONTROVERSY: Long Count Correlations

By the time of contact, the Maya were no longer using the Long Count to record specific days in history. Instead, they were using an abbreviated version known as the Short Count. This count could give an accurate date within a 256-year span, after which year names began to repeat. There is a recorded correlation of the founding of Mérida, Yucatan, on 6 January 1542 CE in the K'atun 13 Ajaw. The question is: how many Short Count cycles of 256 years had gone by since that cycle had been connected with the Long Count (assuming continuous date-keeping)? Today the so-called GMT (Goodman-Martinez-Thompson) correlation (584,283) is probably the most-accepted correlation between the Maya Long Count and the Gregorian calendar. Joseph T. Goodman (an American newspaper man who hired a young Samuel Clemens) proposed the first version of this correlation (584,280), which was slightly amended by Juan Martínez Hernández (584,281) and later by J. Eric S. Thompson (584,283). This correlation, placing the start of the Long Count at 11 August 3114 BCE, most accurately accords with archaeological and astronomical evidence from sites and codices. Some still advocate other correlations, such as those proposed by Herbert J. Spinden (489,384) or George C. Vaillant (679,183), which would move the end of the Classic from around 900 CE to 640 CE or 1156 CE, respectively. Floyd Lounsbury proposed a correlation two days greater than GMT (584,285) using precomputer Venus tables, but his correlation was generally discounted when more accurate astronomical modeling became available.

The correlation coefficients in table 3.6 refer to the numbers of days that must be added to the Day Number to reach the Julian Day Number in the calculations.

Another anomaly you may notice is that some dates are given in Julian and others are given in Gregorian. The Julian calendar was started by Julius Caesar in 46 BCE and consisted of a 365-day year with one leap day every four years. Over time, it was observed that the calendar year had begun to run longer than the solar year (the equinoxes came earlier and earlier). In 1582 Pope Gregory XIII amended the system by not counting leap years at the turn of a century if it was not divisible by 400, giving a close approximation to the true solar year (Julian year: 365.25 days, Gregorian year: 365.2425 days, solar year: 365.2422 days). The countries (mostly strongly Catholic) that initially adopted the reform skipped ten days in October 1584. People went to sleep on 4 October 1584 and woke up on 15 October 1584. This calendar was not immediately adopted by all countries. Indeed the "October Revolution" in Russia took place on 25 October 1917 of the Julian calendar, which was 7 November 1917 for most of the rest of Europe. Some Orthodox Christian churches still use the Julian calendar for liturgical purposes, explaining why my Greek friend celebrates Easter at a different time than my other Christian friends. For the purposes of Maya epigraphy, this is important. Some prefer to calculate dates in Julian and others in Gregorian, so you should always specify which you are using. Most calendar programs give you a choice of either date. I prefer Gregorian and use it throughout this book unless otherwise noted.

Table 3.6. List of Correlation Coefficients

Willson	438,906
Smiley	482,699
Makemson	489,138
Spinden	489,384
Goodman	584,280
Martínez Hernández	584,281
Thompson	584,283
Lounsbury	584,285
Pogo	588,626
Kreichgauer	626,927
Hochleitner	674,265
Schultz	677,723
Escalona Ramos	679,108
Vaillant	679,183
Weitzel	774,078

3.3. CALENDAR ROUND

If we expressed dates as "the 84th day of the 603rd year" we could identify any day in history; but we can identify this day in a number of other ways, such as Wednesday, 23 March. The Maya had similar cycles of day names and numbers as well as months and month days. The combination of these names and numbers is known as the **Calendar Round**. Although the Long Count alone can specify any day that the Maya needed to express, the Calendar Round often proves essential to understanding eroded or partial dates. Two series make up the Calendar Round: a ritual cycle of 260 days and a "vague" year of 365 days.

The first cycle, known as the **Tzolk'in** (ritual cycle), has 20 Day Names, which combine with 13 Day Numbers in 260 unique combinations. The names and numbers cycle independently, much as the seven-day cycle of one week continues regardless of the year or month. The Day Names (in order) are commonly given as Imix, Ik', Ak'bal, K'an, Chikchan, Kimi, Manik', Lamat, Muluk, Ok, Chuwen, Eb, Ben, Ix, Men, Kib, Kaban, Etz'nab, Kawak, and Ajaw. These are based on the Yucatec pronunciation and spelling of these Day Names in the colonial period, which is not necessarily how they were pronounced in Classic Mayan (note the lack of glottalization on the *b*s). Furthermore, these names are sometimes spelled differently, depending on the orthography of some authors. Traditionally, for instance, *ajaw* has been spelled *ahau,* but they are pronounced the same by scholars. Although these may not have been the Classic Mayan names, they are still the preferred names. Here I have adopted the convention of phonetically transcribing each name, transliterating the reconstructed pronunciation, and translating it into the Yucatec name used by most scholars:

Transcription: AK'AB
Transliteration: ak'ab
Translation: Ak'bal

Figure 3.3 shows each Day Name for which there is a reconstructed spelling and pronunciation.

These twenty Day Names repeat in an unending cycle alongside a rotation of numbers from one to thirteen. The rotation would start with 1 Imix, 2 Ik', 3 Ak'bal, 4 K'an, and so on until 13 Ben, when the numbers start over at 1 Ix. The names continue until 7 Ajaw, while the numbers continue to 8 Imix as the Day Names recycle. This continues through 260 unique combinations before returning to 1 Imix. It is unclear why a 260-day cycle was used. This length of time has been equated with the time for human gestation or corn maturation as well as a number of astronomical arguments. **Table 3.7** can be used for calculating the Tzolk'in for any given day.

The Maya had 20 Day Names and the Maya numeral system is base-20, producing a one-for-one correspondence between the Long Count and the accompanying Day Name. Specifically, the number of K'in corresponds to the Day Name in order (1 K'in corresponds to Imix, 2 K'in corresponds to Ik', and so on until the K'in starts over at 0, corresponding to Ajaw). The Tzolk'in Day Number is slightly harder to calculate. The Day Number must be calculated in **table 3.7** and 4 must be added (because the first day, 0.0.0.0.0, was 4 Ajaw, 8 Kumk'u). This number is divided by 13. The decimal of that quotient is then multiplied by 13 to give the Day Number for that date (it may come out with

---
Table 3.7. Calculating Tzolk'in Position
---

1. Use the number of K'in (the last position) of the Long Count to identify the Day Number in the first column of the table below:
   09.08.09.13.00 Long Count Day corresponds to <u>Ajaw</u> Day Name from the table below.

K'in	Day	K'in	Day	K'in	Day	K'in	Day	K'in	Day
0	Ajaw	4	K'an	8	Lamat	12	Eb'	16	Kib'
1	Imix	5	Chikchan	9	Muluk	13	Ben	17	Kaban
2	Ik'	6	Kimi	10	Ok	14	Ix	18	Etz'nab'
3	Ak'bal	7	Manik	11	Chuwen	15	Men	19	Kawak

2. Add 4 to the converted Day Number (from table 3.3) and divide by 13:
   <u>1,357,100</u> (Day Number) + 4 = <u>1,357,104</u> / 13 = <u>104,392.6154</u>

3. Multiply the decimal by 13:
   <u>.6154</u> × 13 = <u>8.0002</u> ~ <u>8</u> Tzolk'in Day Number

4. Use the Tzolk'in Day Number and Name:
   The day <u>09.08.09.13.00</u> corresponds to <u>8</u> (Day Number) <u>Ajaw</u> (Day Name) in the Tzolk'in.

---

a decimal .9999 repeating, which can be rounded to the nearest integer, because this is due to truncated decimals in calculation).

The second cycle of the calendar round, called the **Haab'**, "vague year," consists of eighteen 20-day months and one 5-day month for a total of 365 total days, as shown in **figure 3.4**. This operates much in the same way as the months in the Gregorian calendar. The nineteen month names, again derived from Yucatec pronunciation and spelling and used by scholars, are Pop, Wo, Sip, Sotz', Sek, Xul, Yaxk'in, Mol, Ch'en, Yax, Sak, Keh, Mak, K'ank'in, Muwan, Pax, K'ayab, Kumk'u, and Wayeb. The majority of these names, unlike the Tzolk'in Day Names, can be read phonetically, as shown in **figure 3.4**. Each month lasts 20 days except Wayeb, the last month, which is only 5 days long. Wayeb is considered an unlucky and transitional time of the year, somewhat akin to Friday the 13th. Maya months start counting days at zero and end at 19. The zero is not always expressed as a number in inscriptions; instead the **CHUM,** "seating," glyph is used to indicate the beginning or seating of the new month. The Haab' date is usually found at the very end of the Supplementary Series (see section 3.4), when the inscription starts with a full Long Count. In other parts of the inscription, the Haab' comes directly after the Tzolk'in.

Finding the corresponding Haab' date for any given Long Count date is relatively straightforward, as shown in **table 3.8**. Using this information, complete **exercises 3.2 and 3.3**, where you must find, calculate, and read Tzolk'in and Haab' dates.

3.3. CALENDAR ROUND

Figure 3.3. Tzolk'in Day Names

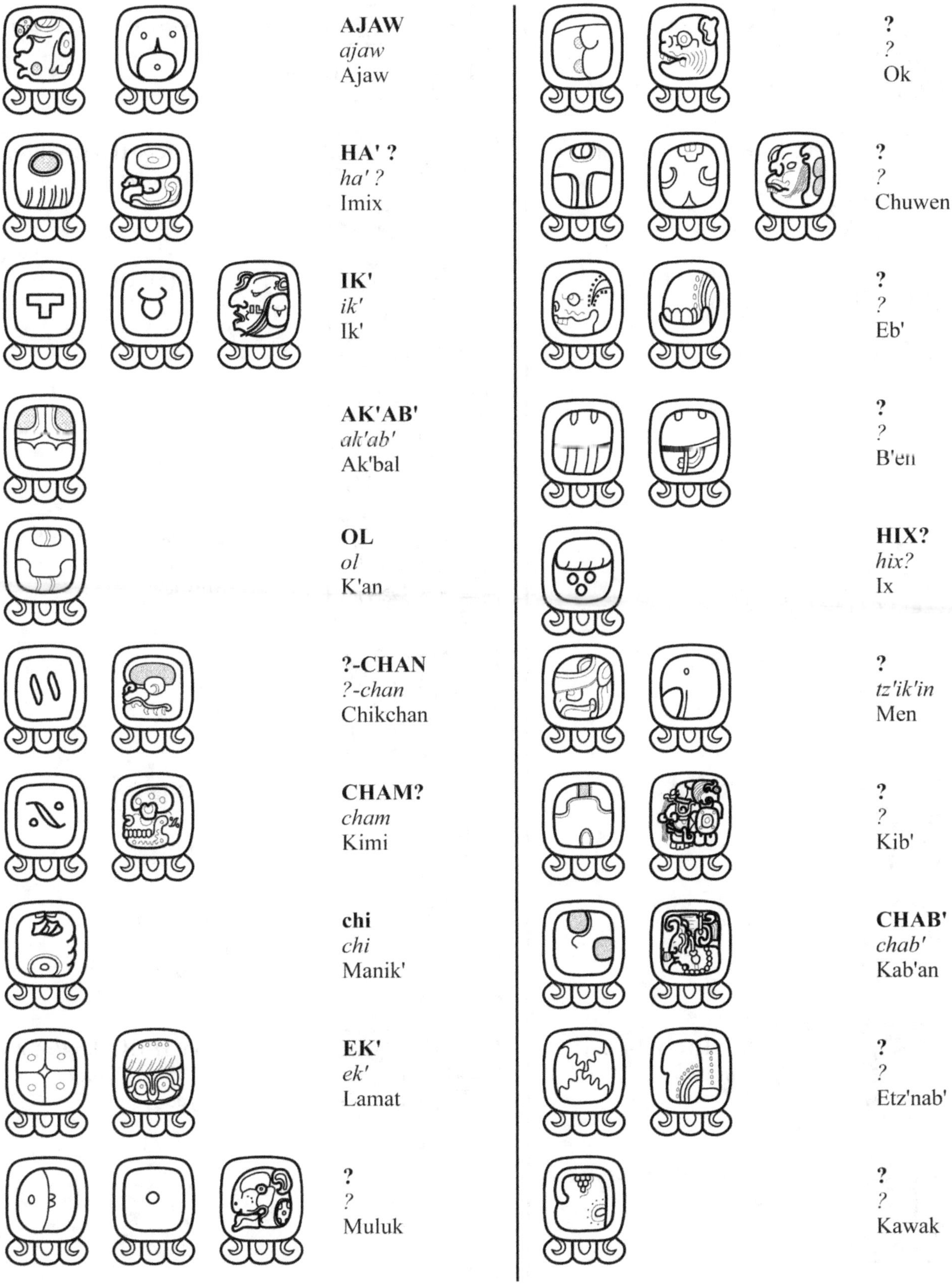

Glyphs	Name		Glyphs	Name
	AJAW / *ajaw* / Ajaw			**?** / ? / Ok
	HA'? / *ha'?* / Imix			**?** / ? / Chuwen
	IK' / *ik'* / Ik'			**?** / ? / Eb'
	AK'AB' / *ak'ab'* / Ak'bal			**?** / ? / B'en
	OL / *ol* / K'an			**HIX?** / *hix?* / Ix
	?-CHAN / *?-chan* / Chikchan			**?** / *tz'ik'in* / Men
	CHAM? / *cham* / Kimi			**?** / ? / Kib'
	chi / *chi* / Manik'			**CHAB'** / *chab'* / Kab'an
	EK' / *ek'* / Lamat			**?** / ? / Etz'nab'
	? / ? / Muluk			**?** / ? / Kawak

Figure 3.4. Haab' Month Names

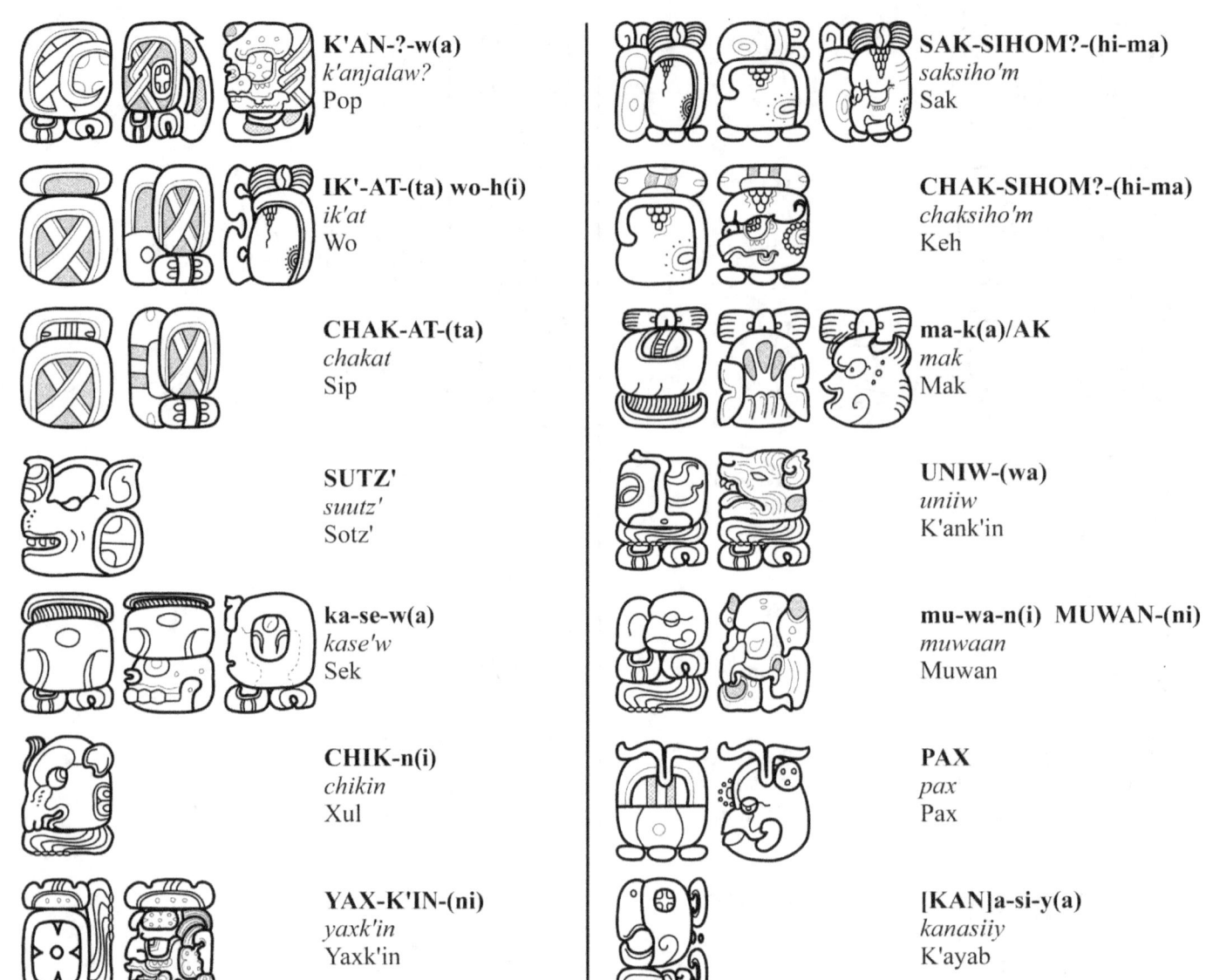

Table 3.8. Calculating Haab' Position

1. Add 348 to the converted Day Number (from table 3.3) and divide by 365:
   09.08.09.13.00 Long Count → 1,357,100 (Day Number) + 348 = 1,357,448 / 365 = 3,719.0356

2. Multiply the decimal by 365 (round if needed):
   .0356 × 365 − 12.994 ~ 13 Haab' Day Number

3. Find the largest Day Number that is less than the days calculated above.
   0 Day Number, Month of Pop

Month	Day Number	Month	Day Number	Month	Day Number
Pop	0	Yaxk'in	120	Mak	240
Wo	20	Mol	140	K'ank'in	260
Sip	40	Ch'en	160	Muwan	280
Sotz'	60	Yax	180	Pax	300
Sek	80	Sak	200	K'ayab	320
Xul	100	Keh	220	Kumk'u	340
				Wayeb	360

4. Subtract the Day Number from the days calculated above:
   13 Haab' Days − 0 Day Number = 13 Month Day

5. Use the Haab' Month Name and Day:
   The day 09.08.09.13.00 corresponds to 13 (month day) Pop (month name) in the Haab'.

92 DATES AND NUMBERS

Exercise 3.2. Calculate Calendar Round Dates

1. Calculate the Calendar Round dates for the following Long Counts.

	Day Number	Tzolk'in	Haab'
8.0.0.0.0	_____	_____	_____
8.2.12.13.0	_____	_____	_____
9.3.15.2.14	_____	_____	_____
9.8.0.3.0	_____	_____	_____
9.19.14.9.19	_____	_____	_____
10.4.0.0.0	_____	_____	_____
13.0.0.0.0	_____	_____	_____

2. Calculate the Calendar Round dates for the Long Counts from exercise 3.1.

	Day Number	Tzolk'in	Haab'
Palenque Tablet of the Sun	_____	_____	_____
Piedras Negras Stela 1	_____	_____	_____
Yaxchilan Lintel 21	_____	_____	_____
Tonina Monument 139	_____	_____	_____
Tikal Stela 31	_____	_____	_____

3. Identify the associated calendar round for the Long Counts from exercise 3.1 using the calculations in exercise 3.2.2.

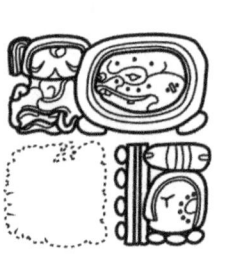

Exercise 3.3. Identify Calendar Round Dates

1. Identify the following Tzolk'in number and Day Name or number and Haab' Month.

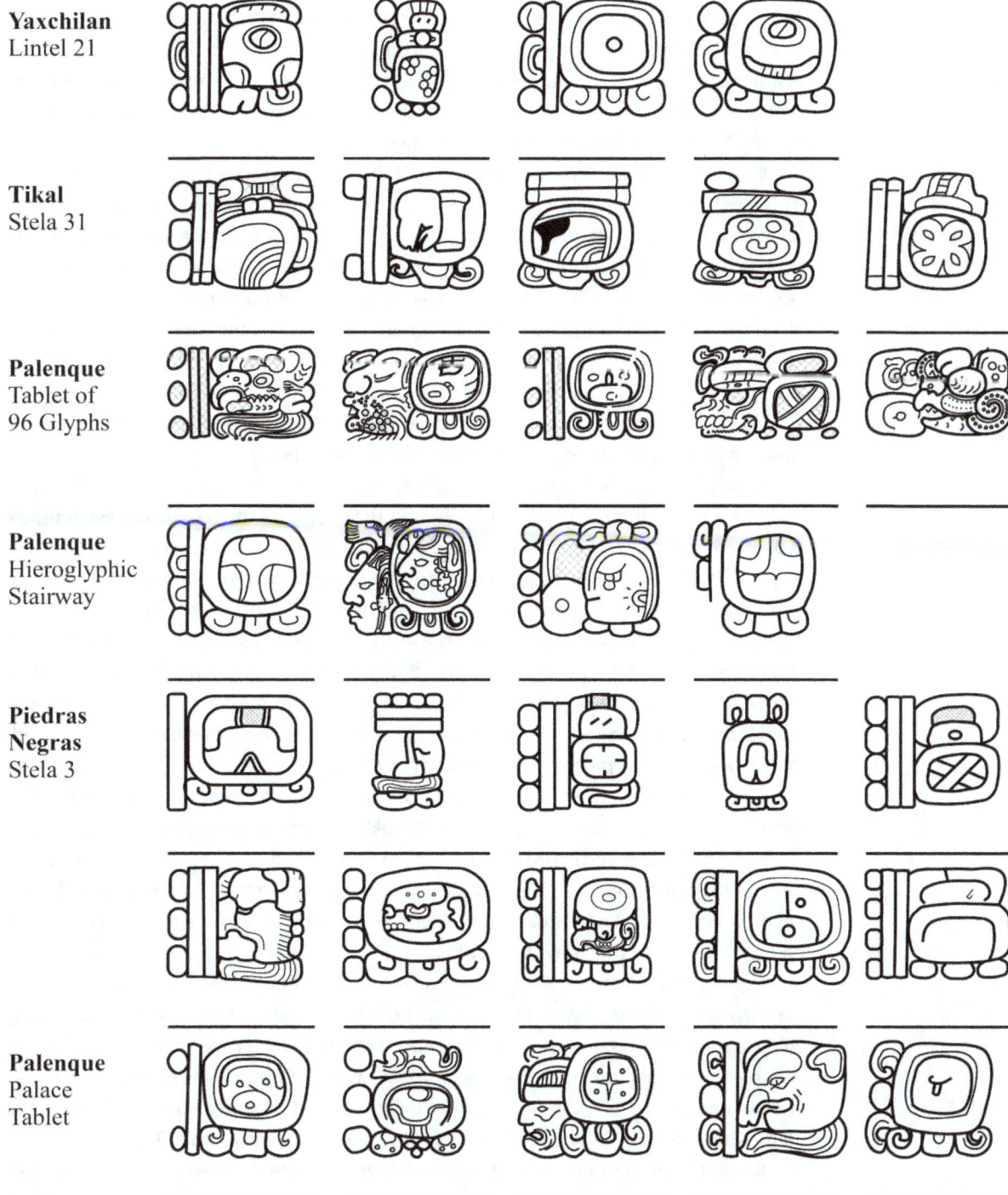

3.4. SUPPLEMENTARY SERIES

The **Supplementary Series** is the group of glyphs that commonly occurs after the Long Count and between the Tzok'in and Haab' glyphs in an inscription. As the name suggests, it contains information supplemental to the Long Count date. The most common glyphs of the series contain lunar information but may also include information relating to cycles of 7 or 819 days. Before they could be read phonetically, each glyph was assigned a letter, in descending order starting after the Tzolk'in: G, F, E, D, C, B, and A. A few more glyphs of the Supplementary Series were identified and assigned the letters X, Y, and Z. The complete order (although these glyphs rarely appear all at once) is G, F, Z, Y, E, D, C, X, B, and A. Let's look at each glyph in turn.

Glyph G represents the so-called Lord of the Night and directly follows the Tzolk'in. This glyph has nine versions, each denoting a different patron deity that rules over that specific day in the calendar. Because they have not been read yet, they are assigned numbers prefixed with *G:* G1–G9. Examples of each Lord of the Night are given in **figure 3.5**. Some of them (G1, G4, G5, and G6) have a bar-and-dot number (9, 7, 5, and 9, respectively) that has nothing to do with their label or order. G9 is the most common Lord of the Night, as it coincides with major period endings. It is thought that the nine lords represented in Glyph G are indicative of each of the nine lords of the underworld (one for each level). Because this is a continuous cycle, it can be easily calculated from the Winal and K'in of any given Long Count date, as shown in **table 3.9**.

Glyph F directly follows Glyph G and appears to be connected to it. Indeed, Glyphs G and F are sometimes combined, such as in the examples for G3, G7, and G8 in **figure 3.5**, where you can see that some of the elements from Glyph F are added to Glyph G. Glyph F is made up of three components. The top and bottom parts are the same for all five versions of this glyph. The top part can be read **TI'** and pronounced *ti'*, meaning "mouth," "lips," "speaking," or "edge." The last part is a **na** syllable. The central element, which varies, can be read as **HUN** or **hu** depending on the version (**see fig. 3.6**). As a whole, Glyph F can be read **TI'-HUN-(na)** or **TI'-hu-n(a)**, both of which can be transliterated *ti' hu'n*, which I argue is translated as "speaker of the book" or more literally "mouth of the book." In the past it was thought that this glyph referred to the "headdress" or "burden" of the current Lord of the Night or possibly "at the margin" (Stuart 2005). The word *hu'n* can be glossed as "paper" or "book" in many languages but not usually as "headdress." Together, Glyphs G and F may be translated as "Lord of the Night GX [is] the mouth of the book," suggesting that the current Lord of the Night is responsible for reciting, perhaps out of a ritual codex. Glyph F has no cycle, and the variant used seems to be the choice of the individual scribe.

Glyphs Z and **Y** occur rarely and indicate the current position in a cycle of seven days. As seen in **figure 3.7**, Glyph Z is made up of a number from 1 to 7, indicating the day in the cycle, followed by the optional component **b'i-xi-y(a)**, pronounced *b'ixiiy*, which is a numeral classifier for "counts of five or seven" with an intransitive verbal maker; it may mean "it happened after." Glyph Y is not fully readable but appears to be related to the deity K'awil, possibly in one of his baby forms (see Yasugi and Saito 1991).

Glyphs E and **D** indicate the number of days since the last new moon (**see fig. 3.8**). Glyph E, which represents 20 days, may or may not be present. Glyph D begins with a number, between zero and 19, indicating the days of the current lunation. Any number

Figure 3.5. Glyph G (Lords of the Night)

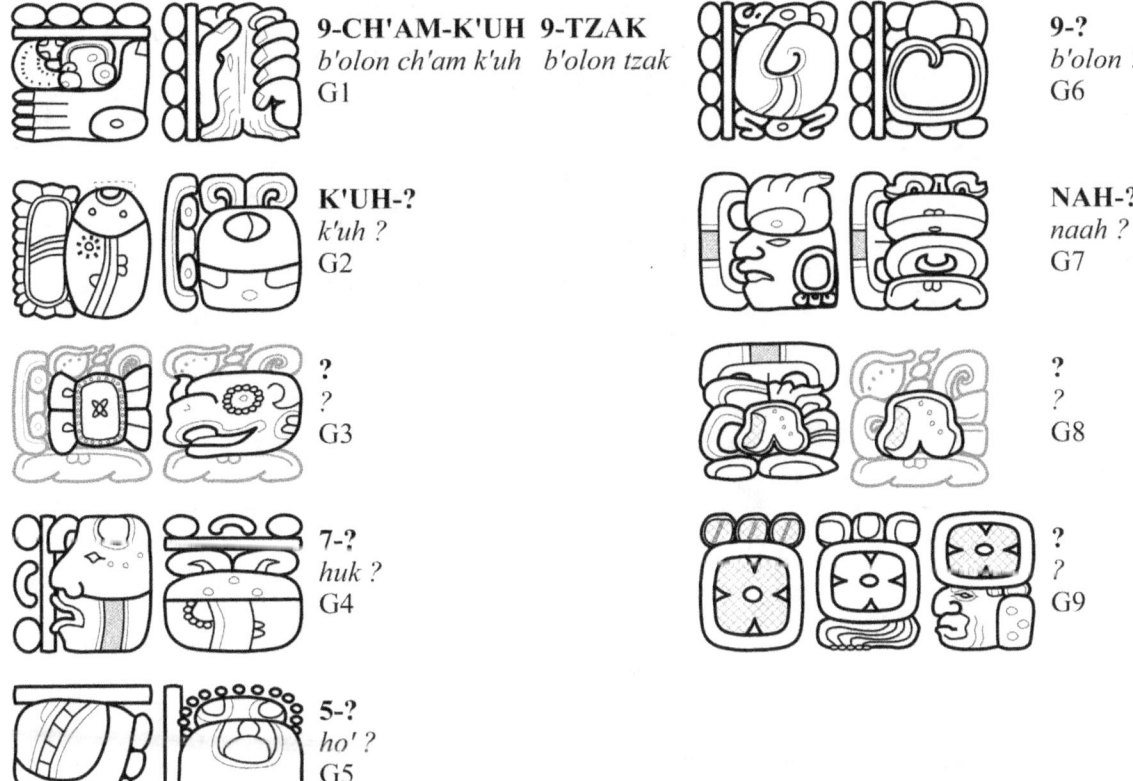

Table 3.9. Calculating Lord of the Night Position

1. Convert the K'in and Winal to a decimal number:

   14 Winal × 20   (1 × 20) = 280
   07 K'in × 1   =   7 +
                                 287 days

2. Divide this number by nine:
   287 / 9 = 31.8888

3. Multiply the decimal by nine and round up:
   0.8888 × 9 = 7.9992 ~ 8 Lord of the Night (if zero, it corresponds to the 9th Lord of the Night)

4. The Lord of the Night is G8.

Figure 3.6. Glyph F

 **TI'-hu-n(a)**
ti' hu'n
reader of the book

  **TI'-HUN-(na)**
ti' hu'n
reader of the book

Figure 3.7. Glyphs Z and Y

 **#-b'i-xi-y(a)**
?
?

 **?**
?
?

Figure 3.8. Glyphs E and D

 **20**
winik
twenty

  **#-hu-li-y(a)**
huliiy
days ago [the moon] arrived

  **#-HUL-li-y(a)**
huliiy
days ago [the moon] arrived

Figure 3.9. Glyph C

  **#-?-K'AL-ja**
? *k'ahlaj*
? was bound

over 19 is indicated by the 20 of Glyph E and the numbers indicated by Glyph D to add up to 29 days. This is followed by glyphs spelling either **hu-li-y(a)** or **HUL-li-y(a)**, both read as *huliiy*, meaning "[days] ago it [the new moon] arrived."

Glyph C tells the position of the current lunation within a "lunar semester" (cycle of six lunations). Six lunations of 29.5 days equals 177 days, which is half a day short of a half-year. The glyph is started with a number from one to six, indicating which lunation is meant. Sometimes the number one is replaced by the **NAH,** "house," glyph (pronounced *naah*). The main part of the glyph block is either a female head or skull atop a hand, followed by a **ja** verbal marker, as seen in **figure 3.9**. This may be read **#-?-K'AL-ja**, read *# ? k'ahlaj*, literally "# ? was bound," but this reading may be proven incorrect.

Glyph X follows Glyph C and modifies it. Glyph X seems to represent the patron deity for that lunation within the lunar semester. The variants occur in several types and are not yet readable, as shown in **figure 3.10**. Each is identified by an X-number, starting with X1 and ending with X6. The presiding deity changes halfway through the lunation (apparently during the full moon).

Glyph B is an epithet following Glyph X, which describes (or possibly modifies) it. Usually it reads **u-ch'ok-K'AB'A'** or **u-K'UH-K'AB'A'** (although the initial **u** is optional), as shown in **figure 3.11**. This is pronounced *uch'ok k'ab'a'* or *uk'uh k'ab'a'*, meaning "its princely name" or "its holy name," referring to the deity in Glyph X.

Figure 3.10. Glyph X

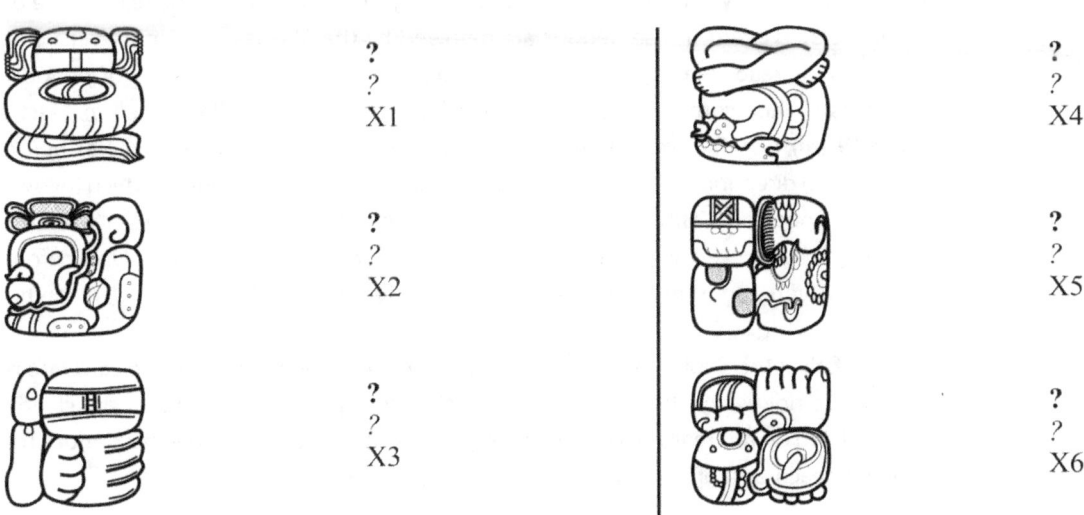

Figure 3.11. Glyph B

ch'o[k(o)]-K'AB'A'
ch'ok k'ab'a'
its princely name

K'UH-K'AB'A'
k'uh k'ab'a'
its holy name

Glyph A indicates the length of the current lunation, either 29 or 30 days. Because the Maya did not use fractions, measuring astronomical events that do not coincide with the length of a day must be indicated by different cycles of greater and lesser days to equal the right length of time. For instance, the solar year is 365.2425 days long. Therefore the Western calendar has three years of 365 days, followed by one year of 366 days (leap year). This brings us to a 365.25-day year, which is 0.0075 days too long. That is mitigated by not having a leap year at the turn of a century, unless it is divisible by 400. The Maya had a similar practice for measuring and calculating the length of a lunation. Generally, 29- and 30-day lunations were alternated to give an average lunation of 29.5 days. Corrections and patterns produced a more accurate average. Suffice it to say that Glyph A indicates whether the current lunation is 29 or 30 days through a large glyph similar to **ja,** with a large circle in the upper central area, usually containing three smaller circles. It represents **WINIK,** *winik,* meaning "20." This is followed by a bar-and-dot number of 9 (*b'olon*) or 10 (*laju'n*). Added together this gives either 29 or 30, reading *winik b'olon* or *winik laju'n,* and can be translated as "twenty-nine [-day lunation]" or "twenty [and] ten [-day lunation]," as seen in **figure 3.12**.

Finally, the **819-Day Cycle** is indicated by a dedicatory verb, a cardinal direction, an associated color, and a reference to the deity K'awil. All of these glyphs are shown in **figure 3.13**. This cycle is thought to come from 9 × 7 × 13 (the levels of the underworld, earth, and heavens, respectively), all of which have important cultural meaning to the Maya. The cycle begins with a series of numbers and calendrical period glyphs found in the Long Count. In this case, they function as a Distance Number (see section 3.5). The date reached by counting backward that many periods indicates the occurrence of a K'awil-related event. These periods are followed by the 819-day dedicatory verb, not currently fully read: **?-ja-ji-ya,** *?ajiiy,* indicating a previous event: "[number of periods] ago it was ?" Then comes one of the four cardinal directions: **EL-K'IN-(ni),** *elk'in,* "east"; **OCH-K'IN-(ni),** *ochk'in,* "west"; **xa-MAN-(na),** *xaman,* "north"; and **no-NOJOL?-(la),** *nojo'l,* "south." Each direction is associated with a color and unread head variant, which follows in the next position: **CHAK-?,** *chak ?,* "red ?"; **IK'-?,** *ik' ?,* "black ?"; **SAK-?,** *sak ?,* "white ?"; and **K'AN-?,** *k'an ?,* "yellow ?" After the direction color comes an unknown glyph before the K'awil glyph, together referred to as a K'awil reference: **? K'AWIL,** *? k'awiil,* meaning "? K'awil."

Out of all of the Supplementary Series cycles, the only one that is easy to calculate is Glyph G. Do not worry about reconstructing the lunar series or others: they are clearly indicated and do not really have any bearing on the date or events of the inscription. Try to identify each part of the Supplementary Series in **exercise 3.4**.

Figure 3.12. Glyph A

20-9
winik b'olon
twenty-nine [-day lunation]

20-10
winik laju'n
twenty- and ten [-day lunation]

Figure 3.13. 819-Day Cycle

819-day dedicatory verb

 **?-ja-ji-ya**
?ajiiy
it was ?

Quadrant Direction

 **EL-K'IN-(ni)**
elk'ihn
east

 **OCH-K'IN-(ni)**
ochk'ihn
west

 **xa-MAN-(na)**
xaman
north

 **no-NOJOL?-(la)**
nojo'l
south

Direction Color

 **CHAK-?**
chak ?
red ?

 **IK'-?**
ik' ?
black ?

 **SAK-?**
sak ?
white ?

 **K'AN-?**
k'an ?
yellow ?

K'awil reference

 ?
?
?

 **K'AWIL**
k'awiil
K'awil

100 DATES AND NUMBERS

Exercise 3.4. Identify Supplementary Inscription Elements

1. Identify the following Supplementary Series elements (e.g., "Glyph F") and their current positions if applicable; (e.g., "G2" or "27th day").

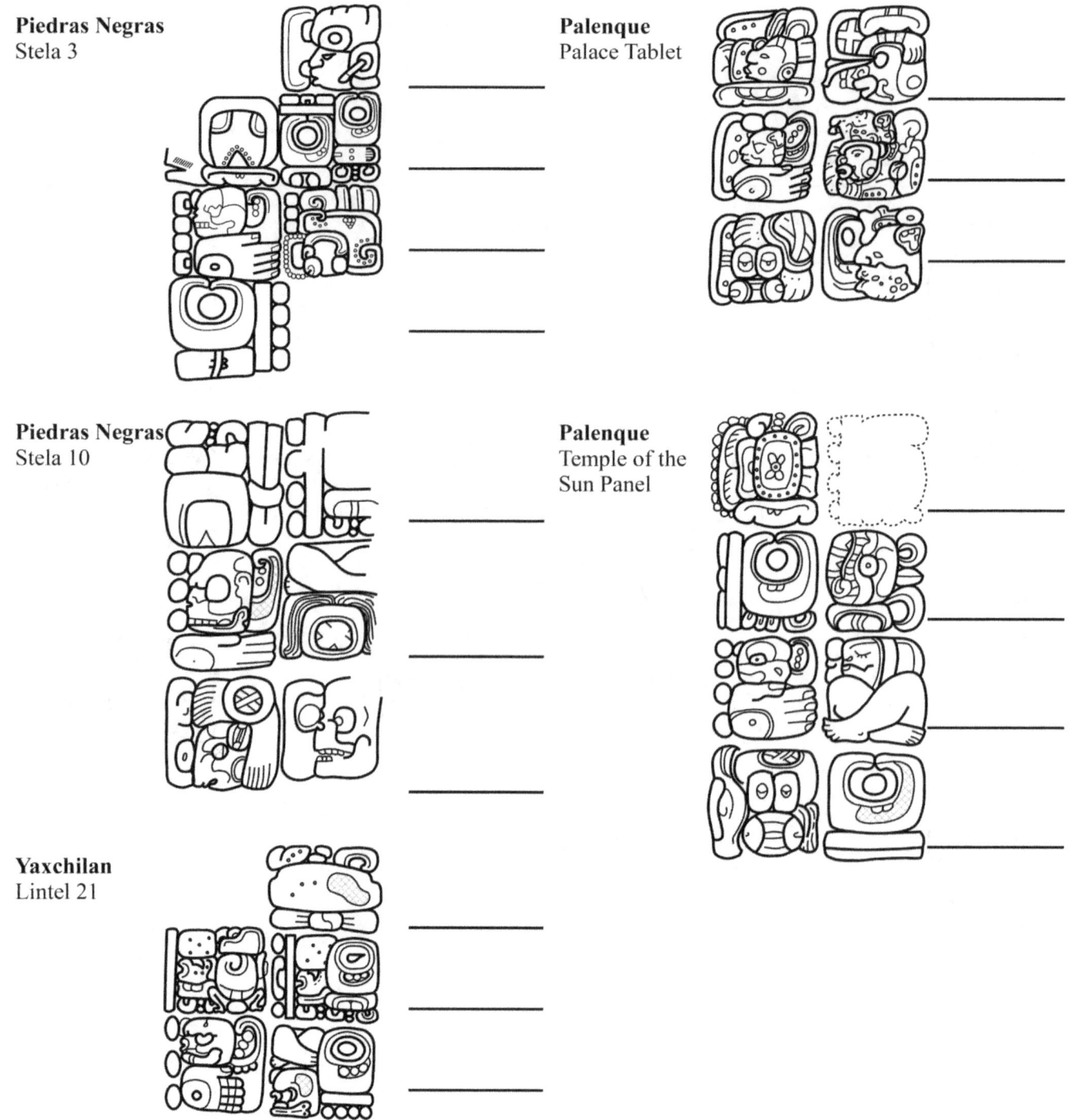

Piedras Negras
Stela 3

_____
_____
_____
_____

Piedras Negras
Stela 10

_____
_____
_____

Yaxchilan
Lintel 21

_____
_____
_____

Palenque
Palace Tablet

_____
_____
_____

Palenque
Temple of the
Sun Panel

_____
_____
_____
_____

3.5. DISTANCE NUMBERS

Now that we are familiar with the Maya Long Count calendar and other cycles, it is time to learn about Distance Numbers. A **Distance Number** gives the number of days between events and dates on an inscription. If the Long Count basically says, "On this day, this happened," the Distance Number says, "This many days later [or earlier], this happened." Distance Numbers do not function as stand-alone dates; they always refer to another event. A Distance Number usually counts the days between one event and a previously written date. Sometimes a Distance Number calculates the number of days from the initial Long Count each time. Rarely, a Distance Number refers to the amount of time between the current event and a well-known event not even indicated on the inscription; luckily this is not very common. A Distance Number is composed of four parts: Distance Number Introductory Glyph, Number of Days, Date Indicator, and Calendar Round date. Let's take them one at a time.

The **Distance Number Introductory Glyph** (DNIG) is an optional component of the Distance Number that basically introduces it: "You are about to read a Distance Number." It has three main variants, seen in **figure 3.14**. The first, **u-TZ'AK-ka-AJ**, read *utz'akaj*, means "it was set in order." The second version, **u-K'IN-AK'AB'-AJ**, may be read *uk'ihnak'ab'aj*; it derives a verb out of the noun "day-and-night," giving something like "it day-and-nighted." Another version, **u-IK'-NAB'-AJ**, read *uik'naab'aj*, also derives a verb from a noun, in this case "black-lily," producing "it black-lilied." This probably had a euphemistic meaning similar to the first two versions of the DNIG. The second and third DNIGs presented here are not perfectly understood and may not be verbs at all but ritualistic phrases dealing with the passage of time.

The **Number of Days** is the count of days between indicated events. For instance, if the Long Count of an inscription is 9.0.0.0.0, a Distance Number may indicate that 1.10.3 days (563 days) have elapsed since that date, giving a new date of 9.0.1.10.3. Because this Long Count date is not explicitly given in the inscription, it should be placed in brack-

---

Figure 3.14. Distance Number Introductory Glyph and K'in Variants

Distance Number Introductory Glyph

 **u-TZ'AK-ka-AJ**
utz'akaj
it was set in order

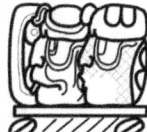 **u-K'IN-AK'AB'-AJ**
uk'inak'ab'aj
it day-and-nighted (?)

 **u-IK'-NAB'-AJ**
uik'naab'aj
it black-lilied (?)

K'in Variants

 **K'IN**
k'ihn
day(s)

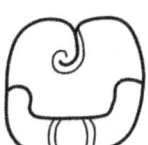 **he**
he
day(s)

 **?-w(a)**
?w
day(s)

 **PAS**
pas
dawn

 **K'IN**
k'ihn
day(s)

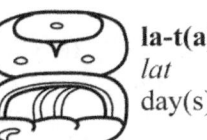 **la-t(a)**
lat
day(s)

 **b'i-xi-y(a)**
b'ixiiy
5 or 7 days

ets: [9.0.1.10.3]. Unlike a Long Count, where units decrease in size (B'aktun, K'atun, Tun, Winal, and K'in), Distance Numbers are indicated in the reverse order: K'in, Winal, Tun, K'atun, B'aktun, and so on. As seen in **figure 3.15**, the K'in glyph is usually absent altogether and two numbers accompany the Winal glyph, the first of which is the number of K'in. In cases where only a few days are meant, a number of *k'ihn* sign variants are used, also shown in **figure 3.14**. In our example above, the Distance Number would likely read **3-10-WINIK 1-HAB'** (see fig. 3.15) and read aloud as *ox laju'n winik, ju'n haab'*. You might translate this as "three [days], ten months, and one year." Often the English "day, month, year, score, and era" may be used to stand for "K'in, Winal, Tun, K'atun, and B'aktun," respectively. Other scholars simply use the traditional Maya terms.

Remember that the second place (Winal) of calendar dates only reaches 18 instead of 20. For instance, if you add 14.14 as the Distance Number to 9.0.0.4.4, you should get 9.0.1.0.18, *not* 9.0.0.18.18. This can be tricky, so take care. Luckily, the Calendar Round dates indicated after a Distance Number usually serve to double check your math.

The **Date Indicator** (DI) tells you to count the given number of days forward or backward. The DI has two main forms. The first is the **Posterior Date Indicator** (PDI), which indicates that an event took place after the base date: therefore you must count forward the number of days given in the Distance Number. The usual form of this is shown in **figure 3.16**, transcribed as **i-u-ti**, read *iuti*, "and then it happened." This is sometimes reconstructed as *iuht, iuuht, iuut*, or *iuhti*. Those transliterations that drop the final **i** and double the preceding **u** in accordance with the spelling rules of disharmony ignore the fact that *ut* is a root intransitive verb and that the **-Ci** ending is verbal and should be transliterated *-Ci*, not dropping the sound. The transliteration choice does not change the overall meaning, which is clear: count forward this many days to reach the new date. In our preceding example, a PDI after the Distance Number 1.10.3 from the base date of 9.0.0.0.0 gives 9.0.1.10.3, as seen in **figure 3.17**. The **Anterior Date Indicator** (ADI) indicates a backward count from the base date. In **figure 3.16**, you can see that it is similar to the PDI except for two glyphs. The initial **i-** is dropped off and a **-y(a)** is added to the end,

---

Figure 3.15. Distance Number Examples

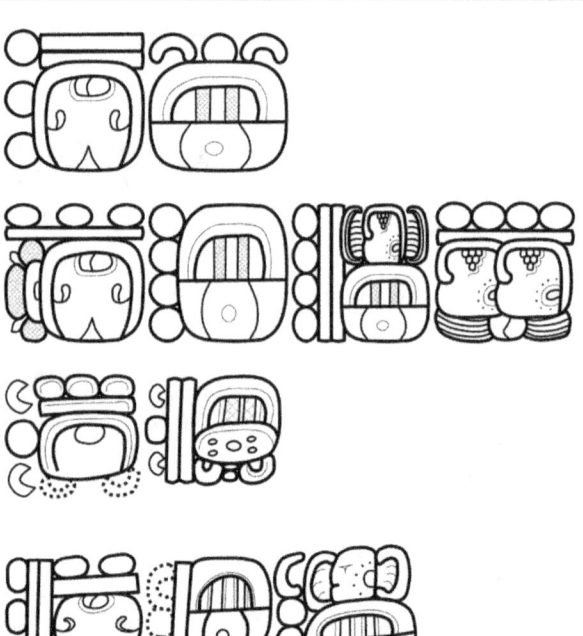

3-10-WINIK 1-HAB'
ox laju'n winik ju'n haab'
3 [days], 10 months, and 1 year

8-0-WINIK 4-HAB' 14-WINIK-HAB' 9-pi-h(i)
waxak mih winik chan haab' chanlaju'n winikhaab' b'olon pih
8 [days], 0 months, 4 years, 4 score, 9 eras

1-8-WINIK-y(a) 11-HAB'-(b'i)-y(a)
ju'n waxak winik-iiy b'uluk haab'-iiy
1 days, 8 months, and 11 years
(modified Naranjo Stela 24)

13-7-WINIK-y(a) 6-HAB'-y(a) 1-WINIK-HAB'-[pl.]
oxlaju'n huk winik-iiy wak haab'-iiy ju'n winikhaab'
13 [days], 7 months, 6 years, 1 score
(modified Palenque Temple of the Cross Tablet)

resulting in **u-ti-y(a)**. This should be pronounced *utiiy*, but you may also see *uutiiy*, *uhtiiy*, or *uuhtiiy*. Again, the transliteration does not change the meaning: count backward this many days to reach the new date. In our example, an ADI after 1.10.3 indicates a backward count from 9.0.0.0.0, giving 8.19.18.7.17 (remember that the Winal only reaches 18, not 20). An easy way to display this relationship is seen in **table 3.10**. The direction of counting can also be indicated by a small snake that may be facing forward or backward, usually over the Tzolk'in. A snake facing backward is an ADI; a snake facing forward one is a PD (both are shown in **figure 3.16**).

Finally, most Distance Numbers are completed by giving the **Calendar Round (CR)** for the new date. The Tzolk'in and Haab' cycle positions are often used to make sure that your Distance Number calculations are correct. This is especially useful if parts of the dates or Distance Numbers are eroded. Because they only repeat every 52 years, it is often easy to pin down the correct date by using calendar programs (see appendix V). This information is shown in **table 3.10**. Write out the Distance Numbers and whether or not they should be added (+) or subtracted (–) from the preceding date in **exercise 3.5**.

Figure 3.16. Date Indicators and Period Completions

Posterior Date Indicator

  **i-u-ti**
iuti
and then it happened

  **UTI**
uti
and then it happened

Anterior Date Indicator

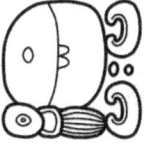  **u-ti-y(i)**
utiiy
it happened ... ago

  **UTIY**
utiiy
and then it happened ... ago

Future Date Indicator

 **u-to-m(a)**
uto'm
it will happen

General Completion

 **TZUTZ-y(i)**
tzutzuuy
got completed

Half-Period Completion

 **TAN-LAM-mi-j(a)**
tan lahmaj
it was half-diminished

Tun Completion

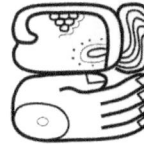 **K'AL-TUN-(ni)**
k'al tuun
the bound stone

 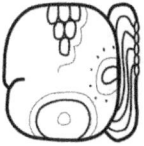 **CHUM-TUN-(ni)**
chum tuun
the seated stone

DATES AND NUMBERS

Figure 3.17. Date Examples

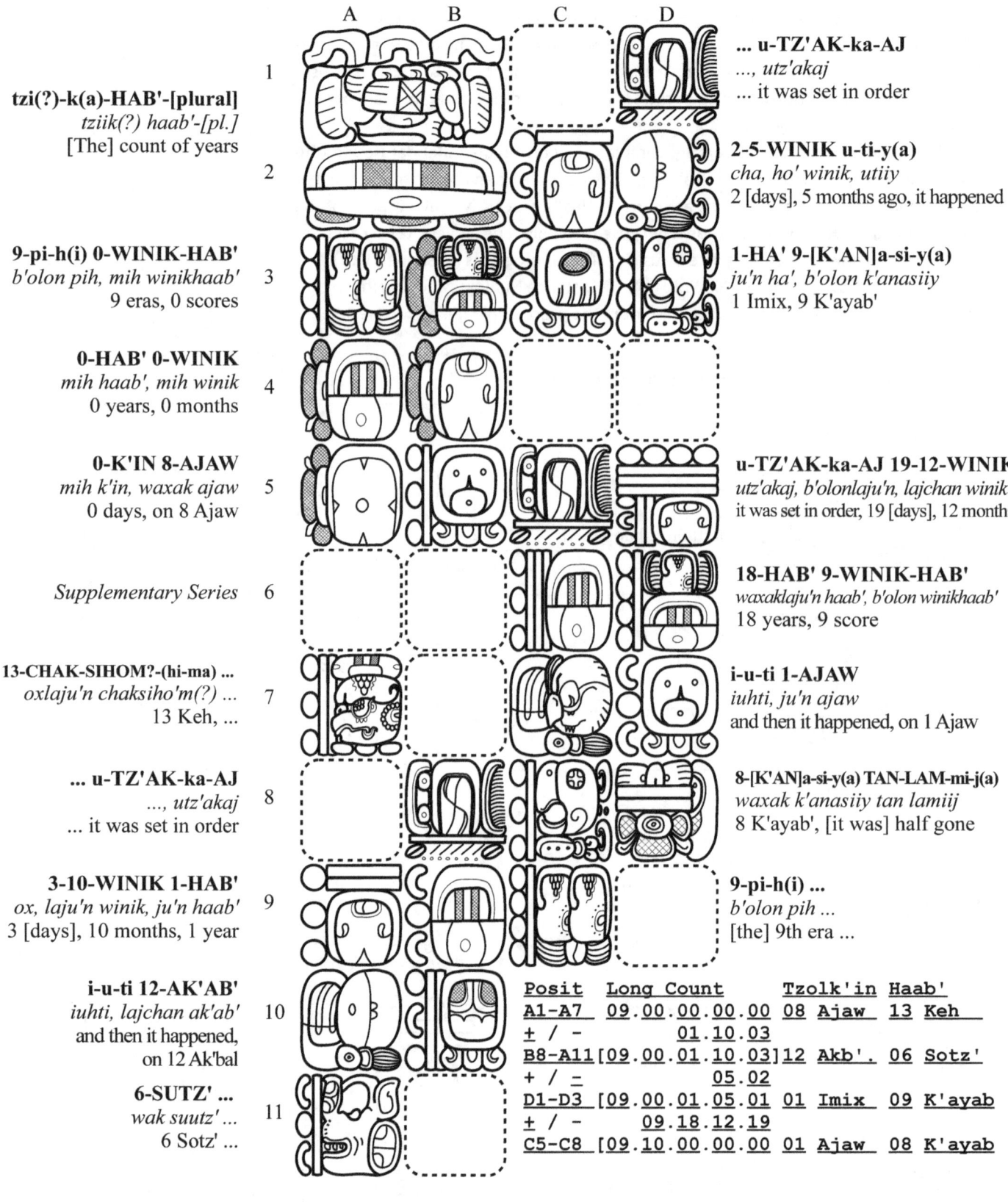

3.5. DISTANCE NUMBERS

Table 3.10. Indicating Dates through an Inscription

This is an example of the dates from an inscription displayed in a table. Note that many of the Long Counts are in brackets, because they are not given expressly, only through calculation from Distance Numbers. This example is illustrated in figure 3.17.

Position:	Counts:	Calendar Round:	Gregorian Date:
A1–A7	09.00.00.00.00	8 Ajaw 13 Keh	9 December 435 CE
+/−	01.10.03		
B8–A11	[09.00.01.10.03]	12 Akb'al 6 Sotz'	24 June 437 CE
+/−	05.02		
D1–D3	[09.00.01.05.01]	1 Imix 9 K'ayab	14 March 437 CE
+/−	09.18.12.19		
C5–C8	[09.10.00.00.00]	1 Ajaw 8 K'ayab	25 January 633 CE

Maya scribes often gave other clues to indicate the Long Count date, even if they did not indicate it directly. Period endings such as 9.0.0.0.0 or 9.10.0.0.0, for example, are often commemorated by saying in effect "the period is complete" or "the period is half-complete." This is done in four main ways in inscriptions, all shown in **figure 3.16**. First, the verb "to complete" is **TZUTZ** or *tzutz*. It is usually inflected with a **-y(i)** syllable, giving *tzutzuuy*, which is translated as "got completed." This is usually followed by a statement like *u b'olon pih*, "his 9th B'aktun"; or *u waxak winikhaab'*, "his 8th K'atun," indicating a date such as 9.0.0.0.0 or 9.8.0.0.0, respectively. Sometimes a period is half completed. This is indicated by the glyph spelled **TAN-LAM-mi-ja,** or *tan lahmaj*, meaning "half-diminished" (*tan* means "center" and *lam* means "to disappear"). This could be used to indicate the middle of a K'atun or B'aktun, such as 9.7.10.0.0 as *tan lamiij wuk winikhaab'* or 9.10.0.0.0 as *tan lamiij b'olon pih:* each period (7 K'atun and 9 B'aktun) is half completed. The completion of a significant period is also commemorated. It seems that great pomp and circumstance surrounded the completion of each K'atun, which happened about every twenty years. Part of this ritual involved erecting and binding stelae. This is reflected in the words used to describe the end of a period: **K'AL-TUN-(ni)**, read *k'al tuun*, meaning something like "bound stone" or "stone binding." The glyph *tuun* is used for stone but also for a stela, sometimes described as *lakam tuun*, "large/great stone." The erection of a stela was described as a stone "seating," using the same verb that rulers used when they took the throne: *chum*. **CHUM-TUN-(ni)**, or *chum tuun*, meaning "seated stone" or "stone seating," suggests the erection of a stela commemorating the ending of a significant period.

Look at the real examples in **figures 3.18 and 3.19. Figure 3.18** represents Lintel 21 from Yaxchilan. It starts with the ISIG in A1, followed by the B'aktun, K'atun, Tun, Winal, and K'in glyphs in B1, A2, B2, A3, and B3, respectively. This date is 9.0.19.2.4, corresponding to 14 October 454 CE. In B4, the Tzolk'in day 2 K'an can be seen, followed by Glyphs G8 and F conflated in B4. Glyphs X and Y are squeezed into glyph A5, indicating the fifth day in the seven-day cycle of uncertain meaning. Glyph D follows in B5, telling us that the current lunation started 7 days ago, but Glyph E is not seen in this inscription because the current lunation is less than 20 days. Glyphs C and X follow in A6 and B6, indicating the coefficient 3 in Glyph C and X4. Glyph B is absent, but Glyph A, indicating that the current lunation is 29 days long, is behind Glyph X in B6. The Supplementary Series is complete: A7 has the Haab' date 2 Yax. This is followed by a brief statement about "Moon

106   DATES AND NUMBERS

Exercise 3.5. Identify Distance Numbers

1. Identify the following Distance Numbers and whether they are a forward or backward count on the line provided (e.g., "+ 2.14.3").

Palenque
Hieroglyphic
Stairway
+ _____

Palenque
Hieroglyphic
Stairway
+ _____

Piedras Negras
Stela 3
_____

Piedras Negras
Stela 3
_____

Palenque
Palace Tablet
_____

Palenque
Palace Tablet
_____

Palenque
Tablet of the
96 Glyphs
_____

Palenque
Tablet of the
96 Glyphs
_____

Piedras Negras
Stela 3
_____

Yaxchilan
Lintel 21
_____

3.5. DISTANCE NUMBERS

Figure 3.18. Dates and Distance Numbers from Yaxchilan, Lintel 21

tzi(?)-k(a)-HAB' 9-pi-h(i)
tziik(?) haab' b'olon pih
On the day, 9 eras,

0-WINIK-HAB' 19-HAB'-[pl.]
mih winikhaab' b'olonlaju'n haab'-[pl.]
0 score, 19 years,

2-WINIK-(ki) 4-K'IN-(ni)
cha' winik, chan k'in
2 months, and 4 days,

2-OL TI'-?-HUN
cha' ol ? ti' hu'n
on 2 K'an, G8 [was the] speaker of the book,

5-b'i-xi-ya-? 7-bi-xi-ya-HUL-li-ya
ho' bixiiy ? huk bixiiy huliiy
it happened after 5 days (?),
[the moon] arrived 7 days ago.

3-?-K'AL-aj ?-20-9
ox ? k'alaj, ? winik b'olon
3 ? was bound, X4, a 29 [-day lunation]

2-YAX-SIHOM?-(hi-ma)
cha' yax siho'm
2 Yax

5-16-WINIK-ya 1-HAB'-ya
ho', waklaju'n winik-iiy, ju'n haab'-iiy
5 [days], 16 months, 1 years

15-WINIK-HAB'-ya i-u-ti
ho'laju'n winikhaab'-iiy iuhti
15 scores [later] it happened

7-? 17-ka-se-w(a)
huk ?, huklaju'n kase'w
on 7 Muluk, 17 Sek

Posit	Long Count	Tzolk'in	Haab'	DD	MMM	YYYY	E
A1-A7	09.00.19.02.04	02 K'an	02 Yax	14	OCT	454	CE
+/-	15.01.16.05						
C3-D5	[09.]16.01.00.09]07 Muluk	17 Sek	10	MAY	752	CE

108 DATES AND NUMBERS

Figure 3.19. Dates and Distance Numbers from Naranjo, Stela 24

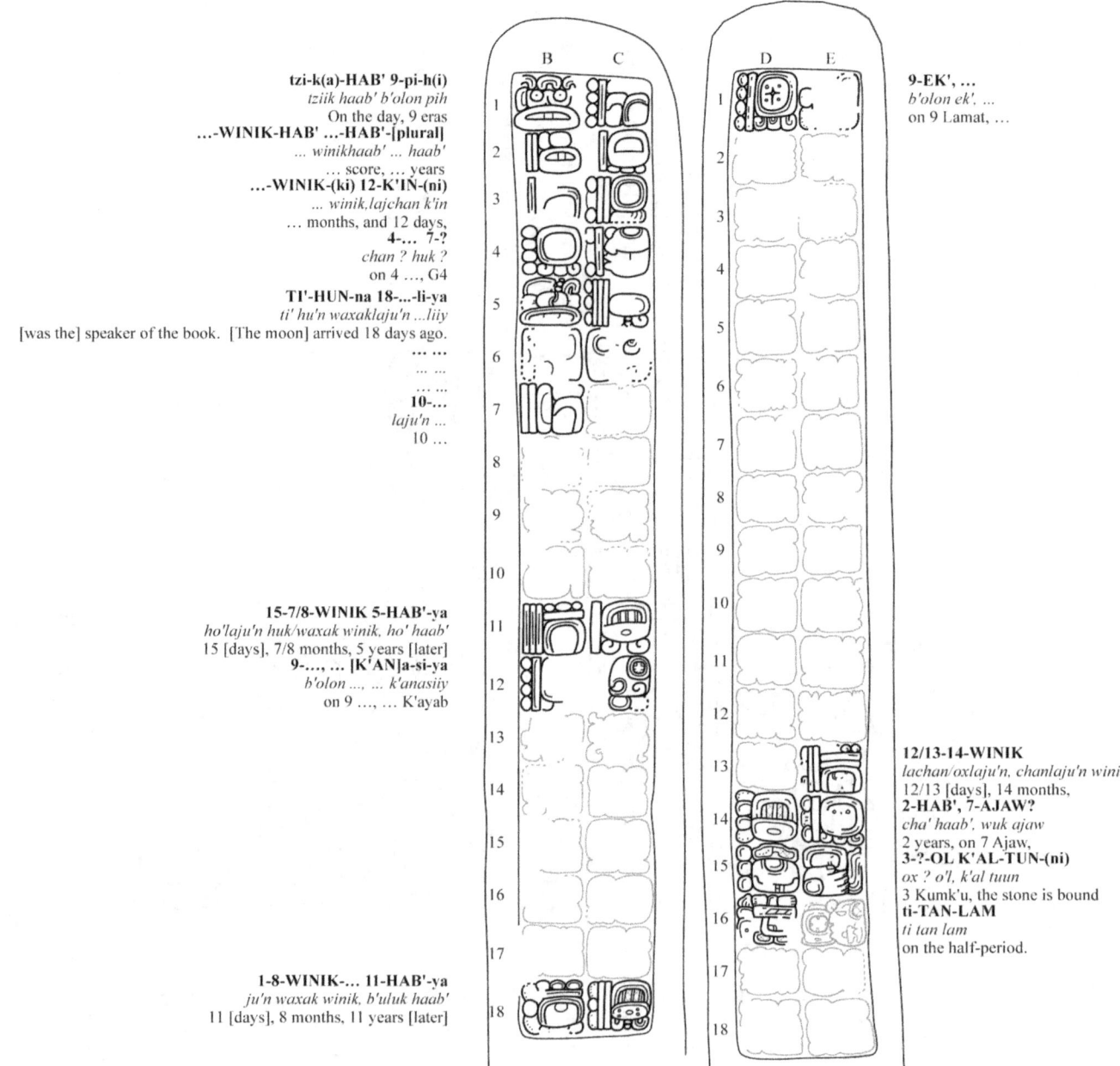

Posit	Long Count	Tzolk'in	Haab'	DD	MMM	YYYY	E
B01-B07	09[12.10.05]12	04 [Eb']	10 [Yax]	28	AUG	682	CE
+/-	05[07]15						
B11-C11	[09.12.15.13.07]	09 [Manik	00]K'ayab	04	JAN	688	CE
+/-	11.08.01						
B18-E02	[09.13.07.03.08]	09 Lamat	[01 Sotz']	17	APR	699	CE
+/-	02.14[12]						
E13-D16	[09.13]00.00.00	07 Ajaw	03 Kumk'u	16	MAR	692	CE

Skull," the seventh ruler of Yaxchilan. A Distance Number follows in glyph blocks C3–C4. Remembering that the periods increase in size in a Distance Number, we can read the number 15.1.16.5. The PDI in glyph block D4 indicates that we must add the Distance Number to our base date. This works out to 9.16.1.0.9, 10 May 752 CE. Following the PDI, the Calendar Round of 7 Muluk, 17 Sek (C5 and D5, respectively) matches the calculated Long Count date. This is followed by a statement about the fifteenth ruler of Yaxchilan, Bird Jaguar IV. Reconstructing the date on Lintel 21 is relatively straightforward.

It is harder but still possible to reconstruct the dates on Naranjo's Stela 24. The Initial Series is introduced by the ISIG, followed by the B'aktun through K'in periods. Only the B'aktun period number is clearly readable, however. The K'atun is more than ten and the Tun and Winal are more than five: the bars on each period are visible, but the dots and/or remaining bars are eroded. There may be 11, 12, or 13 K'in, but it is impossible to tell whether or not any of the apparent dots are placeholders. Furthermore, the Tzolk'in Day Name is unreadable in B4. Usually it is possible to reconstruct a difficult K'in count by using the one-for-one comparison with the Tzolk'in. The day Ajaw always corresponds to zero K'in, Imix corresponds to 1 K'in, and so on. With the unreadable Haab' month in B7, we can reconstruct this date as 9.?.?.?.11/12/13 4 ?, 10 ? (where numbers separated by a forward slash indicate equally viable possibilities). Even though we do not know our base date, we may be able to reason it out from later dates and Distance Numbers. The Distance Number in B11–C11 can be read as 5.7/8.15, but no ADI or PDI is present to indicate a forward or backward count. The Calendar Round in B12–C12 is no great help, being readable only as 9 ?, ? K'ayab. With the next Distance Number and Calendar Round, we are able to fill in some of our unknown values. In B18–C18, the Distance Number is given as 11.8.11. The Calendar Round can be read as 9 Lamat, ?. For now, without an ADI or PDI, it is best to assume that the Distance Number should be added (as if a PDI were present), as is usually the case. We can use the Distance Number's K'in coefficient of 1 to subtract from the Tzolk'in Day Name (with 20 K'in and 20 Day Names, there is a correlated relationship). One day less than Lamat is Manik, so the Day Name in C12 is 9 [Manik]. If we then subtract 15 K'in (from the first Distance Number) from Manik, we can reconstruct the initial Tzolk'in as 4 [Eb']. The final Distance Number, Calendar Round, and other clues will allow us to reconstruct the entire sequence. In glyph blocks E13–D14, the Distance Number 2.14.12/13 can be reconstructed. The following Calendar Round appears to be 7 Ajaw, 3 K'umku. The next two glyphs (E15–D16) show the ending of a half-period (first the stone-binding glyph, followed by the half-period glyph). This suggests that the date is ?.?.0.0.0 (or possibly ?.?.?.0.0) 7 Ajaw, 3 Kumk'u. A calendar program or date chart quickly identifies 9.13.0.0.0 7 Ajaw, 3 Kumk'u as the only possible date. Now we can work backward to calculate the rest of the dates. 9.13.0.0.0 minus 2.14.12/13 can give either [9.13.7.3.8] or [9.13.7.3.7]. This Tzolk'in is known to be Lamat, so it must be the former, making the Distance Number 2.14.[12], and the previous Calendar Round 9 Lamat, [1 Sotz']. Subtracting 11.8.1 from 9.13.7.3.8, we arrive at [9.12.15.13.7] 9 [Manik] [0] K'ayab. Finally, we can subtract either 5.7.15 or 5.8.15 from this date to reconstruct our base date. Only the former Distance Number will allow us to arrive at a date with a 4 Eb' Tzolk'in date: 9.[12.10.5.12] 4[Eb'] 10 [Yax]. Reconstructing the complete date for such an inscription can be a fun and challenging puzzle or absolutely frustrating. If you get really stuck, set it aside for a few hours and come back by starting over from the beginning. Often I find that I made a simple transcription error early in the first attempt that stymied my progress. Try your luck on exercises 3.6–3.12. Some are easy, while others are difficult. **Exercise 3.12** is particularly hard. Do not be discouraged if you have trouble. Take a break and come back to it later.

Exercise 3.6. Reconstruct Dates: Yaxchilan, Hieroglyphic Stairway 3 (easy)

1. Identify all calendar-related glyphs by drawing a square around them.

2. Reconstruct the Long Count date, Calendar Round, Distance Numbers, and Gregorian date for each clause in the inscription, using the form above. Remember to put brackets around anything reconstructed.

Posit	Long Count	Tzolk'in	Haab'	DD	MMM	YYYY	E
	__.__.__.__.__	____	____	__	__	__	__
+/−	__.__.__.__.__						
	__.__.__.__.__	____	____	__	__	__	__

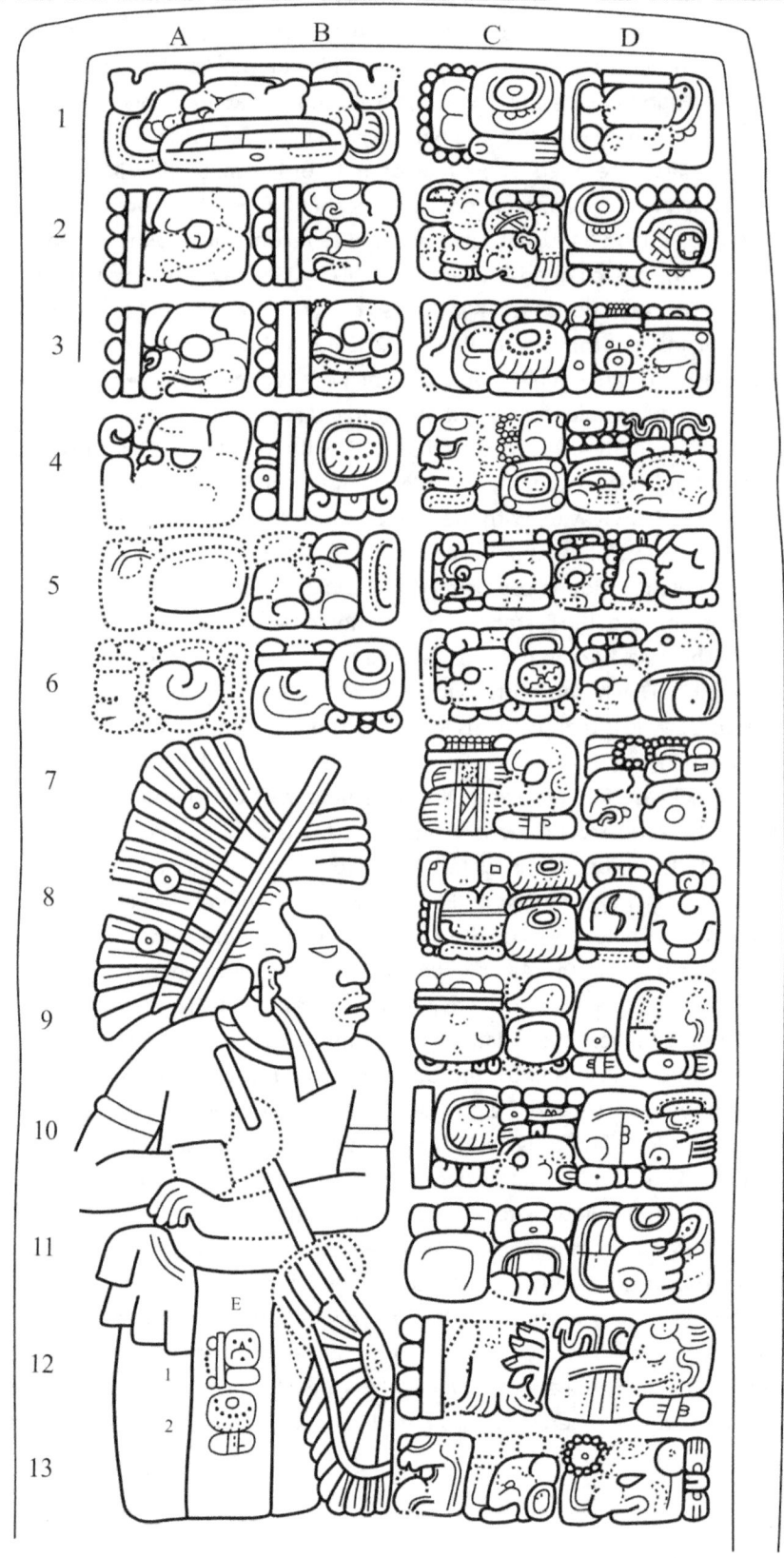

3.5. DISTANCE NUMBERS

Exercise 3.7. Reconstruct Dates: Piedras Negras, Stela 3 (medium)

1. Identify all calendar-related glyphs by drawing a square around them.

2. Reconstruct the Long Count date, Calendar Round, Distance Numbers, and Gregorian date for each clause in the inscription, using the form above. Remember to put brackets around anything reconstructed.

Posit	Long Count	Tzolk'in	Haab'	DD	MMM	YYYY	E
___	__.__.__.__.__	_____	_____	__	___	____	_
+ / -	__.__.__.__.__	_____	_____	__	___	____	_
+ / -	__.__.__.__.__	_____	_____	__	___	____	_
+ / -	__.__.__.__.__	_____	_____	__	___	____	_
+ / -	__.__.__.__.__	_____	_____	__	___	____	_

Exercise 3.8. Reconstruct Dates: Palenque, Tablet of 96 Glyphs (medium)

1. Identify all calendar-related glyphs by drawing a square around them.

2. Reconstruct the Long Count date, Calendar Round, Distance Numbers, and Gregorian date for each clause in the inscription, using the form to the right. Remember to put brackets around anything reconstructed. If any Distance Numbers are not calculated from the previous date, use an arrow to indicate the point from which it should be calculated.

Note: Many of the numbers are head variants. The first date is a K'atun ending.

Posit	Long Count	Tzolk'in	Haab'	DD	MMM	YYYY	E
+/−	_ . _ . _ . _ . _	_	_	_	_	_	_
+/−	_ . _ . _ . _ . _	_	_	_	_	_	_
+/−	_ . _ . _ . _ . _	_	_	_	_	_	_
+/−	_ . _ . _ . _ . _	_	_	_	_	_	_

3.5. DISTANCE NUMBERS

Exercise 3.9. Reconstruct Dates: Piedras Negras, Altar 2 (easy)

1. Identify all calendar-related glyphs by drawing a square around them.

2. Reconstruct the Long Count date, Calendar Round, Distance Numbers, and Gregorian date for each clause in the inscription, using the form below. Remember to put brackets around anything reconstructed. If any Distance Numbers are not calculated from the previous date, use an arrow to indicate the point from which it should be calculated.

Note: You must first figure out the order of the four legs (inscription blocks). You will have to work backward to get the initial date.

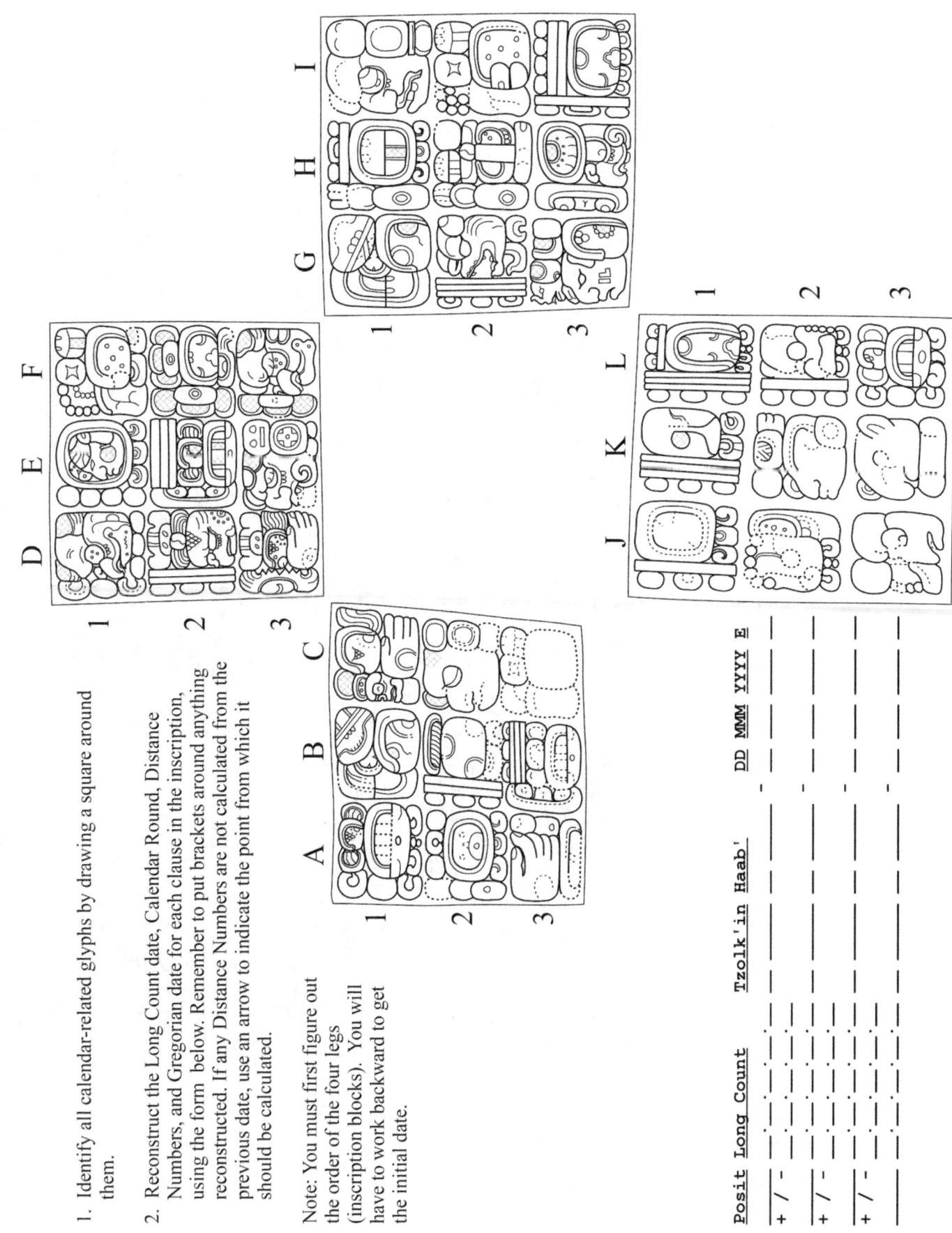

114 DATES AND NUMBERS

Exercise 3.10. Reconstruct Dates: Palenque, Hieroglyphic Stairway (medium)

1. Identify all calendar-related glyphs by drawing a square around them.

2. Reconstruct the Long Count date, Calendar Round, Distance Numbers, and Gregorian date for each clause in the inscription, using the form below. Remember to put brackets around anything reconstructed. If any Distance Numbers are not calculated from the previous date, use an arrow to indicate the point from which it should be calculated.

Note: Not all dates are consecutive.

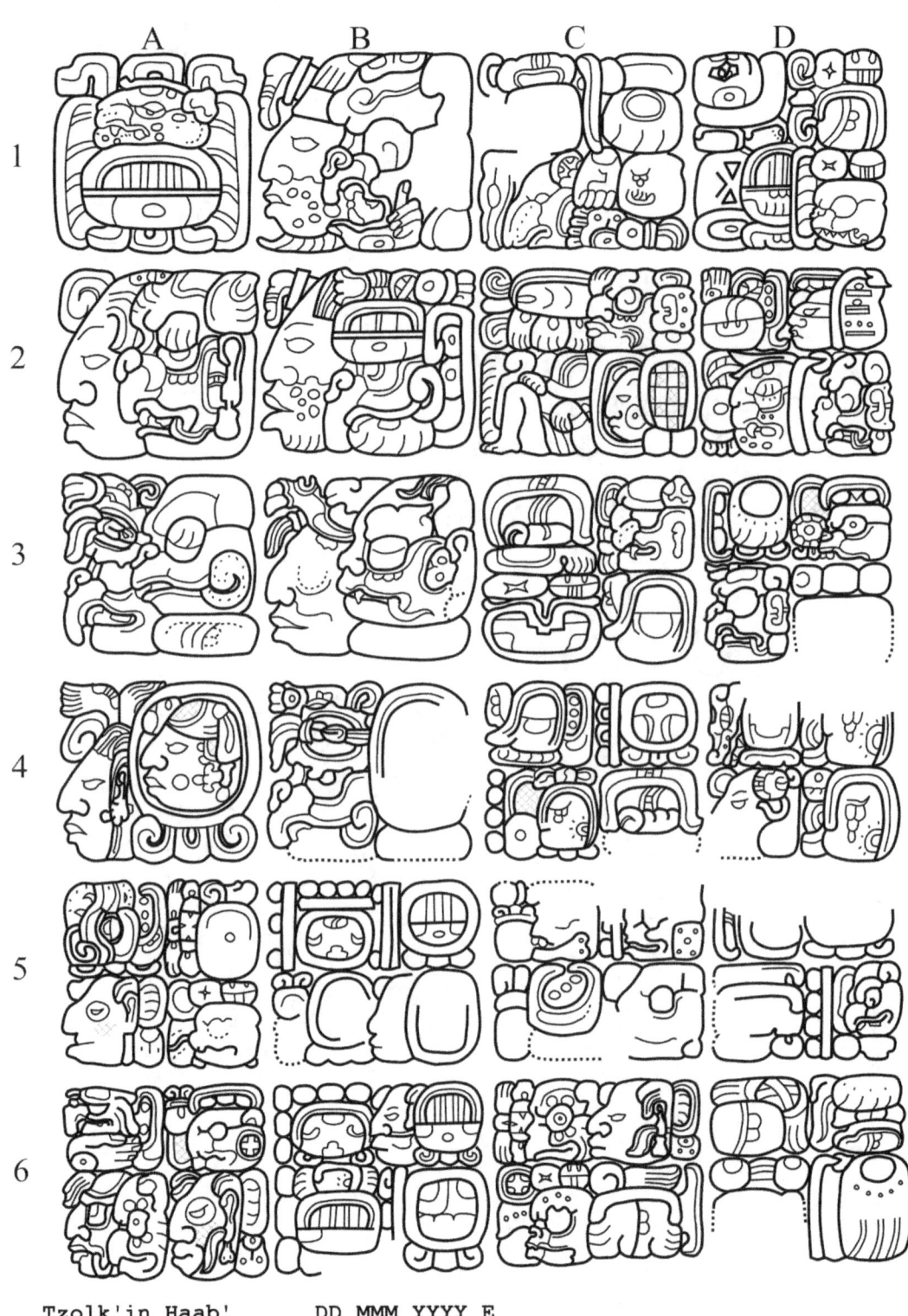

```
Posit  Long Count       Tzolk'in Haab'      DD MMM YYYY E
_____  __.__.__.__.__   __ ____   __ ____   __ ___ ____ _
 + / - __.__.__.__.__
_____  __.__.__.__.__   __ ____   __ ____   __ ___ ____ _
 + / - __.__.__.__.__
_____  __.__.__.__.__   __ ____   __ ____   __ ___ ____ _
 + / - __.__.__.__.__
_____  __.__.__.__.__   __ ____   __ ____   __ ___ ____ _
```

Exercise 3.11. Inscription Date Reconstruction: Palenque, Sarcophagus (medium) (page 1 of 2)

1. Identify all calendar-related glyphs by drawing a square around them.
2. Reconstruct the Long Count date, Calendar Round, Distance Numbers, and Gregorian date for each clause in the inscription, using the chart below, remembering to put brackets around anything reconstructed. If any Distance Numbers are not calculated from the previous date, use an arrow to indicate from where it should be calculated.

Note: This inscription starts by describing the life of K'inich Janab' Pakal (d. 680 CE) and then his ancestors. The **earliest** date is in glyphs 16 and 17. Each following date is consecutive and moves linearly through time (from earliest to latest). Use the *chum tuun* glyphs in positions 24a and 45a to anchor these dates to the Long Count (remember that the *chum tuun* glyph is used to commemorate the end of a K'atun period, so the associated Long Count date should be X.X.0.0.0). Some of you may have noticed the *chum tuun* glyph in position 6, but this example only refers to the fact that K'inich Janab' Pakal was in his 4th K'atun of life.

Posit	Long Count	Tzolk'in	Haab'	DD	MMM	YYYY	E

[blank reconstruction chart with rows for multiple dates, each with +/− Distance Number entry]

DATES AND NUMBERS

Exercise 3.11. (page 2 of 2)

3.5. DISTANCE NUMBERS

Exercise 3.12. Reconstruct Dates: Palenque, Palace Tablet (very difficult) (page 1 of 2)

1. Identify all calendar-related glyphs by drawing a square around them.

2. Reconstruct the Long Count date, Calendar Round, Distance Numbers, and Gregorian date for each clause in the inscription, using the form below. Remember to put brackets around anything reconstructed. If any Distance Numbers are not calculated from the previous date, use an arrow to indicate the point from which they should be calculated.

Note: If you cannot reconstruct or read a given date or number, move on and keep working. Often it is possible to work backward once you get the next date. Not all dates are consecutive. For example, some clauses calculate the new date not from the previous date but from a date earlier in the inscription or history.

Posit	Long Count	Tzolk'in	Haab'	DD	MMM	YYYY	E
___	__.__.__.__.__	__ ___	__ ____	__	___	____	_
+/−	__.__.__.__.__						
___	__.__.__.__.__	__ ___	__ ____	__	___	____	_
+/−	__.__.__.__.__						
___	__.__.__.__.__	__ ___	__ ____	__	___	____	_
+/−	__.__.__.__.__						
___	__.__.__.__.__	__ ___	__ ____	__	___	____	_
+/−	__.__.__.__.__						
___	__.__.__.__.__	__ ___	__ ____	__	___	____	_
+/−	__.__.__.__.__						
___	__.__.__.__.__	__ ___	__ ____	__	___	____	_
+/−	__.__.__.__.__						
___	__.__.__.__.__	__ ___	__ ____	__	___	____	_
+/−	__.__.__.__.__						
___	__.__.__.__.__	__ ___	__ ____	__	___	____	_
+/−	__.__.__.__.__						
___	__.__.__.__.__	__ ___	__ ____	__	___	____	_
+/−	__.__.__.__.__						
___	__.__.__.__.__	__ ___	__ ____	__	___	____	_
+/−	__.__.__.__.__						
___	__.__.__.__.__	__ ___	__ ____	__	___	____	_

118 DATES AND NUMBERS

Exercise 3.12. (page 2 of 2)

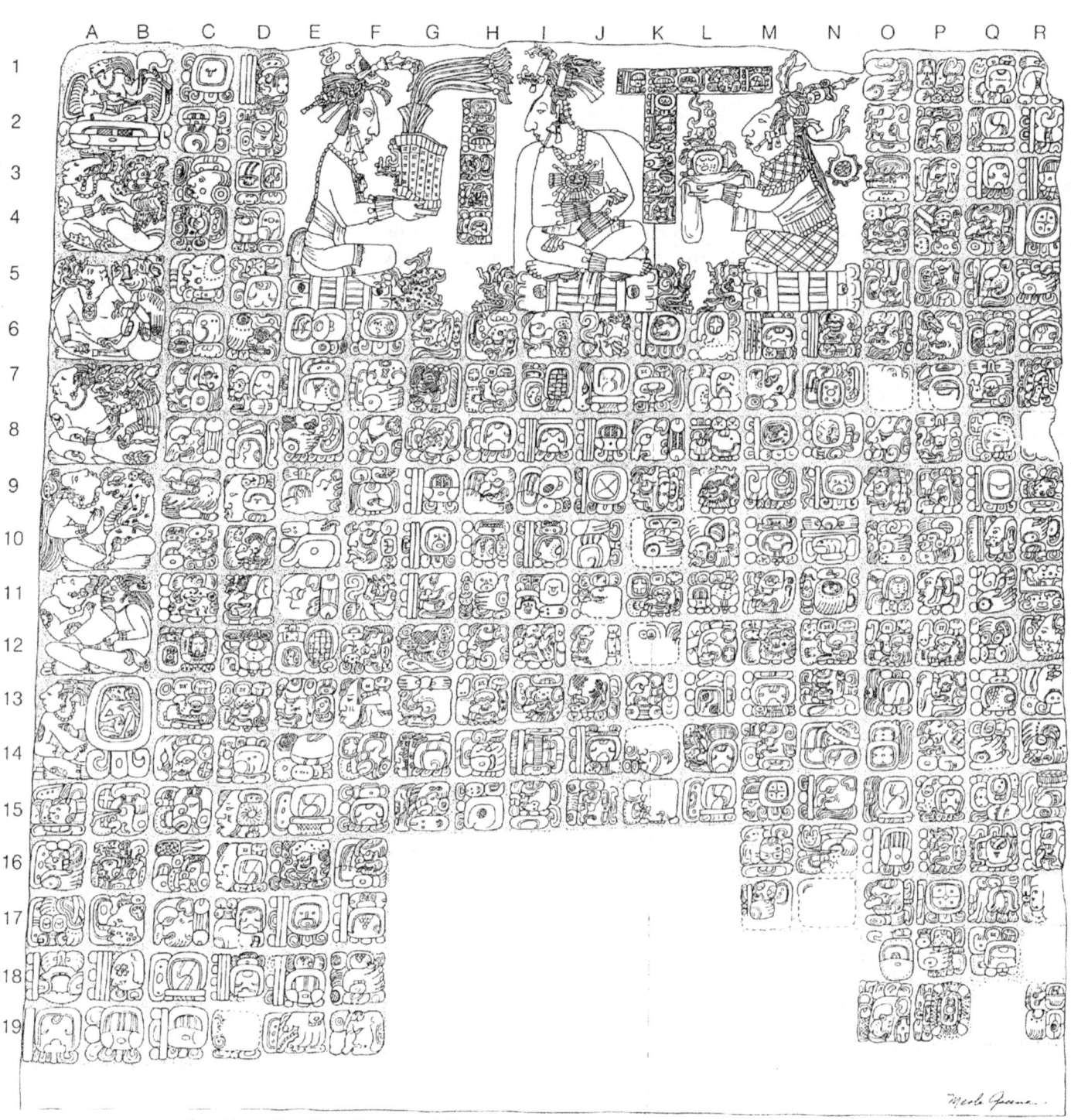

Image copyright Merle Greene Robertson, 1976.

3.6. SHORT COUNTS

The minutely exact Long Count date was occasionally abbreviated starting in the Late Classic and was severely truncated by the contact period. At first dates were given in relation to the ending of a K'atun (ca. 20-year period). The date 9.10.0.0.0 1 Ajaw, 8 K'ayab (25 January 623 CE) would be recorded as K'atun 10, 1 Ajaw, 8 K'ayab. This abbreviation is still accurate enough to indicate any day within the course of Maya history. Glyphically, it appears as **u-10-WINIK-HAB' 1-AJAW 8-[K'AN]a-si-y(a),** or *u laju'n winikhaab' ju'n ajaw waxak k'anasiiy,* meaning "its 10th K'atun, on 1 Ajaw, 8 K'ayab," as shown in **figure 3.20**.

By the time of contact, the calendar had been further abbreviated. At this point only the Tzolk'in day that ended a particular K'atun was given. Only "1 Ajaw" would be given to indicate our example date of 9.10.0.0.0 1 Ajaw, 8 K'ayab (although this system was probably not in use until the twelfth or thirteenth century). This may seem drastically short, but the K'atun names did not repeat for about 256 years (13 numbers of Ajaw × ca. 20 years). The debate over the correct correlation of the Maya and European calendars often centered on the founding of Mérida (1542 CE) in the K'atun ending on 11 Ajaw and other similar dates. The question became "How many cycles of 256 years had elapsed since the Classic period?" This is why the Spinden correlation puts all dates 256 years earlier than the Goodman-Martinez-Thompson correlation coefficient. These 20-year periods were used in the annals to summarize events that happened during that time. As long as all of the periods were listed in succession, events could be recorded for thousands of years without ambiguity. Indeed, the Spanish records indicate a history going back 62 K'atuns, to the fifth century CE. **Table 3.11** can be used to indicate the beginning date for any given Short Count date.

The Maya calendar is rich and complex. Most dates recorded on monuments can be quickly understood and even converted into Gregorian dates with a little practice. Dates form the basic framework of inscriptional content and should be fairly well understood before moving on to the actual content of the inscriptions.

Figure 3.20. Short Count Date

u-10-WINIK-HAB' 1-AJAW
u laju'n winikhaab' ju'n ajaw
[it is] its 10th K'atun, on 1 Ajaw

8-[K'AN]a-si-y(a)
waxak k'anasiiy
8 K'ayab'

Table 3.11. Short Count Names and Their Equivalent Long Counts

The Short Count name, given as the Tzolk'in Day, is in the left column. The possible Long Count coefficients are given in the same row to the right.

Short Count	435–692 CE	692–928 CE	928–1185 CE	1185–1441 CE	1441–1697 CE
1 Ajaw	9.10.0.0.0	10.3.0.0.0	10.16.0.0.0	11.9.0.0.0	12.2.0.0.0
2 Ajaw	9.3.0.0.0	9.16.0.0.0	10.9.0.0.0	11.2.0.0.0	11.15.0.0.0
3 Ajaw	9.9.0.0.0	10.2.0.0.0	10.15.0.0.0	11.8.0.0.0	12.1.0.0.0
4 Ajaw	9.2.0.0.0	9.15.0.0.0	10.8.0.0.0	11.1.0.0.0	11.14.0.0.0
5 Ajaw	9.8.0.0.0	10.1.0.0.0	10.14.0.0.0	11.7.0.0.0	12.0.0.0.0
6 Ajaw	9.1.0.0.0	9.14.0.0.0	10.7.0.0.0	11.0.0.0.0	11.13.0.0.0
7 Ajaw	9.7.0.0.0	10.0.0.0.0	10.13.0.0.0	11.6.0.0.0	11.19.0.0.0
8 Ajaw	9.0.0.0.0	9.13.0.0.0	10.6.0.0.0	10.19.0.0.0	11.12.0.0.0
9 Ajaw	9.6.0.0.0	9.19.0.0.0	10.12.0.0.0	11.5.0.0.0	11.18.0.0.0
10 Ajaw	9.12.0.0.0	10.5.0.0.0	10.18.0.0.0	11.11.0.0.0	12.4.0.0.0
11 Ajaw	9.5.0.0.0	9.18.0.0.0	10.11.0.0.0	11.4.0.0.0	11.17.0.0.0
12 Ajaw	9.11.0.0.0	10.4.0.0.0	10.17.0.0.0	11.10.0.0.0	12.3.0.0.0
13 Ajaw	9.4.0.0.0	9.17.0.0.0	10.10.0.0.0	11.3.0.0.0	11.16.0.0.0

4. BASIC GRAMMAR

Just like English and other languages of the world, Classic Mayan had prepositions, pronouns, nouns, adjectives, adverbs, and grammatical organization. This chapter introduces some of the vocabulary and the important parts of speech used in Classic Mayan inscriptions. The basic vocabulary presented here, especially the nouns, will be useful to you in the next chapter when verbal morphology is introduced.

4.1. PREPOSITIONS

Prepositions are used before a noun, pronoun, or verb to indicate the relationship of that word to others. This relationship is usually spatial or temporal. In Classic Mayan inscriptions, one preposition is used more than any other. The preposition **ti**, pronounced *ti-*, can mean "in, into," "with," "by," "at," "on," or "to." For instance, the phrase **ti-sa-ja-la-le**, probably read *ti-sajale[l]*, means "into lordship," as in "the lord was installed into lordship," a phrase used for royal ascension. This preposition may also take the form **ta** or **tu**. The former is the elision of the *i* in the *ti* syllable before an *a*-initial word, such as *ajaw*: **ta-AJAW-le** is read as *tajawle[l]*, "into rulership." The *i* is dropped for ease of pronunciation (although **ti-AJAW-le** also occurs, the **ti** syllabogram may be being used out of habit and can still be transliterated *tajawle[l]*, not *tiajawle[l]*). In some cases, **ta-** may also be a regional variant of **ti-**. The preposition **tu-** is a contraction of **ti** and **u**, which can mean "his," "hers," or "its," giving readings such as "in his," "on her," "to its," and others depending on context. **Figure 4.1** shows **ti** and all of the other prepositions discussed here.

Although *ti* makes up the majority of the prepositions used in Classic inscriptions, other prepositions have also been identified. There are two prepositions meaning "within": **i-chi-l(a)** or *ichiil* and **ma-l(a)** or *mal*. The preposition **TAN**, pronounced *tan*, means "in the center of"; similarly, **xi-n(i)**, or *xin*, means "in" or "inside." The word **ti-i-l(i)**, or *ti'il*, seems to mean "pertaining to." The final preposition (which is probably the second most common), **yi-chi-NAL-(la)**, pronounced *yichnal* (or possibly *yichonal*), means "with" in the sense of "in front of" another person. This preposition is most commonly used when talking about an action performed by somebody who is accompanied by another person, usually a subordinate or superordinate ruler. Using **figure 4.1**, try to identify the different forms of prepositions in **exercise 4.1**.

Figure 4.1. Prepositions

i-chi-l(a)
ichiil-
within

ma-l(a)-
mal-
within

ta-
ta-
in/with/by/at/on/to

TAN-
tan-
in-the-center-of

ti-
ti-
in/with/by/at/on/to

ti-i-li
ti'il
pertaining to

tu- [ti + u]
tu- [ti + u]
in/with/by/at/on/to his/her/its

xi-n(i)-
xin-
in/inside

yi[chi]-NAL
yichinal
with/in-the-presence-of

Exercise 4.1. Identify Prepositions

1. Identify the following prepositions, with appropriate transcriptions, transliterations, and translations.

Aguateca
Stela 1

_____ _____   **Palenque**
_____ _____   Palace Tablet   _____ _____ _____
_____ _____   _____ _____ _____
                                      _____ _____ _____

Palenque
Tablet of
the 96
Glyphs

_____ _____ _____   _____
_____ _____ _____   _____
_____ _____ _____   _____

Hypothetical

_____ _____ _____ _____ _____
_____ _____ _____ _____ _____
_____ _____ _____ _____ _____

Piedras
Negras
Stela 3

_____ _____
_____ _____
_____ _____

4.2. PRONOUNS

Pronouns in Classic Mayan, just as in English and other languages, represent nouns in certain contexts. In the case of Classic Mayan, pronouns are most often found before verbs and possessed objects. It has two sets of related personal pronouns, whereas English has three: for example, "he/him/his" and "she/her/hers." One English pronoun is used as the subject, one as the object, and one as the possessor. In Classic Mayan, one set (Set A) is used for the subject and possessor, while the other (Set B) is used as a subject or object, depending on context (the terms "agent" and "patient" are used in chapter 5 for these functions, because the concepts "subject" and "object" do not appropriately convey the meaning of pronouns in the Classic Maya system). The first set of pronouns is most commonly seen in Classic inscriptions. The second group is often present but rarely seen, as we'll discover.

The pronouns in the first set, called **Set A** or **ergative** pronouns, are used as the subject of transitive verbs and to possess nouns. The word "ergative" simply refers to a language that uses pronouns with transitive verbs that are different from those used with intransitive verbs. Ergative pronouns in Classic Mayan are prefixes and are always appended to the beginning of the word with which they are associated (either a transitive verb or a possessed noun). We will discuss transitive verbs and their morphology in chapter 5. Suffice it to say here that a transitive verb is one that is used with both a subject and an object. For instance, the verb "runs" in "he runs" is not transitive because it takes only a subject, no object, while the verb "hugs" in "he hugs her" is transitive because it takes both a subject and an object. With a transitive verb, Classic Mayan uses pronouns from Set A to indicate the subject. Set A pronouns are also used to show possession. In this case, they are simply attached to the front of the noun they possess.

The vast majority of inscriptions use only third-person singular pronouns. This may have to do with narrative traditions and conventions of the Classic Maya. A few examples of first- and second-person singular pronouns are found in inscriptions, but the plural pronouns discussed in this chapter and shown in **figure 4.2** are largely reconstructed based on existing Maya languages. Nonetheless, the full set of pronouns is presented here.

4.2. PRONOUNS

Figure 4.2. Personal Pronouns

Personal pronouns stand in for a noun or noun phrase. They are used with nouns and verbs to indicate possession and action roles, respectively.

		Ergative: Subject of transitive verbs and possessor of nouns ( ) indicates vowel-initial version	**Absolutive:** Object of transitive verbs and subject of intransitive verbs * = not well attested
Singular	First Person	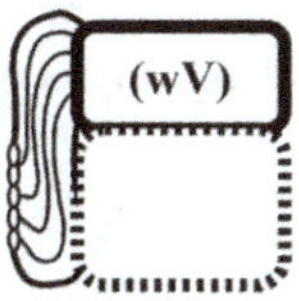 **ni(w)-** *ni(w)-* I or my	 **-Ce-n(a)** *-een* (or *-e'n*) I or me
	Second Person	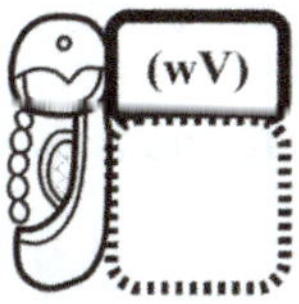 **'a-(wV)-** *a(w)-* you or your	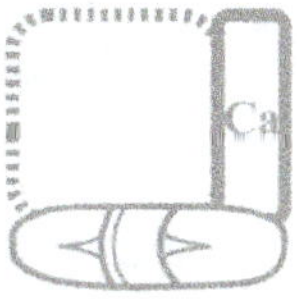 **-Ca-t(a)** *-at** you
	Third Person	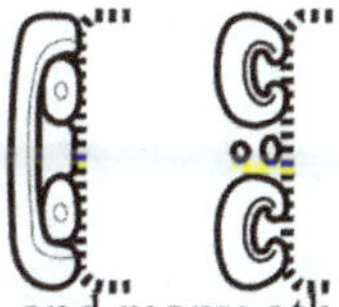 **'u- (yV-)** *u- (yV-)* he/she/it or his/her/its and many others	**-ø** he/she/it or him/her/it
	Demonstrative	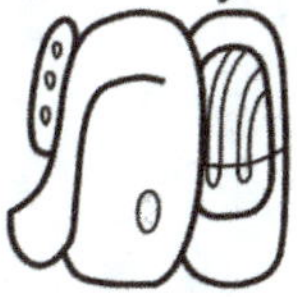 **ha-(i)** *haa* this or that	
Plural	First Person	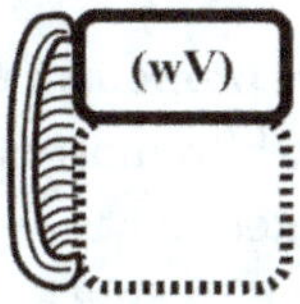 **ka-(wV)-** *ka(w)-* we or our	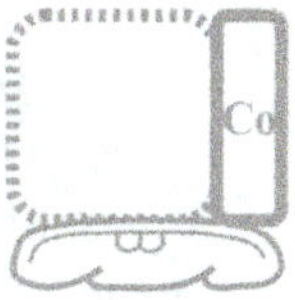 **-Co-n(a)** *-o'n** we or us
	Second Person	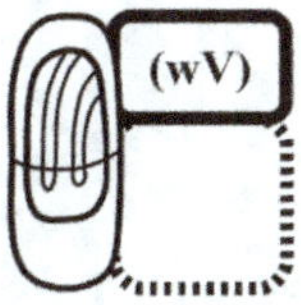 **i-(wV)-** *i(w)-* you (pl.) or your (pl.)	 **-Co-x(o)** *-ox** you (pl.)
	Third Person	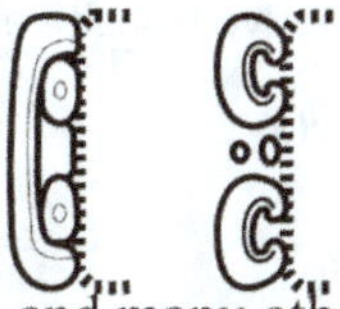 **'u- (yV-)** *u- (yV-)* they or their and many others	 **-Co-b'(a)** *-o'b'** they or them
	Demonstrative	 **ha-o-b'(a)** *hao'b'* these or those	

Ergative pronouns are shown in the left half of **figure 4.2**. Just as with English, we find the usual pronouns: "I," "you," "we," "you" (plural), and "they," but Classic Mayan combines "he," "she," and "it" into one pronoun. The **first-person singular ergative pronoun** is written **ni-**, pronounced *ni-*, and means either "I" before a verb or "my" before a noun. If the verb or noun begins with a vowel, **ni-wV-** is used (the **V** is the vowel that begins the noun or verb), read *niw-*. This is easy to see in the following examples. The transitive verbs "to plant" (*pak'*) and "to drop" (*akt*) (see chapter 5 for the *-aw* following the verbs) as well as the nouns "plate" (*lak*) and "ruler" (*ajaw*) can serve as examples:

Transcription:	**ni-pa-k'a-w(a)**			
Transliteration:	*nipak'aw*			
Translation:	I planted it			
Simplified Analysis:	*ni-*	*pak'-*	*aw-*	ø
	I-	plant-	active.transitive.verb.marker-	him/her/it

Transcription:	**ni-wa-k(a)-ta-w(a)**			
Transliteration:	*niwaktaw*			
Translation:	I dropped it			
Simplified Analysis:	*niw-*	*akt-*	*aw-*	ø
	I-	drop-	active.transitive.verb.marker-	him/her/it

and

Transcription:	**ni-la-k(a)**	
Transliteration:	*nilak*	
Translation:	my plate	
Simplified Analysis:	*ni-*	*lak*
	my-	plate

Transcription:	**ni-w(a)-AJAW**	
Transliteration:	*niwajaw*	
Translation:	my ruler	
Simplified Analysis:	*niw-*	*ajaw*
	my-	ruler

The **second-person singular ergative pronoun** is written **a-** if it occurs before a verb or noun that begins with a consonant (which most do) or **a-wV** before a noun or verb that starts with a vowel. These are transliterated as *a-* or *aw-*, respectively; but both can mean either "you" (before a verb) or "your" (before a noun). For example:

Transcription:	**a-pa-k'a-w(a)**			
Transliteration:	*apak'aw*			
Translation:	you planted it			
Simplified Analysis:	*a-*	*pak'-*	*aw-*	ø
	you-	plant-	active.transitive.verb.marker-	him/her/it

Transcription:	**a-wa-k(a)-ta-w(a)**			
Transliteration:	*awaktaw*			
Translation:	you dropped it			
Simplified Analysis:	*aw-*	*akt-*	*aw-*	ø
	you-	drop-	active.transitive.verb.marker-	him/her/it

and

Transcription:	**a-la-k(a)**
Transliteration:	*alak*
Translation:	your plate
Simplified Analysis:	*a- lak*
	your- plate

Transcription:	**a-w(a)-AJAW**
Transliteration:	*awajaw*
Translation:	your ruler
Simplified Analysis:	*aw- ajaw*
	your- ruler

The **third-person singular ergative pronoun** is by far the most commonly seen pronoun in Classic Maya inscriptions. Most passages are written in third-person narrative: "he went forth and did such-and-such." This pronoun is written **u-** and read *u-* unless the following verb or noun begins with a vowel, in which case it is written **yV-** and pronounced *yV-*. Both can mean "he," "she," or "it" (before a verb) or "his," "hers," or "its" (before a noun); you must decide which English pronoun to use from the context. For example:

Transcription:	**u-pa-k'a-w(a)**
Transliteration:	*upak'aw*
Translation:	he planted it
Simplified Analysis:	*u- pak'- aw- ø*
	he- plant- active.transitive.verb.marker- him/her/it

Transcription:	**ya-k(a)-ta-w(a)**
Transliteration:	*yaktaw*
Translation:	he dropped it
Simplified Analysis:	*y- akt- aw- ø*
	he- drop- active.transitive.verb.marker- him/her/it

and

Transcription:	**u-la-k(a)**
Transliteration:	*ulak*
Translation:	his plate
Simplified Analysis:	*u- lak*
	his- plate

Transcription:	**y(a)-AJAW**
Transliteration:	*yajaw*
Translation:	his ruler
Simplified Analysis:	*y- ajaw*
	his- ruler

Plural pronouns are rather rare in Classic inscriptions. The **first-person plural ergative pronoun** is **ka-**, read *ka-* (or **ka-wV-**, read *kaw-* before a word beginning with a vowel). Again, this can mean either "we" (before a verb) or "our" (before a noun). For example:

Transcription:	**ka-pa-k'a-w(a)**
Transliteration:	*kapak'aw*
Translation:	we planted it
Simplified Analysis:	*ka- pak'- aw- ø*
	we- plant- active.transitive.verb.marker- him/her/it

Transcription:	**ka-wa-k(a)-ta-w(a)**
Transliteration:	*kawaktaw*
Translation:	we dropped it
Simplified Analysis:	*kaw- akt- aw- ø*
	we- drop- active.transitive.verb.marker- him/her/it

and

Transcription:	**ka-la-k(a)**
Transliteration:	*kalak*
Translation:	our plate
Simplified Analysis:	*ka- lak*
	our- plate

Transcription:	**ka-w(a)-AJAW**
Transliteration:	*kawajaw*
Translation:	our ruler
Simplified Analysis:	*kaw- ajaw*
	our- ruler

The **second-person plural ergative pronoun** is written **i-** and pronounced *i-* (or **i-wV-**, read *iw-*, before a verb or noun starting with a vowel). It can be translated as "you" (before verbs) or "your" (before nouns). Remember that this is the plural form of "you," sometimes expressed as "you guys" or "y'all" in American English. Here are a few examples:

Transcription:	**i-pa-k'a-w(a)**
Transliteration:	*ipak'aw*
Translation:	you planted it.
Simplified Analysis:	*i- pak'- aw- ø*
	you- plant- active.transitive.verb.marker- him/her/it

Transcription:	**i-wa-k(a)-ta-w(a)**
Transliteration:	*iwaktaw*
Translation:	you dropped it
Simplified Analysis:	*iw- akt- aw- ø*
	you- drop- active.transitive.verb.marker- him/her/it

and

Transcription:	**i-la-k(a)**
Transliteration:	*ilak*
Translation:	your plate
Simplified Analysis:	*i- lak*
	your- plate

Transcription: **i-w(a)-AJAW**
Transliteration: *iwajaw*
Translation: <u>your</u> ruler
Simplified Analysis: *iw-   ajaw*
　　　　　　　　　<u>your-</u> ruler

The **third-person plural ergative pronoun** is identical to the third-person singular pronoun: **u-** before consonant-initial nouns or verbs and **yV-** before vowel-initial ones. You must infer from the context that more than one person is meant. In that case, they are often named in the sentence. Here are a few examples:

Transcription: **u-pa-k'a-w(a)**
Transliteration: *upak'aw*
Translation: <u>they</u> planted it
Simplified Analysis: *u-   pak'-   aw-*   ø
　　　　　　　　　<u>they-</u> plant- active.transitive.verb.marker- him/her/it

Transcription: **ya-k(a)-ta-w(a)**
Transliteration: *yaktaw*
Translation: <u>they</u> dropped it
Simplified Analysis: *y-   akta- w-*   ø
　　　　　　　　　<u>they-</u> drop- active.transitive.verb.marker- him/her/it

and

Transcription: **u-la-k(a)**
Transliteration: *ulak*
Translation: <u>their</u> plate
Simplified Analysis: *u-   lak*
　　　　　　　　　<u>their-</u> plate

Transcription: **y(a)-AJAW**
Transliteration: *yajaw*
Translation: <u>their</u> ruler
Simplified Analysis: *y-   ajaw*
　　　　　　　　　<u>their-</u> ruler

The second set of pronouns in Classic Mayan, the so-called **Set B** or **absolutive** pronouns, can be the object of transitive verbs and the subject of intransitive verbs. Do not worry too much about knowing the difference between the two right now. Each one is dealt with in detail in chapter 5. The word "absolutive" is simply the counterpart to the term "ergative" for Set A. English has nominative pronouns ("I," "you," "he," "she," "it," "we," "you" [plural], and "they") as well as accusative pronouns ("me," "you," "him," "her," "it," "us," "you" [plural], and "them"). Classic Mayan absolutive pronouns are used as the object when there is an ergative pronoun marking the subject (remember that transitive verbs take both a subject and an object) or as the subject when it is used with an intransitive verb. In short, an intransitive verb can only take one actor, such as "he sits." Absolutive pronouns always appear as suffixes, attached after the verbal root and marker. They can occur with nouns only as part of a stative clause (see the discussion in section 4.6).

Absolutive pronouns are shown in the right half of **figure 4.2**. In this figure, most of them appear with gray lines instead of black. This is because most of them are not found in Classic inscriptions and are reconstructed from modern Maya languages. The main reason for this is that the vast majority of inscriptions use third-person pronouns. Furthermore, ergative pronouns serving as possessors of nouns are the most common use of first- or second-person pronouns in inscriptions. As far as absolutive pronouns are concerned, verbs rarely indicate anything other than the third person. Just as ergative pronouns could be translated as "I/my," "you/your," and "he/his" depending on the context, absolutive pronouns can be translated as "I/me," "you/you," and "he/him" in context.

The **first-person singular absolutive pronoun** is written **-Ce-n(a)**, resulting in *-een* (or possibly *-e'n*) appended to the end of a verbal marker. When this follows a transitive verb, it should be translated as "me." After an intransitive verb, it means "I." If it follows a noun, it forms a stative compound similar to simple English statements with the verb "to be" (such as "I am large"). In many cases, an absolutive pronoun that follows a vowel may mask the first vowel to avoid aggregated vowels. For example, "I arrived" could have been *hulieen,* but the close proximity of *i* and *ee* may have caused the word to be pronounced *huleen*. Unfortunately, we have so few non-third-person examples that this is difficult to assess. The transitive verb "to wound" (*jatz'*); the intransitive verb "to arrive" (*hul*); and the noun "ruler" (*ajaw*) may serve as examples of this principle:

Transcription:	**u-ja-tz'a-we-n(a)**
Transliteration:	*ujatz'aween*
Translation:	he wounded me
Simplified Analysis:	u- jatz'- aw- een
	he wound- active.transitive.verb.marker- me

Transcription:	**hu-li-e-n(a)**
Transliteration:	*huleen* or *hulieen*
Translation:	I arrived
Simplified Analysis:	hul- i- een
	arrive- root.intransitive.verb.marker- I

Transcription:	**AJAW-(w)e-n(a)**
Transliteration:	*ajaween*
Translation:	I [am] ruler
Simplified Analysis:	ajaw een
	ruler- I

The **second-person singular absolutive pronoun** is rarely seen glyphically and was reconstructed from extant Maya languages. It should appear as **-Ca-t(a)**, pronounced *-at*. This is read as "you" as either an object (transitive verb) or a subject (intransitive verb).

Transcription:	**u-ja-tz'a-wa-t(a)**
Transliteration:	*ujatz'awat*
Translation:	he wounded you
Simplified Analysis:	u- jatz'- aw- at
	he wound- active.transitive.verb.marker- you

Transcription:	**hu-li-a-t(a)**
Transliteration:	*hulat* or *huliat*
Translation:	you arrived
Simplified Analysis:	*hul-* *i-* *at*
	arrive- root.intransitive.verb.marker- you

Transcription:	**AJAW-(w)a-t(a)**
Transliteration:	*ajawat*
Translation:	you [are] ruler
Simplified Analysis:	*ajaw* *at*
	ruler- you

The **third-person singular absolutive pronoun** is by far the most common Set B pronoun seen—or rather not seen: it is implied, not written, after a verb. This is usually represented by an empty set: ø. Although it appears that a verb without an object should be translated without a definite object (e.g., "he hugs" instead of "he hugs her"), specific verbal markers indicate a passive condition. Often the object of a transitive verb is explicitly named following the verb, so there is no ambiguity in the inscriptions themselves. Many people do not write the empty set in the transcription and transliteration, but it could be added to help remind the reader that an object is implied: -ø. It is not pronounced but should be translated as "him/her/it" (after transitive verbs) or "he/she/it" (after intransitive verbs).

Transcription:	**u-ja-tz'a-w(a)**
Transliteration:	*ujatz'aw*
Translation:	he/she/it wounded him/her/it
Simplified Analysis:	*u-* *jatz'-* *aw-* ø
	he/she/it wound- active.transitive.verb.marker- him/her/it

Transcription:	**hu-li**
Transliteration:	*huli*
Translation:	he/she/it arrived
Simplified Analysis:	*hul-* *i-* ø
	arrive- root.intransitive.verb.marker- he/she/it

Transcription:	**AJAW**
Transliteration:	*ajaw*
Translation:	he/she [is] ruler
Simplified Analysis:	*ajaw* ø
	ruler- he/she/it

The **first-person plural absolutive pronoun** is not often found in Classic inscriptions. Like all of the plural absolutive pronouns, it is reconstructed from modern Maya languages. The first-person plural absolutive pronoun should appear as **-Co-n(a)**, resulting in *-o'n*. This should be translated as "us" (after transitive verbs) or "we" (after intransitive verbs).

Transcription:	**u-ja-tz'a-wo-n(a)**
Transliteration:	*ujatz'awo'n*
Translation:	he wounded us
Simplified Analysis:	*u-* *jatz'-* *aw-* *o'n*
	he wound- active.transitive.verb.marker- us

Transcription:	**hu-li-o-n(a)**
Transliteration:	*hulo'n* or *hulio'n*
Translation:	we arrived
Simplified Analysis:	*hul- i- o'n*
	arrive- root.intransitive.verb.marker- we

Transcription:	**AJAW-(w)o-n(a)**
Transliteration:	*ajawo'n*
Translation:	we [are] ruler[s]
Simplified Analysis:	*ajaw o'n*
	ruler- we

The **second-person plural absolutive pronoun** should appear as **-Co-x(o)**, read as *-ox*, translated as "you" (plural), as either an object (after transitive verbs) or a subject (after intransitive verbs).

Transcription:	**u-ja-tz'a-wo-x(o)**
Transliteration:	*ujatz'awox*
Translation:	he wounded you (plural)
Simplified Analysis:	*u- jatz'- aw- ox*
	he wound- active.transitive.verb.marker- you (plural)

Transcription:	**hu-li-o-x(o)**
Transliteration:	*hulox* or *huliox*
Translation:	you (plural) arrived
Simplified Analysis:	*hul- i- ox*
	arrive- root.intransitive.verb.marker- you (plural)

Transcription:	**AJAW-(w)o-x(o)**
Transliteration:	*ajawox*
Translation:	you (plural) [are] ruler[s]
Simplified Analysis:	*ajaw ox*
	ruler- you (plural)

The **third-person plural absolutive pronoun** should appear as **-Co-b'(a)**, resulting in *-o'b'*. This can be translated as "them" (after transitive verbs) or "they" (after intransitive verbs). We will see this ending again: some suggest that it is a plural marker on nouns.

Transcription:	**u-pa-k'a-wo-b'(a)**
Transliteration:	*ujatz' awo'b'*
Translation:	he wounded them
Simplified Analysis:	*u- jatz'- aw- o'b'*
	he wound- active.transitive.verb.marker- them

Transcription:	**hu-li-o-b'(a)**
Transliteration:	*hulo'b'* or *hulio'b'*
Translation:	they arrived
Simplified Analysis:	*hul- i- o'b'*
	arrive- root.intransitive.verb.marker- they

Transcription:	**AJAW-(w)o-b'(a)**
Transliteration:	*ajawe'n*
Translation:	they [are] ruler[s]
Simplified Analysis:	*ajaw o'b'*
	ruler- they

Finally, **demonstrative pronouns** serve to highlight a specific item in discourse. "This," "that," "these," and "those" serve this purpose in English. It appears that **ha-(i)** and **ha-o-b'(a),** or *haa* and *hao'b',* in Classic Mayan might be translated as "this" and "these" as the singular and plural demonstrative pronouns, respectively. **Independent pronouns** are used to emphasize a person or thing already mentioned as part of a verbal or noun phrase. For instance, in English a pronoun can occur independently: "Whom did Sally see? Him?!" In Classic Mayan, they are formed by adding an absolutive pronoun to the base *haa'*. Elision can occur, dropping abutting vowels: *hiin* (or possibly *he'n*) as "I" (*haa'-e'n*); *hat* as "you" (*haa'-at*); *haa'* as "he/she/it" (*haa'-ø*); *haa'-o'n* as "we"; *haa'-o'x* as "you" (plural); and *ha'-o'b'* as "they." These "stand alone" pronouns can also take prepositions, just as in English: *ti-hiin,* "with me." Practice identifying pronouns in **exercise 4.2** and then try translating the phrases in **exercises 4.3 and 4.4**.

134 BASIC GRAMMAR

Exercise 4.2. Identify Pronouns

1. Identify the following pronouns, with appropriate transcriptions, transliterations, and translations.

Exercise 4.3. Pronouns

1. Using the following vocabulary, translate the phrases below into English (refer to fig. 4.2 for pronouns). The first column of exercises contains nouns, and the second column has verbs.

ajaw	ruler (n)	*chuk-aw*	to catch (tv)	*lak*	plate (n)
atan	wife (n)	*hul-i*	to arrive (iv)	*muk-aw*	to bury (tv)
b'aak	captive (n)	*il-aw*	to witness (tv)	*sajal*	lord (n)

u-b'aak _____   hul-i-ox _____

ni-lak _____   ka-muk-aw-ø _____

i-sajal _____   a-chuk-aw-een _____

y-ajaw _____   i-muk-aw-ø _____

niw-atan _____   hul-i-et _____

a-lak _____   niw-il-aw-o'b' _____

kaw-atan _____   u-chuk-aw-o'n _____

haa-b'aak _____   a-muk-aw-o'b' _____

2. Using the vocabulary, translate the following English phrases into Classic Mayan.

cham-i	to die (iv)	*ju'n tan*	cherished one (n)	*mam*	ancestor (n)
itz'aat	sage (n)	*koj-aw*	to hit (tv)	*otoot*	house (n)
ixik	lady, woman (n)	*k'ohaw*	helmet (n)	*uk'ib'*	drinking vessel (n)

my helmet _____   You die. _____

their house _____   We die. _____

his cherished one _____   You (pl.) hit them. _____

our drinking vessel _____   I die. _____

your (pl.) sage _____   You hit him. _____

this lady _____   He hit us. _____

your ancestor _____   They die. _____

his lady _____   I hit you. _____

BASIC GRAMMAR

Exercise 4.4. Pronouns II

1. Using the figures from chapter 4 and vocabulary, transcribe, transliterate, and translate the following phrases. The five exercises on the left are nouns, while those on the right are verbs. Remember the third-person singular ergative pronoun is unmarked.

ak'-aw	to give (tv)	jub'-aw	to take down (tv)	naw-aw	to display (tv)
al-aw	to say (tv)	kakaw	chocolate (n)	tzul	dog (n)
ch'ok	heir (n)				

4.3. NOUNS, NOUN SUFFIXES, AND MORPHOSYLLABLES

Nouns are generally known as people, places, things, or ideas. They are one of the two most basic categories of words: verbs are the other. Most other parts of speech modify or are related to nouns or verbs. Like many Maya words, most nouns appear as CVC or CVCVC words: alternating consonant-vowel combinations that are easily written syllabically. Classic Mayan appears to have two types of nouns. First are the pure nouns, which describe, a person, place, thing, or idea at the most basic level. Second are derived nouns, which come from a different part of speech (verbs, adjectives, or even other nouns), usually with the addition of a suffix. Nouns can be possessed or unpossessed (indicated by prefixes and suffixes), depending on the type or class of noun.

Pure nouns are nouns whose root cannot be reduced to anything less than a simple noun. They can appear as affixes or main signs, depending on the scribal preference. Some examples of pure nouns are given in **figure 4.3**. As you can see, some pure nouns can be represented with a single logogram (not counting phonetic complements). This distinguishes some pure nouns from derived ones (which require a suffix), but note that pure nouns can also be spelled phonetically with syllabograms. Pure nouns are not inherently better than derived nouns. For instance, the pure English noun "song" is clearly no better than the derived noun "singer" (where the -er agentive suffix is added to the verb "sing" to imply "one who sings").

Figure 4.3. Pure Nouns

Pure nouns are not derived from other parts of speech and are not suffixed in their basic state. Some can be represented by a single logogram, but they may also be spelled phonetically.

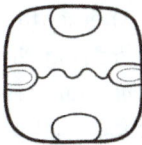
B'AK
b'aak
captive, bone (n)

ch'o[k(o)]
ch'ok
youth, heir (n)

i-tz'a-t(i)
itz'aat
sage (n)

IXIK
ixik
woman (n)

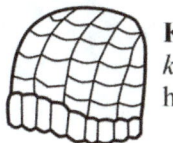
KO'HAW
ko'haw
helmet (n)

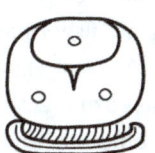
la-k(a)
lak
plate (n)

MAM
mam
ancestor (n)

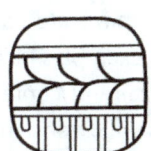
OTOT
otoot
house (n)

tzu-l(u)
tzul
dog (n)

Derived nouns are created from other parts of speech, such as verbs, adjectives, suffixes, or even other nouns. They consist of a non-noun with a derivational suffix or a noun with a modifying suffix, usually an instrumental (although nouns can also be derived into new nouns of related meanings). Noun-deriving suffixes are shown in **figure 4.4**.

Transitive verbs can become nouns through the addition of -*b'al*, usually from the addition of **-b'a-l(a)** or possibly just **-b'a** after a transitive verb. For example, *k'ochb'al tuun* means "container" (from the transitive verb *k'och*, "to carry") and *chub'al che'eb'* means "quill/brush container." A transitive verb may be suffixed with -*lay*, spelled **-la-y(a)**, to form a derived noun, such as *ch'amlay*, "grasper," from the root noun *ch'am*, meaning "to grasp." They may also be suffixed by -*o'l*, spelled **-Co-l(a)**, as in *poko'l*, "washbowl," from *pok*, meaning "to wash."

Nouns can be derived from intransitive verbs by adding -*al*, usually spelled **-Ca-l(a)** or just **-la**. The word *payal*, "guide," comes from the verb *pay*, meaning "to lead," with the -*al* derivational suffix. Intransitive verbs can also be made into title-like nouns by adding the -*o'm* or -*no'm* suffix. This is an agentive suffix, which basically serves the same purpose as -*er* in English words such as "singer," "runner," and "writer." Maya intransitive verbs, such as *pas, jatz'*, and *kok* ("to open," "to strike," and "to guard," respectively) can be made into the derived nouns *pasno'm, jatz'o'm*, and *kokno'm* ("opener," "striker," and "guardian," respectively) by adding **-no-m(a)** or **-Co-m(a)**.

Positional verbs can become derived nouns by adding -*ib'*, spelled **-Ci-b'(i)** or simply **-b'i**. For example, the verb *chum*, "to sit," becomes *chumib'*, spelled **CHUM-b'i**, "seat." The suffix -*ib'* can also be added to intransitive verbs, such as *uk*, "to drink," to create nouns such as *uk'ib'*, spelled **u-k'i-b'(i)**, "drinking vessel." Derivational suffixes are shown glyphically in **figure 4.4**, along with further examples.

Nouns can also be modified by suffixes to derive a new, related noun. As noted, the agentive suffix -*o'm* indicates a person who does that particular thing. For example, the noun *kayo'm*, "fisherman," is derived from the noun *kay*, "fish." It is unclear whether the noun *k'ayo'm*, "singer," comes from the noun *k'ay*, "song," or the verb *k'ay*, "to sing"; in either case, -*o'm* is acting as an agentive suffix. Just as the English suffix -*ship* indicates a noun of office or condition (making a concrete noun abstract), such as "leadership" or "hardship," Classic Mayan expressed this condition with the suffix -*lel*. The most well-known example of this is *ajawlel*, "rulership," from the noun *ajaw*, "ruler." This is often spelled **AJAW-le-l(e)**, but the final -**le** may also be left off. Other examples include *ch'oklel* (youth-hood or heirship) and *sajalel* (lordship, from the title *sajal*, which is close to the English title "lord"), as shown in **figure 4.4**. Finally, **toponyms** (place-names) can be derived from a wide variety of words. The clearest toponymic suffix is -*nal*, meaning "place-of." Examples include *k'ahk'nal*, "fire-place" (a toponym mentioned at Uxmal and Chichen Itza), and *k'ante'nal*, "yellow-tree-place," in the Dresden Codex. Using **figure 4.4**, do **exercise 4.5**, translating the given derived nouns from Mayan into English.

4.3. NOUNS, NOUN SUFFIXES, AND MORPHOSYLLABLES

Figure 4.4. Noun Suffixes (page 1 of 3)

These suffixes derive nouns from nouns, verbs, and other parts of speech.

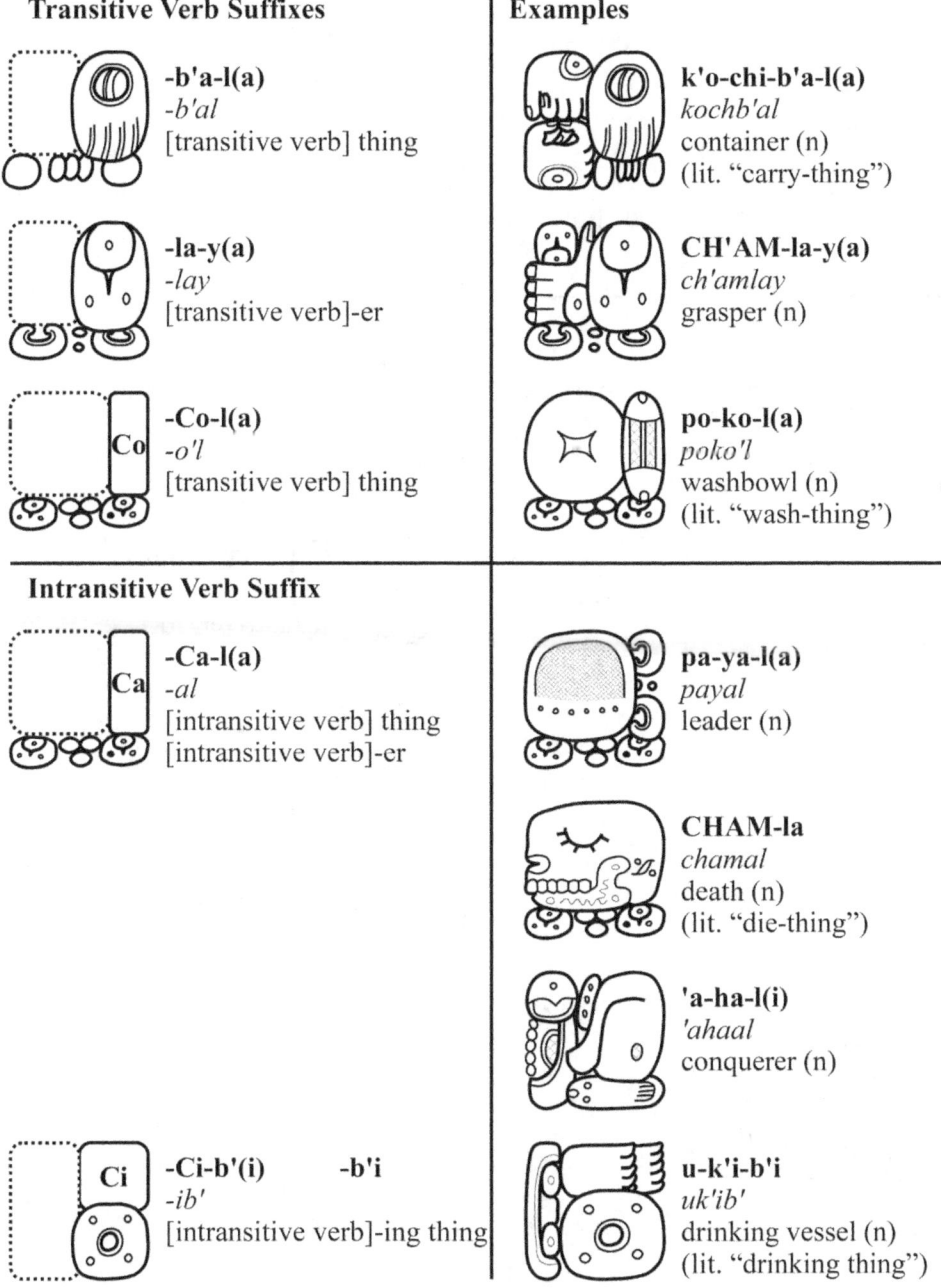

Figure 4.4. Noun Suffixes (page 2 of 3)

Positional Verb Suffix	Examples
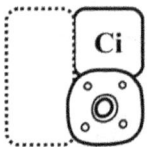 **-Ci-b'(i)** -b'i -ib' [positional verb]-ing thing	 **CHUM[b'i]** chumib' seat (n) (lit. "sitting thing")
 **-ya-j(a)** -yaj [positional verb]-ing thing	

Verb Suffix	
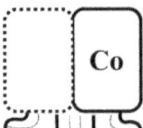 **-Co-m(a)** -no-m(a) -o'm -no'm [verb]-er	 **pa-sa-no-m(a)** pasno'm opener (n)  **JATZ'-m(a)** jatz'[o]'m striker (n)  **ko-ko-no-m(a)** kokono'm guardian (n)  **k'a-yo-m(a)** k'ayo'm singer (n)
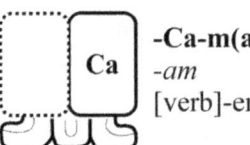 **-Ca-m(a)** -am [verb]-er	

4.3. NOUNS, NOUN SUFFIXES, AND MORPHOSYLLABLES

Figure 4.4. Noun Suffixes (page 3 of 3)

Noun Suffixes	Examples
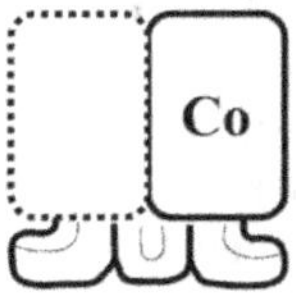 **-Co-m(a)** **-no-m(a)** *-o'm* *-no'm* [noun]-er	 **ka-yo-m(a)** *kayo'm* fisherman (n)
	**ch'a-ho-m(a)** *ch'aho'm* incense scatterer (n)
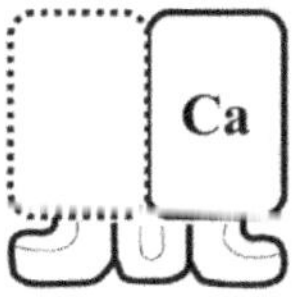 **-Ca-m(a)** *-am* [noun]-er	
 **-le-l(e)** **-le** *-lel* [noun]-ship	 **AJAW-le** *ajawle[l]* rulership (n)
	**ch'o[k(o)]-le-l(e)** *ch'oklel* heirship (n)
	**sa-ja[la]-le** *sajalel* lordship (n)
-NAL **-Ca-l(a)** *-nal* *-al* [noun]-place	 **K'AK'-nal** *k'ahk'nal* fire-place (n)
	**K'AN-TE'-nal** *k'ante'nal* yellow-tree-place (n)

Exercise 4.5. Derived Nouns

1. Using the following vocabulary, translate the nouns below into English (refer to fig. 4.4 for suffixes).

ajaw	ruler (n)	kok	to guard (tv)	pok	to wash (tv)
ak'	to give (tv)	k'ak'	fire (n)	sajal	lord (n)
chak	to tie up (pv)	k'an	yellow (n)	taj	obsidian (n)
cham	to die (iv)	k'ay	to sing (iv)	te'	tree (n)
chok	to scatter (tv)	k'ihn	sun (n)	til	to burn (iv)
ch'am	to grasp (tv)	mak	to cover (tv)	toj	to pay (tv)
ch'ok	youth (n)	muk	to bury (tv)	tz'ib	to paint (tv)
ch'um	to seat (pv)	naab'	water (n)	witz	mountain (n)
hix	jaguar (n)	pas	to open (tv)	yab'	abundance (n)
jatz'	to strike (tv)	pay	to lead (iv)		

ch'amlay _____   ak'nom _____

chokno'm _____   jatz'o'm _____

kokno'm _____   makno'm _____

tz'ib'al _____   ajawlel _____

pasno'm _____   hixnal _____

chamal _____   tajnal _____

ch'oklel _____   yab'nal _____

tilo'm _____   payal _____

k'ak'nal _____   poko'l _____

k'an-nal _____   tojol _____

te'nal _____   k'ayo'm _____

witznal _____   chakib' _____

k'ihn-nal _____   sajalel _____

ch'umib' _____   muknal _____

naab'nal _____

4.3. NOUNS, NOUN SUFFIXES, AND MORPHOSYLLABLES 143

> **BOX 4.1. KEY CONTROVERSY: Plural Markers**
>
> **Plural nouns** are a controversial point of modern Maya epigraphy. It was once thought that plurals were not necessarily marked in the script. As odd as this sounds to an English speaker, a plural marker is not always needed; some languages, such as Japanese, indicate the plural only through context. More recently, Stuart et al. (1999) have suggested that the glyph **TAK**, read *-taak*, is a plural-marking suffix appended to nouns, specifically living or supernatural things. Furthermore, they posit that the three dots that often occur below the **HAB'** glyph should be read *-o'b'*, a favorite plural marker among Mayanists. This plural marker is well known to scholars accustomed to the Yucatecan pronunciation and spelling of glyphs and vocabulary (such as the Tzolk'in Day Names). The reconstructed reading of *-o'b'* for the "three dots" suggested by Stuart et al. might not be fully accepted for conservative reasons. First, this suffix is arguably related to the third-person plural absolutive pronoun of the same spelling. Remember that this is a reconstructed pronoun not strongly attested in the glyphic corpus. Second, although the modern Ch'olti' *-ob'* plural marker is a clear cognate of the suggested reading, we have no demonstrated substitution pattern, such as **-Co-b'(a)**, to indicate the *-o'b'* reading. Usually there are completely logographic and syllabic spellings in identical contexts to support a specific reading, something not yet demonstrated in this case. Although the hypothesis is plausible and I think it will be proven correct, it may be premature to assign this pronunciation to the "three dots."

Possessed nouns come in three major classes. Each class has a different suffix when the noun is not explicitly possessed. First are **body-part nouns,** which must be possessed in some way; these are sometimes referred to as "inalienable nouns" because they must belong to somebody. A "nonpossessed" body-part noun, such as *b'aak*, "bone," adds the suffix *-is*, resulting in *b'aakis*, which can be translated "a bone." The ending drops off when a body-part word is used with any of the ergative pronouns above, such as *ub'aak*, "his/her bone." This also happens with other words, such as *way*, "companion spirit"; *k'ab'*, "hand"; *ti'*, "mouth"; *o'l*, "heart"; and *ut*, "face." All of these nouns must have either an *-is* suffix or a clear ergative pronoun possession (usually *u-*). **Personal property nouns have the** suffix *-aj* when formally unpossessed: body-part and personal-property nouns, along with kinship nouns, form a group of nouns with "intimate possession" in many Maya languages (see Further Reading). This group of nouns includes items that can be worn and counted. For example *u'h*, "collar," either carries this suffix (*u'haj*, "a collar") or is formally possessed (*yu'h*, "his/her collar") This pattern holds true for *b'aah*, "image"; *sih*, "gift"; and *tu'p*, "earflare": they must be formally possessed by a pronoun or suffixed with *-aj*. The last and largest group of nouns, **independent nouns**, can stand alone without possessive suffixes, such as *tuun*, "stone." Someone might possess a stone (*utuun*, "his/her stone"), but a stone by itself does not require a suffix (some epigraphers append a *-ø* suffix to indicate this). Finally, an *-il* suffix may be added to words possessed by a pronoun, such as *utuunil*, "his stone"; but this does not change the meaning as currently understood. Furthermore, this *-il* suffix is not always present. These noun suffixes are shown in **figure 4.5** along with examples.

144 BASIC GRAMMAR

Figure 4.5. Noun Suffixes Showing Possession

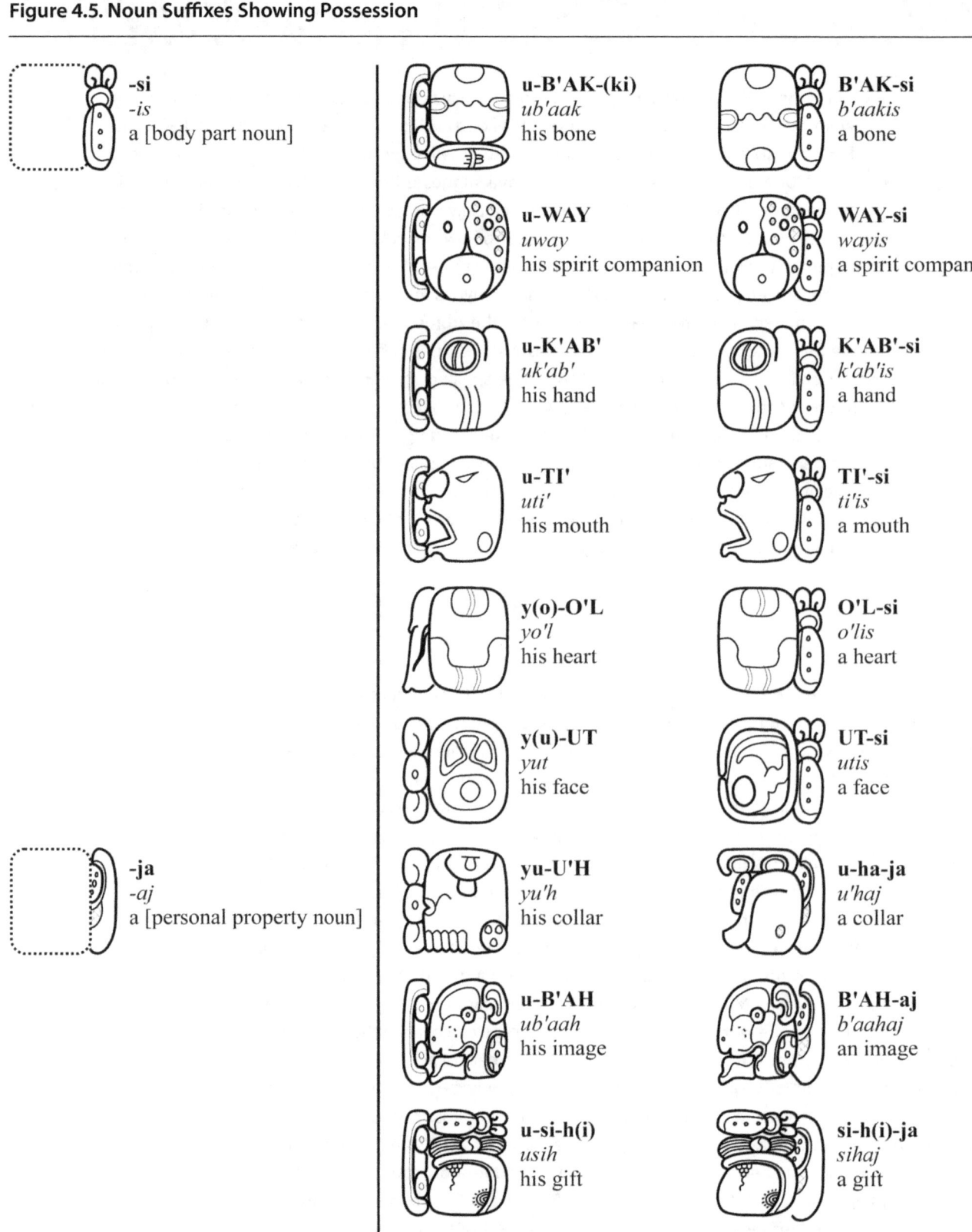

BOX 4.2. KEY CONTROVERSY: Morphosyllables

Morphosyllables are thought to be syllables that can be used to add meaning to verbs, adjectives, and nouns. Originally outlined by Houston, Robertson, and Stuart (2001), morphosyllables reverse their reading order to supply verbal and adjectival endings. For instance, the syllable **-b'i**, as in the positional verb derivational suffix, could represent *-ib'*. Sometimes the indicated vowel is dropped, and the preceding vowel is reconstructed based on vowel harmony. Because of their special nature, Houston et al. (2001) suggest that these syllables, when used in this way, should be written in capital letters, as logograms: **-IB'**. Morphosyllables are thought to be both semantic and phonetic, are inflectional or derivational, and suspend disharmonic principles. Six morphosyllables were proposed originally.

Table 4.1. Morphosyllables

Syllable	Morphosyllable	Result	Use
-wa	-WA	*-Vw*	active transitive verbs declarative mood
-yi	-YI	*-Vy*	mediopassive transitive verbs
-li	-IL	*-Vl*	"-ness"
-b'i	-IB'	*-Vb'* (*-ib'*)	instrumental
-si	-IS	*-Vs*	nominalizer
-ja	-AJ	*-aj*	passive transitive verb

Although these syllables are usually present in the contexts described, it is unclear whether they are actually reversing their value. It is evident, however, that some syllables are consistently present as suffixes in specific contexts (passive transitive verbs are almost always specified as **-ja**). Whether or not these syllables are truly morphosyllables or just the traditional syllable used for a particular suffix, the meaning and transliteration are the same. The final meaning does not change whether or not we accept the morphosyllable hypothesis. For the purposes of this book, the syllables are transliterated as syllabograms (lowercase, boldface), and the transliterated suffix is reconstructed. That is, the result of transliterations is often the same as the morphosyllabic hypothesis, but the transcription differs.

In learning Maya hieroglyphs, you do not have to memorize thousands of symbols. Concentrate on committing to memory a core vocabulary of about 60 calendrical components, 100 nouns, 30 verbs, and 20 grammatical glyphs. I hesitate to provide lists of these glyphs, because lists are by nature incomplete. **Figure 4.6**, for instance, shows some but not all of the most common titles found in inscriptions. You can test your knowledge in **exercise 4.6**, where you must identify titles. I have also included glyphs for common animals (**fig. 4.7**), emblem glyphs (**fig. 4.8**), and family relationship glyphs (**fig. 4.9**), although these do not represent the entire core vocabulary. Appendix III contains a more complete compendium of commonly used Maya words. Appendix IV provides a comprehensive lexicon. Many of these figures include brief notes on the significance of these titles or relationships; but for more on the life and culture of the Classic Maya elite, see Coe (2005), Martin and Grube (2008), Schele and Miller (1986), and Sharer and Traxler (2006). My goal here is to give you the building blocks to use these different parts of speech to achieve a better understanding of the written record of these elites.

Figure 4.6. Titles (page 1 of 3)

It is safe to say that Classic Maya elites were prolific boasters. Major inscriptions mentioning the deeds and events of a particular ruler were typically rife with names, titles, and epithets of that person. It was not sufficient for a ruler to say "Yax B'alam erected the stela," but instead "Yax B'alam, holy ruler of such-and-such-a-place, he of many captives, the incense scatterer, erected the stela." This may sound pompous and overly dramatic, but compare the Duke of York's complete title: "His Royal Highness The Prince Andrew Albert Christian Edward, Duke of York, Earl of Inverness, Baron Killyleagh, Knight Companion of the Most Noble Order of the Garter, Knight Commander of the Royal Victorian Order, Canadian Forces Decoration, Aide-de-Camp to Her Majesty." Many of these titles are presented here glyphically, with their accompanying transcription, transliteration, and translation and a few notes on the most common, interesting, or contentious titles (see the more comprehensive list in appendix III.4).

AJ- *aj-* one who …
This agentive is commonly used to create titles out of nouns, such as "captives," "writing," or "carving."

used in:

AJ-K'UH-n(a) *aj k'uhu'n* one who venerates (n)
This title has been read a number of ways, including "he of the holy books," but Jackson and Stuart (2001) argue that it means "he who keeps, guards, venerates, or worships."

AJ-tz'i-b(a) *ajtz'iib'* he of writing (n)

AJ-yu-xu-l(u) *ajyuxul* he of carving (n)

AJAW *a-ja-w(a)* *ajaw* ruler (n)
This title is ubiquitous and probably the most common title found in texts.

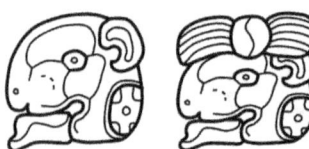

B'AH *b'a-h(i)* *b'aah* self, image, first, head (n)

used in:

B'AH-AJAW *b'aah ajaw* head ruler (n)

4.3. NOUNS, NOUN SUFFIXES, AND MORPHOSYLLABLES

Figure 4.6. Titles (page 2 of 3)

 **B'AH-TE'**   *b'aah te'*   first tree (?) (n)

 **b'a-ka-b'(a)**   *b'aahkab'*   first of the earth (?) (n)
This title is not well understood. Although translated as "first of the earth," it is spelled syllabically, never as **B'AH-KAB'**, which might have been expected if this was the meaning.

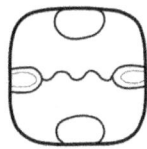  **B'AK**   **b'a-k(i)**   *b'aak*   bone, captive (n)
This title is often seen in name tags accompanying captives on inscriptions, identifying them as captives, usually of the dominant individual in the scene.

 **ch'a-ho-m(a)**   *chaho'm*   incense scatterer (n)
Incense was important for Maya rituals. Rulers were often responsible for dropping it into fires and incense burners.

 **ch'o[k(o)]**   *ch'ok*   youth, heir (n)
This title is often given to an individual who will later become an ajaw: the heir apparent.

 **1-TAN**   *ju'n tan*   cherished one (n)

  **[i]tz'a-t(i)**   **i-tz'a-t(a)**   *itz'aat (itz'at)*   sage (n)

 **IXIK**   *ixik*   woman (n)

 **IX-**   *ix-*   lady (n)
This appears to be the female counterpart to the male agentive *aj-*.

used in:

 **IX-sa-ja-l(a)**   *ix sajal*   female lord (n)

Figure 4.6. Titles (page 3 of 3)

 **KALOM-TE'** ka-lo-m(a)-TE' *kalo'mte'* Kalomte' "he of wood?" (n)
This title is not fully understood. It appears to be a supreme-ruler title. Only ajaws (but not all of them) become Kalomte'. A stela at Copan records four Kalomte' (one for each cardinal direction) at Palenque, Tikal, Calakmul, and Copan.

 **K'INICH** *k'inich* sun-faced [one] (n)
This title associates the bearer with the sun deity and is very common.

  **K'UH** *k'uh* god, deity (n)

used in:

 **K'UHUL-AJAW** *k'uhul ajaw* holy ruler (n)

 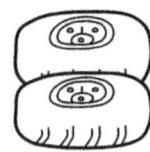 **MAM** ma-m(a) *mam* grandfather, ancestor (n)

 **pi-tzi-l(i)** *pitzil* ballplayer (n)

 **sa-ja-l(a)** *sajal* lord, rank subordinate to ajaw (n)

 **WAY** *way* companion spirit (n)

4.3. NOUNS, NOUN SUFFIXES, AND MORPHOSYLLABLES

Figure 4.7. Animals

The Maya mentioned a number of animals. Many of these animals are shown here glyphically, with their accompanying transcription, transliteration, and translation and a note or two on the most common or interesting animals (see more comprehensive list in appendix III.5).

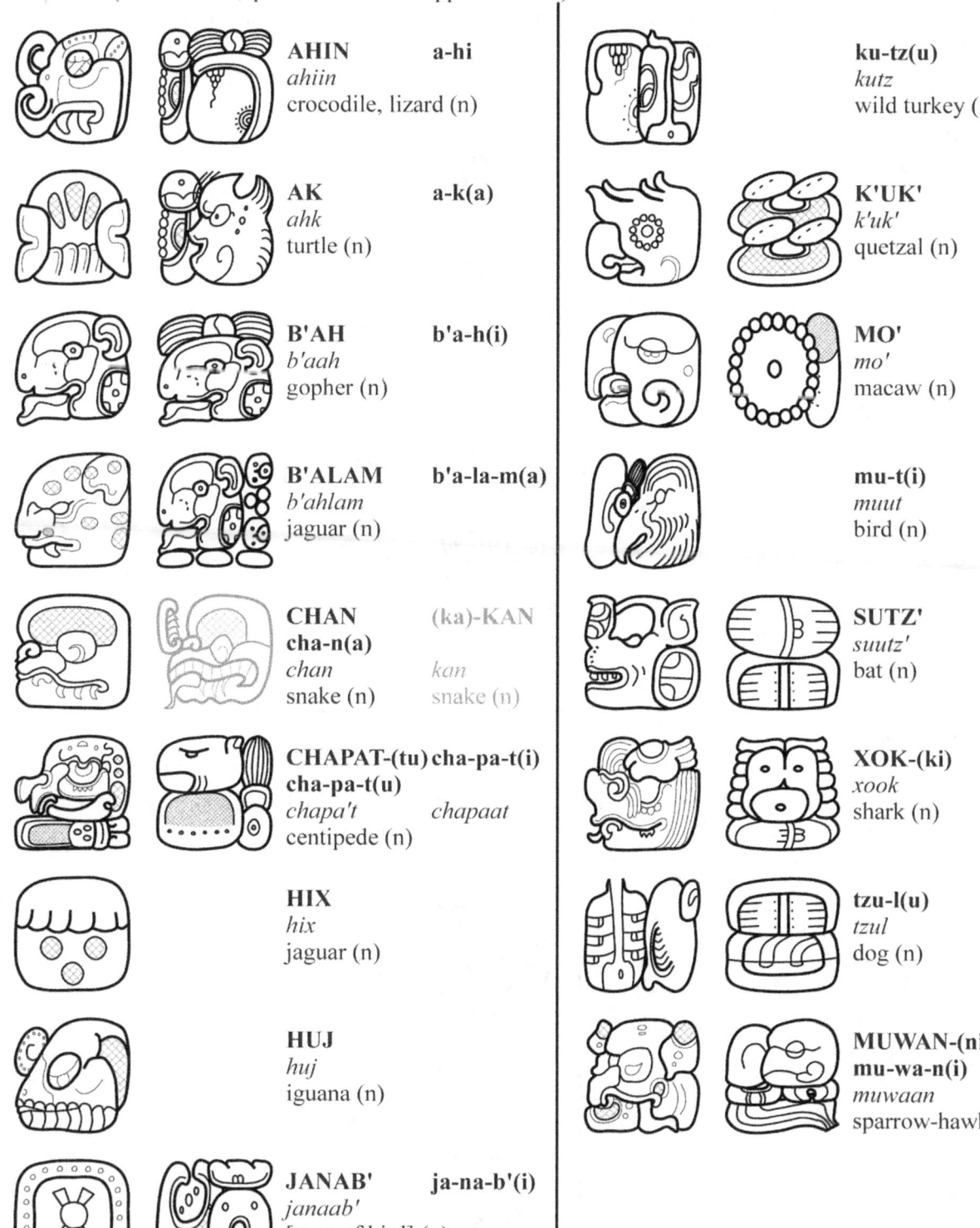

Figure 4.8. Emblem Glyphs

In the mid-1900s Heinrich Berlin noticed that certain glyphs appeared most frequently at specific sites. Each of these glyphs shared a common element, the "ben ich" affix. It is now thought that each emblem glyph is really naming the ruling dynasty, as it moves from city to city when a royal dynasty moves. The most common emblem glyphs are shown below, with their transcription, transliteration, and translation along with a few notes (see the more comprehensive list in appendix III.7).

K'UHUL ... AJAW
k'uhul ... ajaw
holy ... ruler

(ka)-KAN
kan
Calakmul
(lit. "snake")

SUTZ/xo?-pi
koxoop or *xuk pip*
Copan
(lit. "?")

yo-ki-b'(i)
[yo]yokib'
Piedras Negras
(lit. "[his] canyon")

B'AK
b'aak
Palenque
(lit. "bone")

MUTUL
mutul
Tikal
(lit. "bundle")

?-?-y(i)
?
Naranjo
(lit. "?")

PA'CHAN
pa'chan
Yaxchilan
(lit. "split-sky")

Figure 4.9. Family Relations

Family ties are often included in Classic Maya inscriptions, which offer dynastic and biographical information. The most common relational glyphs are shown here (see the more comprehensive list in appendix III.6).

'AL
'al
child of (mother) (n)

'ATAN
'atan
wife (n)

ch'o[k(o)]
ch'ok
youth, heir (n)

1-TAN-na
ju'ntan
cherished one (n)

MIJIN?
mijiin
child of (father) (n)

(y)u-n(e)
une[n]
child of (n)

4.3. NOUNS, NOUN SUFFIXES, AND MORPHOSYLLABLES

Exercise 4.6. Identify Titles

1. Identify the following titles, with appropriate transcriptions, transliterations, and translations.

Aguateca
Stela 1

_____ _____
_____ _____
_____ _____

Naranjo
Stela 24

_____ _____ _____
_____ _____ _____
_____ _____ _____

Palenque
Tablet of the 96 Glyphs

_____ _____ _____ _____ _____
_____ _____ _____ _____ _____
_____ _____ _____ _____ _____

_____ _____
_____ _____
_____ _____

4.4. ADJECTIVES AND ADVERBS

Adjectives in Classic Mayan (see appendix I.4) are either pure adjectives or derived adjectives, just as with nouns. Adjectives modify nouns. In Classic Mayan sentences and word phrases, adjectives appear directly before the noun they modify: adjective-noun. If that noun is possessed, the ergative possessive pronoun appears first: possessive. pronoun–adjective–noun.

Derived adjectives are simply nouns with a -Vl suffix, as seen in **figure 4.10**. The vowel in the suffix is harmonic with the preceding vowel in the noun. For example, *k'ahk'al* is the adjective "fiery," derived from the word *k'ahk'*, "fire"; *ha'al*, meaning "wet," comes from the word *ha'*, "water." In both cases, the nouns are followed by **-la**, which can be transliterated as *-al*. *K'uhul*, "divine," can be spelled **K'UH-lu**, where the final **-lu** indicates the *-ul* adjectival suffix. Practice deriving adjectives in **exercise 4.7**.

Pure adjectives cannot be reduced to constituent parts (they do not require a suffix). **LAKAM** or **la-ka-m(a)**, read *lakam*, means "big, great, or wide" and does not require the *-Vl* adjectival suffix. A number of these pure adjectives have one meaning, such as *lab'*, "ugly or evil"; *ch'ok*, "young"; and *chel*, "high," which only serve as adjectives. Other pure adjectives have multiple meanings, usually an adjectival meaning and a color. Most col-

Figure 4.10. Adjectival Endings

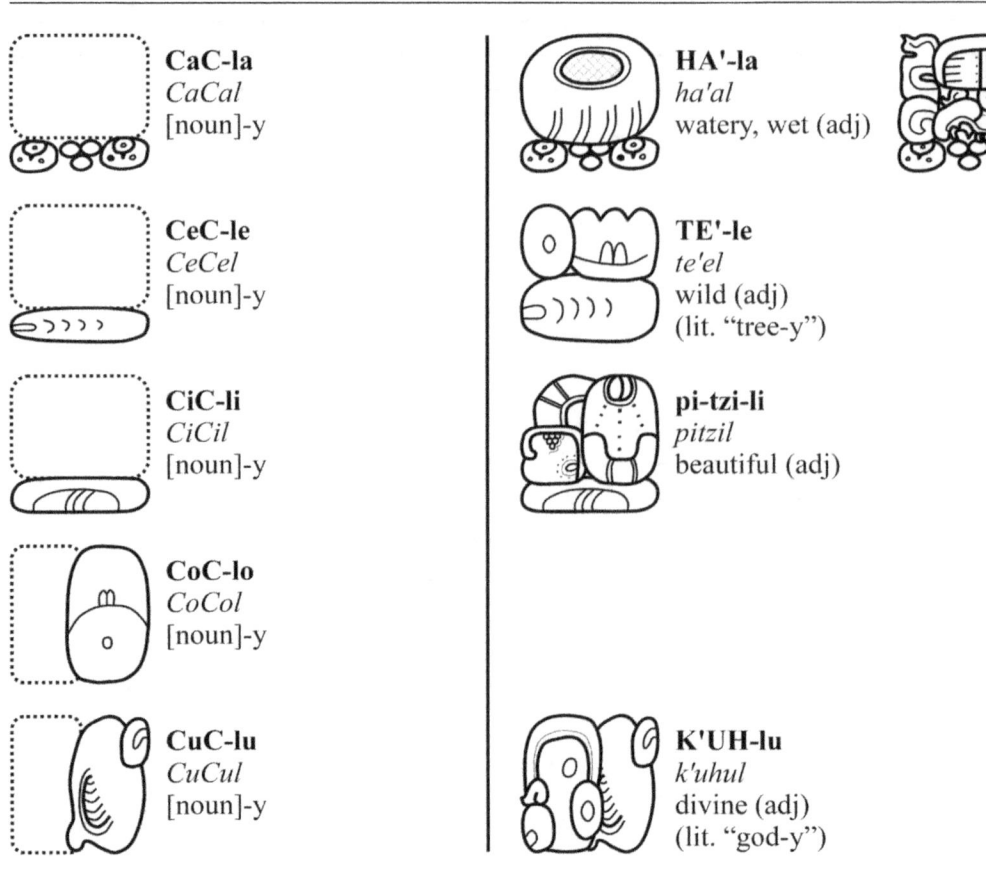

ors in Mayan are also associated with a particular adjectival meaning. For instance, *k'an* can mean "yellow" but also "ripe" or "precious," and *yax* can mean "first" or "blue-green." Although it may seem difficult to translate such an ambiguous adjective, you should remember that the meaning was not separated in Mayan. Colors had properties that could be applied to other things when used as adjectives. This happens in English as well. We might say that somebody who cannot fail is "golden," meaning not that the person is that color but that he or she is highly talented and successful. Colors, though, can also be independent nouns; it can be difficult at first to determine if the scribe meant *k'an* as a noun or adjective. Adjectives are never possessed, cannot be the subject or object of a sentence, and do not appear without a noun to modify them. Therefore, if *k'an* appears directly before another noun, such as the common name *b'alam,* "jaguar," we might read "precious jaguar," not necessarily "yellow jaguar." Some common adjectives and colors are shown in **figure 4.11**.

Classic Mayan includes a few adverbs. They form an important part of glyphic discourse, but their exact nature is still hotly debated. Chapter 5 discusses how time is expressed in Maya texts (the equivalent of past, present, and future tense). For now, imagine that all Maya texts are in the narrative past. This means that everything is inflected for the past tense, just like stories that begin "Once upon a time." The best way to put events in order if all the verbs are in the past tense is to use adverbs, such as "be

---

Exercise 4.7. Derived Adjectives

1. Using the following vocabulary, derive the nouns below into an adjective by adding -*Vl* and then translate into English.

ak	turtle (n)	*kakaw*	chocolate (n)	*taj*	obsidian or torch (n)
ha'	water (n)	*k'ahk'*	fire (n)	*te'*	tree (n)
kab'	earth (n)	*k'uh*	god (n)		

Mayan Root	Mayan Adjective	English Translation
kab' →	_____	_____
taj →	_____	_____
te' →	_____	_____
ha' →	_____	_____
k'uh →	_____	_____
ak →	_____	_____
k'ahk' →	_____	_____
kakaw →	_____	_____

fore," "ago," "then," and "already." Some but not all scholars believe that this is what is happening in Ancient Maya texts. We'll discuss this debate later (see section 5.7). For now, let's talk about the adverbs used in Maya hieroglyphic writing. You have already seen these adverbs in the context of the Posterior and Anterior Date Indicators in chapter 3. The vowel **i-**, pronounced *i-*, is appended to verbs and can be translated as "then," as in *iuti*, "and then it happened," indicating something that happened later. Similarly, **-ya** can be postfixed to verbal phrases to mean "ago" or "already," indicating an event that took place in the past. We saw this in the *-iiy* of *utiiy*, ". . . ago it happened." Another version of this is spelled **-ji-ya**, written *-jiiy*, and may suggest something that happened in the distant past, perhaps as ". . . long ago." These adverbs may be better described as enclitics (see chapter 5).

Figure 4.11. Adjectives and Colors

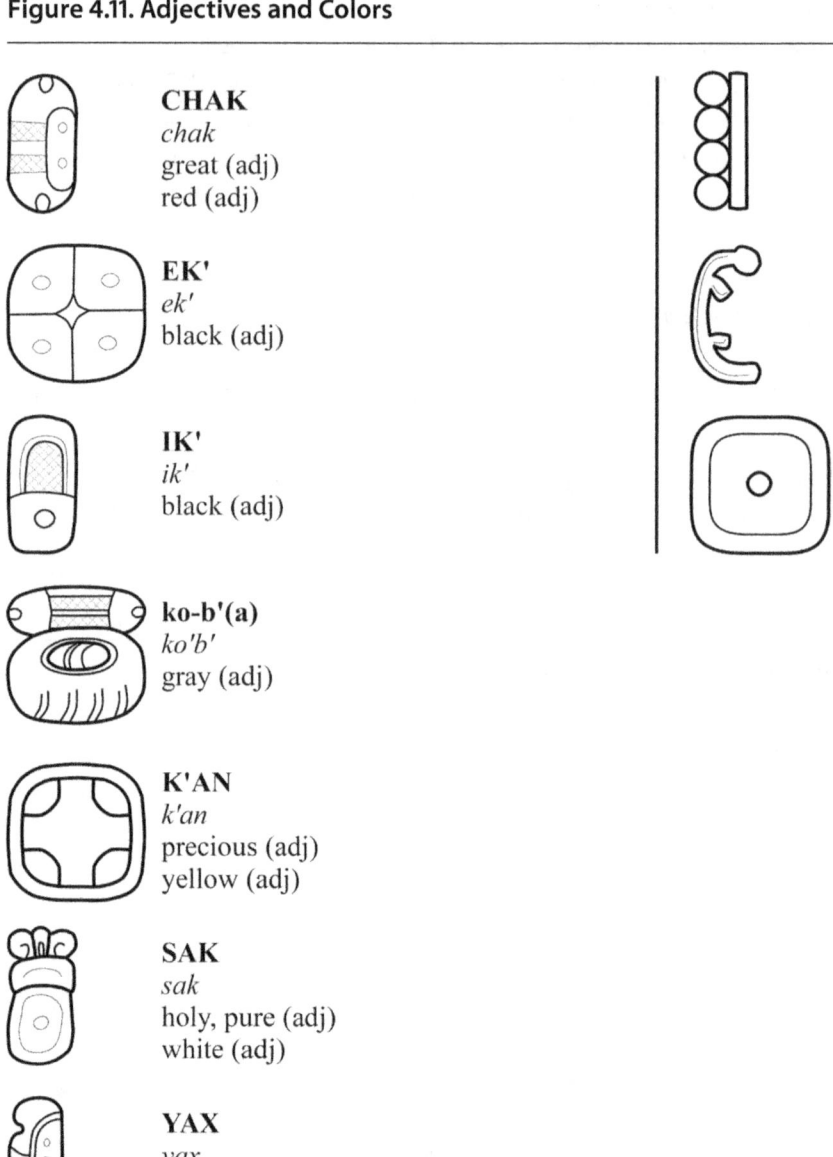

4.5. WORD ORDER IN CLASSIC MAYAN

Words occur in regular patterns in most Classic Mayan sentences. Each sentence or clause can be made up of pronouns, adjectives, nouns, verbs, prepositions, and dates. Nouns and verbs form small phrases that are put in a specific order. Let's take it one at a time with nouns and verbs and then move on to larger clauses.

Parts of speech occur in regular positions. Nouns and verbs are built up into small noun-and-verb phrases that can include pronouns, prepositions, adjectives, and verbal and temporal markers. Unlike English, where the sentence fragment "in his white house" is four distinct words, Mayan combines connected particles: *tusaknaah* (dashes can be added for intelligibility: *t-u-sak-naah,* literally "in his white house"). The proper word order for a noun phrase is preposition–possessive.pronoun–adjective–noun–suffix. All elements but the noun are optional in a noun phrase. Another noun phrase might read *yichnal-u-k'uhul-ajaw,* literally "in front of his divine ruler." You might think of each noun and verb phrase as being built up like a train, with each part of speech as a car. **Figure 4.12** shows this schematically: you can choose a preposition, pronoun, adjective, noun, and suffix to build a complete noun phrase.

Verb phrases (discussed at length in chapter 5) generally follow a similar format. Most verbs incorporate information that is usually given through independent words in an English sentence. For example, "I eat it" is three words in English, but the equivalent verb phrase in Mayan consists of elements combined into one verb phrase: *nik'ux-uw-ø,* where the pronouns for "I" (*ni-*) and "it" (*-ø*: remember that the empty set [ø] is the third-person singular absolutive pronoun for "him/her/it" in some verbs) are combined with the verb "to eat" (*-k'ux-*) and verbal marker *-Vw.* For verbs with an explicit subject and object, the order is adverb–ergative.pronoun–verb–suffix–verbal.marker–absolutive.pronoun–temporal.marker. Other verbs, which appear to have only one explicit subject or object (a patient), drop the initial ergative pronoun. The temporal marker is not always visible (see chapter 5).

As in other Mesoamerican languages, the basic word order of Maya inscriptions is verb, object, and then subject (usually abbreviated VOS). There are exceptions to every rule, of course, but this basic word order holds true in the majority of cases. A literal translation of a text reading *uchokow ch'aaj ajaw* would be "he-scattered incense, the ruler," meaning "the ruler scattered incense." The object or subject is omitted in many cases (intransitive verbs and certain forms of transitive verbs), but the verb is almost always the first part of speech, directly after a date or temporal indicator. Possessed objects, again as in other Mesoamerican languages, occur before their possessor. For example, instead of saying "the man's dog," a Maya inscription would literally say "his-dog, the man."

Using these building blocks, a complete example can look something like this:

Transcription:
3-AJAW 4-YAX-K'IN-(ni) u-tz'a-pa-w(a) u-LAKAM-TUN-(ni) K'UH-lu-AJAW

Transliteration:
cha' ajaw chan yaxk'ihn u-tz'ap-aw-ø u-lakam-tuun k'uhul-ajaw

Literally:
3 Ajaw, 4 Yaxk'in he-planted-it his-great-stone divine-ruler

Translation:
[On] 3 Ajaw, 4 Yaxk'in, the divine ruler erected his stela.

Try to translate the phrases found in **exercise 4.8**.

Figure 4.12. Noun Phrase Construction

Choose a preposition, ergative pronoun, adjective, and/or noun in this order to create a noun phrase.

Examples:

yichnal-	ka-	ch'ok-	ajaw		yichnalkach'okajaw	in front of our young ruler
	ni-	k'ahk'-al-	k'ab'		nik'ahk'alk'ab'	my fiery hand
		k'ab'-		is	k'abis	[the] hand
t-	u-	k'uh-ul-	ajaw		tuk'uhulajaw	to his holy ruler
t-	a-	k'uh-ul-	ch'um-ib'		tak'uhulch'umib'	on your holy throne

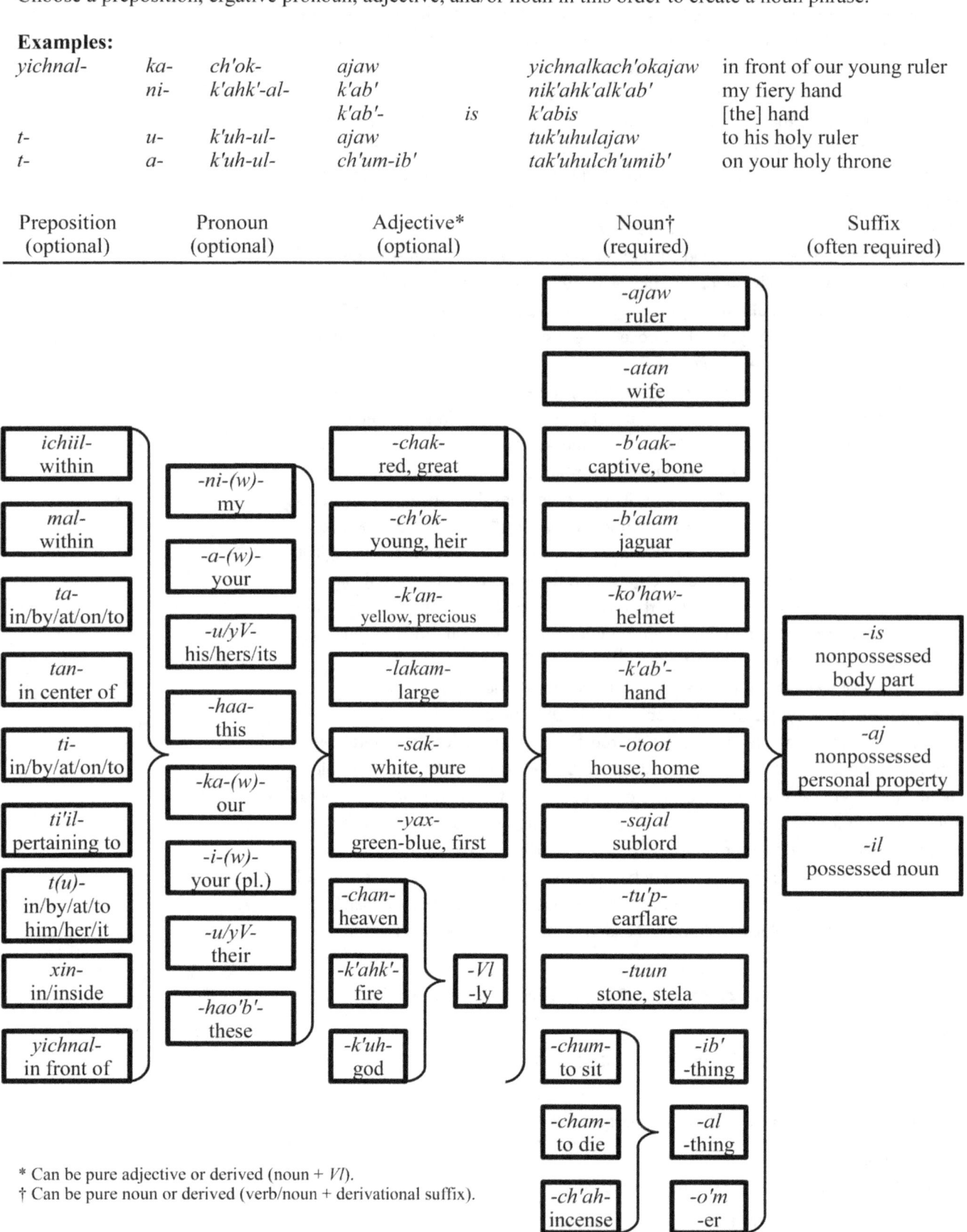

* Can be pure adjective or derived (noun + Vl).
† Can be pure noun or derived (verb/noun + derivational suffix).

Exercise 4.8. Noun Phrases

1. Using figure 4.12, translate the following phrases into English or Mayan.

Mayan Noun Phrase	English Translation
yichnal-u-sajal	_____
ichiil-a-lakam-ko'haw	_____
t-u-chan-al-otoot	_____
tan-k'an-tu'p-aj	_____
ka-sak-otoot	_____
ti-y-ajaw	_____
yichnal-u-k'uh-ul-ajaw	_____
_____	to his ruler
_____	at your large stela
_____	with my fiery hand
_____	with [a] fiery hand

4.6. STATIVE CLAUSES AND PARTICLES

Maya languages have no real verb "to be." Instead, a noun or adjective can form a stative sentence when coupled with an absolutive pronoun: noun-ABS. Remember that the third-person singular pronoun *-ø* is not actually shown glyphically in the vast majority of cases. Therefore *ajaw-ø* might be used to say "he is ruler," but this is not necessarily distinguishable from the noun *ajaw*, as both would be spelled **AJAW.** "I am ruler" would be expressed as *ajaween*, where the *-een* absolutive pronoun is expressed. The correct identification of a stative clause depends on the context and often does not really change the meaning. For instance, it is common to find titles after a ruler's name, such as *k'uhul ajaw*, meaning "holy ruler"; but this could also be translated as "[he is the] holy ruler." Either reading is acceptable and basically means the same thing.

A stative clause may also be created is by appending *-liiy* to make an adjective. The formal shape of this particle is **CVC-Vl-i-ABS,** meaning a CVC-root followed by the adjectival suffix *-Vl* plus *-i* and an absolutive pronoun. Most of the time this is seen as a **-li-y(a)** suffix (the absolutive pronoun in this case is *-ø* again: $CV_iC\text{-}V_il\text{-}i\text{-}ø$). The most commonly cited example of this stative particle is *hamliiy* (or perhaps *hamaliiy*), meaning "[it was in an] opened state" (*ham* is the transitive verb "to open"). Examples of these clauses are seen in **figure 4.13**.

4.6. STATIVE CLAUSES AND PARTICLES

Figure 4.13. Stative Clauses and Particles

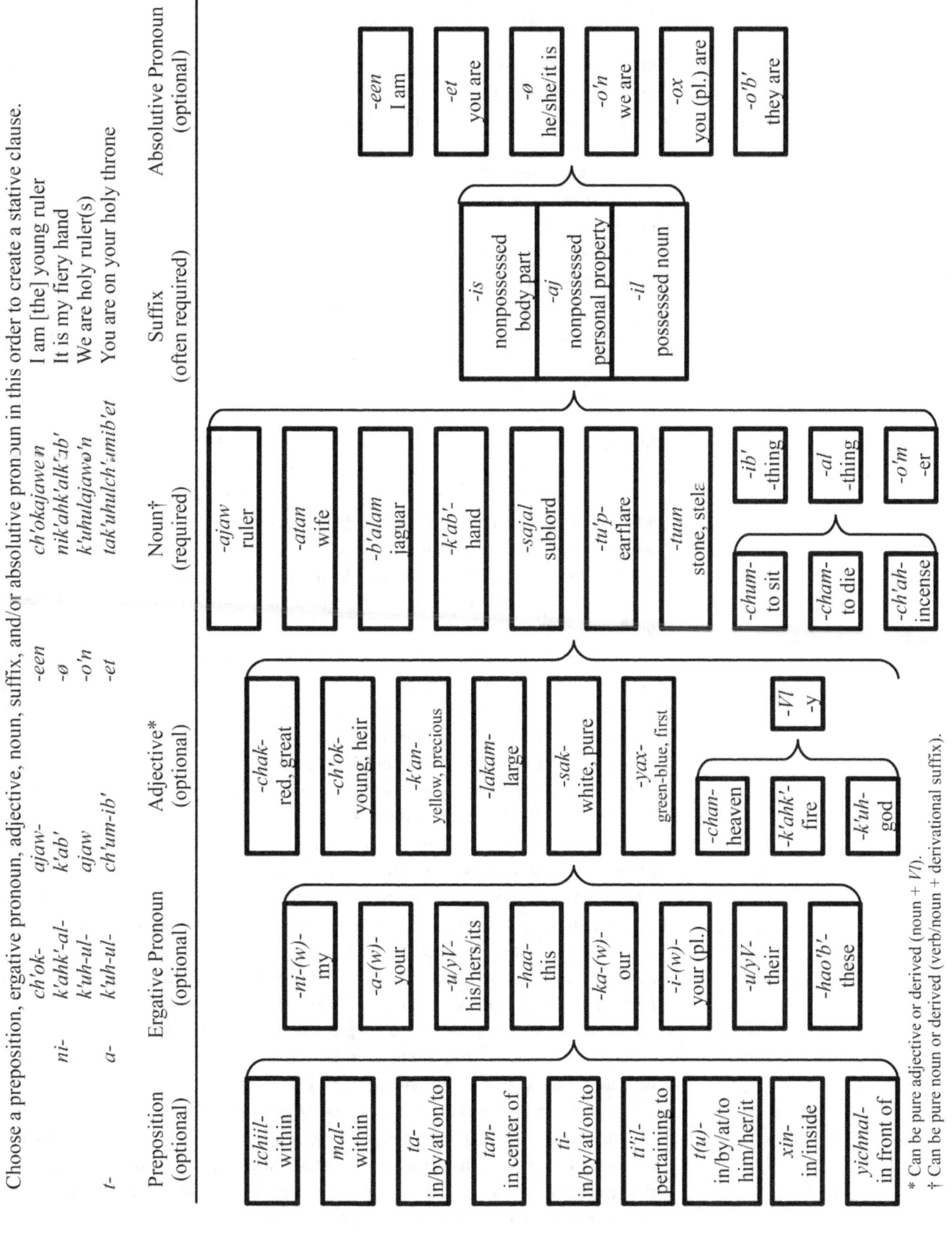

4.7. COMPLETE EXAMPLES

In the next chapter we will get into verbal morphology in earnest. But for the moment let's take a look at simple sentences that make use of pronouns, nouns, adjectives, and adverbs. Some of these examples are drawn directly from the inscriptions. Others are hypothetical, especially those that use pronouns other than the third-person singular.

Let's look first at Piedras Negras, Panel 3. In this scene, a ruler sits on a raised dais, above a number of subservient lords. Near one of them we find the phrase **a-wi-na-ke-n(a)** (see fig. 4.14), which would have been pronounced *awinakeen*. You will recognize the second-person ergative pronoun *a-:* because it is found in front of a noun, it can be read as "your." This is followed by *winak*, a different spelling of the word *winik*, meaning "man" or "person." Next comes the first-person absolutive pronoun *-een*, which is part of a stative clause because it follows a noun, translated as "I am." Putting it together literally, this phrase might translate as "your-man I am." This phrase is usually read as "I am your man," where "man" may mean "servant" or "subject."

Another example of first-person dialog is from the so-called Rabbit Vase, shown in **figure 4.14**. It is a two-scene story of insult and thievery. In the first scene, shown in this figure, the evil rabbit steals God L's things and insults him. Look for first- and second-person pronouns in the two accompanying texts. In B1 we see **a-JOL,** read *a-jol*, which means "your head." Two glyph blocks away in D1 we see **a-wi-ti,** spelled *aw-it*, which translates to the charming construction "your anus." The rabbit is telling the deity to hit his head and smell his own anus. In his hand the rabbit holds the clothing and hat of God L, who complains about the theft, using first-person dialog in H1: **ni-b'u-k(u),** *ni-buhk*, "my clothes."

These are two examples of first- and second-person pronouns used in inscriptions. This is exceedingly rare. For the most part, we see only third-person singular pronouns used with nouns and verbs in inscriptions. In order to show a few more examples, I have created a few phrases at the bottom of **figure 4.14**.

In the first example, we have **ni-pi-tzi-l(i) ATAN-na-t(a),** which contains both ergative and absolutive pronouns as well as an adjective and noun. This is transliterated as *nipitzilatanat*. We can separate it out as *ni-pitzil-atan-at,* which would translate literally as "my-beautiful-wife-you" or more regularly as "you are my beautiful wife." The next phrase, **ha-i u-xi-n(i)-tzu-l(u) PAKAL-(la),** would be pronounced *haa' u-xin-tzul pakal*. Here we have a demonstrative pronoun as well as a possessive construction, literally "that his-stinking-dog, Pakal," which might best be translated as "That is Pakal's stinking dog." Remember that the possessive construction in Classic Mayan is literally "his-thing, John," meaning "John's thing." Finally, **ha-i MAM i-tz'a-t(i)** can be read as *haa' mam itz'aat*. If we had just *itz'aat,* "wise man," we might translate this as "he is a wise man," as if the third-person singular absolutive pronoun was attached to the noun: *itz'aat-ø*. The addition of the clause "this old man" at the beginning specifies that "this old man is a wise man" (literally, "this old-man, wise-man").

For the final exercises in this chapter (**exercises 4.9 and 4.10**), let's go back to Piedras Negras, Stela 3 and Altar 2. Although all of the pronouns are third-person singular, it is still worth going through an inscription systematically to look for nouns and other parts of speech that you can now recognize. We will also use the information about pronouns, nouns, and word order in the next chapter, as we look at verbal morphology.

4.7. COMPLETE EXAMPLES   161

Figure 4.14. Pronoun Examples (from real and hypothetical texts)

a-wi-na-ke-n(a)
a-winak-een
I am your subject
(lit. "I am your man")
Piedras Negras, Panel 3

pu-lu a-JOL u-tz'u a-wi-ti   **ha-ta** …   **ni-bu-ku**
pul-u a-jol utz'-u aw-it   *hat* …   *ni-buhk*
hit your head, smell your anus   you …   my clothes
Naranjo-area Vessel

ni-pi-tzi-l(i) ATAN-na-t(a)
ni-pitzil-atan-at
you are my beautiful wife

ha-i u-xi-n(i)-tzu-l(u) PAKAL-(la)
haa' u-xin-tzul pakal
that is Pakal's stinking dog.

ha-i MAM i-tz'a-t(i)
haa' mam itz'aat-ø
this old man is a wise man

162 BASIC GRAMMAR

Exercise 4.9. Piedras Negras, Stela 3

1. Identify and circle all pronouns, noncalendrical nouns, titles, prepositions, or adjectives in this inscription.

2. Correctly transcribe, transliterate, and translate them in the space provided.

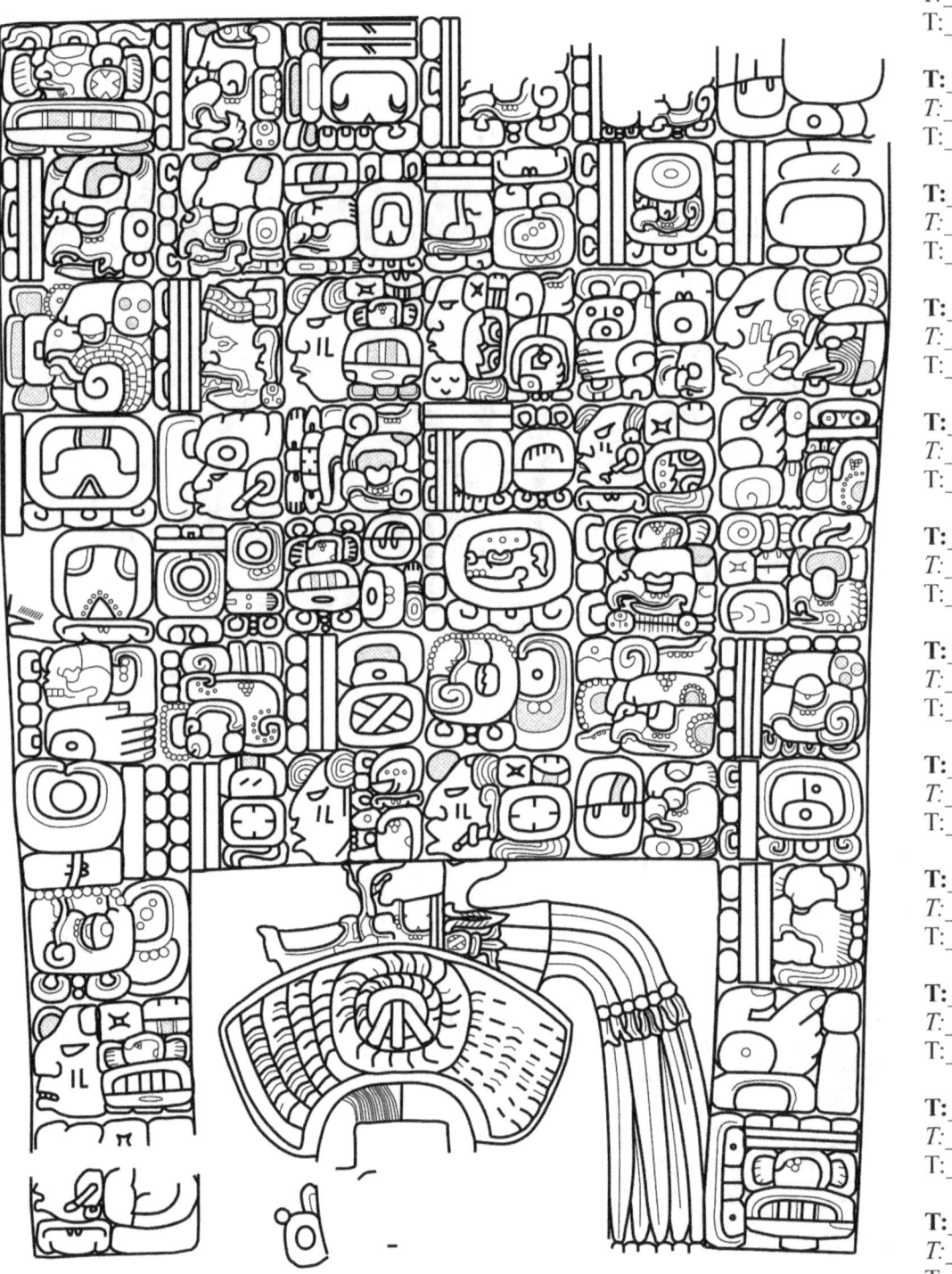

T:_____
T:_____
T:_____

T:_____
T:_____
T:_____

T:_____
T:_____
T:_____

T:_____
T:_____
T:_____

T:_____
T:_____
T:_____

T:_____
T:_____
T:_____

T:_____
T:_____
T:_____

T:_____
T:_____
T:_____

T:_____
T:_____
T:_____

T:_____
T:_____
T:_____

T:_____
T:_____
T:_____

T:_____
T:_____
T:_____

Exercise 4.10. Piedras Negras, Altar 2

1. Identify (noncalendrical) pronouns, titles, nouns, prepositions, adjectives, and adverbs, labeling them nearby.

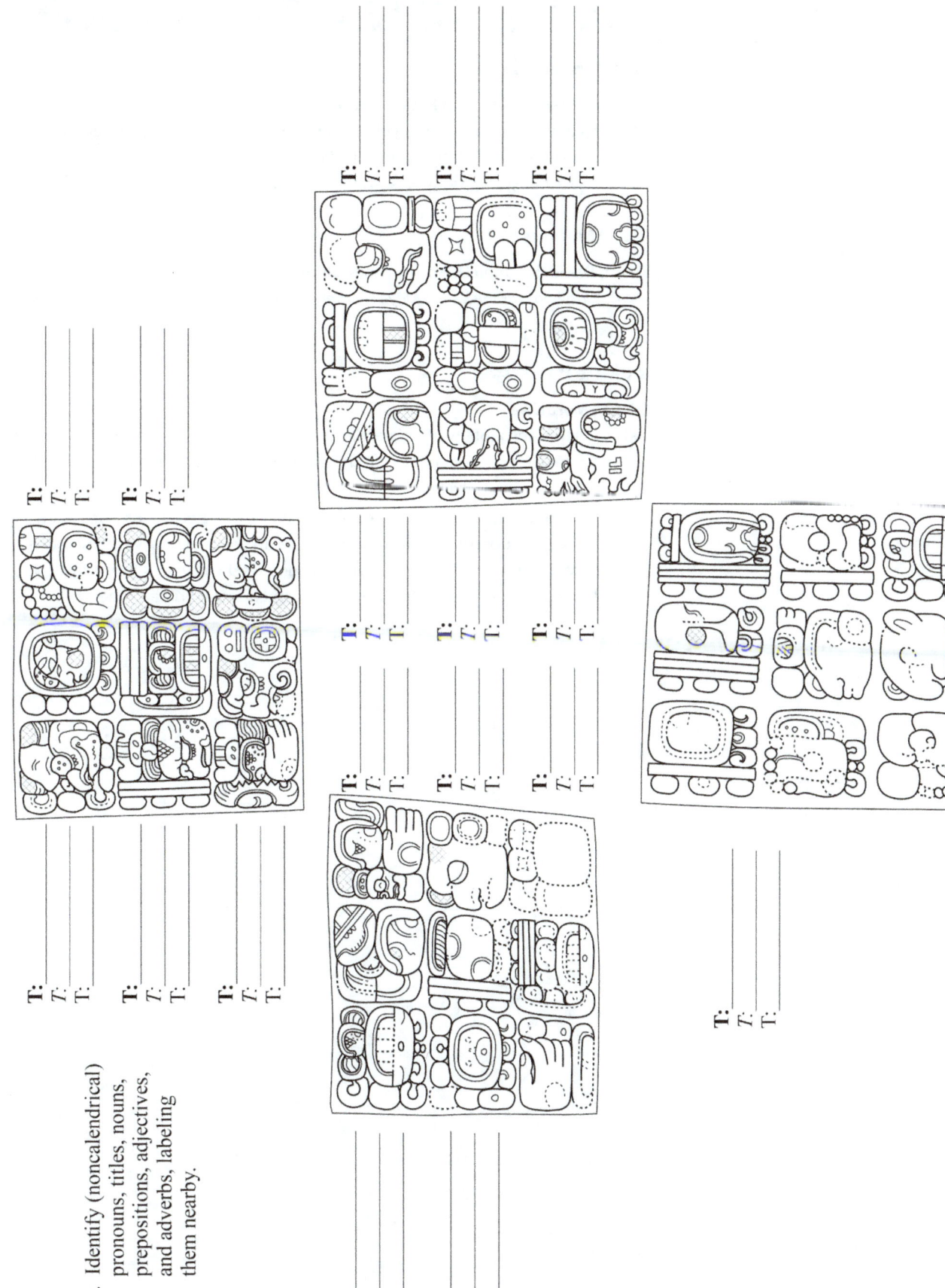

FURTHER READING

Morphosyllables

Houston, Stephen D., John Robertson, and David Stuart
2001   Quality and Quantity in Glyphic Nouns and Adjectives. *Research Reports on Ancient Maya Writing* 47. Washington, D.C.: Center for Maya Research.

The original exposition of morphosyllables.

Plural Markers

Stuart, David, Stephen D. Houston, and John Robertson
1999   *Notebook for the XXIIIrd Maya Hieroglyphic Forum at Texas.* Austin: Maya Workshop Foundation.

Intimate Possession

Zender, Marc Uwe
2004   On the Morphology of Intimate Possession in Mayan Languages and Classic Mayan Grammar. In *The Linguistics of Maya Writing,* edited by S. Wichmann, pp. 195–210. Salt Lake City: University of Utah Press.

Zender discusses the evidence for intimately possessed nouns (such as body parts, personal property, and kinship) and clears up the use of -*aj* (which is also used as a verbal ending) as a noun suffix. He also defines the use of -*is* to indicate unpossessed body parts and cites historical linguistic and hieroglyphic arguments.

5. VERBAL GRAMMAR

Like any language, verbs and their inflections are a vital part of expression. Verbs in Classic Mayan inscriptions are built up of many constituent parts. Unlike English, where a verb has a root and a final inflection, a Mayan verb has pronouns, verbal markers, and temporal information all bound together. English constructs phrases with auxiliary verbs to flesh out specific verbal expression or voices, such as the differences among "the glass was raised," "the glass got raised," and "he raised the glass." Instead of using helper-verb constructions, a Mayan verb can be "colored" with particular markers that indicate a particular voice. In this chapter we will take a look at transitive, intransitive, positional, and other verb types.

Before introducing the verbs and their voices, let's briefly discuss agglutinating verbal phrases. An agglutinating verbal phrase is simply a verbal root with numerous affixes attached in a systematic way. For example, the English sentence "he painted it" has three separate words. This would all be combined into one Mayan verb-phrase, *utz'ib'iw* (which can be divided as *u-tz'ib'-iw-ø*), literally translated as "he-painted-it." Each verbal phrase is constructed in a specific order that is given for each inflection and voice description. Abbreviations for each part of speech are often used to describe the morphology of verb and noun phrases. The most common abbreviations are given in **table 5.1**.

In the case of the *utz'ib'iw* example, an active transitive verb is constructed in the following manner: ERG-CV$_1$C-V$_1$w-ABS. This means that an ergative pronoun (such as *u-*) is prefixed to a CVC verb root (such as *-tz'ib'-*), which is affixed by the *-Vw-* active-transitive marker (in this case *-iw-*), and completed with the ergative pronoun (invisible in this example as *-ø*). This may be written glyphically as **u-tz'i-b'i-w(a)**. Note that the rules of disharmony are not followed: the final **a** does not cause the preceding **i** to lengthen. It is currently thought that the rules of disharmony and synharmony are suspended in the case of verbal markers. A **-wa** is used to mark active transitive verbs, regardless of the vowel in the CVC root; the correct vowel for the *-Vw-* marker is supplied by the CVC root. In other voices and verb types, the vowel is independent of the verb root: for example, a passive transitive verb is always marked by *-aj*.

Table 5.1. Common Abbreviations

Abbreviation	Meaning	Abbreviation	Meaning	Abbreviation	Meaning
ABS	Absolutive Pronoun	ENC	Enclitic	$V_1...V_1$	Identical Vowels
ERG	Ergative Pronoun	CVC	Consonant–Vowel–Consonant Verb	$V_1...V_2$	Nonidentical Vowels
MRK	Verbal Marker	non.CVC	Non-Consonant–Vowel–Consonant Verb	ADV	Adverb

5.1. TRANSITIVE VERBS

A transitive verb takes an agent and a patient: that is, two arguments. Usually in English we refer to these as the subject and object of a sentence. Technically, a subject performs a verb on an object, but the object becomes emphasized in some voices, turning it into the subject of the sentence. For example, in the sentence "Mary grows tomatoes," Mary is the subject and agent while the tomatoes are the object and patient. In the sentence "the tomatoes grow," the tomatoes have become the subject but are still the patient of the verb. The patient and agent are marked with two groups of pronouns (absolutive and ergative, respectively) in Classic Mayan, whereas the subject and object are marked by different classes (nominative and accusative, respectively) in English.

Transitive verbs can take an active, passive, mediopassive, antipassive, or imperative voice. This simply means that the same transitive verb can have slightly different meanings or expression. This is similar to the differences seen in the English sentences "Pakal captured B'alam," "B'alam was captured," "B'alam got captured," "Pakal captured," and "Capture B'alam!" The verb's meaning is the same, but the expression varies. In all transitive verbs, the ergative pronoun is acting as the agent (Pakal) and the absolutive pronoun represents the patient (B'alam). Transitive verbs can be made up of a string of elements: ADV-ERG-verb-MRK-ABS-ENC. It is rare that a verb would have all of these elements at once, however; some are optional, and others vary by voice. **Figure 5.1** provides quick reference for the different transitive verb voices as well as a list of the most common transitive verbs. For the glyphs that represent these verbs, see appendix III.2.

5.1.1. Active

The active transitive voice is a "complete" transitive verb. It has the full expression of the ergative and absolutive pronouns, indicating the agent and patient. "Mary grows tomatoes" is an active transitive sentence. The verbal marker for the active transitive voice is -Vw-. An active transitive verb is always in the form ERG-CV_1C-V_1w-ABS. Remember that most inscriptions use third-person singular pronouns, u- for the ergative and -$ø$ for the absolutive. Therefore most active transitive verbs look like u-CV_1C-V_1w-$ø$ and are pronounced uCV_1CV_1w. Glyphically, this looks like **u-CVC-w(a)** or **u-CV₁-CV₁-w(a)**, where the vowel before the final w is the same as the root verb's vowel. The giveaway for this voice is the **u-** (or **yV-** before a vowel) prefix and the **-wa** suffix (**see fig. 5.1**). These sentences are easy to translate directly into English as "the *actor verb*ed the *patient*."

Four examples of the active transitive verb form are shown in **figure 5.2**. The first two come from the site of Palenque. The verb *ch'am* means "to grasp" or "to take" and is seen here in the form **u-CH'AM-w(a)**, which would have been read *uch'amaw*. The next example uses a vowel-initial verb, *'ak'*, "to give." This requires a *y*-initial ergative pronoun: in this case **ya-** matches the initial *a* of the verb. The form **ya-ka-w(a)**, read as *yakaw*, means "he/she gave it." Example 3 comes from Tikal and reads **u-TZUTZ-w(a)**, pronounced *utzutzuw*, meaning "he finished it" or in this case "he finished the 14th K'atun." Even though **wa** is the final syllabogram, the verb's vowel is repeated, giving -*uw* as the verbal marker. The final **a** does not lengthen or glottalize the preceding vowel. Finally, the fourth example, from Yaxchilan, has the verb *tzak*, meaning "to conjure," in the phrase *utzakaw*. In this case, the god K'awil is being called upon.

Figure 5.1. Transitive Verb Markers

Transitive verbs (verbs that can take two arguments) can express five separate moods.

Voice: **Paradigm:** **Common Glyphic Expression:**

Active:
– 2 named arguments
– agent-focused

ERG-CV_1C-V_1w-ABS
u-CV_1C-V_1w-ø
agent verbed patient.

u-CVC-w(a)
uCV_1CV_1w
He/she/it verbed him/her/it.

Giveaway: **u-** and **-wa** syllables

Passive:
– 1 named argument
– patient-focused

CVhC-aj-ABS
CVhC-aj-ø
patient was verbed.

CVC-ja
CVhCaj
He/she/it was verbed.

Giveaway: **-ja** syllable

Mediopassive:
– 1 named argument
– patient-focused

CV_1C-$V_1(V_1)$y-ABS
CV_1C-V_1y-ø
patient got verbed.

CVC-y(i)
CV_1CV_1y or $CV_1CV_1V_1y$
He/she/it got verbed.

Giveaway: **-yi** syllable

Antipassive:
– 1 named argument
– agent-focused

CV_1C-$V_1(V_1)$w-ABS
CV_1C-V_1w-ø
agent verbed.

CVC-w(i)
CV_1CV_1w or $CV_1CV_1V_1w$
He/she/it verbed.

Giveaway: **-wi** syllable

Imperative:
– 1 named argument
– patient-focused

CV_1C-V_1-ABS
CV_1C-V_1-ø
verb!

CV_1C-V_1
CV_1CV_1
verb it!

Giveaway: copy cat **-V** syllable

Common Transitive Verbs:

'ak	to give	joy	to encircle	pas	to open, dawn	tz'akb'u	to put in order
'al	to say, throw	jul	to throw, shoot	pat	to form, build	tz'ap	to plant, erect
a'l	to say	kab'	to supervise	puk	to scatter	tz'ib'	to write, paint
b'aak	to capture	kuch	to carry	pul	to sprinkle	'ub'	to hear
chab'	to supervise	k'al	to bind	sat	to lose, die	'uk'	to drink
chan	to watch over	k'am	to grasp, take	taj	to strike, split	'utz'	to smell, sniff
chok	to scatter	k'ul	to venerate	toj	to pay	uxul	to carve, sculpt
chuk	to capture, seize	muk	to bury	tok	to burn	we'	to eat (bread)
ch'ak	to decapitate, cut	nak	to conquer	t'ab'	to anoint, polish	wi'	to create carnage
ch'am	to grasp, take	naw	to adorn	tzak	to grab, conjure	yal	to throw, demolish
'il	to see	nup	to join, marry	tzik	to count, honor		
jatz'	to strike, wound	pak'	to plant, form	tzutz	to end, join		

Figure 5.2. Transitive Verb Examples

Active: prefixed by the ergative third-person singular pronoun **u-** and suffixed by **-wa**.

u-CH'AM-w(a)
uch'amaw-ø
He grasped it.
(Palenque, Palace Tablet)

u-TZUTZ-w(a) 14-WINIK-HAB'-[pl.]
utzutzuw-ø chanlaju'n winikhaab'-[pl.]
He finished it, the 14th K'atun.
(Tikal, Stela 31)

ya-ka-w(a)
yakaw-ø
She gave it.
(Palenque, Temple of Inscriptions)

u-TZAK-w(a) u-K'AWIL-(la-li)
utzakaw-ø uk'awiil
He conjured it, his K'awil.
(Yaxchilan, Lintel 25, reversed)

Passive: verb suffixed by **-ja**.

TZUTZ-j(a) u-5-HAB'-ta
tzuhtzaj-ø uho'haab'
It was finished, his 5th year.
(Yaxchilan, Lintel 2)

K'AL-j(a)
k'ahlaj-ø
It was bound.
(Naranjo, Stela 29)

na-wa-j(a)
nahwaj-ø
It was adorned.
(Aguateca, Stela 2)

ch'a-ka-j(a)
ch'ahkaj-ø
It was cut.
(Palenque, Temple of the Inscriptions)

TZAK-j(a)
tzakhkaj-ø
It was conjured.
(Yaxchilan, Lintel 14)

Mediopassive: verb suffixed by **-yi**.

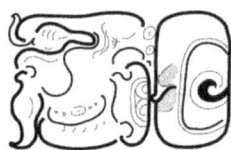
TZUTZ-y(i)
tzutzuy-ø
It got finished.
(Palenque, Tablet of 96 Glyphs)

i-TZUTZ-y(i)
itzutzuy-ø
And then it got finished.
(Palenque, Tablet of 96 Glyphs)

K'AL-y(i)-u-HUN
k'alay-ø uhu'n
It got bound, his headdress.
(Palenque, Temple of the Cross)

Antipassive: verb suffixed by **-wi**.

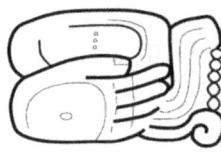
K'AL-w(i)-?
k'alaw-ø ?
It bound ?
(Naranjo, Stela 29)

5.1.2. Passive

The passive transitive voice is well known as the bane of beginning English students (a better construction, of course, would be "Beginning English students detest the passive voice"). There seems to be no prohibition against this construction in Maya inscriptions. Unlike the active voice, the passive voice emphasizes the patient: the agent is not directly named. These verbal phrases are best translated as "the *patient* was *verb*ed." In describing Mary's garden, we might say "the tomatoes were grown." The agent can be named in a subordinate clause, even though it is not included in the verbal phrase: for example, "the tomatoes were grown by Mary." Only the absolutive pronoun is necessary in this verb, and it follows the *-aj* passive transitive verbal marker. The full form of this construction is CVhC-aj-ABS. Note the infixed (and reconstructed) *h* within the CVC verbal root. Unlike the active transitive voice, the vowel of the verbal marker is always *a*. Glyphically, this appears as **CVC-ja** or **CV-Ca-j(a)**, reconstructed as *CV[h]C-aj-ø* and pronounced *CVhCaj*, expressing the third-person singular absolutive pronoun (as shown in **fig. 5.1**). The telltale sign for this voice is the **-ja** suffix, just as in the case of the derived intransitive verb discussed below. Unlike the derived intransitive verb, however, the CVC root in the passive transitive voice is a transitive verb, not any other part of speech.

Figure 5.2 has five examples of passive transitive constructions. In the first example, we see the verb *tzutz*, "to finish," again. This was translated as "he finished it" in the active voice. But in the passive voice **TZUTZ-j(a)**, or *tzuhtzaj*, is translated as "it was finished." The agent is removed, and the patient is emphasized. The same holds true for the next example, **na-wa-j(a)**, or *nahwaj*, which can be translated as the innocuous-sounding phrase "it was adorned." This verb can be used whenever somebody or something might have been decorated with ornaments. You might see it when new wives or children are displayed, probably adorned in fancy regalia. We have already seen the verb in the third example in the Supplementary Series: *k'al*, "to bind." In this case, **K'AL-j(a)**, pronounced *k'ahlaj*, means "it was bound." This verb can be used for "binding" stela on K'atun endings or "binding" the ruler's crown on his or her head. The fourth example, **ch'a-ka-j(a)**, would have been pronounced *ch'ahkaj* and means "it was cut" or "it was decapitated." This passive construction would then be followed by the name of an important captive taken in war. Finally, we see the verb *tzak* again in the fifth example, but this time in the passive voice, **TZAK-j(a)**, giving *tzahkaj*, which means "it was conjured."

5.1.3. Mediopassive

The patient again becomes the focus of the sentence in the mediopassive voice, appearing as the subject. English has no real mediopassive voice, but it is usually translated using the axillary verb "got," as in "the tomatoes got grown." Although the tomatoes (the patient) are being acted upon by the verb, there is no named agent doing the growing: the person or thing that is being affected by the verb is emphasized. Children might say "the window got broken," instead of the whole truth (active transitive voice), "my ball broke the window" or (passive transitive voice) "the window was broken [by my ball]." In the same way, the defeat of a city may be recorded in this "middle" voice. Mediopassive constructions are formed CV_1C-V_1y-ABS (or possibly $CV_1C-V_1V_1y$-ABS). Glyphically, this appears as either **CVC-y(i)** or **CV$_1$-CV$_1$-y(i)**. Again the vowel preceding the final *y* is supplied by the verb's central vowel. Because the third-person absolutive pronoun is usually used, it is reconstructed as $CV_iC-V_i(V_i)y$-ø and pronounced $CV_iCV_i(V_i)y$. The giveaway for this voice is the **-yi** glyph, which always indicates the mediopassive regardless of synharmony with the preceding vowel. Mediopassive clauses can be translated as "the *patient* got *verb*ed."

Three examples of the mediopassive voice (using verbs that we have seen before) are shown in **figure 5.2**. **TZUTZ-y(i)** can be read as *tzutzuy*, as the *u* in the *-uy* verbal marker comes from the root verb's central vowel and is not affected by the final *i* in the **-yi** postfix. It means "it got finished." The second example also uses the *tzutz* verb with the mediopassive construction but has the adverb *i-* attached to the front, adding "and then" to the translation of the phrase. You might remember this adverb from the Posterior Date Indicator, *iuti*. This adverb is important for indicating time and chronological relationships in Classic Mayan written discourse, as discussed below (see section 5.7). Finally, we see the verb *k'al* again, this time in the mediopassive voice, describing the crowning of a ruler. This phrase is especially illustrative of the fusion of art and writing in this script. A headdress (the equivalent of a crown in Western cultures) is resting on the binding-hand *k'al* glyph. Artistic values trump reading order in this case: this phrase should be read **K'AL-y(i)-u-HUN**, not **u-HUN-K'AL-y(i)**. It may be translated most literally as "it got bound, his headdress" or, more meaningfully, "his headdress got bound."

5.1.4. Antipassive

The antipassive voice fronts the agent and removes the patient, the opposite of the passive voice. An example of this may be "Mary grew," not in the sense of Mary growing larger but as Mary growing things, although this sounds incomplete as an English sentence. Antipassives are formed by appending **-wi** to a transitive verb—either **CVC-w(i)** or **CV$_1$-CV$_1$-w(i)**—followed by an absolutive pronoun: CV$_1$C-V$_1$V$_1$w-ABS (early inscriptions) or CV$_1$C-V$_1$w-ABS (later inscriptions). Sometimes the form CVC-oon-ABS is also seen. The antipassive construction results in $CV_1C\text{-}V_1V_1w\text{-}ø$, pronounced $CV_1CV_1V_1w$. This differs from the similar-appearing active transitive voice (uCV_1CV_1w) in two ways. First, the active transitive is always indicated by the **-wa** syllable, while the antipassive uses **-wi**. Second, the active transitive verb is prefixed by an ergative pronoun, usually **u-**, while the antipassive never takes an ergative pronoun. This can be translated as *"agent verb*ed" or "it *verb*ed."

Figure 5.2 includes an example of the antipassive voice from an inscription at Naranjo, using the verb *k'al* again: **K'AL-w(i)**, resulting in *k'alaw*. As the agent is not named, it can be translated as "it bound."

5.1.5. Imperative

The "command form" imperative voice urges the agent to perform some action on a patient (with a transitive verb). The form is simple. A copycat vowel, V_1, and absolutive pronoun are added to the end of the verb: CV$_1$C-V$_1$-ABS. Because texts are primarily third-person singular, this appears as $CV_1C\text{-}V_1\text{-}ø$, pronounced CV_1CV_1. It can be translated as "*verb* it" or, if the actor and patient are named after the verb, "*agent, verb* the *patient*." An example of this is shown in **figure 4.14**, where the rascally rabbit commands God L *pulu ajol*, "hit your head," and *utz'u awit*, the ever-colorful "smell your [own] anus." As far as we can tell, the hortative, where many are extolled to undertake an action, is the same as the imperative in Classic Mayan. Now that you have seen the five voices that transitive verbs take, please complete the verbal conjugations in **exercise 5.1**. **Figure 5.3** includes a chart diagram that allows for the easy construction of transitive verbs and may be useful in these exercises. You can now also translate from and to Mayan in **exercises 5.2 and 5.3**.

5.1. TRANSITIVE VERBS

Figure 5.3. Transitive Verb Construction

Choose an ergative pronoun, verb, verbal marker, absolutive pronoun, and/or suffix in order to create a transitive verb phrase.

niw-	ak-	aw-	et		niwakawet	I gave you
a-	chok-	ow-	ø-	iiy	achokawiiy	You had scattered it / You already scattered it
	chuhk-	aj-	o'n		chukajo'n	We were captured
	jatz-	ay-	ø-	iiy	jatzayiiy	He had gotten hit / He already got hit

Ergative Pron. (for active voice)	Verb (required)	Verbal Marker (required)	Absolutive Pronoun (required)	Suffix (often required)

Ergative Pronouns:
- ni(w)- I
- a(w)- you
- u/yV- him/her/it
- ka(w)- we
- i(w)- you (pl.)
- u/yV- they

Verbs:
- -'ak- gave
- -'al- said
- -chok- scattered
- -chuk- captured
- -ch'ak- cut
- -ch'am- grasped
- -'il- saw
- -jatz- struck
- -joy- encircled
- -k'al- bound
- -naw- adorned
- -tzutz- ended
- -tz'ap- planted
- -tz'ib'- wrote

Verbal Markers:
- -Vw- (Active)
- (CVhC)-aj- was (Passive)
- -Vy- got (Mediopassive)
- -Vw- (Antipassive)
- -V- ! (Imperative)

Absolutive Pronouns:
- -een me / I
- -et you / you
- -ø him/her/it / he/she/it
- -o'n us / we
- -ox you (pl.) / you (pl.)
- -o'b' them / they

Suffixes:
- -ø (Unmarked)
- -iiy / -jiiy ago (Prior Event)
- -o'm will (Future Event)

VERBAL GRAMMAR

Exercise 5.1. Transitive Verb Voices

1. Conjugate and translate each of the following verbs for the given arguments for each voice.

Active: ERG-CV$_1$C-V$_1$w-ABS
Passive: CVhC-aj-ABS
Mediopassive: CV$_1$C-V$_1$(V$_1$)y-ABS
Antipassive: CV$_1$C-V$_1$(V$_1$)w-ABS
Imperative: CV$_1$C-V$_1$-ABS

chuk to catch (tv)

Pronouns	Active (3rd pers.)	Passive	Mediopassive	Antipassive	Imperative
1st Person Sing.	*u-chuk-uw-een* he caught me				
2nd Person Sing.		*chuhk-aj-et* you were caught			
3rd Person Sing.			*chuk-uy-ø* he got caught		
1st Person Plural				*chuk-uw-o'n* they caught	
2nd Person Plural					*chuk-u-ox* catch you (pl.)!
3rd Person Plural	*u-chuk-uw-o'b'* he caught them				

ch'ak to cut (tv)

	Active	Passive	Mediopassive	Antipassive	Imperative
3rd Person Sing.				*ch'ak-aw-ø* he cut	

'il to see (tv)

	Active	Passive	Mediopassive	Antipassive	Imperative
3rd Person Sing.		*'ihl-aj-ø* it was seen			

Exercise 5.2. Transitive Verb Voices II

1. Using the following vocabulary and pronouns, translate the verbs below into English. Refer to figure 5.1 for transitive verb voices. Remember sentences are generally verb-object-subject order. Refer to chapter 4 for noun vocabulary.

chok	to scatter (tv)	*chuk*	to catch (tv)	*ch'ab'*	to do penance (tv)
ch'ak	to chop (tv)	*ch'am*	to grasp (tv)	*'il*	to see, witness (tv)
jatz'	to strike (tv)	*joy*	to encircle (tv)	*jub'*	to take down (tv)
jul	to spear, pierce (tv)	*koj*	to hit (tv)	*k'al*	to bind (tv)
k'a'y	to end (tv)	*muk*	to bury (tv)	*naw*	to display (tv)
pul	to burn (tv)	*sat*	to diminish, lose (tv)	*siy*	to bear (children) (tv)
tzak	to conjure (tv)	*tzutz*	to end (tv)	*tz'ak*	to count, order (tv)
tz'ap	to plant (tv)	*yak'*	to give (tv)	*yal*	to say (tv)
we'	to eat (tv)				

u-tzutz-uw-at it ended you

ch'ab'-ay-een _____

tzahk-aj-ø _____

ch'ahm-aj-een _____

tz'ak-aw-een _____

tz'ap-ay-een _____

jatz'-ay-at _____

ni-pul-uw-at _____

ni-k'al-aw-at _____

a-chuk-uw-ø _____

k'a'y-a-ø _____

muk-uw-een _____

koj-o-ø _____

u-chok-ow-ø _____

jul-uw-ø _____

jub'-u-ø _____

we'-ew-at _____

nahw-aj-een I was displayed

ch'ahk-aj-een _____

joy-oy-at _____

sat-a-ø _____

yahk'-aj-ø _____

'il-iw-at _____

siy-iy-ø _____

yal-a-ø _____

u-chok-ow-ø b'ahlam pakal _____

u-tz'ap-aw-ø lakam-tuun u-ajaw _____

u-ch'am-aw-ø k'awiil u-k'uhul-ajaw _____

ch'ahk-aj-ø b'alham _____

jub-uy u-to'k-u-pakal _____

Exercise 5.3. Transitive Verb Voices III

1. Using the following vocabulary and pronouns, translate the verbs below into Classic Mayan. Refer to figure 5.1 for transitive verb voices. Remember that sentences are generally in the order verb-object-subject. Refer to chapter 4 for noun vocabulary.

ak'	to give (tv)	joy	to encircle (tv)	pul	to burn (tv)
al	to say (tv)	jub'	to take down (tv)	sat	to diminish (tv)
chok	to scatter (tv)	jul	to spear, pierce (tv)	siy	to bear (children) (tv)
chuk	to catch (tv)	koj	to hit (tv)	tzak	to conjure (tv)
ch'ab'	to do penance (tv)	k'al	to bind (tv)	tzutz	to end (tv)
ch'ak	to chop (tv)	k'a'y	to end (tv)	tz'ak	to count, order (tv)
ch'am	to grasp (tv)	muk	to bury (tv)	tz'ap	to plant (tv)
'il	to see, witness (tv)	naw	to display (tv)	we'	to eat (tv)
jatz'	to strike (tv)				

jatz'-ay-ø	It got hit	_____	It got counted
_____	He saw it	_____	I was speared
_____	You got conjured	_____	You (pl.) were bound
_____	I planted it	_____	They conjured us
_____	Eat it!	_____	You were encircled
_____	It was taken down	_____	It got bound
_____	You buried us	_____	You said it
_____	It got ended	_____	They got caught
_____	You scatter it	_____	He ended it
_____	They struck us	_____	I was diminished
_____	He was caught	_____	It got grasped
_____	You gave me		
_____	I hit them		

_____ B'alam captured my ruler.

_____ I buried your sajal.

_____ I ate my blue-green turtle.

_____ You caught the big jaguar.

_____ Bob saw the red dog.

5.2. INTRANSITIVE VERBS

An intransitive verb can only take one argument. An intransitive verb in English can only take a subject, while in Classic Mayan it only takes a patient (and therefore only uses absolutive pronouns). Verbs such as "arrive," "sleep," and "smile" cannot take an object in English and are considered intransitive. When "Mary grows tomatoes," she is the agent (subject) and the tomatoes are the patient (object). In the sentence "tomatoes grow," the tomatoes are still the patient (as discussed above) but are now the subject. The verb "grow" has changed from transitive (when it had two arguments) to intransitive (when it only has one). This is similar to a some transitive verb voices; remember that the agent is deleted in passive and mediopassive voices. The difference is that intransitive verbs can never take an agent, while transitive verbs can do so when they are expressed in the active voice. Indeed, you will notice that the derived intransitive and passive transitive verbs are both marked by **-ja**. The different forms of intransitive verbs are shown with their verb markers in **figure 5.4**.

5.2.1. Root

A root intransitive verb is much like a pure noun in that its most basic CVC form is an intransitive verb (no derivational suffixes are needed; nor is the root a noun or adjective). In English this would be similar to "the tomatoes hang [from the vine]." Root intransitive verbs are marked simply by the addition of an absolutive pronoun. The complete form is CVC-ABS. In the case of the third-person singular absolutive pronoun, ø is replaced with an *i*. This is represented with an *i*-final syllabogram, such as **-b'i**, **-chi**, or **-ch'i**. Because most expressions are third-person singular, these are often expressed as **CV-Ci** or **CVC₁-(C₁)i** (the final verb-root consonant is echoed by the syllabogram and therefore dropped in transliteration). This gives *CVC-i,* which is pronounced simply as *CVCi*. Note that in this case the word-final vowel *i* is not silent, as it is in most other instances. This can be translated as "the *patient verb*ed."

Root intransitives are fairly common in Classic inscriptions. Indeed, in **figure 5.5** you will recognize *iuti,* the Posterior Date Indicator, in the first example. Technically, the initial *i-* is an adverb, followed by the root intransitive verb *'ut* and the verb-marker *-i.* The second example, from Piedras Negras, Stela 3's Supplementary Series, is the verb *hul,* meaning "to arrive," marked with the third-person singular absolutive replacement, *-i.* The third and fourth examples are commonly used root intransitives, *cham* and *och,* meaning "to die" and "to enter," respectively. Just as in the second example, the final consonant of the verb root is echoed by the *i*-final syllabogam: **CHAM** is followed by **mi** and **OCH** by **chi**. This results in *chami* and *ochi,* "he died" and "she entered," respectively.

5.2.2. Derived

Derived intransitive verbs are a noun or adjective used as a verb. This may sound strange, but a number of verbs do the same in English, such as "to tar and feather." Classic Mayan nouns or adjectives can be suffixed by **-ja,** resulting in **CVC-ja, CV-Ci-ja,** or **CV-Ca-ja.** The paradigm of derived transitive verbs is CVC-Vj-ABS, where the CVC-root (or sometimes CVCVC-root) is either a noun or an adjective. This usually either results in *CVC-iij-ø* or *CVC-aj-ø,* depending on the syllabic spelling. This is pronounced *CVCiij* or *CVCaj* and can be translated as "the *patient noun*ed." Note that the noun or adjective can also be a

176 VERBAL GRAMMAR

Figure 5.4. Intransitive Verb Markers

Intransitive verbs (verbs that only take one argument) can be derived or root verbs.

Type: **Paradigm:** **Common Glyphic Expression:**

Root:
—only one argument
—agent-focused
—"pure" verb (not formed from any other part of speech)

CVC-ABS ø → i
CVC-ø, usually CVC-i
*agent verb*ed.

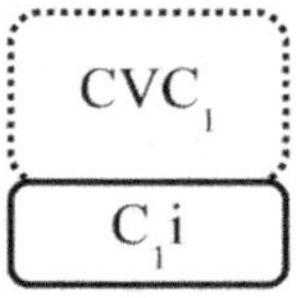

CVC_1-(C_1)i
CVCi
He/she/it *verb*ed.

Giveaway: **-Ci** syllable

Common Root Intransitive Verbs:

cham	to die	*lok'*	to emerge, leave, escape	*tal*	to come
che'	to say	*och*	to enter	*til*	to burn, stir
hul	to arrive	*pas*	to come out	*t'ab'*	to move, go up
jatz'	to strike	*pay*	to guide, lead	*'ut*	to happen, occur
jub'	to fall, descend	*puk*	to scatter fire	*xan*	to walk

Derived:
—only one argument
—agent-focused
—derived verb (from another part of speech)

CVC-Vj-ABS
CVC-aj-ø or CVC-iij-ø
*agent noun*ed.

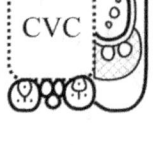

CVC-ja
CVCaj or *CVCiij*
He/she/it *noun*ed.

Giveaway: **-ja** syllable on a noun or adjective

Common Derived Intransitive Verbs:

'ah	to conquer	*otot*	to be housed	*siy*	to bear (children)
'ak't	to dance	*pitz*	to (play) ball	*uk'*	to drink
em	to go down, descend	*pul*	to burn	*way*	to sleep
				witz	to pile up

Positional:
—only one argument
—agent-focused

CVC-laj-ABS or -waan-ABS
CVC-laj-ø or CVC-waan-ø
*agent verb*ed.

CVC-la-j(a) or **CVC-wa-n(i)**
CVClaj or *CVCwaan*
He/she/it *verb*ed.

Giveaway: **-la-j(a)** or **-wa-n(i)** syllables

Causative:
—two arguments
—agent forcing patient

ERG-CVC-b'u-ABS
u-CVC-b'u-ø
agent made *patient verb*.

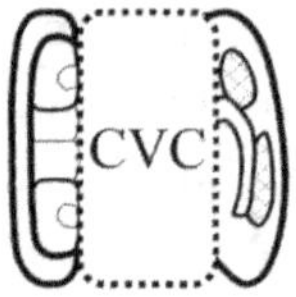

u-CVC-b'u
uCVCb'u
He/she/it made him/her/it *verb*.

Giveaway: **-b'u** syllable

Common Positional Verbs:

b'uch	to be seated	*ham*	to lie down	*pat*	to form, build
chak	to tie up	*lam*	to go down, disappear	*tz'ak*	to add, accumulate
chum	to seat				

5.2. INTRANSITIVE VERBS 177

Figure 5.5. Intransitive Verb Examples

Root: suffixed by an *i*-final syllabogram (**-Ci**).

i-u-ti
iut-i
and then it happened
(Palenque, Tablet of 96 Glyphs)

CHAM-mi
cham-i
he died

HUL-li
hul-i
it arrived
(Piedras Negras, Stela 3)

OCH-chi
och-i
she entered

Derived: suffixed by **-ja**.

SIY-ya-j(a)
siyaj-ø
he was born
(Piedras Negras, Stela 3)

OTOT-ja
ototaj-ø
he was housed

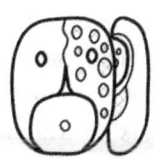
WAY-ja
wayaj-ø
she slept/dreamt

pi-tzi-ja
pitzaj-ø
he played ball

Positional: suffixed by **-la-j(a)** or **-wa-n(i)**, resulting in *-laj* or *-waan*.

CHUM[mu]-la-j(a)
chumlaj-ø
he was seated
(Palenque, Tablet of 96 Glyphs)

pa-ta-la-j(a)
patlaj-ø
it was formed

CHUM[mu]-wa-n(i)
chumwaan-ø
she was seated

Causative: suffixed by **-b'u**, resulting in *-b'u*.

u-TZ'AK-b'u
utz'akb'u-ø
he made it become accumulated
(modified Yaxchilan, Lintel 21)

u-pa-t(a)-b'u
upatb'u-ø
she made it become formed

derived noun or adjective. This can result in constructions such as CV₁C-V₁l-ja, where the -Vl- is a derivational suffix on a noun or adjective. For this reason the next category, positional verbs, may be subsumed into the derived intransitive verb category.

Derived intransitive verbs are also common (**see fig. 5.5**). One of the most common verbs is "to be born," written *siy* in Classic Mayan. In this example, the form **SIY-ya-j(a)** results in *siyaj*, which can best be translated as "he/she was born." In reality, the root of this verb comes from the noun *siy*, "gift." The bearing of children is equated with giving a gift. Other examples come from the nouns *otoot*, "house"; *way*, "spiritual co-essence"; and *pitz*, "ball game." From these nouns, suffixed with *-aj*, come the verbs *ototaj*, "he was housed"; *wayaj*, "she slept/dreamt"; and *pitzaj*, "he played ball."

5.3. POSITIONAL (AND CAUSATIVE)

A positional verb refers to a physical state that a person or animal can take, such as sitting, standing, or lying. These verbs can only take one argument, which is again the patient and therefore uses the absolutive pronoun. There are two forms that differ loosely by region: CVC-laj-ABS (eastern) and CVC-waan-ABS (western). These can be spelled as **CVC-la-j(a)** or **CVC-wa-n(i)**. Taking the usual third-person singular, this results in *CVC-laj-ø* or *CVC-waan-ø*. These are pronounced *CVClaj* and *CVCwaan*, respectively. In either case, this can be translated as "the *patient* verbed."

Although they are generally considered intransitive, the causative form of positional verbs can take two arguments: ERG-CVC-b'u-ABS. In the causative voice, an agent forces or causes a patient to perform a verb. The **-b'u** syllable is appended to a CVC positional verb to cause it to happen, with the third-person singular form expressed as **u-CVC-b'u**, resulting in *u-CVC-b'u-ø*, read *uCVCb'u*. This can be translated into English as "the *actor* made the *patient* verb."

Positional verbs including the "seating" verb *chum* can be seen in **figure 5.5**. The first example, **CHUM[mu]-la-j(a)**, is one pattern of the phrase "he was seated," pronounced *chumlaj*. This might also have been written **CHUM[mu]-wa-n(i)** and pronounced *chumwaan* but translated the same, as shown in the third example. This phrase is usually followed by a clause saying **ti-AJAW-le**, *tajawlel*, meaning "into rulership," to record royal ascensions. The second example, **pa-ta-la-j(a)**, *patlaj*, meaning "it was formed," can also be turned into the causative statement **u-pa-t(a)-b'u**, pronounced *upatb'u*, which means "she made it become formed." The most common example of this causative form is **u-TZ'AK-b'u**, read *utz'akbu*, "he made it accumulate." This verb *tz'ak* means "to count or accumulate" and is often used in dynastic statements, such as "he is the 13th ruler." Please complete **exercises 5.4 and 5.5**, in which you must translate intransitive verbs to and from Classic Mayan.

5.3. POSITIONAL (AND CAUSATIVE)

Exercise 5.4. Intransitive Verbs

1. Conjugate and translate each of the following verbs for the given arguments for each voice.

Root: CVC-ABS*   *ø → i
Derived: CVC-aj-ABS
Positional: CVC-laj-ABS   CVC-waan-ABS
Causative: ERG-CVC-b'u-ABS

	cham to die	*ak'* to dance	*chum* to seat	
Pronouns	Root	Derived	Positional	Causative (3rd pers.)
1st Person Sing.	cham-een I died			
2nd Person Sing.	_____	ak'-aj-at you danced		
3rd Person Sing.	_____	_____	chum-waan-ø he sat	_____
1st Person Plural	_____	_____	_____	u-chum-b'u-o'n he made us sit
2nd Person Plural	cham-ox you (pl.) died	_____	_____	_____
3rd Person Plural	_____	ak'-aj-o'b they danced	_____	_____

hul to arrive *tz'ib'* to write *lam* to disappear

3rd Person Sing.	_____	_____	lam-waan-ø he disappeared	_____

'och to enter *pul* to burn *pat* to disappear

3rd Person Sing.	_____	_____	_____	u-pat-b'u-ø he made it form

VERBAL GRAMMAR

Exercise 5.5. More Intransitive Verbs

1. Using the following vocabulary and pronouns, translate the verbs below into English. Refer to figure 5.4 for intransitive verb endings.

'ak't	to dance (div)	*lok'*	to emerge, leave (riv)	*tal*	to come (riv)
cham	to die (riv)	*och*	to enter (riv)	*tz'ib'*	to write (div)
chum	to sit (pv)	*pat*	to form, make (pv)	*'uk'*	to drink (riv)
hul	to arrive (riv)	*pitz*	to (play) ball (div)		

hul-at	you arrived	*pitz-aj-at*	_____
och-at	_____	*'uk'-een*	_____
och-i	_____	*lok'-o'n*	_____
tal-o'n	_____	*u-chum-b'u-ø*	_____
hul-i	_____	*chum-laj-o'b'*	they sat
pat-waan-een	_____	*tal-i*	_____
hul-een	_____	*'uk'-i*	_____
cham-een	_____	*'ak't-aj-een*	_____
pitz-aj-ø	_____	*tal-i*	_____
ni-pat-b'u-ø	_____	*cham-at*	_____
tz'ib'-aj-een	_____	*lok'-ox*	_____
tz'ib'-aj-at	_____	*cham-i*	_____
'ak't-aj-ø	_____	*'uk'-i*	_____

5.4. INCHOATIVE

Much like the derived intransitive verbs, the inchoative action derives a verb from a noun or adjective. Inchoative is a grammatical aspect (not a voice) expressing the beginning of an action or state. We might say "the man became ruler." In Maya hieroglyphics, the inchoative is used to indicate the act of becoming. It is indicated by the addition of -*Vj* or -*Vn* to the noun or adjective root: CV_1C-V_1j-ABS or CV_1C-$V_1(V_1)n$-ABS. This is usually expressed in the third person singular as CV_1C-V_1j-ø or CV_1C-$V_1(V_1)n$-ø. It is spelled **CVC-j(a)** or **CVC-n(i)**, resulting in CV_1CV_1j or $CV_1CV_1(V_1)n$. Although it may be possible to translate

Figure 5.6. Other Verb Markers

Type:	Paradigm:		Common Glyphic Expression:
Inchoative: –only one argument –patient-focused –derived verb (formed from noun or adjective)	CV_1C-V_1j-ABS or -V_1n-ABS CV_1C-V_1j-ø or CV_1C-$V_1(V_1)n$-ø *patient* became *noun*.	CVC  CVC	**CVC-j(a)** or **CVC-n(i)** CV_1CV_1j or $CV_1CV_1(V_1)n$ He/she/it became *noun*. *Giveaway:* **-ja** or **-ni** syllable

Common Inchoative Verbs:
ajaw   ruler (n)   b'aak   captive (n)   kalo'mte'   Kalomte' (title) (n)
ch'ok   heir (n)   b'akab' first of the earth (?) (n)

Affective: –only one argument –agent-focused –derived verb (from another part of speech)	CVC-laj-ABS CVC-laj-ø *noun*ing.	CVC 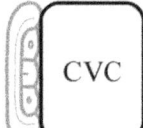	**CVC-la-j(a)** *CVClaj* *noun*ing. *Giveaway:* **-la-ja** syllable on a noun or adjective

Common Affective Verbs:
b'aj   hammer (n)

Stative: –one argument –possession possible –implied verb (no verb "to be" in Mayan) plus noun	(ERG)-CVC-ABS (u)-CVC-ø *patient* was *noun*.	CVC	**CVC** *CVC* He/she/it was *noun*. *Giveaway:* no real giveaway.
	(ERG)-CV_1C-(V_1l)-ABS (u)-CV_1C-(V_1l)-ø *patient* was (*possessor*) *noun*.	CVC	**(u)-CVC-l(i)** $uCV_1C[V_1]l$ He/she/it was [his/her/its] *noun*. *Giveaway:* **-li** syllable on a noun.

this as "the *patient noun*ed" (much like a derived intransitive verb), it is better expressed as "the *patient* became *noun*." For example, "Yax B'alam became ruler," but not "the tomatoes ripen," which is a derived intransitive construction. The inchoative differs from derived intransitive verbs in that it can take a *-Vn* marker and the nouns and adjectives used are those of states of being or positions, such as "ruler." Derived intransitives suggest that the agent is performing a noun; inchoatives suggest that the agent is becoming one. Inchoatives and other verb types are shown in **figure 5.6**.

This is seen in accession statements as individuals become rulers or heirs, as shown in **figure 5.7**. The first example is yet another way in which royal ascension was recorded. **AJAW-n(i)**, read *ajawaan*, could be translated as "he/she became [the] ruler." Other examples include derivations of the nouns *ch'ok*, "heir"; and *b'aak*, "captive." By adding *-Vj* or *-VVn*, we see *ch'okoj* and *b'aakaj* in examples 2 and 3. It might also be suggested that the derived intransitive verb *siy*, "to bear [children]," which derives from the root noun "gift," might be reclassified as an inchoative, giving the identical form *siyaj* but translated literally as "he/she became a gift."

Figure 5.7. Other Verb Examples

Inchoative: a noun suffixed by **-ja** or **-ni**.

AJAW-n(i)
ajawaan-ø
he/she became ruler
(Aguateca, Stela 15)

ch'o-ko-j(a)
ch'okoj-ø
he/she became heir

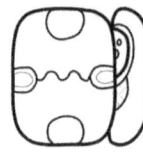
B'AK-j(a)
b'aakaj-ø
he/she became [a] captive

Affective: a noun suffixed by **-la-j(a)**.

b'a-la-j(a)
b'alaj-ø
hammering
(Dos Pilas, Hieroglyphic Stair 4)

Stative: a noun suffixed by nothing (ø) or **-li**.

ya-AJAW-(wa)
yajaw-ø
he/she was his/her ruler
(Palenque, Tablet of 96 Glyphs)

MAM
mam-ø
he/she was [an] ancestor

u-MAM
umam-ø
it was his/her ancestor

5.5. AFFECTIVE

An affective verb is one that describes phenomena such as bright lights, loud sounds, or strong smells. It is rare and is formed by adding *-laj*, which is the same **-la-j(a)** ending seen on positional verbs. They differ, however, in the type of verb being expressed: affective verbs are not positions that a human or animal can take. The form of this verbal phrase is CVC-laj-ABS, usually expressed as *CVC-laj-ø*, read *CVClaj*. This is usually translated as "*noun*ing." The most prominent example of this is from the name *b'alaj* (or *b'a[j] laj*) *chan k'awiil*, "hammering sky K'awil" (**see fig. 5.7**).

5.6. STATIVE PARTICLES

Stative particles are discussed in chapter 4 but bear repetition here because they act as verbs. Classic Mayan has no verb "to be." Instead, noun phrases can include an absolutive pronoun to act in this stative sense. As the third-person absolutive pronoun is invisible (ø), most noun phrases (discussed in chapter 4) can also be interpreted as "he/she/it was the *noun*." This is can be formed simply as CVC-ABS, usually giving *CVC-ø*, which can look like just a noun. It can also be possessed through an ergative pronoun (ERG-CVC-ABS), usually *u-*, translated as "he/she/it was his/her/its *noun*." Remember that nouns can be pure or derived from other parts of speech, often by adding a suffix. In this instance, it may still be translated as "he/she/it was the *noun*." In all honesty, many of the titles seen in inscriptions may well be subclauses. For instance, the sentence *siyaj pakal k'uhul b'aak ajaw* might correctly be translated as "Pakal, the holy ruler of Palenque, was born." If the *k'uhul b'aak ajaw* phrase was meant to be interpreted as a stative clause, however, we might better translate the same sentence as "Pakal was born, he was the holy ruler of Palenque." The meaning does not really change. **Figure 5.7** has just a few examples of this stative form. The first example, **ya-AJAW-(wa)**, read *yajaw*, means "it/he was his ruler." The second and third examples use the same noun, *mam*, meaning "grandfather" or "ancestor." In the second example (*mam*), this may simply be saying "he was [an] ancestor." The third example (*umam*), may mean "it was his ancestor."

5.7. EXPRESSING TIME

The preceding discussion has focused on transitive and intransitive verbs and their various voices without bringing up the question of time and tense. In each explanation, however, the suggested English translation has been given in the past tense. It is likely that the Classic Maya were not using a tense-based system but rather an aspectual one. This point is currently debated by the field's top epigraphers and is discussed in inset box 5.1. Generally speaking, the English system has three tenses: past, present, and future. Each tense has different aspects that can affect the exact meaning of the verb: simple, progressive, perfect simple, and perfect progressive. Examples of the most common are shown in **table 5.2**.

Most modern Maya languages are not tense based. They employ an aspectual system that is not based on the time of an action's occurrence but rather on the completion of that action. In this system, an action can be either completive or incompletive, depending on its current state. For instance, say that Mary grew beans last year and this year she is growing tomatoes. A tense-based system might say "Mary picked beans" and "Mary picks tomatoes." In an aspectual system, the verbs would be marked to show that Mary is no longer picking beans (completive aspect) and that she is currently or still picking tomatoes (incompletive). In the case of one-time actions (such as birth, death, and marriage), past tense and completive aspect correspond, as do the present tense and incompletive aspect. For repetitive or durational actions, tense and aspect differ. For instance, "Mary picked beans" is past tense and completive aspect, while "Mary was picking beans" is past tense but may be incompletive, depending on the context.

In English we mark the past tense. An event in the past takes on specific grammatical markers to indicate the past tense, often *-ed,* as in "I walk" (present) versus "I walked" (past). It is likely that Classic Mayan did the opposite (just like many extant Maya languages), marking the incompletive action while leaving the completive unmarked. In the verbal morphology presented in sections 5.1 and 5.2, there does not seem to be any marking for aspect; therefore it is thought that the verbs are expressing the completive (unmarked) aspect. This may sound strange, but inscriptions on stone monuments were formal and historical. Because the texts describe past events, it should not be surprising that the completive aspect is used. This is the reason why the suggested English translation is in the past tense. There is no exact correspondence between tense and aspect

Table 5.2. English Tense and Voice

Tense and Voice	Past	Present	Future	Meaning
Simple	Mary grew beans	Mary grows tomatoes	Mary will* grow squash	Statement of action
Progressive	Mary was growing beans	Mary is growing tomatoes	Mary will* be growing squash	Recurring or continual action
Perfect Simple	Mary had grown beans	Mary has grown tomatoes	Mary will* have grown squash	Action occurring before another action
Perfect Progressive	Mary had been growing beans	Mary has been growing tomatoes	Mary will* have been growing squash	Statement about length of action

*First- and third-person singular may also use "shall" as the auxiliary verb.

BOX 5.1. KEY CONTROVERSY: Aspect versus Tense

Some languages use tense to describe the occurrence of events as past, present, or future, such as the English pattern of "ate," "eat," and "will eat." Other languages use aspect, which describes events as complete or incomplete (ongoing). Aspect is difficult to translate into English, because it is a fundamentally different system, but it might sound something like "already eaten" as completive and "eating" as incompletive. Maya languages today primarily use an aspect-based system. Noted epigraphers Houston, Stuart, and Robertson (2004) have proposed that Classic Mayan discourse used a tense-based system.

Houston et al. point out that in Maya languages today the incompletive aspect is marked, while the completive is not. We "mark" the past tense in English by adding an *-ed* to the end of verbs (or using a different form of the verb, such as "ate"). In hieroglyphic texts, we see that the earlier events (those that should be in the completive aspect) are marked, in opposition to the pattern of modern Maya languages. Houston et al. therefore suggest that there was a shift to a tense system, which they support with complex linguistic arguments. In their model, the **-ya** suffix works in the same way as *-ed* in English, to mark the past tense, and unmarked verbs are in the present tense. Other scholars (e.g., Wald 2004) take issue with this model. The linguistic arguments that Houston et al. muster to support their hypothesis are possibly too complex, suggesting a shift from aspect to tense and then to aspect again. Although they have found a singular example of an aspectual system shifting to a tense-based one, the entire scenario seems to be overly complicated and unlikely. The simplest answer often proves to be the correct one in science, and their linguistic argumentation is far from simple. Time will tell (no pun intended) if this hypothesis receives broad-based support and fosters improved argumentation. As outlined in this chapter, this textbook uses the more conservative, aspect-based approach.

An alternative proposal by Wald (2004) suggests that the *-jiiy/-iiy* elements are enclitics, as described in this chapter. Although some suggest that *-iy* and *-jiiy* inflect verbs, this does not make sense, because they are attached to nouns, such as *winik* and *haab'*. It would make sense, however, if these variables were adjectives or enclitics, similar to "ago" in English.

It is important to note, though, that there is really little difference between the model of Houston et al. and the enclitic-based one. Everybody agrees that **-ya** marks a previously occurring event, whether it was expressed with completive aspect or past tense. As long as this is recognized, the English translation of Maya texts should be largely the same. Epigraphers are gaining a clearer understanding of the linguistics of Maya hieroglyphic writing through debates such as this, even though we already have a decent understanding of the content.

forms, so a translation from one system to another must choose the most appropriate approximation. In the case of most events described in glyphic inscriptions, the past tense can approximate the completive aspect.

The Maya did have a way to indicate the chronological occurrence of events, however, by way of enclitics. A clitic is a phonetically dependent but grammatically independent morpheme. Its meaning is independent of the word it modifies, but it must be attached to it. An enclitic attaches to the end of a word (a proclitic attaches to the front). For instance, in English, -s can be attached to the end of a noun to indicate plurality: "one bean," "two beans." Enclitics are grammatically independent but must be attached to a word in order to have meaning. Temporal indicators in Classic Mayan seem to work in the same way to signal the relative chronological occurrence of events. The chronological scheme of ancient Maya inscriptions has been debated, as summarized in inset box 5.1.

Think of it this way: if you could only use past tense to tell a story in English, how would you describe events that happened one after the other? You could use words such as "then," "until," "already," "before," "earlier," and "ago." For example, "He was born twenty years *before* he was installed as the ruler, and *then* he died thirty five years later."

To indicate an event in the recent or distant past, the Classic Maya attached *-iiy* or *-ijiiy* to the complete verb phrase, as shown in **figure 5.8**. It is usually given by **-y(a)** alone or the **-ji-y(a)** syllable combination. This indicates that an event occurred before a later event and used to be called the Anterior Event Indicator (before its phonetic value was known). For instance, in the sentence *siyajiiy b'olonlaju'n haab' chumwaan tajawlel,* "he was born nineteen years before he was seated into rulership," somebody must be born before he can be seated in rulership. The derived intransitive verb from *siy,* "to bear [children]," must be given as *siy-aj-ø-iiy,* pronounced *siyajiiy,* because the ruler must have been born before he was seated into office (note that the latter event is not marked with an adverb). This may also be translated as "he was born before . . . " It does not seem to be a marker like the English *-ed,* which can only be appended to verbs. The enclitic *-iiy/-ijiiy* can be attached to other parts of speech. It is commonly attached to the glyphs expressing units in distance numbers, such as *winik, haab',* and *winikhaab'.* In many cases, the *-iiy/-ijiiy* can best be translated as a separate English word, such as "before," "ago," "earlier," or "already." In other cases, it may be possible to translate this as the English past perfect simple aspect: "he/she/it had *verb*ed." A full example of this paradigm is shown in **table 5.3**.

Sequential events may also be indicated by adding an adverb or enclitic to the verb. In chapter 4 *i-* is presented as an adverb meaning "and then," which is one way to indicate the temporal relationship of two completive verbs: *siyaj i-chami,* "he was born, and then he died." Another way is through the future-marking enclitic *-o'm.* It is attached to the end of the verbal phrase, just like *-iiy.* While *i-* is best translated as "and then," *-o'm* can use the common English helper-verb "will," as in *siyaj chami-o'm,* "he/she was born and he/she will die." The use of *-o'm* is rare, often pertaining to events projected far into the future, while *i-* is common, used not only in many Posterior Date Indicators but also in general verbal discourse.

5.7. EXPRESSING TIME

Table 5.3. Verb Paradigm Indicating Relative Time

Verb	Anterior Event	Unmarked	Posterior Event	Future Event
Transitive Active	**u-JATZ'-w(a)-y(a)** *u-jatz'-aw-ø-iiy* *ujatz'awiiy* He hit it already/ago He had hit it	**u-JATZ'-w(a)** *u-jatz'-aw-ø* *ujatz'aw* He hit it	**i-u-JATZ'-w(a)** *i-u-jatz'-aw-ø* *iujatz'aw* And then he hit it	**u-JATZ'-wo-m(a)** *u-jatz'-aw-ø-o'm* *ujatz'awo'm* He will hit it
Passive	**JATZ'-j(a)-y(a)** *jahtz'-aj-ø-iiy* *jahtz'ajiiy* It was hit already/ago It had been hit	**JATZ'-j(a)** *jahtz'-aj-ø* *jahtz'aj* It was hit	**i-JATZ'-j(a)** *i-jahtz'-aj-ø* *ijahtz'aj* And then it was hit	**JATZ'-jo-m(a)** *jahtz'-aj-ø-o'm* *jahtz'ajo'm* It will be hit
Mediopassive	**JATZ'-yi-y(a)** *jatz'-ay-ø-iiy* *jatz'ayiiy* It got hit already/ago It had gotten hit	**JATZ'-y(i)** *jatz'-ay-ø* *jatz'ay* It got hit	**i-JATZ'-y(i)** *i-jatz'-ay-ø* *ijatz'ay* And then it got hit	**JATZ'-yo-m(a)** *jatz'-ay-ø-o'm* *jatz'ayo'm* It will get hit
Antipassive	**JATZ'-wi-y(a)** *jatz'-aw-ø-iiy* *jatz'awiiy* It hit already/ago It had hit	**JATZ'-w(i)** *jatz'-aw-ø* *jatz'aw* It hit	**i-JATZ'-w(i)** *i-jatz'-aw-ø* *ijatz'aw* And then it hit	**JATZ-wo-m(a)** *jatz'-aw-ø-o'm* *jatz'awo'm* It will hit
Intransitive Root	**OCH-i-y(a)** *och-i-iy* *ochiiy* He arrived already/ago He had arrived	**OCH-i** *och-i* *och-i* He arrived	**i-OCH-i** *i-och-i* And then he arrived	**OCH-o-m(a)** *och-o'm* *ocho'm* He will arrive
Derived	**pi-tzi-j(a)-y(a)** *pitz-ij-ø-iiy* *pitzijiiy* He ball-played already/ago He had ball-played	**pi-tzi-j(a)** *pitz-iij-ø* *pitziij* He ball-played	**i-pi-tzi-j(a)** *i-pitz-iij-ø* *ipitziij* And then he ball-played	**pi-tzi-jo-m(a)** *pitz-ij-ø-o'm* *pitzijo'm* He will ball-play
Positional	**CHUM-wa-ni-y(a)** *chum-waan-ø-iiy* *chumwaaniiy* He sat already/ago He had sat	**CHUM-wa-n(i)** *chum-waan-ø* *chumwaan* He sat	**i-CHUM-wa-n(i)** *i-chum-waan-ø* *ichumwaan* And then he sat	**CHUM-wa-no-m(a)** *chum-waan-ø-o'm* *chumwaano'm* He will sit
Causative	**u-CHUM-b'i-y(a)** *u-chum-b'-iiy* *uchumb'iiy* He made her sit already/ago He had made her sit	**u-CHUM-b'u** *u-chum-b'u-ø* *uchumb'u* He made her sit	**i-u-CHUM-b'u** *i-u-chum-b'u-ø* *iuchumb'u* And then he made her sit	**u-CHUM-b'o-m(a)** *u-chum-b'-o'm* *uchumb'o'm* He will make her sit
Inchoative	**AJAW-ni-y(a)** *ajaw-aan-iiy* *ajawaaniiy* He became king already/ago He had become king	**AJAW-n(i)** *ajaw-aan-ø* *ajawaan* He became king	**i-AJAW-n(i)** *i-ajaw-aan-ø* *iajawaan* And then he became king	**AJAW-no-m(a)** *ajaw-aan-o'm* *ajawaano'm* He will become king
Affective		**b'a-ja-la-j(a)** *baj-laj* *balaj* hammering		

VERBAL GRAMMAR

Table 5.3. Verb Paradigm Indicating Relative Time (continued)

Verb	Anterior Event	Unmarked	Posterior Event	Future Event
Imperative		**JATZ'-a** jatz'-a-ø jatz'a Hit it!	**JATZ'-a** jatz'-a-ø jatz'a Hit it!	
Stative	**ha-ma-li-y(a)** ham-liiy hamliiy It was open already/ago It had been open	**ha-ma-l(a)** ham-al hamal It was open	**ha-ma-l(a)** ham-al hamal It was open	**ha-ma-lo-m(a)** ham-al-o'm hamalo'm It will be open

Figure 5.8. Temporal Verb Markers or Adverbs

Relative chronology and temporal relationships are indicated by clitics and adverbs.

Type: | **Paradigm:** | **Common Glyphic Expression:**

Posterior Event Indicator:
—describes next event in a series
—adverb prefixed to a verb

i-VERB
i-VERB
and then *verb*ed

i-CVC...
iCVC...
And then he/she/it *verb*ed

Giveaway: **i-** syllable

Future Event Indicator:
—describes future event
—enclitic suffixed to a verb

VERB-o'm
VERB-o'm
will *verb*

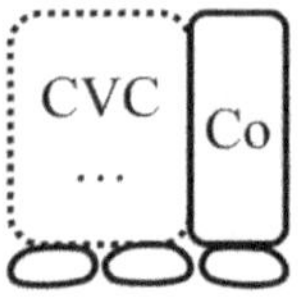

CVC...Co-m(a)
CVC...o'm
will *verb*

Giveaway: **-Co-ma** syllables

Anterior Event Indicator:
—describes previous event
—enclitic suffixed to a verb

VERB-iiy
VERB-iiy
ago/already *verb*ed

CVC...-y(a)
CVC...iiy
already *verb*ed

Giveaway: **-ya** syllables

Extreme Anterior Event Indicator:
—describes significantly earlier event
—enclitic suffixed to a verb

VERB-jiiy
VERB-jiiy
long ago *verb*ed

CVC...-ji-y(a)
CVC...jiiy
long ago *verb*ed

Giveaway: **-ji-ya** syllables

The top of **figure 5.9** shows examples of the four common temporal indicators, all from Tortuguero, Monument 6. In the first example, **i-CH'AK-(k)a-ja**, the *ch'ak* verb ("to decapitate or chop," which is often used to indicate military defeat) is given in the transitive passive voice, plus the adverb *i-*, resulting in *ich'ahkaj*, "And then he was defeated or decapitated." The next example, **u-to-m(a)**, is the same verb as the Posterior and Anterior Date Indicators, *ut*. In this case, the future event indicator, *-o'm*, is suffixed, giving *uto'm*, meaning "it will happen." This suffix can be attached to other glyphs to indicate a future event. Unlike the adverb *i-*, this enclitic is usually used to indicate dates far into the future and is often used in prophecy. The next example, **CHUM[mu]-wa-ni-y(a)**, results in *chumwaaniiy*. In this case, the enclitic *-iiy* is attached to the positional verb *chum*, "to seat." This verb is commonly used in royal ascension statements. The entire phrase can be translated in a few ways, depending on the context. If it appears before a Distance Number, it can be translated as "he was seated in rulership X days before . . ." followed by the next event. Without a Distance Number between events, it may look more like "he had already been seated in rulership when he . . ." and then the next event. The final example, **SIY-ja-[ji]y(a)**, shows the *-jiiy* enclitic, which may indicate a much earlier event, similar to the difference between "ago" and "long ago" in English. The translation of this enclitic is also dependent on context but in practice is similar to the *-iiy* enclitic. In this case, *siyaj-jiiy* may be translated as "he was born X days before . . ." or "he had been born before he . . ." It is worth noting that both *-iiy* and *-jiiy* are often appended to Distance Number units, such as *winik* and *haab'*. If these enclitics were verbal markers, it would be strange for them to be attached to nouns; if they are taken as something akin to adverbs, however, the forms *winikiiy* and *haab'iiy* are easily translated as "month(s) ago" and "year(s) ago."

Let's look at two examples of this expression of time in Maya hieroglyphic writing. **Figure 5.9** shows drawings of Palenque's Hieroglyphic Stairway (top) and Piedras Negras Stela 8 (bottom). The inscription from Piedras Negras reads:

Transcription:
. . . 9-? 9-UNIW-(wa) ma-AK-ja-ji-y(a) IXIK-(na)-MAN-(ni)-AJAW u-KAB'-ji-y(a) [K'AN]AK 4-WINIK-HAB'-AJAW-(wa) 2-la-t(a) [11-? 11-UNIW]-(wa) [K'A'-y(i)]-u-SAK[?]-IK'-li [K'AN]AK K'UHUL-yo-ki[b'(i)]-AJAW-(wa)

Transliteration:
. . . b'olon ? b'olon uniiw mahkaj-iiy ixik namaan ajaw uk'ab-jiiy k'an ahk chan winikhaab' ajaw cha' lat b'uluk ? b'uluk uniiw k'a'ay u sak ? ik'il k'an ahk k'uhul yokib' ajaw

Translation:
. . . on 9 Chuwen, 9 K'ank'in Lady Ruler of La Florida was betrothed when Ruler 2, the 4-K'atun ruler, had supervised it two days before, on 11 B'en, 11 K'ank'in, Ruler 2's white wind got diminished [he died], the holy ruler of Yaxchilan.

Let's look at the verbal morphology in this sentence. The verbs are *mak*, "to betroth"; *k'ab*, "to supervise"; and *k'a'*, "to diminish." The first two are marked with the *-iiy* Anterior Event Indicator, and the second is unmarked. If we look at where they occur in the sentence and in overall time (as given by the dates), we see that "Lady Ruler of La Florida" (see chapter 6) was betrothed under the supervision of Ruler 2 two days before Ruler 2 died. It is no coincidence that the events that occurred earlier were marked. If

Figure 5.9. Verb Time Examples

Future Event Indicator: a verb suffixed by **-Co-ma**.

u-to-m(a)
ut-ø-o'm
it will happen
(Tortuguero, Monument 6)

Posterior Event Indicator: a verb prefaced by **i-**.

i-CH'AK-(k)a-ja
i-ch'ahkaj-ø
and then he was decapitated
(Tortuguero, Monument 6)

Anterior Event Indicator: a verb suffixed by **-y(a)**.

CHUM[mu]-wa-ni-y(a)
chumwaan-ø-iiy
he became ruler before ...
(Tortuguero, Monument 6)

Extreme Anterior Event Indicator: a verb suffixed by **-ji-y(a)**, *-jiiy*.

SIY-ja-[ji]y(a)
siyaj-ø-jiiy
he was born ... long ago
(Tortuguero, Monument 6)

SIY-ja-y(a)-K'INICH-PET-NAL
siyaj-iiy k'inich pet nal
... was born Sun-Faced Round-Place

pa-ka-l(a)-K'UHUL-B'AK-la-AJAW
pakal k'uhul b'aakal ajaw
Shield, holy ruler of Palenque

8-9-WINIK-12-HAB'
waxak b'olon winik lajchan haab'
8 days, 9 months, and 12 years

tu-[HO'-EK'-JUN-mo-l(o)]
tu [ho' ek' ju'n mol]
on 5 Lamat, 1 Mol

K'AL-ja-HUN-tu-u-B'AH
k'ahlaj hu'n tub'aah
the headdress was bound to his head

K'INICH-JANAB'-pa-ka-l(a)
k'inich janaab' pakal
Sun-Faced [bird name] Shield

(Palenque, Modified Hieroglyphic Stairway)

9-?
b'olon ?
[On] 9 Chuwen

9-UNIW-(wa) ma-AK-ja-ji-y(a)
b'olon uniiw mahkaj-iiy
9 K'ank'in, was betrothed

IXIK-na-MAN-(ni)-AJAW u-KAB'-ji-y(a)-[K'AN]AK
ixik namaan ajaw ukab'-jiiy k'an ahk
Lady Ruler of La Florida was supervised by Ruler 2,

4-WINIK-HAB'-AJAW-(wa) 2-la-t(a)
chan winikhaab' ajaw cha' lat
the 4-K'atun ruler. Two days later

11-? 11-[UNIW-(wa)]
b'uluk ? b'uluk uniiw
11 B'en, 11 K'ank'in

[K'A'-y(i)]-u-SAK[?]-IK'-li [K'AN]AK
k'aay usak ? ik'il k'an ahk
died Ruler 2 [Yellow Turtle]

K'UHUL-yo-ki[b'(i)]-AJAW-(wa)
k'uhul yokib' ajaw
holy ruler of Yaxchilan.

(Piedras Negras, Stela 8)

we shorten this translation, it says: "Lady Ruler of La Florida was betrothed under Ruler 2's supervision two days *before* he died." There is no *iuti* Posterior Date Indicator to tell us that the *cha' lat,* "two days," indicates a forward count (although the Calendar Round would indicate this forward count). The use of this enclitic is consistent with the context.

Now let's turn to Palenque's Hieroglyphic Stairway:

Transcription:
. . . WAXAK-AJAW OXLAJU'N-[K'AN-?-w(a)]* SIY-ja-y(a) K'INICH-PET(?)-NAL pa-ka-l(a) K'UHUL-B'AK-la-AJAW 8-9-WINIK-12-HAB'-[HO'-EK'-JUN-mo[l(o)]] K'AL-ja-HUN tu-u-B'AH K'INICH-JANAB' pa-ka-l(a)
* not shown in figure

Transliteration:
. . . *waxak ajaw oxlaju'n k'anjalaw(?)* siyaj-iiy k'inich pet nal pakal k'uhul b'aakal ajaw waxak b'olon winik lajchan haab' tu [ho' ek' ju'n mol] k'ahlaj hu'n tub'aah k'inich janaab' pakal*
* not shown in figure

Translation:
. . . 8 Ajaw, 13 Pop,* Sun-Faced Round-Place Shield, holy ruler of Palenque, was born 8 days, 9 months, and 12 years before the headdress was bound onto Sun-Faced [bird name] Shield's head.
* not shown in figure

In this sentence, we have the birth and crowning of Pakal, Palenque's most famous ruler. Of course his birth must precede his assumption of rulership, and the verbal morphology bears this out: *siyaj-iiy* precedes *k'ahlaj,* "he was born *before* he was crowned."

We will continue examining inscriptions in chapter 6, translating all or most of the inscriptions and tracing the lives of a few rulers. This will not only illustrate the process that professional epigraphers have gone through to reconstruct Classic Maya history but also highlight all of the aspects of Maya hieroglyphic writing covered in this book.

6. PUTTING IT ALL TOGETHER

In 1960 Russian-born scholar Tatiana Proskouriakoff, working for the Peabody Museum at Harvard University, published a ground-breaking article proving that Maya inscriptions held historical information. At the site of Piedras Negras, where she was working, many stelae had the image of a seated person surrounded by glyphs. She noticed that two glyphs were used repeatedly and were associated with particular dates. The first glyph was the "upended frog" glyph, and the second was the "toothache" glyph. By plotting these glyphs and their associated dates, Proskouriakoff was able to show that the upended frog glyph always appeared before the toothache glyph on each monument. Furthermore, the toothache glyph on one monument usually occurred shortly after the last date on another monument. When she worked out the length of time between the toothache-glyph events, it averaged 29.5 years. Using this information, she concluded that the upended frog glyph represented the birth and the toothache glyph represented assumption of rulership of the individual pictured. The length of time between toothache-glyph events was the average length of a ruler's reign. Although Proskouriakoff did not know that these glyphs were pronounced *siy* and *joy,* she was able to infer their meaning correctly. Until this time, few had accepted the idea that monuments recorded historical information. If we jump forward forty years, the historical nature of glyphs was showcased in *Chronicles of the Maya Kings and Queens* by Simon Martin and Nikolai Grube (2008). Martin and Grube trace the royal history of major Maya sites, such as Tikal, Calakmul, Yaxchilan, Copan, and Piedras Negras. They reconstruct Maya history using monumental inscriptions, deciphered using the same methods described in this book. In this final chapter, we will walk through a few inscriptions from Piedras Negras and Palenque, showing the work that goes into tracing Maya history. Much of the supplemental information here comes from the *Chronicles of the Maya Kings and Queens*, but the glyphic dissection of each monument is done independently.

Try to attack each inscription systematically. Start with the most visually identifiable glyphs: dates. The bar-and-dot numbers, the Tzolk'in cartouche, and the ISIG are easy to find by simply scanning the entire inscription. They are also useful because dates form the framework of the inscription. Divide the inscription into clauses using these dates. Remember that most Mayan clauses on monumental inscriptions begin with a date followed by a verb and then objects and subjects. I suggest printing a copy of the inscription to draw on with colored pencils, delineating the clauses. Other scholars prefer to cut out each glyph block and arrange them in clauses from left to right, like an English sentence.

Using the dates, work out as much of the chronology as you can. Do not spend a long time trying to work out points in the chronology if they are proving too difficult. Move on to the next section and come back later. You might not be able to work out every date from chronological data, such as Distance Numbers. Sometimes important dates (such as the ruler's birth) are referred to without any notice. This practice was not confusing to the readers of this text, who were as familiar with these dates as we are with 9/11 (we do not need to specify 2001). Other dates may rely on textual clues for identification, such as the completion of a K'atun.

Once you have tried to work out the entire chronology, move on to the inscription's content. Look for the verb directly following the Calendar Round in each clause. It is not always there, but that is usually where it will be found. If you are not familiar with a lot of verb glyphs, look for the verbal markers from chapter 5: the most common are **-wa** and **-ja.** Because many clauses refer to one person doing something to another person, names often follow the verb. Remember that for transitive verbs with two individuals named the first one is the patient (to whom the action is being done) and the second is the actor (the one who is performing that action). Names can be difficult to read because they are not always constructed of nouns or verbs that you have learned. It may be worth picking up a copy of the *Chronicles of Maya Kings and Queens* as a handy reference volume. Names, especially those of the local ruler (who is usually the actor in these clauses), are often followed by a string of titles generally ending with an emblem glyph (see chapter 4). Using this systematic approach, let's look at a few inscriptions. If you would like an extra challenge, try to analyze and translate as much of these inscriptions as you can before reading each section of the text and then compare your results.

6.1. PIEDRAS NEGRAS: K'INICH YO'NAL AHK II AND LADY K'ATUN AJAW

K'inich Yo'nal Ahk II is a well-documented ruler of Piedras Negras. He is mentioned on a number of stelae. To trace his life history we will be using Stelae 1, 3, and 8. Yo'nal Ahk II had a famous wife and daughter, Lady K'atun Ajaw and Lady Ju'n Tan Ahk, who are also mentioned on his monuments. Briefly, Yo'nal Ahk II was born on 9.11.12.7.2 2 Ik', 10 Pax (30 December 644 CE), a date that we will see a number of times. He was married at about twenty-two, around the time of the death of his father, Ruler 2. Yo'nal Ahk II ascended to the throne shortly after his father's death and presided over many K'atun and half-K'atun endings.

6.1.1. Piedras Negras, Stela 1

The chronology of Piedras Negras, Stela 1 is relatively straightforward. Let's start with the first Long Count, on the left side of **figure 6.1** (A1–J1). The Long Count reads 9.13.15.0.0 13 ?, 18 Pax (29 December 706 CE). This brings us to the right side of the monument. Because this is an even three-quarter K'atun (X.X.15.0.0), we know that the eroded Tzolk'in day must be Ajaw, which can be confirmed by using a calendar program. A Distance Number follows in J9–J11, moving us backward 19 days and 6 months. This brings us to 9.13.14.11.1 4 Imix, 19 Ch'en (12 August 706 CE). We will get to the events that happened on these days later. The front of Stela 1 also begins with a Long Count date (C1–E2). Beware the irregular reading order here: Column C is read straight down, and then the regular paired-column reading order takes over. The date is 9.12.2.0.16 5 Kib', 14 Yaxk'in (5 July 674 CE). The Distance Number follows in F2–I1, moving the date forward 12 years, 9 months, and 15 days, to 9.12.14.10.11 9 Chuwen, 9 K'ank'in (14 November 686 CE). Careful readers may have noticed that the Distance Number Indicator is *utiiy*, which usually tells us to count backward with the Distance Number. In this case, the Tzolk'in and Haab' are

6.1. PIEDRAS NEGRAS

Figure 6.1. Piedras Negras, Stela 1

196 PUTTING IT ALL TOGETHER

Table 6.1. Piedras Negras, Stela 1 Chronology

Position:	Counts:	Calendar Round:	Gregorian:
(Sides)			
A1–J1	09.13.15.00.00 − 06.19	13 [Ajaw] 18 Pax	29 December 706 CE
J9–J11	[09.13.14.11.01]	04 Imix 19 Ch'en	12 August 706 CE
(Front)			
C1–E2	09.12.02.00.16 + 12.09.15	05 Kib' 14 Yaxk'in	5 July 674 CE
F2–I1	[09.12.14.10.11] + 05	09 Chuwen 09 K'ank'in	14 November 686 CE
H3–I4	[09.12.14.10.16] + 01.00.02.05	01 Kib' 14 K'ank'in	19 November 686 CE
I6–I9	[09.13.14.13.01]	05 Imix 19 Sak	21 September 706 CE

clearly 9 Chuwen, 9 K'ank'in, which only works if the Distance Number is counted forward. This may be a scribal error or be mitigated by the phrase in G3, *ipas,* which can mean "on the next dawn." The most likely reason, however, is that it refers back to the previous event (as shown in the translation here). At any rate, it is clear that this later date is meant. The next Distance Number is abbreviated in H3–I4. Moving 5 days forward, to 9.12.14.10.16 1 Kib', 14 K'ank'in (19 November 686 CE), we come to an important date that also occurs on another monument. Stela 1 ends by jumping forward 5 days, 2 months, 0 years, and 1 score to 9.13.14.13.1 5 Imix, 19 Sak (21 September 706 CE) in I6–I9. Now that we have gotten through the chronology, let's lay it out in a quick-reference table (**table 6.1**) and move on to formal analysis and translation of the inscription on the monument.

Now we can divide the inscription into clauses based on the chronology that we just worked out. The first clause runs from A1 to K8 and includes a Long Count date, a calendar-period commemoration, and the name of Yo'nal Ahk II's father:

Transcription:
tzi(?)-k(a)-HAB'-[pl.] 9-PIH 13-WINIK-HAB' 15-HAB 0-WINIK 0-K'IN 13-[AJAW]
... ...3-?-K'AL-ja... ...-K'AB'A' 20-10 19-PAX-ma(?)...
-5-[TUN-n(i)]... ... ...-AJ K'UH-... u-MIJIN-(na)
...-ti ? [K'AN]AK K'UHUL-yo-ki[b'(i)]-AJAW

Transliteration:
tziik(?) haab'-[pl.] b'olon pih oxlaju'n winikhaab' ho'laju'n haab' mih winik mih k'ihn oxlaju'n [ajaw]... ... ...ox ? k'ahlaj... ...k'ab'a' winik laju'n b'olonlaju'n pax... ho' [tuun]... ... ...aj k'uh umijiin.... ti ? k'an ahk k'uhul yokib' ajaw

Translation:
On the day 9 eras, 13 scores, 15 years, 0 months, and 0 days, on 13 Ajaw,... ... ...3 ? was bound,..., its... name, [of a] 30-day lunation, on the 19th of Pax, 5 years [before the completion of the K'atun, observed by K'inich Yo'nal Ahk II, holy ruler of Piedras Negras]; he is the son of... Ruler 2, holy ruler of Piedras Negras.

This clause first commemorates the relatively minor calendrical holiday of the completion of three-quarters of a K'atun. In five years the more significant K'atun completion will be celebrated on other monuments. Although his name is eroded, we can be sure that it is Yo'nal Ahk II observing this rite as the ruler of Piedras Negras at this time. Further proof follows in the subclause starting in K6, which names Yo'nal Ahk II's father, still only known as Ruler 2. His full name is *? chaahk itzam(?) k'an ahk*, or "? rain deity iguana precious turtle," but only part of his name is visible in this instance. The next clause (J9–K16) commemorates the death of Yo'nal Ahk II's father:

Transcription:
u-TZ'AK-AJ 19-6-WINIK-y(a)(?) u-ti-y(a) 4-HA'(?) 14-IK'-SIHOM(?)-(ma) PUL(?) u-tzi-hi-li(?) ? . . . u-?-CH'AM-wa ? . . . -?-NAL . . . ti-1-WINIK-HAB' . . . [K'AN]AK

Transliteration:
utz'ahkaj b'olonlaju'n wak winik-iiy utiiy chan ha'(?) chanlaju'n ik' siho'm(?) pul(?) u-tzihil(?) ? . . . uch'amaw . . . ? . . .?nal . . . ti ju'n winikhaab' . . . k'an ahk

Translation:
It was set in order, it happened 19 days and 6 months ago, on 4 Imix, 14 Ch'en, his fresh-thing(?) [was] burned(?) . he grasped . . . ? ? . . . on 1 score . . . Ruler 2.

Even though many key words are eroded, the date can give us a clue as to what is going on. This clause refers to the date 9.13.14.11.1. The phrase *ti ju'n winikhaab'*, "on 1 score," and Ruler 2's name might hint at a date referring to the previous ruler. If we look back twenty years from this date, we come within seven days of Ruler 2's death on 9.12.14.10.13 11 B'en, 11 K'ank'in (16 November 686 CE). It has been suggested that the verb in K12 is related to fire, probably *pul*, "to burn," indicating that this may have been some rite involving a burned offering on the anniversary of the death of Yo'nal Ahk II's father. This date will come up again. In summary the sides of Piedras Negras, Stela 1 say: "On 9.13.15.0.0 13 Ajaw, 19 Pax the three-quarter K'atun is completed, [by K'inich Yo'nal Ahk II] son of Ruler 2. About 7 months earlier, on 4 Imix, 14 Ch'en, the 1-K'atun anniversary of Ruler 2's death was celebrated."

For now, let's continue with this inscription, moving to the front of the stela and a new Long Count (C1–G1):

Transcription:
tzi(?)-k(i)-HAB'-[pl.] 9-PIH 12-WINIK-HAB' 2-HAB' 0-WINIK 16-K'IN 5-? . . . TI'-HUN-(na) 8-HUL-li-y(a) 3-?-K'AL-ja ? u-ch'o[ko]-K'AB'A' 20-10 14-YAX-K'IN-(ni) SIY-ja-ji-y(a) IXIK-WINIK-HAB'-[pl.] (a)-[AJAW] IXIK-NAMAN(?)-(ni)-AJAW

Transliteration:
tziik(?) haab'-[pl.] b'olon pih lajchan winikhaab' cha' haab' mih winik waklaju'n k'ihn ho' ? . . . ti' hu'n waxak huliiy ox ? k'ahlaj ? u-ch'ok k'ab'a' winik laju'n chanlaju'n yaxk'ihn siyajiiy ixik winikhaab'-[pl.] ajaw ixik namaan(?) ajaw

Translation:
On the day 9 eras, 12 score, 2 years, 0 months, and 16 days, 5 Kib', . . . is the reader of the book, 8 days ago [the moon] arrived, 3 ? was bound, X4, its princely name, [of a] 30-day lunation, on the 14th of Yaxk'in Lady K'atun Ajaw, Lady Ruler of La Florida, was born.

This clause simply states the birthday of a woman named *ixik winikhaab' ajaw ixik namaan ajaw,* "Lady K'atun Ajaw, Lady Ruler of La Florida." We will soon see that she is the wife of Yo'nal Ahk II. We can glean from this first passage, though, is that she is a royal woman from another site, *namaan,* now thought to be La Florida.

The next two passages are quite interesting in terms of site history and ancient Maya politics:

Transcription:
15-9-WINIK-ji-y(a) 12-HAB'-[pl.] u-ti-y(a) i-PAS 9-? 9-UNIW-(wa) ma-ka-ja IXIK-NAMAN(?)-AJAW-(wa)

Transliteration:
ho'laju'n b'olon winik-jiiy lajchan haab'-[pl.] utiiy ipas b'olon ? b'olon uniiw mahkaj ixik namaan ajaw

Translation:
Then it happened 15 days, 9 months, and 12 years ago, it dawned [her birth?], on 9 Chuwen, 9 K'ank'in Lady Ruler of La Florida was betrothed.

The first notable thing about this clause (F2–I2) is the Distance Number Indicator. Although *utiiy* is specified, meaning that we should count back the indicated number of days, the glyph following it, *ipas,* means "then dawns" and can be used for the birth of deities. In essence, this date is saying "15 days, 9 months, and 12 years ago she was born, and now, today, on 9 Chuwen, 9 K'ank'in . . ." The second interesting point of this clause is her betrothal and the day on which it falls: 9.12.14.10.11, only two days before the death of Ruler 2. Although the passive transitive verb *mahkaj* does not say to whom Lady K'atun Ajaw is betrothed (he is specified in the next clause), it is significant that she is betrothed just before Ruler 2's death (we will come back to this point in a moment). The last interesting tidbit in this clause is her name. Almost everywhere else she is known as *ixik winikhaab' ajaw,* whereas here she is only referred to as *ixik namaan ajaw,* "Lady Ruler of La Florida." This phrasing may be used to emphasize her foreign ancestry and the newly strengthened connection between her site and Piedras Negras. Two days after her betrothal, Ruler 2 dies.

In the next clause (H3–I5), taking place five days after her betrothal and three days after Ruler 2's death, we see her marriage to Yo'nal Ahk II:

Transcription:
u-5-la-t(a) 1-? 14-UNIW-(wa) na-wa-j(a)

Transliteration:
u-ho' lat ju'n ? chanlaju'n uniiw nahwaj

Translation:
[It was] 5 days, on 1 Kib', 14 K'ank'in, she was adorned.

In contrast to the fancy wedding invitations sent out today, this clause exemplifies the short shrift that the Classic Maya gave to many seemingly important events. On Stela 3 we will see that Lady K'atun Ajaw indeed married Yo'nal Ahk II. It is interesting that the betrothal and wedding bracket the death of the previous ruler. Perhaps Yo'nal Ahk II needed to be married to be installed as ruler after his father's death. This might explain the otherwise strange connection of his death with the royal couple's marriage.

The final clause (I6–I12) may refer to the construction of this monument:

Transcription:
5-2-WINIK-ji 1-WINIK-HAB'-[pl.] 5-HA'(?) 19-SAK-SIHOM-(hi) u-b'a-h(i) ti-?-. . .-mi-. . . IXIK-WINIK-HAB'-AJAW IXIK-(na)-NAMAN-(ni)-[AJAW]

Transliteration:
ho' cha' winik-jii[y] ju'n winikhaab' ho' ha'(?) b'olonlaju'n sak siho'm(?) ub'aah ti-? ixik winikhaab' ajaw ixik namaan ajaw

Translation:
5 days, 2 months, [0 years,] and 1 score [later], on 5 Imix, 19 Sak, it is Lady K'atun Ajaw, Lady Ruler of La Florida's image, ?

The possessed noun *ub'aah* is in the place where we would expect to find a verb. Remember that there is no verb "to be" in Classic Mayan and that a noun standing alone can be the equivalent of the short stative sentence "it is this noun." In this case, we find "it is her image," referring to the main figure on this stela, Lady K'atun Ajaw. The glyph block at I11 is eroded and difficult to read. It begins with the preposition *ti-* and contains the syllable *mi*. It is interesting to note that this date is the latest on the inscription, except for the three-quarter-complete K'atun date. This last sentence may be saying simply, "This is Lady K'atun Ajaw on this day, as the stela was carved." In summary, the front of Piedras Negras, Stela 1 reads: "On 9.12.2.0.16 5 Kib', 14 Yaxk'in Lady K'atun Ajaw was born. About 12½ years later, on 9 Chuwen, 9 K'ank'in she was betrothed [to Yo'nal Ahk II] and 5 days later, on 1 Kib', 14 K'ank'in she was married [to him]."

6.1.2. Piedras Negras, Stela 3

You have worked out the chronology for the back of Piedras Negras, Stela 3 as an exercise in chapter 3. Here we will use this monument to trace the lives of Yo'nal Ahk II; his wife, Lady K'atun Ajaw; and their daughter, Lady Ju'n Tan Ahk. The inscription on Stela 3 covers the left, right, and back sides (**fig. 6.2**). Let's start on the left side, because it begins with a Long Count date. From A1 to B8, the Long Count date is given as 9.14.0.0.0 6 Ajaw, 13 Muwan (3 December 711 CE). The next date is found after the Distance Numbers in B14–B15 and the verb in A16. Normally the Calendar Round would be found directly after the Distance Number, but in this case the construction is irregular. The Distance Number reads 18 days, ? months, 7 years, and 2 score but does not give a Posterior or Anterior Date Indicator. The Calendar Round can be read as 2 ?, 10 Pax. If we know that the Long Count must end in either an 18 (if the Distance Number is added) or a 2 (if the Distance Number is subtracted), you can enter 9.?.?.?.2 2 ?, 10 Pax and 9.?.?.?.18 2 ?, 10 Pax into a calendar program. The second option is an impossible combination, so the program should return an error. Now we know that the Distance Number must be subtracted and the Tzolk'in day name is Ik' (which always corresponds to a Long Count ending in 2). Again using the calendar program, the only date with the 2 Ik', 10 Pax Calendar Round that is 2 score before the 9.14.0.0.0 K'atun ending is 9.11.12.7.2 (30 December 644 CE), making 10 the missing number of months in the Distance Number. The original 6 Ajaw, 13 Muwan is repeated in A19–B19 but may not be delineating a new clause (the next glyph is eroded). We know that the inscription now continues on the right side of the stela, because the back begins with its own Long Count, not a Distance Number. The first glyph on the right side is eroded, but a Distance Number follows in J1–J2: ? days, 3

Table 6.2. Piedras Negras, Stela 3 Chronology

Position:	Counts:	Calendar Round:	Gregorian:
(Sides)			
A1–B8	09.14.00.00.00 − 02.07[10]18	06 Ajaw 13 Muwan	3 December 711 CE
B14–B15	[09.11.12.07.02] + 01.02.03[11]	02 [Ik'] 10 Pax	30 December 664 CE
K1–I3	[09.12.14.10.13] + 02[08]	11 Ben 11 K'ank'in]	16 November 686 CE
I5–J6	[09.12.14.13.01] + 01.05.00[00]	[7 Imix] 19 Pax	3 January 687 CE
I8–J10	[09.13.19.13.01] + 04.19	11 [Imix] 14 Yax	26 August 711 CE
I15–J16	[09]14.00.00.00	06 Ajaw 13 Muwan	3 December 711 CE
(Back)			
C1–D7	[09]12.02.00.16 + 12.10.00	05 Kib' 14 Yaxk'in	5 July 674 CE
E1–F2	[09.12.14.10.16] + 01.01.11.10	01 Kib' 14 K'ank'in	19 November 686 CE
F4–E6	[09.13.16.04.06] + [03.08.15]	04 Kimi 14 Wo	19 March 708 CE
G1–H2	[09.13.19.13.01] + 04.19	11 Imix 14 Yax	26 August 711 CE
H6–H8	[09]14.00.00.00	06 Ajaw 13 Muwan	3 December 711 CE

months, 2 years, and 1 score later. The Posterior Date Indicator is eroded, but the silhouette clearly indicates that it must be **i-u-ti**, not **u-ti-ya.** This leads to an eroded Calendar Round in I3. Although the number of days in the Distance Number is eroded, we can see that it should be 11, 12, or 13. Using the available Distance Numbers, we can calculate three possible dates. But first let's see if we can work backward from the next date. The next Distance Number (in I5–J5) is 8 days and 2 months later (again using the silhouette of the Posterior Date Indicator), with a Calendar Round of 7 ?, 19 Pax. Using our known values from the last date, only one date works for this clause: 9.12.14.13.1, corresponding to 7 Imix (which is eroded in I6) and 19 Pax (which is readable in J6) (3 January 687 CE). Working backward, we now reach the date of 9.12.14.10.15 11 Ben, 11 K'ank'in (16 November 686 CE) for the preceding clause. The next Distance Number starts in I8 but is eroded. Glyphs J8–I9 give the rest of the Distance Number, leaving us with 1.5.0.?, followed by a Posterior Date Indicator in J9. The eroded Calendar Round follows in I10 and J10: 11 ?, 14 Yax. Using a calendar program, we can add the known values to our previous Long Count date and solve with the known Calendar Round data, leaving 9.13.19.13.01 11 Imix, 14 Yax (26 April 711 CE) as the only date that fits. The last Distance Number on the side is found in J15 and clearly reads 4.19, followed by the Posterior Date Indicator. Adding this to the previous Long Count, we reach the K'atun ending of 9.14.0.0.0 6 Ajaw, 11 Muwan (3 December 711 CE). Even if more glyphs were eroded, we could have used the clue in I17, which reads **u-14-WINIK-HAB'-[pl.],** *uchanlaju'n winikhaab',* meaning "[it is] his 14th K'atun [period ending]." You have already worked out the chronology of the back in chapter 3, so I will not describe it in detail; but the dates are given in **table 6.2.**

Using the chronology we have just worked out, let's split the inscription into phrases and translate them. Starting with the first phrase, which begins in A1 and runs through A14, the inscription reads:

6.1. PIEDRAS NEGRAS

Figure 6.2. Piedras Negras, Stela 3

tzi(?)-k(a)-HAB'-[pl.] 9-PIH 14-WINIKHAB' 0-HAB' 0-WINIK 0-K'IN 6-[AJAW] K'IN(?)-NAL u-TI'-... 17-HUL-li-y(a) 3-?-K'AL-[ja] ? u-[CH'OK-K'AB'A'] 20-10 13-[MUWAN] u-IL-w(a) 14-WINIK-HAB'-[pl.] yo-o-NAL a-AK [K'UHUL-yo-ki[b'(i)]-AJAW] a-... ... ...4-...-hi-?

Transliteration:
tziik(?) haab' b'olon pih chanlaju'n winikhaab' mih haab' mih winik mih k'ihn wak ajaw k'ihn(?)nal u-ti'... huklaju'n huliiy ox ? k'ahl[aj] u-ch'ok k'ab'a' winik laju'n oxlaju'n muwaan u-il-iw chanlaju'n winikhaab'... yo'nal ahk k'uhul yokib' ajaw a... ... ...chan...

Translation:
On the day 9 eras, 14 scores, 0 years, 0 months, and 0 days, on 6 Ajaw, Lord G9 is the reader [of the book], 17 days ago [the moon] arrived, 3 ? was bound, X2(?), its princely name, [of a] 30-day lunation, on the 13th of Muwan, Yo'nal Ahk, holy ruler of Piedras Negras [among other eroded titles], observed [the completion of] the 14th K'atun.

This opening clause simply says that Yo'nal Ahk II observed the ending of the 14th K'atun. That event may have included a ceremony in which the ruler publicly commemorated the end of this period. In other contexts, the verb *il,* "to observe," is used for rulers observing their vassals in a ceremony to add legitimacy to their subordinates and their relationship to them. Other verbs are also used to commemorate the end of the K'atun, as we will see later in this inscription.

The next phrase picks up in block B14 and continues through J1:

Transcription:
18-?-[WINK]-y(a) 7-HAB'-y(a) 2-WINIK-HAB'-[pl.] SIY-ya-j(a) 2-[IK'] 10-PAX... ... u-... 6-[AJAW] 13-MUWAN ...

Transliteration:
waxaklaju'n ? winik-iiy huk haab'-iiy cha' winikhaab'-[pl.] siyaj cha' ik' laju'n pax... ... u... wak [ajaw] oxlaju'n muwaan...

Translation:
18 days, ? months, 7 years, and 2 score ago he was born, on 2 Ik, 10 Pax ... on 6 Ajaw, 13 Muwan ... on 6 [Ajaw], 13 Muwan.

This clause is a little confusing because the verb is placed between the Distance Number and Calendar Round. It counts back the time between the 14th K'atun ending of the preceding clause to the ruler's date of birth. This is followed by an eroded phrase ending in the Calendar Round of the 14th K'atun ending; it may be a second reference to that K'atun ending. Simply stated, this clause reads: "about 47 years earlier Yo'nal Ahk II was born, before he commemorated the period ending on 6 Ajaw, 13 Muwan." The next clause begins on J1 and continues through J4:

Transcription:
[11]-3-WINIK-y(a) 2-HAB'-... 1-WINIK-HAB'-y(a)-[i-u-ti] [11-?-11-UNIW-(wa)] ... ... K'UHUL-AJAW-(wa)

Transliteration:
[b'uluk] ox winik-iiy cha' haab'... ju'n winikhaab'iiy [iuhti b'uluk ? b'uluk uniiw]... ... k'uhul ajaw

Translation:
Then it happened 11 days, 3 months, 2 years, and 1 score later, on 11 Ben, 11 K'ank'in ... ... the holy ruler.

Unfortunately the verb is eroded in this clause. It names a significant date in the history of Piedras Negras that takes place about 22 years after Yo'nal Ahk II's birth: the death of his father. We only know this from other contexts, however, because the verb and name are eroded. It probably read something like "about 22 years after [Yo'nal Ahk II's birth], Ruler 2 [his father], holy ruler, died." Logically, after the father dies, the son must be installed as the new ruler: precisely what we see in the next clause from I5–J7:

Transcription:
8-2-WINIK-y(a) [i-u]-ti 7-[HA'(?)] 19-PAX-[pl.] ...-AJAW yo-...-NAL ...

Transliteration:
waxak cha' winik-iiy iuhti huk [ha' (?)] b'olonlaju'n pax... ajaw yo[']nal...

Translation:
Then it happened 8 days and 2 months later, on 7 Imix, 19 Pax, ... ruler Yo'nal ...

Although the inscription is eroded, we know from context that this is probably Yo'nal Ahk II's ascension, reading something like "about 2 months later, Yo'nal Ahk II became the ruler of Piedras Negras." The next clause from I8 to I15d is largely eroded:

Transcription:
... 0-5-HAB'-y(a) 1-WINIK-HAB'-y(a) i-u-ti 11-[HA'(?)] 14-YAX-SIHOM(?)-(ma) ...-u-... 1-... ... ... KOJ-...

Transliteration:
... mih ho' haab'-iiy ju'n winikhaab'-iiy iuhti b'uluk [ha'(?)] 14 yax siho'm ... u ... ju'n... ... ... koj...

Translation:
Then it happened [0 days], 0 months, 5 years, and 1 score later, on 11 [Imix], 14 Yax ... ... puma ...

This passage is eroded beyond recognition, but we will see this date again on the back of the monument and reconstruct some of its meaning there. We know that the passage refers to Yo'nal Ahk II because *koj*, "puma," is part of his complete regal name.

The next clause starts on J15 and finishes the rest of the side:

Transcription:
19-4-WINIK-y(a) [i-u]-ti 6-[AJAW]-13-MUWAN u-14-WINIK-HAB'-[pl.] u-K'AL-w(a)-TUN-(ni) ... K'UHUL-[yo-ki[b'(i)]]-AJAW-(wa) ... ma-5-AK'AB'(?)-NAH ...-ti ...

Transliteration:
b'olonlaju'n chan winik-iiy iuhti wak [ajaw] oxlaju'n muwaan u-chanlaju'n winikhaab'-[pl.] uk'alaw tuun ... k'uhul yokib' ajaw ... ma ho' ak'ab'(?) naah ... ti ...

Translation:
Then it happened 19 days and 4 months later, on 6 Ajaw, 13 Muwan [it was] its 14th K'atun, [Yo'nal Ahk II], the holy ruler of Piedras Negras, bound the stone . . . the "not-5-darkness" (?) house . . .

This final clause brings us back to the 14th K'atun ending and the "stone-binding" ritual performed to commemorate it. This may refer to the ritual bundling or wrapping of cloth around important stelae at Maya sites. Apparently this specific binding was done in association with a particular house, named in J19. In summary, the inscription on the left and right sides of Piedras Negras, Stela 3 reads: "On 9.14.0.0.0, the 14th K'atun completion was witnessed by Yo'nal Ahk II, about 47 years after he was born on 2 Ik', 10 Pax. About 22 years after his birth, his father died on 11 Ben, 11 K'ank'in. About 2 months later Yo'nal Ahk II became the ruler of Piedras Negras. About 25 years later [eroded action] took place. About 5 months after that, Yo'nal Ahk II commemorated the completion of the 14th K'atun by binding a stone."

Now we can turn to the back of Piedras Negras, Stela 3, which starts with a Long Count date. The first clause runs from C1 to C10:

Transcription:
tzi-k(a)-HAB'-[pl.] 9-PIH 12-WINIKHAB' 2-HAB' 0-WINIK 16-K'IN 5-? NAH-2 . . . -HUN-(na) 7-20-(li)-HUL-li-y(a) 2-?-K'AL-j(a) 3-?-K'UH-K'AB'A'(?) 20-(ki)-9 14-YAX-K'IN-(ni) SIY-ya-j(a) IXIK-WINIK-HAB'-AJAW [IXIK]-na-MAN-[(ni)-AJAW]

Transliteration:
tziik haab' b'olon pih lajchan winikhaab' cha' haab' mih winik mih k'ihn ho' ? naah cha . . . hu'n huk winik huliiy cha' ? k'ahlaj ox ? k'uh k'ab'a' winik b'olon chanlaju'n yax k'ihn siyaj ixik winikhaab' ajaw ixik namaan ajaw

Translation:
On the day 9 eras, 12 scores, 2 years, 0 months, and 16 days, on 5 Kib', Lord G7 is the [reader] of the book, 27 days ago [the moon] arrived, 2 ? was bound, X2, its holy name, [of a] 29-day lunation, on the 14th of Yaxk'in, Lady K'atun Ajaw, Lady Ruler of La Florida, was born.

The Long Count and supplementary information is followed by the "birth" verb, *siy*, and the name *ixik winikhaab' ajaw*, "Lady K'atun Ajaw." As we have seen, she possesses another title that describes her city of origin: **IXIK-na-MAN-ni-AJAW,** "Lady Ruler of La Florida." This clause reads: "On this day, Lady K'atun Ajaw was born."

The next clause begins at E1 and continues through E4:

Transcription:
0-10-WINIK-ji-y(a) 12-HAB'-y(a) i-u-ti-1-? 14-UNIW-(ni-wa) na-wa-j(a) IXIK-WINIK-HAB'-[pl.] IXIK-na-MAN-(ni)-AJAW-yi-chi-NAL-(la) K'INICH-yo-NAL-AK

Transliteration:
mih laju'n winik-jiiy lajchan haab'-iiy iuhti ju'n ? chanlaju'n uniiw nahwaj ixik winik haab'-[pl.] ixik namaan ajaw yichnal k'inich yo'nal ahk

Translation:
Then it happened 0 days, 10 months, and 12 years later, 1 Kib', 14 K'ank'in Lady K'atun Ajaw, Lady Ruler of La Florida, was adorned [by] K'inich Yo'nal Ahk II.

This "adorning" event took place 12½ years after Lady K'atun Ajaw's birth. This event appears to be the marriage of Yo'nal Ahk II to Lady K'atun Ajaw.

The marriage was fruitful, as shown in the next passage, beginning on F1 and continuing through F7:

Transcription:
10-11-WINIK-y(a)-1-HAB'-y(a) 1-WINIK-HAB'-y(a)-i-u-ti 4-CHAM 14-IK'-AT SIY-ya-j(a) IXIK-1-ta-n(a)-a-k(u) IXIK-K'IN-(ni)-AJAW

Transliteration:
laju'n b'uluk winik-iiy ju'n haab'-iiy ju'n winikhaab'-iiy iuhti chan cham chanlaju'n ik'at siyaj ixik ju'n tan ahk ixik k'ihn ajaw

Translation:
Then it happened 10 days, 11 months, 1 year, and 1 score later, on 4 Kimi, 14 Wo Lady Ju'n Tan Ahk, Lady Sun Ruler, was born.

About 21½ years after their "adorning" event, Yo'nal Ahk II and Lady K'atun Ajaw's daughter, whose name means "Lady Cherished Turtle," was born.

We can now return to the event mentioned on the right side of the stela in eroded glyphs from 11 Imix, 14 Yax:

Transcription:
15-8-WINIK-y(a)-3-HAB'-y(a) i-u-ti 11-HA'(?) 14-YAX-SIHOM-(ma) u-CH'AM-w(a)-te-m(u) IXIK-WINIK-AJAW-(wa) IXIK-(na)-NAMAN-(ni)-AJAW TZUTZ-y(i) u-5-tu-k(u) 1-WINIK-HAB'-la-t(a) ti-AJAW-le-yo-(o) NAL-a-k(u)

Transliteration:
ho'laju'n waxak winik-iiy ox haab'-iiy iuhti b'uluk ha'(?) chanlaju'n yax siho'm u-ch'am-aw teem ixik winik ajaw ixik namaan ajaw tzutzuy u-ho' tuk ju'n winikhaab' lat ti ajawle[l] yo' nal ahk

Translation:
Then it happened 15 days, 8 months, 3 years later, on 11 Imix, 14 Yax Lady K'atun Ajaw, Lady Ruler of La Florida, took the throne, Yo'nal Ahk II's 5th year and 1st score in rulership got completed.

This clause, running from G1 to G6, has two phrases. In the first, Lady K'atun Ajaw takes the throne. In the second, Yo'nal Ahk II notes his 25th year anniversary of attaining the office of ruler on this same date.

Finally, about five months later, the inscription is closed, just as it was opened, with the commemoration of the 14th K'atun:

Transcription:
19-4-WINIK-ji-y(a) i-u-ti 6-AJAW 13-MUWAN-(ni) TZUTZ-y(i) u-14-WINIK-HAB'-[pl.]

Transliteration:
b'olonlaju'n chan winik-jiiy iuhti wak ajaw oxlaju'n muwaan tzutzuy u-chanlaju'n winikhaab'-[pl.]

Translation:
Then it happened 19 days and 4 months later, on 6 Ajaw, 13 Muwan, the 14th K'atun got completed.

Table 6.3. Piedras Negras, Stela 8 Chronology

Position:	Counts:	Calendar Round:	Gregorian:
(Sides)			
A1–B8	09.11.12.07.02	02 Ik' 10 Pax	30 December 664 CE
	+ 01.02.03.09		
A17–A19	[09.12.14.10.11]	09 Chuwen 09 K'ank'in	14 November 686 CE
	+ 02		
B24–N2	[09.12.14.10.13]	11 [B'en] 11 K'ank'in	16 November 686 CE
(Front)			
G2–H2	09.12.14.13.01	07 Imix 19 Pax	3 January 687 CE

In summary, the back of Piedras Negras Stela 3 reads: "On 9.12.2.0.16 Lady K'atun Ajaw was born. About 12½ years later, Yo'nal Ahk II married Lady K'atun Ajaw. About 21½ years later, Lady Ju'n Tan Ahk was born. Three years later, Lady K'atun Ajaw received a throne and Yo'nal Ahk II completed his 25th year as ruler. Almost 5 months later, the 14th K'atun was completed."

6.1.3. Piedras Negras, Stela 8 (Partial)

To illustrate the repetition of significant events on Maya monuments, let's look briefly at parts of Piedras Negras, Stela 8 (**fig. 6.3**). In just a few sentences, we will see the birth, betrothal, and ascension of Yo'nal Ahk II and the death of his father. This monument is heavily eroded, so here I will only cherry-pick the pertinent clauses, most of which come from the left side. The chronology, shown in **table 6.3**, starts with the ISIG in A1, with the Long Count continuing through B9: 9.11.12.7.0 2 Ik', 10 Pax (30 December 664 CE). We have seen this date before and recognize it as Yo'nal Ahk II's birth date. The Distance Number is located in A17–A19, moving 9 days, 3 months, 2 years, and 1 score forward in time to 9.12.14.10.11 9 Chuwen, 9 K'ank'in (14 November 686 CE), which we recognize as Yo'nal Ahk II and Lady K'atun Ajaw's betrothal date. Two days later, as shown in B21–B22, we reach the date 9.12.14.10.13 11 B'en, 11 K'ank'in (16 November 686 CE), which we saw before as the death date of Yo'nal Ahk II's father, Ruler 2. Jumping to the front of the inscription, we can barely make out the date of Yo'nal Ahk II's ascension. The verb was eroded on Stela 3; the date is eroded here, but enough of the inscription is intact to reconstruct the date as 9.12.14.13.1 7 Imix, 19 Pax (3 January 687 CE). Although we have already seen these events, let's look at the different ways in which they are expressed on this stela.

The first clause starts at A1 and continues through B16. It is unusually long, including a Long Count and more than one event:

Transcription:
tzi(?)-k(a)-HAB'-[pl.] 9-PIH 12-WINIK-HAB' 12-HAB' 7-WINIK 2-K'IN 2-IK' ? TI'-HUN-(na) 6-HUL-li-y(a) 5-?-K'AL-ja ? ch'o[k(o)]-K'AB'A' 20-10 10-PAX SIY-ya-j(a) ch'o[k(o)] ? K'UHUL-yo-ki[b'(i)]-AJAW-(wa) ya-AL [fem.]- . . . IXIK-SAK- . . . u-MIJIN(?)-(na) AJAW(?)-li ?-[K'AN]AK K'UHUL-yo-ki[b'(i)]-AJAW-(wa) . . .-hu-li-y(a) ch'o-k(o) IXIK-MAN-(ni)-AJAW ya-? B'ALAM[. . .]-ji ch'o- . . .

Transliteration:
tziik(?) haab'-[pl.] b'olon pih lajchan winikhaab' lajchan haab' huk winik cha' k'ihn cha' ik' ? ti' hu'n wak huliiy ho' ? k'ahlaj ? ch'ok k'ab'a' winik laju'n laju'n pax sihyaj ch'ok ?

6.1. PIEDRAS NEGRAS

Figure 6.3. Piedras Negras, Stela 8

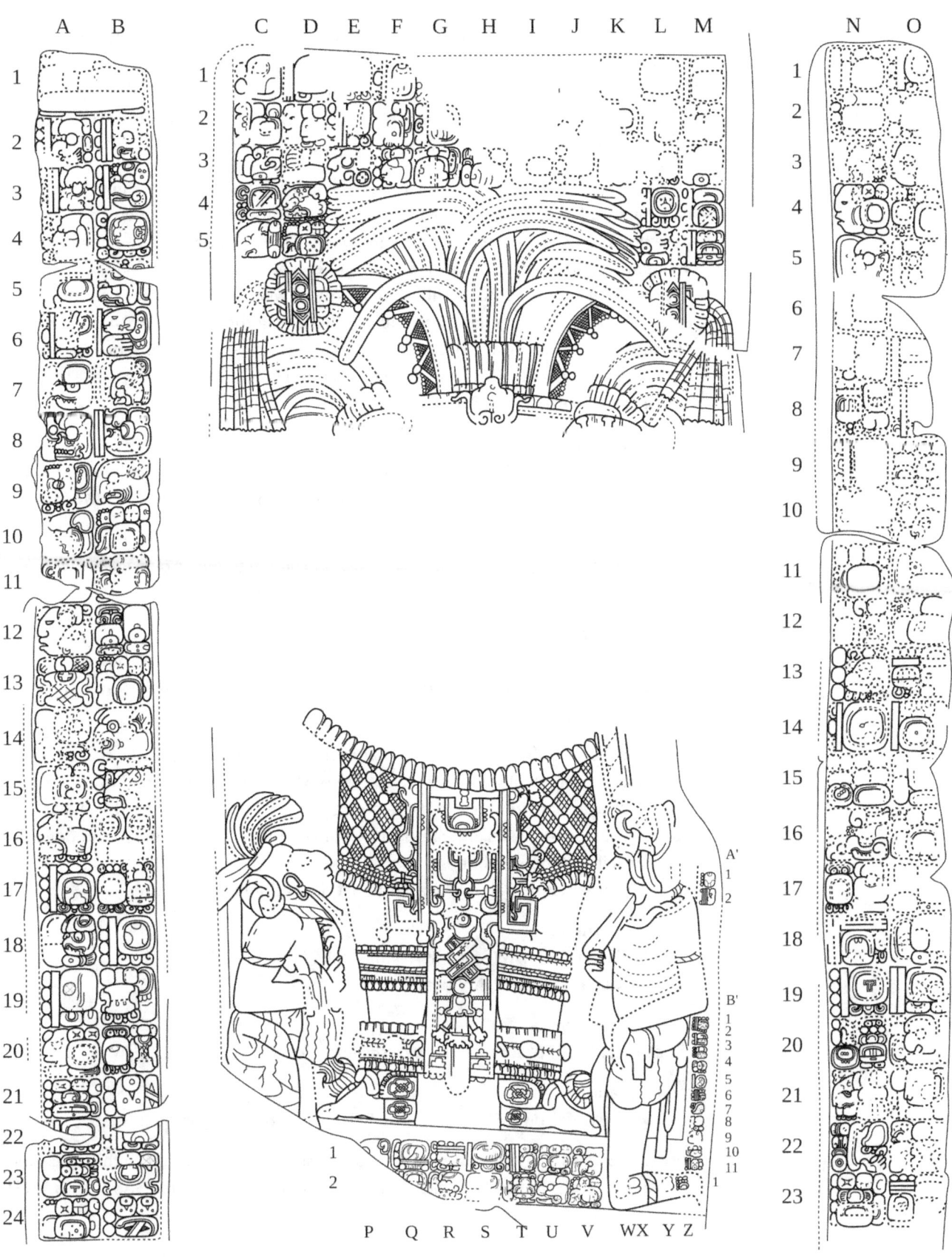

k'uhul yokib' ajaw y-al [fem.]-... ixik sak... u-mijiin ajaw(?) k'an ahk k'uhul yokib' ajaw ... huliiy ch'ok ixik [na]maan ajaw ya-? b'ahlam(?)... j ch'o...

Translation:
On the day 9 eras, 12 score, 12 years, 7 months, 2 days 2 Ik', G6 was the reader of the book, 6 days ago [the moon] arrived, 5 ? was bound, X5, its princely name, [of a] 30 day lunation, on 10 Pax [predynastic name of Yo'nal Ahk II], holy ruler of Piedras Negras, was born, son of the mother . . . Lady White . . . , son of father Ruler 2; the youth (heir) Lady Ruler of La Florida, ? Jaguar ?, arrived.

These clauses recount the birth of Yo'nal Ahk II, using his preregnal name, which may have been *koj*, "puma." It also names his mother, whose name is eroded here but may have been Lady White Bird. His father (whom we already know) is also named. Finally, an interesting bit of foreshadowing is given here, as a female ruler from La Florida arrives on Yo'nal Ahk II birthday. This is not his future wife, who would not be born for another ten years, but may have been her mother or another royal woman from the site of *namaan*. The relationship between these sites would be further strengthened by the later marriage between this woman's daughter and Ruler 2's son.

The next clause (A7–A21), fittingly, notes this betrothal:

Transcription:
9-3-WINIK-y(a) 2-HAB'-y(a)-1-WINIK-HAB'-y(a) i-u-ti 9-? 9-UNIW-(wa) ma-AK-ja-ji-y(a) IXIK-na-MAN-(ni)-AJAW u-KAB'-ji-y(a) [K'AN]AK 4-WINIK-HAB'-AJAW-(wa)

Transliteration:
b'olon ox winik-iiy cha' haab'-iiy ju'n winikhaab'-iiy iuti b'olon ? b'olon uniiw mahkaj-iiy ixik namaan ajaw uk'ab-jiiy k'an ahk chan winikhaab' ajaw

Translation:
Then it happened 9 days, 3 months, 2 years, and 1 score later, on 9 Chuwen, 9 K'ank'in Lady Ruler of La Florida was betrothed when Ruler 2, the 4-K'atun ruler, had supervised it.

This passage contains interesting verbal morphology, as discussed in chapter 5. We know that Yo'nal Ahk II was about twenty-two when he was betrothed to Lady K'atun Ajaw. In this version, we learn that the betrothal was directly supervised by Ruler 2. As both the sacred and secular head of state, Ruler 2 may have performed the betrothal rites himself from his deathbed.

In the next clause (B21–A24) we learn that he died shortly thereafter:

Transcription:
2-la-t(a) [11-? 11-UNIW]-(wa) [K'A'-y(i)]-u-SAK[?]-IK'-li [K'AN]AK K'UHUL-yo-ki[b'(i)]-AJAW-(wa)

Transliteration:
cha' lat b'uluk ? b'uluk uniiw k'a'ay u sak ? ik'il k'an ahk k'uhul yokib' ajaw

Translation:
Two days later, on 11 B'en, 11 K'ank'in, Ruler 2's white wind got diminished.

Just as in English, the Maya often used euphemisms to express death. In this case, Ruler 2's "white breath" (possibly "white flower breath" if the questioned **SAK** infix is **NICH**, read *nich,* meaning "flower") got diminished. Note the mediopassive transitive construction, which removes the actor who caused this action.

Let's now jump to the front of the stela and the ascension clause found from G2 to H3:

Transcription:
7-[HA'(?) 19-PAX] JOY[. . .]-ja ti-AJAW-le

Transliteration:
huk [ha'(?) b'olonlaju'n pax] johyaj ti-ajawle[l]

Translation:
On 7 [Imix, 19 Pax] he was bound into rulership.

Unfortunately, the front is eroded and we do not have the complete date; but from the context and previous inscriptions, we know that Yo'nal Ahk II must be the subject of this sentence.

In summary, the most legible parts of this inscription read: "On 9.11.12.7.2 Yo'nal Ahk II was born, son of Lady White Bird and Ruler 2, who was visited by a Lady Ruler from La Florida. About 22 years later, Lady K'atun Ajaw was betrothed [to Yo'nal Ahk II], which was supervised by Ruler 2, 2 days before he died . . . About 2 months later, Yo'nal Ahk II was bound into rulership."

6.2. PALENQUE: DYNASTY AND K'INICH JANAAB' PAKAL

The best-known ruler from the site of Palenque is K'inich Janaab' Pakal. He is one of the longest-lived rulers that we know of, living for over eighty years. His reign is also interesting in that his father did not precede him as king. For the most part, Maya rulers seemed to prefer passing rulership directly to their sons. This was not always possible, however. Pakal inherited the right to rule at Palenque from his mother, while his father's pedigree was not mentioned with any great detail. In other inscriptions not discussed here, Pakal draws a comparison between his divine right to rule and patron deities who founded the site of Palenque thousands of years earlier, in the mythical past. In the following inscriptions, we will see a list of previous rulers found etched on the side of Pakal's sarcophagus lid and some events from Pakal's life from the inscription found on Palenque's Hieroglyphic Stairway. Again, feel free to try to work out the chronology and translation of these inscriptions before reading the following sections.

6.2.1. Palenque, Sarcophagus Lid

This inscription, shown in **figure 6.4**, comes from the edge of a large limestone lid for the ruler Pakal's sarcophagus. The front of this lid is well known in popular culture. It depicts Pakal falling down into or rising up out of a large Earth-monster, with a world-tree sprouting from the same spot. The inscription around the edge traces over 100 years of the local royal dynasty (**table 6.4**). There are no Long Count dates to anchor the Calendar Rounds in time; but other clues such as period endings and the linear progression of rulers can allow us to re-create these dates. The first date, in positions 1 and 2, reads 8 Ajaw, 13 Pop, a date that we know from many contexts as Pakal's birth date (9.8.9.13.0; 24 March 603 CE). This date is so important that the Long Count would be known by anybody reading this text (much like George Washington's birthday for a professional American historian). The next date (4–5) jumps forward to Pakal's death on 6 Etz'nab', 11 Yax (9.12.11.5.18; 29 August 683 CE), another date with which everybody was familiar. Now we jump back in time, although it would be impossible to know this right away. One way to attack this problem is to start at the end, with Pakal's mother and father, and work backward, calculating the date for the death of each consecutive ruler. Otherwise, the Calendar Rounds are floating in time; although we know the relative distance between them (5 Kab'an, 5 Mak to the next 7 Kib', 4 K'ayab' is always 2.0.13.19), we do not know where the dates are in absolute time unless we know on which date the inscription started. Another way would be to identify the period endings and use these dates to anchor the surrounding dates. In 24 and 45 we see the *u-chum-tuun* phrase, meaning that a stela commemorating a period ending was erected on these days. Using a calendar program, we find that 9.7.0.0.0 (5 December 573 CE) is a period ending matching the Calendar Round 7 Ajaw, 3 K'ank'in, found in positions 22–23. Also, 9.10.0.0.0 (25 January 633 CE) matches the 1 Ajaw, 8 K'ayab' Calendar Round in 43–44. Using these dates, we can work out the remaining Calendar Rounds as shown in **table 6.4**. Remember that this is a king-list and should therefore be in chronological order (each king's death should be after his predecessors but before his successors). The only remaining tricky spot in this inscription is the dates from 42 to 46. A Tzolk'in is followed by another Tzolk'in and Haab', a *u-chum-tuun* phrase, and then another Haab'. A subclause is being stuffed in the space between the Tzolk'in and Haab' of the Calendar Round of the death of Pakal's mother. The first Tzolk'in matches the last

6.2. PALENQUE

Figure 6.4. Palenque, Pakal's Sarcophagus Lid

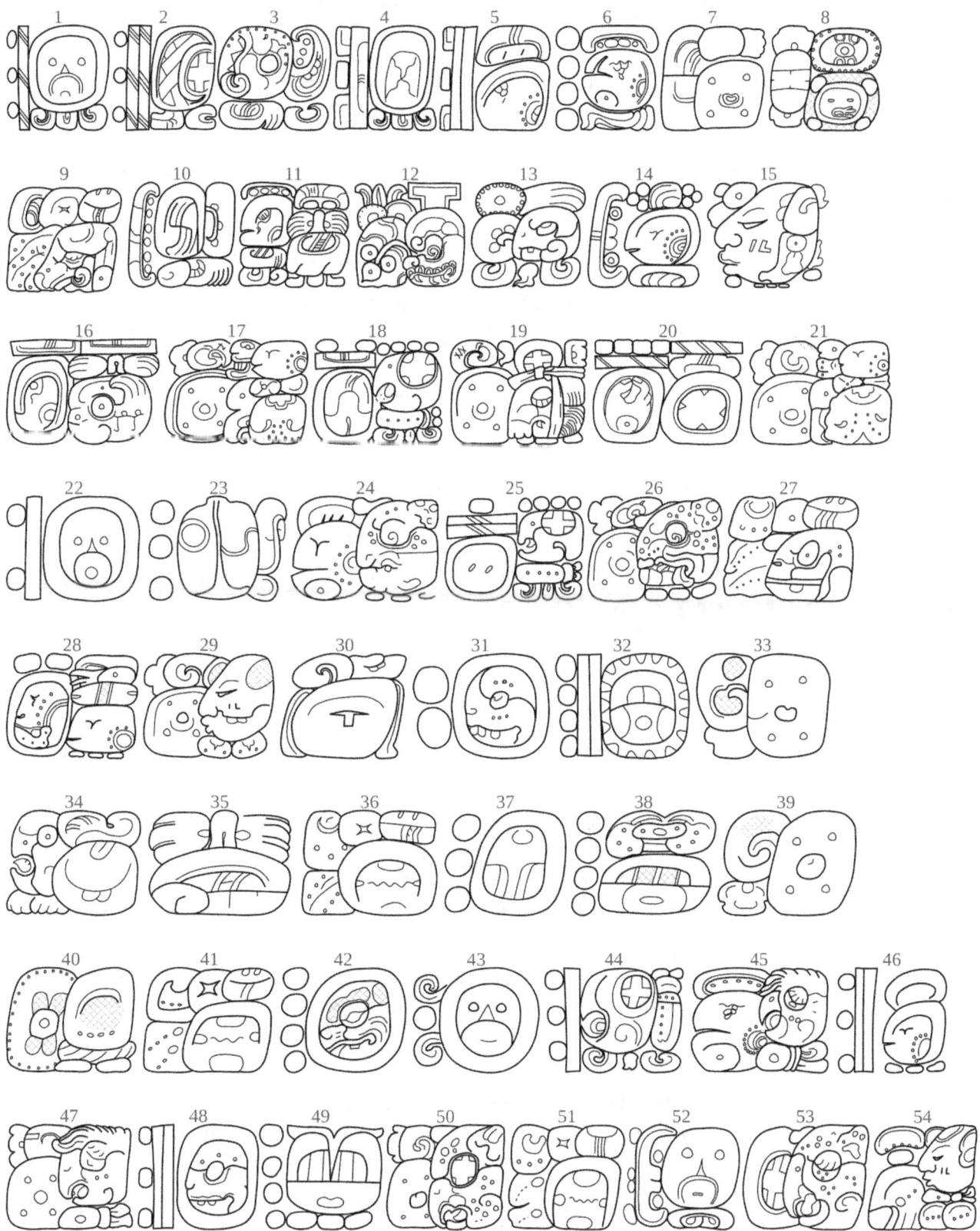

212 PUTTING IT ALL TOGETHER

Table 6.4. Palenque, Pakal's Sarcophagus Lid Chronology

Position:	Counts:	Calendar Round:	Gregorian:
1–2	[09.08.09.13.00] [+ 04.02.10.18]	08 Ajaw 13 Pop	24 March 603 CE
4–5	[09.12.11.05.18] [− 08.01.01.01]	06 Etz'nab 11 Yax	29 August 683 CE
16	[09.04.10.04.17] [+ 02.00.13.19]	05 Kab'an 05 Mak	29 November 524 CE
18	[09.06.11.00.16] [+ 05.09.11]	07 Kib 04 K'ayab	6 February 565 CE
20	[09.06.16.10.07] [+ 03.07.13]	09 Manik' 05 Yaxk'in	21 July 570 CE
22–23	[09.07]00.00.00 [+ 09.05.05]	07 Ajaw 03 K'ank'in	5 December 573 CE
25	[09.07.09.05.05] [+ 01.02.01.07]	11 Chikchan 03* K'ayab	1 February 583 CE
28	[09.08.11.06.12] [+ 07.15.14]	02 Eb' 00 Mak†	5 November 604 CE
31–32	[09.08.19.04.06] [− 7.15]	02 Kimi 14 Mol	9 August 612 CE
37–38	[09.08.18.14.11] [+ 01.01.03.09]	03 Chuwen 04 Wayeb	7 March 612 CE
43–44	[09.10.]00.00.00 [+ 07.13.05]	01 Ajaw 08 K'ayab	25 January 633 CE
42–46	[09.10.07.13.05] [+ 02.06.01]	04 Chikchan 13 Yax	10 September 640 CE
48–49	[09.10.10.01.06]	13 Kimi 04 Pax	30 December 642 CE

* The inscription reads 4 K'ayab.
† The inscription reads 20 Keh.

Haab', and the central Tzolk'in and Haab' are one Calendar Round commemorating a period ending.

Let's look at this inscription clause by clause. The beginning of the first phrase (1–15) is easiest to understand and contains the most relevant information:

Transcription:
8-AJAW 13-K'AN-?-w(a) SIY-ja-ji-y(a) 6-? 11-YAX-SIHOM(?) 4-u-CHUM[TUN]-(ni)
i-OCH-b'i K'INICH-JANAB'-PAKAL K'UHUL-AJAW u-TZ'AK-b'u-y(i) u-CH'AB-ji-?-
u-ma tzi(?)-?-CH'AN-NAH pa-b'u-y(i) u-?-TUN-li IXIK(?)-la

Transliteration:
*waxak ajaw oxlaju'n k'anjalaw(?) siyaj-iiy wak ? b'uluk yax siho'm(?) chan u chum-tuun
i-och b'ih k'inich janaab' pakal k'uhul ajaw utz'akb'uy uch'ab? ? ? chan naah pab'uy
utuunil ixik(?)*

Translation:
Before, on 8 Ajaw, 11 Pop he was born, and on 6 Etz'nab', 11 Yax, in his 4th K'atun, Sun-Faced [bird name] Shield, the holy ruler, entered the road [died], it got set in order ? [at the (?)] snake house ?, his stela ?

Here we have interesting verbal morphology. The first part of the phrase states that Pakal was born on 8 Ajaw, 11 Pop. The verb is *siyaj-iiy,* suggesting that this action is considered to have taken place well before the following one. Instead of translating it "On 8 Ajaw, 11 Pop he was born. On 6 Etz'nab', 11 Yax" as if the verb had been simply *siyaj*, we are forced to indicate the temporal relationship between these two clauses by adding the word "before" (or "earlier") and making it a two-clause sentence instead of two separate ones. The second part of the phrase includes *u-chum-tuun,* but it is used differently here, commemorating Pakal's fourth K'atun of life. Pakal was eighty-three when he died, an action that follows directly after this statement about his age. Throughout the inscription the euphemism *och b'ih,* "enter the road," is used to describe the death of each ruler. The remainder of the clause is difficult to parse but may discuss Pakal's ritual role, his place in the local dynasty, and a local building. The inscription now jumps back over 150 years to the third known ruler at Palenque, Ahku'ul Mo' Naahb' (Turtle-like Macaw Pool) (16–17):

Transcription:
5-?-5-ma-k(a) OCH-b'i-a-ku-MO'-NAB'

Transliteration:
ho' ? ho' mak och b'ih ahku['ul] mo' naahb'

Translation:
On 5 Kawak, 5 Mak Turtle-like Macaw Pool entered the road [died].

This simple statement of Ahku'ul Mo' Naahb's death contains no surprises or irregularities. The same is true of the information on the next two rulers (18–19 and 20–21):

Transcription:
7-?-4-[KAN]a-si-y(a) OCH-b'i-K'AN-(na)-JOY[CHITAM]-(ma)

Transliteration:
huk ? kanasiiy och b'ih k'an joy chitam

Translation:
On 7 Kib', 4 K'ayab Precious[/Yellow] Bound Peccary entered the road [died].

and

Transcription:
9-chi-5-YAX-K'IN OCH-b'i-a-ku-MO'-NAB'

Transliteration:
b'olon chi ho' yaxk'in och bi'h ahku['ul] mo' naahb'

Translation:
On 9 Manik, 5 Yaxk'in Turtle-like Macaw Pool entered the road [died].

We now see the commemoration of the 9.7.0.0.0 K'atun by Snake-Jaguar, who then shuffled off this mortal coil in the second clause of this phrase (22–27):

Transcription:
7-AJAW-3-UNIW-(wa) u-CHUM[TUN]-CHAN[B'ALAM]-(ma) 11-?-CHAN-4-[KAN]a-si-y(a) OCH-b'i-CHAN[B'ALAM]-(ma) K'UHUL-B'AK-AJAW

Transliteration:
huk ajaw ox uniiw u-chum-tuun chan b'ahlam b'uluk ?chan chan kanasiiy och b'ih chan b'ahlam k'uhul b'aak ajaw

Translation:
On 7 Ajaw, 3 K'ank'in Snake-Jaguar's stone [stela] was seated; on 11 Chikchan, 4 K'ayab Snake-Jaguar, holy ruler of Palenque, entered the road [died].

Snake-Jaguar is followed by his daughter, Lady Ik'nal (Wind-Place), who appears to be the first ruling queen of Palenque:

Transcription:
2-?-CHUM-CHAK-SIHOM(?)-(ma) OCH-b'i-IXIK[OL]-(la) IK'-NAL

Transliteration:
cha' ? chum chak siho'm(?) och b'ih ixik o'hl ik' nal

Translation:
On 2 Eb', 0 Keh(?) Lady Wind-Place-Heart entered the road [died].

Although rulers often passed their office through the male line (patrilineal), this is an example of a few instances in which women formed a link in the chain of rulership. We will see this again with Pakal's mother. There is a slight date discrepancy here. The Haab' is clearly Keh, but the superfixed element is difficult to see. It may indeed be the *chum* glyph, indicating a 0 Keh date, but we know that it should be the beginning of the next month, Mak. This may be another glyph indicating the end of a month, but it is difficult to read.

Two more deaths follow:

Transcription:
2-CHAM(?) 14-mo-l(o) OCH-b'i a-je-ne-OL ma-t(a) K'UHUL-B'AK-AJAW

Transliteration:
cha' cham(?) chanlaju'n mol och b'ih ajen(?) o'hl mat k'uhul b'aak ajaw

Translation:
On 2 Kimi, 14 Mol ?[Awakened(?)]-Heart Cormorant, holy ruler of Palenque, entered the road [died].

and

Transcription:
3-? 4-WAY-HAB' OCH-b'i PAKAL-(pa-ka-la) K'UHUL-B'AK-AJAW

Transliteration:
ox ? chan wayhaab' och b'ih pakal k'uhul b'ak ajaw

Translation:
On 3 Chuwen, 4 Wayab' Shield, holy ruler of Palenque, entered the road [died].

Now we come to Pakal's parents. First, his mother's death date is interrupted in an irregular fashion:

Transcription:
4-?-CHAN 1-AJAW 8-[KAN]a-si-y(a) u-CHUM[TUN]-K'UK'-SAK 13-YAX-SIHOM(?)-(ma) OCH-b'i K'UK' SAK

Transliteration:
chan ?chan ju'n ajaw waxak kanasiiy u-chum-tuun k'uk' sak oxlaju'n yax siho'm(?) och b'ih k'uk' sak

Translation:
On 4 Chikchan, 13 Yax Resplendent[/White] Quetzal entered the road [died], having had her stone [stela] seated on 1 Ajaw, 8 K'ayab.

We can imagine the stonecutters having already carved the 4 Chikchan glyph when the scribal artist caught the mistake, saying, "Oh no, we forgot her period ending, *u-chum-tuun* statement! Where can we add it?" Or perhaps they wanted to break up the monotonous repetition with something novel.

At any rate, Pakal's father is mentioned next, described in poignant terms:

Transcription:
13-CHAM(?) 4-PAX-(ma) OCH-b'i-[KAN]MO'[HIX] K'UHUL-B'AK-AJAW u-AJAW-le(?) K'AN-MO'[HIX] u-1-ta-na-SAK-ku-k(u)

Transliteration:
ox cham(?) chan pax och b'ih kan mo' hix k'uhul b'aak ajaw u-ajawlel(?) k'an mo' hix u-ju'n tan sak k'u[k']

Translation:
On 3 Kimi, 4 Pax Precious[/Yellow] Macaw Jaguar, holy ruler of Palenque, entered the road [died]; it was Precious[/Yellow] Macaw Jaguar's rulership(?); he was Lady Resplendent[/White] Quetzal's beloved one.

The last phrase is intriguing. We do not know much about Pakal's father, K'an Mo' Hix (Precious Macaw Jaguar), but he is described here as the "beloved" of Pakal's mother. Usually we see wives labeled as *ju'n tan* ("beloved") or *'it* ("companion"), but it is unusual to see such an overt statement of endearment from a woman.

6.2.2. Palenque, Hieroglyphic Stairway (Partial)

Palenque's Hieroglyphic Stairway mentions events in Pakal's life and Itzamnaaj B'ahlam's capture (shown in **fig. 6.5**). As usual, we'll start with the chronology (**table 6.5**). This inscription utilizes head-variant numbers for the initial Long Count date (A1–B4) of 9.8.9.13.0 8 Ajaw, 13 Pop (24 March 603 CE), a touchstone date for Palenque, because it is Pakal's birthday. The Distance Number follows in B5, moving us forward 8 days, 9 months, and 12 years to 9.9.2.4.8 5 Lamat, 1 Mol (27 July 615 CE), the date of Pakal's accession (A1–A6).

Transcription:
tzi(?)-k(a)-HAB'-[pl.] B'OLON-PIH WAXAK-WINIKHAB' B'OLON-HAB' OXLAJU'N-WINIK-(ki) MIH-K'IN-[ni] WAXAK-AJAW OXLAJU'N-[K'AN-?-w(a)] SIY-ja-y(a) K'INICH-PET(?)-NAL pa-ka-l(a) K'UHUL-B'AK-AJAW 8-9-WINIK-12-HAB'-[HO'-EK'-JUN-mo[l(o)]] K'AL-ja-HUN tu-u-B'AH K'INICH-JANAB' pa-ka-l(a)

Transliteration:
tziik(?) haab' b'olon pih waxak winikhaab' b'olon haab' oxlaju'n winik mih k'ihn waxak ajaw oxlaju'n k'anjalaw(?) siyaj-iiy k'inich pet nal pakal k'uhul b'aak ajaw waxak b'olon winik lajchan haab' ho' ek' ju'n mol k'ahlaj hu'n t-u-b'aah k'inich janaab' pakal

Translation:
On the day 9 era, 8 score, 9 months, 13 months, and 0 days, 8 Ajaw, 13 Pop, Sun-Faced Round-Place Shield, holy ruler of Palenque, was born 8 days, 9 months, and 12 years before, on [5 Lamat, 1 Mol] the headdress was bound onto Sun-Faced [bird name] Shield's head.

216 PUTTING IT ALL TOGETHER

Figure 6.5. Palenque, Hieroglyphic Stairway

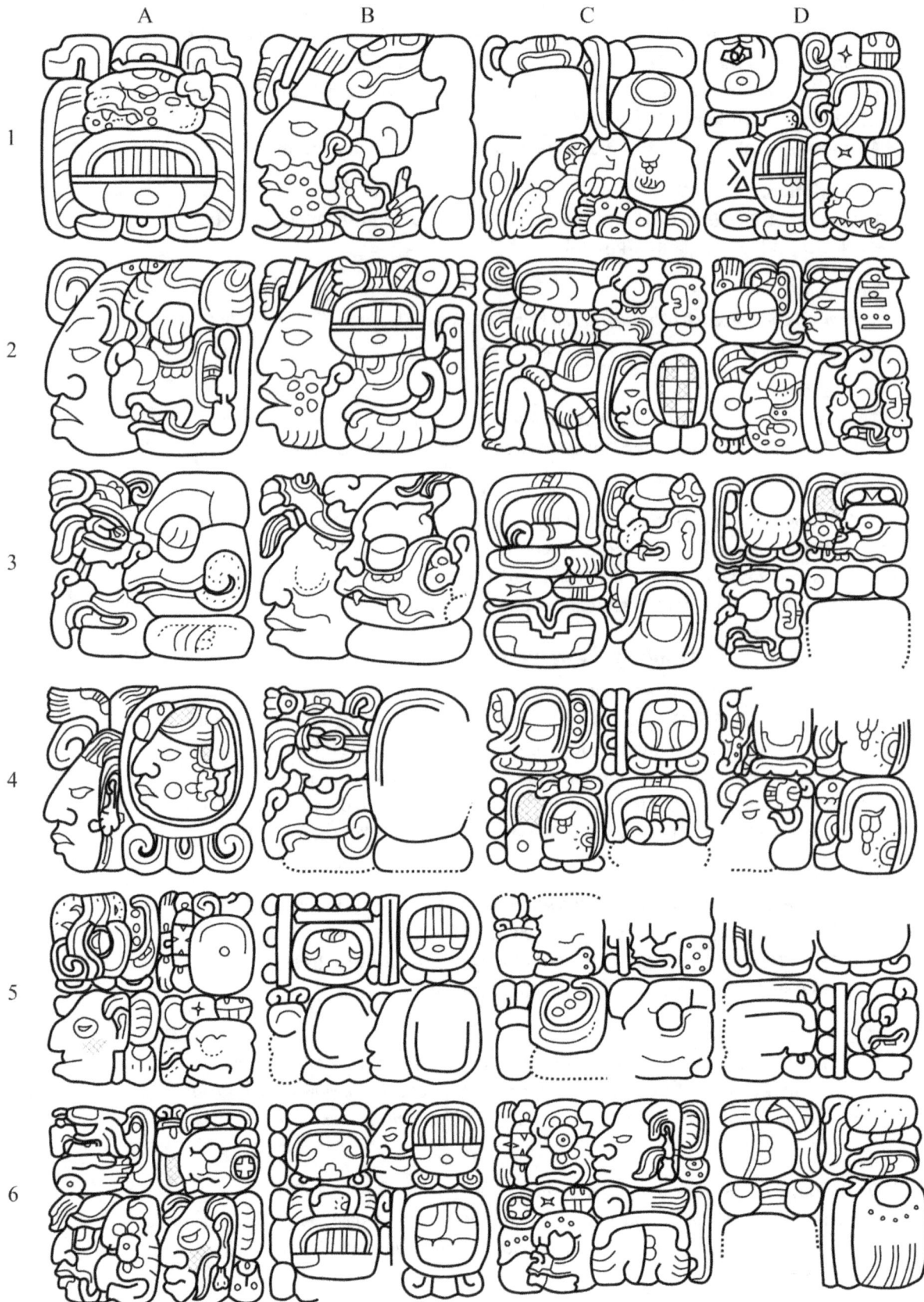

Table 6.5. Palenque, Hieroglyphic Stairway Chronology

Position:	Counts:	Calendar Round:	Gregorian:
A1–B4	09.08.09.13.00	08 Ajaw 13 Pop	24 March 603 CE
	+ 12.09.08		
B4	[09.09.02.04.08]	05 Lamat 01 Mol	27 July 615 CE
	[09.08.09.13.00]	08 Ajaw 13 Pop]	24 March 603 CE
	+ 03.00.02.03		
B5–C1	[09.11.09.15.03]	06 Ak'bal 01 [Yaxk'in]	25 June 622 CE
	[− 02.16.12]		
C4	[09.11.06.16.11]	07 Chuwen 04 Ch'en	8 August 659 CE

The verbal morphology here is interesting and is best explained if these two clauses are combined. After the Long Count, we have the verb *siyaj-iiy*. If the phrase meant "on this day, Pakal was born," we would expect just *siyaj*. The additional *-iiy* suggests that this event is being cast as having occurred well before the next event: his coronation, twelve years later. Therefore the passage is best translated as "Pakal was born about 12 years before he was crowned as ruler," combining the two clauses. The text becomes more difficult to read after this point. Palenque may have been defeated by Calakmul, as evidenced by the phrase *ch'ak lakam ha'*, meaning "great water defeat" in C1 ("great water" was a toponym used at Palenque), with the perpetrator named as the ruler of Calakmul (*kan ajaw*) in D1 (probably in 599 CE). This is followed by the "throwing" (*yalej*) of the patron deities of Palenque: GI, GII, and GIII (C2). Times improve, and the stairway goes on to name six captives (*b'aak*) who were captured (*chukaj*) by Pakal in 659 CE (C4–C6).

By examining these inscriptions systematically, we can trace the history of ancient Maya rulers in their own words. For the most part, we have looked at large, public monuments that contain brief passages. This history is an austere record of complex interpersonal, political, and ritual relationships among real people. It is almost certain that we are missing many other types of written information, such as songs, poems, and dialogs, which may have been written on perishable media like codices. Even with the paltry number of surviving texts, a complex picture of Classic Maya history can be reconstructed. As archaeologists work to uncover new inscriptions and passages in the coming years, even more of this complex history will come to light. Our understanding of the past will become even more accurate as epigraphers continue to advance the field of Maya hieroglyphics and we strive to understand the exact words uttered by the scribes responsible for these texts.

APPENDIX I. GRAMMAR

I.1. Pronouns

Personal pronouns stand in for a noun or noun phrase in a sentence. In Classic Mayan they are used with nouns and verbs to indicate possession and action roles, respectively.

		Ergative: Subject of transitive verbs and possessor of nouns. ( ) indicates vowel-initial version		**Absolutive:** Object of transitive verbs and subject of intransitive verbs. * = not well attested	
Singular	First Person	(wV)	**ni(w)-** *ni(w)-* I or my	Ce	**-Ce-n(a)** *-een (or -e'n)* I or me
	Second Person	(wV)	**'a-(wV)-** *a(w)-* you or your	Ca	**-Ca-t(a)** *-at** you
	Third Person	and many others	**'u- (yV-)** *u- (yV-)* he/she/it or his/her/its		*-ø* he/she/it or him/her/its
	Demonstrative		**ha-(i)** *haa* this or that		
Plural	First Person	(wV)	**ka-(wV)-** *ka(w)-* we or our	Co	**-Co-n(a)** *-o'n** we or us
	Second Person	(wV)	**i-(wV)-** *i(w)-* you (pl.) or your (pl.)	Co	**-Co-x(o)** *-ox** you (pl.)
	Third Person	and many others	**'u- (yV-)** *u- (yV-)* they or their	Co	**-Co-b'(a)** *-o'b'** they or them
	Demonstrative		**ha-o-b'(a)** *hao'b'* these or those		

I.2. Verbs

Verbs denote action and are inflected with various affixes.

Transitive Verbs:

Transitive verbs take more than one argument (both an agent and a patient). In other words, an *agent* is *verb*ing a *patient*.

Active: In active voice, the subject and object are directly named in the sentence. Their positions indicate who is doing what to whom. Any transitive sentence with an actor and object is generally a completive transitive sentence. "Pakal captured B'alam."

u-____-wa
u____Vw-ø
He ____ ed

ERG-CV₁C-V₁w-ABS

Passive: In passive voice, the actor is not named directly and the object appears to be the main subject. The passive voice is retained even if the actor is named in a subordinate clause:
"B'alam was captured."

____-ja
____h_aj-ø
It was ____ ed

CVhC-aj-ABS

Mediopassive: In mediopassive voice, the agent is not stated and the patient appears to be the subject. The mediopassive is used for an unclear cause, such as raining or burning. The patient cannot take a preposition. The mediopassive is a way of talking about an event without assigning blame. It has a stative meaning: "B'alam got decapitated."

____-yi
____Vy-ø
He got ____ ed

CV₁C-V₁y-ABS or
CV₁C-V₁V₁y-ABS

Antipassive: In antipassive voice, the patient is not named directly. Basically this fronts the agent and creates a passive-like form: "Pakal decapitated."

____-wi
____Vw-ø
____ ed

Early: CV₁C-V₁V₁w-ABS
Late: CV₁C-V₁w-ABS

Imperative: In the imperative voice, a patient is ordered to do something. This is also called the command form: "Decapitate B'alam!"

____-V
____V-ø
____ it!

CV₁C-V₁-ABS

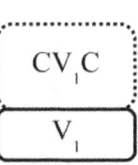

I.2. Verbs (continued)

Intransitive Verbs:
Intransitive verbs do not take a *patient* and have only one argument (they need only an *agent* and cannot take an object).

Root Intransitives: For root intransitives a verb is used only with an actor. "He arrived."

____-Ci
____i
He/she ____ed

CVC-ABS*
ø → i

Derived Intransitives: Derived intransitives are verbs formed from nouns that take an actor but no object: "He danced."

____-ja
____j-ø
He/she ____ed

NOUN/ADJ-Vj-ABS
(usually -aj or -iij)

Positionals: Positional verbs refer to physical states or positions (such as sitting or standing) that can be assumed by people or animals: "He/she/it sat."

____-la-ja
____laj
He/she ____

Eastern: CVC-l-aj-ABS

____-wa-ni
____waan
He/she ____

Western: CVC-waan?-ABS

Causative: Causative verbs describe an agent forcing a patient to perform an action. All are derived from nouns or adjectives. "He/she made him/her sit."

u-____-b'u
u____b'u-ø
He/she made him/her ____

ERG-CVC-b'u-ABS

Inchoatives: Inchoative verbs are verbs of becoming, explaining a change in the subject. All are derived from nouns or adjectives: "He/she became king."

____-ja
____j-ø
He/she became ____

CVC(Noun/Adj.)-Vj-ABS

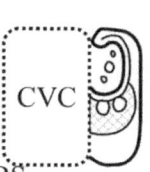

____-ni
____n-ø
He/she became ____

CVC(Noun/Adj.)-Vn-ABS

I.3. Prepositions

i-chi-l(a)
ichiil-
within

ma-l(a)-
mal-
within

ta-
ta-
in/with/by/at/on/to

TAN-
tan-
in the center of

ti-
ti-
in/with/by/at/on/to

ti-i-li
ti'il
pertaining to

tu- [ti + u]
tu- [ti + u]
in/with/by/at/on/to his/her/its

xi-n(i)-
xin-
in/inside

yi[chi]-NAL
yichinal
with/in the presence of

I.4. Adjectives

Adjectives modify and/or describe nouns.

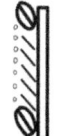 **AJ** *aj* one who

 **ch'a-j(i)** *ch'aaj* bitter

 **k'a** *k'a'* abundant

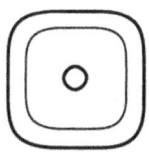 **PET** *pet* round

 **a-ku-l(a)** *aku'l* turtle-like

 **ch'o[k(o)]** *ch'ok* young

 **K'AK'-la** *k'ak'al* fiery

 **pi-tzi-li** *pitzil* beautiful

 **9** *b'olon* many (also "nine")

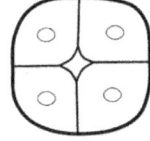 **EK'** *ek'* black

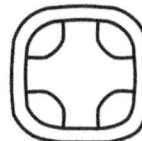 **K'AN** *k'an* precious yellow

 **SAK** *sak* holy, pure white

 **b'u-b'u-l(u)** *b'ub'ul* frothy

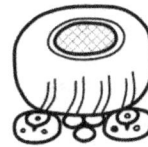 **HA'-la** *ha'al* watery, wet

 **K'INICH** *k'inich* sun-faced heated

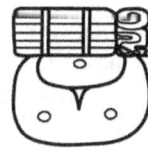 **TAJ-l(a)** *tajal* obsidian-like

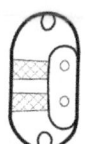 **CHAK** *chak* great red

 **IK'** *ik'* black

 **K'UH-lu** *k'uhul* divine (lit. "god-y")

 **TE'-le** *te'el* wild (lit. "tree-y")

 **CHAN-la** *chanal* heavenly

 **KAB'-l(a)** *kab'al* low, earth-like

 **LAKAM** *lakam* great

 **tzi-hi-l(i)** *tzihil* new, fresh

 **cha** *cha'* dark

 **²ka-wa-l(a)** *kakawal* chocolaty

 **ma-tzi-l(i)** *matzil* bad

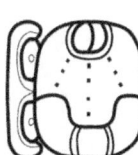 **u-tz(i)** *uutz* good

 **che-l(e)** *chel* high

 **KELEM** *kele'm* strong

 **nu-k(u)** *nuk* big, great

 **xi-n(i)** *xin* stinking

 **chi-h(i)** *chih* sweet

 **ko-b'(a)** *ko'b'* grey

 **o-n(a)** *o'n* many

 **YAX** *yax* first blue-green

I.5. Adverbs and Enclitics

Verbs and enclitics modify and/or describe verbs. Enclitics can also modify nouns.

Posterior Event Indicator: This adverb is prefixed to the front of a complete verb-phrase. It indicates that this event comes after the event that was mentioned before it. It can be added to any verb. "And then Pakal captured B'alam."

i-____
*i*____
And then ____

i-VERB

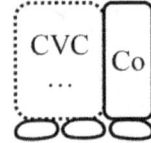

Future Event Indicator: This enclitic is suffixed to the end of a complete verb-phrase. It indicates that this verb will occur in the future, often the mythical or foretold future. It can be added to any verb. "Pakal will capture B'alam."

____**Co-m(a)**
____*o'm*
____will

VERB-o'm

Anterior Event Indicator: This enclitic is suffixed to the end of a complete verb-phrase or noun. It indicates that this verb occurred before the next event or adds the English adverb "ago." It can be attached to any verb or noun. "Pakal captured B'alam before ..."

____**-y(a)**
____*iiy*
____already

VERB-iiy

Extreme Anterior Event Indicator: This enclitic is suffixed to the end of a complete verb-phrase or noun. It indicates that this verb occurred well before the next event, even as far back as the mythical past, or adds the English adverb "long ago." It can be attached to any verb or noun. "Pakal captured B'alam long before ..."

____**-ji-y(a)**
____*jiiy*
____long ago

VERB-jiiy

APPENDIX II. CATALOG CORRESPONDENCE

II.1. Catalog Numbers and Drawings (page 1 of 7)

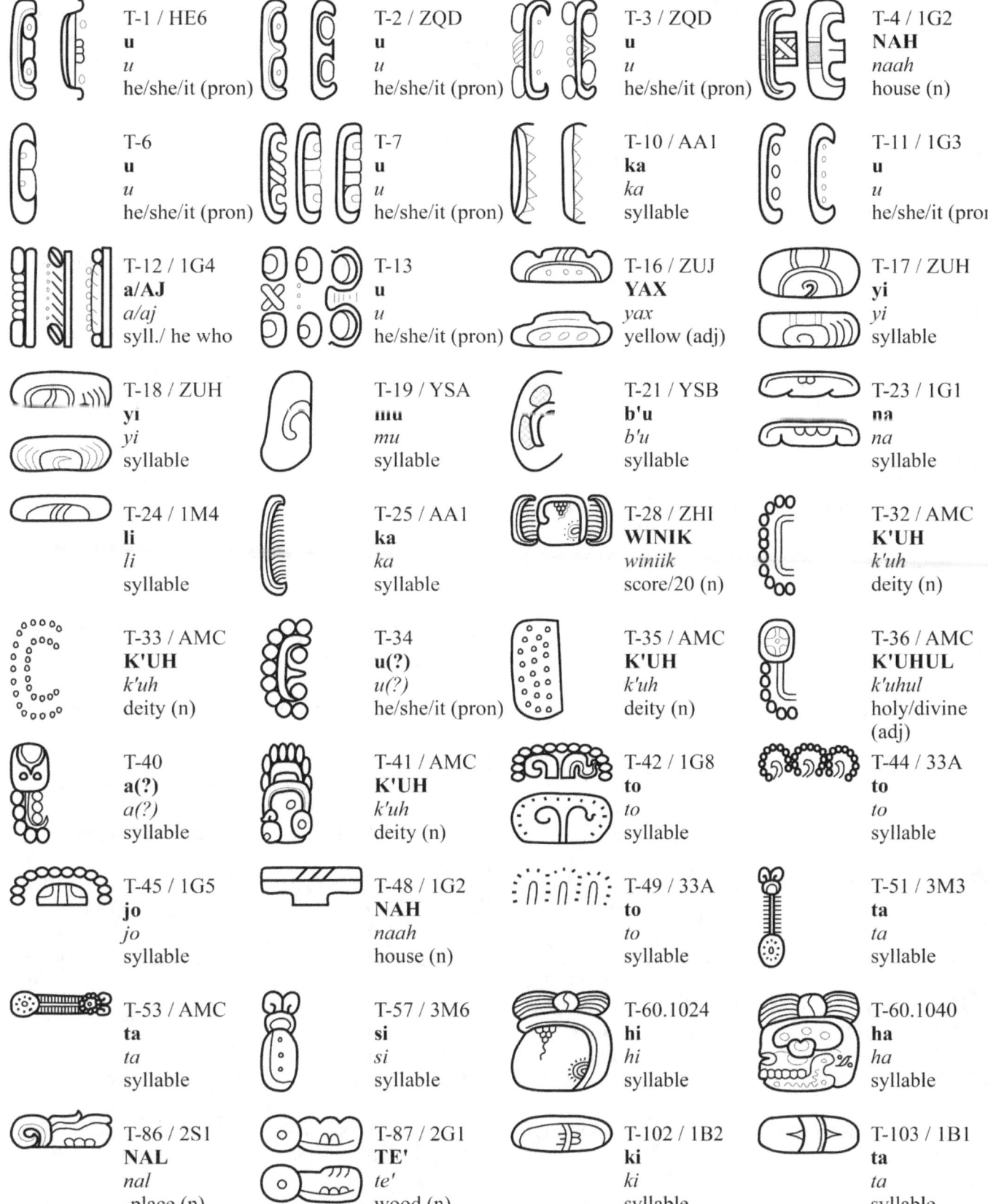

II.1. Catalog Numbers and Drawings (page 2 of 7)

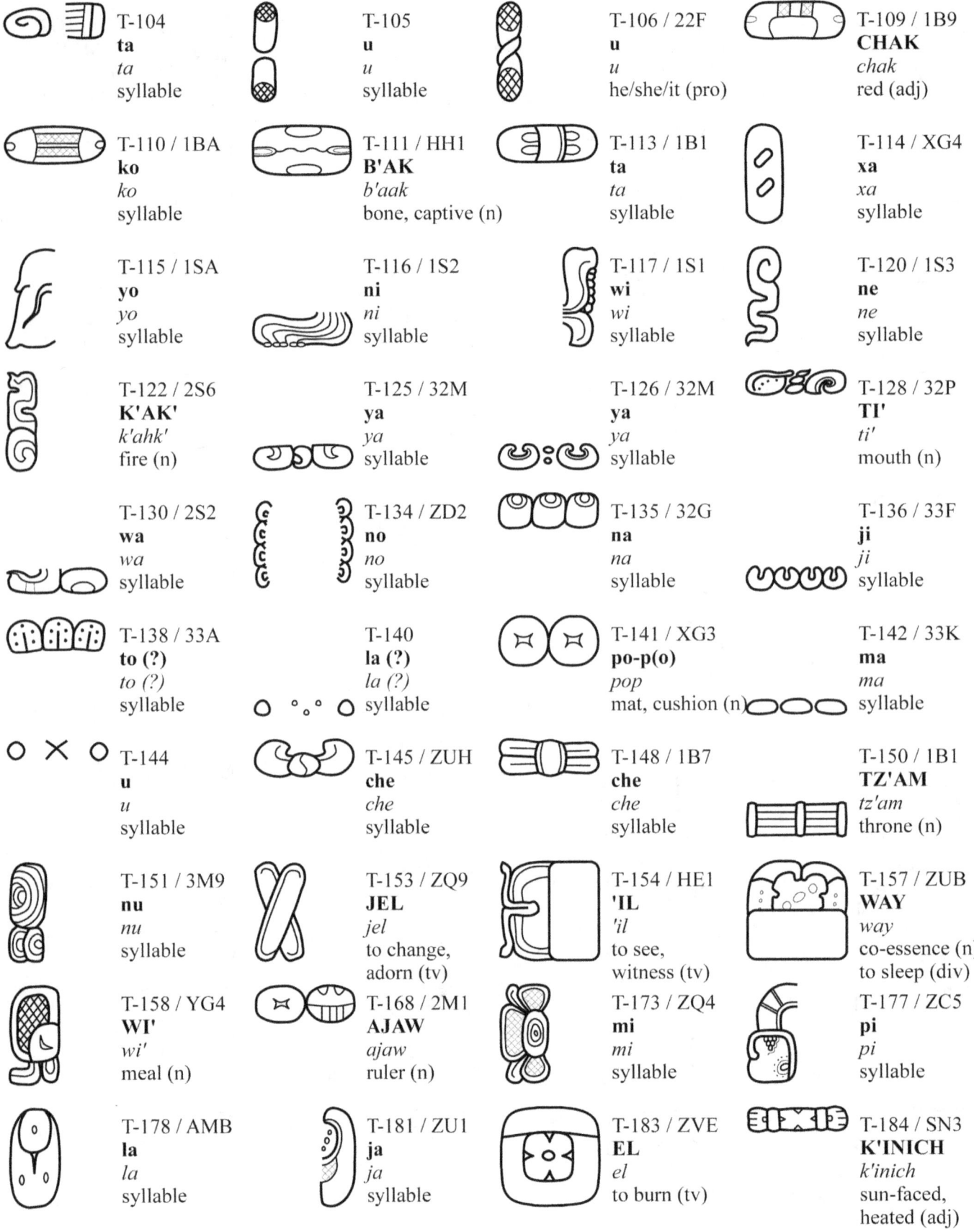

II.1. Catalog Numbers and Drawings (page 3 of 7)

 T-187 / ZE1
K'AB'A
k'ab'a
name (n)

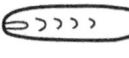 T-188 / 1SC
le
le
syllable

 T-191 / HE6
u
u
he/she/it (pron)

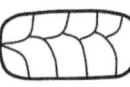 T-192 / ZY6
OTOT
otoot
house (n)

 T-198 / 1S3
ne
ne
syllable

 T-200 / ZC5
pi
pi
syllable

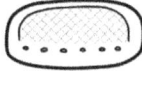 T-202 / XD1
pa (?)
pa (?)
syllable

 T-204 / AA4
u
u
he/she/it (pron)

 T-205
u
u
he/she/it (pron)

 T-207 / ACN
OCH
och
to enter (riv)

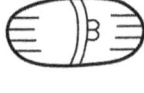 T-216 / 1B3
su
su
syllable

 T-220 / MZA
ke
ke
syllable

 T-221 / MZ6
OCH
och
to enter (riv)

 T-222 / MZ2
PAS
pas
to open (tv)

 T-227 / HT4
EM
em
to go down, descend (div)

 T-228 / AL2
a
a
syllable

 T-229 / AL2
a
a
syllable

 T-232 / HE6
u
u
syllable

 T-238 / BP3
a
a
syllable

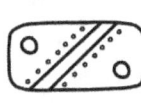 T-245 / 1M5
TOK (?)
to'k'
flint (n)

 T-246
ji-ya
jiiy
(long) ago (adv)

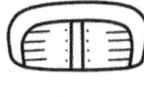 T-248 / XV1
tz'i
tz'i
syllable

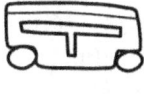 T-254
nu (?)
nu
syllable

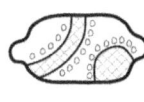 T-257 / 1C1
TOK'
to'k'
flint (n)

 T-258
tu
tu
syllable

 T-262 / ZS8
LAKAM
lakam
big, great, wide (adj)

 T-266 / 1G5
pu
pu
syllable

 T-274
TAL
tal
count of days (ncl)

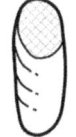 T-279 / BT1
o
o
syllable

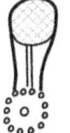 T-280 / BT1
o
o
syllable

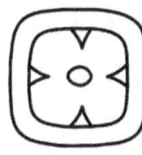 T-281 / XQ1
K'AN
k'an
yellow (adj)

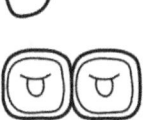 T-287 / HE5
ch'o
ch'o
syllable

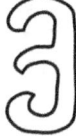 T-291 / AV5
XUKUB'
xukub'
horn (n)

 T-297 / 22E
o
o
syllable

 T-324 / 2S3
NAB' (?)
naahb'
large body of water (n)

 T-327 / AC3
LOK'
lok'
to emerge, escape (riv)

 T-333 / 2M7
CH'AK
chak
to cut (tv)

 T-358 / HTB
YAJ
yaaj
at same time (adv)

 T-361 / MZM
JATZ'OM
jatz'o'm
striker, spear thrower (n)

 T-370 / ZS4
tzu
tzu
syllable

APPENDIX II. CATALOG CORRESPONDENCE

II.1. Catalog Numbers and Drawings (page 4 of 7)

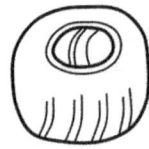
T-501 / XE1
b'a
b'a
syllable

T-502 / XE3
ma
ma
syllable

T-503 / XQ6
IK'
ik'
wind, air (n)

T-504 / XH9
AK'AB'
ak'ab'
night (n)

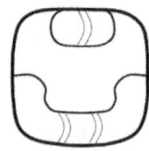
T-506 / XH4
OL/WAJ
o'l/waaj
middle/tortilla (n)

T-507 / XH5
tzi
tzi
syllable

T-508 / XG4
xa
xa
syllable

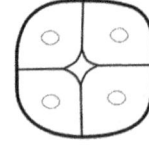
T-510 / ZQD
EK'
eek'
star (n) / black (adj)

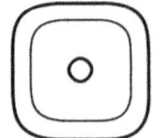
T-511 / XG1
PET
pet
round (adj)

T-512 / ZY7
ye
ye
syllable

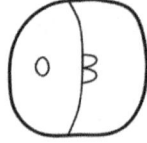
T-513 / YG2
u
u
syllable

T-514 / ZZ5
ETE'
e[b]tej (?)
work (n)

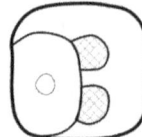
T-516 / YG5
AK'
ak'
dance (n), to dance (div)

T-518c / 2M1
TE'
te'
tree, wood (n)

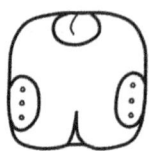
T-519 / HM1
b'o
b'o
syllable

T-520 / XS3
se
se
syllable

T-521 / XS1
WINAL
winal
20-day period (n)

T-522 / XS2
HUN
hu'n
book, paper (n)

T-524 / AT7
HIX
hix
jaguar (n)

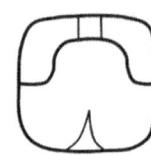
T-525 / XH6
ka
ka
syllable

T-526 / YS1
KAB'/xo
kab'/xo
earth, bee (n)/syllable

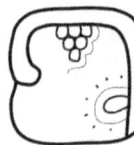
T-528 / ZC1
TUN/ku
tuun/ku
stone (n)/syllable

T-529 / ZC2
WITZ
witz
mountain (n)

T-531 / ZC2
WITZ (?)
witz
mountain (n)

T-532 / ZC1
TUN (?)
tuun
stone (n)

T-533 / AM1
AJAW
ajaw
ruler (n)

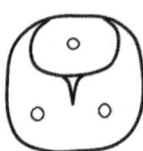
T-534 / AMB
la
la
syllable

T-535 / AM4
MIJIN (?)
mijiin (?)
child of father (n)

T-536 / AM6
xo
xo
syllable

T-537 / PX4
na
na
syllable

T-539 / AM7
WAY
way
co-essence (n) / to sleep (div)

T-542 / PX4
e
e
syllable

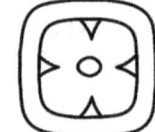
T-544 / XQ3
K'IN
k'ihn
sun, day (n)

T-546 / XVC
EL-K'IN
el k'ihn
east (n)

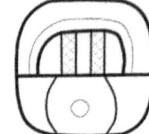
T-548 / XH2
HAB'
haab'
vague year (n)

T-552 / XQB
AT
aat
penis (n)

T-553 / 32R
K'AT
k'at
pottery bowl (n)

T-554 / AC2
AT
aat
penis (n)

T-556 / XE2
HA'
ha'
water (n)

T-559 / ZS4
UNIW
uniiw
avocado (n)

II.1. Catalog Numbers and Drawings (page 5 of 7)

 T-560 **tzu** *tzu* syllable

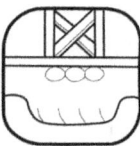 T-561 / XH3 **CHAN** *chan* sky (n)

 T-562 **PA'CHAN** *pa'chan* "Split Sky," Yaxchilan (n)

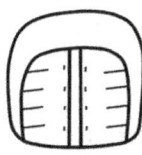 T-563 / XV1 **tz'i** *tz'i* syllable

 T-565 / YM2 **ta** *ta* syllable

 T-566 / ACL **HA'** *ha'* water (n)

 T-568 / ZUG **lu** *lu* syllable

 T-569 / HB1 **MUT** *mut[u'l]* "knot," Tikal (n)

 T-570 / HH1 **B'AK** *b'aak* bone, captive (n)

 T-571 / HH2 **CH'EN** *ch'e'n* cave (n)

 T-573 / YS6 **TZ'AK** *tz'ak* to add (pv)

 T-574 / ZU8 **he** *he* syllable

 T-577 / ZUP **ne** *ne* syllable

 T-578 / ZUP **ne** *ne* syllable

 T-580 / XGA **lo** *lo* syllable

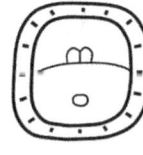 T-581 **mo-lo** *mol* Mol month name (n)

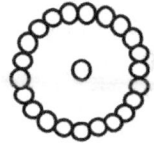 T-582 / BP5 **mo** *mo* syllable

 T-583 / XGG **JANAB'** *janaab'* [bird name] (n)

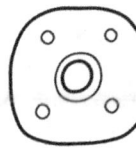 T-585 / XGE **b'i** *b'i* syllable

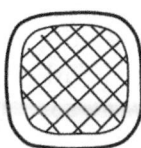 T-586 / XD1 **pa** *pa* syllable

 T-589 **CH'EN** *ch'e'n* cave (n)

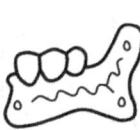 T-590 / HJ1 **cho** *cho* syllable

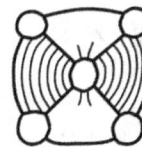 T-592 / 22F **nu** *nu* syllable

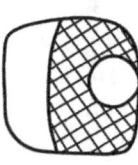 T-599 / HH2 **CH'EN** *ch'e'n* cave (n)

 T-600 / ZQB **WI' (?)** *wi' (?)* root (n)

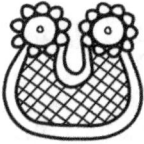 T-603 / 2G2 **K'U / k'u** *k'u / k'u* nest (n) / syllable

 T-604 / 22B **K'U / k'u** *k'u / k'u* nest (n) / syllable

 T-606 / YM3 **TAN** *tahn* in (prep) / front (n)

 T-607 / ZUF **jo** *jo* syllable

 T-608 **tz'u** *tz'u* syllable

 T-609a / XHA **TZ'AM** *tz'am* throne (n)

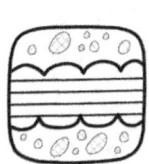 T-609b / XHB **HUN** *hu'n* book, paper (n)

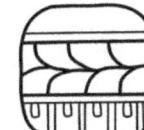 T-614 / ZY5 **OTOT** *otoot* house (n)

 T-618 / HE3 **UT** *ut* eye (n)

 T-624 / XQC **PAKAL** *pakal* shield (n)

 T-626 / AL3 **AK** *ahk* turtle (n)

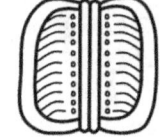 T-630 / XV4 **sa** *sa* syllable

 T-632 / XGK **MUYAL** *muyaal* cloud (n)

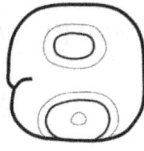 T-644 / HT8 **CHUM** *chum* to seat (pv)

 T-645 / ZSF **WAY** *way* co-essence (n) / to sleep (div)

APPENDIX II. CATALOG CORRESPONDENCE

II.1. Catalog Numbers and Drawings (page 6 of 7)

 T-646 / XQ2
NIK
nik
flower (n)

 T-649 / ZUA
pa
pa
syllable

 T-650
UT
ut
eye (n)

 T-653 / ZYD
JUL
jul
spear (n),
to throw (tv)

 T-668 / MZ9
cha
cha
syllable

 T-669 / MZ3
k'a
k'a
syllable

 T-670 / MZD
CH'AM
ch'am
to take, grab (tv)

 T-671 / MR7
chi
chi
syllable

 T-672 / MZ4
ho
ho
syllable

 T-673 / MZC
yo
yo
syllable

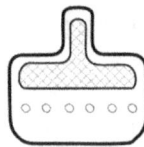 T-674 / ZZ8
TAL
tal
count of periods (ncl)

 T-678 / ZD5
KOHAW
ko'haw
helmet (n)

 T-679 / YM1
i
i
syllable

 T-683a / ZU2
K'AL
k'aal
twenty (num)

 T-683b / ZU1
ja
ja
syllable

 T-684 / ZB1
JOY
joy
to encircle (tv)

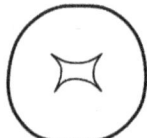 T-687 / XG3
po / TZ'AM
po / tz'am
syllable /
throne (n)

 T-696 / ZSE
UNIW
uniw
avocado (n)

 T-699 / ZZA
tza
tza
syllable

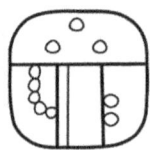 T-709 / YGA
SAB'AK
sab'aak
ink, soot (n)

 T-710 / MZS
ye / CHOK
ye / chok
syllable /
to throw (tv)

 T-712 / ZYC
CH'AB'
ch'ahb'
sacrifice (n),
to fast (tv)

 T-713a / MR2
K'AL
k'al
to bind (tv)

 T-713b / MRA
HUL
hul
to arrive (riv)

 T-714 / MZK
TZAK
tzak
to grab,
conjure (tv)

 T-716 / HB1
MUT
mut[u'l]
"knot," Tikal (n)

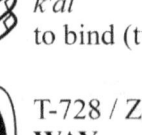 T-728 / ZUB
WAY
way
co-essence (n) /
to sleep (div)

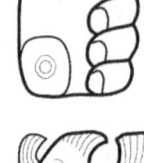 T-738 / AA1
ka / CHAY
ka / chay
syllable /
fish (n)

 T-740 / AL8
hu
hu
syllable

 T-741a / AL1
e
e
syllable

 T-741c
HUJ
huj
iguana (n)

 T-743 / BP1
a
a
syllable

 T-744 / BP7
K'UK'
k'uk'
quetzal (n)

 T-747 / BV1
AJAW
ajaw
ruler (n)

 T-751 / AT1
B'ALAM
b'ahlam
jaguar (n)

 T-753 / AP2
TZ'I
tz'i'
dog (n)

 T-754 / APH
CHITAM
chitam
peccary (n)

 T-756a / APM
SUTZ'
suutz'
bat (n)

 T-756c / APM
xu
xu
syllable

 T-757 / AP9
B'AH / b'a
b'aah / b'a
first, head (n) / syllable

II.1. Catalog Numbers and Drawings (page 7 of 7)

 T-758a / APB
ch'o[k(o)]
ch'ok
young (adv), heir (n)

 T-758b / APC
CHIK / ch'o
chi'k / ch'o
coatimundi (n) / syllable

 T-759 / AP7
CHIT
chit
father, patron (n)

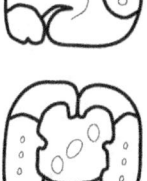 T-761 / AM2
AT
aat
penis (n)

 T-764 / AC6
CHAN
chan
snake (n)

 T-765
OK
ook
dog, foot (n)

 T-766 / AV1
CHIJ
chij
deer (n)

 T-769 / ZUB
WAY
way
co-essence (n) to sleep (div)

 T-770
ke
ke
syllable

T-778 / HB1
MUT
mut[u'l]
"knot," Tikal (n)

 T-783
MAT
mat
cormorant (n)

T-785 / ZY7
AT
aat
penis (n)

 T-790
SAB'IN
sab'in
weasel (n)

 T-793a / BM7
MAT
mat
cormorant (n)

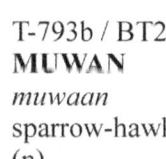 T-793b / BT2
MUWAN
muwaan
sparrow-hawk (n)

 T-832 / AT6
B'ULAY (?)
b'ulaay
small jaguar (n)

 T-843 / ZY1
T'AB'
t'ab'
to polish (tv) to go up (riv)

 T-844 / AL6
AHIN
ahiin
crocodile, lizard (n)

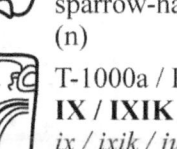 T-1000a / PC1
IX / IXIK / JUN / na
ix / ixik / ju'n / na
female (n) / woman (n) / one (num) / syllable

 T-1000e / PT7
AJAW
ajaw
ruler (n)

 T-1002
IXIK
ixik
woman (n)

 T-1004 / PM1
sa
sa'
syllable

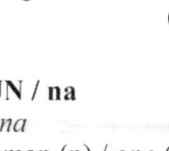 T-1004a / PM1
sa[ja-l(a)]
sajal
sajal, title (n)

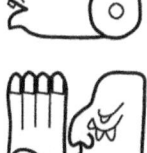 T-1008 / PC4
XIB'
xib'
male, young man (n)

 T-1010 / SN4
K'INICH
k'inich
sun-faced, heated (adj)

 T-1011 / SN1
CHAK
chaahk
Chak, rain-deity (n)

 T-1016 / AMC
K'UH
k'uh
god, deity (n)

T-1028c
KELEM
kele'm
strong (adj) young boy (n)

T-1030e / SSF
K'AWIL
k'awiil
K'awil, deity (n)

 T-1030h / SSF
K'AWIL
k'awiil
K'awil, deity (n)

 T-1030m / SS2
CHAK
chaahk
Chak, rain-deity (n)

II.2. Transcriptions and Catalog Numbers (page 1 of 4)

The most common hieroglyphs and their corresponding Thompson Numbers and New Catalog Codes are listed alphabetically.

Transcription	T-Number(s)	NC Code(s)
a	12/40?/228/229/238/743	AL2/AMG/BP1/MB1/1G4/BP3
AHIN	844	AL6
AJ	12/181/683b	ZU1/AL2/1G4
AJAW	168/533/747/1000d	AM8/AX1/BV1/BV2/PT7/XD4/ZB3/2M1/AM1
AK	516/626	AL1/AL3/SNN
AK'AB'	504	XH9
AT	552/554/761/785	XQB/AC2/HM2
b'a	501/757	AP9/AT1/PCB/PT9/SC2/SCM/XE1/XE2/ZX5/33H
B'AH	757/501	AP9/XE1
B'AK	111/570	HH1/HJ1/SCM/SC2
B'ALAM	751	AT1/PT9
b'i	585	HTF/AC6/XGE
b'o	519	HM1
b'u	20	YSB
B'ULAY?	832	AT6
cha	668	MZ9/XS3/2S4?/32F?
CHAK	109/1011/1030i-o	SS1/HJ2/1B9
CHAN	561/764	XH3/SB2/AC6/ACH/004/SN4/SN1
CHAY	738	AA1
che	145/148	1B7
chi	671	AV1/MR7/SC9
CHIJ	766	AV1
CHIK	758b	APC
CHIT	759	AP7
CHITAM	754	APH
cho	590	HJ1
CHOK	170/710	2M2/MZS
CHUM	644	HT8/HTA/HT9?
CH'AB'	712	PTC/ZYC
CH'AK	333	2M7
CH'AM	670	MZD
CH'EN	571/589/599	MB8/BT6/HH2/ZC4
ch'o	287/758b	APB
CH'OK	758a	APB/HE5ZQB?
e	542/741a	AA7
EK'	510	ZQD
EL	183	ZVE
EL-K'IN	546	ZVC
EM	227	HT4
ETE'	514	ZZ5
ha	60-1024/1040	SC3/ZYB
HA'	556/566	XE2/ZUP/33G/SS6/SS5?/SB5
HAB'	548	SB5/SS8/XH2/SB4

II.2. Transcriptions and Catalog Numbers (page 2 of 4)

Transcription	T-Number(s)	NC Code(s)
he	574	ZU8
hi	60	32K
HIX	524	AT1/AT7
ho	672	MZ4
hu	740	AL8
HUJ	741c	AL9
HUL	713b	HTE/MRA/ZU3/1G5
HUN	522/609b	SSC/XHB/XS2/1B5/AM3
i	679	BV8/YM1
IK'	503	ZQ6/PT3/XG8
IL	154	HE1
IX	1000a	PC1
IXIK	1000a/1002	PC1
ja	181/683b	ZU1
JANAB'	583	BT7/XGG
JATZ'OM	361	MZM
JEL	153	ZQ9
ji	136	APC/1M1/33F
ji-ya	246	—
jo	607	ZUF
JOY	684	ZB1
ju	45	1G5
JUL	653	ZYD
JUN	1000a	MBA/001/PC1
ka	10/25/525/738	AA1/AA2
KAB'	526	PE1/YS1
ke	220/770	MZA
KELEM	1028c	MZB
ki	102	BT5/1B2
ko	110	HJ3/1BA
KOHAW	678	ZD5
ku	528	ZC1
k'a	669	MZ3/2S6/SSB?/ZS9?/32P?
K'AB'A	187	ZB1
K'AK'	122	2S6/
K'AL	683a/713a	ZU2/MR2
K'AN	281	ZQ1
K'AT	553	XQB
K'AWIL	1030a–h	SSF
k'i	76/77	BM1/BM2
K'IN	544	XQ3
K'INICH	184/1010	SN3
k'u	603/604	2G2/22B
K'U	603/604	2G2/22B
K'UH	32/33/35/41/1016	AMC/PH1
K'UHUL	36	PH1
K'UK'	744	BP7

II.2. Transcriptions and Catalog Numbers (page 3 of 4)

Transcription	T-Number(s)	NC Code(s)
la	178/534/140?	AMB
LAKAM	262	ZS8
le	188	ZSD/1SC
li	24	BV5/1G3/1M4/1SB
lo	580	XGA
LOK'	327	AC3
lu	568	ZUG
ma	42?/142/502	XE3/32A/32U/33K
MAT	783/793a	BM7
mi	173/807	MR1/ZQ4/PM7?
MIJIN (?)	535	AM4
mo	582	BP5
mo-lo	581	—
mu	19	YSA
MUT	569/716/778	HB1/PE4
MUWAN	793b	BT2
MUYAL	632	XGK
na	23/135/537/1000a	PC1/PX4/XD5/1G1/1G2/1M3/2M4/34A
NAB' (?)	324	MR5/SCA/XD6/2S3/XG7?/XQ9?/SS5?
NAH	4/48	PC1/1G2/ZY5
ne	120/198/577/578	ATB/1S3
ni	116	1S2
NIK	646	XQ2/AM1?/AM4?
no	134	ZD2
nu	151/254?/592	22F/3M9
o	279/280/297	BT1/1SJ/32E
OCH	207/221	ACN/MRC
OK	765	AP5
OL	506	XH4
OTOT	192/614	ZY5/ZY6/1G7
pa	202?/586/649	XD1/ZUA
PAKAL	624	XD2/XQC
PAS	222	ZX2/MZ2/SCP
PA'CHAN	562	—
PET	511	XG1
pi	177/200	SB1/ZC5
po	687	XG3
po-po	141	
pu	266	XH7
sa	630/1004/1004b	PM1/XV4/32C/32R
SAB'AK	709	YGA
SAB'IN	790	—
sa-ja-la	1004a	—
se	520	XS3
si	57	3M6/1B3
su	216	1B3

II.2. Transcriptions and Catalog Numbers (page 4 of 4)

Transcription	T-Number(s)	NC Code(s)
SUTZ'	756a/756b	APM
ta	51/53/103/104/113/565	SCG/XQB/YM2/ZS1/1B1/3M3
TAL	274/674	YS7
TAN	606	YM3
TE'	518c	XGC/YG1/2G1/ZZ5
ti	59	BV3/3M2
TI'	128	32P
to	44/49/138?	33A
TOK'	257/245?	1C1/22E
tu	258	3M4
TUN	532?/528	ZC1
T'AB'	843	ZY1
tza	699	ZZA
TZAK	714	MZK
tzi	507	BVA/XH5/ZU5/32J
tzu	370/560	SSJ/ZS4
TZ'AK	573	YS6/ZX6
TZ'AM	150/609a	XHA?/XQ7?
tz'i	248/563	AP1/XV1/APM
TZ'I	753	AP1
tz'u	608	AA3
u	1/2/3/6/7/11/13/34?/105/106/191/204/205/232/513	AA4/AMF/AT8/HE6/PC7/PE5/YG2/33D
UNIW	559/696	ZS4/ZSE
UT	618/650	HE3
wa	130	ACK/PX3/2S2/XH4?/ZUB?
WA'	588	SSL
WAJ	506	XH4
WAY	157/539/645/728/769	AM7/AT2/YS8/ZSF/PE4/ZUB?
wi	117/600	1S1
WI'	158	ZQB
WINAL	521	AA7/AM2/AM9/XS1
WINIK-HAB'	28	SB4/SB3/SB3/ZH1
WITZ	29/531?	ZC2
xa	114/144/508	XG4
XIB'	1008	HT2/PC4
xo	526/536	AM6
xu	756c	APM
XUKUB'	291	AV5
ya	125/126	SCJ/32M
YAJ	358	HTB
YAX	16	PT9/YUJ
ye	512/710	MZR/PH3/ZY7
yi	17/18	ZUH
yo	115/673	MZC/1SA
yu	61	32D

APPENDIX III. BASIC VOCABULARY

III.1. Classic Maya Calendar (page 1 of 8)

Numbers

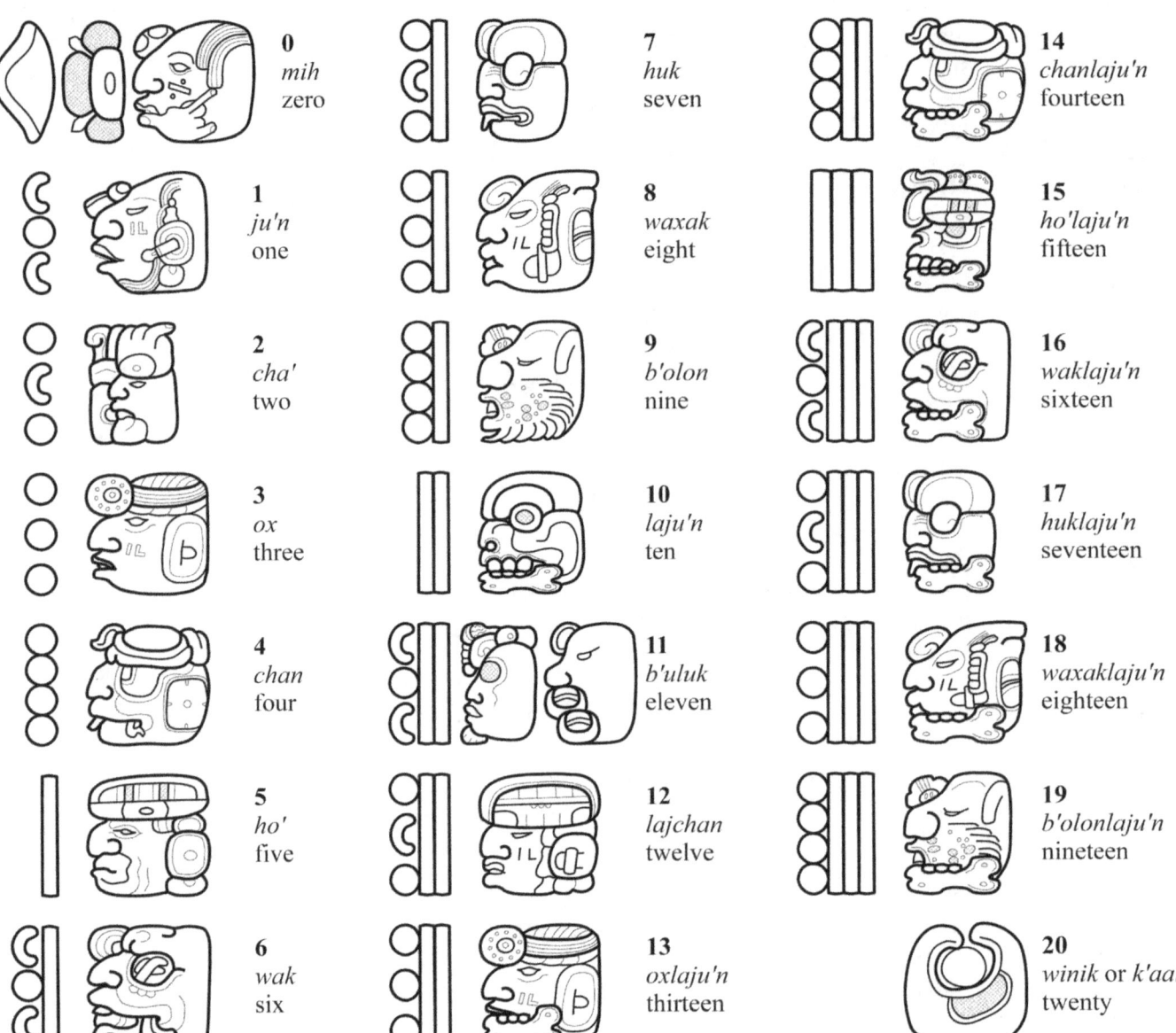

III.1. Classic Maya Calendar (page 2 of 8)

Long Count Glyphs and Head Variants

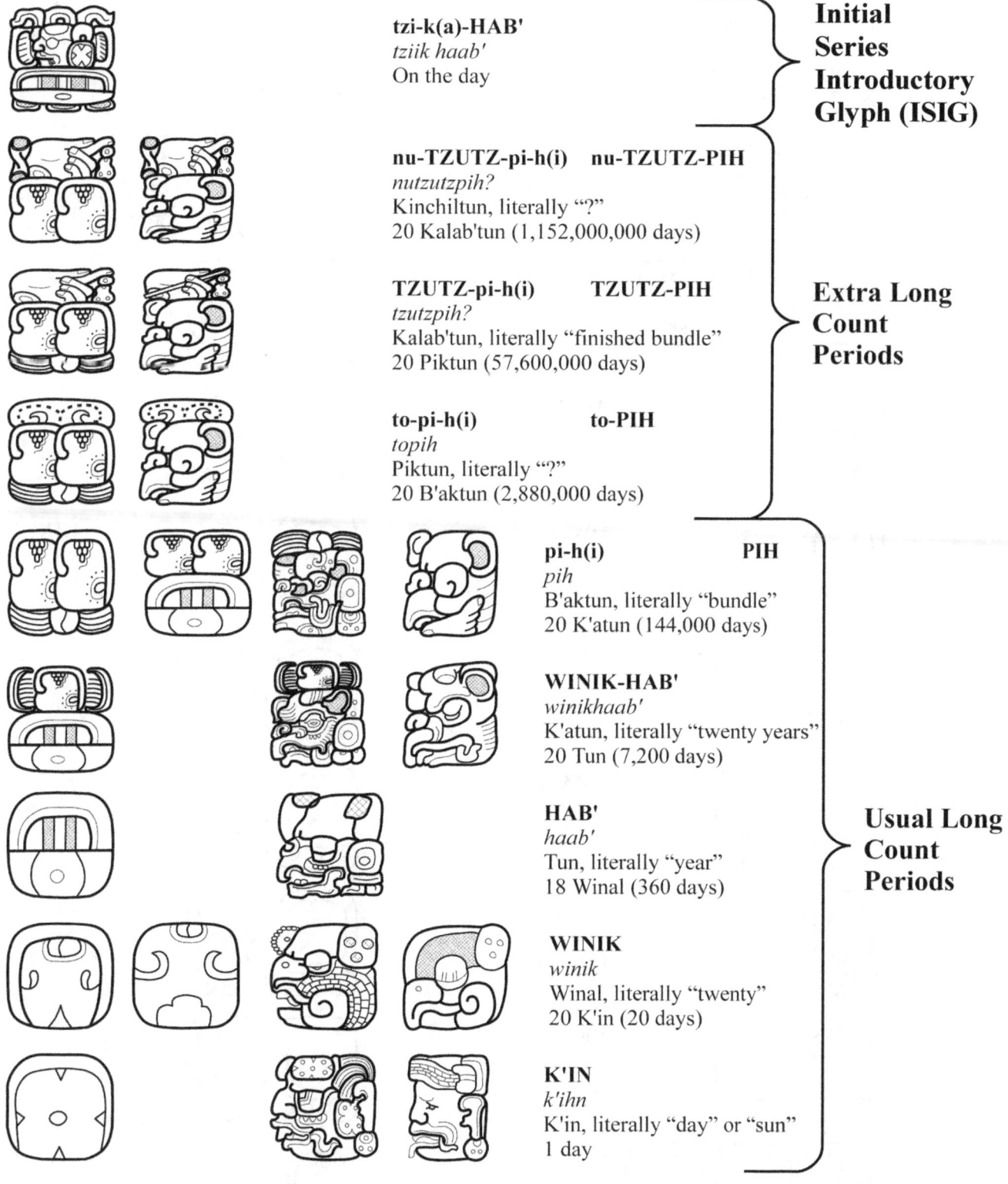

III.1. Classic Maya Calendar (page 3 of 8)

Tzolk'in Day Names

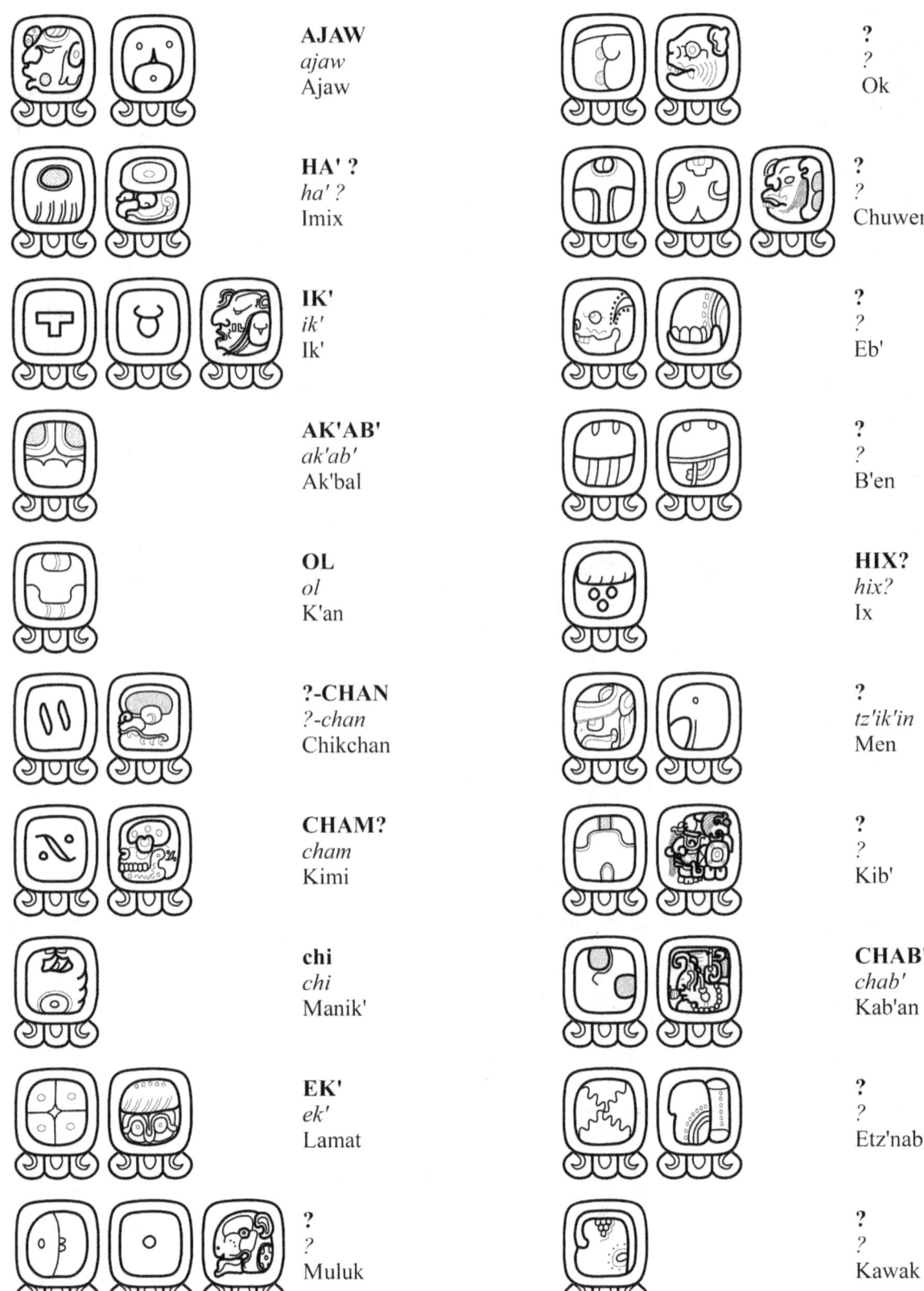

Glyph	Reading	Day
	AJAW / *ajaw*	Ajaw
	HA' ? / *ha' ?*	Imix
	IK' / *ik'*	Ik'
	AK'AB' / *ak'ab'*	Ak'bal
	OL / *ol*	K'an
	?-CHAN / *?-chan*	Chikchan
	CHAM? / *cham*	Kimi
	chi / *chi*	Manik'
	EK' / *ek'*	Lamat
	? / *?*	Muluk
	? / *?*	Ok
	? / *?*	Chuwen
	? / *?*	Eb'
	? / *?*	B'en
	HIX? / *hix?*	Ix
	? / *tz'ik'in*	Men
	? / *?*	Kib'
	CHAB' / *chab'*	Kab'an
	? / *?*	Etz'nab'
	? / *?*	Kawak

III.1. Classic Maya Calendar (page 4 of 8)

Haab' Month Names

 **K'AN-?-w(a)**
k'anjalaw?
Pop

 **SAK-SIHOM?-(hi-ma)**
saksiho'm
Sak

 **IK'-AT-(ta) wo-h(i)**
ik'at
Wo

 **CHAK-SIHOM?-(hi-ma)**
chaksiho'm
Keh

 **CHAK-AT-(ta)**
chakat
Sip

 **ma-k(a)/AK**
mak
Mak

 **SUTZ'**
suutz'
Sotz'

 **UNIW-(wa)**
uniiw
K'ank'in

 **ka-se-w(a)**
kase'w
Sek

 **mu-wa-n(i) MUWAN-(ni)**
muwaan
Muwan

 **CHIK-n(i)**
chikin
Xul

 **PAX**
pax
Pax

 **YAX-K'IN-(ni)**
yaxk'in
Yaxk'in

 **[KAN]a-si-y(a)**
kanasiiy
K'ayab

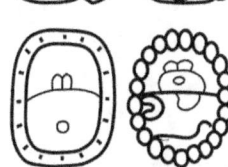 **mo-l(o)**
mol
Mol

 **?-OL-(la)**
o'l
Kumk'u

 **IK'-SIHOM?-(ma)**
ik'siho'm
Ch'en

 **WAY-HAB'**   **ko-l(o)-AJAW**
wayhaab'   *kol ajaw*
Wayeb

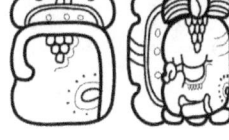 **YAX-SIHOM?-(hi-ma)**
yaxsiho'm
Yax

APPENDIX III. BASIC VOCABULARY

III.1. Classic Maya Calendar (page 5 of 8)

Glyph G, Lords of the Night

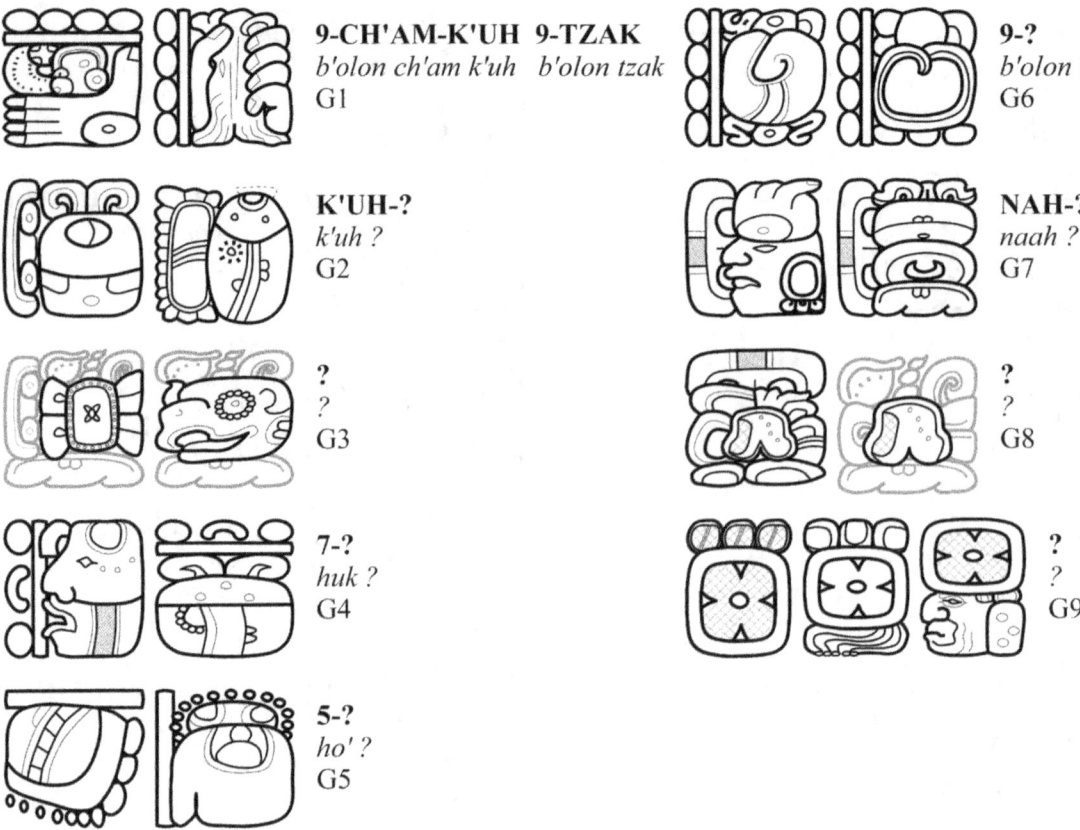

Glyph F

TI'-hu-n(a)
ti' hu'n
reader of the book

TI'-HUN-(na)
ti' hu'n
reader of the book

Glyphs Z and Y

#-b'i-xi-y(a)
?
?

?
?
?

III.1. Classic Maya Calendar (page 6 of 8)

Glyphs E and D

20
winik
twenty

#-hu-li-y(a)
huliiy
days ago [the moon] arrived

#-HUL-li-y(a)
huliiy
days ago [the moon] arrived

Glyph C

#-?-K'AL ja
? *k'ahlaj*
? was bound

Glyph X

?
?
X1

?
?
X4

?
?
X2

?
?
X5

?
?
X3

?
?
X6

Glyph B

ch'o[k(o)]-K'AB'A'
ch'ok k'ab'a'
its princely name

K'UH-K'AB'A'
k'uh k'ab'a'
its holy name

III.1. Classic Maya Calendar (page 7 of 8)

Glyph A

 **20-9**
winik b'olon
twenty-nine [day lunation]

 **20-10**
winik laju'n
twenty and ten [day lunation]

819-Day Cycle
819-day dedicatory verb

 **?-ja-ji-ya**
?ajiiy
it was ?

Quadrant Direction

 **EL-K'IN-(ni)**
elk'ihn
east

 **OCH-K'IN-(ni)**
ochk'ihn
west

 **xa-MAN-(na)**
xaman
north

 **no-NOJOL?-(la)**
nojo'l
south

Direction Color

 **CHAK-?**
chak ?
red ?

 **IK'-?**
ik' ?
black ?

 **SAK-?**
sak ?
white ?

 **K'AN-?**
k'an ?
yellow ?

K'awil reference

 ?
?
?

 **K'AWIL**
k'awiil
K'awil

APPENDIX III. BASIC VOCABULARY

III.1. Classic Maya Calendar (page 8 of 8)

Distance Number Introductory Glyph and K'in Variants

Distance Number Introductory Glyph

 **u-TZ'AK-ka-AJ**
utz'akaj
it was set in order

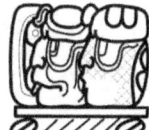 **u-K'IN-AK'AB'-AJ**
uk'inak'ab'aj
it day-and-nighted (?)

 **u-IK'-NAB'-AJ**
uik'naab'aj
it black-lilied (?)

K'in Variants

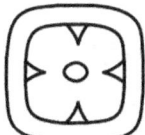 **K'IN**
k'ihn
day(s)

 **he**
he
day(s)

 **?-w(a)**
?w
day(s)

 **PAS**
pas
dawn

 **K'IN**
k'ihn
day(s)

 **la-t(a)**
lat
day(s)

 **b'i-xi-y(a)**
b'ixiiy
5 or 7 days

Date Indicators and Period Completions

Posterior Date Indicator

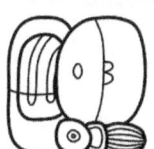  **i-u-ti**
iuti
and then it happened

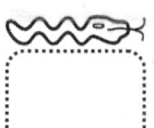 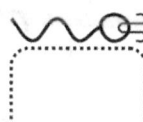 **UTI**
uti
and then it happened

Anterior Date Indicator

  **u-ti-y(i)**
utiiy
it happened ... ago

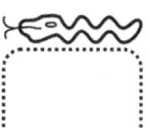 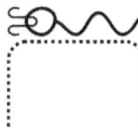 **UTIY**
utiiy
and then it happened ... ago

Future Date Indicator

 **u-to-m(a)**
uto'm
it will happen

Tun Completion

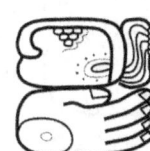 **K'AL-TUN-(ni)**
k'al tuun
the bound stone

General Completion

 **TZUTZ-y(i)**
tzutzuuy
got completed

Half-Period Completion

 **TAN-LAM-mi-j(a)**
tan lahmaj
it was half-diminished

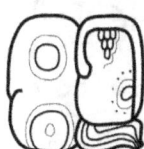 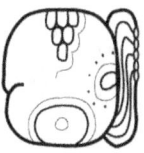 **CHUM-TUN-(ni)**
chum tuun
the seated stone

III.2. Classic Maya Verbs

Birth

SIY
siy
to be born (div)

PAS-KAB'
pas kab'
earth opening (div)

Accession

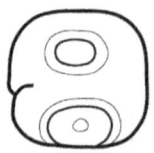
CHUM
chum
to sit/be seated (pv)

JOY
joy
to encircle (tv)

K'AL-SAK-hu-n(a)
k'al sak hu'n
to bind white headdress (tv)

AJAW-ni
ajawaan
to become ajaw (in)

K'AL-MAY
k'al may
to bind the offering (tv)

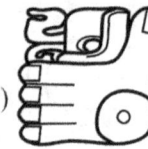
CH'AM-K'AWIL
ch'am k'awiil
to grasp the k'awiil scepter (tv)

Death

CHAM
cham
to die (riv)

mu-k(a)
muk
to bury (tv)

sa-ta
sat
to diminish (tv)

OCH-B'IH
och b'ih
to enter the road (riv)

OCH-HA'
och ha'
to enter the water (riv)

K'A'-SAK-IK-li
k'a' sak ikiil
to diminish white wind (tv)

Ritual

TZAK
tzak
to conjure (tv)

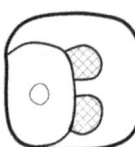
AK'
ak'
to dance (div)

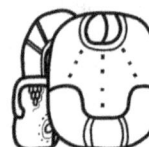
pi-tzi
pitz
to play ball (div)

tz'a[pa]
tz'ap
to plant (tv)

tz'i-b'(a)
tz'ib'
to write (div)

CH'AB'
ch'ab'
to do penance (tv)

CHOK
chok
to scatter (tv)

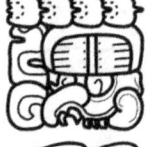
OCH-K'AK'
och k'ahk'
to enter fire (riv)

nu-pu
nup
to marry (tv)

K'AL
k'al
to bind (tv)

k'u-lu
k'ul
to venerate (div)

TZUTZ
tzutz
to end (tv)

APPENDIX III. BASIC VOCABULARY 245

III.2. Classic Maya Verbs (continued)

Capture

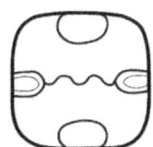 **B'AK** *b'aak* to capture (tv)

 **chu-ka** *chuk* to catch (tv)

 **na-wa** *naw* to display (tv)

Military Action

 **CH'AK-ka** *ch'ak* to chop, cut (tv)

 **to-ko** *tok* to burn (tv)

 **a-ha** *'ah* to conquer (div)

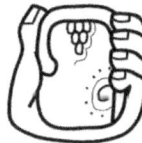 **JATZ'** *jatz'* to strike, wound (tv)

 **wi** *wi'* to create carnage (tv)

 **CH'AY(?)** *ch'ay (?)* to be defeated (riv)

 **na-ka** *nak* to conquer (div)

 **JUL** *jul* to throw, shoot (tv)

 **ya-la** *yal* to throw, demolish (tv)

 **ko-jo** *koj* to hit (tv)

 **ju-b'u** *jub'* to take down (tv)

 **pu-lu** *pul* to sprinkle (tv)

Other Verbs

 **a-ka** *'ak* to give (tv)

 **u-b'u** *'ub'* to hear (tv)

 **OCH** *'och* to enter (riv)

 **a-la** *'al* to say (tv)

 **u-k'u** *uk'* to drink (tv)

 **T'AB'** *t'ab'* to ascend (riv)

 **cha-b'a** *chab'* to supervise (tv)

 **u-tz'u** *'utz'* to smell, sniff (tv)

 **CH'AM** *ch'am* to grasp, take (tv)

 **'IL** *'il* to see (tv)

 **WE'** *we'* to eat (tv)

 **HUL** *hul* to arrive (riv)

APPENDIX III. BASIC VOCABULARY

III.3. Classic Maya Colors

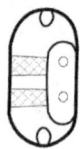 **CHAK** *chak* red

 **IK'** *ik'* black

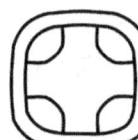 **K'AN** *k'an* yellow

 **YAX** *yax* blue-green

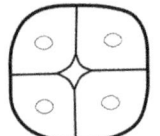 **EK'** *ek'* black

 **ko-b'(a)** *ko'b'* gray

 **SAK** *sak* white

III.4. Classic Maya Titles

Royal Titles

 **AJAW**
ajaw
ruler (n)

 **AJAW**
ajaw
ruler (n)

 **AJAW**
ajaw
ruler (n)

 **AJAW**
ajaw
ruler (n)

 **AJAW-TE'**
ajaw te'
tree ruler (n)

 **B'AH-AJAW**
b'aah ajaw
head ruler (n)

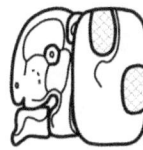 **B'AH-KAB'**
b'aah kab'
first of the earth (n)

 **B'AH-lo-m(u)**
b'aah lo'm
first spear (n)

 **B'AH-lo-m(u)-sa-ja-l(a)**
b'aah lo'm sajal
first spear lord (n)

 **B'AH-pa-ka-l(a)**
b'aah pakal
first shield (n)

 **B'AH-sa-ja-l(a)**
b'aah sajal
first lord (n)

 **B'AH-TE'**
b'aah te'
first tree (n)

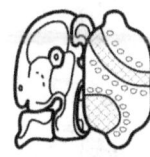 **B'AH-TOK'**
b'aah to'k
first flint (n)

 **b'a-ka-b'(a)**
b'akab'
first of the earth (n)

 **ch'o[k(o)]**
ch'ok
heir (n)

 **KALOM-TE'**
kalo'm te'
supreme ruler (n)

 **ka-na-ka-TE'**
kanak te'
second tree (n)

 **K'INICH**
k'inich
sun-faced (adj),
sun-faced one (n)

 **K'INICH**
k'inich
sun-faced (adj),
sun-faced one (n)

 **K'UHUL-AJAW**
k'uhul ajaw
holy ruler (n)

 **sa-ja-l(a)**
sajal
lord (n)

 **yo-K'IN-(ni)**
yok'ihn
sun foot (n)

 **yu-ku-no-m(a)**
yukno'm
shaker (n)

III.4. Classic Maya Titles (continued)

Female Titles

 **IXIK**
ixik
woman, lady (n)

 **IX-sa-ja-l(a)**
ix sajal
lady lord (n)

 **IX-KALOM-TE'**
ix kalo'm te'
Lady supreme ruler (n)

 **IX**
ix
woman, lady (n)

 **B'AH-IXIK**
b'aah ixik
first lady (n)

 **?[K'AN]**
?[k'an]
[female title] (n)

 **IX-AJAW**
ix ajaw
Lady ruler (n)

 **IXIK-b'a-ka-b'(a)**
ixik b'akab'
first of the earth (n)

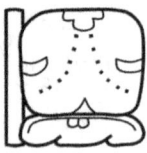 **5-HUN-(na)**
ho' hu'n
five book (n)

Occupational Titles

 **AJ-[#]-B'AK**
aj [#] b'aak
he of [#] captives (n)

 **B'AK**
b'aak
captive (n)

 **MAM**
mam
ancestor, grandfather (n)

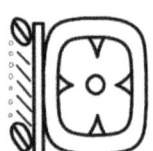 **AJ-K'IN**
aj k'ihn
priest (n)

 **che-b'(u)**
che'ehb'
painter (n)

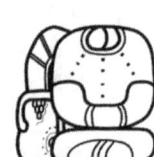 **pi-tzi-l(i)**
pitzil
ball player (n)

 **AJ-K'UH-n(a)**
aj k'uhu'n
one who venerates (n)

 **CHUWEN**
chuwen
artist (n)

 **TI'-SAK-hu-n(a)**
ti' sak hu'n
speaker of the white book (n)

 **AJ-na-b'(i)**
aj naahb'
sculptor (n)

 **ch'a-ho-m(a)**
chaho'm
incense scatterer (n)

 **u-xu-l(u)**
uxul
carver (n)

 **AJ-tz'i-b'(a)**
aj tz'iib'
scribe (n)

 **[i]tz'a-t(i)**
itz'aat
sage, wise man (n)

 **WI'-TE'-NAH**
wi' te' naah
founder (lit. "house root") (n)

 **AJ-yu-xu-l(u)**
ajyuxul
sculptor (n)

 **1-TAN**
ju'n tan
cherished one (n)

 **WINIK**
winik
human, man

III.5. Classic Maya Animals (page 1 of 3)

Mammals

B'AH
b'aah
gopher (n)

CHITAM
chitam
peccary (n)

OK
ook
dog (n)

B'ALAM
b'ahlam
jaguar (n)

ch'a-ma-k(a)
ch'amak
fox (n)

SAB'IN
sab'in
weasel (n)

b'a-tz'(u)
b'a'tz'
howler monkey (n)

CH'O
ch'o
rat (n)

SUTZ'
suutz'
bat (n)

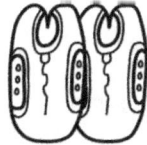
b'o-b'(o)
b'ohb'
coyote (n)

EM-ma-ch(a)
emach
racoon (n)

TIL
tihl
tapir (n)

b'o-la-y(i)
b'olay
small jaguar (n)

HIX
hix
jaguar (n)

T'UL
t'ul
rabbit (n)

B'ULAY (?)
b'ulaay (?)
small jaguar (n)

KOJ
koj
puma (n)

tzu-l(u)
tzul
dog (n)

chi-j(i)
chij
deer (n)

ma-m(a)
mam
possum (n)

tz'i-(i)
tz'i'
dog (n)

CHIK
chi'k
coatimundi (n)

MAY
may
deer (n)

tz'u-tz'(i)
tz'uutz'
coatimundi (n)

chi-l(i)-ka-y(u)
chilka'y
manatee (n)

MAX
maax
spider monkey (n)

wa-x(i)
waax
fox (n)

III.5. Classic Maya Animals (page 2 of 3)

Birds

 **a-k'a-ch(a)**
ak'ach
turkey hen (n)

 **K'UK'**
k'uk'
quetzal (n)

 **to-t(o)**
tot
robin, lark (n)

 **I**
i'
hawk (n)

 **MAT**
mat
cormorant (n)

 **tu-ku-n(u)**
tukun
dove, pigeon (n)

 **i-chi-y(a)**
ichiiy
hawk, heron (n)

 **MO'**
mo'
macaw (n)

 **tz'u-²nu**
tz'unun
hummingbird (n)

 **JANAB'**
janaab'
[type of bird] (n)

 **mu-t(i)**
muut
bird (n)

 **u-ku-m(u)**
ukum
dove, pigeon (n)

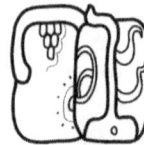 **ku-tz(u)**
kutz
(wild) turkey (n)

 **MUWAN**
muwaan
sparrow-hawk (n)

 **u-lu-m(u)**
ulum
turkey hen (n)

 **KUH / KUY**
kuh / kuy
owl (n)

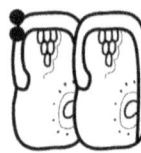 **²pi**
pip
[bird of prey] (n)

 **u-si-j(a)**
usiij
vulture (n)

 **k'u-ch(i)**
k'uuch
vulture (n)

 **pu-y(i)**
puuy
roadrunner (n)

 **ya-xu-n(a)**
yaxu'n
cotinga (n)

Fish

 **KAY**
kay
fish (n)

 **XOK**
xook
shark (n)

III.5. Classic Maya Animals (page 3 of 3)

Reptiles and Amphibians

 **AHIN** *ahiin* crocodile, lizard (n)

 **CHAN** *chan* snake (n)

 **ITZAM** *itzam* lizard, iguana (n)

 **AK** *ahk* turtle (n)

 **HUJ** *huj* iguana (n)

 **mu-ch(i)** *muuch* toad (n)

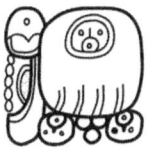 **a-ma-l(a)** *amal* toad (n)

 **i-b'a-ch(a)** *ib'ach* armadillo (n)

Insects and Invertebrates

 **CHAPAT** *chapa't* centipede (n)

 **pu-y(i)** *puuy* snail (n)

 **chi-wo-j(o)** *chiwoj* tarantula (n)

 **b'u-b'u-l(u)-HA'** *b'ub'ul ha'* water insect (n)

 **sa-y(u)** *sa'y* ant (n)

 **(y)u-ch'(a)** *u'ch'* louse (n)

 **KAB'** *kab'* earth, bee (n)

 **si-na-n(a)** *sinan* scorpion (n)

 **xu** *xu'* ant (n)

 **ma-s(u)** *ma's* cricket (n)

III.6. Classic Maya Family Relations

Parentage Statements

'AL
'ahl
child of (mother) (n)

MIJIN?
mijiin
child of (father) (n)

(y)u-n(e)
une[n]
child of (n)

ni-ch(i)
nich
child of man (n)

Relationship Titles

'AT-n(a)
'atan
wife (n)

ki-t(i)
kit
father (n)

su-ku-n(a)
suku'n
older brother (n)

B'AH-AL
b'aah ahl
first child (n)

1-ta-n(a)
ju'n tan
cherished one (n)

²ta
tat
father (n)

chi-t(i)
chit
father (n)

MAM
mam
grandfather, ancestor (n)

yu-m(u)
yum
father (n)

ch'o[k(o)]
ch'ok
youth, heir (n)

mi-m(i)
mim
grandmother (maternal) (n)

i-tzi-n(i)
ihtz'iin
younger brother (n)

sa-ku-n(a)
saku'n
older brother (n)

Deities

CHAK
chaahk
Chak
(rain-deity) (n)

K'INICH
k'inich
K'inich
(sun deity) (n)

ITZAMNAJ
itzamnaaj
Itzamnaj
(creator-deity) (n)

K'AWIL-(la)
k'awiil
K'awil (deity) (n)

K'UH
k'uh
god, deity (n)

WAY
way
co-essence
spirit (n)

III.7. Classic Maya Emblem Glyphs

Emblem Glyphs

 **K'UHUL ... AJAW**
k'uhul ... ajaw
Holy Ruler of ...

 **ne-?**
ne-?
Altun Ha'
(lit. "?")

 **?**
?
Lamanai
(lit. "?")

 **MUTUL**
mutul
Tikal
(lit. "bundle")

 **b'i-TAL**
b'ital
Bital (at Naranjo)
(lit. "?")

 **AT-t'o-s(u) (?)**
?
Machaquila
(lit. "?")

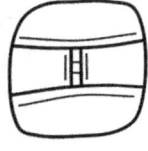 **po**
po[po']
Tonina
(lit. "?")

 **(ka)-KAN**
kan
Calakmul
(lit. "snake")

 **SA-AT-y(i)**
?
Naranjo
(lit. "?")

 **K'AN-(na)-WITZ-NAL**
k'an witznal
Ucanal
(lit. "yellow mountain place")

 **AK**
ahk
Cancuen
(lit. "turtle")

 **B'AK**
b'aak
Palenque
(lit. "bone")

 **YAX-a**
yax [h]a'
Yaxha
(lit. "green water")

 **K'AN-tu-ma[k(i)]**
k'antu' maak
Caracol
(lit. "yellow-thing person")

 **yo-ki-b'(i)**
[yo]yokib'
Piedras Negras
(lit. "[his] canyon")

 **PA'CHAN**
pa'chan
Yaxchilan
(lit. "split-sky")

 **xu[k(u)]-pi**
xuk pi'
Copan
(lit. "dance staff"?)

 **tzu (?)**
tzu ?
Quirigua
(lit. "gourd"?)

 **PET (?)**
pet (?)
Yaxchilan
(lit. "round")

 **MUTUL**
mutul
Dos Pilas
(lit. "bundle")

 **?**
?
Seibal
(lit. "?")

III.8. Classic Maya Objects (page 1 of 3)

Vessels

 **cha-ch(i)** *chaach* basket

 **la-k(a)** *lak* plate

 **WE'-b'i** *we'ib* plate (lit. "eating thing")

 **ja-y(i)** *jaay* bowl

 **le-k(e)** *lek* calabash

 **ja-wa-TE'** *jawa[n]te'* plate with legs

 **(y)u-k'i-b'(i)** *(y)uk'ib'* (his) drinking vessel (lit. "drinking thing")

Ritual Objects

 **CH'AB'** *ch'ahb'* fast, penance

 **ja-sa-w(a)-CHAN-(na)** *jasaw chan* dance staff

 **po-p(o)** *pop* mat

 **K'AN-(na)-TUN-(ni)** *k'an tuun* seat, bench

 **k'u-tz(i)** *k'uutz* tobacco

 **ta-j(i)** *taaj* obsidian, bloodletter

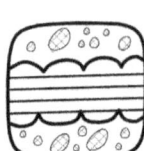 **HUN** *hu'n* book, paper, bark

 **NEN** *neen* mirror

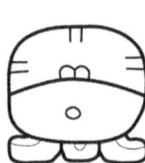 **te-m(a)** *te'm* throne, bench

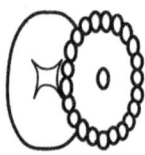 **po-m(o)** *pom* incense, copal

 **TZ'AM** *tz'am* throne

Monuments

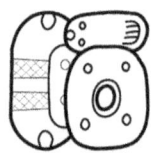 **CHAK-li-b'(i)** *chaklib'* panel

 **(LAKAM)-TUN-(ni)** *(lakam) tuun* stela (lit. "(great) stone")

 **u-xu-l(u)** *uxul* carving

 **ka-y(a)-wa-k(a)** *kaywak* jade

 **pa-ka-b'(a)-TUN-(ni)** *pakab' tuun* lintel (lit. "face-down stone")

III.8. Classic Maya Objects (page 2 of 3)

Warfare-Related Objects

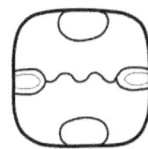
B'AK
b'aak
captive (n)

JUL
jul
dart, spear (n)

PAKAL
pakal
shield (n)

chu-ni-k'(u)
chuni'k'
drum (n)

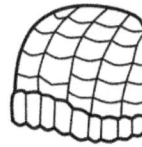
KOHAW
ko'haw
helmet, headdress (n)

TOK'
to'k'
flint (n)

ju-b'(i)
juub'
conch shell trumpet (n)

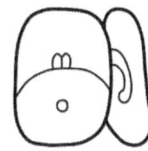
lo-m(u)
loom (?)
lance (n)

Plants

CHAK-la-TE'
chakalte'
cedar (n)
(lit. "reddish tree")

ha-n(a)
han
flower (n)

NAL
nal
ear of corn, place, person (n)

chi-h(i)
chih
maguey (n)

K'AN-TE'
k'ante'
yellow tree (n)

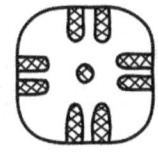
NICH
nich
flower (n)

EK'-TE'
ek'te'
black tree (n)

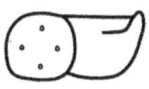
NAB'
naahb'
water lily (n)

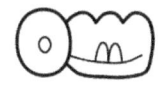
TE'
te'
tree (n)

Structures

a-la-w(a)
alaw
ball court (n)

HALAB'
halaab'
ball court (n)

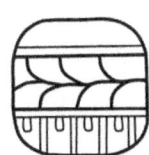
OTOT
otoot
house, home, building (n)

chi-ti-n(a)
chitiin
sweatbath, oven (n)

MUK-NAL
muknal
tomb (n)
(lit. "bury place")

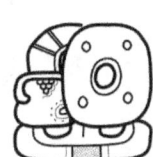
pi-b'(i)-NAH
pib'naah
sweatbath, oven (n)

e-b'(a)
e'b'
staircase, ladder (n)

NAH
naah
house, building (n)

WAY
way
co-essence, spirit, dormitory (n)

III.8. Classic Maya Objects (page 3 of 3)

Landforms

 **CH'EN** *ch'e'n* cave, well (n)

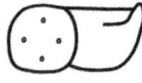 **NAB'** *naahb'* pool, sea (n)

 **WITZ** *witz* mountain, hill (n)

 **KAB'** *kab'* earth, dirt (n)

 **PET-n(e)** *peten* island, district (n)

 **yo-ki-b'(i)** *yokib'* canyon (n)

 **lu-m(a)** *lu'm* earth, soil (n)

 **TUN-(ni)** *tuun* stone (n)

Food

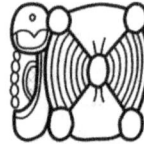 **a-n(u)** *a'n* spring maize (n)

 **NAL** *nal* ear of corn (n)

 **u-l(u)** *ul* atole (n)

 **b'u-l(a)** *b'u'l* bean (n)

 **ON-(ni)** *oon* avocado (n)

 **UNIW** *uniiw* avocado (n)

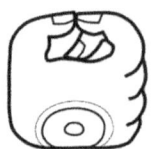 **chi** *chi'* pulque (n)

 **pa** *pa* food (n)

 **UT** *uut* fruit (n)

 **i-ch(i)** *ich* chili (n)

 **sa** *sa* atole (n)

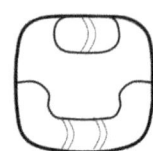 **WAJ** *waaj* tamale, tortilla (n)

 **²ka-w(a)** *kakaw* chocolate (n)

 **SAK-HA'** *sak ha'* atole (n) (lit. "white water")

 **WE'-l(a)** *we'el* food, meat (n)

 **ko-b'a-l(a)** *kob'al* atole (n)

APPENDIX IV.1. CLASSIC MAYAN TO ENGLISH LEXICON

Glyphic Expression

Each logogram specific to an entry is drawn in the first column. Entries that are only spelled phonetically are not usually drawn. Using the syllabary, it is possible to "spell out" pure syllabic words.

Transcription

The second column gives some of the known glyphic spellings for each entry. Usually the logographic spellings are given first, and then any possible syllabic spellings are listed.

> B'ALAM
> b'a-la-ma

Standard transcription conventions are used (except that final vowels or phonetic compliments are not placed in parenthesis to aid in searching this database). Logographic spellings are often accompanied by syllabic phonetic compliments in inscriptions, but in this lexicon, superfluous phonetic compliments are not given.

> B'ALAM not b'a-B'ALAM-ma
> b'a-la-ma not b'a-la-m(a)

Transliteration

Many entries have more than one suggested transliteration. This is because of the variability of historical reconstruction and the current debate surrounding the complex vowel spelling rules outlined in Chapter 2. In this lexicon, the third column has most of these suggested transliterations. The first spelling is the one used in this book. The following spellings are from Lacadena and Wichman (2004), Robertson et al. (2007), as indicated by the note attached to each, or other sources such as Boot (2002), Mathews and Biro (2006), or Montgomery (2002). Sometimes there are discrepancies among the dictionaries, but remember that the transliteration is not required for translation; it is a reconstruction of the sound only. For the most part, the spellings used in this book follow a simplified version of Lacadena and Wichmann (2004), but will be updated as the field advances. For example, "shell," glyphically spelled as **ju-ch(i)**, is reconstructed as *juu[h]ch* by Lacadena and Wichmann (2004) but as *ju[h]ch* by Robertson et al. (2007). As mentioned before, spelling rules are still hotly debated. In this lexicon, the entry for "shell" lists the spellings as follows, indicating the variety of reconstructed transcriptions:

> *juu[h]ch* [1]
> *(ju[h]ch* [2])
> *(juch)*
> *(juuch)*

[1] Lacadena and Wichmann 2004

[2] Robertson, Houston, Stuart 2004 or Robertson, Houston, Stuart, and Zender 2007 (2007 spellings trump 2004 spellings)

For the purposes of this lexicon, an infixed *h* is indicated within brackets for the root entry, but in compound words, the brackets are left off. This is done to show that the *h* is indeed artificially inserted when the root word entry is checked, but to make names and other compound words easier to read:

> *b'a[h]lam*

but

> *yax b'ahlam*

APPENDIX IV.1 CLASSIC MAYAN TO ENGLISH LEXICON

Translation

For each item, one or more acceptable translations is given in the last column. Sometimes more than one meaning may be derived from a single word. Context may be required to choose the correct meaning. For each entry, the translation is given first, followed by the literal translation in quotation marks. Sometimes a description of where or how this term is used. Finally, the part of speech is indicated by one of the following abbreviations:

n	noun
adj	adjective
adv	adverb
tv	transitive verbs
div	derived intransitive verbs
riv	root intransitive verbs
pv	positional verbs
icv	inchoative verbs
ncl	numeral classifiers
num	numeral

Transcription	*Transliteration*	Translation
A		
a	*a*	1) you, your, yours (prep.) 2) focus marker
'AB'AK' (y)a-b'a-ki	*ab'ak* *(ab'ak'* [2]*)*	1) soot, ink (n)
(H)AB'-ta	*ab'at*	1) servant (n)
a-ha-	*ah-*	1) to conquer (div)
AHAL a-ha-li	*ahaal*	1) conquest (n)
AHIN-na **AHIN-ni** a-hi	*ahiin* [1,2]	1) crocodile/lizard (n)
AHIN-CHAN-na-a-ku **AHIN-CHAN-AK**	*ahiin chan ahk*	1) Ahin Chan Ak, "crocodile snake/sky(?) turtle", name (elite at Pomona) (n)
AJ a	*aj*	1) he who (adj)

APPENDIX IV.1 CLASSIC MAYAN TO ENGLISH LEXICON

Transcription	*Transliteration*	Translation
-a-ja- -a-je-	*-aj-*	1) to wake up (tv)
a-ja-la a-ja-li	*ajal*	1) awakening (n) 2) dawn (n) 3) conquest (?) (n) 4) manifested (?) (adj)
AJAW a-ja-wa	*ajaw* *(ajaaw ?)*	1) lord, king, ruler (n) 2) 20th day name (n)
AJAW-li a-ja-wa-li	*ajawil*	1) reign, kingship, lordship (n)
AJAW-le-le **AJAW-le** **AJAW-2le**	*ajawlel*	1) reign, kingship, lordship (n)
AJAW-TE'	*ajaw te'*	1) Ajaw Te', "tree lord", title (n)
AJ-b'i-K'A'?-la	*ajb'ik'al*	1) scribbler (n)
a-CHAK-ma-xi	*aj chak maax*	1) Aj Chak Maax, "he of the red spider monkey", name (at Laxtunich) (n)
AJ-CHAK-SUTZ'-k'u-ti-ma	*aj chak suutz' k'utiim*	1) Aj Chak Sutz' K'utim, "he of red bat ?", name (sajal at El Cayo) (n)
AJ-'CHE-le-wa-ji **AJ-'CHE-le-wa-WAJ**	*aj chel waaj*	1) Aj Chel Waj, "he of the high tamale", title (at Chichen Itza) (n)
AJ-chi-ji **AJ-chi**	*ajchij*	1) drunkard (n) 1) hunter, "he of the deer" (n)
AJ-ch'a-ma	*ajch'ama[k]*	1) fox (n)
a-je-se	*ajes-*	1) to make awake (div)
AJ-ha-ma-li-b'i	*aj hamlib*	1) Aj Hamlib', "he of the laid-down-thing", title (at Yaxchilan) (n)
AJ-HUN-K'IN-ni-K'AK'	*aj hu'n k'ihn k'ahk'*	1) Aj Hun K'in K'ak', "he of the sun fire book (?)", name (ruler at Seibal) (n)
AJ-K'AK'-MUWAN-CHAK-ki	*aj k'ahk' muwaan chaahk*	1) Aj K'ak' Muwan Chak, "he of the fiery sparrow-hawk rain-deity", name (deity) (n)
AJ-K'AK'-o-CHAK-ki **AJ-K'AK'-o-cha-ki**	*aj k'ahk' o chaahk*	1) Aj K'ak' O Chak, "he of the fiery rain-deity", name (deity)(n)

APPENDIX IV.1 CLASSIC MAYAN TO ENGLISH LEXICON

Transcription	Transliteration	Translation
AJ-K'A'?-mi-la-yu	aj k'amla'y	1) Aj K'amlay, "he who receives", title (n)
AJ-K'AN-b'a-tz'u	aj k'an b'a'tz'	1) Aj K'an B'atz', "he of the yellow howler monkey", name (n)
AJ-K'AN-ma-xi	aj k'an maax	1) Aj K'an Max, "he of the yellow spider monkey", name (ruler at El Chorro) (n)
AJ-K'AN-na-to-ko-mu-ku-yi	aj k'an tok mukuuy	1) Aj K'an Tok Mukuy, "he of the yellow cloud dove", name (at Calakmul) (n)
AJ-K'AN-na-tu-MUWAN	aj k'antu' muwaan	1) Aj K'antu Muwan, "he of the yellow-thing sparrow-hawk", name (at Bonampak) (n)
AJ-K'AN-na-u-si-ja	aj k'an usiij	1) Aj K'an Usih, "he of the yellow vulture", name (ruler at B'uktun) (n)
AJ-K'IN	aj k'ihn	1) priest, "he of the sun", title (n)
AJ-K'UH-na AJ-K'UH-HUN-na AJ-K'UH-HUN AJ-K'UH-hu-na a-K'UH-na	aj k'uhu'n (aj k'uhuun)	1) He who venerates (he of the headband/holy books), title (n)
AJ-la-tzi	aj laatz	1) He of the stack, title (n)
AJ-la-tzi-HUN-na AJ-la-tzi-u-HUN-na	aj laatz hu'n	1) He of the stack of books, title (n)
a-mu-chi	a[j]muuch [1,2]	1) toad (n)
AJ-pa-ka-la-TAN-na	aj pakal tan	1) Aj Pakal Tan, "he of the shield center", name (of court official at Comalcalco) (n)
AJ-po-k'o-chi-ji-la-ka-ma-YAX-le-ke-HIX	aj pok' chij lakam yax lek hix	1) Aj Pok' Chij Lakam Yax Lek Hix, "he of ? deer large blue/green calabash jaguar", name (on Kerr 5722) (n)
AJ-si-k'a-b'a	aj si[h] k'ab'	1) Aj Sih K'ab', "he of offering hand", name (at Palenque) (n)
AJ-si-ya-i-chi	aj siya[j] ich	1) Aj Siyaj Ich, "he of the born chili (?)", name (deity on Codex-style vessel) (n)
AJ-tz'i-b'i a-tz'i-b'i AJ-tz'i-b'a	aj tz'ihb'	1) scribe, "he of writing" (n)
a-tz'i-b'a-la	aj tz'ihb'aal	1) painter, artist (n)
AJ-u-b'u	aj [j]ub'	1) trumpeter, "he of the conch trumpet" (n)
AJ-WAK-TUN-ni-ya-YAXUN?-B'ALAM-ma	aj wak tuun yaxu'n b'ahlam	1) Aj Wak Tun Yaxun B'alam, "he of the upright stone cotinga jaguar", name (ruler of Yaxchilan) (n)
AJ-yu-lu	aj yul	1) polisher (?) (n)

APPENDIX IV.1 CLASSIC MAYAN TO ENGLISH LEXICON

Transcription	*Transliteration*	Translation
AK **a-ka**	*a[h]k* [1] *(ak)*	1) turtle (n)
AKAN **AJ-AKAN-na**	*a[h]kan* [1,2] *(akan)*	1) Akan, name (deity of visions, alcohol, enemas; God A) (n), roaring (adj) 2) roaring, groan (n)
AKAN-CHIJ	*ahkan chij*	1) Akanchij, "roaring deer (?)", toponym (Yucatan) (n)
AKAN-SUTZ	*ahkan suutz'*	1) Akan Sutz', "roaring bat (?)", name (scribe on Kerr 1599) (n)
AKAN-na-YAX-ha	*ahkan yaxha'*	1) Akan Yaxha, name (deity) (n)
(y)a-ka-ta	*-akta-*	1) to lose, drop (tv)
AK-la **a-ku** **a-ku-la** **AJ-lu**	*a[h]ku'l* *(a[h]ku'ul* [1]*)* *(aku'l)* *(aku'ul)* *(a[h]kuul)*	1) Akul, "turtle place", toponym (area of Usamacinta/Petexbatun) (n) 2) turtle-like (adj)
a-AK-MO' **AK-ku-MO'-o** **a-ku-MO'** **a-ku-lu-MO'-o**	*ahku'l mo'*	1) Akul Mo', "turtle-like macaw", name (captive at Yaxchilan, LTL 10)
a-ku-la-MO'-NAB' **AK-la-MO'-NAB'** **a-ku-la-MO'-na-b'i** **a-ku-la-MO'-NAH-b'i**	*ahku'l mo' naahb'*	1) Akul Mo' Nab', "turtle-like macaw pool", name (ruler at Palenque) (n)
a-ku-NIK-TE'	*ahku'l nikte'*	1) Akul Nikte, "turtle-like mayflower", name (scribe) (n)
a-k'a **a-AK'**	*ak'* *-ak'-* *(a[h]k')*	1) tongue (n) 2) to give (tv)
AK'AB' **a-k'a-b'a**	*ak'ab'* [1] *(a[h]k'ab'* [2]*)*	1) night (n) 2) darkness (n)
a-k'a-b'a-ka-yo-ma	*ak'ab' kayo'm*	1) Ak'ab' Kayom, "night fisherman", name (deity) (n)
AK'ACH **a-k'a-cha**	*ak'ach*	1) turkey hen (n)

APPENDIX IV.1 CLASSIC MAYAN TO ENGLISH LEXICON

Transcription	*Transliteration*	Translation
a-k'e	*ak'e*	1) Ak'e, emblem glyph (Bonampak) (n) 2) Ak'e, emblem glyph (Nimli Punit) (n)
a-AK'-no-ma	*ak'no'm*	1) giver (n)
AK'-ta- AK'-TAJ	*ak't-* *(a[h]k't)*	1) to dance (div)
AK'-ta a-k'a-ta	*ak'[o]t (?)* *(a[h]k'[u]t ²)* *(a[h]k'[o]t)*	1) dance (n)
(y)a-k'u-tu-u	*ak'tu'* *(a[h]k'tu')*	1) gift (n)
AL (y)a-AL (y)a-la	*a[h]l ¹* *(al)* *(aal)* *-al-*	1) child of mother (n) 2) woman's offering (n) 3) to say (tv) 4) to throw (tv)
(C)a-la	*-al*	1) derives nouns from transitive verbs (suf) 2) possessive suffix 3) toponym suffix, "place of …"
a-la-wa	*alaw*	1) ballcourt (n)
a-LAY-ya a-la-ya	*alay*	1) hereby, thus (adv)
(C)a-ma	*-am*	1) participial suffix 2) agentive suffix
a-ma-la	*amal*	1) toad (n)
a-ni	*an-* *(a[h]n-)*	1) to run (div)
a-nu	*a'n ¹,²*	1) spring maize, young corn (n) 2) An, title (deity impersonator) (n) 3) carving (n) 4) to be (as in deity impersonator) (iv)
a-na-yi-TE'	*anayte'*	1) Anayte', toponym (area of Tonina) (n)
AT-ti AT-ta	*aat ¹,²*	1) penis (n)
(y)a-AT-na (y)a-ta-na	*atan ²*	1) wife (n)

Transcription	Transliteration	Translation
(y)a-ATI (y)a-ti	-ati-	1) to bathe (tv)
(y)a-ATOT-ti (y)a-to-TE'	(atoot [1,2])	1) house (n) see *otoot*
a-wi a-wo	aw-	1) your (pro)
(y)a-a-la (y)a-la	-a'l-	1) to say (tv)
a-na-b'i (y)a-a-na-b'i-	ajnaahb'	1) sculptor, title (n)

B

Transcription	Transliteration	Translation
-b'a	-b'a	1) causative suffix
b'a-hi B'AH b'a	b'aah[2]	1) self (suffix) 2) face, self, image (n) 3) first, head (n) 4) gopher (n)
B'AH-AJAW	b'aah ajaw	1) head lord, title (n)
B'AH-AL	b'aah ahl	1) first child, title (n)
B'AH-che-b'u	b'aah che'[eh]b'	1) first painter, title (n)
b'a-ch'o	b'aah ch'o	1) gopher rat (n)
B'AH-ja B'AH-hi-ja b'a-hi-ja	b'ahiij b'ahaj	1) image (n)
B'AH-li b'a-hi-li	b'aahil	1) portrait (n)
B'AH-si	b'aahis	1) head (n)
B'AH-ka-b'a b'a-ka-b'a b'a-KAB'	b'aahkab'	1) first of the earth, title (n)
B'AH-ITZ'AT	b'aah itz'at	1) first sage, title (n)
B'AH-IXIK-ki	b'aah ixik	1) first lady, title (n)
B'AH-lo-mu-sa-ja-la	b'aah lo'm sajal	1) first spear sajal, title (n)
B'AH-pa-ka-la	b'aah pakal	1) first shield, title (n)
B'AH-sa-ja-la	b'aah sajal	1) first sajal, title (n)

Transcription	Transliteration	Translation
B'AH-TE' b'a-TE'	b'aah te'	1) first tree?, title (n)
B'AH-TE'-pi-tzi-la	b'aah te' pitzal	1) B'ah Te' Pitzal, "first tree ballplayer," classic title (n)
B'AH-TOK' B'AH-to-k'a	b'aah to'k'	1) first flint, title (n)
B'AH-tz'a-ma b'a-hi-tz'a-ma	b'aahtz'am	1) down (n)
B'AH-u-xu-lu	b'aah uxul	1) first carver, title (n)
B'AJ b'a-ja	b'aj-	1) to hammer, beat (icv)
B'AK b'a-ki	b'aak [1,2] -b'ak-	1) captive (n) 2) bone (n) 3) heron (n) 4) cascade of water (n) 5) to capture, seize (tv)
b'a-ku	b'a'k [1]	1) child (n)
B'AK-la	b'aakal (b'aak[ii]l) (b'aak[u'u]l)	1) abundance of herons (n) 2) B'akal, emblem glyph (at Palenque) (n)
B'AK-ke-la B'AK-le b'a-ke-le	b'aakel b'aakeel b'aake'l	1) bone (of the body) (n)
B'AK-le-wa-WAY-la (B'AK-la-WAY-ya-la)	b'aakel wayal	1) B'akel Wayal, "dormitory bone," title (at Palenque) (n)
B'AK-JOL	b'aakjol	1) skeleton (n)
b'a-la B'AL b'a-la-ha	b'al -b'al-	1) participal suffix 2) to hide (tv) 3) to double (tv)
B'AL-CHAN-na-K'AWIL	b'alaj chan k'awiil	1) B'alaj Chan K'awil, "hammering sky k'awil," name (ruler at Dos Pilas) (n)
B'ALAM b'a-la-ma	b'a[h]lam [1,2] (b'alam)	1) jaguar (n)
B'ALAM-ma-AJAW	b'ahlam ajaw	1) B'alam Ajaw, "jaguar ruler," name (Tortuguero) (n)
B'ALUN-i-pi	b'alu'n ip-	1) to banish (pv)
b'a-ni	b'aan	1) oneself, alone (pn)

APPENDIX IV.1 CLASSIC MAYAN TO ENGLISH LEXICON

Transcription	*Transliteration*	Translation
b'a-TUN-na	*b'atun*	1) root of plant (n) 2) B'atun, name (at Xcalumkin) (n)
b'a-tz'u B'ATZ'?	*b'a'tz'* [1,2]	1) howler monkey (n)
b'a-ya	*b'ay*	1) where (part.) 2) as such (adv) 3) fat (?) (n)
b'i	*b'i'*	1) name (n)
B'I b'i-hi	*b'ih* [2] (*b'iih* [2])	1) road (n) 2) line (of writing) (n)
b'i-K'A'	*b'ik'-*	1) to scribble (div)
b'i-TAL-la b'i-ta-la	*b'ital*	1) B'ital, emblem glyph (at Naranjo) (n)
b'i-TUN-ni	*b'ihtuun*	1) road, prepared surface (n)
b'i-xi	*b'ix*	1) units of five and seven (nc)
B'IX-na B'IX-ni	*b'ixVn-*	1) to go away (div)
b'o-b'o	*b'o[h]b'* [1] (*b'ob'*)	1) coyote (n)
b'o-ja	*-b'oj-*	1) to nail (tv)
b'o?-la-yi B'OL?-la-u	*b'olay*	1) small jaguar (n)
9	*b'olon* (*b'alu'n*) (*b'aluun*)	1) nine (num) 2) many (adj)
9-AJAW-NAH	*b'olon ajaw naah*	1) B'olon Ajaw Nah, "nine ruler house," structure name (at Tikal) (n)
9-CHAN-na-yo-(OK)- K'IN-ni-18-(yo)-OK- K'IN-ni	*b'olon chan yok'ihn waxaklaju'n yok'ihn*	1) B'olon Chan Yok'in Waxaklajun Yok'in, "nine sky his-sun, eighteen his-sun," name (deity) (n)
9-KAL-ne-la 9-ka-la-ne-la	*b'olon kal ne'l**	1) B'olon Kal Ne'l, "nine mouth ?," name (at Yaxchilan) (n)
9-K'AWIL	*b'olon k'awiil*	1) B'olon K'awil, "nine k'awil," name (ruler at Calakmul) (n)

APPENDIX IV.1 CLASSIC MAYAN TO ENGLISH LEXICON

Transcription	Transliteration	Translation
9-K'IN-ni-b'a	b'olon k'ihn b'aah	1) B'olon K'in B'ah, "nine first sun," name (deity) (n)
9-ta-CHAB'-K'INICH	b'olon ta chaab' k'inich	1) B'olon Ta Chab' K'inich, "nine in beehive sun-faced [one] ?," ruler (area of Campeche) (n)
9-TE'-NAH	b'olon te' naah	1) B'olon Te' Nah, "nine tree house," structure name (at Palenque) (n)
9-TE'-WITZ	b'olon te' witz	1) B'olon Te' Witz, "nine tree mountain," toponym (area of Copan) (n)
9-tz'a[pa]-la-K'UH	b'olon tz'apal k'uh	1) B'olon Tz'apal K'uh, "nine planted deity," name (deity) (n)
9-yo-'OK-TE'-K'UH	b'olon yokte' k'uh	1) B'olon Yokte' K'uh, "nine ? deity," name (deity) (n)
19	b'olonlaju'n (b'alu'nlaju'n)	1) 19 (num)
b'u	-b'u	1) causative suffix (suf)
b'u-b'a	b'u'b' (b'ub')	1) cylinder (n)
b'u-lu b'u-b'u-lu ²b'u-lu	b'ub'ul	1) frothy (adj) 1) cylinder (n)
b'u-lu-HA' b'u-b'u-lu-HA'	b'ub'ul ha'	1) water insect (n) 2) B'ub'ul Ha', toponym (area of Piedras Negras) (n)
b'u-B'UCH	b'uch-	1) to be seated (pv)
b'u-ku	b'u[h]k [1,2] (b'uk) -b'uk-	1) clothing (n) 2) B'uk, emblem glyph (Los Alacranes) (n) 3) to dress (tv)
b'u-ku-TUN-ni	b'uhktuun (b'uktuun)	1) B'uktun, "dressed stone," toponym (area of Yaxchilan) (n)
b'u-ku-tzi	b'ukuutz	1) B'ukutz, name (n)
b'u-ku-tzu	b'ukutz	1) B'ukutz, foodstuff name
b'u-la	b'u'l (b'u'ul [1]) (b'u'l [2])	1) bean (n)
b'u-lu	-b'ul-	1) to submerge (tv)

Transcription	Transliteration	Translation
B'ULAY? b'u?-la-yi	*b'ulaay*	1) small jaguar (n)
11 [b'u]-lu-ku	*b'uluk* [1,2]	1) eleven (num)
b'u-t'u	*-b'ut'-*	1) to fill, cover, bury (tv)
b'u-tz'a b'u-tz'a-ha	*b'u'tz'* *(b'uutz')*	1) smoke (n)
b'u-tz'a-ja-SAK-chi-ku	*b'u'tz'aj sak chi'k*	1) B'utz'ah Sak Chik, "smoking? white bird [lark]", name (at Palenque) (n)

CH

Transcription	Transliteration	Translation
cha-b'a	*cha[n]b'a[h]*	1) festival, celebration (n)
CHAB' cha-b'i	*chaab'* [1,2] *-chab'-*	1) beehive, bee, honey (n) 2) anteater (n) 3) to supervise (tv)
cha-chi	*chaach* [1]	1) basket (n)
cha-hu-ku	*chahuk* [1,2]	1) thunder (n)
cha-hu-ku-NAH	*chahuk naah*	1) Chahuk Nah, "thunder house", structure name (at Piedras Negras) (n)
CHAK **CHAK-ki** cha-ki	*chaa[h]k* [1] *(cha[h]k* [2]*)* *(chaak)*	1) Chak, rain-deity (n) 2) rain (n)
CHAK	*chak* [2] *-chak-*	1) red (adj) 2) great, big (adj) 3) to tie up (pv)
CHAK-la	*chakal*	1) reddish, ruddy (adj)
CHAK-la-TE' **CHAK-TE'-e**	*chakalte'* *(chakte')*	1) chicozapote (n) 2) cedar (n) 3) title (n)

APPENDIX IV.1 CLASSIC MAYAN TO ENGLISH LEXICON

Transcription	*Transliteration*	Translation
CHAK-AT CHAK-a-ta CHAK-AT-na	*chakat* *(chakatan)*	1) 3rd *haab'* month name (n)
CHAK-B'ALAM-ma	*chak b'ahlam*	1) puma (n)
CHAK-b'a-ya-ka-KAN	*chak b'ay kan*	1) Chak B'ay Kan, "great where snake ?", name (Vision Serpent) (n)
CHAK-che-le	*chak chel*	1) Chak Chel, "great rainbow", name (deity) (n)
CHAK-ch'o-ko-'IXIK	*chak ch'ok ixik*	1) girl, "great unripe woman" (n)
CHAK-ch'o-ko	*chak ch'ok*	1) infant, youth, youngster, "great heir" (n)
CHAK-EK'	*chak ek'*	1) Chak Ek, "great star", name (Venus) (n)
CHAK-HA'	*chak ha'*	1) Chak Ha', "great water", toponym (area of Petexbatun) (n)
CHAK-ha-lu	*chak ha'l*	1) "great rain" (n)
cha-la-ma	*chalam*	1) jawbone (n)
CHAK-li-b'i	*chaklib'*	1) tied-up thing (n) 2) panel (n)
CHAK-SIHOM-ma	*chak siho'm*	1) 12th *haab'* month name (n)
CHAK-tzu-la-ha-CHAN-na-to-'AT-ta-K'AK'-OL-la-K'IN-ni-chi	*chak tzu'l ha' chan to[j]at k'ahk' o'l k'inich*	1) Chak Tzul ha' Chan Tojat K'ak' Ol K'inich, "?", name (deity at Yotz) (n)
CHAK-u-pa-ka-la-K'INICH-K'IN-ni-chi-K'AN-na-JOY?-CHITAM-ma	*chak upakal k'inich k'an joy chitam*	1) Chak U Pakal K'inich K'an Joy Chitam, "great his-shield sun-faced [one] yellow encircled peccary", name (at Palenque) (n)
CHAK-XIB'-CHAK	*chak xib' chak*	1) Chak Xib' Chak, "great young man great ?", name (deity) (n)
CHAK-xi-wi-te-i	*chak xiwite'i*	1) Chak Xiwite'i, "great xiwite'i", foreign deity (in Dresden Codex) (n)
CHAM CHAM-mi	*cham-*	1) to die (riv)
CHAM-la	*chamal*	1) death (n)
4 CHAN cha-na	*chan* *(cha'n²)*	1) four (num) 2) snake (n) 3) sky (n)

APPENDIX IV.1 CLASSIC MAYAN TO ENGLISH LEXICON

	Transcription	Transliteration	Translation
	CHAN **cha-nu**	cha'n (cha'an ¹) (cha'n ²) -chan-	1) guardian, overseer (n) 2) to watch over, own (tv)
	CHAN-na-a-ku	chan ahku['l]	1) Chan Akul, "great turtle-like", title (at Naj Tunich) (n)
	CHAN-la	chanal	1) celestial, heavenly, sky-like (adj)
	CHAN-NAL-la-K'UH **CHAN-la-K'UH**	chanal k'uh	1) Chanal K'uh, "sky-like god", deity (n)
	CHAN-CHAK **cha-na-cha-ki**	chan chaahk	1) Chan Chak, "heavenly rain-deity", ruler title (n)
	CHAN-na-CH'EN-na **CHAN-CH'EN**	chan ch'e'n	1) Chan Ch'en, "Sky Cave", toponym (symbolic reference) (n)
	CHAN-ch'o-ko-wa- **WAY-b'i-xo-ki**	chan ch'ok wayib' xook	1) Chan Ch'ok Wayib' Xok, "sky young sleeping-place shark ?", name (artist at Piedras Negras) (n)
	CHAN-na-K'INICH	chan k'inich	1) Chan K'inich, "sky sun-faced [one]", title (common for rulers) (n)
	14	chanlaju'n (chanlajuun)	1) fourteen (num)
	CHAN-TE'-AJAW	chante' ajaw	1) Chante' Ajaw, "sky-tree ruler", name (patron deity at Copan) (n)
	CHAN-TE'-SUTZ'	chante' suutz'	1) Chante' Sutz', "sky-tree bat", structure name (at Yaxchilan) (n)
	CHAN-wi-ti-ki	chan witik	1) Chan Witik, "sky plant", emblem glyph (at Copan) (n)
	CHAPAT-tu **cha-pa-tu** **cha-pa-ta** **CHAPAT-ti**	chapa't (chapa[a'h]t ¹) (chapa[h]t ²) (chapa'[h]t)	1) centipede (n)
	CHAPAT-CHAN	chapa't chan	1) large centipede, "snake centipede", (n)
	cha-ta **cha-TAN**	chatan	1) Chatan, toponym (on Codex-style vessel) (n)
	CHAY **cha-ya**	chay ²	1) fish (n)

APPENDIX IV.1 CLASSIC MAYAN TO ENGLISH LEXICON

Transcription	*Transliteration*	Translation
CHA' **2**	*cha'* *(cha)*	1) again, second time (adv) 2) two (num)
cha	*cha'* *-cha-*	1) dark, obscure (adj) 2) to do (tv)
CHA'-b'i-ji	*cha'b'ij*	1) day after tomorrow (adv)
che	*che*	1) thus (adv)
che-le	*chel*	1) high (adj) 2) rainbow (n)
che-le-te	*chele[h]t* [1] *(che[']le[h]t* [1]*)* *(chelet)*	1) place on (adv)
che-le-**TE'**-**CHAN**- na-**K'INICH**- **ITZAMNAJ**- **B'ALAM**	*chelte' chan k'inich itzamnaaj b'ahlam*	1) Chelte' Chan K'inich Itzamnaj B'alam, "high-tree sky sun-faced itzamnaj jaguar", ruler (at Yaxchilan, on LTL 52 and 58) (n)
che-b'u che-e-b'u	*che'e[h]b'* [1] *(che[h]b')* *(che'eeb')* *(che'e[h]b')*	1) quill (n) 2) bamboo (n)
che-e-na che-na che-he-na	*chehe'n* *(cheen)* *(cheheen)*	1) so, so it says (part.)
che-e che-he	*(che')* *(che'-)*	1) tree (n) 2) to say (riv) see: *te'*
chi	*chi* *(chi[h])* *(chi')*	1) pulque (n) 2) ring (?) (n)
chi-chi	*chich*	1) word, reason (n)
CHICH?-che?	*chich (?)*	1) rabbit ? (n)
chi-hi	*chiih* [2]	1) maguey, sweet (adj)
chi-ji chi **CHIJ**-ji	*chij* [1] *(chi[h]j* [2]*)*	1) deer (n)
CHIJ-ji-li chi-ji-li	*chijil*	1) deer-like

APPENDIX IV.1 CLASSIC MAYAN TO ENGLISH LEXICON

Transcription	Transliteration	Translation
chi-ji-li-ta-CHAN-na **chi-ji-TAL-CHAN-na**	*chijil tal chan*	1) Chijil Tal Chan, "deer-like days? sky?", *way* name (at Calakmul) (n)
chi-ji-la-ma	*chijlam*	1) translator, spokesman (n)
CHIK-ki **chi-ku**	*chi'k* *(chi'ik* [1,2]*)* *(chi'[h]k)* *(chi[h]k)*	1) coatimundi (n)
chi-ku	*chi'k* *(chiik)* *(chi[h]k)*	1) bird (n)
chi-ka-ja	*chikaj*	1) chikaj, "?", tree name (n)
CHIK-ni **CHIK-ki-ni**	*chikin*	1) 6th *haab'* month name (n)
chi-ki	*chiki[n]*	1) ear (n)
chi-ku-NAB'	*chi'k naahb'*	1) Chik Nab', "? pool", toponym (at Calakmul) (n)
chi-K'IN-ni	*chik'ihn*	1) west (n) 2) east, PSC? (n)
chi-la-ma	*chilam*	1) spokesman (n)
chi-li-ka-yu	*chilka'y* *(chilkaay)*	1) manatee (n)
chi-li-K'UH	*chi'il k'uh*	1) Chi'il K'uh, "? god", toponym (at Naj Tunich) (n)
CHIT-ta **CHIT-ti** **chi-ti**	*chit* *(chiit)*	1) father (n) 2) patron (n) 3) rabbit (?) (n)
CHITAM	*chitam* *(chitaam* [2]*)*	1) peccary (n)
chi-ti-na	*chitiin*	1) sweatbath (n) 2) oven (n)
chi-wo-jo **chi-wo**	*chiwoj* [2] *(chiwo[']j* [1]*)*	1) tarantula (n)
cho-cho	*choch*	1) intestines (n)

APPENDIX IV.1 CLASSIC MAYAN TO ENGLISH LEXICON

Transcription	Transliteration	Translation
CHOK cho-ka cho-ko	-chok-	1) to throw, scatter (tv)
CHOK-no-ma	chokno'm (choknoom)	1) scatterer (n)
chu-b'a-la-che-b'u	chub'al che'eb'	1) quill pen/brush container (n)
chu-chu	chuch	1) loom (n) 2) cloth (n)
chu-ka chu-ku	-chuk-	1) to capture, catch, grab, seize, fetch (tv)
?	chuluk	1) lizard (n)
CHUM **CHUM[mu]**	chum-	1) to seat (pv)
CHUM[mu]-b'i	chumib' (chumuub')	1) seat (n)
CHUM-mu-ta-li	chumtaal	1) sitting (n)
chu-ni	-chun-	1) to conjure (tv)
chu-ni-k'u	chuni'k' (chuniik)	1) drum (n)
CHUWEN	chuwen (chuwe'n) (chuween)	1) artist (?) (n) 2) title at Naranjo (n)
chu-yu	-chuy-	1) to sew, weave (tv)

CH'

Transcription	Transliteration	Translation
CH'AB' ch'a-b'a	ch'a[h]b' [1,2] -ch'ab'- (ch'ab')	1) fasting, penance, sacrifice (n) 2) to fast (tv)
ch'a-b'a	-ch'ab'-	1) to create (tv)
ch'a-ha	ch'ah	1) bitter (adj)
ch'a-ja ch'a-ji ch'a-ha	ch'aaj [1,2] (ch'aj)	1) roasted maize flour (n) 2) drop, droplet (n) 3) bitter (adj)

APPENDIX IV.1 CLASSIC MAYAN TO ENGLISH LEXICON

Transcription	Transliteration	Translation
ch'a-ho-ma (ch'a-jo-ma)	*ch'aho'm* (ch'ahoom) (ch'ajo'm) (ch'ajoom)	1) incense scatterer (n)
ch'a-ja-TE'	*ch'aj te'*	1) type of incense, drink (n)
CH'AK ch'a-ka	*-ch'ak-*	1) to injure, chop, cut, decapitate (tv)
CH'AK?-TE'-le	*ch'akte'el*	1) palanquin, litter (n)
CH'AK?-TE'-le-HIX-NAL	*ch'akte'el hixnal*	1) Ch'akte'el Hixnal, "palanquin jaguar place", *way* name (n)
CH'AM ch'a-ma	*-ch'am-*	1) to take, grab, receive (tv)
ch'a-ma-ka	*ch'amak*	1) fox (n)
ch'a-ti ch'a-ta	*ch'aat* [1,2] (ch'at)	1) dwarf, hunchback (n)
CH'EN CH'EN-na CH'EN-ni CH'EN-ne	*ch'e'n* [1,2] (ch'een) (ch'en)	1) cave, well (n)
CH'O ch'o	*ch'o* (ch'o[h])	1) rat (n)
ch'o-ko **CH'OK**	*ch'ok* [1,2]	1) unripe, young (adj) 2) heir to the throne (n)
ch'o-CHAK-li-b'i	*ch'o[k] chaklib'*	1) Ch'ok Chaklib', "young bound-thing", name (captive at Tonina) (n)
CH'OK-ko-le-le	*ch'oklel*	1) youth-hood (n) 2) unripeness (n)
ch'o-ko-WINIK-ki	*ch'ok winik*	1) Ch'ok Winik, "young man", title (n)
ch'o-ma	*-ch'om-*	1) to hit, pierce (tv)

APPENDIX IV.1 CLASSIC MAYAN TO ENGLISH LEXICON

Transcription	Transliteration	Translation
E		
e **(E)**	*e'*	1) tooth (n)
e-b'a **e-b'u** **(y)e-b'a-li** **(y)e-b'u-li**	*e'b', e'b'aal, e'b'uul* *(e[h]b', e[h]b'aal,* *e[h]b'uul* [2]*)*	1) staircase, stair, ladder (n)
(y)e-b'e-ta **(y)e-b'e-te**	*eb'et* [2] *(eb'e't)*	1) messenger (n)
(y)e-je	*ej*	1) tooth (n)
e-ke	*ek-* *([h]ek)*	1) to place, enter, insert (pv) 2) to hang up, be stuck (pv)
e-ke-li-b'i	*eklib'* *([h]eklib')*	1) placed/inserted object (n) 2) vertical panel (n)
EK-TE'	*ek'te'* *eek'te'*	1) Ek' Te', "black tree", tree name (n)
EK' **e-k'e**	*ek'* *(eek')*	1) star (n) 2) black (adj)
EK'-MUYAL-la-CHAN	*ek' muyal chan*	1) Ek' Muyal Chan, "black cloud snake", toponym (Chak-related) (n)
EL **EL-le** **(EL)**	*-el-*	1) to burn (tv)
le **(EL)**	*-el*	1) body part suffix 2) instrumental suffix
EL-K'IN	*elk'ihn* *(elk'iin)*	1) east (n)
EM-mi **e-mi**	*em* *(e[h]m)*	1) to go down, descend (div)
EM-ma **EM-ma-cha**	*emach*	1) raccoon (n)
(y)e-ma-la	*emal* *(e[h]mal)*	1) descent (n)
Ce-na	*-een*[2] *(-e'n)*	1) I, first person pronominal postfix (pro)

Transcription	Transliteration	Translation
(y)e-TE' (y)e-he-TE'	-et- (ehet)	1) to work together (?) (tv)
ETE' ETE'-TE' ETE'-TE'-je	e[b']tej (?)	1) work, office (n)
	et'kab'a'	1) namesake (n)
e-tz'e	etz'- ([h]etz')	1) to set down (pv)
e-wi-tzi	ewitz	1) Ewitz, "? mountain", toponym (related to Uxmal) (n)
H		
HAB' HAB'-b'i HAB'-b'a	haab'¹ (ha'b'²) (hab')	1) 365-day year (n) 2) shrub, plant (n)
HAB'-li	haab'il	1) year, time, period (n)
HAB'-na-la	haab'nal	1) Hab'nal, "year place/person", toponym (at Chichen Itza) (n)
ha-chi ha-cha	haach hach	1) incised thing (n)
HAL	-hal-	1) to say, manifest (tv)
HAL HAL-le	-hal-	1) to weave (tv)
HAL-b'u	hal[a]b' (?)	1) weaving (n)
HALAB' HALAB'-b'i	halaab'	1) ballcourt (n) 2) throwing stick (n)
HALAB'-KUH HALAB'-ma-KUH	halaab' kuh (halaab'om kuh)	1) Halab' Kuh, "Spearthrowing Owl", name (at Tikal) (n)
HALAW ?	halaw (?)	1) ballcourt (n)

APPENDIX IV.1 CLASSIC MAYAN TO ENGLISH LEXICON

Transcription	Transliteration	Translation
ha-ma	*ham-* *-ham-*	1) to lie down (pv) 2) to open, untie (tv)
ha-ma-li-b'i	*hamlib'*	1) lied-down-thing (n)
ha-na	*han*	1) flower (n)
ha-wa	*haw*	1) 18th *haab'* month name (n)
HA' **HA'-a** **a**	*ha'*	1) water (n)
ha-i **ha-a**	*haa'* *(ha')* *(ha'i')*	1) he, she, it, this, that (pr)
HA' **HA'-la** **ha-la**	*ha'al* *(hal)*	1) wet, rainy (adj)
HA'-a-la **HA'-la**	*ha'al [winik]*	1) Ha'al Winik, "rainy man", *way* name (n)
HA'-K'IN-XOK-ki	*ha' k'ihn xook*	1) Ha' K'in Xok, "water sun shark", name (ruler at Piedras Negras) (n)
ha-o-b'a	*ha'o'b'* [2] *(haa'oob')*	1) they, those (pr)
he-na	*heen* *(he'n)*	1) count of single days (n)
he-wa	*he'w* *(heew)*	1) count of single days (n)
hi-li	*hil-*	1) to rest, plant (riv)
hi-na	*hiin*	1) I (pro)
hi-na-ja **hi-na**	*hinaj*	1) seed (n)
HIX	*hix*	1) jaguar (n)
HIX-li	*hixil*	1) Hixil, "jaguar (possessed)", toponym (area of Tikal) (n)
HIX-WITZ **HIX-wi-tzi**	*hix witz*	1) Hix Witz, "jaguar mountain", emblem glyph (at El Pajaral) (n)

APPENDIX IV.1 CLASSIC MAYAN TO ENGLISH LEXICON

	Transcription	Transliteration	Translation
	5 **HO'**	*ho'*	1) five (num)
	5-CHAN-na	*ho' chan*	1) Ho' Chan, "Five Sky", toponym (in Dresden Codex) (n)
	5-HUN-na	*ho'hu'n*	1) Ho' Hun, "five book/paper", female title (n)
	5-KAB'	*ho'kab'*	1) Ho' Kab', "Five Earth", toponym (at Ixtutz) (n)
	15 **HO'LAJUN**	*ho'laju'n* *(ho'lajuun)*	1) fifteen (num)
	5-TUN-ni	*ho'tuun*	1) Five-Tun period
	HUJ	*huj*	1) iguana (n)
	7 **HUK**	*huk*	1) seven (num)
	17 **HUKLAJUN**	*huklaju'n* *(huklajuun)*	1) seventeen (num)
	7-si-pu	*huk si'p* [1]	1) "Seven Sins", name (deity) (n)
	HUL-li **hu-li**	*hul-*	1) to arrive (riv)
	HUN **HUN-na** **hu-na**	*hu'n* [1,2] *(huun)*	1) book, paper, bark (n) 2) headband ? (n)

Transcription	Transliteration	Translation
hu-na-la **HUN-la**	*hunal*	1) headband (n)

I

Transcription	Transliteration	Translation
i	*i*	1) and then (part.)
I	*i'*	1) hawk (n)
-Ci-b'i **-b'i** **(-IB')**	*-ib'*	1) derives insturmentals from positional verbs (suffix)
i-b'a-cha	*ib'ach*	1) armadillo (n)
i-b'i-li	*ib'il*	1) Ib'il, "?", toponym (area of Naj Tunich) (n)
i-chi	*ich*	1) chili (n) 2) eye, face (n)
-Ci-chi	*-ich*	1) intensifier (suffix)
(y)i-cha-ni	*ichaan* [1,2]	1) maternal uncle (n)
i-chi-ki	*ichik*	1) bathe (iv?)
i-chi-la	*ichiil*	1) in, within (prep)
i-chi-li	*ichil*	1) bathe (iv?)
i-chi-ya	*ichiiy*	1) hawk (n) 2) heron (n)
(y)i-chi-NAL **(a-w)i-chi-NAL** **(y)i-chi-na-la**	*ichnal* *(ichVn)*	1) presence (n) 2) with, "in the company of", (prep)
ICH'AK **(y)i-ch'a-ki**	*ich'aak* *(i[h]ch'aak)*	1) claw (n)
i-ka-tzi	*ikaatz*	1) load, bundle, tribute (n)
i-ki **i-ki-ku-yu**	*iki[m] (?)* *iki[m] kuy*	1) small owl (n)
i-ki-tzi	*ikitz*	1) load, bundle, tribute (n)

Transcription	Transliteration	Translation
IK' **i-ki**	*ik'*	1) black (adj)
IK'	*ik'*	1) wind, air (n)
IK'-la	*ik'al* [2]	1) one day later (adj)
IK'-AT **IK'-AT-na**	*ik'at* *ik'atan*	1) 2nd *haab'* month name (n)
IK'-chi-ji	*ik' chij*	1) Ik' Chij, "black deer", name (ruler at Lakamtun, captive) (n)
IK'-SIHOM? **i-ki-SIHOM?**	*ik' siho'm*	1) 9th *haab'* month name (n)
IL **IL-la** **i-la**	*-il-*	1) to see, witness (tv)
-li **-Ci-li** **(-IL)**	*-il*	1) possessive suffix (suf) 2) place name suffix (suf)
IL-TUN-ni	*iltuun*	1) stone seat name (n) 2) throne (n)
i-ni	*in-*	1) first person singular, "I" (pronoun) 1) first-person possessive, "my" (pronoun)
i-pi	*ip*	1) strength (n)
-si	*-is*	1) body part absolutive suffix (suf)
(y)i-ta	*it* *-it-*	1) companion (n) 2) to accompany (tv)
i-tza	*iitz*	1) enchanted (adj)
(a-w)i-tzi	*itz*	1) pitch, sap (n) 2) urine (n)

Transcription	Transliteration	Translation
i-tza-a [i]tza-a [i]tza	*itza'*	1) Itza, toponym (Central Peten) (n)
ITZAM	*itzam*	1) lizard, iguana (n)
ITZAM-K'AN-AK	*itzam k'an ahk*	1) Itzam K'an Ak, "lizard yellow turtle", name (Ruler A at Piedras Negras) (n)
ITZAMNAJ	*itzamnaaj*	1) Itzamnaj, name (deity) (n)
ITZAMNAJ-B'ALAM-ma	*itzamnaaj b'ahlam*	1) Itzamnaj B'alam, "Itzamnaj jaguar", name (ruler at Yaxchilan) (n)
ITZAMNAJ-B'ALAM-che-le-TE'-CHAN-na-K'INICH	*itzamnaaj b'ahlam chelte' chan k'inich*	1) Itzamnaj B'alam Chelte' Chan K'inich, "Itzamnaj jaguar high-tree sky?", ruler (ruler at Yaxchilan, on LTL 52 and 58) (n)
ITZAMNAJ-K'AWIL	*itzamnaaj k'awiil*	1) Itzamnaj K'awil, "itzamnaj k'awil", name (ruler at Naranjo) (n)
i-tz'a-ti i-tz'a-ta	*itz'aat* *itz'at*	1) wise man (n)
ITZ'AT-ti-K'INICH-chi-b'a	*itz'aat k'inich b'a'*	1) Itz'at K'inich B'a', "wise-man sun-faced one", name (on Copan vessel) (n)
ITZ'AT-ti-to-AT-ti-B'ALAM	*itz'aat tojat b'ahlam*	1) Itz'at Tohat B'alam, "wise-man ? jaguar", name (on codex-style vessel) (n)
i-tz'i i-tz'i-ni	*i[h]tz'iin* [1,2] *(i[h]tz'in)*	1) younger brother (n)
IX i-xi	*ix*	1) she, female agentive (prefix) 2) plant name (n)
IX-che-le	*ix chel* [1]	1) Ix Chel, "high woman", name (deity) (n)
IXIK i-xi-ki	*ixik* [2]	1) woman (n)
IXIK-ch'o-ko	*ixik ch'ok*	1) young female "unripe woman" (n)
IXIM	*ixim*	1) maize (n)

APPENDIX IV.1 CLASSIC MAYAN TO ENGLISH LEXICON

Transcription	Transliteration	Translation
IXIM-TE'	*iximte'*	1) Iximte', "maize tree", tree name (n)
IX-KALOM	*ix kalo'm*	1) she who (adj)
IX-KALOM-TE'	*ix kalo'mte'*	1) Ix Kalomte, "female Kalomte'", title (n)
IX-K'AWIL-la-ka-KAN	*ix k'awiil kan*	1) Ix K'awil Kan, "female sky k'awil", name (woman at Tonina) (n)
IX-ma-b'a-lu-ma	*ix mab' lu'm*	1) Ix Mab' Lum, "female earth box?", name (woman at Xcalumkin, wife of Kit Pa') (n)
IX-ma-ya-MO'-o-K'UK'	*ix may mo' k'uk'*	1) Ix May Mo' K'uk', "female offering macaw quetzal", name (woman at Piedras Negras) (n)
IX-NIK?-ki-u-k'u-cha-na	*ix nik uk'uu[w] chan*	1) Ix Nik Uk'uw Chan, "female flower ? snake/sky", name (woman at Chichen Itza on Monjas LTL 7A) (n)
IX-3-ka-KAN	*ix ox kan*	1) Ix Ox Kan, "female three snake", name (woman at Site Q on panel) (n)
IX-pa-ka-la-TUN-wi-tzi	*ix pakal tuun witz*	1) Ix Pakal Tun Witz, "lady shield stone mountain", name (woman at Comalcalco) (n)
IX-sa-ja-la	*ix sajal*	1) Ix Sajal, "female Sajal", female title (n)
IX-SAK-b'i-ya-ni	*ix sak b'iyaan*	1) Ix Sak B'iyan, "female white ?", name (woman at Yaxchilan, wife of Itzamnaj B'alam) (n)
IX-TE'-wi-tzi-k'u-k'u-IX-k'a-ya-ma	*ix te' witz k'uk' ix k'ayam*	1) Ix Te' Witz K'uk' Ix K'ayam, "female tree mountain quetzal, female ?", name (at Chichen Itza) (n)
IX-TUN-ni-ka-ya-wa-ka	*ix tuun kaywak*	1) Ix Tun Kaywak, "female stone jade plaque", name (woman at Topoxte') (n)
IX-u-ne-B'ALAM-ma	*ix une' b'ahlam*	1) Ix Une' B'alam, "female child of jaguar ?", name (woman at Naranjo) (n)
IX-yo-K'IN	*ix yok'ihn*	1) Ix Yok'in, "female sun-foot", title (n)
Ci-ya	*-iy*	1) deictic clitic: "ago, already, after" 2) completive aspect
i-yu-wa-la	*iyuwal*	1) progressive aspect-marking prefix, "ongoing"

J

ja-chi	*jaach*	1) incision (n)
ja-ka-WITZ-li	*jakawitzil*	1) Jakawitzil, emblem glyph (at Seibal) (n)
-ja-la	*-jal*	1) "-like", adjectival suffix (suf)

APPENDIX IV.1 CLASSIC MAYAN TO ENGLISH LEXICON

Transcription	Transliteration	Translation
JANAB' ja-na-b'i	*janaab'*	1) bird name ? (n)
ja-sa	*-jas-*	1) to open, clear (tv)
ja-sa-wa-CHAN-na	*jasaw chan*	1) dance staff (n)
ja-sa-wa-CHAN-K'AWIL	*jasaw chan k'awiil*	1) Jasaw Chan K'awil, "k'awil dance-staff (scepter?)", name (ruler at Tikal) (n)
JATZ' ja-tz'i ja-tz'a	*jatz'-* *-jatz'-*	1) to strike (riv) 2) to wound, split (tv)
ja-tz'a-la ja-tz'a-li	*jatz'al* *jatz'aal*	1) struck (adv)
JATZ'-ni JATZ'-no-ni	*jatz'noon*	1) striking (adv)
JATZ'OM ja-tz'o-ma	*jatz'o'm* *(jatz'oom)*	1) striker, spear thrower (n)
ja-wa	*jaw-*	1) to lie face up (pv)
ja-wa-TE'	*jawa[n]te'* *jawte'*	1) pottery dish (n)
ja-yi ja-ya	*jaay* [1] *(ja[h]y* [2]*)* *(jay)*	1) clay bowl (n)
je-le JEL	*-jel-*	1) to replace, change (tv) 2) to adorn (tv)
ji-chi	*jich*	1) surface (?) (n) 2) derivational suffix (?) (suf)
jo-ch'o jo-ch'a	*-joch'-*	1) to drill, perforate (tv)
JOL	*jo'l* [1,2]	1) head (n) 2) doorway, portal (n)
JOL-K'UH	*jo'l k'uh*	1) skull deity, "head god" (n)
JOL-mi jo-lo-mi	*jo'loom* *(jooloom* [2]*)*	1) skull (?) (n)

Transcription	*Transliteration*	Translation
jo-mo	*-jom-*	1) to collapse, sink (tv) 2) to end (tv) 3) to destroy (tv)
jo-po	*jop-*	1) to stake (pv)
JOY	*-joy-*	1) to encircle (tv)
JOY-ye-la	*joye'l* *(joyeel)*	1) encirclement (n)
ju-b'u	*jub'-*	1) to fall, descend (riv)
ju-b'i	*juub'* [1]	1) conch (n) 2) conch trumpet (n)
ju-b'u-li	*jub'uul*	1) descent (n)
ju-chi **ju-chu**	*juuch* *(juu[h]ch* [1]*)* *(ju[h]ch* [2]*)* *(juch)*	1) conch shell (n)
JUKUB' **ju-ku-b'i**	*jukuub'* [1,2]	1) canoe (n)
JUL **ju-lu**	*jul* *-jul-*	1) perforator, dart, spear (n) 2) to throw, shoot (tv)
ju-li-b'a-ki	*ju[l]il b'aak*	1) perforator bone (n)
1 **JUN**	*ju'n* [1] *(juun* [2]*)*	1) one (num)
JUN-JUN-AJAW	*ju'n ju'n ajaw*	1) Jun Jun Ajaw, "one one ruler", name (deity) (n)
JUN-ye-NAL-ye	*ju'n ye nal*	1) Jun Ye Nal, "one revealed corn/person", name (deity) (n)
1-pi-si-TUN-ni	*ju'n pis tuun*	1) first Tun, "one [count of periods] stone" (n)
1-pu-wa	*ju'n pu'w* [1]	1) Jun Pu'w, "one blowgun", name (n)

APPENDIX IV.1 CLASSIC MAYAN TO ENGLISH LEXICON

Transcription	Transliteration	Translation
1-TAN 1-ta-na	*ju'n tan*	1) beloved, cherished one, "front/center one" (n)
ju-su	*-jus-*	1) to plaster over (tv)

K

Transcription	Transliteration	Translation
ka	*ka'-* *ka-*	1) we (pro) 2) our (pro) 3) then (adv) 4) Ka, "?", emblem glyph (area of Kayal) (n)
2 **ka**	*(ka)* *(ka')*	1) two (num) 2) second (num) see: *cha'*
KAB' ka-b'a ka-b'i	*kab'* ² *(kaab'* ²*)* *-kab'-*	1) earth (n) 2) bee (n) 3) to make it happen, supervise (tv)
KAB' **KAB'-la**	*kab'al*	1) low (adj) 2) earth-like (adj)
KAB'-la-K'UH	*kab'al k'uh*	1) Kab'al K'uh, "Earth-like god," title (n)
KAB'-la-pi-tzi-la	*kab'al pitziil*	1) Kab'al Pitzil, "Earth-like ballplayer," title (Kerr No. 7749) (n)
ka-cha	*kach* *-kach-*	1) knot, tie (n) 2) to tie, bundle up (tv)
ka-ka-tu-na-la	*kak(a)tunal*	1) Kakatunal, "?", name (foreign deity in Dresden [Acantonal?]) (n)
ka-ka-wa ²**ka-wa** **ka-wa**	*kakaw* ²	1) cacao (n)
ka-ka-wa-la	*kakawal*	1) cacao-like (adj)
ka-la	*kal*	1) opening, mouth (n) 2) drunkenness (n)
KAL **ka-la** **ka-lo**	*-kal-*	1) to open (tv)

APPENDIX IV.1 CLASSIC MAYAN TO ENGLISH LEXICON

Transcription	Transliteration	Translation
ka-la-ke-ji-to-TOK'	kal keej to'k'	1) Kalkejtok', "open deer flint", toponym (Yula/Chichen Itza) (n)
KAL-ma KALOM-ma	kalo'm (kaloom)	1) he/she who (n)
KAL-ma-TE' ka-lo-ma-TE' KALOM-TE'	kalo'mte'	1) Kalomte', "he of wood ?", title (n)
KAL-ma-TE'-u-k'u-wi-CHAN-na-cha-ki	kalo'mte' uk'uuw chan chaahk	1) Kalomte' Uk'uw Chan Chak, "he of wood, ? heavenly rain-deity", name (ruler at Dzibilchaltun) (n)
ka-le-TUN	kal tuun	1) stone effigy (n) 2) stone opener (?) (n)
4 ka-na	(kan [1,2])	1) four (num) see *chan*
KAN	(kan [1,2])	1) snake (n) see *chan*
ka-na-ka-TE' ka-na-ka-te-e	kanak te' (ka'nak te')	1) Ka'nak Te', "Second Tree", title (n)
ka-KAN KAN-la	kanal (kanu[u']l)	1) Kanal, "snake-like", emblem glyph (at Calakmul) (n)
KAN-NAL-la KAN-la-K'UH	kanal k'uh	1) Kanal K'uh, "sky/snake-like God," name (deity) (n)
KAN-chi-wo-jo	kan chiwoj	1) Kan Chiwoj, "snake tarantula", name (artist at Piedras Negras) (n)
KAN-e-k'e KAN-EK'	kan ek'	1) Kan Ek', "sky star", name (ruler at Xultun) (n)
KAN-PET	kan pet	1) Kan Pet, "snake round", name (at Seibal and Edzna) (n)
KAN-wi-ti-ki	kan witik	1) Kan Witik, "sky planet?", emblem glyph (at Copan) (n) see: *chan witik*
ka-se-wa	kase'w [1] (kaseew)	1) 5th *haab'* month name (n)

Transcription	Transliteration	Translation
KAY ka-ya	(kay)	1) fish (n) see: *chay*
ka-yo-ma	kayo'm (kayoom)	1) fisherman (n)
ka-ya-wa-ka	kaywak	1) jade (plaque) (n)
ke-ji	(ke[h]j ²) (keej)	1) deer (n) see: *chij*
KELEM ke-le-ma	kele'm (keleem ²)	1) strong (adj) 1) young boy (n)
ki	ki	1) heart (n)
ki-si-ni	kisin ²	1) Kisin, name (deity) (n)
ki-ti ki-ta	(kit) (kiit)	1) father (n) 2) patron (n) see: *chit*
ki-WI'L	kiwi'l	1) Kiwi'l, "?", tree name (n)
ko	ko (ko[h])	1) tooth (n)
ko-b'o	-kob'-	1) to procreate (tv)
ko-b'a	ko'b' (koob')	1) grey (adj)
ko-b'a-a	kob'a'	1) Kob'a, toponym (area of Coba) (n)
ko-b'a-la	kob'al	1) atole (n)
ko-b'a-na	kob'an	1) Kob'an, toponym (area of Dos Pilas) (n)
KOHAW ko-ha-wa ko-o-ha-wa	ko'haw	1) helmet, headdress (n)
KOJ ko-jo	koj (kooj)	1) puma (n)
ko-jo	koj-	1) to finish (?) (riv)

Transcription	Transliteration	Translation
ko-ko	kok (ko[h]k) kok- -kok-	1) trogon, small turtle (n) 2) to hear (riv) 3) to watch, guard (tv)
ko-ko-no-ma	kokno'm (ko[h]kno'm ²) (koknoom)	1) guardian (n)
ko-ko-ma	koko'm (kokoom ²)	1) hearer, auditor (n)
ko-la	ko'l (kool)	1) Kol, toponym (area of Palenque) (n)
ko-lo-AJAW	kol ajaw	1) 19th *haab'* month name (n)
ko-lo-lo-TE' ko-lo-TE' ko-²lo-TE'	kololte'	1) Kololte', toponym (mentioned at Tonina) (n) 2) arbor (n)
ko-TE'	ko[l]te'	1) Kolte', toponym (area of Yaxchilan) (n)
ko-xo-pi	koxoop	1) Koxop, toponym (area of Copan) (n)
ko-yi	kooy	1) Koy, name (possible patronym at Chichen Itza) (n)
KUCH ku-chu	kuch (kuuch ²) -kuch-	1) burden (n) 2) to carry (tv)
KUH ku	kuh	1) owl (n)
²ku-la ku-la	kuku'l (kukal (?))	1) Kukul, toponym (mentioned at Tikal) (n)
ku-lu	kul	1) count of tun periods (at Palenque) (nc)
ku-k'u ku-K'UH	ku[m]k'u ku[m]k'uh	1) 18th *haab'* month name (n)
ku-nu	kun	1) oven (n) 2) platform (?) (n)
ku-se-wa	kuse'w ¹ (kuseew)	1) 5th *haab'* month name (n)
ku-tzu	kutz (kuutz ²)	1) (wild) turkey (n)
KUY ku-yu	kuy ¹	1) (large) owl (n)

APPENDIX IV.1 CLASSIC MAYAN TO ENGLISH LEXICON

Transcription	Transliteration	Translation
K'		
k'a	k'a	1) abundant (adj)
K'AB' k'a-b'a	k'ab'- [1,2]	1) hand, arm (n)
K'AB'A k'a-b'a-a	k'ab'a' (k'ab'a)	1) name (n)
K'AB'-si k'a-b'a-si	k'ab'aas k'ab'is	1) hand (n)
K'AB'-CHAN-TE' k'a-b'a-CHAN-TE'	k'ab' chan te'	1) K'ab' Chan Te', "hand sky tree", name (ruler at Sak Tz'i') (n)
K'AK' k'a-k'a	k'a[h]k' [1,2] (k'ak')	1) fire (n)
K'AK'-la	k'ahk'al (k'ak'al)	1) fiery (adj)
k'a-k'a-si	k'ahk'aas (k'ak'is) (k'ak'aas) (k'ahk'is)	1) fire (n)
K'AK'-NAB'	k'ahk' naahb'	1) sea, ocean (n)
K'AK'-jo-po-la-ja-KAN-na-K'AWIL	k'ahk' joplaj kan k'awiil	1) K'ak' Joplaj Kan K'awil, "fire stakes yellow K'awil", name (ruler at Copan) (n)
K'AK'-NAL K'AK'-na-la	k'ahk'nal	1) place of fire (n) 2) K'ak'nal, "fire place", toponym (Uxmal and Chichen Itza) (n)
K'AK'-ne-tz'u-tz'i	k'ahk' ne' tz'uutz'	1) K'ak' Ne' Tz'utz', "fire tail coatimundi", *way* name (n)
K'AK'-OL-la	k'ahk' o'l	1) K'ak' Ol, "fire heart", name (ruler at Yotz) (n)
K'AK'-TE'	k'ahk'te'	1) k'ak'te, "fire tree", tree name (n)
K'AK'-TILIW-CHAN-na K'AK'-ti-li-wi-CHAN-na	k'ahk' tiliw chan	1) K'ak' Tiliw Chan, "fire-burned sky", name (ruler at Quirigua) (n)

APPENDIX IV.1 CLASSIC MAYAN TO ENGLISH LEXICON

Transcription	Transliteration	Translation
K'AK'-TILIW-CHAN-na-CHAK-ki K'AK'-ti-li-wi-CHAN-na-CHAK-ki	k'ahk' tiliw chan chaahk	1) K'ak' Tiliw Chan Chak, "fire-burned sky rain-deity", name (ruler at Naranjo) (n)
K'AK'-k'u-PAKAL	k'ahk'upakal (?)	1) K'ak'upakal, "rire-his-shield", name (Chichen Itza) (n)
K'AK'-WE'-CHITAM	k'ahk' we' chitam	1) K'ak' We' Chitam, "fire eating? peccary", *way* name (n)
K'AK'-yi-pi-ya-ja-KAN-na-K'AWIL-la	k'ahk' yipyaj kan k'awiil	1) K'ak' Yipyaj Kan K'awil, "fire filled? yellow K'awil", name (ruler at Copan) (n)
20 K'AL	k'aal	1) twenty (num) 2) completion (n) see: *winik*
k'a-li k'a-le	k'aal	1) enclosure, room, quarters (n)
K'AL	-k'al-	1) to bind (tv)
K'AL-TUN-ni	k'altuun	1) stone-binding (n)
k'a-ma K'AM	(-k'am-)	1) to receive (tv) 2) to take, grasp (tv) see: *ch'am*
K'AN K'AN-na	k'an [1,2]	1) yellow (adj) 2) seat, bench (n) 3) precious (n) 4) ripe (n) 5) jewel, collar (n)
K'AN-a-si-ya K'AN-a-si K'AN-a-ya	k'anasiiy	1) 17th *haab'* month name (n)
K'AN-a-wa	k'anaw	1) 17th *haab'* month name (n)
K'AN-na-b'a	k'an b'a'	1) K'an Ba', "yellow gopher/image", *way* name (n)
K'AN-na-b'a-CH'O	k'an b'a' ch'o	1) K'an Ba' Ch'o, "yellow gopher rat", name (Tonina) (n)
K'AN-CHITAM	k'an chitam	1) K'an Chitam, "yellow peccary", name (ruler at Tikal) (n)

Transcription	Transliteration	Translation
K'AN-na-CHIT-li	k'an chitil	1) K'an Chitil, "yellow father-place?", toponym (area of Naranjo) (n)
K'AN-ni-la k'a-ni-la	k'aniil (k'anal)	1) K'anil, "yellow place?", name (on Fenton Vase) (n)
K'AN-ja-la-mu-ku-yi	k'anjal mukuuy	1) K'anjal Mukuy, "yellow-like dove", name (on British Museum vessel) (n)
K'AN-na-ja-la-NAH	k'anjal naah	1) K'anjal Nah, "yellow-like house", structure name (n)
K'AN-JAL-b'u K'AN-JAL-wa K'AN-JAL-wa-b'u	k'anjalawb'u(?) k'anjalab' k'anjalaw	1) 1st *haab'* month name (n)
K'AN-JOY-CHITAM	k'an joy chitam	1) K'an Joy Chitam, "yellow bound peccary", name (ruler at Palenque) (n)
K'AN-na-ju-b'a-ma-ta-wi-la	k'an ju'b' matawiil	1) K'an Jub' Matawil, "yellow ? ?", name (mythological ruler at Palenque) (n)
K'AN-K'IN	k'ank'ihn (k'ank'iin)	1) 14th *haab'* month name (n)
K'AN-na-le-ke	k'an lek	1) K'an Lek, "yellow calabash", name (on looted panel) (n)
K'AN-na-MO'-o-B'ALAM-ma	k'an mo' b'ahlam	1) K'an Mo' B'alam, "yellow macaw jaguar", name (ruler at Seibal) (n)
K'AN-NAL-la-e-b'u	k'an nal eb'	1) K'an Nal Eb', "yellow place stair", toponym (Copan) (n)
K'AN-TE'	k'ante'	1) K'ante', "yellow tree", tree name (n) 2) seat (n)
K'AN-TE'-NAL	k'ante' nal	1) K'ante' Nal, "yellow tree place", toponym (in Dresden Codex) (n)
K'AN-na-to-ko-mo-o	k'an tok mo'	1) K'an Tok Mo', "yellow smoke macaw", name (artist at El Peru) (n)
K'AN-na-tu	k'antu'	1) K'antu', "yellow thing", emblem glyph (Caracol) (n)
K'AN-na-TUN-ni	k'antuun (k'ahntuun)	1) stone bench, panel, "yellow stone" (n)
K'AN-WITZ-NAL	k'an witznal	1) K'an Witznal, "yellow mountain-place", toponym (Ucanal) (n)
k'a-sa	-k'as-	1) to break (tv)
K'AT	k'at	1) crosswise (n) 2) pottery bowl (n)
k'a-ti	-k'at-	1) to want (tv)

APPENDIX IV.1 CLASSIC MAYAN TO ENGLISH LEXICON

Transcription	Transliteration	Translation
K'AWIL-la k'a-wi-li	k'awiil (k'awil)	1) K'awil, name (deity) (n)
K'AWIL-CHAN-K'INICH	k'awiil chan k'inich	1) K'awil Chan K'inich, "k'awil sky sun-faced [one]", name (ruler at Pusilha) (n)
K'AWIL-K'INICH	k'awiil k'inich	1) K'awil K'inich, "k'awil sun-faced [one]", name (ruler at Dos Pilas) (n)
K'AWIL-la-MO'-o	k'awiil mo'	1) K'awil Mo', "k'awil macaw", name (Palenque captive at Tonina) (n)
k'a-ya k'a-yo	k'ay -k'ay-	1) song (n) 2) to sing (tv)
k'a-b'a	k'a[y]ab'	1) 17th *haab'* month name (n)
k'a-ya-ma	k'ayam	1) K'ayam, name (at Chichen Itza) (n)
k'a-yo-ma	k'ayo'm (k'ayoom)	1) singer (n)
K'EB'	-k'eb'-	1) to kneel down (tv)
K'IN	k'i[h]n [1] (k'iin [2]) (k'in)	1) hot (n) 2) sun (n) 3) day (n) 4) festival (n)
K'IN-AJAW-wa	k'ihn ajaw	1) K'in Ajaw, "sun ruler", title (deity) (n)
K'IN-ni-B'ALAM	k'ihn b'ahlam	1) K'in B'alam, "sun jaguar", name (ruler at Dos Pilas) (n)
K'INICH K'IN-chi	k'inich (k'i[h]nich)	1) sun-faced, heated (adj)
K'INICH-a-ku-la-MO'-NAB'	k'inich ahku'l mo' naahb'	1) K'inich Akul Mo' Nab', "sun-faced turtle-place macaw pool", name (ruler at Palenque) (n)
K'INICH-B'AK-NAL-la-CHAK-ki	k'inich b'aaknal chaahk	1) K'inich B'aknal Chak, "sun-faced bone-place rain-deity", name (ruler at Tonina) (n)
K'INICH-B'ALAM-ma	k'inich b'ahlam	1) K'inich B'alam, "sun-faced jaguar", name (ruler at El Peru) (n)
K'INICH-B'ALAM-CHAPAT	k'inich b'ahlam chapa't	1) K'inich B'alam Chapat, "sun-faced jaguar centipede", name (ruler at Tonina) (n)
K'IN-chi-li-KAB'	k'inichil kab'	1) K'inichil Kab', "sun-faced-place? earth", toponym (area of Naranjo) (n)

Transcription	Transliteration	Translation
K'INICH-JANAB'-PAKAL	k'inich janaab' pakal	1) K'inich Janab' Pakal, "sun-faced bird shield", name (ruler at Palenque) (n)
K'INICH-JOY-K'AWIL-li	k'inich joy k'awiil	1) K'inich Joy K'awilil, "sun-faced bound k'awil-place?", name (ruler at Caracol) (n)
K'INICH-KAN-B'ALAM	k'inich kan b'ahlam	1) K'inich Kan B'alam, "sun-faced snake jaguar", name (ruler at Palenque) (n)
K'INICH-K'AN-to-ko-mo-o	k'inich k'an tok mo'	1) K'inich K'an Tok Mo', "sun-faced yellow smoke macaw", name (ruler at Comalcalco) (n)
K'INICH-K'OCH-B'ALAM	k'inich k'ooch b'ahlam	1) K'inich K'och B'alam, "sun-faced carrying? jaguar", structure name (at Comalcalco) (n)
K'IN-ni-chi-K'UK'-NAH	k'inich k'uk' naah	1) K'inich K'uk' Nah, "sun-faced quetzal house", structure name (n)
K'INICH-LAKAM-TUN	k'inich lakam tuun	1) K'inich Lakam Tun, "sun-faced great stone", name (ruler at Rio Azul) (n)
K'INICH-LAM-EK' K'INICH-ni-la-ma-wa-EK'	k'inich lamaw ek'	1) K'inich Lamaw Ek', "sun-faced disappearing star", name (rulers at Ik' and Rio Azul) (n)
K'INICH-TAJAL-CHAK	k'inich tajal chaahk	1) K'inich Tajal Chak, "sun-faced obsidian-like rain-deity", name (ruler at Naranjo) (n)
K'INICH-²ta-b'u-JOL K'INICH-ta-b'u-JOL	k'inich tatb'u jol	1) K'inich Tatb'u Jol, "sun-faced father-b'u head", name (ruler at Yaxchilan) (n)
K'INICH-to-b'i-li-yo-AT-ti	k'inich tob'il yo[p] aat	1) K'inich Tob'il Yopat, "sun-faced ? helmet", name (ruler at Caracol) (n)
K'INICH-TUN-ni-CHAPAT	k'inich tuun chapa't	1) K'inich Tun Chapat, "sun-faced stone centipede", name (ruler at Tonina) (n)
K'INICH-wi-WITZ	k'inich witz	1) K'inich Witz, "sun-faced mountain", toponym (at Aguateca) (n)
K'INICH-YAX-K'UK'-MO'	k'inich yax k'uk' mo'	1) K'inich Yax K'uk' Mo', "sun-faced blue/green quezal macaw", name (founder and ruler at Copan) (n)
K'IN-ni-li-ka-yo-ma	k'inil kayo'm	1) K'inil Kayom, "sun's? fisherman", name (deity) (n)
K'IN-LAKAM-ma-cha-ki	k'ihn lakam chaahk	1) K'in Lakam Chak, "sun great rain-deity", name (artist at Piedras Negras) (n)
K'IN-MUWAN-wa-ni	k'ihn muwaan	1) K'in Muwan, "sun sparrow-hawk", name (at Naj Tunich) (n)
K'IN-NAL	k'ihn nal	1) K'in Nal, "sun place", toponym (Piedras Negras) (n)

Transcription	Transliteration	Translation
K'IN-TUN-ni	*k'ihntuun*	1) drought, "sun stone" (n)
k'i-wi-ki	*k'iwik*	1) market (n)
k'o-b'a	*k'o'b'* (*k'oob'*)	1) hearth (n)
K'OCH-chi	*-k'och-*	1) to carry (tv) 2) to contain (tv)
K'OCH-b'a-TUN	*k'ochb'a'tuun*	1) container (n) -b'a is causitive suffix.
K'OCH-chi-tu	*k'oochtu'*	1) container (n)
k'o-jo	*k'oj*	1) mask, image (n)
k'o-b'a	*k'o[j]b'a'*	1) mask (n)
K'U (k'u)	*k'u*	1) nest (n)
k'u-b'a	*-k'ub'-*	1) to deliver, give (tv) 2) to present (tv)
k'u-chi	*k'uuch*	1) vulture (n)
K'UH **k'u-hu**	*k'uh* ² (*k'uuh* ²)	1) god, deity (n)
K'UH **K'UH-lu** **K'UH-HUL** **K'UH-hu-lu** **K'UH-JUL-lu**	*k'uhul* (*k'u'ul* ¹) (*k'uuhul* ²)	1) divine, sacred (adj) 2) god-like (adj)
K'UH-lu-AJAW-wa	*k'uhul ajaw*	1) K'uhul Ajaw, "divine ruler", royal title (n)
K'UH-lu-ITZ'AT-ta	*k'uhul itz'at*	1) K'uhul Itz'at, "divine wise-man", royal title (n)
K'UH-lu-KALOM-ma	*k'uhul kalo'm*	1) K'uhul Kalom, "divine doer?", royal title (n)
K'UH-lu-WINIK-ki	*k'uhul winik*	1) K'uhul Winik, "divine person", royal title (n)
K'UK' **k'u-k'u**	*k'uk'* ¹	1) quetzal (n)

Transcription	Transliteration	Translation
K'UK'-B'ALAM	k'uk' b'ahlam	1) K'uk' B'alam, "quetzal jaguar", name (founder at Palenque) (n)
K'UK'-CHAN-na	k'uk' chan	1) K'uk' Chan, "quetzal snake?", name (sajal on Uaxactun vessel) (n)
K'UK'-LAKAM-wi-WITZ	k'uk' lakam witz	1) K'uk Lakam Witz, "quetzal great mountain", mountain name (n)
K'UK'-MO'-AJAW	k'uk' mo' ajaw	1) K'uk Mo' Ajaw, "quetzal macaw ruler", name (founder at Copan, pre-accession) (n)
K'UH-le	-k'ul-	1) to venerate (tv)
k'u-li	k'uul	1) penis (n)
k'u-ti-ma k'u-ti	k'utiim	1) K'utim, "?", name (at El Cayo) (n)
k'u-tzi K'UH-tzi	k'uutz (k'uu[h]tz ¹) (k'u[h]tz ²)	1) tobacco (n)
k'u-xa	-k'ux-	1) to torture, hurt (tv) 2) to eat (tv) 3) to grind (tv)
k'u-yu-NIK-AJAW	k'uy nik ajaw	1) K'uy Nik Ajaw, "? flower ruler", name (deity at Copan) (n)
L		
LAB' la-b'a	lab'	1) ugly, evil (adj)
12	lajchan (lajcha')	1) twelve (num)
10	laju'n ¹ (lajuun)	1) ten (num) 2) Laju'n, "ten", name (deity) (n)
10-YAX-HA'	laju'n yax ha'	1) Lajun Yax Ha' "ten blue/green water", name (deity) (n)
LAK la-ka	lak ¹,²	1) plate (n) 2) clay object (n)

Transcription	Transliteration	Translation
LAKAM la-ka-ma	*lakam* [1]	1) big, great, wide (adj)
LAKAM-HA'	*lakam ha'*	1) Lakam Ha', "big water", toponym (Palenque) (n)
LAKAM-TUN-ni la-ka-ma-TUN-ni	*lakam tuun*	1) stela, "great stone" (n) 2) Lakam Tun, "great stone", toponym (area of Peten) (n)
la-K'IN	*lak'ihn*	1) east (n)
[2]**la-ka**	*lalak*	1) plate, dish (n)
LAM la-ma	*lam-*	1) to go down, disappear (pv)
la-ta	*-lat*	1) count of elapsed periods, ordinals, days (ncl) 2) later (suffix)
la-tzi	*laatz*	1) stack (n)
LAY	*lay*	1) here (adv, n)
la-ya **la-yu**	*-lay* *-la'y* *(-laay)*	1) "-er", instrumental marker (suf)
le-e	*le'*	1) noose (n)
le-ke **le-ku**	*lek* *(leek)*	1) calabash (n)
le-k'a	*le'k'* *(leek')*	1) elevation (n)
le-k'e	*-lek'-*	1) to elevate (tv)
-le-le -[2]**le** **-le**	*-lel*	1) "-ship", instrumental suffix (suf)
li-pi	*lip-*	1) to climb (pv)
lo-che	*looch (?)*	1) twisted, bent, flexed (adj)
LOK	*lok'-*	1) to emerge (riv) 2) to escape (riv) 3) to leave (riv)
lo-mu	*loom (?)*	1) lance (n)
lo-ta	*lo't* *(loot)*	1) twin, companion (n)

Transcription	Transliteration	Translation
lu-k'u	*luuk'* [2] *(luk')*	1) stucco, mud (n)
lu-ma lu-mi	*lu'm* [1,2] *(luum)*	1) earth, soil (n)
lu-mi-li-pi-tzi-la	*lumil pitzal*	1) Lumil Pitzal, "Earth-like ballplayer", Kerr 7749 (n)

M

Transcription	Transliteration	Translation
ma ma-a	*ma'* *ma*	1) not, no (part.)
ma-b'i ma-b'a	*maab'* *mab'*	1) box, cache (n) 2) Mab', "box", *way* name (n)
ma-b'a-B'ALAM-ma	*mab' b'ahlam* *(mab'alam (?))*	1) Mab' B'alam, "box jaguar", name (at Xcalumkin) (n)
ma-cha	*-mach-*	1) to grab (tv)
ma-cha-ja	*machaj*	1) no, negative (part.)
ma-ka ma-AK	*-mak-*	1) to promise, betroth (tv) 2) to cover, close (tv)
ma-ka ma-AK ma-AK-ka	*mak* [1]	1) 13th *haab'* month name (n)
MAK-ka ma-ka	*ma[h]k* [2]	1) turtle carapace (n)
ma-ka ma-ko	*mak*	1) cover, capstone (n)
ma-ki	*maak*	1) person (n)
ma-k'a	*-mak'-*	1) to eat (soft food) (tv)
ma-ka-no-ma	*makno'm*	1) closer, coverer (n)
ma-la	*mal*	1) within (prep.)
MAM ma-ma	*mam* [2]	1) grandfather, grandson, old man, ancestor (n)
ma-ma	*mam*	1) possum (n)
MAN-ni	*maan* [1]	1) Man, "?", toponym (la Florida) (n)

Transcription	Transliteration	Translation
ma-su	ma's (maas)	1) goblin, dwarf (n)
ma-su	ma's (maas) (ma[h]s)	1) cricket (n)
ma-su ma-su-la	masu'l (masuul) (ma'sal)	1) Masul, "cricket place?", emblem glyph (at Naachtuun ?) (n)
MAT ma-ta	mat	1) cormorant (n)
MAT MAT-la	mat matal	1) Matal, "cormorant place?", emblem glyph (at Palenque ?) (n)
ma-ta-na	matan (ma[h]taan ²)	1) gift, offering (n)
ma-ta-wi-la	matawi'l (matawiil)	1) Matawil, "?", emblem glyph (at Palenque, mythical) (n)
ma-TUN-a (matunha)	matunha	1) Matunha', "no-stone? water", toponym (area of Bonampak and Yaxchilan) (n)
ma-tza	matz	1) wise man (n)
ma-tzi-li	matzil (ma[u]tzil)	1) bad (adj)
MAX ma-xi	maax ¹ (ma'x ²)	1) spider monkey (n)
ma-xu	ma'x (maax)	1) shield (n)
ma-xa-ma	maxam	1) Maxam, "?", toponym (at Naranjo) (n)
MAY ma-ya	may	1) deer (n)
MAY ma-yi-ji	maay	1) gift, offering, tobacco (n)
ma-yu-yu	mayuy ¹	1) fog, haze (n)

APPENDIX IV.1 CLASSIC MAYAN TO ENGLISH LEXICON

Transcription	Transliteration	Translation
ma-yu-yu-K'AWIL	mayuy k'awiil	1) Mayuy K'awil, "fog k'awil", name (sculptor of Laxtunich lintel) (n)
me-k'e	-mek'-	1) to embrace, hug, rule (tv)
0 mi	mi[h] ² (mi)	1) nothing, no (adv) 2) zero (num)
MIJIN (?)	mijiin (?)	1) child of father (n)
mi-mi	mim (miim ²)	1) (maternal) grandmother (n)
mi-si	-mis-	1) to sweep (tv)
mi-xi-NAL	mixnal	1) Mixnal, "? place", toponym (at Yaxchilan) (n)
mi-ya-tzi	miyaatz ¹	1) wise man (n)
MO' mo-o	mo'	1) macaw (n)
MO-o-AK-CHAK	mo' ahk chaahk	1) Mo' Ak Chak, "macaw turtle rain-deity?", name (ruler at Piedras Negras) (n)
mo-lo mo[lo]	mol	1) 8th *haab'* month name (n)
mo-lo-la	molo'l (molool)	1) 8th *haab'* month name (n)
mo-lo-wa	molo'w (moloow)	1) 8th *haab'* month name (n)
mo-ni	moon	1) sweet (?) (adj)
mo-o-la	mo'ol ¹	1) paw (?)
mo-pa-na mo-pa-ni	mopan mopaan	1) Mopan, "?", toponym (area of Naj Tunich) (n)
MO-wi-WITZ mo-o-wi-tzi	mo' witz	1) Mo' Witz, "macaw mountain", toponym (at Copan) (n)
mu-chi	muuch¹,²	1) toad (n)
mu-ka	mu'k ¹ (mu'uk ²) (muuk)	1) omen, announcement (n)

APPENDIX IV.1 CLASSIC MAYAN TO ENGLISH LEXICON 299

Transcription	*Transliteration*	Translation
MUK mu-ku mu-ka	*-muk-*	1) to bury (tv)
MUK-NAL	*muknal*	1) tomb, "bury place" (n)
mu-ku-yi	*mukuuy* [1,2]	1) dove, pigeon (n)
mu-lu	*mul-*	1) to stack, pile up (pv)
mu-lu	*-mul*	1) count of stacked/mounted objects (ncl)
mu-ti	*muut* [1,2]	1) bird (n) 2) omen (n)
MUT-ti-ITZAMNAJ-ji	*muut itzamnaaj*	1) Mut Itzamnaj, "bird itzamnaj" name (avian itzamnaj) (n)
MUT **MUT-la** **MUT-tu**	*mutu'l* *(mutuul)*	1) knot of hair (n) 2) Mutul, "knot", emblem glyph and toponym (at Tikal) (n)
mu-wa	*mu[']wa[k]* [1] *(muwa[k])*	1) tidings (n)
MUWAN-ni mu-wa-na	*muwaan* [2] *(muwaa[h]n* [1]*)*	1) 15th *haab'* month name (n) 2) sparrow-hawk (n)
MUYAL **MUY-ya-la**	*muyaal* [1,2]	1) cloud (n)
N		
NA na	*na'*	1) lady (n)
NA'? na	*na'*	1) property of animate objects (n)
na-i	*na'*	1) house, structure (n)
NAB'	*na[h]b'* [1,2] *(nab')*	1) handspan (n) 2) palm (n)

Transcription	Transliteration	Translation
NAB-b'i NAH-b'i na-b'a na-b'i	naa[h]b' [1] (na[h]b' [2]) (naab')	1) large body of standing water (n) 2) water lily (n)
NAB'-NAL-la-K'INICH	naahb' nal k'inich	1) Nab' Nal K'inich, "water place sun-faced", name (dynasty at Tikal) (n)
na-chi	naach	1) far (adv)
NAH	naah [1,2]	1) first (num) 2) great, large (adj)
NAH na-hi na-ha	naah [1,2] (nah)	1) house, building (n)
NAH-CHAPAT na-ha-cha-pa-ta	naah chapat	1) Nah Chapat, "great centipede" (n)
NAH-5-CHAN	naah ho' chan	1) Nah Ho' Chan, "great five snake/sky?", toponym (supernatural location) (n)
na-ka-KAN NAH-ka-KAN	naah kan	1) Nah Kan, "great snake" (n)
na	naj	1) full, satisfied, satiated (adj)
na-ja	-naj-	1) to fill up (tv)
na-ka	-nak nak	1) count of living beings (ncl) 2) captives (n)
na-ka	-nak-	1) to conquer (tv)
NAL na-la	nal [1]	1) ear of corn (n) 2) place (n) 3) person (n)
NAL na-la na-li	naal [1] (nal)	1) native (n)
NAL NAL-la	nal	1) north (n)

APPENDIX IV.1 CLASSIC MAYAN TO ENGLISH LEXICON

Transcription	Transliteration	Translation
na-ta	*nat*	1) understanding, reason (n)
na-wa	*-naw-*	1) to adorn (tv)
ne	*ne* *(ne[h])*	1) tail (n)
NEN **ne-na**	*neen* *(ne'[h]n [1])* *(ne[h]n [2])*	1) mirror (n)
ni	*ni* *(in)*	1) my (prep)
ni	*ni'*	1) nose (n)
ni-b'i	*nib'*	1) place (n)
NICH **ni-chi**	*nich* [1,2]	1) flower (n) 2) child of man (n)
NIK	*(nik)*	1) flower (n) 2) child of man (n) see *nich*
NIK-TE'	*nikte'*	1) mayflower (n)
NIK-TE'-NAH	*nikte' ha'(?)* *(nikte' naah)*	1) Nikte' Ha', "mayflower water [house]", structure name (n)
NOJ **no**	*noj*	1) grand (adj)
NOJOL	*nojo'l* [1] *(nojool)*	1) south (n)
nu-chu	*nuch*	1) joined, together (adv)
nu-chu-jo-lo	*-nuchjol-*	1) to speak together (tv)
nu-ku	*nuk*	1) big, great (adj) 2) coat, cover (n)
nu-ku	*nu[h]ku[l]* [1] *(nuku[l])*	1) skin, pelt (n)
nu-mu	*num-*	1) to pass (riv)

Transcription	Transliteration	Translation
NUN nu-na nu-u-na	*nu'un* [1] *(nuun)*	1) deluge (?) (n) 2) intermediary, ritual speaker (n)
NUN-u-JOL-CHAK-ki	*nu'n uhol chaahk*	1) Nun Ujol Chak, "ritual-speaker head/portal? rain-deity", name (ruler at Tikal) (n)
NUN-u-JOL-K'INICH	*nu'n uhol k'inich*	1) Nun Ujol K'inich, "ritual-speaker head/portal? sun-faced [one]", name (ruler at Tikal) (n)
NUN-YAX-AHIN	*nu'n yax ahiin*	1) Nun Yax Ahin, "ritual-speaker blue/green crocodile", name (ruler at Tikal) (n)
nu-pu	*-nup-*	1) to join, marry (tv)
nu-pu-lu	*nupul*	1) counter, familiar (adj)
nu-pu-lu-**B'ALAM**-ma	*nupul b'ahlam*	1) Nupul B'alam, "familiar jaguar", *way* name (n)

O

Transcription	Transliteration	Translation
OCH o-chi	*och-*	1) to enter (riv)
OCH-B'IH	*och- b'ih*	1) to die, "enter the road" (riv)
o-chi-**CHAN**-nu	*och cha'n*	1) Och Chan, "enter the guardian", *way* name (n)
	ochel	1) entrance (n)
OCH-HA'	*och- ha'*	1) to die, "enter the water" (riv)
OCH-K'AK' o-chi-**K'AK'**	*och- k'ahk'*	1) to enter fire, "enter fire" dedication ritual (riv)
OCH-K'IN	*ochk'ihn*	1) west, "sun enter" (n)
o-chi-ma-xi	*och maax*	1) Och Max, "enter spider-monkey", *way* name (n)
-o-ka	*[h]o'ok* [1]	1) valley (?) (n)
OK o-ki	*ook* [1,2] *(ok)*	1) foot (n) 2) dog (n)
o-ki-b'i (y)o-ko-b'i-li	*okib'* *(okib'il)*	1) pedestal (n)

APPENDIX IV.1 CLASSIC MAYAN TO ENGLISH LEXICON

Transcription	Transliteration	Translation
o-ki-b'i-a-'OX-TE'-K'UH	okib' aj oxte' k'uh	1) Okib' Aj Oxte' K'uh, "pedestal he of three time-period deity", name (at Palenque) (n)
OL OL-la o-la	o'l (o'[h]l ¹) (o[h]l ²)	1) middle, center, heart (n) 2) game ball (n) 3) opening (n) 4) 18th *haab'* month name (n)
Co-lo	-ol	1) possessive suffix (suf)
o-OL-si o-la-si	o'laas (o'[h]lis) (o'[h]laas)	1) heart, middle (n)
OL-si-K'UH OL-si-k'u-hu o-la-si-K'UH	o'laas k'uh	1) Olis K'uh, "heart deity", name (deity) (n)
o-lo-mo	olom	1) lineage (n)
Co-mo Co-ma	o'm (-oom ²)	1) resultative of intransitive verbs, future (suf) 2) "-er", adjective suffix (?) (suf)
o-mo yo-ma	o'm oom	1) foam (n)
o-mi-b'i	omib'	1) whisk (?) (n)
o-mo-tzi	omootz	1) Omotz, "?", name (at Piedras Negras) (n)
o-na	o'n ¹ (oon ²)	1) many (adj)
ON-ni	oon	1) avocado (n)
(y)o-o-NAL	o'nal	1) stomach (n)
(y)o-to-chu (y)o-to-che	(otooch)	1) house, home, building (n) see: *otoot*
OTOT (y)o-to-ti o-to-ti	otoot ¹ otot-	1) house, home, building (n) 2) to be housed (div)
	otoy	1) poisonous (adj)
OX?-xo	ox (oox ²)	1) three (num) 2) jaguar paw (n) 3) many (adj)

APPENDIX IV.1 CLASSIC MAYAN TO ENGLISH LEXICON

Transcription	Transliteration	Translation
3	ox (oox ?)	1) three (num)
3-a-ja-la-AJAW-wa	ox ajal ajaw	1) Ox Ajal Ajaw, "many conquest ruler", name (at Copan) (n)
3-a-ha-la-e-b'u **3-a-ha-li-EB'**	ox ajal eb'	1) Ox Ajal Eb', "many conquest stair", toponym (ballgame-related) (n)
3-a-ja-li-K'UH	ox ajal k'uh	1) Ox Ajal K'uh, "many conquest deity", epithet (of Palenque Triad) (n)
3-B'ALAM	ox b'ahlam	1) Ox B'alam, "many jaguar", name (ruler at Comalcalco) (n)
3-9-CHAK	ox b'olon chaahk	1) Ox B'olon Chak, "many rain-deity", name (deity at Palenque) (n)
3-HAB'-TE'	ox hab'te	1) Ox Hab'te', "three years", title and toponym (at Rio Azul) (n)
3-HUN-na	ox hu'n	1) Ox Hun, "three book/paper", structure name (at Yaxchilan) (n)
3-JOL-TE'	ox jol te'	1) Ox Jol Te', "many head tree", structure name (at Chichen Itza) (n)
3-TE'-HA'	oxte' ha'	1) Oxte' Ha', "three-period water", name (deity) (n)
3-TE'-TUN-ni	oxte' tuun	1) Oxte' Tun, "three-period 360-day-period", toponym (at Calakmul) (n)
3-TE-K'UH	oxte' k'uh	1) Oxte' K'uh, "three-period deity", toponym (area of Palenque and Tortuguero) (n)
3-WI'	ox wi'il	1) abundance of food, "many food" (n)
3-wi-ti-ki	ox witik	1) Ox Witik, "three [plant-name]", toponym (at Copan) (n)
3-WITZ	ox witz	1) Ox Witz, "many mountain", toponym (area of Caracol) (n)
3-WITZ-tzi-a	ox witz ha'	1) Ox Witz Ha', "many mountain water", toponym (area of Caracol) (n)
3-yo-HUN	ox yo'h'un	1) Ox Yo'hun, "many ? headband", headband? name (at Palenque) (n)
13	oxlaju'n (oxlajuun)	1) thirteen (num)

APPENDIX IV.1 CLASSIC MAYAN TO ENGLISH LEXICON

Transcription	Transliteration	Translation
13-CHAN-KUY	*oxlaju'n chan kuy*	1) Oxlajun Chan Kuy, "thirteen sky owl", celestial bird name (n)

P

Transcription	Transliteration	Translation
pa	*pa*	1) food (n)
pa-chi	*paach* [2] *-pach-*	1) skin (n) 2) to choose, select, take possession of (tv)
pa-ka	*pak-*	1) to be face down (pv)
pa-ka-b'a	*pakab'*	1) lintel, "face-down" (n)
pa-ka-b'a-TUN-ni pa-ka-b'u-TUN-ni	*pakab' tuun*	1) lintel stone, "face-down stone" (n)
pa-ka-b'u-la pa-ka-b'u	*pak(a)b'ul*	1) Pakab'ul, emblem glyph (at Pomona) (n)
PAKAL pa-ka-la	*pakal* [1]	1) shield (n)
pa-ka-xa pa-ka-xi	*pakax-*	1) to return (div)
pa-k'a	*-pak'-*	1) to plant (tv) 2) to form, mold (tv) 3) to hoist (tv)
	pal	1) child (n) (Yukatek)
pa-na	*pan-*	1) to dig (?) (pv)
pa-pa-ma-li-li	*papamalil*	1) Papamalil, name (person from Ucanal mentioned at Caracol) (n)
pa-si	*paas*	1) opening (n)
PAS	*pas* *pas-*	1) on the next day (adv) 2) to come out (riv)

Transcription	Transliteration	Translation
PAS pa-sa	-pas-	1) to open, dawn (tv)
PAS-sa-ja PAS pa-sa-ja	pasaj [1]	1) dawn (n) 2) after (adv)
pa-sa-no-ma	pasno'm	1) opener (n)
pa-si-li	pasil	1) door, opening (n)
PAS-ka-b'a	pas kab'	1) deity birth, "earth opening" (n)
pa-ti	paat	1) back, shoulders, skin (n) 2) after, later (adv)
PAT pa-ta	pat- -pat-	1) to form, build (pv) 2) to form, build (tv)
pa-ta	pat	1) hat (n)
pa-ta-ha	pataah [1] (patah)	1) guava (n)
pa-ta-na pa-ta	pataan [1] (patan)	1) tribute, work, burden (n)
pa-xi pa-xa	paax [1] (pax)	1) 16th *haab'* month name (n)
pa-ya	pay-	1) to guide, lead (riv)
pa-ya-la pa-ya-li pa-ya	payal (payil)	1) guide, leader (n)
pa-ya-LAKAM-CHAK	pay lakam chaahk	1) Pay Lakam Chak, "guide great rain-deity", name (ruler at *wakab'*) (n)
pa-yi-ku-na	-paykun-	1) to attract with enchantments (tv)
pa pa-a	pa'	1) wall, mural, fortress (n) 2) cleft, split (n)
PA'CHAN	pa'chan	1) Pa'chan, "split sky", emblem glyph (at Yaxchilan) (n)
pa-a-la	pa'al	1) creek, lagoon, stream (n)
pe-ka	-pek-	1) to call, order (tv)

Transcription	Transliteration	Translation
PET	pet [2] -pet pet-	1) round (adj) 2) count of round things (ncl) 3) to round (riv)
PET-ne PET-ni	pet[e]n [2]	1) island, land, district (n)
pi-b'i-NAH	pib'naah	1) sweatbath (n) 2) oven (n)
pi-chi	-pich-	1) to perforate (tv)
pi pi-hi	pih	1) bundle (n) 2) 144,000 day period, "b'aktun" (n)
PIK μi (pik)	pik	1) 144,000 day period, "b'aktun" (n)
PIK pi-ki	pik [1]	1) skirt (n)
pi-ki	-pik pik	1) counts of 8,000 (ncl) 2) skirt (n)
[2]pi pi	pip	1) bird of prey (n)
[2]pi-a pi-a	pipha'	1) Pipha', "bird of prey water", toponym (at Pomona) (n)
pi-si	pis [1]	1) count of periods (n) 2) count in 20-day period (n)
pi-tzi	pitz [1] pitz-	1) ballgame (n) 2) beautiful (adj) 3) to play ball (div)
pi-tzi-la pi-tzi-li	pitziil (pitzil) (pitzal)	1) ballplayer (n) 2) ballplaying (adj) 3) beautiful, well-adorned (adj)
pi-xo-la	pixo'l [1,2]	1) hat (n)
pi-xo-ma	pixo'm (pixoom)	1) hat, headdress (n)
pu	pu[j]	1) cattail reed (n)
po-ko	-pok-	1) to wash (tv)

APPENDIX IV.1 CLASSIC MAYAN TO ENGLISH LEXICON

Transcription	Transliteration	Translation
po-ko-la **po-ko-lo**	*pokol* *(poko'l)* *(pokool)*	1) wash bowl (n)
po-ko-lo-che-b'u **po-ko-lo-che-e-b'u**	*pokol che'eeb'* *(pokol che[h]b')* *(pokol che'e[h]b')*	1) quill bowl (n)
POL	*pol*	1) sculptor (n)
po-lo	*-pol-*	1) to carve (tv)
po-mo **po**	*pom* *(poom* [2]*)*	1) incense, copal (n)
po-mo-yo	*pomoy*	1) Pomoy, "?", toponym (area of Tonina) (n)
po-po	*po[h]p* [1,2] *(pop)*	1) mat (n) 1) 1st *haab'* month name (n)
po-po-TUN-ni	*pohp tuun*	1) Pop Tun, "mat stone", toponym (mentioned at Calakmul) (n)
po-po-o **po-o**	*popo'*	1) Popo', "?", emblem glyph (at Tonina) (n)
po-o-a	*popo' ha'*	1) Popo' Ha', toponym (at Tonina) (n)
po-o-NAL	*popo' nal*	1) Popo' Nal, "? place", toponym (variant at Tonina) (n)
po-po-la	*popo'l* *(popal)*	1) roasted (adj)
po-po-lo-cha-ya [2]**po-lo-cha-ya**	*popol chay*	1) type of fish, "mat-like fish" (n)
pu	*pu[j]*	1) cattail reed (n)
pu-chi	*puuch*	1) intestines (n)
PUK-ki	*puuk* *-puk-* *puk-*	1) spine, sting, goad (n) 2) to scatter, distribute (tv) 3) to scatter fire (riv)
pu-lu	*pul-*	1) to burn (div)
pu-la **pu-lu**	*-pul-*	1) to sprinkle (tv)
pu-tz'i	*puutz'* *(puu[h]tz'* [1]*)* *(pu[h]tz'* [2]*)*	1) (sewing) needle (n)
pu-tz'i-b'a-ki	*puutz' b'aak*	1) bone needle (n)

APPENDIX IV.1 CLASSIC MAYAN TO ENGLISH LEXICON

Transcription	Transliteration	Translation
pu-wa	pu'w [1] (puuw)	1) blowgun (n)
pu-yi	puuy [2]	1) snail (n) 2) roadrunner (n)

S

Transcription	Transliteration	Translation
sa	sa	1) atole (n)
SAB'AK sa-b'a-ka sa-b'a-ki	sab'aak (sab'ak)	1) ink, soot (n) 2) Sab'ak, toponym (at Chichen Itza) (n)
SAB'IN sa-b'i	sab'in	1) weasel (n)
sa-ja-la sa-ja	sajal	1) Sajal, title (n)
sa-ja-la-li	sajalaal (sajalil)	1) sajal-ship (n)
sa-ja-le-le	sajalel	1) sajal-ship (n)
SAK	sak [1,2]	1) white (adj) 2) resplendent (adj) 3) pure (adj)
SAK-la	sakal	1) white (adj) 2) resplendent (adj) 3) pure (adj)
SAK-b'a-**WITZ**-li	sak b'aah witzil	1) Sak B'ah Witzil, "white/pure first mountain", name (ruler at Caracol, pre-accession) (n)
SAK-B'AK-NAH-CHAPAT **SAK**-b'a-ki-na-ha-cha-pa-ta	sak b'aak nah chapaat	1) Sak B'ak Nah Chapat, "white bone great centipede", name (deity) (n)
SAK-cha-pa-tu	sak chapa't	1) Sak Chapat, "white centepede", name (at Rio Azul) name (n)

Transcription	Transliteration	Translation
SAK-chi-ji-li-WAJ SAK-ki-CHIJ-ji-li-WAJ-ji	sak chijil waaj	1) Sak Chijil Waj, "white venison bread", foodstuff name (n)
SAK-chi-ku	sak chi'k	1) lark, "white bird" (n)
SAK-HA'	sak ha'	1) atole, "white water" (n) 2) Sak Ha', "white/pure water", toponym (area of Naranjo) (n)
SAK-ha-la	sakhal	1) white-like (adj)
SAK-ha-la-SUTZ'	sakhal suutz'	1) Sakhal Sutz', "white-like bat", name (n)
SAK-HA'-WITZ-NAL	sak ha' witznal	1) Sak Ha' Witznal, "white/pure water mountain-place", toponym (at Rio Azul) (n)
SAK-IXIK	sak ixik	1) Sak Ixik, "white/pure woman", name (deity) (n)
SAK-KAB'-b'a	sak kab'	1) sascab, "white earth" (n)
SAK-ka-ya	sak kay	1) Sak Kay, "white fish", toponym (area of Zacpeten) (n)
SAK-LAK	sak lak	1) incensario, "white/pure plate" (n)
SAK-LAK-TUN-ni	sak lak tuun	1) stone incensario, "white/pure stone plate" (n)
SAK-mo-o	sak mo'	1) Sak Mo', "white/pure macaw", name (on Kerr 1256) (n)
SAK-MUWAN-ni	sak muwaan	1) Sak Muwan, "white/pure sparrow-hawk", name (on Dumbarton Oaks vessel) (n)
SAK-NIK-TE'	sak nikte'	1) Sak Nikte', "white/pure mayflower", emblem glyph (at La Corona) (n)
SAK-nu-ku-NAH	sak nuku[l] naah	1) Sak Nukul Nah, "white skin house", structure name (at Palenque) (n)
SAK-OL-WAY-si	sak o'l wayaas	1) Sak Ol Wayas, "white/pure heart spirit-companion", title (on codex-style vessels) (n)
SAK-3-OK	sak ox ook	1) Sak Ox Ok, "white/pure three dog", *way* name (n)
SAK-SIHOM?-ma	sak siho'm	1) 11th *haab'* month name (n)
SAK-SUTZ'-K'IN-ni-KALOM-cha-ki	sak suutz' k'ihn k'alo'm chaahk	1) Sak Sutz' K'in Kalom Chak, "white/pure bat sun, he the rain-deity ?", name (captive at La Mar) (n)
SAK-TZ'I' SAK-tz'i-i	sak tz'i'	1) Sak Tz'i', "white/pure dog", emblem glyph (area of Usumacinta) (n)

APPENDIX IV.1 CLASSIC MAYAN TO ENGLISH LEXICON

Transcription	*Transliteration*	Translation
sa-ku-na **sa-ku**	*saku'n* [2] *(sakuun)*	1) older brother (n)
SAK-u-NAL	*sakunal*	1) Sakunal, "white/pure place?", toponym (area of Oxkintok') (n)
sa-sa	*sas*	1) stucco, plaster (n) 2) brilliant, resplendent (adj)
sa-ta	*-sat-*	1) to got lost (tv) 2) to diminished (tv) 3) to die (tv)
sa-ya	*say*	1) outside (n)
sa-yu	*sa'y* *(saay)*	1) ant (n) 2) Say, toponym (n)
sa-ya-HUN	*sayhu'n*	1) book cover (n)
SA'? **SA'?-li**	*sa'il*	1) Sa'il, toponym (at Naranjo) (n)
sa-mi-ya **sa-a-mi-ya**	*sa'miiy*	1) earlier today (adv)
se-ka	*se'k* [1] *(se'ek* [2]*)* *(sek)*	1) 5th *haab'* month name (n)
se-wa	*se'w* *(seew)*	1) 5th *haab'* month name (n)
SIH **si-hi** **si-li ?** **si**	*(sih)*	1) offering, gift (n) see: *siy*
si-hi-ja	*sihiij* *sihaj*	1) gift (n)
SIHOM-ma **SIHOM-mo**	*siho'm* [1] *(sihoom)* *(sihom)*	1) winter maize crop (n)
	-sil-	1) to split (tv)
si-na	*-sin-*	1) to spread out, extend (tv)
si-na-na	*sinan* [1] *(siina'n* [2]*)*	1) scorpion (n)
si-pu	*si'p* *(siip)*	1) sin (n)
si	*si[p]*	1) 3rd *haab'* month name (PST CLA) (n)

Transcription	Transliteration	Translation
si-tz'i	*sitz'*	1) glutton, appetite (n)
SIY	*siy-* *siy*	1) bear (as in child) (ivd) 2) gift (n)
SIY-CHAN	*siyaj chan*	1) Siyaj Chan, "sky-born", emblem glyph (at Yaxchilan) (n)
SIY-ya-CHAN-a-ku	*siyaj chan ahku'l*	1) Siyaj Chan Akul, "sky-born turtle-like", name (sculptor of Altar 4 at El Cayo) (n)
SIY-ya-CHAN-na-ja-yi	*siyaj chan jaay*	1) Siyaj Chan Jay, "sky-born pot", painted pottery name (n)
SIY-HA'-EK'	*siyaj ha' ek'*	1) Siyaj Ha' Ek', "water-born star", name (at Tamarindito) (n)
SIY-ya-ja-K'AK'	*siyaj k'ahk'*	1) siyaj k'ak', "fire-born", name (at Tikal) (n)
SIY-K'IN-CHAK-ki SIY-ya-ja-K'IN-cha-ki	*siyaj k'ihn chaahk*	1) Siyaj K'in Chak, "sun-born sun rain-deity", name (at Piedras Negras and Machaquila) (n)
SIY-ja-TUN	*siyaj tuun*	1) Siyaj Tun, "stone-born", toponym (area of Nebaj) (n)
so-ti	*soot*	1) sound (n)
so-ti-li-hi-HIX	*sotil hix*	1) Sotil Hix, "sounding? jaguar", *way* name (n)
SOTZ' so-tz'i	*(sootz')*	1) 4th *haab'* month name (n) 2) bat (n) see: *suutz'*
su-ju-yu	*suujuy* [1,2] *(sujuy)*	1) virgin, clean (adj)
su-ku	*suku'[n]* [2] *(sukuu[n])*	1) elder brother (n)
su-ku-ku	*sukuk*	1) ground bean tortilla (n)
su-K'IN	*suk'ihn*	1) fast, fasting, abstinence (n)
su-lu	*sul*	1) dependent (n)
su-sa	*-sus-*	1) to clean, peel off (tv) 2) to crush (tv)
SUTZ' su-tz'i	*suutz'* [1,2]	1) 4th *haab'* month name (n) 2) bat (n)

APPENDIX IV.1 CLASSIC MAYAN TO ENGLISH LEXICON

Transcription	Transliteration	Translation
T		
ta	ta	1) in, at, by, with, to, on (prep)
ta-ji ta-ja	taaj [1] (taj [2])	1) obsidian, bloodletter (n)
TAJ ta-ja ta	taj [2]	1) pitch-pine, torch (n)
ta-jo	-taj-	1) to strike, split (tv)
TAJ TAJ-la ta-ja-la	tajal	1) obsidian-like (adj) 2) torch-like (adj)
TAJ-MO'-o TAJ-ja-MO-o ta-ja-la-MO ta-ja-MO-o	tajal mo'	1) Tajal Mo', "torch-like macaw", name (captive) (n)
ta-ja-NAL	tajnal	1) Tajnal, "obsidian/torch-place", court name (n)
ta-jo-ma ta-jo-mo	tajo'm (tajoom)	1) he/she who strikes (n)
ta-jo-ma-u-K'AB'-K'AK'	tajo'm u k'ab' k'ahk'	1) Tajom U K'ab' K'ak', "earth fire striker ?", name (ruler at Calakmul) (n)
ta-jo-ma-u-k'a-b'a-TUN-ni	tajo'm u k'ab' tuun	1) Tajom U K'ab' Tun, "?", wooden box name (at Piedras Negras and Tabasco) (n)
TAK ta-ki ta-ka	-taak [2] (-tak)	1) plural suffix for living or supernaturals (suf)
ta-k'a	-tak'-	1) to glue, paste, plaster (tv)
TAL ta-la	-tal	1) count of elapsed periods, ordinals, days (ncl)
ta-li	tal-	1) to come (riv)

APPENDIX IV.1 CLASSIC MAYAN TO ENGLISH LEXICON

	Transcription	*Transliteration*	Translation
	TAL **TAL-lo**	*talol*	1) Talol, emblem glyph (at Ek' B'alam) (n)
	TAN	*ta[h]n* [1,2] *(tan)*	1) in, in the center of (prep) 2) front (of building) (n)
	TAN-la	*tanal*	1) stomach, chest (n)
	TAN-na-LAM-wa	*tahn lamaw*	1) half-period (n)
	ta-pa	*-tap-*	1) to douse (tv) 1) to adorn, decorate (tv)
	ta-pa-la	*tapal*	1) dousing (adj)
	ta-ta	*tat* [2]	1) dense, thick, fat (adj)
	[2]**ta** **ta**	*tat*	1) father (?) (n)
	[2]**ta-b'u** **ta-b'u**	*tatb'u*	1) Tatb'u, "?", name (at Yaxchilan) (n)
	ta-wi-si-ka-la	*tawiskal*	1) Tawiskal," Tlahuizcalpantecuhtli?", foreign deity (in Dresden Codex) (n)
	te-k'a	*-tek'-*	1) to step on (tv)
	te-k'a-ja	*tek'aj*	1) stepping (n)
	te-le	*tel*	1) crest (n)
	te-ma **te-mu** **te-me**	*te'm (?)* [1] *temul (?)* [1] *(teem* [2]*)* *(tem)*	1) throne, bench (n)
	TE' **TE'-e** **te** **te-e**	*-te'* *te'*	1) count of time periods (ncl) 2) tree, wood (n)
	TE'-b'a	*te'b'a*	1) tree-thing (n)
	TE'-le **TE'-e-le**	*te'el*	1) wild, "of the tree" (adj) 2) tree (n)
	TE'-li **(te'il)**	*te'il*	1) wild, "of the tree" (adj)
	TE'-k'a-b'a-cha-ki	*te'k'ab'chaahk*	1) Te' K'ab' Chak, "red-earth tree", name (ruler at Caracol) (n)

Transcription	Transliteration	Translation
TE'-ku-yu	*te'kuy*	1) Te' Ku, "tree owl", title (at Yaxchilan) (n)
TE'-ni-b'i	*te'nib'*	1) tree-place, "tree place" (n)
ti	*ti*	1) in, at, by, with, on (prep)
ti-ho-i **ti-ho**	*tiho'*	1) Tiho, emblem glyph (at Dzibilchaltun) (n)
ti-ki-li	*-tikil*	1) beings, count of beings (ncl)
TIL **ti-li**	*-til-* *til-*	1) to untie (tv) 2) to burn (riv) 3) to stir (fire) (riv)
TIL **ti-li** **ti-la**	*ti[h]l* [1,2] *(tɪl)* *(tiil)*	1) tapir (n)
TIL-B'AK	*tilb'ak*	1) lightning bone, "burning bone" (n)
TIL-wi **ti-li-wi**	*tiliw*	1) Tiliw, name (n)
ti-lo-ma	*tilo'm* *(tiloom)*	1) burner, "he/she who burns" (n)
ti-mi **ti-ma**	*-tim-*	1) to appease (tv) 2) to fasten (tv) 3) to stretch (tv)
ti-si	*tis* [1] *(tiis* [2]*)*	1) fart (n) 2) body liquid (n)
TIWOJ **ti-wo**	*tiwoj*	1) poisonous spider (n)
TIWOJ-KAN-na-MAT **ti-wo-KAN-na-ma-MAT**	*tiwoj kan mat*	1) Tiwoj Kan Mat, "poisonous spider snake cormorant ?", name (at Palenque) (n)
TI' **ti** **ti-i**	*ti'*	1) mouth, opening, edge (n)
ti-i-li	*ti'il*	1) pertaining to (prep)
TI'-si	*ti'is*	1) mouth (n)
TI'-pa-a	*ti' pa'*	1) river-sore (n)

APPENDIX IV.1 CLASSIC MAYAN TO ENGLISH LEXICON

Transcription	*Transliteration*	Translation
TI'-SAK-HUN **TI'-SAK-hu-na**	*ti' sak hu'n*	1) speaker of the white book, "white/book mouth", title (n)
to-b'o-ti-B'ALAM	*tob'oo[h]t b'ahlam* [1]	1) Tob'ot B'alam, "jumping jaguar", name (n)
to-jo	*toj* *-toj-*	1) tribute, payment (n) 2) to pay (tv)
to-jo-a-AT-[KAN] **to-'AT-ti-KAN-na**	*toj aat kan*	1) Toj At Kan, "payment? penis snake", founder title (n)
to-jo-la **to-jo-li**	*tojo'l* *(tojool* [2]*)*	1) price, payment, tribute (n)
to-jo-ma-B'ALAM-ma	*tojo'm b'ahlam*	1) Tojom B'alam, "paying? jaguar", name (at Yaxchilan) (n)
TOK?-ko **to-ko**	*-tok-*	1) to burn (tv)
to-ko	*tok*	1) cloud (n) 2) smoke (n)
to-ko-TAN	*tok tan*	1) Tok Tan, "in [the] cloud/smoke", emblem glyph (at Palenque) (n)
TOK-la **to-ka-la**	*tokal* [1]	1) cloud (n) 2) smoke (n)
TOK' **to-k'a**	*to'k'* *(too'k'* [1]*)* *(took'* [2]*)*	1) flint (n)
TOK'-b'a	*to'k'b'a'*	1) flint-thing (n)
to-TOK'-ni-b'i	*to'k'nib'*	1) flint-place (n)
TOK'-PAKAL **to-k'a-pa-ka-la**	*to'k' pakal*	1) flint [and] shield, "flint-shield", war emblem or battle standard (n)
to-TOK'-ya-si-AJAW-wa	*to'k yaas ajaw*	1) Tok' Yas Ajaw, "flint ? lord", title (at Yula) (n)
TOK'-ya-si-K'INICH	*to'k yaas k'inich*	1) Tok' Yas K'inich, "flint ? sun-faced [one]", name (on Kerr 1728) (n)
TOT	*tot*	1) robin or lark, bird name (n)
tu	*tu*	1) in/with/at/to his/her/its (contraction of *ti+u*) (prep)
tu **tu-u**	*-tu'*	1) thing (n)

Transcription	Transliteration	Translation
tu-b'a-la tu-b'a	*tub'al*	1) Tub'al, toponym (area of Naranjo) (n)
tu-ku	*-tuk*	1) piles, count of piles (20) (ncl)
tu-ku-la	*tuku'l*	1) heaped up (n)
tu-ku-nu	*tukun* [1]	1) dove or pigeon (n)
tu-ku-nu-wi-WITZ	*tukun witz*	1) Tukun Witz, "dove mountain", toponym (Copan) (n)
TUN-ni	*tuun* [1,2]	1) stone (n) 2) 360 days, "stone", period of 360 days (n) 3) year (n)
TUN-ni-chi	*tunich*	1) stone (n)
TUP tu-pa tu-pi	*tu'p* (*tuu'p* [1]) (*tuup* ?)	1) earflare (n)
tu-pa-ja	*tu'paj* (*tuu'paj*) (*tuupaj*)	1) earflare (n)
[2]tu tu-tu tu-ta	*-tut-*	1) to visit (?) (tv)
tu-ta	*tu't* (*tuut*)	1) ? (n)
tu-ta-li	*tutaal*	1) adornment (?) (n)
tu-tu-K'IN-ni-CHAK-ki	*tutu[l] k'ihn chaahk*	1) Tutul K'in Chak, "? sun/hot rain", name (on Kerr 7524) (n)
tu-tu-ma tu-tu	*tutu'm* (*tutuum*)	1) Tutum, "?", name (n)
tu-tu-ma-yo-'OL-K'INICH	*tutu'm yo'l k'inich*	1) Tutum Yol K'inich, "? his center, the sun-faced [one]", name (dynasty founder at Quirigua and Caracol, person at Naj Tunich) (n)

T'

Transcription	Transliteration	Translation
T'AB' t'a?-b'a	*-t'ab'-* *t'ab'-*	1) to anoint, burnish, polish (tv) 2) to cover with stucco (tv) 3) to move, go up (riv)

APPENDIX IV.1 CLASSIC MAYAN TO ENGLISH LEXICON

Transcription	*Transliteration*	Translation
T'UL t'u-lu	*t'ul* [1] *(t'u'l* [2]*)*	1) rabbit (n)

TZ

Transcription	*Transliteration*	Translation
TZAK tza-ku	*tza'k* [1] *-tzak-*	1) conjurer (n) 2) to grab, conjure (tv)
tzi-hi-li tzi-hi	*tzihil*	1) new, fresh, raw (adj)
TZIK tzi-ka	*-tzik-*	1) to count (tv) 2) to honor, sanctify (tv)
TZIK-la	*tzikal*	1) honored, sanctified, venerated (adj)
tzu-ku	*tzuk*	1) partition, division, segment, province (n)
tzu-lu	*tzul*	1) dog (n)
TZUTZ tzu-tza tzu-tzu	*-tzutz-*	1) to end, terminate (tv) 2) to join (tv)
TZUTZ-no-ma	*tzutzno'm* *(tzutznoom)*	1) finisher (n)
TZU' tzu	*tzu'*	1) gourd, calabash (n)

TZ'

Transcription	*Transliteration*	Translation
tz'a	*-tz'a'-*	1) to give (tv)
TZ'AK	*tz'a[h]k* [1] *(tz'ak)* *t'zak-* *-tz'ak*	1) whole (adj) 2) to add, accumulate (pv) 3) things, count of things (ncl)

APPENDIX IV.1 CLASSIC MAYAN TO ENGLISH LEXICON

Transcription	Transliteration	Translation
TZ'AK-ka-ja TZ'AK-ja TZ'AK-a	-tz'akaj	1) count, completing (ncl)
TZ'AK-ka-la	tz'ahkal	1) accumulated (adj)
TZ'AK-b'u	-tz'akb'u-	1) to put in order (tv)
TZ'AK-b'u-li tz'a-ka-b'u-li	tz'ahkb'u'l (tz'akb'uul)	1) successor (n)
TZ'AM tz'a-ma	tz'am	1) throne (n)
tz'a-nu	-tz'an-	1) to destroy (tv)
tz'a-pa	-tz'ap-	1) to drive into ground, plant, erect (tv)
tz'a-ya	-tz'ay-	1) to come down, descend, win (tv)
tz'a-ya-ja-K'AN-na-tu-ma-ki	tz'ayaj k'ahk' k'antu' maak	1) Tz'ayaj K'ak' K'antu' Mak, "fire descended, Caracol person", name (of Caracol person at Naj Tunich) (n)
TZ'I tz'i-i	tz'i'	1) dog (n)
tz'i-b'i	tz'i[h]b' [1,2] (tz'ib')	1) writing, painting (n)
tz'i-b'a	-tz'ib'-	1) to write, paint (tv)
tz'i-b'a-li tz'i-b'a-la	tz'i[h]b'al (tz'ib'aal) (tz'i[h]b'al)	1) painting, color (n)
tz'i-b'a-la-NAH	tz'ihb'al naah	1) Tz'ib'al Nah, "painted(?) house", structure name (n)
tz'i-b'a-ma-TUN-ni	tz'ihb'am tuun	1) Tz'ib'am Tun, "painted(?) stone", name (ruler at Ek B'alam) (n)
tz'i-b'a-a-AT	tz'ihb' aat	1) Tz'ib' At, "painted(?) penis", structure name (n)
tz'i-b'a-CHAK-ki	tz'ihb' chaahk	1) Tz'ib' Chak, "painted(?) rain-deity", name (at Yaxchilan) (n)
tz'i-b'a-NAH	tz'ihb' naah	1) Tz'ib Nah, "painted(?) house", structure name (n)
tz'i-b'i-na-ja-la	tz'ihb'najal	1) painting, writing (n)

Transcription	Transliteration	Translation
tz'i-ku	tz'i[h]k [1] (tz'i'k)	1) clay (n)
tz'u-lu	-tz'ul-	1) to skin, peel (tv)
tz'u-lu-B'AK	tz'ul b'aak	1) skinning bone (n)
TZ'UNUN tz'u-[2]nu tz'u-nu	tz'unun [1] (tz'uunu'n [2])	1) hummingbird (n)
tz'u-tz'i	tz'uutz'	1) coatimundi (n)

U

Transcription	Transliteration	Translation
u-b'u	-ub'-	1) to hear (tv)
(y)u-b'a	u'b'	1) painted/smeared object (n)
(y)u-b'u-te	ub'te'	1) tribute (n)
u-CHAN-ni u-cha-ni	uchaan	1) Uchan, "his snake", emblem glyph (at Calakmul) (n)
u-cho-cho-yo-ko-pu-yi	uchoch yokpuuy	1) Uchoch Yokpuuy, "his intestines(?) ?", name (deity at Chichen Itza) (n)
(y)u-ch'a	u'ch' (uuch')	1) louse (n)
UH (y)u-UH (y)u-UH-(li) (y)u-ha	uh [1] (uuh [2])	1) necklace, collar (n) 2) bead (n)
UH/U'	uh (u')	1) moon (n)
UH-CHAPAT	uh chapa't	1) Uh Chapat, "moon centipede", name (ruler at Tonina) (n)
UH-IXIK u-IXIK	uh ixik	1) Uh Ixik, "moon woman", name (deity) (n)
UH-ja u-ha-ja	uhaj (u'haj)	1) necklace (n)
u-ka-KAN	ukan	1) Ukan, "his snake", emblem glyph (at Calakmul) (n)

Transcription	*Transliteration*	Translation
u-ku **u-ku-la** **UK?-la**	*uku'ul* *uku'l* *(ukuul)*	1) ?, "abundance of uk?" (n) 2) Ukul, "?", toponym (area of Yaxchilan) (n)
u-ku-mu **u-ku-ma**	*ukum* *uku'm* *(ukuum)*	1) dove, pigeon (n)
u-ki-ti-KAN-le-ku-TOK' **u-ki-ti-ka-na-le-ku-TOK'**	*ukit kan lek to'k'*	1) U Kit Kan Lek Tok', "his father four calabash flint (?)", name (ruler at Ek Balam) (n)
u-ki-ti-ko-yi	*ukit kooy*	1) U Kit Koy, "his father ?", name (at Chichen Itza) (n)
u-ki-ti-TOK'	*ukit to'k'*	1) U Kit Tok', "flint's father", name (ruler at Copan) (n)
UK'	*uk'* *-uk'-* *uk'-*	1) drinking vessel (n) 2) to drink (tv) 2) to drink (div)
u-K'A-b'i **(y)u-K'A-b'i** **(y)u-UK-b'a**	*uk'aab'*	1) drinking vessel (n)
(y)u-k'e-sa	*uk'e's* *(uk'ees)*	1) trumpet-shell (n)
u-k'i-b'i **UK-b'i** **UK**	*uk'ib'*	1) drinking vessel (n)
u-K'IN	*uk'ihn*	1) U K'in, "his sun", toponym (area of Bonampak, Sak Tz'i') (n)
u-K'INICH-chi-NAL-la	*uk'inich nal*	1) U K'inich Nal, "his sun-faced ear of corn(?)", name (of shield) (n)
u-lu	*ul* ¹ *(uul* ²*)*	1) atole (n)
u-li	*-ul-*	1) to arrive (tv)
u-lu-mu	*ulum* *(uulum* ²*)*	1) turkey, hen (n)
u-ma-na	*uman*	1) Uman, toponym (El Peru) (n)
UN **u-ni**	*uun*	1) avacado (n)
u-²ne **(y)u-ne**	*unen*	1) child of father (n)

Transcription	Transliteration	Translation
UNIW	uniiw	1) avocado (n)
UNIW-wa UNIW-ni-wa	uniiw	1) 14th *haab'* month name (n)
u-pa-ka-la	upakal	1) U Pakal, "his shield", name part (n)
u-pa-ka-la-EL-K'INICH	upakal elk'inich	1) U Pakal El K'inich, "his shield, burning sun-faced [one]", name (ruler at Comacalco) (n)
u-PAKAL-la-K'INICH-chi	upakal k'inich	1) U Pakal K'inich, "his shield, sun-faced [one]", name (at Naj Tunich) (n)
u-PAKAL-la-K'INICH-ja-na-b'i-pa-ka-la	upakal k'inich janaab' pakal	1) U Pakal K'inich Janab' Pakal, "his shield, sun-faced ? shield", name (ruler at Palenque) (n)
u-si-ja u-si	usiij [1]	1) vulture (n) 2) aura (n)
UT-tu UT-si u-ti (y)u-ta	ut utis uut	1) eye (n) 2) face (n) 3) fruit (n)
UH-ti u-ti	ut-	1) to happen, occur (riv)
u-tzi (y)u-tzi	uutz	1) good (adj)
u-tz'u	-utz'- (u[h]tz')	1) to smell, sniff (tv)
u-tzi-li	utzil	1) goodness (n)
u-6-pu-AK-na-hi	uwak pu[j] ahk naah	1) U Wak Puh Ak Nah, "his six reed turtle house", name (building at Chichen Itza) (n)
3	(ux) (u[h]x)	1) three (num) see: ox

Transcription	Transliteration	Translation
13	(uxlaju'n) (u[h]xlaju'n) (uxlajuun)	1) thirteen (num) see: oxlaju'n
13-CHAN-na-KUY	(uxlaju'n chan kuy)	1) Uxlajun Chan Kuy, "thirteen sky owl", name (bird associated with God L) (n) see: oxlaju'n chan kuy
3-lu-ti-K'UH	ux luut k'uh	1) Ux Lut K'uh, "three ? deity", epithet (of the Palenque triad) (n)
3-wi-ti-ki	ux witik	1) Ux Witik, "three [plant]", emblem glyph (at Copan) (n)
3-WITZ	ux witz	1) Ux Witz, "three mountain", emblem glyph (at Copan) (n)
3-WITZ-tzi-a	ux witz ha'	1) Ux Witz Ha', "three mountain water", emblem glyph (at Caracol) (n)
3-TE'-HA'	uxte' ha'	1) Uxte' Ha', "three-wood/period water" name (of deity) (n)
3-TE'-TUN-ni	uxte' tuun	1) Uxte' Tun, "three-period year", emblem glyph (at Calakmul) (n)
u-xu-lu	uxul	1) carving, sculpture (n)
u-xu-lu	-uxul-	1) to carve, sculpt (tv)
(y)u-xu-lu-li	uxuluul uxulil	1) his carving (n)
(y)u-xu-lu-na-ja-la	uxulnajal	1) carving, sculpture (n)
(y)u-xu-wa-ja-la	uxulwajal	1) carving, sculpture (n)
u-yu-b'u	uyub'	1) auditor (n)
W		
-wa	-wa	1) active transitive verb marker (suf)
wa	wa-	1) to erect (pv)
WACH	wach-	1) to erect (pv)
WAJ wa-ji	waaj [1,2]	1) tamale, tortilla (n)

APPENDIX IV.1 CLASSIC MAYAN TO ENGLISH LEXICON

Transcription	Transliteration	Translation
6	wak	1) six (num)
WAK	wak	1) upright (adj)
6-AJAW-NAH	wak ajaw naah	1) Wak Ajaw Nah, "six ruler house", structure name (at Calakmul) (n)
wa-KAN	wakan	1) Wakan, name (on Early Classic celtiform plaques) (n)
6-CHAN-na-MUYAL-ya-la-WITZ	wak chan muyal witz	1) Wak Chan Muyal Witz, "six sky cloud mountain", toponym (mythical) (n)
6-KAB'-NAL	wak kab'nal	1) Wak Kab'nal, "six earth place", emblem glyph (at Naranjo)
16	waklaju'n (waklajuun)	1) sixteen (num)
WAK'AB' **wa-k'a-b'i**	wak'aab'	1) Wak'ab', toponym (area of Yaxchilan, Santa Elena) (n)
WAL	wal -wal-	1) now (adv) 2) to set up (tv)
-wa-ni	-waan	1) positional verb marker (suf)
wa-t'u-lu-cha-te-le	wat'ul chatel	1) Wat'ul Chatel, "?", name (ruler of Seibal) (n)
wa-xi	waax	1) fox (n)
8 **wa-xa-ka**	waxak	1) eight (num)
18	waxaklaju'n (waxaklajuun)	1) eighteen (num)
18-u-B'AH-CHAN-na-K'AWIL	waxaklaju'n ub'aah chan k'awiil	1) Waxaklajun Ub'ah Chan K'awil, "18 hevenly k'awil's image", name (ruler at Copan and war serpent)

APPENDIX IV.1 CLASSIC MAYAN TO ENGLISH LEXICON

	Transcription	*Transliteration*	Translation
	WAY	*way* *(wa[h]y* [2]*)* *way-*	1) *nawal*, co-essence, animal companion spirit, malign spirit (n) 2) room, quarter (n) 3) to sleep (div)
	wa-ya	*way* *way-*	1) here (adv) 2) here (n) 3) to sleep (div)
	WAY-HAB'	*wayhaab'*	1) final 5-day period of 365-day year (n)
	WAY-b'i **wa-ya-b'a**	*wayib'* *(wayaab')*	1) sleeper, dreamer (n) 2) sleeping room, sanctuary, dormitory, domicile (n)
	WAY-ya-si	*wayis* *(wayaas)*	1) spirit companion (n)
	WE	*-we-*	1) to eat (bread) (tv)
	WE-i-b'i	*we'ib'*	1) eating instrument, food plate (n)
	WE'-la	*we'el* [1]	1) food, meat (n)
	WE-ma	*we'em*	1) eating instrument, food plate (n)
	wi-i-li	*wi'il* [1]	1) after, last (adj)
	(a)-wi-na-ke-(na)	*winak*	1) servant (n)
	WINAL-la	*winal*	1) 20-day period (n)
	WI-ni-B'AH-hi **WI-ni-b'a**	*winb'aah*	1) image (n)
	WINIK **wi-ni-ki**	*winik* [1,2]	1) human being, man (n) 2) 20-day period (n)
	WINIK **20**	*winik*	1) twenty (num)

APPENDIX IV.1 CLASSIC MAYAN TO ENGLISH LEXICON

Transcription	Transliteration	Translation
WINIK-HAB'	winikhaab'	1) 20-year period/k'atun (n)
WINIK-li	winikil	1) 20-day period (at Tila) (n)
WINIK-ki-li-b'a-TE'-pi-tzi-la	winikil b'ate' pitziil	1) Winikil B'ate Pitzil, "20-day tree-image ballplayer", title (Kerr 7749) (n)
wi-ti-ki	witik	1) plant name (n) 2) Witik, toponym (area of Copan) (n)
WITZ **wi-tzi**	witz [1,2] witz-	1) mountain, hill (n) 2) to pile up (div)
WITZ-NAL	witznal	1) mountain-place (n)
wi	wi' -wi'-	1) root (n) 2) to create carnage (tv)
wi-TE'-NAH	wi' te' naah	1) Wi' Te' Nah, "tree root house", structure name (at Copan) (n)
WI'	wi'	1) meal (n)
WI' **wi-i-li**	wi'il	1) last, for the last time (adj) 2) after (adj)
WI'-NAL	wi'nal	1) hunger, famine (n)
wo **wo-i** **wo-hi**	wooh [1]	1) 2nd *haab'* month name (n)
wo-o-ja **wo-ja** **wo-jo** **wo-jo-li** **wo-jo-le**	wo'oj [1] (wooj) (woj)	1) hieroglyph (n)
wo-lo	wol -wol-	1) round object (n) 2) to wrap up, round (tv)
7	wuk	1) seven (num)

Transcription	Transliteration	Translation
7-CHAPAT-CHAN-K'INICH-AJAW 7-CHAPAT-tu-CHAN-na-K'INICH-AJAW-wa	wuk chapa't chan k'inich ajaw	1) Wuk Chapat Chan K'inich Ajaw, "seven centipede sky sun-faced ruler", name (war serpent) (n)
7-IK'-K'AN-NAL	wuk ik' k'an nal	1) Wuk Ik' K'an Nal, "seven black bench place", toponym (mythical) (n)
7-si-pu	wuk si'p	1) Wuk Sip, "Seven Sins", name (deity) (n)
17	wuklaju'n (wuklajuun)	1) seventeen (num)
17-K'IN-ni-b'a	wuklaju'n k'ihn b'aah	1) Wuk K'in B'aah, "seven sun image", name (deity) (n)
7-ye-to-k'a	wukye' to'k'	1) Wukye' Tok', "seven divine-objects flint", name (deity) (n)

X

Transcription	Transliteration	Translation
xa	xa	1) already (adv)
xa	xa	1) iterative aspect marker (?) (suf)
xa-k'u	xak'-	1) to be posted (riv)
xa-MAN-na xa-ma-na	xaman ²	1) north (n)
XAN	xan-	1) to go, walk (riv)
XIB' xi-b'i	xib' (xiib' ²)	1) male person, young man (n)
xi-ki-b'a-le xi-ki-b'a-le-le	xikb'alel	1) ? (war object) (n)
xi-ni	xin	1) stinking (adj) 2) in, inside (prep)

Transcription	Transliteration	Translation
XOK-ki xo-ki	xook [1]	1) shark (n)
xo-ko	xok	1) count (n)
xo-ko-TUN-ni	xoktuun	1) counting-stone (n)
xo	xo[l]	1) cylindrical (adj)
xo-TE'	xo[l]te'	1) cylindrical piece of wood (n)
xu-ka	xu'k (xu[h]k)	1) corner (n)
xu-ku-pi	xuk(?) pi'	1) proper name of dance staff (n)
xu-ka-la	xukal (xu[h]kal)	1) cornered, square (n)
xu-ka-la-NAH xu-ka-NAH	xukal naah	1) cornered-house, "corner/square house", structure name(n)
XUKUB' xu-ku-b'u	xukub'	1) horn (n)
xu-ku-pi-pi xu-ku-pi-pu xu-ku-pu xu-pu	xuk pip (?) xuk pi' xukup	1) Xukpip(?), emblem glyph (Copan) (n)
XUL-WITZ xu-lu-WITZ	xul witz	1) Xul Witz, "? mountain", toponym (Naj Tunich Xultun) (n)
xu	xu'	1) ant (n)

Y

ya	ya	1) there (adv)

Transcription	*Transliteration*	Translation
ya-b'a	*yab'*	1) abundance (n)
ya-b'a-NAL	*yab'nal*	1) Yab'nal, "place of abundance", emblem glyph (at Chichen Itza) (n)
YAJ ya-ji	*yaaj*	1) at the same time (?) (adv)
ya-ja	*-yaj*	1) derives nouns from positionals (suffix)
ya-AJAW ya-ja-wa	*yajaw*	1) vassal, subordinate ruler, "his ruler" (n)
ya-AJAW-CHAN-MUWAN-ni	*yajaw chan muwaan*	1) Yajaw Chan Muwan, "sky sparrow-hawk's ruler", name (ruler at Bonampak)
ya-ja-wa-KALOM	*yajaw kalom*	1) Yajaw Kalom, "?'s ruler", name (artist at Piedras Negras) (n)
ya-AJAW-K'AK' ya-ja-wa-k'a-k'a	*yajaw k'ahk'*	1) Yajaw K'ak', fire servant, "fire's ruler", elite title (n)
ya-AJAW-TE' ya-ja-wa-TE'	*yajawte'*	1) Yajaw Te', spear-lord (?), "wood's ruler", elite title (n)
ya-AJAW-TE'-pi-tzi-la	*yajawte' pitziil*	1) Yajaw Te' Pitzil, "wood's ruler, ballplayer", elite title (n)
ya-la	*-yal-*	1) to throw, demolish (tv)
YATIK ya-ti-ki	*yatik*	1) flower (?) (n)
YAX ya-xa	*yax* *(ya'x ?)*	1) blue/green (adj) 2) first (adj) 3) precious, sacred (adj) 4) Yax, toponym (mentioned at Caracol) (n)
YAX-a-ku	*yax ahku['l]*	1) Yax Akul, "blue/green turtle-like", name (ruler at Anayte') (n)
YAX-a-ku-la-HA'	*yax ahku'l ha'*	1) Yax Akul Ha', "blue/green turtle-like water", emblem glyph (at El Cayo) (n)
YAX-AM-TE'	*yax amte'*	1) Yax Amte', "new ?-tree", name (tree erected during New Year ceremony) (n)
YAX-B'ALAM	*yax b'ahlam*	1) Yax B'alam, "precious/first jaguar", name (Classic hero twin and ruler at Santa Elena Poco Uinic) (n)
YAX-EB'-XOK	*yax e'b' xok*	1) Yax Eb' Xok, "precious/first stair shark", name (founder of Tikal dynasty) (n)
YAX-a YAX-HA'	*yax ha'*	1) Yax Ha', toponym (area of Peten/Usamacinta/Petexb'atun)

APPENDIX IV.1 CLASSIC MAYAN TO ENGLISH LEXICON

Transcription	*Transliteration*	Translation
YAX-HA' YAX-HA'-la YAX-ha-la	*yaxha'l* *(yaxha'al)*	1) blue/green water-like (adj)
YAX-HA'-CHAK YAX-HA'-la-CHAK-ki	*yaxha'l chaahk*	1) Yaxhal Chak, "blue/green water-like rain-deity", name (deity) (n)
YAX-ha-la-wi-tzi YAX-ha-la-wi-tzi-na-la	*yaxha'l witznal*	1) Yaxhal Witznal, "blue/green water-like mountain-place", toponym (mythical) (n)
YAX-ITZAM-AT	*yax itzam aat*	1) Yax Itzam At, "blue/green iguana penis?", name (court official at Palenque) (n)
YAX-KALOM-ma	*yax kalo'm*	1) Yax Kalom, "blue/green (or first) ?", title (n)
YAX-KALOM-TE'	*yax kalo'mte'*	1) Yax Kalomte', "first wood lord", title (n)
YAX-k'a-ma-la-ya	*yax k'amlay*	1) Yax K'amlay, "first grasper", title (ruler at Copan) (n)
YAX-K'IN	*yax k'ihn*	1) 7th *haab'* month name (n)
YAX-ma-yu-CHAN-CHAK-ki YAX-ma-yu-yu-CHAN-na-CHAK YAX-ma-yu-CHAN-na-CHAK	*yax mayuy chan chaahk*	1) Yax Mayuy Chan Chak, "blue/green fog sky rain-deity", name (ruler at Naranjo) (n)
YAX-MUT	*yax mutu'l*	1) Yax Mutul, "blue/green (or first/precious) knot", emblem glyph (at Tikal) (n)
YAX-NAH-hi-ITZAMNAJ-ji	*yax naah itzamnaaj*	1) Yax Nah Itzamnaj, "first house Itzamnaj", name (paramount deity at Palenque) (n)
YAX-ni-la	*yax niil*	1) Yax Nil, "first ?", emblem glyph (at El Cayo) (n)
YAX-PAS-CHAN-na YAX-PAS-sa-ja-CHAN-na YAX-pa-sa-ja-CHAN-na YAX-pa-sa-CHAN-na	*yax pasaj chan*	1) Yax Pasaj Chan, "first sky dawn", name (ruler at Copan) (n)
YAX-SIHOM?-ma	*yax siho'm*	1) 10th *haab'* month name (n)
YAX-TE'	*yax te'*	1) ceiba tree, "blue/green (or first) tree" (n)
YAXUN ya-xu-na	*yaxu'n* *(yaxuun)*	1) cotinga, song bird name (n)
ya-xu-nu-B'ALAM-ma	*yaxu'n b'ahlam*	1) Yaxun B'alam, "cotinga jaguar", name (ruler at Ixtutz) (n)
ya-YAX	*yayax*	1) very blue/green (adj)

Transcription	Transliteration	Translation
ye	-ye	1) divine-objects (ncl)
ye	ye (ye[h])	1) revealed (adj)
ye-ma-la-K'UK'-LAKAM-wi-WITZ	yemal k'uk' lakam witz	1) Yemal K'uk' Lakam Witz, "quetzal's descent large mountain", toponym (area of Palenque) (n)
ye-te	yet	1) insignia, costume (n)
yi-b'a-na	yib'an	1) Yib'an, "?", name (at Jaina and Xcalumkin) (n)
YICH'AK-B'ALAM YICH'AK-ki-B'ALAM-ma yi-ch'a-ki-B'ALAM	yich'aak b'ahlam	1) Yich'ak B'alam, "jaguar's claw", name (ruler at Seibal) (n)
yi-pi	yip-	1) to fill (riv)
yo-chi-ni	yochin	1) Yochin, "?", toponym (area of Peten) (n)
yo-ke	yook	1) Yok, "?", emblem glyph (at Aguacatal) (n)
yo-ki-b'i	yokib'	1) Yokib', "canyon", emblem glyph (at Piedras Negras) (n) 2) canyon (n) 3) entrance (n)
yo-ko-MAN-na	yokman	1) Yokman, toponym (area of Tikal) 2) pillar (n)
yo-K'IN-ni	yok'ihn	1) Yok'in, "sun foot", title (n)
yo-OL-la-a-ku	yo'l ahku'l	1) Yol Ak, "turtle's center", toponym (mythological) (n)
yo-mo-po yo-mo-pi	yomop yomoop	1) Yomop, "?", toponym (area of Tonina/Tortuguero) (n)
yo-NAL	yo'nal	1) relative (n)
yo-o-NAL-AK yo-o-NAL-a-ku	yo'nal ahk	1) Yo'nal Ak, "turtle's stomach", name (dynasty at Piedras Negras) (n)
yo-po?-AT-ti yo-AT-ti yo-AT-ta	yopaat	1) mitre, crown, type of helmet (n)
yo-po-'AT-ti-CHAN-na yo-'AT-ta-CHAN-na	yopaat chan	1) Yopat Chan, "sky helmet ?", title (rulers) (n)

Transcription	Transliteration	Translation
yo-YOTZ-tzi yo-tzi	yootz	1) Yotz, "?", toponym (area of Naranjo) (n)
YOTZ-tzi-KAN-PET	yootz kanpet	1) Yotz Kanpet, "? round sky?", name (deity in Campeche area) (n)
yu-b'u-TE'	yub'te'	1) tribute cloth (n)
yu-ch'a-ma-xi	yu'ch' maax (yuuch' maax)	1) Yuch' Max, "spider monkey's louse", *way* name (n)
yu-ku	-yuk-	1) to shake (tv) 2) to join, unite (tv)
yu-ku-no-ma	yukno'm (yu[h]kno'm) (yuknoom) (yu[h]knoom)	1) shaker, one who shakes (n) 2) Yuknom, "shaker", title (at Calakmul) (n)
yu-ku-no-yi-ICH'AK-K'AK'	yukno'm yich'aak k'ahk'	1) Yuknom Yich'ak K'ak', "shaker claw fire", name (ruler at Calakmul) (n)
yu-lu	yul -yul-	1) polished object (n) 2) to polish, brush (tv)
yu-lu-li	yuluul	1) polished object (n)
yu-mu yu-ma	yum [1] (yu'm)	1) family head, father, boss, patron (n)
yu-wa-la	yuwal	1) progressive aspect marker ? (suf) 2) now (adv)

APPENDIX IV.2. ENGLISH TO CLASSIC MAYAN LEXICON

Translation

For each item, one or more acceptable translations are given in the last column. Sometimes more than one meaning may be derived from a single word. Context may be required to choose the correct meaning. For each entry, the translation is given first, followed by the literal translation in quotation marks. A description of where or how this term is used is sometimes included. Finally, the part of speech is indicated by one of the following abbreviations:

adj	adjective
adv	adverb
div	derived intransitive verb
icv	inchoative verb
n	noun
ncl	numeral classifier
num	numeral
partic	participle
prep	preposition
pron	pronoun
pv	positional verb
riv	root intransitive verb
tv	transitive verb

Transcription

The second column gives some of the known glyphic spellings for each entry. The logographic spellings are given first, followed by any possible syllabic spellings.

> B'ALAM
> b'a-la-ma

Standard transcription conventions are used (except that final vowels or phonetic complements are not placed in parentheses to simplify searching). Although logographic spellings are often accompanied by syllabic phonetic complements in inscriptions, superfluous phonetic complements are omitted here.

> B'ALAM not b'a-B'ALAM-ma
> b'a-la-ma not b'a-la-m(a)

Transliteration

Many entries have more than one suggested transliteration because of the variability of historical reconstruction and the current debate on the complex vowel spelling rules (see chapter 2). The third column lists most of these suggested transliterations. The first spelling is the one used in this book. The spellings are from Lacadena and Wichmann (2004: indicated by superscript 1) or Houston et al. (2004; Robertson et al. 2007: indicated by superscript 2; Robertson et al. 2007 spellings trump Houston et al. 2004 spellings). Other sources include Boot (2000), Mathews and Biro (2006), and Montgomery (2002). Sometimes there are discrepancies among the dictionaries, but remember that the transliteration is not required for translation; it is a reconstruction of the sound only. For the most part, the spellings used in this book follow a simplified version of Lacadena and Wichmann (2004). They will be updated as the field advances. For example, "shell," glyphically spelled **ju-ch(i)**, is reconstructed as *juu[h]ch* by Lacadena and Wichmann (2004) but as *ju[h]ch* by Robertson et al. (2007). The entry for "shell" here lists the following spellings, indicating the variety of reconstructed transcriptions:

juu[h]ch [1]
(ju[h]ch) [2]
(juch)
(juuch)

For the purposes of this lexicon, an infixed *h* is indicated within brackets for the root entry but without brackets in compound words to make names and other compound words easier to read:

b'a[h]lam
but
yax b'ahlam.

Translation	Transcription	Transliteration
144,000 day period (n)	**PIK**	*pik*
	pi	
	pi	*pih*
	pi-hi	
20-day period (n)	**WINIK-li**	*winikil*
	WINAL-la	*winal*
	WINIK	*winik* [1,2]
	wi-ni-ki	
	WINIK-HAB'	*winikhaab'*
360 days (n)	**TUN-ni**	*tuun* [1,2]
abstinence (n)	**su-K'IN**	*suk'ihn*
abundance (n)	**ya-b'a**	*yab'*
abundance of food, "many food" (n)	**3-WI'**	*ox wi'il*
abundance of herons (n)	**B'AK-la**	*b'aakal*
abundant (adj)	**k'a**	*k'a*
accompany (tv)	**(y)i-ta**	*-it-*
accumulate (pv)	**TZ'AK**	*t'zak-*
accumulated (adj)	**TZ'AK-ka-la**	*tz'akal*
add (pv)	**TZ'AK**	*t'zak-*
adorn (tv)	**je-le**	*-jel-*
	JEL	
	na-wa	*-naw-*
	ta-pa	*-tap-*
adornment ? (n)	**tu-ta-li**	*tutaal*

Translation	Transcription	Transliteration
after (adv)	**Ci-ya**	*-iiy*
	WI'	*wi'il* [1]
	wi-i-li	
	pa-ti	*paat*
	PAS-sa-ja	*pasaj* [1]
	PAS	
	pa-sa-ja	
again (adv)	**CHA'**	*cha'*
	2	
ago (adv)	**Ci-ya**	*-iiy*
air (n)	**IK'**	*ik'*
alone (adj)	**b'a-ni**	*b'aan*
already (adv)	**Ci-ya**	*-iiy*
	xa	*xa*
ancestor (n)	**MAM**	*mam* [2]
	ma-ma	
and then (partic)	**i**	*i*
animal companion spirit (n)	**WAY**	*way*
announcement (n)	**mu-ka**	*mu'k* [1]
anoint (tv)	**T'AB'**	*-t'ab'-*
	t'a?-b'a	
ant (n)	**sa-yu**	*sa'y*
	xu	*xu'*
anteater (n)	**CHAB'**	*chaab'* [1,2]
	cha-b'i	

APPENDIX IV.2 ENGLISH TO CLASSIC MAYAN LEXICON

Translation	Transcription	Transliteration
appease (tv)	ti-mi ti-ma	-tim-
appetite (n)	si-tz'i	sitz'
arm (n)	K'AB' k'a-b'a	k'ab'- [1,2]
armadillo (n)	i-b'a-cha	ib'ach
arrive (riv)	HUL-li hu-li	hul-
arrive (tv)	u-li	-ul-
artist (n)	CHUWEN a-tz'i-b'a-la	chuwen aj tz'i[h]b'aal
as such (adv)	b'a-ya	b'ay
at (prep)	ta ti	ta ti
at the same time (?) (adv)	YAJ ya-ji	yuuj
atole, "white water" (n)	ko-b'a-la sa u-lu SAK-HA'	kob'al sa ul [1] sak ha'
attract with enchantments (tv)	pa-yi-ku-na	-paykun-
auditor (n)	ko-ko-ma u-yu-b'u	koko'm uyub'
avocado (n)	UN u-ni ON-ni UNIW	uun oon uniiw
awakening (n)	a-ja-la a-ja-li	ajal
back (n)	pa-ti	paat
bad (adj)	ma-tzi-li	matzil
B'aktun (n)	PIK pi (pik) pi pi-hi	pik pih
ball court (n)	a-la-wa HALAB' HALAB'-b'i HALAW?	alaw halaab' halaw?
ballgame (n)	pi-tzi	pitz [1]

Translation	Transcription	Transliteration
ballplayer (n)	pi-tzi-la pi-tzi-li	pitziil
ball-playing (adj)	pi-tzi-la pi-tzi-li	pitziil
bamboo (n)	che-b'u che-e-b'u	che'e[h]b' [1]
banish (pv)	B'ALUN-i-pi	b'alu'n ip-
bark (n)	HUN HUN-na hu-na	hu'n [1,2]
basket (n)	cha-chi	chaach [1]
bat (n)	SOTZ' so-tz'i SUTZ' su-tz'i	(sootz') suutz' [1,2]
bathe (iv?)	i-chi-ki i-chi-li	ichik ichil
bathe (tv)	(y)a-ATI (y)a-ti	-ati-
be face down (pv)	pa-ka	pak-
be posted (riv)	xa-k'u	xak'-
be seated (pv)	b'u-B'UCH	b'uch-
be stuck (pv)	e-ke	ek-
bead (n)	UH (y)u-UH (y)u-UH-(li) (y)u-ha	uh [1]
bean (n)	b'u-la	b'u'l [1]
bear (a child) (div)	SIY	siy-
beat (icv)	B'AJ b'a-ja	b'aj-
beautiful (adj)	pi-tzi pi-tzi-la pi-tzi-li	pitz [1] pitziil
bee (n)	CHAB' cha-b'i KAB' ka-b'a ka-b'i	chaab' [1,2] kab' [2]
beehive (n)	CHAB' cha-b'i	chaab' [1,2]

Translation	Transcription	Transliteration	Translation	Transcription	Transliteration
beings (ncl)	ti-ki-li	-tikil	body part absolutive suffix (suf)	-si (-IS)	-is
beloved (n)	1-TAN 1-ta-na	ju'n tan	bone (n)	B'AK b'a-ki B'AK-ke-la B'AK-le b'a-ke-le	b'aak [1,2] b'aakel
bench (stone) (n)	K'AN-na-TUN-ni te-ma te-mu te-me	k'antuun te'm (?) [1] temul (?) [1]	bone needle (n)	pu-tz'i-b'a-ki	puuhtz' b'aak
bent (adj)	lo-che	looch (?)	book (n)	HUN HUN-na hu-na	hu'n [1,2]
betroth (tv)	ma-ka ma-AK	-mak-	book cover (n)	sa-ya-HUN	sayhu'n
big (adj)	CHAK LAKAM la-ka-ma nu-ku	chak [2] lakam [1] nuk	boss (n)	yu-mu yu-ma	yum [1]
bind (tv)	K'AL	-k'al-	box (n)	ma-b'i ma-b'a	maab'
bird (n)	chi-ku mu-ti	chi'k muut [1,2]	break (tv)	k'a-sa	-k'as-
bird name (?) (n)	JANAB' ja-na-b'i	janaab'	brilliant (adj)	sa-sa	sas
bird of prey (n)	²pi pi	pip	brother (elder) (n)	su-ku	suku'[n] [2]
birth (of deity) (n)	PAS-ka-b'a	pas kab'	brother (younger) (n)	i-tz'i i-tz'i-ni	i[h]tz'iin [1,2]
bitter (adj)	ch'a-ha ch'a-ja ch'a-ji ch'a-ha	ch'ah ch'aaj [1,2]	brush (tv)	yu-lu	-yul-
black (adj)	EK' e-k'e IK' i-ki	ek' ik'	brush container (n)	chu-b'a-la-che-b'u	chub'al che'eb'
bloodletter (n)	ta-ji ta-ja	taaj [1]	build (pv)	PAT pa-ta	pat-
blowgun (n)	pu-wa	pu'w [1]	build (tv)	PAT pa-ta	-pat-
blue/green (adj)	YAX-HA' YAX-HA'-la YAX-ha-la YAX ya-xa	yaxha'l yax	building (n)	(y)o-to-chu (y)o-to-che NAH na-hi na-ha OTOT (y)o-to-ti o-to-ti	(otooch) naah [1,2] otoot [1]
blue/green (intense) (adj)	ya-YAX	yayax	bundle (n)	i-ka-tzi i-ki-tzi pi pi-hi	ikaatz ikitz pih
body liquid (n)	ti-si	tis [1]	bundle up (tv)	ka-cha	-kach-
body of water (n)	NAB-b'i NAH-b'i na-b'a na-b'i	naa[h]b' [1]	burden (n)	ku-chu pa-ta-na pa-ta	kuch pataan [1]

Translation	Transcription	Transliteration
burn (div)	pu-lu	pul-
burn (riv)	TIL	til-
	ti-li	
burn (tv)	EL	-el-
	EL-le	
	(EL)	
	TOK?-ko	-tok-
	to-ko	
burner, "he/she who burns" (n)	ti-lo-ma	tilo'm
burnish (tv)	T'AB'	-t'ab'-
	t'a?-b'a	
bury (tv)	b'u-t'u	-b'ut'-
	MUK	-muk-
	mu-ku	
	mu-ka	
by (prep)	ta	ta
	ti	ti
cacao (n)	ka-ka-wa	kakaw [2]
	[2]ka-wa	
	ka-wa	
cacao-like (adj)	ka-ka-wa-la	kakawal
cache (n)	ma-b'i	maab'
	ma-b'a	
calabash (n)	le-ke	lek
	le-ku	
	TZU'	tzu'
	tzu	
call (tv)	pe-ka	-pek-
canoe (n)	JUKUB'	jukuub' [1,2]
	ju-ku-b'i	
canyon (n)	yo-ki-b'i	yokib'
capstone (n)	ma-ka	mak
	ma-ko	
captive (n)	B'AK	b'aak [1,2]
	b'a-ki	
	na-ka	nak
capture (tv)	B'AK	-b'ak-
	b'a-ki	
	B'AK	-b'ak-
	b'a-ki	
	chu-ka	-chuk-
	chu-ku	
carry (tv)	K'OCH-chi	-k'och-
	ku-chu	-kuch-

Translation	Transcription	Transliteration
carve (tv)	po-lo	-pol-
	u-xu-lu	-uxul-
carving (n)	(y)u-xu-lu-na-ja-la	uxulnajal
	(y)u-xu-wa-ja-la	uxulwajal
	AN	a'n [1,2]
	a-nu	
cascade of water (n)	B'AK	b'aak [1,2]
	b'a-ki	
catch (tv)	chu-ka	-chuk-
	chu-ku	
cattail reed (n)	pu	pu[j]
cave (n)	CH'EN	ch'e'n [1,2]
	CH'EN-na/ni/ne	
cedar (n)	CHAK-la-TE'	chakalte'
	CHAK-TE'-e	
ceiba tree, "blue/green [or first] tree" (n)	YAX-TE'	yax te'
celebration (n)	cha-b'a	cha[n]b'a[h]
celestial (adj)	CHAN-la	chanal
center (n)	OL	o'l
	OL-la	
	o-la	
centipede (n)	CHAPAT-tu	chapa't [1]
	cha-pa-tu	
	cha-pa-ta	
	CHAPAT-ti	
centipede (large, "snake centipede") (n)	CHAPAT-CHAN	chapaa'ht chan
Chak (n)	CHAK	chaa[h]k [1]
	CHAK-ki	
	cha-ki	
change (tv)	je-le	-jel-
	JEL	
cherished one (n)	1-TAN	ju'n tan
	1-ta-na	
chest (n)	TAN-la	tanal
chicozapote (n)	CHAK-la-TE'	chakalte'
	CHAK-TE'-e	
child (n)	b'a-ku	b'a'k [1]
	pa-la	pal
child of father (n)	MIJIN (?)	mijiin (?)
	u-[2]ne	unen
	(y)u-ne	

Translation	Transcription	Transliteration
child of man (n)	**NICH** ni-chi	nich [1,2]
child of mother (n)	**AL** (y)a-**AL** (y)a-la	a[h]l [1]
chili (n)	i-chi	ich
choose (tv)	pa-chi	-pach-
chop (tv)	**CH'AK** ch'a-ka	-ch'ak-
claw (n)	**ICH'AK** (y)i-ch'a-ki	ich'aak
clay (n)	tz'i-ku	tz'i[h]k [1]
clay bowl (n)	ja-yi ja-ya	jaay [1]
clay object (n)	**LAK** la-ka	lak [1,2]
clean (adj)	su-ju-yu	suujuy [1,2]
clean (tv)	su-sa	-sus-
clear (tv)	ja-sa	-jas-
cleft (n)	pa pa-a	pa'
climb (pv)	li-pi	lip-
close (tv)	ma-ka ma-**AK**	-mak-
closer (n)	ma-ka-no-ma	makno'm
cloth (n)	chu-chu	chuch
clothing (n)	b'u-ku	b'u[h]k [1,2]
cloud (n)	**MUYAL** **MUY**-ya-la to-ko	muyaal [1,2] tok
clown (n)	**B'AH**-tz'a-ma b'a-hi-tz'a-ma	b'aahtz'am
coat, cover (n)	nu-ku	nuk
coatimundi (n)	**CHIK**-ki chi-ku tz'u-tz'i	chi'k tz'uutz'
co-essence (n)	**WAY**	way
collapse (tv)	jo-mo	-jom-

Translation	Transcription	Transliteration
collar (n)	**K'AN** **K'AN**-na **UH** (y)u-**UH** (y)u-**UH**-(li) (y)u-ha	k'an [1,2] uh [1]
color (n)	tz'i-b'a-li tz'i-b'a-la	tz'i[h]b'al
come (riv)	ta-li	tal-
come down (tv)	tz'a-ya	-tz'ay-
come out (riv)	**PAS**	pas-
companion (n)	(y)i-ta lo-ta	it lo't
completion (n)	20 **K'AL**	k'aal
conch (n)	ju-b'i	juub' [1]
conch shell (n)	ju-chi ju-chu	juu[h]ch [1]
conch trumpet (n)	ju-b'i	juub' [1]
conjure (tv)	chu-ni **TZAK** tza-ku	-chun- -tzak-
conjurer (n)	**TZAK** tza-ku	tza'k [1]
conquer (div)	a-ha-	ah-
conquer (tv)	na-ka	-nak-
conquest (n)	a-ja-la a-ja-li **AHAL** a-ha-li	ajal ahaal
contain (tv)	**K'OCH**-chi	-k'och-
container (n)	**K'OCH**-b'a-**TUN** **K'OCH**-chi-tu	k'ochb'a'tuun k'oochtu'
copal (n)	po-mo po	pom
cormorant (n)	**MAT** ma-ta	mat
corner (n)	xu-ka	xu'k
cornered (adj)	xu-ka-la	xukal
costume (n)	ye-te	yet

Translation	Transcription	Transliteration
cotinga (song bird name) (n)	**YAXUN** **ya-xu-na**	*yaxu'n*
count (n)	**xo-ko**	*xok*
count (ncl)	**TZ'AK-ka-ja** **TZ'AK-ja** **TZ'AK-a**	*-tz'akaj*
count (tv)	**TZIK** **tzi-ka**	*-tzik-*
count of beings (ncl)	**ti-ki-li**	*-tikil*
count of elapsed periods (ncl)	**la-ta** **TAL** **ta-la**	*-lat* *-tal*
count of living beings (ncl)	**na-ka**	*-nak*
count of mounted objects (ncl)	**mu-lu**	*-mul*
count of periods (n)	**pi-si**	*pis* [1]
count of piles (20) (ncl)	**tu-ku**	*-tuk*
count of round things (ncl)	**PET**	*-pet*
count of single days (n)	**he-na** **he-wa**	*he'n* *he'w*
count of stacked objects (ncl)	**mu-lu**	*-mul*
count of things (ncl)	**TZ'AK**	*-tz'ak*
count of time periods (ncl)	**TE'** **TE'-e** **te** **te-e**	*-te'*
count of Tun periods (at Palenque) (ncl)	**ku-lu**	*-kul*
[numerical-]count (adj)	**nu-pu-lu**	*nupul*
counting-stone (n)	**xo-ko-TUN-ni**	*xoktuun*
counts of 8,000 (ncl)	**pi-ki**	*-pik*
cover (n)	**ma-ka** **ma-ko**	*mak*
cover (tv)	**b'u-t'u** **ma-ka** **ma-AK**	*-b'ut'-* *-mak-*
cover with stucco (tv)	**T'AB'** **t'a?-b'a**	*-t'ab'-*

Translation	Transcription	Transliteration
coverer (n)	**ma-ka-no-ma**	*makno'm*
coyote (n)	**b'o-b'o**	*b'o[h]b'* [1]
create (tv)	**ch'a-b'a**	*-ch'ab'-*
create carnage (tv)	**wi**	*-wi'-*
creek (n)	**pa-a-la**	*pa'al*
crest (n)	**te-le**	*tel*
cricket (n)	**ma-su**	*ma's*
crocodile (n)	**AHIN-na** **AHIN-ni** **a-hi**	*ahiin* [1,2]
crosswise (adj)	**K'AT**	*k'at*
crown (n)	**yo-po?-AT-ti** **yo-AT-ti** **yo-AT-ta**	*yopaat*
crush (tv)	**su-sa**	*-sus-*
cut (tv)	**CH'AK** **ch'a-ka**	*-ch'ak-*
cylinder (n)	**b'u-b'a** **b'u-lu** **b'u-b'u-lu** ²**b'u-lu**	*b'u'b'* *b'ub'ul*
cylindrical (adj)	**xo**	*xo[l]*
cylindrical piece of wood (n)	**xo-TE'**	*xo[l]te'*
dance (div)	**AK'-ta-** **AK'-TAJ**	*ak't-*
dance (n)	**AK'-ta** **a-k'a-ta**	*ak'[o]t*
dance staff (n)	**ja-sa-wa-** **CHAN-na** **xu-ku-pi**	*jasaw chan* *xuk? pi'*
dark (adj)	**cha**	*cha'*
darkness (n)	**AK'AB'** **a-k'a-b'a**	*ak'ab'* [1]
dart (n)	**JUL** **ju-lu**	*jul*
dawn (n)	**a-ja-la** **a-ja-li** **PAS-sa-ja** **PAS** **pa-sa-ja**	*ajal* *pasaj* [1]

Translation	Transcription	Transliteration
dawn, "to open" (tv)	**PAS** pa-sa	*-pas-*
day (n)	**K'IN**	*k'i[h]n* [1]
day after tomorrow (adv)	**CHA'-b'i-ji**	*cha'b'ij*
days (ncl)	la-ta **TAL** ta-la	*-lat* *-tal*
death (n)	**CHAM**-la	*chamal*
decapitate (tv)	**CH'AK** ch'a-ka	*-ch'ak-*
decorate (tv)	ta-pa	*-tap-*
dedicate, "enter fire" ritual (riv)	**OCH-K'AK'** o-chi-**K'AK'**	*och- k'ahk'*
deer (n)	chi-ji chi **CHIJ**-ji **MAY** ma-ya	*chij* [1] *may*
deer-like (adj)	**CHIJ**-ji-li chi-ji-li	*chijil*
deity (n)	**K'UH** k'u-hu	*k'uh* [2]
deliver (tv)	k'u-b'a	*-k'ub'-*
deluge (?) (n)	**NUN** nu-na nu-u-na	*nu'un* [1]
demolish (tv)	ya-la	*-yal-*
dense (adj)	ta-ta	*tat* [2]
dependent (n)	su-lu	*sul*
derivational suffix (?) (suf)	ji-chi	*jich*
descend (div)	**EM**-mi e-mi	*em-*
descend (riv)	ju-b'u	*jub'-*
descend (tv)	tz'a-ya	*-tz'ay-*
descent (n)	(y)e-ma-la ju-b'u-li	*emal* *jub'uul*
destroy (tv)	jo-mo tz'a-nu	*-jom-* *-tz'an-*
die, "diminish" (tv)	sa-ta	*-sat-*
die, "enter the road" (riv)	**OCH-B'IH**	*och- b'ih*
die, "enter the water" (riv)	**OCH-HA'**	*och- ha'*
dig (?) (pv)	pa-na	*pan-*
diminish (tv)	sa-ta	*-sat-*
disappear (pv)	**LAM** la-ma	*lam-*
dish (n)	[2]la-ka	*lalak*
distribute (tv)	**PUK**-ki	*-puk-*
district (n)	**PET**-ne **PET**-ni	*pet[e]n* [2]
divine (adj)	**K'UH** **K'UH**-lu **K'UH-HUL** **K'UH**-hu-lu **K'UH-JUL**-lu	*k'uhul*
divine ruler (n)	**K'UH**-lu-**AJAW**-wa	*k'uhul ajaw*
divine-objects (ncl)	ye	*-ye*
division (n)	tzu-ku	*tzuk*
do (tv)	cha	*-cha-*
dog (n)	**OK** o-ki **TZ'I** tz'i-i tzu-lu	*ook* [1,2] *tz'i'* *tzul*
domicile (n)	**WAY**-b'i wa-ya-b'a	*wayib'*
door (n)	pa-si-li	*pasil*
doorway, portal (n)	**JOL**	*jo'l* [1,2]
dormitory (n)	**WAY**-b'i wa-ya-b'a	*wayib'*
double (tv)	b'a-la **B'AL** b'a-la-ha	*-b'al-*
douse (tv)	ta-pa	*-tap-*
dousing (adj)	ta-pa-la	*tapal*
dove (n)	mu-ku-yi tu-ku-nu u-ku-mu u-ku-ma	*mukuuy* [1,2] *tukun* [1] *ukum* *uku'm*

Translation	Transcription	Transliteration	Translation	Transcription	Transliteration
dreamer (n)	WAY-b'i wa-ya-b'a	wayib'	earth-like (adj)	KAB' KAB'-la	kab'al
dress (tv)	b'u-ku	-b'uk-	east (n)	EL-K'IN la-K'IN	elk'ihn lak'ihn
drill (tv)	jo-ch'o jo-ch'a	-joch'-	eat (tv)	k'u-xa	-k'ux-
drink (div)	UK	uk'-	eat (bread) (tv)	WE	-we-
drink (tv)	UK'	-uk'-	eat (soft food) (tv)	ma-k'a	-mak'-
drink type (n)	ch'a-ja-TE'	ch'aj te'	edge (n)	TI' ti ti-i	ti'
drinking vessel (n)	u-K'A-b'i (y)u-K'A-b'i (y)u-UK-b'a u-k'i-b'i UK-b'i UK UK	uk'aab' uk'ib' uk'	eight (num)	8 wa-xa-ka	waxak
			eighteen (num)	18	waxaklaju'n
			elevate (tv)	le-k'e	-lek'-
			elevation (n)	le-k'a	le'k'
			eleven (num)	11 [b'u]-lu-ku	b'uluk [1,2]
drop (n)	ch'a-ja ch'a-ji ch'a-ha	ch'aaj [1,2]	embrace (tv)	me-k'e	-mek'-
drop (tv)	(y)a-ka-ta	-akta-	emerge (riv)	LOK	lok'-
droplet (n)	ch'a-ja ch'a-ji ch'a-ha	ch'aaj [1,2]	enchanted (adj)	i-tza	iitz
			encircle (tv)	JOY	-joy-
drought, "sun stone" (n)	K'IN-TUN-ni	k'ihntuun	encirclement (n)	JOY-ye-la	joye'l
drum (n)	chu-ni-k'u	chuni'k'	enclosure (n)	k'a-li k'a-le	k'aal
drunkard (n)	AJ-chi-ji AJ-chi	ajchij	end (tv)	jo-mo TZUTZ tzu-tza tzu-tzu	-jom- -tzutz-
drunkenness (n)	ka-la	kal			
dwarf (n)	ch'a-ti ch'a-ta ma-su	ch'aat [1,2] ma's			
ear (n)	chi-ki	chiki[n]	enter (pv)	e-ke	ek-
ear of corn (n)	NAL na-la	nal [1]	enter (riv)	OCH o-chi	och-
earflare (n)	tu-pa-ja TUP tu-pa tu-pi	tu'paj tu'p	enter fire, "enter fire" dedication ritual (riv)	OCH-K'AK' o-chi-K'AK'	och- k'ahk'
			entrance (n)	 yo-ki-b'i	ochel yokib'
earlier today (adv)	sa-mi-ya sa-a-mi-ya	sa'miiy	erect (pv)	wa WACH	wa- wach-
earth (n)	KAB' ka-b'a ka-b'i lu-ma lu-mi	kab' [2] lu'm [1,2]	erect (tv)	tz'a-pa	-tz'ap-
			escape (riv)	LOK	lok'-

Translation	Transcription	Transliteration
evil (adj)	**LAB'** la-b'a	lab'
extend (tv)	**si-na**	-sin-
eye (n)	**i-chi** **UT-tu** **UT-si** **u-ti** **(y)u-ta**	ich ut
face (n)	**b'a-hi** **B'AH** **b'a** **i-chi** **UT-tu** **UT-si** **u-ti** **(y)u-ta**	b'aah [2] ich ut
fall (riv)	**ju-b'u**	jub'-
familiar (adj)	**nu-pu-lu**	nupul
family head (n)	**yu-mu** **yu-ma**	yum [1]
famine (n)	**WI'-NAL**	wi'nal
far (adv)	**na-chi**	naach
fart (n)	**ti-si**	tis [1]
fast (n)	**su-K'IN**	suk'ihn
fast (tv)	**CH'AB'** **ch'a-b'a**	-ch'ab'-
fasten (tv)	**ti-mi** **ti-ma**	-tim-
fasting (n)	**CH'AB'** **ch'a-b'a** **su-K'IN**	ch'a[h]b' [1,2] suk'ihn
fat (?) (n)	**b'a-ya**	b'ay
fat (adj)	**ta-ta**	tat [2]
father (n)	**²ta** **ta** **CHIT-ta** **CHIT-ti** **chi-ti** **ki-ti** **ki-ta** **yu-mu** **yu-ma**	tat chit kit yum [1]

Translation	Transcription	Transliteration
female (young), "unripe woman" (n)	**IXIK-ch'o-ko**	ixik ch'ok
festival (n)	**cha-b'a** **K'IN**	cha[n]b'a[h] k'i[h]n [1]
fetch (tv)	**chu-ka** **chu-ku**	-chuk-
fiery (adj)	**K'AK'-la**	k'ahk'al
fifteen (num)	**15** **HO'LAJUN**	ho'laju'n
fill (riv)	**yi-pi**	yip-
fill (tv)	**b'u-t'u**	-b'ut'-
fill up (tv)	**na-ja**	-naj-
finish (?) (riv)	**ko-jo**	koj-
finisher (n)	**TZUTZ-no-ma**	tzutzno'm
fire (n)	**k'a-k'a-si** **K'AK'** **k'a-k'a**	k'ahk'aas k'a[h]k' [1,2]
first (adj)	**YAX** **ya-xa**	yax
first (n)	**b'a-hi** **B'AH** **b'a**	b'aah [2]
first (num)	**NAH**	naah [1,2]
first carver (title) (n)	**B'AH-u-xu-lu**	b'aah uxul
first child (title) (n)	**B'AH-AL**	b'aah ahl
first flint (title) (n)	**B'AH-TOK'** **B'AH-to-k'a**	b'aah too'k'
first lady (title) (n)	**B'AH-IXIK-ki**	b'aah ixik
first of the earth (title) (n)	**B'AH-ka-b'a** **b'a-ka-b'a** **b'a-KAB'**	b'aahkab'
first painter (title) (n)	**B'AH-che-b'u**	b'aah che'[eh]b'
first sage (title) (n)	**B'AH-ITZ'AT**	b'aah itz'at
first sajal (title) (n)	**B'AH-sa-ja-la**	b'aah sajal
first shield (title) (n)	**B'AH-pa-ka-la**	b'aah pakal
first spear sajal (title) (n)	**B'AH-lo-mu-sa-ja-la**	b'aah lo'm sajal
first tree? (title) (n)	**B'AH-TE'** **b'a-TE'**	b'aah te'

Translation	Transcription	Transliteration
fish (n)	**CHAY**	*chay* [2]
	cha-ya	
	ka-ya	*kay*
fish type, "mat-like fish" (n)	**po-po-lo-cha-ya**	*popol chay*
	[2]**po-lo-cha-ya**	
fisherman (n)	**ka-yo-ma**	*kayo'm*
five (num)	**5**	*ho'*
	HO'	
Five-Tun period (n)	**5-TUN-ni**	*ho'tuun*
flexed (adj)	**lo-che**	*looch (?)*
	lo-che	*looch (?)*
flint (n)	**TOK'**	*took'* [1]
	to-k'a	
flint [and] shield (war emblem or battle standard) (n)	**TOK'-PAKAL**	*took' pakal*
	to-k'a-pa-ka-la	
flint-place (n)	**to-TOK'-ni-b'i**	*took'nib'*
flint-thing (n)	**TOK'-b'a**	*took'b'a'*
flower (n)	**YATIK**	*yatik*
	ya-ti-ki	
	ha-na	*han*
	NICH	*nich* [1,2]
	ni-chi	
	NIK	*(nik)*
foam (n)	**o-mo**	*o'm*
	yo-ma	
fog (n)	**ma-yu-yu**	*mayuy* [1]
food (n)	**pa**	*pa*
	WE'-la	*we'el* [1]
food plate (n)	**WE-i-b'i**	*we'ib'*
	WE-ma	*we'em*
foodstuff name (n)	**b'u-ku-tzu**	*b'ukutz*
foot (n)	**OK**	*ook* [1,2]
	o-ki	
form (pv)	**PAT**	*pat-*
	pa-ta	
form (tv)	**pa-k'a**	*-pak'-*
	PAT	*-pat-*
	pa-ta	
fortress (n)	**pa**	*pa'*
	pa-a	
four (num)	**4**	*chan*
	CHAN	
	cha-na	
	4	*kan* [1]
	ka-na	
fourteen (num)	**14**	*chanlaju'n*
fox (n)	**AJ-ch'a-ma**	*ajch'ama[k]*
	CH'AMAK	*ch'amak*
	ch'a-ma-ka	
	wa-xi	*waax*
fresh (adj)	**tzi-hi-li**	*tzihil*
	tzi-hi	
front (of building) (n)	**TAN**	*ta[h]n* [1,2]
frothy (adj)	**b'u-lu**	*b'ub'ul*
	b'u-b'u-lu	
	[2]**b'u-lu**	
fruit (n)	**UT-tu**	*ut*
	UT-si	
	u-ti	
	(y)u-ta	
full (adj)	**na**	*naj*
game ball (n)	**OL**	*o'l*
	OL-la	
	o-la	
get lost (tv)	**sa-ta**	*-sat-*
gift (n)	**(y)a-k'u-tu-u**	*ak'tu'*
	ma-ta-na	*matan*
	MAY	*maay*
	ma-yi-ji	
	si-hi-ja	*sihiij*
		sihaj
	SIH	*(sih)*
	si-hi	
	si-li ?	
	si	
	SIY	*siy*
girl, "great unripe woman" (n)	**CHAK-ch'o-ko-'IXIK**	*chak ch'ok ixik*
give (tv)	**a-k'a**	*-ak'-*
	a-AK'	
	k'u-b'a	*-k'ub'-*
	tz'a	*-tz'a'-*
giver (n)	**a-AK'-no-ma**	*ak'no'm*
glue (tv)	**ta-k'a**	*-tak'-*

Translation	Transcription	Transliteration
glutton (n)	si-tz'i	sitz'
go (riv)	XAN	xan-
go away (div)	B'IX-na B'IX-ni	b'ixVn-
go down (div)	EM-mi e-mi	em-
go down (pv)	LAM la-ma	lam-
go up (riv)	T'AB' t'a?-b'a	t'ab'-
goad (n)	PUK-ki	puuk
goblin (n)	ma-su	ma's
god (n)	K'UH k'u-hu	k'uh [2]
god-like (adj)	K'UH K'UH-lu K'UH-HUL K'UH-hu-lu K'UH-JUL-lu	k'uhul
good (adj)	u-tzi (y)u-tzi	uutz
goodness (n)	u-tzi-li	utzil
gopher (n)	b'a-hi B'AH b'a	b'aah [2]
gopher rat (n)	b'a-ch'o	b'aah ch'o
gourd (n)	TZU' tzu	tzu'
grab (tv)	CH'AM ch'a-ma chu-ka chu-ku ma-cha TZAK tza-ku	-ch'am- -chuk- -mach- -tzak-
grand (adj)	NOJ no	noj
grandfather (n)	MAM ma-ma	mam [2]
grandmother (maternal) (n)	mi-mi	mim

Translation	Transcription	Transliteration
grandson (n)	MAM ma-ma	mam [2]
gray (adj)	ko-b'a	ko'b'
great (adj)	CHAK LAKAM la-ka-ma nu-ku NAH	chak [2] lakam [1] nuk naah [1,2]
great rain (n)	CHAK-ha-lu	chak ha'l
grind (tv)	k'u-xa	-k'ux-
groan (n)	AKAN AJ-AKAN-na	akan
ground bean tortilla (n)	su-ku-ku	sukuk
guard (tv)	ko-ko	-kok-
guardian (n)	CHAN cha-nu ko-ko-no-ma	cha'n kokno'm
guava (n)	pa-ta-ha	pataah [1]
guide (n)	pa-ya-la pa-ya-li pa-ya	payal
guide (riv)	pa-ya	pay-
half-period (n)	TAN-na- LAM-wa	tan lamaw
hammer (icv)	B'AJ b'a-ja	b'aj-
hand (n)	K'AB'-si k'a-b'a-si K'AB' k'a-b'a	k'ab'aas k'ab'- [1,2]
handspan (n)	NAB'	na[h]b' [1,2]
hang up (pv)	e-ke	ek-
happen (riv)	UH-ti u-ti	ut-
hat (n)	pa-ta pi-xo-la pi-xo-ma	pat pixo'l [1,2] pixo'm
hawk (n)	I i-chi-ya	i' ichiiy
haze (n)	ma-yu-yu	mayuy [1]
he (pron)	ha-i ha-a	haa

Translation	Transcription	Transliteration
he of the headband (title) (n)	AJ-K'UH-na AJ-K'UH-HUN-na AJ-K'UH-HUN AJ-K'UH-hu-na a-K'UH-na	aj k'uhu'n
he of the holy books (title) (n)	AJ-K'UH-na AJ-K'UH-HUN-na AJ-K'UH-HUN AJ-K'UH-hu-na a-K'UH-na	aj k'uhu'n
he of the stack (title) (n)	AJ-la-tzi	aj laatz
he of the stack of books (title) (n)	AJ-la-tzi-HUN-na AJ-la-tzi-u-HUN-na	aj laatz hu'n
he who (adj)	AJ a	aj
he who (n)	KAL-ma KALOM-ma	kalo'm
he who strikes (n)	ta-jo-ma ta-jo-mo	tajo'm
he who venerates (title) (n)	AJ-K'UH-na AJ-K'UH-HUN-na AJ-K'UH-HUN AJ-K'UH-hu-na a-K'UH-na	aj k'uhu'n
head (n)	b'a-hi B'AH b'a B'AH-si JOL	b'aah [2] b'aahis jo'l [1,2]
head lord (title) (n)	B'AH-AJAW	b'aah ajaw
headband (n)	hu-na-la HUN-la HUN HUN-na hu-na	hunal hu'n [1,2]
headdress (n)	KOHAW ko-ha-wa ko-o-ha-wa pi-xo-ma	ko'haw pixo'm
heap (n)	tu-ku-la	tuku'l
hear (riv)	ko-ko	kok-
hear (tv)	u-b'u	-ub'-
hearer (n)	ko-ko-ma	koko'm
heart (n)	ki o-OL-si o-la-si OL OL-la o-la	ki o'laas o'l [1]
hearth (n)	k'o-b'a	k'o'b'
heated (adj)	K'INICH K'IN-chi	k'inich
heavenly (adj)	CHAN-la	chanal
heir (n)	CHAK-ch'o-ko	chak ch'ok
heir to the throne (n)	ch'o-ko CH'OK	ch'ok [1,2]
helmet (n)	KOHAW ko-ha-wa ko-o-ha-wa yo-po?-AT-ti yo-AT-ti yo-AT-ta	ko'haw yopaat
here (adv)	LAY wa-ya	lay way
hereby (adv)	a-LAY-ya a-la-ya	alay
heron (n)	B'AK b'a-ki i-chi-ya	b'aak [1,2] ichiiy
hide (tv)	b'a-la B'AL b'a-la-ha	-b'al-
hieroglyph (n)	wo-o-ja wo-ja wo-jo wo-jo-li wo-jo-le	wo'oj [1]
high (adj)	che-le	chel
hill (n)	WITZ wi-tzi	witz [1,2]
his/her/its carving (n)	(y)u-xu-lu-li	uxulil
hit (tv)	ch'o-ma	-ch'om-
hoist (tv)	pa-k'a	-pak'-

Translation	Transcription	Transliteration
holy ruler (n)	**K'UH-lu-AJAW-wa**	k'uhul ajaw
home (n)	(y)o-to-chu	otooch
	(y)o-to-che	
	OTOT	otoot [1]
	(y)o-to-ti	
	o-to-ti	
honey (n)	**CHAB'**	chaab' [1,2]
	cha-b'i	
honor (tv)	**TZIK**	-tzik-
	tzi-ka	
honored (adj)	**TZIK-la**	tzikal
hot (adj)	**K'IN**	k'i[h]n [1]
house (n)	(y)a-ATOT-ti	atoot [1]
	(y)a-to-TE'	
	(y)o-to-chu	otooch
	(y)o-to-che	
	na-i	na'
	NAH	naah [1,2]
	na-hi	
	na-ha	
	OTOT	otoot [1]
	(y)o-to-ti	
	o-to-ti	
house (div)	**OTOT**	otot-
	(y)o-to-ti	
	o-to-ti	
howler monkey (n)	b'a-tz'u	b'a'tz' [1,2]
	B'ATZ'?	
hug (tv)	me-k'e	-mek'-
human being (n)	**WINIK**	winik [1,2]
	wi-ni-ki	
hummingbird (n)	tz'u-²nu	tz'unun [1]
	tz'u-nu	
hunchback (n)	ch'a-ti	ch'aat [1,2]
	ch'a-ta	
hunger (n)	**WI'-NAL**	wi'nal
hunter, "he of the deer" (n)	**AJ**-chi-ji	ajchij
	AJ-chi	
hurt (tv)	k'u-xa	-k'ux-
I (pron)	Ce-na	-een
	hi-na	hiin
	i-ni	in-
	ni	ni-

Translation	Transcription	Transliteration
iguana (n)	**HUJ**	huj
	ITZAM	itzam
image (n)	b'a-hi	b'aah [2]
	B'AH	
	b'a	
	B'AH-ja	b'ahiij
	B'AH-hi-ja	
	b'a-hi-ja	
	k'o-jo	k'oj
	WI-ni-**B'AH**-hi	winb'aah
	WI-ni-b'a	
in (prep)	i-chi-la	ichiil
	ta	ta
	TAN	ta[h]n [1,2]
	ti	ti
	xi-ni	xin
in the center of (prep)	**TAN**	ta[h]n [1,2]
incensario, "white/pure plate" (n)	**SAK-LAK**	sak lak
incensario (stone), "white/pure stone plate" (n)	**SAK-LAK-TUN**-ni	sak lak tuun
incense (n)	po-mo	pom
	po	
incense scatterer (n)	ch'a-ho-ma	ch'aho'm
	(ch'a-jo-ma)	
incense type (n)	ch'a-ja-**TE'**	ch'aj te'
incised thing (n)	ha-chi	haach
	ha-cha	
incision (n)	ja-chi	jaach
infant (n)	**CHAK**-ch'o-ko	chak ch'ok
injure (tv)	**CH'AK**	-ch'ak-
	ch'a-ka	
ink (n)	**'AB'AK'**	ab'ak
	(y)a-b'a-ki	
	SAB'AK	sab'aak
	sa-b'a-ka	
	sa-b'a-ki	
insert (pv)	e-ke	ek-
inserted object (n)	e-ke-li-b'i	eklib'
inside (prep)	xi-ni	xin
insignia (n)	ye-te	yet

Translation	Transcription	Transliteration
intermediary, ritual speaker (n)	**NUN** **nu-na** **nu-u-na**	nu'un [1]
intestines (n)	**cho-cho** **pu-chi**	choch puuch
island (n)	**PET-ne** **PET-ni**	pet[e]n [2]
it (pron)	**ha-i** **ha-a**	haa
Itzamnaj (deity) (n)	**ITZAMNAJ**	itzamnaaj
Ix Chel, "high woman" (deity) (n)	**IX-che-le**	ix chel [1]
Ix Kalomte', "female Kalomte'" (title) (n)	**IX-KALOM-TE'**	ix kalo'mte'
Ix Yok'in, "female sun-foot" (title) (n)	**IX-yo-K'IN**	ix yok'ihn
Iximte', "maize tree" (tree name) (n)	**IXIM-TE'**	iximte'
jade (plaque) (n)	**ka-ya-wa-ka**	kaywak
jaguar (n)	**B'ALAM** **b'a-la-ma** **HIX**	b'a[h]lam [1,2] hix
jaguar (small) (n)	**b'o?-la-yi** **B'OL?-la-u** **B'ULAY?** **b'u?-la-yi**	b'olay b'ulaay
jaguar paw (n)	**OX?-xo**	ox
jawbone (n)	**cha-la-ma**	chalam
jewel (n)	**K'AN** **K'AN-na**	k'an [1,2]
join (tv)	**nu-pu** **TZUTZ** **tzu-tza** **tzu-tzu** **yu-ku**	-nup- -tzutz- -yuk-
joined together (adv)	**nu-chu**	nuch
K'atun (n)	**WINIK-HAB'**	winikhaab'
K'awil (deity) (n)	**K'AWIL-la** **k'a-wi-li**	k'awiil
king (n)	**AJAW** **a-ja-wa**	ajaw
kingship (n)	**AJAW-le-le** **AJAW-le** **AJAW-2le** **AJAW-li** **a-ja-wa-li**	ajawlel ajawil
kneel down (tv)	**K'EB'**	-k'eb'-
knot (n)	**ka-cha**	kach
knot of hair (n)	**MUT** **MUT-la** **MUT-tu**	mutu'l
ladder (n)	**e-b'a** **e-b'u** **(y)e-b'a-li** **(y)e-b'u-li**	e'b' e'b'aal e'b'uul
lady (n)	**NA** **na**	na'
lagoon (n)	**pa-a-la**	pa'al
lance (n)	**lo-mu**	loom?
land (n)	**PET-ne** **PET-ni**	pet[e]n [2]
large (adj)	**NAH**	naah
lark (n)	**SAK-chi-ku** **TOT**	sak chi'k tot
last (adj)	**WI'** **wi-i-li**	wi'il [1]
later (adv)	**pa-ti** **la-ta**	paat -lat
lead (riv)	**pa-ya**	pay-
leader (n)	**pa-ya-la** **pa-ya-li** **pa-ya**	payal
leave (riv)	**LOK**	lok'-
lie down (pv)	**ha-ma**	ham-
lie face up (pv)	**ja-wa**	jaw-
lied-down-thing (n)	**ha-ma-li-b'i**	hamlib'
line (of writing) (n)	**B'I** **b'i-hi**	b'ih [2]
lineage (n)	**o-lo-mo**	olom
lintel, "face-down" (n)	**pa-ka-b'a**	pakab'

Translation	Transcription	Transliteration
lintel stone, "face-down stone" (n)	pa-ka-b'a-TUN-ni pa-ka-b'u-TUN-ni	pakab' tuun
litter (n)	CH'AK?-TE'-le	ch'akte'el
lizard (n)	? AHIN-na AHIN-ni a-hi ITZAM	chuluk ahiin [1,2] itzam
load (n)	i-ka-tzi i-ki-tzi	ikaatz ikitz
loom (n)	chu-chu	chuch
lordship (n)	AJAW-le-le AJAW-le AJAW-²le AJAW-li a-ja-wa-li	ajawlel ajawil
lose (tv)	(y)a-ka-ta	-akta-
louse (n)	(y)u-ch'a	u'ch'
low (adj)	KAB' KAB'-la	kab'al
macaw (n)	MO' mo-o	mo'
maguey (adj)	chi-hi	chiih [2]
maize (n)	IXIM	ixim
maize crop, winter (n)	SIHOM-ma SIHOM-mo	siho'm [1]
make awake (div)	a-je-se	ajes-
make it happen (tv)	KAB' ka-b'a ka-b'i	-kab'-
malign spirit (n)	WAY	way
man (young) (n)	XIB' xi-b'i	xib'
manatee (n)	chi-li-ka-yu	chilka'y
manifest (tv)	HAL	-hal-
manifested (?) (adj)	a-ja-la a-ja-li	ajal
many (adj)	9 o-na OX?-xo	b'olon o'n [1] ox
market (n)	k'i-wi-ki	k'iwik

Translation	Transcription	Transliteration
marry (tv)	nu-pu	-nup-
mask (n)	k'o-b'a k'o-jo	k'o[j]b'a' k'oj
mat (n)	po-po	po[h]p [1,2]
mayflower (n)	NIK-TE'	nikte'
meal (n)	WI'	wi'
meat (n)	WE'-la	we'el [1]
messenger (n)	(y)e-b'e-ta (y)e-b'e-te	eb'et [2]
middle (n)	o-OL-si o-la-si OL OL-la o-la	o'[h]laas o'l
mirror (n)	NEN ne-na	ne'n
miter (n)	yo-po?-AT-ti yo-AT-ti yo-AT-ta	yopaat
mold (tv)	pa-k'a	-pak'-
moon (n)	UH/U'	uh
mountain (n)	WITZ wi-tzi	witz [1,2]
mouth (n)	ka-la TI'-si TI' ti ti-i	kal ti'is ti'
move (riv)	T'AB' t'a?-b'a	t'ab'-
mud (n)	lu-k'u	luk'
mural (n)	pa pa-a	pa'
my (pron)	ni i-ni	ni in in-
nail (tv)	b'o-ja	-b'oj-
name (n)	b'i K'AB'A k'a-b'a-a	b'i' k'ab'a'
namesake (n)		et'kab'a'

APPENDIX IV.2 ENGLISH TO CLASSIC MAYAN LEXICON

Translation	Transcription	Transliteration
native (n)	**NAL** **na-la** **na-li**	*naal* [1]
nawal (animal companion spirit) (n)	**WAY**	*way*
necklace (n)	**UH-ja** **u-ha-ja** **UH** **(y)u-UH** **(y)u-UH-(li)** **(y)u-ha**	*uhaj* *uh* [1]
needle (sewing) (n)	**pu-tz'i**	*puu[h]tz'* [1]
nest (n)	**K'U** **(k'u)**	*k'u*
new (adj)	**tzi-hi-li** **tzi-hi**	*tzihil*
night (n)	**AK'AB'** **a-k'a-b'a**	*ak'ab'* [1]
nine (num)	**9**	*b'olon*
nineteen (num)	**19**	*b'olonlaju'n*
no (adv)	**0** **mi** **ma-cha-ja** **ma** **ma-a**	*mi[h]* [2] *machaj* *ma* *ma'*
noose (n)	**le-e**	*le'*
north (n)	**NAL** **NAL-la** **xa-MAN-na** **xa-ma-na**	*nal* *xaman* [2]
nose (n)	**ni**	*ni'*
not (partic)	**ma** **ma-a**	*ma* *ma'*
nothing (adv)	**0** **mi**	*mi[h]* [2]
now (adv)	**WAL** **yu-wa-la**	*wal* *yuwal*
obscure (adj)	**cha**	*cha'*
obsidian (n)	**ta-ji** **ta-ja**	*taaj* [1]
obsidian-like (adj)	**TAJ** **TAJ-la** **ta-ja-la**	*tajal*

Translation	Transcription	Transliteration
occur (riv)	**UH-ti** **u-ti**	*ut-*
offering (n)	**ma-ta-na** **MAY** **ma-yi-ji** **SIH** **si-hi** **si-li ?** **si**	*matan* *maay* *(sih)*
office (n)	**ETE'** **ETE'-TE'** **ETE'-TE'-je**	*e[b']tej ?*
old man (n)	**MAM** **ma-ma**	*mam* [2]
omen (n)	**mu-ka** **mu-ti**	*mu'k* [1] *muut* [1,2]
on (prep)	**ta** **ti**	*ta* *ti*
on the next day (adv)	**PAS**	*pas* *pas-*
one (num)	**1** **JUN**	*ju'n* [1]
one day later (adv)	**IK'-la**	*ik'al* [2]
oneself (pron)	**b'a-ni**	*b'aan*
open (tv)	**ha-ma** **ja-sa** **KAL** **ka-la** **ka-lo** **PAS** **pa-sa**	*-ham-* *-jas-* *-kal-* *-pas-*
opener (n)	**pa-sa-no-ma**	*pasno'm*
opening (n)	**ka-la** **OL** **OL-la** **o-la** **pa-si** **pa-si-li** **TI'** **ti** **ti-i**	*kal* *o'l* *paas* *pasil* *ti'*
order (tv)	**pe-ka**	*-pek-*
ordinals (ncl)	**la-ta** **TAL** **ta-la**	*-lat* *-tal*

APPENDIX IV.2 ENGLISH TO CLASSIC MAYAN LEXICON

Translation	Transcription	Transliteration
our (pron)	**ka**	ka-
outside (n)	**sa-ya**	say
oven (n)	**chi-ti-na**	chitiin
	ku-nu	kun
	pi-b'i-NAH	pib'naah
overseer (n)	**CHAN**	cha'n [1]
	cha-nu	
owl (small) (n)	**i-ki**	iki[m] kuy
	i-ki-ku-yu	
own (tv)	**CHAN**	-chan-
	cha-nu	
paint (tv)	**tz'i-b'a**	-tz'ib'-
painted object (n)	**(y)u-b'a**	u'b'
painter (n)	**a-tz'i-b'a-la**	aj tz'ihb'aal
painting (n)	**tz'i-b'a-li**	tz'i[h]b'al
	tz'i-b'a-la	
	tz'i-b'i	tz'i[h]b' [1,2]
	tz'i-b'i-na-ja-la	tz'i[h]b'najal
palanquin (n)	**CH'AK?-TE'-le**	ch'akte'el
palm (n)	**NAB'**	na[h]b' [1,2]
panel (n)	**CHAK-li-b'i**	chaklib'
	K'AN-na-TUN-ni	k'antuun
paper (n)	**HUN**	hu'n [1,2]
	HUN-na	
	hu-na	
partition (n)	**tzu-ku**	tzuk
pass (riv)	**nu-mu**	num-
paste (tv)	**ta-k'a**	-tak'-
patron (n)	**CHIT-ta**	chit
	CHIT-ti	
	chi-ti	
	ki-ti	(kit)
	ki-ta	(kiit)
	yu-mu	yum [1]
	yu-ma	
paw (?) (n)	**mo-o-la**	mo'ol [1]
pay (tv)	**to-jo**	-toj-
payment (n)	**to-jo**	toj
	to-jo-la	tojo'l
	to-jo-li	
peccary (n)	**CHITAM**	chitam

Translation	Transcription	Transliteration
pedestal (n)	**o-ki-b'i**	okib'
	(y)o-ko-b'i-li	
peel (tv)	**tz'u-lu**	-tz'ul-
peel off (tv)	**su-sa**	-sus-
pelt (n)	**nu-ku**	nu[h]ku[l] [1]
penance (n)	**CH'AB'**	ch'a[h]b' [1,2]
	ch'a-b'a	
penis (n)	**AT-ti**	aat [1,2]
	AT-ta	
	k'u-li	k'uul
perforate (tv)	**jo-ch'o**	-joch'-
	jo-ch'a	
	pi-chi	-pich-
perforator (n)	**JUL**	jul
	ju-lu	
perforator bone (n)	**ju-li-b'a-ki**	ju[l]il b'aak
period (360 days) (n)	**HAB'-li**	haab'il
	TUN-ni	tuun [1,2]
person (n)	**ma-ki**	maak
	NAL	nal [1]
	na-la	
pertaining to (prep)	**ti-i-li**	ti'il
pierce (tv)	**ch'o-ma**	-ch'om-
pigeon (n)	**mu-ku-yi**	mukuuy [1,2]
	tu-ku-nu	tukun [1]
	u-ku-mu	ukum
	u-ku-ma	uku'm
pile up (div)	**WITZ**	witz-
	wi-tzi	
pile up (pv)	**mu-lu**	mul-
piles (n)	**tu-ku**	-tuk-
	(a-w)i-tzi	itz
pitch-pine (n)	**TAJ**	taj [2]
	ta-ja	
	ta	
place (n)	**NAL**	nal [1]
	na-la	
	ni-b'i	nib'
place (pv)	**e-ke**	ek-
place of fire (n)	**K'AK'-NAL**	k'ak'nal
	K'AK'-na-la	
placed on (adv)	**che-le-te**	chele[h]t [1]

Translation	Transcription	Transliteration
placed object (n)	e-ke-li-b'i	eklib'
plant (riv)	hi-li	hil-
plant (tv)	pa-k'a	-pak'-
	tz'a-pa	-tz'ap-
plant name (n)	wi-ti-ki	witik
plaster (n)	sa-sa	sas
plaster (tv)	ta-k'a	-tak'-
plaster over (tv)	ju-su	-jus-
plate (n)	²la-ka	lalak
	LAK	lak [1,2]
	la-ka	
platform (?) (n)	ku-nu	kun
play ball (div)	pi-tzi	pitz-
poisonous (adj)		otoy
polish (tv)	T'AB'	-t'ab'-
	t'a?-b'a	
	yu-lu	-yul-
polished object (n)	yu-lu	yul
	yu-lu-li	yuluul
polisher (?) (n)	AJ-yu-lu	aj yul
portrait (n)	B'AH-li	b'aahil
	b'a-hi-li	
possum (n)	ma-ma	mam
pottery bowl (n)	K'AT	k'at
pottery dish (n)	ja-wa-TE'	jawa[n]te'
precious (adj)	YAX	yax
	ya-xa	
	K'AN	k'an [1,2]
	K'AN-na	
prepared surface (n)	b'i-TUN-ni	b'ihtuun
presence (n)	(y)i-chi-NAL	ichnal
	(a-w)i-chi-NAL	
	(y)i-chi-na-la	
present (tv)	k'u-b'a	-k'ub'-
price (n)	to-jo-la	tojo'l
	to-jo-li	
priest, "he of the sun" (title) (n)	AJ-K'IN	aj k'ihn
procreate (tv)	ko-b'o	-kob'-

Translation	Transcription	Transliteration
promise (tv)	ma-ka	-mak-
	ma-AK	
province (n)	tzu-ku	tzuk
pulque (n)	chi	chi
puma (n)	CHAK-B'ALAM-ma	chak b'ahlam
	KOJ	koj
	ko-jo	
pure (adj)	SAK	sak [1,2]
	SAK-la	sakal
put in order (tv)	TZ'AK-b'u	-tz'akb'u-
quarter (n)	WAY	way
	k'a-li	k'aal
	k'a-le	
quetzal (n)	K'UK'	k'uk' [1]
	k'u-k'u	
quill (n)	che-b'u	che'e[h]b' [1]
	che-e-b'u	
quill bowl (n)	po-ko-lo-che-b'u	pokol che'ehb'
	po-ko-lo-che-e-b'u	
quill pen container (n)	chu-b'a-la-che-b'u	chub'al che'ehb'
rabbit (n)	CHIT-ta	chit
	CHIT-ti	
	chi-ti	
	CHICH?-che?	chich?
	T'UL	t'ul [1]
	t'u-lu	
raccoon (n)	EM-ma	emach
	EM-ma-cha	
rain (n)	CHAK	chaa[h]k [1]
	CHAK-ki	
	cha-ki	
rain deity (n)	CHAK	chaa[h]k [1]
	CHAK-ki	
	cha-ki	
rainbow (n)	che-le	chel
rainy (adj)	HA'	ha'al
	HA'-la	
	ha-la	
rat (n)	CH'O	ch'o
	ch'o	

352 APPENDIX IV.2 ENGLISH TO CLASSIC MAYAN LEXICON

Translation	Transcription	Transliteration
raw (adj)	tzi-hi-li tzi-hi	tzihil
reason (n)	na-ta	nat
receive (tv)	CH'AM ch'a-ma	-ch'am-
red (adj)	CHAK	chak [2]
reddish (adj)	CHAK-la	chakal
reign (n)	AJAW-le-le AJAW-le AJAW-²le AJAW-li a-ja-wa-li	ajawlel ajawil
relative (n)	yo-NAL	yo'nal
replace (tv)	je-le JEL	-jel-
resplendent (adj)	sa-sa SAK SAK-la	sas sak [1,2] sakal
rest (riv)	hi-li	hil-
return (div)	pa-ka-xa pa-ka-xi	pakax-
revealed (adj)	ye	ye
ring (?) (n)	chi	chi
ripe (adj)	K'AN K'AN-na	k'an [1,2]
river-shore (n)	TI'-pa-a	ti' pa'
road (n)	b'i-TUN-ni B'I b'i-hi	b'ihtuun b'ih [2]
roadrunner (n)	pu-yi	puuy [2]
roaring (adj)	AKAN AKAN AJ-AKAN-na	a[h]kan akan
roasted (adj)	po-po-la	popo'l
roasted maize flour (n)	ch'a-ja ch'a-ji ch'a-ha	ch'aaj [1,2]
robin (n)	TOT	tot
room (n)	k'a-li k'a-le WAY	k'aal way

Translation	Transcription	Transliteration
root (n)	wi	wi'
root of plant (n)	b'a-TUN-na	b'atun
round (adj)	PET	pet [2]
round (riv)	PET	pet-
round (tv)	wo-lo	-wol-
round object (n)	wo-lo	wol
ruddy (adj)	CHAK-la	chakal
rule (tv)	me-k'e	-mek'-
ruler (n)	AJAW a-ja-wa	ajaw
run (div)	a-ni	an-
sacred (adj)	K'UH K'UH-lu K'UH-HUL K'UH-hu-lu K'UH-JUL-lu YAX ya-xa	k'uhu yax
sajal (title) (n)	sa-ja-la sa-ja	sajal
sajal-ship (n)	sa-ja-la-li sa-ja-le-le	sajalil sajalel
sanctified (adj)	TZIK-la	tzikal
sanctify (tv)	TZIK tzi-ka	-tzik-
sanctuary (n)	WAY-b'i wa-ya-b'a	wayib'
sap (n)	(a-w)i-tzi	itz
satiated (adj)	na	naj
satisfied (adj)	na	naj
say (tv)	(y)a-a-la (y)a-la AL (y)a-AL (y)a-la HAL	-a'l- -al- -hal-
scatter (tv)	CHOK cho-ka cho-ko PUK-ki	-chok- -puk-
scatter fire (riv)	PUK-ki	puk-

Translation	Transcription	Transliteration
scatterer (n)	**CHOK-no-ma**	*chokno'm*
scorpion (n)	**si-na-na**	*sinan* [1]
scribble (div)	**b'i-K'A'**	*b'ik'-*
scribbler (n)	**AJ-b'i-K'A'?-la**	*ajb'ik'al*
scribe, "he of writing" (n)	**AJ-tz'i-b'i** **a-tz'i-b'i** **AJ-tz'i-b'a**	*aj tz'ihb'*
sculpt (tv)	**u-xu-lu**	*-uxul-*
sculptor (n)	**POL**	*pol*
sculptor (title) (n)	**a-na-b'i** **(y)a-a-na-b'i-**	*a'naahb'*
sculpture (n)	**(y)u-xu-wa-ja-la** **u-xu-lu**	*uxulwajal* *uxul*
sea, ocean (n)	**K'AK'-NAB'**	*k'ahk' naahb'*
seat (n)	**CHUM[mu]-b'i** **K'AN-TE'** **K'AN** **K'AN-na**	*chumib'* *k'ante'* *k'an* [1,2]
seat (pv)	**CHUM** **CHUM[mu]**	*chum-*
second time (adv)	**CHA'** **2**	*cha'*
see (tv)	**IL** **IL-la** **i-la**	*-il-*
seed (n)	**hi-na-ja** **hi-na**	*hinaj*
segment (n)	**tzu-ku**	*tzuk*
seize (tv)	**chu-ka** **chu-ku**	*-chuk-*
select (tv)	**pa-chi**	*-pach-*
self (n)	**b'a-hi** **B'AH** **b'a**	*b'aah* [2]
-self (suf)	**b'a-hi** **B'AH** **b'a**	*b'aah* [2]
servant (n)	**(a)-wi-na-ke-(na)** **(H)AB'-ta**	*winak* *ab'at*
set down (pv)	**e-tz'e**	*etz'-*
set up (tv)	**WAL**	*-wal-*

Translation	Transcription	Transliteration
seven (num)	**7** **7** **HUK**	*wuk* *huk*
Seven Sins (name of deity) (n)	**7-si-pu**	*huk si'p* [1]
seventeen (num)	**17** **17** **HUKLAJUN**	*wuklaju'n* *huklaju'n*
sew (tv)	**chu-yu**	*-chuy-*
shake (tv)	**yu-ku**	*-yuk-*
shaker (n)	**yu-ku-no-ma**	*yukno'm*
shark (n)	**XOK-ki** **xo-ki**	*xook* [1]
she (pron)	**ha-i** **ha-a**	*haa*
she who ? (n)	**IX-KALOM** **KAL-ma** **KALOM-ma**	*ix kalo'm* *kalo'm*
she who strikes (n)	**ta-jo-ma** **ta-jo-mo**	*tajo'm*
shield (n)	**ma-xu** **PAKAL** **pa-ka-la**	*ma'x* *pakal* [1]
shoot (tv)	**JUL** **ju-lu**	*-jul-*
shoulders (n)	**pa-ti**	*paat*
shrub, plant (n)	**HAB'** **HAB'-b'i** **HAB'-b'a**	*haab'* [1]
sin (n)	**si-pu**	*si'p*
sing (tv)	**k'a-ya** **k'a-yo**	*-k'ay-*
singer (n)	**k'a-yo-ma**	*k'ayo'm*
sink (tv)	**jo-mo**	*-jom-*
sitting (n)	**CHUM-mu-ta-li**	*chumtaal*
six (num)	**6**	*wak*
sixteen (num)	**16**	*waklaju'n*
skeleton (n)	**B'AK-JOL**	*b'aakjol*
skin (n)	**nu-ku** **pa-chi** **pa-ti**	*nu[h]ku[l]* [1] *paach* [2] *paat*

Translation	Transcription	Transliteration
skin (tv)	tz'u-lu	-tz'ul-
skinning bone (n)	tz'u-lu-B'AK	tz'ul b'aak
skirt (n)	pi-ki PIK pi-ki	pik pik [1]
skull (?) (n)	JOL-mi jo-lo-mi	jo'loom
skull deity, "head god" (n)	JOL-K'UH	jo'l k'uh
sky (n)	4 CHAN cha-na	chan
sky-like (adj)	CHAN-la	chanal
sleep (div)	wa-ya WAY	way- way-
sleeper (n)	WAY-b'i wa-ya-b'a	wayib'
sleeping room (n)	WAY-b'i wa-ya-b'a	wayib'
smell (tv)	u-tz'u	-utz'-
smoke (n)	b'u-tz'a b'u-tz'a-ha to-ko TOK-la to-ka-la	b'u'tz' (b'uutz') tok tokal [1]
snail (n)	pu-yi	puuy [2]
snake (n)	4 CHAN cha-na KAN	chan (kan)
sniff (tv)	u-tz'u	-utz'-
so (partic)	che-e-na che-na che-he-na	chehe'n
soil (n)	lu-ma lu-mi	lu'm [1,2]
song (n)	k'a-ya k'a-yo	k'ay
soot (n)	'AB'AK' (y)a-b'a-ki SAB'AK sa-b'a-ka sa-b'a-ki	ab'ak sab'aak

Translation	Transcription	Transliteration
sound (n)	so-ti	soot
south (n)	NOJOL	nojo'l [1]
sparrow-hawk (n)	MUWAN-ni mu-wa-na	muwaan
speak together (tv)	nu-chu-jo-lo	-nuchjol-
spear (n)	JUL ju-lu	jul
spear thrower (n)	JATZ'OM ja-tz'o-ma	jatz'o'm
spider (poisonous) (n)	TIWOJ ti-wo	tiwoj
spider monkey (n)	MAX ma-xi	maax [1]
spine (n)	PUK-ki	puuk
spirit companion (n)	WAY-ya-si	wayis
split (n)	pa pa-a	pa'
split (tv)	 JATZ' ja-tz'i ja-tz'a ta-jo	-sil- -jatz'- -taj-
spokesman (n)	chi-ji-la-ma chi-la-ma	chijlam chilam
spread out (tv)	si-na	-sin-
spring maize (n)	AN a-nu	a'n [1,2]
sprinkle (tv)	pu-la pu-lu	-pul-
square (n)	xu-ka-la	xukal
stack (n)	la-tzi	laatz
stack (pv)	mu-lu	mul-
stair (n)	e-b'a e-b'u (y)e-b'a-li (y)e-b'u-li	e'b' e'b'aal e'b'uul
staircase (n)	e-b'a e-b'u (y)e-b'a-li (y)e-b'u-li	e'b' e'b'aal e'b'uul
stake (pv)	jo-po	jop-

APPENDIX IV.2 ENGLISH TO CLASSIC MAYAN LEXICON

Translation	Transcription	Transliteration
star (n)	**EK'**	*ek'*
	e-k'e	
stela, "great stone" (n)	**LAKAM-TUN-ni**	*lakam tuun*
	la-ka-ma-TUN-ni	
step on (tv)	**te-k'a**	*-tek'-*
stepping (n)	**te-k'a-ja**	*tek'aj*
sting (n)	**PUK-ki**	*puuk*
stinking (adj)	**xi-ni**	*xin*
stir (fire) (riv)	**TIL**	*til-*
	ti-li	
stomach (n)	**(y)o-o-NAL**	*o'nal*
	TAN-la	*tanal*
stone (n)	**TUN-ni**	*tuun* [1,2]
	TUN-ni-chi	*tunich*
stone binding (n)	**K'AL-TUN-ni**	*k'altuun*
stone effigy (n)	**ka-le-TUN**	*kal tuun*
stone opener (?) (n)	**ka-le-TUN**	*kal tuun*
stream (n)	**pa-a-la**	*pa'al*
strength (n)	**i-pi**	*ip*
stretch (tv)	**ti-mi**	*-tim-*
	ti-ma	
strike (riv)	**JATZ'**	*jatz'-*
	ja-tz'i	
	ja-tz'a	
strike (tv)	**ta-jo**	*-taj-*
striker (n)	**JATZ'OM**	*jatz'o'm*
	ja-tz'o-ma	
striking (adv)	**JATZ'-ni**	*jatz'noon*
	JATZ'-no-ni	
strong (adj)	**KELEM**	*kele'm*
	ke-le-ma	
struck (adj)	**ja-tz'a-la**	*jatz'al*
	ja-tz'a-li	
structure (n)	**na-i**	*na'*
stucco (n)	**lu-k'u**	*luk'*
	sa-sa	*sas*
submerge (tv)	**b'u-lu**	*-b'ul-*
subordinate ruler, "his/her ruler" (n)	**ya-AJAW**	*yajaw*
	ya-ja-wa	
successor (n)	**TZ'AK-b'u-li**	*tz'akb'u'l*
	tz'a-ka-b'u-li	
sun (n)	**K'IN**	*k'i[h]n* [1]
sun-faced (adj)	**K'INICH**	*k'inich*
	K'IN-chi	
supervise (tv)	**CHAB'**	*-chab'-*
	cha-b'i	
	KAB'	*-(kab')-*
	ka-b'a	
	ka-b'i	
surface (?) (n)	**ji-chi**	*jich*
sweatbath (n)	**chi-ti-na**	*chitiin*
	pi-b'i-NAH	*pib'naah*
sweep (tv)	**mi-si**	*-mis-*
sweet (adj)	**mo-ni**	*moon*
	chi-hi	*chiih* [2]
tail (n)	**ne**	*ne*
take (tv)	**CH'AM**	*-ch'am-*
	ch'a-ma	
take possession of (tv)	**pa-chi**	*-pach-*
tamale (n)	**WAJ**	*waaj* [1,2]
	wa-ji	
tapir (n)	**TIL**	*ti[h]l* [1,2]
	ti-li	
	ti-la	
tarantula (n)	**chi-wo-jo**	*chiwoj* [2]
	chi-wo	
ten (num)	**10**	*laju'n* [1]
terminate (tv)	**TZUTZ**	*-tzutz-*
	tzu-tza	
	tzu-tzu	
that (pron)	**ha-i**	*haa*
	ha-a	
then (adv)	**ka**	*ka-*
there (adv)	**ya**	*ya*
they (pron)	**ha-o-b'a**	*ha'o'b'* [2]
thick (adj)	**ta-ta**	*tat* [2]
thing (n)	**tu**	*-tu'*
	tu-u	
things (ncl)	**TZ'AK**	*-tz'ak*

APPENDIX IV.2 ENGLISH TO CLASSIC MAYAN LEXICON

Translation	Transcription	Transliteration
thirteen (num)	13	oxlaju'n
this (pron)	ha-i	haa
	ha-a	
those (pron)	ha-o-b'a	ha'o'b' [2]
three (num)	3	ox
throne (n)	IL-TUN-ni	iltuun
	te-ma	te'm (?) [1]
	te-mu	temul (?) [1]
	te-me	
	TZ'AM	tz'am
	tz'a-ma	
throw (tv)	AL	-al-
	(y)a-AL	
	(y)a-la	
	CHOK	-chok-
	cho-ka	
	cho-ko	
	JUL	-jul-
	ju-lu	
	ya-la	-yal-
throwing stick (n)	HALAB'	halaab'
	HALAB'-b'i	
thunder (n)	cha-hu-ku	chahuk [1,2]
thus (adv)	a-LAY-ya	alay
	a-la-ya	
	che	che
tidings (n)	mu-wa	mu[']wa[k] [1]
tie (tv)	ka-cha	-kach-
tie (n)	ka-cha	kach
tie up (pv)	CHAK	-chak-
tied-up thing (n)	CHAK-li-b'i	chaklib'
time (n)	HAB'-li	haab'il
to (prep)	ta	ta
toad (n)	a-ma-la	amal
	a-mu-chi	a[j]muuch [1,2]
	mu-chi	muuch [1,2]
tobacco (n)	k'u-tzi	k'uu[h]tz [1]
	K'UH-tzi	
	MAY	maay
	ma-yi-ji	
together (adv)	nu-chu	nuch
tomb, "bury place" (n)	MUK-NAL	muknal

Translation	Transcription	Transliteration
tongue (n)	a-k'a	ak'
	a-AK'	
tooth (n)	(y)e-je	ej
	e	e'
	(E)	
	ko	ko
torch (n)	TAJ	taj [2]
	ta-ja	
	ta	
torch-like (adj)	TAJ	tajal
	TAJ-la	
	ta-ja-la	
tortilla (n)	WAJ	waaj [1,2]
	wa-ji	
torture (tv)	k'u-xa	-k'ux-
translator (n)	chi-ji-la-ma	chijlam
tree (n)	TE'-le	te'el
	TE'-e-le	
	TE'	te'
	TE'-e	
	te	
	te-e	
tree-place (n)	TE'-ni-b'i	te'nib'
tree-thing (n)	TE'-b'a	te'b'a
tribute (n)	(y)u-b'u-te	ub'te'
	i-ka-tzi	ikaatz
	i-ki-tzi	ikitz
	pa-ta-na	pataan [1]
	pa-ta	
	to-jo	toj
	to-jo-la	tojo'l
	to-jo-li	
tribute cloth (n)	yu-b'u-TE'	yub'te'
trumpet-shell (n)	(y)u-k'e-sa	uk'e's
trumpeter, "he of the conch trumpet" (n)	AJ-u-b'u	aj [j]ub'
turkey (hen) (n)	AK'ACH	ak'ach
	a-k'a-cha	
turkey (wild) (n)	ku-tzu	kutz
turtle (small) (n)	ko-ko	kok
turtle carapace (n)	MAK-ka	ma[h]k [2]
	ma-ka	

Translation	Transcription	Transliteration	Translation	Transcription	Transliteration
turtle-like (adj)	AK-la a-ku a-ku-la AJ-lu	a[h]ku'l	wake up (tv)	-a-ja- -a-je-	-aj-
twelve (num)	12	lajchan	walk (riv)	XAN	xan-
twenty (num)	20 K'AL WINIK 20	k'aal winik	wall (n)	pa pa-a	pa'
			want (tv)	k'a-ti	-k'at-
			wash (tv)	po-ko	-pok-
twin (n)	lo-ta	lo't	wash bowl (n)	po-ko-la po-ko-lo	pokol
two (num)	CHA' 2	cha'	watch (tv)	ko-ko	-kok-
ugly (adj)	LAB' la-b'a	lab'	watch over (tv)	CHAN cha-nu	-chan-
uncle (maternal) (n)	(y)i-cha-ni	ichaan [1,2]	water (n)	HA' HA'-a a	ha'
understanding (n)	na-ta	nat			
unite (tv)	yu-ku	-yuk-	water insect (n)	b'u-lu-HA' b'u-b'u-lu-HA'	b'uh'ul ha'
units of five and seven (ncl)	b'i-xi	b'ix	water lily (n)	NAB-b'i NAH-b'i na-b'a na-b'i	naa[h]b' [1]
unripe (adj)	ch'o-ko CH'OK	ch'ok [1,2]			
unripeness (n)	CH'OK-ko-le-le	ch'oklel	water-like (adj)	YAX-HA' YAX-HA'-la YAX-ha-la	yaxha'l
untie (tv)	ha-ma TIL ti-li	-ham- -til-			
			we (pron)	ka	ka-
upright (adj)	WAK	wak	weasel (n)	SAB'IN sa-b'i	sab'in
urine (n)	(a-w)i-tzi	itz			
valley (?) (n)	-o-ka	[h]o'ok [1]	weave (tv)	chu-yu HAL HAL-le	-chuy- -hal-
vassal, "his/her ruler" (n)	ya-AJAW ya-ja-wa	yajaw			
			weaving (n)	HAL-b'u	hal[a]b'?
venerate (tv)	K'UH-le	-k'ul-	well (n)	CH'EN CH'EN-na/ni/ne	ch'e'n [1,2]
venerated (adj)	TZIK-la	tzikal			
vertical panel (n)	e-ke-li-b'i	eklib'	well-adorned (adj)	pi-tzi-la pi-tzi-li	pitziil
virgin (adj)	su-ju-yu	suujuy [1,2]			
visit (?) (tv)	²tu tu-tu tu-ta	-tut-	west, "sun enter" (n)	OCH-K'IN	ochk'in
			wet (adj)	HA' HA'-la ha-la	ha'al
vulture (n)	k'u-chi u-si-ja u-si	k'uuch usiij [1]			
			where (partic)	b'a-ya	b'ay

Translation	Transcription	Transliteration
whisk? (n)	o-mi-b'i	omib'
white (adj)	SAK	sak [1,2]
	SAK-la	sakal
white-like (adj)	SAK-ha-la	sakhal
whole (adj)	TZ'AK	tz'a[h]k [1]
wide (adj)	LAKAM	lakam [1]
	la-ka-ma	
wife (n)	(y)a-AT-na	atan [2]
	(y)a-ta-na	
wild, "of the tree" (adj)	TE'-le	te'el
	TE'-e-le	
	TE'-li	te'il
	(te'il)	
win (tv)	tz'a-ya	-tz'ay-
wind (n)	IK'	ik'
wise man (n)	i-tz'a-ti	itz'aat
	i-tz'a-ta	itz'at
	ma-tza	matz
	mi-ya-tzi	miyaatz [1]
with (prep)	ta	ta
	ti	ti
with, "in the company of" (prep)	(y)i-chi-NAL	ichnal
	(a-w)i-chi-NAL	
	(y)i-chi-na-la	
within (prep)	ma-la	mal
	i-chi-la	ichiil
witness (tv)	IL	-il-
	IL-la	
	i-la	
woman's offering (n)	AL	a[h]l [1]
	(y)a-AL	
	(y)a-la	
wood (n)	TE'	te'
	TE'-e	
	te	
	te-e	
word (n)	chi-chi	chich

Translation	Transcription	Transliteration
work (n)	ETE'	e[b']tej?
	ETE'-TE'	
	ETE'-TE'-je	
	pa-ta-na	pataan [1]
	pa-ta	
work together (?) (tv)	(y)e-TE'	-et-
	(y)e-he-TE'	
wound (tv)	JATZ'	-jatz'-
	ja-tz'i	
	ja-tz'a	
wrap up (tv)	wo-lo	-wol-
write (tv)	tz'i-b'a	-tz'ib'-
writing (n)	tz'i-b'i	tz'ihb' [1,2]
	tz'i-b'i-na-ja-la	tz'ihb'najal
year (n)	HAB'-li	haab'il
	TUN-ni	tuun [1,2]
year, 365 days (n)	HAB'	haab' [1]
	HAB'-b'i	
	HAB'-b'a	
yellow (adj)	K'AN	k'an [1,2]
	K'AN-na	
you (pron)	a	a
young (adj)	ch'o-ko	ch'ok [1,2]
	CH'OK	
young boy (n)	KELEM	kele'm
	ke-le-ma	
young corn (n)	AN	a'n [1,2]
	a-nu	
youngster (n)	CHAK-ch'o-ko	chak ch'ok
your (pron)	a	a
	a-wi	aw-
	a-wo	
yours (pron)	a	a
youth (n)	CHAK-ch'o-ko	chak ch'ok
youth-hood (n)	CH'OK-ko-le-le	ch'oklel
zero (num)	0	mi[h] [2]
	mi	

APPENDIX V. CALENDAR PROGRAMS

A number of Maya calendar programs are available. A few are free and available online to download. One iPhone application even displays today's Maya date. I will outline use of a few of them below. Unfortunately, each program has shortcomings, so I suggest that you search the Internet to find out which one you prefer.

Mayacal, Version 2.02.01

http://www.xoc.net/maya/

From Right Brain Software, this Windows program is old but still one of the best. The main screen of this program shows an idealized Initial Series. On either side of the calendar are fields for periods: K'alabtun, Pik'tun, B'aktun, K'atun, Tun, Winal, and K'in. The Lord of the Night, Tzolk'in, and Haab' are also displayed. In the upper right-hand side, you can choose a correlation (this book utilizes GMT [584283]). Both the Gregorian and Julian correlations are also given. Each field has an attached up-arrow and down-arrow to adjust the day or period one step at a time.

To calculate dates, use the options in the "Edit" menu. A Gregorian or Julian date can be converted into a Long Count using the "Edit" ⟶ "Gregorian Date . . . F2" or ⟶ "Julian Date . . . F3," respectively (or simply by pressing F2 or F3). A Julian Day Number can be converted under "Edit" ⟶ "Julian Day Number . . . F4." The most useful option is the Long Count reconstruction, under "Edit" ⟶ "Long Count . . . F5." In this menu, enter whatever Long Count and Calendar Round values are visible. You may leave any fields blank: the program will calculate all possible dates that match the given values. For instance, if the date on an inscription can only be partially read: 9.14.10.?.? ? Ajaw 3 ?. The known values, when entered into the Long Count menu, will result in the following options:

9.14.10.0.0	5 Ahaw, 3 Mak
9.14.10.1.0	12 Ahaw, 3 K'ank'in
9.14.10.2.0	6 Ahaw, 3 Muwan
9.14.10.3.0	1 Ahaw, 3 Pax
9.14.10.4.0	7 Ahaw, 3 K'ayab
9.14.10.5.0	1 Ahaw, 3 Kumk'u
9.14.10.6.0	8 Ahaw, 3 Wayeb

Note that the spellings of some month and day names in this program differ from those used currently. The resulting seven options can then be used to double-check the missing values. Sometimes you can see enough to rule out one or more options. Look particularly at the outline of the Haab' or shape of the missing numerals, which can often rule out or suggest one of the options over the others. Even if the date cannot be fully deciphered, clues from later Distance Numbers or other contexts can sometimes suggest the date.

You may also use this program to calculate dates by using Distance Numbers. Enter the base Long Count date, as described above, and then navigate to "Edit" ⟶ "Distance Number . . . F6" (or simply press F6). When a dialog box appears, enter ± (the default is addition) to indicate a forward or backward count and then the Distance Number. Note that if you use "tab" to navigate through the fields, it will move from the "±" field to the K'in, Winal, Tun (etc.) fields in that order (the reverse of the Long Count). After you click "OK," the new date will appear on the main screen.

This program can provide more in-depth information for any day by going to "View"

⟶ "Summary . . . F7." There you can find information for that day's Lord of the Night, Moon Age, Date, 819-Day Cycle position, and more. Please explore the other options in this program for yourself.

Mayan Calendrics, Version 3.02.00

http://www.wayeb.org/download/resources/mayancalendrics.zip

The first thing you will notice about this Windows program is its DOS interface. Do not be daunted: it is a useful program. Just be aware that you must navigate the various screens using your keyboard's arrow keys. The program itself is rather self-explanatory. You can enter your Long Count and Distance Numbers on the home screen. It can be rather nice to have a series of Long Counts and Distance Numbers displayed on a single page when you are creating your chronology chart for a given inscription. Be sure to specify the correlation and Western date format you want in the "Options" ⟶ "Configure" area or your Western calendar outputs on the home screen will be incorrect.

As in other programs, you can search for partial dates in this program. Find this option under "Calendrics" ⟶ "Missing Parts F3" or by pressing F3. Overall, this program is simple but useful. The DOS interface can be cumbersome, but it won't take you long to get used to it.

Chac, Version 2.1.2

http://www.macupdate.com/app/mac/25773/chac

This program is for Apple Macintosh. It is another straightforward and easy-to-use program that can do Distance Number and Julian Day Number calculations, do basic calendar correlations (based on more than one correlation coefficient), and provide the year bearer of a given date. A stylized Long Count inscription (similar to Maya Cal) is displayed for each search. I have had the least experience with this program but have heard positive things about it from Mac users.

Online Calculators

If you are connected to the Internet, you can make use of a number of online calculators ranging from simple to complex. I am wary of these programs because they vary widely in quality. It might be best to run a few test dates through a calculator before you trust it with fresh data.

http://www.wayeb.org/resourceslinks/wayeb_calendar.php

WAYEB is the website of the European Association of Mayanists. It includes a simple but trustworthy calculator that can give you the Gregorian date, Calendar Round, and Julian Day Number from a Long Count. Be sure to specify the correlation that you are using in the appropriate field.

http://www.pauahtun.org/Calendar/tools.html

This set of online calculators belongs to an individual interested in computer programing and math. The tools are simple (usually calculating between different parts of the calendar) but can provide information on Long Count, Calendar Round, Julian Day Numbers, 819-Day Cycles, Short to Long Count conversions, and more. It has kitschy color rendering of glyphs that often populate your searches.

http://www.diagnosis2012.co.uk/mlink.htm

I provide this link only because it has such a wide variety of links to various calculators. Again, be careful to run sample dates through any calculator with which you are experimenting to be sure it is giving accurate correlations. Be especially careful to try BCE and CE dates, because some calculators do not react well to earlier dates.

Unfortunately, there is no perfect program for calculating Maya dates. Learning to use one of these calculators can save a lot of time in working with inscriptions. Early scholars concentrated heavily on the calendrical information in Maya texts. Today we understand much more of the linguistic content, and calendrics are no longer a major focus of attention. A good understanding of how the Maya calendar works, however, is vital for understanding the historical content of monuments.

APPENDIX VI. HOW TO DRAW MONUMENTS AND TEXTS

Drawings of hieroglyphic texts abound on the Internet and in books, yet no resource for learning how to draw glyphs is readily available in print. Unfortunately, I am only able to provide a minimal explanation here. Although we have no book describing the various modern methods, you can find various resources out there if you have the right library available (e.g., Greene Robertson 1976). In the short space available here, I will describe field recording and computer vectorization.

Field Recording

The first step in creating a drawing is obtaining the base image from which to work. Vector graphic drawings are basically traces of other images, either photos or hand drawings scanned into the computer. In order to study a monument or artifact with a glyphic inscription, good photographs and field drawings are necessary. If you have ever taken photographs of monuments, you know that your naked eye picks out details that a standard photo does not. In order to draw out the details of an inscription for photography, a method of lighting called "raking light" is employed. Instead of a traditional flash that comes from near the camera, a hand-held light is placed at an oblique angle to the monument in a darkened room or at night. This causes shadows to fall in the crevices and lines of a monument, thus increasing the contrast. Photos should be taken as the camera is held so that the back of the camera is parallel to the monument, which decreases distortion. Another tip to decrease distortion is to move away from the monument and zoom in to increase the size of the image. Sometimes long exposures are needed because raking light is done in low-light conditions. In this case, a tripod is necessary to keep images crisp. It is a good practice to move back from the monument and take a full-scale picture for reference and then move in close for detailed shots of areas with intricate carving. Be sure to use a photographic scale, so that you can zoom the photos to the appropriate proportion later. It is not a bad idea also to place a standardized color sheet in the edge of the photo to help you correct for color distortion later; this is especially useful for polychrome pottery vessels. Serious photographers employ "fish-eye" macro lenses with built-in distortion reduction, but this equipment may be financially out of reach for the nonprofessional.

In addition to photographs, detailed drawings are necessary for recording fine detail that cannot be picked up by photographs. Some people prefer to make a life-sized drawing of every section of a monument; others draw only the most complex details by hand, relying on the photographs to fill in the rest. Time can also be an issue: it might be impossible to sketch an entire full-sized monument in the available time. A raking light, such as a strong hand-held flashlight, might be used to help illuminate the finest details while drawing. Be sure to include a scale and note the location of each drawing or glyph on an overall field sketch of a monument. Nothing is more frustrating than returning from the field with a jumble of papers that cannot be put in order.

Computerized Drawing

The illustrations for this book were drawn on a computer graphics program. Pencil drawings were traced with ink in the past and then scanned to make digital files. Unfortunately, even high-resolution scans suffer from pixelation when magnified. This causes lines to appear blurry when magnified. Vector graphics offer a viable alternative to traditional hand drawing. A vector graphic stores the coordinates of points and lines, recalculating their edges as the image is zoomed in or out. This eliminates pixelation and blurriness in drawings.

APPENDIX VI. HOW TO DRAW MONUMENTS AND TEXTS

A number of programs can be used to draw vector graphics, such as Adobe Illustrator, Corel Draw, and Open Office Draw. For this book I used Open Office Draw, because it is free and fully featured. This product is now called Libre Office and is available for download at www.libreoffice.org. While the following instructions are specific for Open Office, the theory is essentially the same for each program.

First you must open the drawing program and insert your base image: a photograph or scanned drawing. After the image is inserted, it can be rotated and scaled by right-clicking on it and selecting "Position and Size." Be sure to link the width and height of this object by checking the "Keep Ratio" box before changing the size. This prevents the image from becoming distorted. Once the base image is in the best size and location for drawing, double-click on the "Layout" tab at the bottom left of the screen. A menu will appear in which you can check "Locked" on this layer. This prevents you from accidentally moving, resizing, or deleting the base image. After clicking "OK" in this menu, you can click in the empty space to the right of the "Layout," "Controls," and "Dimension Line" tabs to create a new layer. You can name this layer whatever you like. I usually call it simply "Lines." Be sure to leave the "Locked" check box unchecked. Click "OK" to close this menu. Now you are ready to start drawing.

A vector line is made up of a number of points and angles. You will start by "connecting the dots" between prominent places along a single line; but first, let's specify how the line will appear. In the upper right, you can select your line thickness, color, and type. I usually draw with a solid, narrow line (0.02 cm) that is colored "Bright Red." If you draw with a thick line or a black line, you often lose sight of the line in the background image. To the right of the line options is the fill option. In the first drop-down menu, select "Invisible": you just want lines, not areas full of color. This drawing program starts each drawing on a grid to help you make straight lines. Because Maya monuments have many curved lines, we need to turn off this grid. Go to "Tools" ⟶ "Options . . . " and click the small triangle in the left-hand area of the new menu next to "Libre Office Draw," which causes more fields to drop down. Select "Grid." You can now make sure that the following boxes are unchecked: "Snap to grid," "Visible grid," "To snap lines," "To page margins," "When creating or moving objects," and "Extend edges." You will want the "To object frame" and "To object points" boxes to be checked. This allows you to connect your new lines with old ones seamlessly. Click "OK" and return to the main screen.

At the bottom is a toolbar of shapes. We will primarily draw with the "Polygon" tool. This is found by clicking the triangle to the right of the small pencil drawing a line and then selecting the figure of the line connecting dots. If you hold your cursor over the image, it will say "Polygon." Once this is selected (make sure you have clicked on the "Lines" tab or you will not be able to draw because the other layers are locked), you should have a crosshair on your screen. If your image is complex, you may have to zoom in to draw accurately. At the bottom right corner, you can double click on the percentage to bring up a menu to change your zoom. Depending on the complexity of the drawing, I work in anywhere from 200 to 3,000 percent zoom. Usually I zoom until a single glyph covers my screen.

Using the polygon cross-hair, click and hold the cursor at the beginning of a line and drag it along the line to the first change of direction. Release the mouse button and continue to the next change of direction, still dragging the line. As you move along the line, click to drop down "points" along the image. When you have reached the end of the line, or come full circle to the beginning of your line, double click to end it. You might now see your line highlighted by green boxes delimiting a square around it. In the same toolbar as the "Polygon" button to the right is another polygon with points. If you hold your mouse over it, it will say "Points (F8)." Click this button so that you see small green squares at each of your points along the line. A small toolbar should have popped up when you clicked "Points." This toolbar has point editing capability. Right now, your line has a lot of sharp corners that you want to make more rounded. With your line selected (you can see the small blue boxes), press "Control-A" to select all of the points. Then click the button on the small toolbar that looks like a red point on a curved line (it will say "Smooth Transition" if you hold your cursor over it). It should smooth out all the sharp points of your line. To draw your next line, click on the "Polygon" button in the lower toolbar and repeat the steps. Drawing each glyph block may take between ten and fifteen minutes. Try varying the thickness of your line for major and minor lines. You can also move the points of a line as needed, but you may need to resmooth the lines after points have been moved. At the end of the drawing, don't forget to change the line color to black. Finally, you can hide the base image by double clicking on the "Layout" tab and unchecking the "Visible" box. Another option would be to delete the base image; but unless absolutely necessary it is usually better to leave the base image in case you need to update or correct something later.

This is a simplified explanation of how to draw vector graphics. The best way to learn is to experiment with the program. Use the "Help" files, which are extensive and informative.

GLOSSARY

Absolutive: A case in an ergative language (one that has the same pronouns for the direct object of a transitive verb and the subject of an intransitive verb) that is the direct object of a transitive verb or the subject of an intransitive verb.

Affective Verb: A verb that describes phenomena such as bright lights, loud sounds, or strong smells.

Affix: A small, often rectangular glyph that is attached to the main sign (or other affixes) in a glyph block.

Anterior Date Indicator: A glyph that indicates an event took place before the previous date.

Calendar Round: The combination of the Tzolk'in and Haab' dates in a 52-year cycle.

Complex Vowel: A vowel that is long (VV), glottalized (V'), or aspirated (Vh).

Conflation: The graphical combination or melding of two signs.

Date Indicator: A glyph that indicates whether a Distance Number should be counted forward or backward.

Day Number: The number of days passed since the beginning of the Maya Long Count Calendar.

Demonstrative Pronoun: Pronoun that highlights a specific item or person.

Derived Adjective: An adjective created from another part of speech.

Derived Noun: A noun created from another part of speech.

Distance Number: The number of days between events and dates on an inscription.

Distance Number Introductory Glyph: The glyph that often precedes a Distance Number.

Enclitic: A phonetically dependent but grammatically independent morpheme attached to the end of a word.

Ergative: A case in an ergative language (one that has the same pronouns for the direct object of a transitive verb and the subject of an intransitive verb) that possesses a noun or represents the subject of a transitive verb.

Glyph Block: A discrete group of glyphs that constitutes an entire word or verb phrase.

Haab': The vague year of 365 days made up of eighteen 20-day months and a single 5-day month.

Head Variant: A glyph that depicts the head of a person, animal, or supernatural creature, which is the personification of the represented word.

Inchoative Verb: A verb describing the agent (or subject) as beginning an action or state of being.

Independent Pronoun: A pronoun that emphasizes and recalls a noun that is mentioned elsewhere.

Infix: An affix or main sign reduced in size and located within another glyph.

Initial Series Introductory Glyph (ISIG): A large glyph block that introduces a Long Count date.

Intransitive Verb: A verb that only has a patient (or subject).

Logogram: A sign that represents a complete word or idea (literally "written word/idea").

Long Count: The primary Maya calendar recording the number of days from the beginning of time on 13 August 3114 BCE.

Main Inscription: The largest and most prominent text of a monument or inscription.

Main Sign: The large (often square) glyph that is one of the largest in a glyph block (more than one may occur in a single glyph block).

Numeral Classifier: A phonetic component appended to a number to indicate what it counts or what class of objects is counted.

Pars Pro Toto: A small part of the main sign is used to stand for the complete meaning (literally "part for the whole").

Phonetic Complement: A syllabic sign used to indicate the pronunciation of a logogram.

Polyphony: A single sign representing multiple words or sounds.

Polyvalence: A single word with multiple meanings.

Positional Verb: A verb referring to the physical state of a person or animal.

Posterior Date Indicator: A glyph that indicates that an event took place after the previous date.

Postfix: A vertical affix located to the right of the main sign.

Prefix: A vertical affix located to the left of the main sign.

Pure Adjective: An adjective whose root cannot be reduced to anything less.

Pure Noun: A noun whose root cannot be reduced to anything less.

Reduction: A main sign scaled down to fit in the space of an affix.

Semantic Determinative: A sign that helps differentiate between two meanings for the same sign.

Subfix: A horizontal affix located below the main sign.

Superfix: A horizontal affix located above the main sign.

Supplementary Inscription: A smaller section of text, often labeling a person or item.

Supplementary Series: A group of glyphs that commonly occurs after the Long Count and between the Tzolk'in and Haab' dates in an inscription.

Syllabogram: A sign that represents a phonetic syllable: in Maya hieroglyphics, a consonant-vowel combination.

Toponym: A place-name.

Transcription: The systematic recording of hieroglyphics in Latin characters.

Transitive Verb: A verb that takes an agent and a patient (or a subject and an object).

Translation: The conversion of the recorded Classic Mayan into English (or any other language).

Transliteration: The conversion of a transcription into the reconstructed spoken Classic Mayan language.

Truncation: An affix that uses part of a main sign but retains the complete meaning.

Tzolk'in: The ritual cycle of 260 days made up of every combination of 20 Day Names and 13 Day Numbers.

REFERENCES

Beetz, Carl P., and Linton Satterthwaite

1981 *The Monuments and Inscriptions of Caracol, Belize.* Philadelphia: University Museum, University of Pennsylvania.

Boot, Erik

2002 *A Preliminary Classic Maya–English/English–Classic Maya Vocabulary of Hieroglyphic Readings.* Electronic document, www.mesoweb.com/resources/vocabulary/vocabulary.pdf *(accessed 1 November 2006).*

Bricker, Victoria

1986 A Grammar of Mayan Hieroglyphs. *Middle American Research Institute Publication,* no. 56. New Orleans: Tulane University.

Calvin, Inga

2004 Maya Hieroglyphics Study Guide. Electronic document, www.famsi.org/mayawriting/calvin/glyph_guide.pdf (accessed 24 August 2011).

Coe, Michael D.

1999 *Breaking the Maya Code.* Revised edition. New York: Thames and Hudson.

2011 *The Maya.* 8th edition. New York: Thames and Hudson.

Demarest, Arthur

2004 *Ancient Maya: The Rise and Fall of a Rainforest Civilization.* Cambridge: Cambridge University Press.

Eberl, Markus

2000 Descubrimiento de nuevas estelas en Aguateca (Petexbatun). In *XIII Simposio de Arqueología Guatemalteca* (1999), edited by Juan Pedro Laporte, Héctor L. Escobedo, Ana Claudia de Suasnavar, and Bárbara Arroyo, vol. 1, pp. 531–43. Quintana: Ministerio de Cultura y Deportes, Instituto de Antropología e Historia, Asociación Tikal, Guatemala.

Graham, Ian

1967 Archaeological Explorations in El Peten, Guatemala. *Middle American Research Institute,* no. 33. New Orleans: Tulane University.

1978 *Corpus of Maya Hieroglyphic Inscriptions.* Vol. 2, Pt. 2. Cambridge, Mass.: Peabody Museum of Archaeology and Ethnology.

1982 *Corpus of Maya Hieroglyphic Inscriptions.* Vol. 3, Pt. 3. Cambridge, Mass.: Peabody Museum of Archaeology and Ethnology.

1996 *Corpus of Maya Hieroglyphic Inscriptions.* Vol. 7, Pt. 1. Cambridge, Mass.: Peabody Museum of Archaeology and Ethnology.

Graham, Ian, and Eric von Euw

1975 *Corpus of Maya Hieroglyphic Inscriptions.* Vol. 2, Pt. 1. Cambridge, Mass.: Peabody Museum of Archaeology and Ethnology.

1977 *Corpus of Maya Hieroglyphic Inscriptions.* Vol. 3, Pt. 1. Cambridge, Mass.: Peabody Museum of Archaeology and Ethnology.

Graham, Ian, and Peter Mathews
1999 *Corpus of Maya Hieroglyphic Inscriptions.* Vol. 6, Pt. 3. Cambridge, Mass.: Peabody Museum of Archaeology and Ethnology.

Graham, Ian, Peter Mathews, Eric Von Euw, and David Stuart
1975–present *Corpus of Maya Hieroglyphic Inscriptions.* Cambridge, Mass.: Peabody Museum of Archaeology and Ethnology.

Greene Robertson, Merle
1976 Methods Used in Recording Sculptural Art at Palenque. Paper presented at the XLII Congrès International des Américanistes, Paris, France.
1983 *The Sculpture of Palenque.* Vol. 1. *Temple of Inscriptions.* Princeton, N.J.: Princeton University Press.
1985 *The Sculpture of Palenque.* Vol. 3. *Late Buildings of the Palace.* Princeton, N.J.: Princeton University Press.
1991 *The Sculpture of Palenque.* Vol. 4. *The Cross Group, the North Group, the Olvidado, and Other Pieces.* Princeton, N.J.: Princeton University Press.

Hammond, Norman
1988 *Ancient Maya Civilization.* New Brunswick, N.J.: Rutgers University Press.

Houston, Stephen D.
1993 *Hieroglyphs and History at Dos Pilas: Dynastic Politics of the Classic Maya.* Austin: University of Texas Press.

Houston, Stephen D., and Takeshi Inomata
2009 *The Classic Maya.* Cambridge: Cambridge University Press.

Houston, Stephen D., David Stuart, and John Robertson
1998 Disharmony in Maya Hieroglyphic Writing: Linguistic Change and Continuity in Classic Society. In *Anatomía de una civilización: Aproximaciones interdisciplinarias a la cultura maya,* edited by A. Ciudad R., Y. Fernández, J. M. García C., M. J. Iglesias Ponce de León, A. Lacadena G. G., and L. T. Sanz C., pp. 275–96. Madrid: Spanish Society of Maya Studies.
2004 Disharmony in Maya Hieroglyphic Writing: Linguistic Change and Continuity in Classic Society. In *The Linguistics of Maya Writing,* edited by S. Wichmann, pp. 83–99. Salt Lake City: University of Utah Press.

Houston, Stephen D., John Robertson, and David Stuart
2000 The Language of the Classic Maya Inscriptions. *Current Anthropology* 41(3): 321–56.
2001 *Quality and Quantity in Glyphic Nouns and Adjectives.* Research Reports on Ancient Maya Writing 47. Washington, D.C.: Center for Maya Research.

Jackson, Sarah, and David Stuart
2001 The Aj K'uhun Title: Deciphering a Classic Maya Term of Rank. *Ancient Mesoamerica* 12: 217–28.

Jespersen, Otto
1907 *A Modern English Grammar on Historical Principles: Part I, Sounds and Spellings.* Heidelberg: Winter Universitätsbuchhandlung.

Kerr, Justin
1998 Maya Vase Database. Electronic document, http://research.mayavase.com/kerrmaya_hires.php?vase=1398 (accessed 24 August 2011).

Kettunen, Harri, and Christophe Helmke

2010   Introduction to Maya Hieroglyphs. Electronic document, http://www.wayeb.org/download/resources/wh2010english.pdf (accessed 24 August 2011).

Knorozov, Yuri Valentinovich

1952   Drevniaia pis'menost' Tsentral'noi Ameriki. *Sovetskaia Etnografiia* 3(2): 100–18.

Krochock, Ruth, and Peter J. Schmidt

1989   *Hieroglyphic Inscriptions at Chichen Itza, Yucatan, Mexico: The Temples of the Initial Series, the One Lintel, the Three Lintels and the Four Lintels.* Washington, D.C.: Center for Maya Research.

Lacadena, Alfonso

2000   Nominal Syntax and the Linguistic Affiliation of Classic Maya Texts. In *The Sacred and the Profane: Architecture and Identity in the Maya Lowlands,* edited by P. R. Colas, K. Delvendahl, M. Kuhnert, and A. Schubart, pp. 111–28. Acta Mesoamericana, Vol. 10. Munich: Verlag Anton Saurwein.

Lacadena, Alfonso, and Søren Wichmann

2004   On the Representation of the Glottal Stop in Maya Writing. In *The Linguistics of Maya Writing,* edited by S. Wichmann, pp. 100–64. Salt Lake City: University of Utah Press.

Landa, Diego de

1938   *Relación de las cosas de Yucatán.* Mérida: Edición Yucateca.

Macri, Martha J., and Gabrielle Vail

2009   *The New Catalog of Maya Hieroglyphs: Volume Two, The Codical Texts.* Norman: University of Oklahoma Press.

Macri, Martha J., and Matthew G. Looper

2003a   Nahua in Ancient Mesoamerica: Evidence from Maya Inscriptions. *Ancient Mesoamerica* 14: 285–97.

2003b   *The New Catalog of Maya Hieroglyphs: Volume One, The Classic Period Inscriptions.* Norman: University of Oklahoma Press.

Marcus, Joyce

1987   *The Inscriptions of Calakmul: Royal Marriage at a Maya City in Campeche, Mexico.* Ann Arbor: University of Michigan, Museum of Anthropology.

1992   *Mesoamerican Writing Systems: Propaganda, Myth, and History in Four Ancient Civilizations.* Princeton, N.J.: Princeton University Press.

Martin, Simon, and Nikolai Grube

2008   *Chronicle of the Maya Kings and Queens.* 2nd edition. New York: Thames and Hudson.

Mathews, Peter, and Peter Biro

2006   Maya Hieroglyph Dictionary. Electronic document, http://research.famsi.org/mdp/mdp_index.php (accessed 24 August 2011).

Montgomery, John

2000   The Montgomery Drawings Collection. Electronic document, http://research.famsi.org/montgomery.html (accessed 24 August 2011).

2002   *How to Read Maya Hieroglyphs.* New York: Hippocrene Books.

Morley, Sylvanus G.

1938   *The Inscriptions of Petén.* Washington, D.C.: Carnegie Institution of Washington.

Pope, Maurice
1999 *The Story of Decipherment: From Egyptian Hieroglyphs to Maya Script.* New York: Thames and Hudson.

Robertson, John, Stephen D. Houston, Marc Zender, and David Stuart
2007 *Universals and the Logic of the Material Implication: A Case Study from Maya Hieroglyphic Spelling.* Research Reports on Maya Hieroglyphic Writing, No. 62. Washington, D.C.: Center for Maya Research.

Robinson, Andrew
1985 *Lost Languages: The Enigma of the World's Undeciphered Scripts.* New York: McGraw-Hill.

Schele, Linda
1996 *Eighth Palenque Round Table, 1993.* Edited by Martha J. Macri and Jan McHargue. San Francisco: Pre-Columbian Art Research Institute.

Schele, Linda, and David Freidel
1990 *A Forest of Kings: The Untold Story of the Ancient Maya.* New York: William Morrow and Company.

Schele, Linda, and Mary Ellen Miller
1986 *The Blood of Kings: Dynasty and Ritual in Maya Art.* New York: George Braziller; Fort Worth: Kimbell Art Museum.

Sharer, Robert J., and Loa P. Traxler
2006 *The Ancient Maya.* 6th edition. Stanford, Calif.: Stanford University Press.

Stephens, John L.
1963 [1843] *Incidents of Travel in Yucatan.* New York: Dover Publications, Inc.
1969 [1841] *Incidents of Travel in Central America, Chiapas and Yucatan.* New York: Dover Publications, Inc.

Stone, Andrea, and Marc Zender
2011 *Reading Maya Art: A Hieroglyphic Guide to Ancient Maya Painting and Sculpture.* London: Thames and Hudson.

Stuart, David
2005 *The Inscriptions from Temple XIX at Palenque.* San Francisco: Pre-Columbian Art Research Institute.

Stuart, David, and Ian Graham
2003 *Corpus of Maya Hieroglyphic Inscriptions.* Vol. 9, Pt. 1. Cambridge, Mass.: Peabody Museum of Archaeology and Ethnology.

Stuart, David, Stephen D. Houston, and John Robertson
1999 *Notebook for the XXIIIrd Maya Hieroglyphic Forum at Texas.* Austin: Maya Workshop Foundation.

Stuart, George
1988 *A Guide to the Style and Content of the Series Research Reports on Maya Hieroglyphic Writing.* Washington, D.C.: Center for Maya Research

Thompson, John Eric Sydney
1950 *Maya Hieroglyphic Writing: An Introduction.* Pub. 589. Washington, D.C.: Carnegie Institution of Washington.
1960 *Maya Hieroglyphic Writing: An Introduction.* Norman: University of Oklahoma Press.
1962 *A Catalog of Maya Hieroglyphics.* Norman: University of Oklahoma Press.

Wald, Robert F.

2004 Telling Time in Classic-Ch'olan and Acalan-Chontal Narrative: The Linguistic Basis of Some Temporal Discourse Patterns in Maya Hieroglyphic and Acalan-Chontal Texts. In *The Linguistics of Maya Writing,* edited by S. Wichmann, pp. 211–58. Salt Lake City: University of Utah Press.

Wichmann, Søren

2002 *Hieroglyphic Evidence for the Historical Configuration of Eastern Ch'olan.* Research Report on Ancient Maya Writing, No. 51. Washington, D.C.: Center for Maya Research.

Yasugi, Yoshiho, and Kenji Saito

1991 *Glyph Y of the Maya Supplementary Series. Research Reports on Ancient Maya Writing* 34. Washington, D.C.: Center for Maya Research.

Zender, Marc Uwe

2004 On the Morphology of Intimate Possession in Mayan Languages and Classic Mayan Grammar. In *The Linguistics of Maya Writing,* edited by S. Wichmann, pp. 195–210. Salt Lake City: University of Utah Press.

EXERCISE ANSWER KEY

Exercise 1.1. Schematic Depiction of Glyph Blocks

1.1.1. Main inscription: columns labeled A–H, left to right; rows labeled 1–8. Inset inscription: column labeled I; rows labeled 1–2.

1.1.2. Vertical lines drawn between B/C, D/E, and F/G; the top row should read, from left to right, 1, 2, 17, 18, 25, 26, 33, 34; each pair of column continues to count as rows descend (as described in the text).

1.1.3. Refer to figure 1.6.

Exercise 1.2. Piedras Negras, Stela 3

1.2.1. Columns labeled A–F; rows labeled 1–10.

1.2.2. Vertical lines drawn between B/C, D/E, and F/G; the top row should read 1, 2, 18, 19, 32, 33; each pair of column continues to count as rows descend (as described in the text).

1.2.3. Refer to figure 1.6.

Exercise 1.3. Palenque, Tablet of the 96 Glyphs

1.3.1. Columns labeled A–L; rows labeled 1–8.

1.3.2. Vertical lines drawn between B/C, D/E, F/G, H/I, and J/K; the top row should read 1, 2, 17, 18, 33, 34, 49, 50, 65, 66, 81, 82; each pair of column continues to count as rows descend (as described in the text).

1.3.3. It would be impractical to label all of the many syllables in this inscription. The first two columns contain **xu, yi, u, ya, la, a, i, ti, ma, ka, nu, ku, ta,** and **yo** at least once, for example.

Exercise 1.4. Main Signs and Affixes from Piedras Negras, Stela 3

1.4.1. The signs are identified in proper reading order. A1: superfix, main sign, subfix, main sign, main sign; B1: main sign, superfix, main sign, subfix; A2: main sign, subfix, superfix, main sign, subfix; B2: main sign, subfix, superfix, superfix, main sign, main sign; A3: prefix, superfix, main sign, subfix; B3: superfix, superfix, main sign, superfix, mains sign; A4: prefix, superfix, main sign; B4: prefix, superfix, main sign, subfix; A5: main sign, main sign, subfix; B5: prefix, mainsign.

1.4.2. Syllables labeled by glyph block. A1: **u, wa, te, mu**; B1: **na, wa**; A2: **na, ni**; B2: **yi, u, ku**; A3: **ta**; B3: **ti, le, yo**; A4: **a, ku**; B4: **ji/ya**; A5: **i, u, ti**; B5: none.

Exercise 1.5. Identify Logograms

**K'AB'A, HA', AJAW, TUN,
TZ'AK, TUN, B'ALAM, CHAN,
NAH, CHUM, TZUTZ, B'AK,
SAK, TUN, AJAW, AJAW.**

EXERCISE ANSWER KEY

Exercise 1.6. Identify Syllables
chi, i, la, ma,
ta, u, a, la,
ch'a, yi, ya, ti,
le, ko, ji, i,
la, ju, na, u,
ma, a, ta, u,
ti, yu, yi, ja,
nu, ni, pi, a,
xu, ku, ta, chu,
ya, u, ta, me,
u, ka.

Exercise 1.7. Identify Syllables II
ja, yu, mi, u,
b'a, hi, i, ja,
chi, li, ti, wi,
b'i,
u, ya, na, la,
b'u, ni, ki, wa,
chi, na, ja, li,
te, u,
yi, ji, pa, hi,
la, lu,
ni, chi, a, ti,
wa, na, ya, ja,
u, ki, mi, a,
ku, i, b'u,
ka, k'u, yo, ni,
a,
ni, o, u, ko,
chi, yi, ku, u,
ta, ti, tu, ma,
u, ki, la.

Exercise 1.8. Syllabic Spellings
a-ja-wa, b'a-la-ma, b'a-ki, cha-na, hu-na, k'a-wi-la.

Exercise 1.9. Transcribe, Transliterate, and Translate

1.9.1. CHUM-la-j(a) ti-AJAW-(wa)-le, CH'AM-y(i) K'AWIL-(la), u-B'AK-(ki) AJAW-(wa), SIY-ja B'ALAM-(ma), na-wa-w(i) (cha)-CHAN-(na), u-b'a-h(i) CHAN-(na)-K'AWIL-(la).

1.9.2. *chumlaj ajawle[l], chamaay k'awiil, ub'aak ajaw, siyaj b'ahlam, nawaaw chan, ub'aah chan k'awiil.*

1.9.3. was seated into rulership, K'awil got grasped, the ruler's captive, jaguar was born, snake adorned, snake K'awil's image.

Exercise 2.1. Synharmonic Transliterations
ajaw, b'akab', ch'ok, ixik, mam, sajal, way, b'a[h]lam, chan, mo', lakam, ak'ab', chak, k'an, chan, kab', kakaw, kohaw, k'i[h]n, lak, pakal, pitz, pom, taj, tz'am, tz'ib', witz, uk'ib', uxul.

Exercise 2.2. Disharmonic Transliterations
b'aak, b'aah, ch'aho'm, itz'aat, ook, suutz', k'awiil, hu'n, naab', naah, o'l, to'k, tuun, otoot.

Exercise 3.1. Numerals

3.1.1. Palenque: 1.18.5.3.6; Piedras Negras: 9.12.2.0.16; Yaxchilan: 9.0.19.2.4; Tonina: 9.13.10.0.0; Tikal: 9.0.10.0.0.

3.1.2. Top left: two bars, one dot and two bars, three dots and three bars; top right: three dots and three bars, four dots, one dot; bottom left: three bars, four dots and three bars, one dot and one bar; bottom right: one dot and three bars, three dots, one bar.

3.1.3. 5,356; 3,528; 5,909; 3,547.

3.1.4. Palenque: ISIG, B'aktun, K'atun, Tun, Winal, K'in; Piedras Negras: ISIG, B'aktun, K'atun, Tun, Winal, K'in; Yaxchilan: ISIG, B'aktun, K'atun, Tun, Winal, K'in; Tonina: ISIG, B'aktun, K'atun, Tun, Winal, K'in; Tikal: B'aktun, K'atun, Tun, Winal, K'in.

3.1.5. Palenque: 1.18.5.3.6; 1 era, 18 score, 5 years, 3 months, 6 days; 275,466; 2360 BCE; 23 October 2359 BCE.
Piedras Negras: 9.12.2.0.16; 9 era, 12 score, 2 years, 0 months, 16 days; 1,383,136; 647 CE; 5 July 674 CE.
Yaxchilan: 9.0.19.2.4; 9 era, 0 score, 19 years, 2 months, 4 days; 1,302,884; 454 CE; 14 October 454 CE.
Tonina: 9.13.10.0.0; 9 era, 13 score, 10 years, 0 months, 0 days; 1,393,200; 701 CE; 23 January 702 CE.
Tikal: 9.0.10.0.0; 9 era, 0 score, 10 years, 0 months, 0 days; 1,299,600; 445 CE; 16 October 445 CE.

Exercise 3.2. Calculate Calendar Round Dates

3.2.1. 8.0.0.0.0: 1,736,283; 9 Ajaw; 3 Sip.
8.2.12.13.0: 1,755,263; 9 Ajaw; 3 Sip.
9.3.15.2.14: 1,907,337; 9 Ix; 17 K'ank'in.
9.8.0.3.0: 1,937,943; 13 Ajaw; 3 Keh.
9.19.14.9.19: 2,022,322; 9 Kawak; 7 Muwan.
10.4.0.0.0: 2,053,083; 12 Ajaw; 3 Wo.
13.0.0.0.0: 2,453,283; 4 Ajaw; 3 K'ank'in.

3.2.2. Palenque: 275,466; 13 Kimi; 19 Keh.
Piedras Negras: 1,383,136; 5 K'ib'; 14 Yaxk'in.
Yaxchilan: 1,302,884; 2 K'an; 2 Yax.
Tonina: 1,393,200; 7 Ajaw; 3 Kumk'u.
Tikal: 1,299,600; 7 Ajaw; 3 Yax.

3.2.3. From left to right, top to bottom: Palenque, Tonina, Tikal, Piedras Negras, Yaxchilan.

Exercise 3.3. Identify Calendar Round Dates

17 Sek, 2 Yax, 7 Muluk, 2 K'an.
13 Keh, 12 Etznab', 10 Kawak, 7 Ajaw, 10 Yaxkin.
8 Muwan, 9 Manik', 13 Ajaw, 15 Wo, 0 Pax.
7 Kib', 14 K'ank'in, 14 Yaxk'in, 1 Kib', 14 Wo.
13 Muwan, 4 Kimi, 11 Imix, 6 Ajaw, 14 Yax.
7 Ajaw, 3 K'umk'u, 5 Lamat, 6 Xul, 1 Ik.

Exercise 3.4. Identify Supplementary Inscription Elements

Piedras Negras, Stela 3: G7, F, E(7) + D, C(2), X2, A(29).
Piedras Negras, Stela 10: G9 + F, E(9) + D, C(3), X4, B, A(30).
Yaxchilan, Lintel 21: G8 + F, Z(5) + Y, E(7) + D, C(3) + X4 + A(29).
Palenque, Palace Tablet: G3 + F, C(2), X(2), B, A(29).
Palenque, Temple of the Sun Tablet: G3 + F, E(26), D, C(4), X4, B, A(30).

EXERCISE ANSWER KEY 375

Exercise 3.5. Identify Distance Numbers

Palenque, Hieroglyphic Stairway (left): + 3.11.3.3
Piedras Negras, Stela 3 (left): + 4.19
Palenque, Palace Tablet (left): − 8.7
Palenque, Tablet of 96 Glyphs (left): + 19.15.14
Piedras Negras, Stela 3: + 12.10.0
Palenque Hieroglyphic Stairway (right): + 12.9.8
Palenque, Palace Tablet (right): + 18.5.18
Palenque, Tablet of 96 Glyphs (right): + 1.0.0.0
Yaxchilan, Lintel 21 (right): + 15.1.16.5.

Exercise 3.6. Reconstruct Dates: Yaxchilan, Hieroglyphic Stairway 3

3.6.1. A1–D2, D8–C10.

3.6.2.	A1–D2	9.12.08.14.01	12 Imix 4 Pop	23 February 681 CE
	+	12.00		
	D8–C10	[9.12.09.08.01]	5 Imix 4 Mak	21 October 681 CE

Exercise 3.7. Reconstruct Dates: Piedras Negras, Stela 3

3.7.1. A1–B7, C1–D2, D4–C6, E1–E2, F6–F10.

3.7.2.	A1–B7	9.12.02.00.16	5 K'ib 14 Yaxk'in	5 July 674 CE
	+	12.10.00		
	C1–D2	[9.12.14.10.16]	1 K'ib 14 K'ank'in	19 November 686 CE
	+	1.01.11.10		
	D4–C6	[9.13.16.04.06]	4 Kimi 14 Wo	19 March 708 CE
	+	[3.08.15]		
	E1–E2	[9.13.19.13.01]	11 Imix 14 Yax	26 August 711 CE
	+	4.19		
	F6–F10	[9]14.00.00.00	6 Ajaw 13 Muwan	3 December 711 CE

Exercise 3.8. Reconstruct Dates: Palenque, Tablet of 96 Glyphs

3.8.1. A1–B1, A5–A7, C2–C5, D8–E3, E7–G2, G6–G8, L1–K3.

3.8.2.	A1–B1	[9]11.00.00.00	12 Ajaw 8 Keh	12 October 652 CE
	+	2.01.11		
	A5–A7	[9.11.02.01.11]	9 Chuwen 8 Mak	2 November 654 CE
	+	2.08.04.17		
	C2–C5	[9.13.10.06.08]	5 Lamat 6 Xul	1 June 702 CE
	+	19.15.14		
	D8–E3	[9.14.10.04.02]	9 Ik' 5 K'ayab'	1 January 722 CE
	+	2.02.14.05		
	E7–G2	[9.16.13.00.07]	9 Manik 15 Wo	6 March 764 CE
	+	1.00.00.00		
	G6–G8	[9.17.13.00.07]	17 Manik 0 Pax	22 November 783 CE
	−	07		
	L1–K3	[9.17.13.00.00]	13 Ajaw 13 Muwan	15 November 783 CE

Exercise 3.9. Reconstruct Dates: Piedras Negras, Altar 2

3.9.1. A1–B2, E1–D2, F2–F3, G1–G2, I3, J1–K1, L1–L2.

3.9.2. J1–K1	[9.13.09.14.15]	7 [Men] 18 K'ank'in	20 November 701 CE
	+ 1.08.06.18		
L1–G2	[9.14.18.03.13]	7 Ben 16 [K'ank'in]	11 November 729 CE
	+ 1.14.07		
I3–E2	[9]15.00.00.00	4 Ajaw 13 Yax	20 August 731 CE
	+ 1.00.00.00		
F2–B2	[9]16.00.00.00	2 Ajaw 13 Sek	7 May 751 CE

Exercise 3.10. Reconstruct Dates: Palenque, Hieroglyphic Stairway

3.10.1. A1–B4, B5, B6–C1, C4

3.10.2. A1–B4	9.08.09[13]00	8 Ajaw [13 Pop]	24 March 603 CE
	+ 12.09.08		
B5	[9.09.02.04.08]	5 Lamat 1 Mol]	27 July 615 CE
	[9.08.08.13.00]		
	+ [2.12]03.03		
B6–C1	[9.11.01.16.03]	6 Ak'bal 1 Yax	26 August 654 CE
	[+ 5.00.08]		
C4	[9.11.06.16.11]	7 Chuwen 4 Ch'en	8 August 659 CE

Exercise 3.11. Reconstruct Dates: Palenque, Sarcophagus

3.11.1. 1–2, 4–5, 15–16, 18, 20, 22–23, 25, 28, 31–32, 37–38, 42 and 46, 43–44, 48–49.

3.11.2. 1–2	[9.08.09.13.00]	8 Ajaw 13 Pop	26 March 603 CE
	[+ 4.02.10.18]		
4–5	[9.12.11.05.18]	6 Etz'nab 11 Yax	31 August 683 CE
15–16	[9.04.10.04.17]	5 Kab'an 5 Mak	1 December 524 CE
	[+ 2.00.13.19]		
18	[9.06.11.00.16]	7 Kib 4 K'ayab	8 February 565 CE
	[+ 5.09.11]		
20	[9.06.16.10.07]	9 Manik' 5 Yaxk'in	23 July 570 CE
	[+ 3.09.13]		
22–23	[9.07]00.00.00	7 Ajaw 3 K'ank'in	7 December 573 CE
	[+ 9.05.05]		
25	[9.07.09.05.05]	11 Chikchan 3 K'ayeb*	3 February 583 CE
	[+ 1.02.01.07]		
		* Scribe wrote 4	
28	[9.08.11.06.12]	2 Eb 0 Mol	7 November 604 CE
	[+ 7.17.14]		
31–32	[9.08.19.04.06]	2 Kimi 14 Mol	11 August 612 CE
	[− 10.15]		
37–38	[9.08.18.14.11]	3 Chuwen 4 Wayeb	9 March 612 CE
	[+ 1.08.16.14]		

42–46	[9.10.07.13.05] [– 7.13.05]	4 Chikchan 13 Yax	10 September 640 CE
43–44	[9.10]00.00.00 [+ 10.01.06]	1 Ajaw 8 K'ayab	27 January 633 CE
48–49	[9.10.10.01.06]	13 Kimi 4 Pax	1 January 643 CE

Exercise 3.12. Reconstruct Dates: Palenque, Palace Tablet

3.12.1. A1–A18, A19–D1, C18–E7, E15–E18, G8–G11, J7–I10, J12–L6, L15–N8, M9–N10, M13–N15, O15–O18, Q2–Q13.

3.12.2. A1–A18	9.10[11]17.00 – 1.05.18	[11] Ajaw 8 Mak	3 November 644 CE
A19–D1	[9.10.10.11.02] [9.10.11.17.00] + 7.00.19	1 Ik' 15 Yaxk'in	14 July 643 CE
C18–E7	[9.10.18.17.19] + 1.00.01	2 Kawak 12 [Keh]	17 October 651 CE
E15–E18	[9]11.00.00.00 + 13.00.00	12 Ajaw 8 Keh	12 October 652 CE
G8–G11	[9.11]13.00.00 + 18.05.18	12 Ajaw 3 Ch'en	5 August 665 CE
J7–I10	[9.12.11.05.18] + 6.12	6 Etznab' 11 Yax	29 August 683 CE
J12–L6	[9.12.11.12.10] + 18.06.15	8 Ok 3 K'ayab	8 January 684 CE
L15–N8	[9.13.10.01.05] – 1.05	6 Chikchan 3 Pop	18 February 702 CE
M9–N10	[9.13]10.00.00 [9.13.10.01.05] + 5.03	7 Ajaw 3 Kumku	24 January 702 CE
M13–N15	[9.13.10.06.08] – 4.08.02.00	5 Lamat 6 Xul	1 June 702 CE
O15–O18	[9.09.02.04.08] [9.13.10.06.08] + 18.08.07	5 Lamat 1 Mol	27 July 615 CE
Q2–Q13	[9.14.08.14.15]	9 Men 3 Yax	12 August 720 CE

Exercise 4.1. Identify Prepositions

Aguateca, Stela 1: **yi-chi-NAL-(la)**, *yichnal,* in front of; **ti**, *ti,* to, with, for.
Palenque, Palace Tablet: **TAN-(na)**, *tan,* in the center of; **ti**, *ti,* to, with, for; **YICH-NAL-(la)**, *yichnal,* in front of; **yi-chi-NAL-(la)**, *yichnal,* in front of.
Palenque, Tablet of 96 Glyphs: **TAN-(na)**, *tan,* in the center of; **ta**, *ta,* to, with, for; **ti**, *ti,* to, with, for.
Hypothetical: **i-chi-l(a)**, *ichiil,* within; **ti-i-l(i)**, *ti'il,* pertaining to; **ma-l(a)**, *mal,* within; **ma-l(a)**, *mal,* within; **ti-i-l(i)**, *ti'il,* pertaining to.
Piedras Negras, Stela 3: **yi[ch(i)]-NAL-(la)**, *yichnal,* in front of; **ti**, *ti,* to, with, for.

Exercise 4.2. Identify Pronouns

ni-, *ni-*, my; **ye-**, *ye-*, he/she/it; **-Ca-t(a)**, *-[a]t*, you; **ka-**, *ka-*, our; **yu-**, *yu-*, he/she/it; **-Ce-n(a)**, *-een*, I; **ya-**, *ya-*, his/hers/its; **yi-**, *yi-*, he/she/it; **u-**, *u-*, his/hers/its; **yo-**, *yo-*, his/hers/its;
i-, *i-*, your (pl.); **a-**, *a-*, you; **a-**, *a-*, your; **yi-**, *yi-*, he/she/it; **u-**, *u-*, he/she/it;
yi-, *yi-*, he/she/it; **u-**, *u-*, his/hers/its; **ya-**, *ya-*, he/she/it; **ya-**, *ya-*, his/hers/its.

Exercise 4.3. Pronouns

4.3.1. Left column: his captive, my plate, your (pl.) lord, his ruler, my wife, your plate, our wife, this captive.

Right column: you arrived, we buried him/her/it, you caught me, you (pl.) buried him/her/it, you arrived, I witnessed them, he caught us, you buried them.

4.3.2. Left column: *ni-k'ohaw, y-otoot, u-ju'ntan, kaw-uk'ib', iw-itz'aat, haa'-ixik, a-mam, y-ixik.*

Right column: *cham-at, cham-o'n, i-koj-ow-o'b', cham-een, a-koj-ow-ø, u-koj-ow-o'n, cham-o'b', ni-koj-ow-at.*

Exercise 4.4. Pronouns II

Left column: **ni-ka-ka-w(a)**, *ni-kakaw*, my cacao; **a-tzu-l(u)**, *a-tzul*, your dog; **i-ch'o[k(o)]**, *i-ch'ok*, your (pl.) heir; **ka-ch'o[k(o)]**, *ka-ch'ok*, our heir; **u-tzu-l(u)**, *u-tzul*, his/her/its dog.

Right column: **ni-wa-la-w(a)**, *niw-al-aw-ø*, I said it; **ya-k'a-wo-b'(a)**, *y-ak'-aw-o'b'*, he gave them; **i-wa-k'a-w(a)**, *iw-ak'-aw-ø*, you (pl.) gave it; **a-ju-b'u-wo-x(o)**, *a-jub'-uw-ox*, you take down you (pl.); **ka-na-wa-we-n(a)**, *ka-naw-aw-een*, we displayed me.

Exercise 4.5. Derived Nouns

Left column: grasper, scatterer, guardian, painter, opener, death, heirship/youthship, burner, fire-place, yellow-place, tree-place, mountain-place, sun-place, seat, water-place.

Right column: giver, striker, cover/coverer, rulership, jaguar-place, obsidian-place, abundance-place, leader, wash-thing/washbowl, pay-thing/payment, singer, tied-up-thing, lordship, burial-place.

Exercise 4.6. Identify Titles

Aguateca, Stela 1: **AJ-2-B'AK-(ki)**, *aj ch'a b'aak*, he of two captives; **K'UHUL-MUTUL-AJAW**, *k'uhul mutul ajaw*, holy ruler of Dos Pilas (bundle).

Naranjo, Stela 1: **b'a/B'AH-ka-b'(a)**, *b'aah kab'*, first of the earth; **K'UHUL-MUTUL-AJAW**, *k'uhul mutul ajaw*, holy ruler of Tikal (bundle); **?-K'UHUL-IXIK**, *? k'uhul ixik*, ? holy lady.

Palenque, Tablet of 96 Glyphs: **sa-ja[l(a)]**, *sajal*, lord/sajal; **5-WINIK-HAB'-AJAW**, *ho' winikhaab' ajaw*, 5-K'atun ajaw; **K'UHUL-B'AK-la-AJAW**, *k'uhul b'aakal ajaw*, holy ruler of Palenque (bony); **b'a-ka-b'(a)**, *b'aah kab'*, first of the earth; **u-1-ta-n(a)**, *u-ju'n-tan*, his/her cherished one; **5-WINIK-HAB'-[pl.]-AJAW**, *ho' winikhaab'-[pl.] ajaw*, 5-K'atun ajaw; **a-pi-tzi-l(a)**, *ajpitzil*, ballplayer.

Exercise 4.7. Derived Adjectives

kab'al, low/earth-like; *tajal*, torch-/obsidian-like; *te'el*, wild/tree-like; *ha'al*, watery/root; *k'uhul*, holy/divine; *akal*, turtle-like; *k'ak'al*, fiery; *kakawal*, chocolaty.

Exercise 4.8. Noun Phrases

in front of his lord; within your large helmet; to/in his heavenly house; in the center of [the] precious earflare; our white house; to/from his ruler; in front of his holy ruler; *ti-y-ajaw, t-a-lakam-tuun, ti-ni-k'ak'-al-k'ab', ti-k'ak'-al-k'ab'-is*.

Exercise 4.9. Piedras Negras, Stela 3

4.9.1. A9, A10, C3, D3, C4, C7, D7, E3, F3, E4, F4, F5.

4.9.2. IXIK-WINIK-HAB'-[pl.]-AJAW, *ixik winikhaab'-[pl.] ajaw*, Lady K'atun Ruler; **[IXIK]-na-MAN-[(ni)-AJAW]**, *ixik namaan ajaw*, Lady Ruler of La Florida; **IXIK-WINIK-HAB'-[pl.]**, *ixik winik haab'-[pl.]*, Lady K'atun [Ruler]; **IXIK-na-MAN-(ni)-AJAW**, *ixik namaan ajaw*, Lady Ruler of La Florida; **yi-chi-NAL-(la)**, *yichnal*, in the presence of; **K'INICH**, *k'inich*, sun-faced; **IXIK-1-ta-n(a)**, *ixik ju'n tan*, Lady Cherished One; **IXIK-K'IN-(ni)-AJAW**, *ixik k'ihn ajaw*, Lady Sun Ruler; **IXIK-WINIK-AJAW-(wa)**, *ixik winik ajaw*, Lady K'atun Ruler; **IXIK-(na)-NAMAN-(ni)-AJAW**, *ixik namaan ajaw*, Lady Ruler of La Florida; **u**, *u*, his; **u**, *u*, his; **u**, *u*, his.

Exercise 4.10. Piedras Negras, Altar 2

Top block: **u**, *u*, his/her/its; **u**, *u*, his/her/its; **YAX**, *yax*, first; **TUN-(ni)**, *tuun*, stone/stela; **K'UHUL-B'AK-AJAW-(wa)**, *k'uhul b'aak ajaw*, holy ruler of Palenque (Bone).
Left block: **ti**, *ti*, in/at/on; **u**, *u*, his/her/its; **u**, *u*, his/her/its; **TUN-(ni)**, *tuun*, stone/stela; **K'UHUL- . . . -AJAW**, *k'uhul . . . ajaw*, holy ruler of . . .
Right block: **ti**, *ti*, in/at/on; **ti**, *ti*, in/at/on; **AJAW-le**, *ajawlel*, rulership; **IXIK**, *ixik*, lady; **u**, *u*, his/her/its; **K'UHUL-yo-ki[b'(i)]-AJAW-(wa)**, *k'uhul yokib' ajaw*, holy ruler of Piedras Negras (his canyon).
Bottom block: **ch'o-k(o)**, *ch'ok*, heir.

Exercise 5.1. Transitive Verb Voices

1st Pers. Sing.: *chuhk-aj-een*, I was caught; *chuk-uy-een*, I got caught; *chuk-uw-een*, I caught; *chuk-u-een*, catch me!
2nd Pers. Sing.: *u-chuk-uw-et*, he caught you; *chuk-uy-et*, you got caught; *chuk-uw-et*, you caught; *chuk-u-et*, catch you!
3rd Pers. Sing.: *u-chuk-uw-ø*, he caught him; *chuhk-aj-ø*, he was caught; *chuk-uw-ø*, he caught; *chuk-u-ø*, catch him/it!
1st Pers. Pl.: *u-chuk-uw-o'n*, he caught us; *chuhk-aj-o'n*, we were caught; *chuk-uy-o'n*, we got caught; *chuk-u-o'n*, catch us!
2nd Pers. Pl.: *u-chuk-uw-ox*, he caught you (pl.); *chuhk-aj-ox*, you (pl.) were caught; *chuk-uy-ox*, you (pl.) got caught; *chuk-uw-ox*, you (pl.) caught.
3rd Pers. Pl.: *chuhk-aj-o'b'*, they were caught; *chuk-uy-o'b'*, they got caught; *chuk-uw-o'b'*, they caught; *chuk-u-o'b'*, catch them!
3rd Pers. Sing.: *u-ch'ak-aw-ø*, he chopped him/her/it; *ch'ahk-aj-ø*, he was chopped; *ch'ak-ay-ø*, we got chopped; *ch'ak-a-ø*, chop it!
3rd Pers. Sing.: *y-il-iw-ø*, he saw him/her/it; *'il-iy-ø*, it got seen; *'il-iw-ø*, it saw; *'il-i-ø*, see it!

Exercise 5.2. Transitive Verb Voices II

Left column: I got penanced; it was conjured; I was grasped; I counted; I got planted; you got struck; I burned you; I bound you; you caught him/her/it; end it!; I buried; hit it!

Right column: he scattered it; he speared it; take it down!; you ate; I was chopped; you got encircled; lose it!; he was given; you saw; he got born; say it!

Lower section: Pakal scattered B'alam; His ruler planted the stela/great stone; His holy ruler grasped the K'awil scepter; B'alam was chopped; It got downed, his flint and shield.

Exercise 5.3. Transitive Verb Voices III

Left column: *y-il-iw-ø, tzak-ay-at, ni-tz'ap-aw-ø, we'-e-ø, juhb'-aj-ø, a-muk-uw-o'n, tzutz-uy-ø, a-chok-ow-ø, u-jatz'-aw-o'n, chuk-aj-ø, aw-ak-aw-een, ni-koj-ow-o'b'.*

Right column: *tz'ak-ay-ø, juhl-aj-een, k'ahl-aj-ox, u-tzak-aw-o'n, johy-aj-at, k'al-ay-ø, aw-al-aw-ø, chuk-uy-o'b', u-tzutz-uw-ø, saht-aj-een, ch'am-ay-ø.*

Lower section: *u-chuk-uw-ø niw-ajaw-b'ahlam; ni-muk-uw-ø a-sajal; ni-we'-ew-ø ni-yax-ahk; a-chuk-uw-ø lakam-b'ahlam; y-il-iw-ø chak-tzul Bob.*

Exercise 5.4. Intransitive Verbs

1st Pers. Sing.: *ak'-aj-een*, I danced; *chum-waan-een*, I sat; *u-chum-b'u-een*, he made me sit.

2nd Pers. Sing.: *cham-at*, you died; *chum-waan-at*, you sat; *u-chum-b'u-at*, he made you sit.

3rd Pers. Sing: *cham-i*, he died; *ak'-aj-ø*, he danced: *u-chum-b'u-ø*, he made him/her/it sit.

1st Pers. Pl.: *cham-o'n*, we died; *ak'-aj-o'n*, we danced; *chum-waan-o'n*, we sat.

2nd Pers. Pl.: *ak'-aj-ox*, you (pl.) danced; *chum-waan-ox*, you (pl.) sat; *u-chum-b'u-ox*, he made you (pl.) sit.

3rd Pers. Pl.: *cham-o'b'*, they died; *chum-waan-o'b'*, they sat; *u-chum-b'u-ø*, they made it sit.

3rd Pers. Sing.: *hul-i*, he arrived; *tz'ib'-aj-ø*, he wrote; *u-lam-b'u-ø*, he made it disappear.

3rd Pers. Sing.: *och-i*, he entered; *pul-aj-ø*, he burned; *pat-waan-ø*, he formed.

Exercise 5.5. More Intransitive Verbs

Left column: you entered; he entered; we came; he arrived; I formed; I arrived; I died; he played ball; I made him form; I wrote; you wrote; he danced.

Right column: you played ball; I drank; we emerged; he made it sit; he came; he drank; I danced; he came; you died; you (pl.) left; he died; he drank.

INDEX

References to illustrations are in italic type.

Absolutive pronouns, *125*, 129–33, *219*; first-person plural, *125*, 131–32, *219*; first-person singular, *125*, 130, *219*; passive transitive verbs and, 169; second-person plural, *125*, 132, *219*; second-person singular, *125*, 130–31, *219*; stative clauses and, *159*; third-person plural, *125*, 132–33, *219*; third-person singular, *125*, 131, *219*; transitive verbs and, *171*
Abstract main signs, 25
Accession, verbs relating to, *244*
Active transitive verbs, 166, *167*, *168*, 187, 220
ADIs (Anterior Date Indicators), 102–103, *103*, 105, *243*
Adjectives, *152*, 152–53, *223*; colors and, *154*, *246*; derived, 152, *153*, 379; pure, 152–53; stative clauses and, *159*; T-numbers, *New Catalog* codes, and drawings for, *225–28*, *231*
Adverbs, 153–54, *224*; temporal, *188*; T-numbers, *New Catalog* codes, and drawings for, *227*
Affective verbs, *181*, *182*, 183, 187
Affixes, 25; equivalent main signs and, 25, *29*; from Piedras Negras, *28*, 372; T-numbers and, 28
Agglutinating verbal phrases, 165
Agriculture, 7
Aguateca: Stela 1 at, *123*, 151, *377*, *378*; Stela 3 at, *42*, 373
Ahku'ul Mo' Naahb', 213
Altar 1 at Naranjo, *44*, 373
Altar 2 at Piedras Negras: dates exercise and, *113*, 376; grammar exercise and, *163*, 379
Amphibians, *251*
Ancient Maya, The (Sharer and Traxler), 5
Animal glyphs, *149*; birds, *250*; fish, *250*; insects and invertebrates, *251*; mammals, *249*; reptiles and amphibians, *251*
Anterior Date Indicators (ADIs), 102–103, *103*, 105, *243*
Anterior Event Indicators, 186, 187, *188*, 224
Antipassive transitive verbs, *167*, *168*, 170, 187, 220
Archaic period (8000–2000 BCE), 7
Aspirated vowel, 61
Aztec empire, 8

Bar-and-dot numbers, 74, *75*, *79*, 373–74
Belize, *6*, 7
Berlin, Heinrich, 150
Birds, *250*

Birth, verbs relating to, *244*
Body-part nouns, 143, *144*
Boot, Eric, 11
Brasseur de Bourbourg, Abbé Charles-Étienne, 9
Breaking the Maya Code (Coe), 8
Bricker, Victoria, 11

Caesar, Julius, 86
Calakmul, 8, 69, *69*
Calculators for Maya dates, online, 360–61
Calendar. *See* Maya calendar
Calendar Round (CR), 87–88, *89*, *90*, 91, 194; Distance Numbers and, 103, 105; exercises on, *92–93*, 374; Haab' Month Names and, 88, *90*, 91, *93*, *239*, 374; Tzolk'in Day Names and, 45–46, 87, *89*, *93*, *238*, 374
Cancuen, 8
Capture, verbs relating to, *245*
Catalog of Maya Hieroglyphs, A (Thompson), 28, 30
Catherwood, Frederick, 9
Causative verbs, *176*, *177*, *178*, *179*, 187, 221, 300
Chac, Version 2.1.2, 360
Chichen Itza, 8, *44*, 373
Ch'olan languages, 55, 71
Ch'olti', 71
Christianity, 9
Chronicle of the Maya Kings and Queens (Martin and Grube), 5, 11, 193, 194
Classic (250–900/1100 CE) period, 7–8
Classic Ch'olti'an, 71
Clemens, Samuel, 86
Cocom, Juan Nachi, 9, 10
Codex style, 12
Codices, 12
Coe, Michael, 11; *Breaking the Maya Code*, 8; *The Maya*, 5; *Reading the Maya Glyphs*, 4
Colors, *154*, *246*
Complex vowels, 60–61, 62–64, 65–66
Computer vectorization, 362–64
Conflations, 25, *27*
Consonants, 59–60
Controversies: aspect vs. tense in verbs, 185; current epigraphic, 3, 4, 5; disharmonic spellings of complex vowels, 60–61, 62–64; Long Count correlations, 86; morphosyllables, 145; plural markers, 143
Copan, 8

Corpus of Maya Hieroglyphic Inscriptions, The (Peabody Museum), 12, 57
Corpus Project, 12
CR. *See* Calendar Round (CR)
"Cracking the Maya Code" (*Nova* episode), 8

Date Indicators (DIs), 102–103, *103*, 105; Anterior, 102–103, *103*, 105, *243*; Future, *103*, 187, *188*, 224, *243*; Posterior, 102, *103*, 186, *188*, 224, *243*
Dates: exercise on, *80*, 374; in inscription formats, 33, 73; programs for calculating, 359–61; Short Counts and, 86, *119*, 119–20. *See also* Calendar Round (CR); Distance Numbers; Long Counts; Maya calendar; Numbers; Supplementary Series
Day Names, Tzolk'in. *See* Tzolk'in Day Names
Day Number conversion to Gregorian calendar dates, 83–85, 86
Death, verbs relating to, *244*
Decipherment of Maya hieroglyphic writing, short history of, 8–11
Deities, glyphs for, *252*
Demonstrative pronouns, *125*, 133, *219*
Derived adjectives, 152, *153*, 379
Derived intransitive verbs, 175, *176*, *177*, 178, 186, 221; exercise on, 179, 380; relative time and, 187; T-numbers, *New Catalog* codes, and drawings for, *226–31*
Derived nouns, 138, *139–41*, 142, 378
Determinatives, semantic, *45*, 45–46, *46*, *47*
DIs. *See* Date Indicators (DIs)
Disharmonic spelling, 62–64, 72; controversy on, 60–61, 62–64; exercise on, 66, *68*, 373
Distance Number Introductory Glyph (DNIG), 101, *101*, *243*
Distance Numbers, 101–103; Calendar Round and, 103, 105; Date Indicators and, 102–103, *103*, *104*, 105, *243*; Distance Number Introductory Glyphs and, 101, *101*, *243*; exercises on, *106*, 110–18, 375; from Naranjo, Stela 24, *108*, 109; Number of Days and, 101–102, *102*; from Yaxchilan, Lintel 21, 105, *106*, *107*, 109, 375
DNIG (Distance Number Introductory Glyph), 101, *101*, *243*
Doubling mark, 52
Drawing monuments and texts, 362–64
Dresden Codex, 12

Eberl, Markus, 11
819-Day Cycle, 98, *99*, *242*
El Baúl, 8
Ellipses to indicate eroded glyphs, 55
El Mirador, 7
El Salvador, *6*, 7
Emblem glyphs, *150*, *253*
Enclitics, 186, 224
English to Maya lexicon, 333–58

Epigraphers' current debates on Maya hieroglyphics, 3, 4, 5, 60–61, 64–66
Ergative pronouns, 124, *125*, 126, *219*; examples of, 160, *161*; first-person plural, *125*, 127–28, *219*; first-person singular, *125*, 126, *219*; second-person plural, *125*, 128–29, *219*; second-person singular, *125*, 126–27, *219*; stative clauses and, *159*; third-person plural, *125*, 129, *219*; third-person singular, *125*, 127, *219*; transitive verbs and, *171*
Eroded glyphs, ellipses to indicate, 55
European Association of Mayanists, 12, 360
European Maya Conference, 3
Extra long count periods, *82*, 237
Extreme Anterior Event Indicators, 224

Family relations glyphs, *150*, *252*
Female titles, *248*
Field recording, 362
First-person absolutive pronouns, 160, *161*, *219*; plural, *125*, 131–32, *219*; singular, *125*, 130, *219*
First-person ergative pronouns: plural, *125*, 127–28, *219*; singular, *125*, 126, *219*
Fish, *250*
Food, *256*
Förstemann, Ernst, 9
Foundation for the Advancement of Mesoamerican Studies Incorporated, 3, 12
Full-figure variant numbers, 76, *77*
Future Date Indicators, *103*, 187, *188*, 224, *243*

Glottalized consonants, 59–60
Glottalized vowels, 60–61, 63
Glottal stops, 36, 60, 64, 70
Glyph A, 98, *99*, *242*
Glyph B, 97, *97*, *241*
Glyph blocks: from Palenque, Hieroglyphic Stairway, 16, *17*, 21, *24*, 31, *32*; from Palenque, Tablet of 96 Glyphs, 20, *20*, 372; from Piedras Negras, Stela 3, 19, *19*, 372; reading order within, 25, *26*, *27*, 28, *29*, 30–31, *32*, 33; schematic depiction and, 18, *18*, 372; T-numbers and, 28, 30, *30*; traditional labeling scheme for, 15–16, *16*
Glyph C, *96*, 97, *241*
Glyph D, 94, *96*, 97, *241*
Glyph E, 94, *96*, 97, *241*
Glyph F, 94, *96*, *240*
Glyph G (Lord of the Night), 94, 95, *95*, 98, *240*
Glyphs: drawing, 362–64; *New Catalog* codes for, 30, *225–31*, *232–35*; regional differences in, 72; syllabary of currently deciphered, *37–41*; T-numbers for, 28, 30, *30*, *225–31*, *232–35*
Glyph X, 97, *97*, *241*
Glyph Y, 94, *96*, *240*
Glyph Z, 94, *96*, *240*

Goodman, Joseph T., 86
Goodman-Martinez-Thompson (GMT), 84–85, 86
Greene Robertson, Merle, 57
Gregorian calendar dates, 83–85, 86
Gregory XIII, Pope, 86
Grube, Nikolai, 5, 11, 193
Guatemala, *6*, 7
Guide to the Style and Content of the Series Research Reports on Ancient Maya Writing, A (Stuart), 56, 57
Gunter, Stanley, 11

Haab' Month Names, 88, *90*, 91, *93*, *239*, 374
Head-variant numbers, 74, *75*, *77*
Head variants, 25, 28, *237*
Helmke, Christophe, 11
Hernández, Juan Martínez, 86
Hieroglyphic Stairway at Palenque: Calendar Round dates and, *93*, 374; Distance Numbers and, *106*, *114*, 375, 376; K'inich Janaab' Pakal chronology at, 215, *216*, 217; logograms, *34*, 372; reading order of inscription from, 16, *17*, 21, *24*, 31, *32*; temporal indicators from, 109, *190*, 191
Hieroglyphic Stairway 3 at Yaxchilan, *110*, 375
Hieroglyphic texts, drawing, 362–64
Hiragana syllabary, 36
Honduras, *6*, 7
Houston, Stephen, 11, 64, 66, 72
How to Read Maya Hieroglyphs (Montgomery), 3
Humbolt, Alexander von, 9

Ideograms. *See* Logograms
Ideographs. *See* Logograms
Imperative transitive verbs, *167*, 170, 187, 220, 379
Inchoative verbs, *181*, 181–82, *182*, 187, 221
Incidents of Travel in Central America, Chiapas, and Yucatan (Stephens and Catherwood), 9
Incidents of Travel in Yucatan (Stephens and Catherwood), 9
Independent nouns, 143, *144*
Infixes, 25, *26*; examples of, *27*; transcription of, *50*, 52
Initial Series Introductory Glyph (ISIG), 81, *82*, *237*
Inscriptions, 11; common format of, 33; most common titles found in, 146–48; reading order within, 21, *22*, *23*, *24*, 155, *156*, *157*, 379; recognizing numbers in, 73–74, *75*; systematic strategy for deciphering, 193–94
Inscriptions of Petén, The (Morley), 57
Insects, *251*
Intransitive verbs, 175, 221; causative, *176*, *177*, 178, *179*, 187, 221, 380; derived (*see* Derived intransitive verbs); exercises on, 179–80, 380; nouns derived from, 138, *139*; positional (*see* Positional verbs); relative time and, 187; root (*see* Root intransitive verbs)
Invertebrates, *251*
ISIG (Initial Series Introductory Glyph), 81, *82*, *237*

Julian calendar, 86
Julian Day Number, 84–85
Ju'n Tan Ahk, Lady, 194, 199, *201*, 205, 206
Justeson, John, 11

Kaminaljuyu, 7
K'an Mo' Hix, 215
Katakana syllabary, 36
K'atun Ajaw, Lady, 194; in Piedras Negras, Stela 1 chronology, *195*, 197–99; in Piedras Negras, Stela 3 chronology, 199, *201*, 204–205, 206; in Piedras Negras, Stela 8 chronology, *207*, 208–209
Kaufman, Terrence, 11
Kettunen, Harri, 11
K'inich Janaab' Pakal: background of, 210; in Palenque, Hieroglyphic Stairway chronology, 215, *216*, 217; in Palenque, Sarcophagus Lid chronology, 210, *211*, 212–15
K'inich Yo'nal Ahk II: background of, 194; in Piedras Negras, Stela 1 chronology, 194, *195*, 196–99; in Piedras Negras, Stela 3 chronology, 199–200, *201*, 202–206; in Piedras Negras, Stela 8 chronology, 206, *207*, 208–209
K'in Variants, *101*, *243*
Knorozov, Yuri Valentinovich, 10, 62
K'uhul ajaw ("holy ruler"), 8

Lacadena, Alfonso, 11, 62, 64, 65, 66, 72
Ladyville (Belize), 7
Landa, Diego de, 9, 12
Landforms, *256*
Language: changes in pronunciation over time, 66; represented glyphically, 71, 72
Linguistics of Maya Writing, The (Wichmann), 3–4
Lintel 2 at Piedras Negras, *43*, 373
Lintel 21 at Yaxchilan: Calendar Round dates and, 93, 374; Distance Numbers from, 105, *106*, *107*, 109, 375; logograms, *34*, 372; numeral exercises on, *78–80*, 373–74; Supplementary Series elements at, *100*, 374; syllables, *44*, 373
Lintels, 12
Logograms, 34, *34*, 35, 372
Logographs. *See* Logograms
Long Counts, 81, *237*; after the Initial Series Introductory Glyph (ISIG), 81, *82*, *237*; calendar periods based on vigesimal system, 81, *82*, 83; conversion to Gregorian calendar, 83–85, 86; correlations, 86; Day Name and, 87–88, *238*; exercises on, *92*, 374; Haab' Month Names and, 88, 91, *239*; Short Counts and, 119. *See also* Supplementary Series
Looper, Matthew, 30
Lounsbury, Floyd, 86
Lunation, 98

MacLeod, Barbara, 11
Macri, Martha, 11, 30
Madrid Codex, 12
Main inscriptions, 21
Main signs, 25, *26*; equivalent affixes and, 25, *29*; numbering of, 28; from Piedras Negras, *28*
Maize agriculture, 7
Mammals, *249*
Map of major Maya sites, *6*
Martin, Simon, 5, 11, 193
Maya, The (Coe), 5
Mayacal, Version 2.02.01, 359–60
Maya calendar, 73; numbers and, *236*; programs for, 359–61; Short Counts and, 86, *119*, 119–20. *See also* Calendar Round (CR); Dates; Long Counts; Supplementary Series
Maya culture, 12–13; brief history of, 5, *6*, 7–8; passing of rulership in, 210
Maya hieroglyphic decipherment, short history of, 8–11
Maya Hieroglyphic Writing (Thompson), 10
Mayan Calendrics, Version 3.02.00, 360
Maya to English lexicon, 257–332
Mediopassive transitive verbs, *167*, *168*, 169–70, 187, 220, 379
Mérida, Yucatan, 86
Mexico, *6*, 7
Military action, verbs relating to, *245*
Missionaries, 8–9
Montgomery, John, 3
Month Names, Haab', 88, *90*, *91*, *93*, *239*, 374
Monument 139 at Tonina, *78–80*, 373–74
Monument 6 at Tortuguero, *189*, *190*
Monuments, *254*, 365–64
Mora-Marín, David, 11
Morley, Sylvanus Griswold, 5, 57
Morphosyllables, 145, 164
Murals, 12

Nakbe, 7
Names, 194
Naranjo: Altar 1 at, *44*, 373; Stela 21 at, *43*, 373; Stela 24 at, *108*, 109, 151, 378
New Catalog of Maya Hieroglyphs, The (Macri and Looper 2003; Macri and Vail 2009), 30, *225–31*, *232–35*
Nouns, 137; animals, *149*; derived, 138, *139–41*, 142, 378; emblem glyphs, *150*; family relations glyphs, *150*; morphosyllables and, 145, 164; objects, *254–56*; order of, 155, *156*, 157, 379; plural, 143; possessed, 143, *144*, 164; pure, 137, *137*; stative clauses and, *159*; T-numbers, *New Catalog* codes, and drawings for, *225–31*. *See also* Pronouns; Titles
Nova, 8
Numbering of glyphs, Thompson's, 28, 30, *30*, *225–31*, *232–35*

Number of Days, 101–102, *102*
Numbers, 73–74, 76, *236*; bar-and-dot, 74, *75*, 79, 373–74; exercises on, *78–80*, 373–74; full-figure variant, 76, *77*; head-variant, 74, *75*, *77*; in inscriptions, 73–74, *75*; T-numbers, *New Catalog* codes, and drawings for, *230*, *231*. *See also* Dates; Distance Numbers; Vigesimal system
Numeral classifiers, 48, *49*, *227*, *230*

Objects: food, *256*; landforms, *256*; monuments, *254*; plants, *255*; ritual, *254*; structures, *255*; vessels, *254*; warfare-related, *255*
Occupational titles, *248*
October Revolution in Russia, 86
Online calculators for Maya dates, 360–61
Open Office Drawing, 363–64
Orthography, 70

Pakal, K'inich Janaab'. *See* K'inich Janaab' Pakal
Pakal's Sarcophagus Lid at Palenque, 210, *211*, 212–15
Palace Tablet at Palenque: Calendar Round dates and, *93*, 374; Distance Numbers at, *106*, *117–18*, 375, 377; prepositions and, *123*, 377; Supplementary Series elements at, *100*, 374
Palenque, 8, 10, 57; Hieroglyphic Stairway at (*see* Hieroglyphic Stairway at Palenque); Pakal's Sarcophagus Lid at, 210, *211*, 212–15; Palace Tablet at (*see* Palace Tablet at Palenque); Sarcophagus at, *115–16*, 376–77; Tablet of 96 Glyphs at (*see* Tablet of 96 Glyphs at Palenque); Temple of the Sun Tablet at, *78–80*, *100*, 373–74
Paleoindian period (11,000–8000 BCE), 7
Panel 3 at Piedras Negras, 160, *161*
Parentage statements, *252*
Paris Codex, 12
Pars pro toto ("part for the whole"), 25, *29*
Passive transitive verbs, *167*, *168*, 169, 187, 220, 379
PDIs (Posterior Date Indicators), 102, *103*, 186, *188*, 224, *243*
Peabody Museum, 12, 193
Personal property nouns, 143, *144*
Phonetic complements, 69, *69*. *See also* Syllabograms
Piedras Negras, 8; Altar 2 at, *113*, *163*, 376, 379; Lintel 2 at, *43*, 373; Panel 3 at, 160, *161*; Proskouriakoff and dynasty of, 10; Stela 1 at (*see* Stela 1 at Piedras Negras); Stela 3 at (*see* Stela 3 at Piedras Negras); Stela 8 at, 189, *190*, 206, *207*, 208–209; Stela 10 at, *100*, 374
Plants, *255*
Plural nouns, 143
Polyphyonic glyphs, 45, *45*
Polyvalent glyphs, 45, *46*
Positional verbs, *176*, *177*, 178, 221; as derived nouns, 138, *140*; exercise on, 179, 380; relative time and, 187; T-numbers, *New Catalog* codes, and drawings for, *229*

Possessed nouns, 143, *144*, 164
Postclassic period, 8
Posterior Date Indicators (PDIs), 102, *103*, 186, *188*, 224, *243*
Postfix, 25, *26*
Pottery, 11, 12
Preclassic (Formative) period (2000 BCE–250 CE), 7
Prefixes, 25, *26*, 124
Prepositions, 121, *122*, 222; exercise on, *123*, 377; stative clauses and, *159*
Primary Standard Sequence, 11
Pronouns, 124, *125*, 126, 133, *219*; absolutive (see Absolutive pronouns); demonstrative, *125*, 133, *219*; ergative (see Ergative pronouns); examples of, 160, *161*; exercises on, *134–36*, 378; T-numbers, *New Catalog* codes, and drawings for, *225–27*
Pronunciation: changes over time in, 66; logograms and, 34
Proskouriakoff, Tatiana, 10, 193
Pure adjectives, 152–53
Pure nouns, 137, *137*

Quadruple glyph blocks, 31
Quirigua, 8

Rabbit Vase, 160, *161*
Rafinesque, Constantine Samuel, 9
Reading order: within glyph blocks, 25, *26*, *27*, 28, *29*, 30–31, *32*, *33*; within inscriptions, 21, *22–24*
Reading the Maya Glyphs (Coe and Van Stone), 4
Reductions of main sign, 25, *29*
Relación de las cosas de Yucatán (A Relation of the Things of Yucatan: Landa), 9
Relationship titles, *252*
Reptiles, *251*
Right Brain Software, 359
Ritual, verbs relating to, *244*
Ritual objects, *254*
Robertson, John, 11, 64, 72
Root intransitive verbs, 175, *176*, *177*, 179, 221, 380; relative time and, 187; T-numbers, *New Catalog* codes, and drawings for, *227*, *230*, *231*
Rosny, Léon de, 9
Royal titles, *247*
Russia, 86

San Bartolo site (Guatemala), 7
Sarcophagus at Palenque, *115–16*, 376–77
Sarcophagus Lid at Palenque, 210, *211*, 212–15
Schele, Linda, 10
Sculpture of Palenque, The (Greene Robertson), 57
Second-person absolutive pronouns: plural, *125*, 132, *219*; singular, *125*, 130–31, *219*

Second-person ergative pronouns, 160, *161*, *219*; plural, *125*, 128–29, *219*; singular, *125*, 126–27, *219*
Sedentism, 7
Seibal, 44, 373
Semantic determinatives, *45*, 45–46, *46*, *47*
Sharer, Robert, 5
Short Counts, 86, *119*, 119–20
Sounds in Classic Mayan, 59–61, 64–66; consonants, 59–60; vowels, 60–61
Spanish conquest of Latin America, 8–9
Spelling: disharmonic, 60–66, *68*, 72, 373; "new" vs. "old" orthography, 70; sounds and, 59–61, 64–66; synharmonic, 62, 63, *67*, 72, 373; variability over time, 59, 65
Spinden, Herbert J., 86
Stative clauses and particles, 158, *159*
Stative particles, *181*, *182*, 183, 187
Stelae, 11, 12
Stela 8 at Piedras Negras: K'inich Yo'nal Ahk II chronology at, 206, *207*, 208–209; temporal indicators from, 189, *190*
Stela 1 at Aguateca, *123*, 151, 377, 378
Stela 1 at Piedras Negras: K'inich Yo'nal Ahk II chronology at, 194, *195*, 196–99; numeral exercises on, *78–80*, 373–74
Stela 10 at Piedras Negras, *100*, 374
Stela 10 at Seibal, 44, 373
Stela 31 at Tikal: Calendar Round dates at, *93*, 374; numeral exercises and, *78–80*, 373–74
Stela 3 at Aguateca, *42*, 373
Stela 3 at Piedras Negras, 16, 19, *19*, 372; Calendar Round dates and, *93*, 374; Distance Numbers at, *106*, *111*, 375; grammar exercise and, *162*, 379; K'inich Yo'nal Ahk II chronology at, 199–200, *201*, 202–206; main signs and affixes from, *28*; prepositions at, *123*, 377; Supplementary Series elements at, *100*, 374; syllables, *43*, 373; transcription, transliteration, and translation of, *51*
Stela 24 at Naranjo, *108*, 109, 151, 378
Stela 21 at Naranjo, *43*, 373
Stephens, John Lloyd, 9
Structures, *255*
Stuart, David, 10–11, 64, 72
Stuart, George, 56, 57
Subfixes, 25, *26*
Suffixes: noun-deriving, 138, *139–41*; possessed nouns and, 143, *144*; stative clauses and, *159*; transitive verbs and, *171*
Superfixes, 25, *26*
Supplementary inscriptions, 21
Supplementary Series, 94, 97–98; 819-Day Cycle, 98, *99*; exercise on identifying elements of, *100*, 374; Glyph A, 98, *99*, *242*; Glyph B, 97, *97*, *241*; Glyph C, *96*, 97, *241*; Glyph F, 94, *96*, *240*; Glyph G (Lord of the Night), 94, 95, *95*, 98, *240*; Glyphs E and D, 94, *96*, 97, *241*; Glyphs Z and Y, 94, *96*, *240*; Glyph X, 97, *97*, *241*

Syllabary, modern Maya, 36, *37–41*
Syllabic signs. *See* Syllabograms
Syllabic spellings, 52, *53*, 373
Syllables. *See* Syllabograms
Syllabograms, 36, *36*, *37–41*, 69, *69*; exercises on, 36, *42*, *43–44*, 373; T-numbers, *New Catalog* codes, and drawings for, *225–31*
Synharmonic spelling, 62, 63, *67*, 72, 373

Tablet of 96 Glyphs at Palenque, 16, 20, *20*, 372; Calendar Round dates and, *93*, 374; Distance Numbers at, *106*, *112*, 375; logograms, *34*; prepositions at, *123*, 377; syllables, *42*, 373; titles at, 151, 378
Temple of the Initial Series, *44*, 373
Temple of the Sun Tablet, *78–80*, *100*, 373–74
Texas Maya Meetings, 3
Third-person absolutive pronouns: plural, *125*, 132–33, *219*; singular, *125*, 131, *219*
Third-person ergative pronouns: plural, *125*, 129, *219*; singular, *125*, 127, *219*
Thompson, John Eric Sydney: *A Catalog of Maya Hieroglyphs*, 28, 30; GMT and, 86; *Maya Hieroglyphic Writing*, 10; T-numbers of, 28, 30, *30*, 225–31, 232–35
Tikal, *78–80*, *93*, 373–74
Time, verbs and expressing, 56, 184–89, *188*
Titles: exercise on, 151, 378; female, *248*; most common, 146–48; occupational, *248*; relationship, *252*; royal, *247*
T-numbers, 28, 30, *30*, 225–31, 232–35
Tokovinine, Alexandre, 11
Tonina, *78–80*, 373–74
Tortuguero, 189, *190*
Totum pro parte ("whole for a part"), 36, *36*
Transcription, 50, 52; in English to Maya lexicon, 333, 334–58; example of, *50*; exercises, 52, *53*, *54*, 373; of Long Count dates, 83; in Maya to English lexicon, 257, 258–332; of Piedras Negras, Stela 3, *51*
Transitive verbs, 166, *167*, *171*, 220; active, 166, *167*, *168*, 187, 220; antipassive, *167*, *168*, 170, 187, 220; ergative pronouns and, 124; exercises on, 172–74, 379, 380; imperative, *167*, 170, 187, 220, 379; mediopassive, *167*, *168*, 169–70, 187, 220, 379; names and, 194; as nouns, 138, *139*; passive, *167*, *168*, 169, 187, 220, 379; relative time and, 187–88; T-numbers, *New Catalog* codes, and drawings for, *226–27*, *230*
Translation, 56; in English to Maya lexicon, 333, 334–58; example of, *50*; exercises, *54*, 373; in Maya to English lexicon, 258–332; of Piedras Negras, Stela 3, *51*

Transliteration, 55; in English to Maya lexicon, 333–58; example of, *50*; exercises, *54*, 373; in Maya to English lexicon, 257, 258–332; of Piedras Negras, Stela 3, *51*. *See also* Spelling
Traxler, Loa, 5
Tres Zapotes (Stela C), 8
Truncations, 25, *29*
Tzolk'in Day Names, 87, *89*, *238*; cartouche surrounding, 45–46; exercise on, *93*, 374

Usual long count periods, 82, *237*

Vail, Gabrielle, 30
Vaillant, George C., 86
Van Stone, Mark, 4
Vector graphic drawings, 362
Verbs: affective, *181*, *182*, 183, 187; agglutinating verbal phrases, 165; as aspectual vs. tense based, 184–89, *188*, 189, *190*, 191; causative, *176*, *177*, *178*, *179*, 187, 221, 380; common, 244–45; inchoative action, *181*, 181–82, *182*, 187, 221; intransitive (*see* Intransitive verbs); order of, 155; positional (*see* Positional verbs); stative particles, *181*, *182*, 183; transitive (*see* Transitive verbs)
Vessels, *254*
Vigesimal system: calendar periods based on, 81, *82*, 83; vigesimal math and conversion, 73, 74, *79*, 373–74
Vowels: Classic Mayan vowel sounds, 60–61; complexity in old orthography, 70; disharmonic spellings of, 60–61, 64–66, 72; glottalized, 60–61, 63; synharmonic spelling and, 62

Wald, Robert, 11
Waldeck, Jean-Frédéric Maximilien de, 9
Warfare-related objects, *255*
Wichmann, Søren, 11; on disharmonic spellings, 62, 64, 65, 66, 72; *The Linguistics of Maya Writing*, 3–4; on regional differences in the glyphs, 72
Word order, 155, *156*, 157, 379

Yaxchilan, 8; Hieroglyphic Stairway 3 at, *110*, 375; Lintel 21 at (*see* Lintel 21 at Yaxchilan)
Yo'nal Ahk II, K'inich. *See* K'inich Yo'nal Ahk II
Yucatan, 86

Zender, Marc, 11, 72, 164